ORCHESTRAL MUSIC: AN ARMCHAIR GUIDE

ORCHESTRAL MUSIC: AN ARMCHAIR GUIDE

LAWRENCE GILMAN

EDITED BY EDWARD CUSHING

NEW YORK · OXFORD UNIVERSITY PRESS · 1951

The book that follows is a compilation of the program notes that Lawrence Gilman wrote over a period of many years for the concerts of several American orchestras—the National Symphony Orchestra, the Philharmonic (later the Philharmonic-Symphony) Orchestra of New York, the Philadelphia Orchestra. There seem to be two reasons why it has been worth while to compile and publish such a book. First, it should be useful to many persons; second, it is distinguished.

It is evident from the antiquity of the program note (Percy Scholes tells us that it dates from the last quarter of the eighteenth century), from its universality (program notes are now everywhere and always distributed among audiences at orchestral concerts), and from its wide range of type, that listeners of every sort find it valuable in some sense and degree. It tells us something—perhaps much, perhaps little—that we did not know and that is interesting about the music we are to hear or have heard, about the man who wrote it, about the circumstances attending its writing. All of this can be relevant to our understanding and enjoyment of what we hear.

Sometimes the analytic note (a distinct type) assists us to a quicker comprehension of the composer's technique of communication. Illustrated with examples in musical notation, it identifies 'ideas,' describes the development to which these are subjected, the forms into which they evolve. But such notes are for those in the know—for the professional musician, the qualified or at least ambitious amateur. The best are Donald Tovey's and B. H. Haggin's, and they are very good indeed. But they will not benefit *l'homme moyen musicale*, except quite incidentally. For him—and he is in a majority in any concert audience, and certainly in that much vaster audience that listens to serious music on the air and on records—the program note that offers historical and biographical information, interpretation and insight, is more helpful. The essential qualifications for an author of such notes—assuming, of course, that he is a musician—are ardor, insight, scholarship, and style. The more usual qualifications, unfortunately, seem to be indifference, ignorance, and illiteracy.

v

Lawrence Gilman was a qualified musician. But music, while it absorbed him chiefly, did not absorb him wholly. He was interested in and responsive to all the arts through which men communicate to other men the meaning and the value that they have found in life and experience. And writing about music he drew on his experience of literature, of painting, of philosophic speculation, and mystical thought to communicate his insights and enrich his interpretations. He did this, as the pages that follow testify, quite simply and unpretentiously. He wrote neither up nor down to his audience. He assumed that its interest in his subject—the masterpieces of music and their creators—was genuine; that it was intelligent; that its taste was not debased (the contrary assumptions apparently dictate the tone of many program notes). He did not write for musicians, though he was himself one. He did not parade his scholarship, though he was a scrupulous scholar. He had a sense of humor and he indulged it; he knew the importance of the irrelevant detail and included it. He knew that allusions open many doors; his pockets were full of such keys and he distributed them generously. Yet his manner, as a writer of program notes (and it was as such, and as a musical journalist, that, despite his many books, he made his greatest contribution) was always casual and urbane: he told you in a program note what he might have told you, without condescension or pedantry, at dinner. It is in this sense that the editor of this compilation risks calling it distinguished.

The notes in the following pages have been compiled from the program books of the Philharmonic-Symphony Society of New York and of the Philadelphia Orchestral Association, whose co-operation is gratefully acknowledged, and from the columns of the *New York Herald-Tribune*, in which much of the material used by Gilman in his program notes was printed in the form of reviews and Sunday articles. (Lawrence Gilman was music critic of the *New York Tribune* (later the *Herald-Tribune*) from 1923 until his death in 1939.) Some material has been added by the editor. This additional material is indicated by the signs ‡ ‡ which precede and follow the interpolations. These interpolations have been made only where material appropriate to the scheme of this book was not available in Gilman's writings. Footnotes, often used by Gilman, have been largely eliminated, and the information contained in them has been, where essential, incorporated in the text of the notes.

A word about the range of these notes. They cover—incompletely, of course, but more comprehensively than is usual in such compilations—what may be described as the 'standard symphonic repertory.' No definition of this repertory can be made that will satisfy the opinion of all readers. The editor is prepared to accept with humility the strictures that may be made on his own judgement, as evidenced by his selections. Practical considerations have, however, imposed certain limitations on him. The available material would have made a book two or three times the bulk of this one. It was necessary to eliminate much. Contemporary music has been largely excluded: the permanence in the repertory of particular works by living composers is always questionable. What at a given time is popular with performers or audiences may not always or even long endure. The editor has played safe by going no farther back than Purcell and coming no farther forward than Schönberg, Stravinsky, Prokofieff and Shostakovich. He has risked something by including extensive notes on— among other 'debatable' works—symphonies by Bruckner and Mahler not often programmed, though recorded and frequently broadcast. These aberrations should be charged, by those who consider them such, to him alone. Unfortunately, American composers are conspicuous by their absence from this compilation. Only two are represented. But American works were seldom performed by our major orchestras in the 'twenties and 'thirties. For the most part, those then heard have passed into obscurity, while those popular today were then unknown.

Lawrence Gilman was an allusive writer and his notes are sometimes a texture of quotations. His references are for the most part identified in his text, but a selected bibliography including the most important of his sources, along with other standard works and some recent valuable additions to musical literature, will be found in this volume.

The editor wishes, finally, to acknowledge his indebtedness for encouragement and much practical aid in his task to the editorial staff of Oxford University Press, to Miss Gladys Chamberlain, Music Librarian of the 58th Street Branch of the New York Public Library, and to Mrs. Lawrence Gilman, Mrs. Elizabeth L. Anderson, and Mr. G. L. Watson.

Edward Cushing

COMPOSERS

ORCHESTRAL MUSIC: AN ARMCHAIR GUIDE

Johann Christian Bach

1735-82

B

Johann Christian Bach, youngest son of Johann Sebastian and Anna Magdalena Bach, was fourteen when his father died. He went to Berlin to live with his brother Carl Philipp Emanuel, with whom he studied composition and clavier playing. 'A certain gaiety of disposition, possibly increased by his acquaintance with Italian singers,' writes Maczewska, 'led him to Italy.' In 1754 he became a pupil of Padre Martini at Bologna. He dwelt in Naples from 1757, and from 1760 to 1762 he was organist of the Milan Cathedral. In Italy he became an opera composer *à la mode* and a writer of church music as well. In 1762 he went to London, and in the spring of 1763, after the success of his second London opera, *Zanaida*, he was appointed music master to the Queen and the Royal Family. When the eight-year-old Mozart visited London in 1764, Bach made a delightful fuss over him. He took Wolfgang on his knee and went through a piece with him, 'each in turn playing a bar or so with so much precision that no one would have suspected two performers.' About this time he entered into his famous partnership with the prodigious Karl Friedrich Abel, that pupil of Johann Sebastian Bach at the Thomasschule in Leipzig who settled in London in middle life and amazed the English of Queen Charlotte's day by performing with equal skill upon the viola da gamba, the harpsichord, the horn, and 'upon new instruments never heard in public before.' He and Johann Christian conducted jointly Mrs. Cornelys' subscription concerts from 1765. Bach lived in London almost continuously for twenty years, and died there on New Year's Day, 1782, in his forty-seventh year.

The eminent Herr Professor Hugo Riemann in his great *Musiklexicon* refers sternly to Johann Christian Bach as 'light-minded.' Doubtless at times he was; but in a twelve-line notice of a composer who cut a considerable figure in Europe a century and a half ago the epithet seems unnecessarily Draconian. Charles Burney, father of the famous Fanny, and a shrewd and appreciative observer of his contemporaries, speaks with warm admiration of Johann Christian in his *General History of Music* (1776-89): 'He possessed,' says Dr. Burney, 'every requisite for a great

3

musician.' He was one of the chief exponents of the *galant* style, that essentially Italian instrumental idiom which was the issue of a revolt against the severer musical manner of the Handelian period. There is a blend of grace and expressiveness, of sensibility and *élan*, in the instrumental writing of Johann Christian which inclines one to echo Burney's praise. It was Mozart who, delighted by Bach's music, wrote from Paris in 1778: 'I love him with all my heart!'

● Sinfonia in B-flat major

The Sinfonia in B-flat was composed about 1770. Four years later, Bach employed it as the overture to his opera *Lucio Silla*. The original work exists in three forms: in a MS. copy of the score of *Lucio Silla* once in the *Hessiche Landesbibliothek* at Darmstadt; in a set of manuscript parts in the library of the monastery at Einsiedeln, in Switzerland; and in a set of printed parts in the British Museum. After the manner of its period, Bach's Sinfonia is in the 'Italian overture' form, and the three movements of the score, played without pause, are an opening 'Allegro assai' (B-flat, 2-2), an Andante (E-flat, 3-4), and a final Presto (B-flat, 3-8).

In the history of the development of the modern symphony, the 'Italian overture,' or 'overture in the Italian style,' became of greater importance than its Gallic brother, the 'French' overture (*ouverture à la manière Française*), the invention of which is credited to that remarkable Franco-Italian, Jean-Baptiste Lully. The form of the 'French,' or 'Lullian,' overture consisted of a slow Introduction, followed by a quicker movement in lighter style, and concluding with another slow movement, not so grave in character as the first. Sometimes there were only two divisions: the slow opening movement, followed by a short, free, fugal quick movement; or there was the extended variety of this 'Lullian' overture, which added to the other divisions one or more movements in the dance forms of the period. (It was this 'French' model that Johann Sebastian Bach followed in his four orchestral suites, which he did not call 'suites,' but 'overtures.')

The 'Italian' overture reversed the order of the first two sections: the quick movement came first, the slow movement second. The 'French' overture proceeded from sobriety to exhilaration, and often danced itself to bed. The 'Italian' overture began the evening in high spirits, sobered down and became meditative, and brightened up for the party's end—but there was, as a rule, no dancing. Professor Parry gave up the question of the identity of the originator of this form: 'It certainly came into vogue very soon after the French Overture, and quickly supplanted it to a great extent.' But E. J. Dent asserts that the form of overture known as the 'Italian' was introduced in 1696 for the revival of an early opera of Alessandro Scarlatti's, *Dal male il bene*. Scarlatti (1659-1725) generally wrote his overtures in three or four short movements, distributed in the order which is familiar in the modern symphony. 'When he used three movements, the first was a solid allegro; the second a short slow movement aiming at expression; and the third a lively allegro. This scheme came to be universally adopted even until the time of Mozart, who wrote his early opera overtures in this form.'

The first Allegro of Johann Christian's Sinfonia in B-flat is interesting as foreshadowing the classic sonata form. It has its chief theme—the vigorous opening subject for strings and wind—and a contrasting second theme (in the tonic, not the dominant). The third measure of this second theme is curiously like the third measure of the Andante theme of Haydn's 'Clock' Symphony, composed a quarter of a century later. In the Andante we are reminded at once of the young Mozart by the contour of the suave and charming tune for oboe and strings, twice repeated, with rondo-like implications. A curious feature of this movement is the appearance at the thirty-second measure of a portion of the second theme of the preceding movement. The concluding Presto is a merry Rondo, Haydnish in spirit.

Johann Sebastian Bach

1685-1750

B

‡Johann Sebastian Bach, whose pre-eminence as a composer in the history of Western music few will challenge, was born at Eisenach in 1685 and died at Leipzig in 1750, at the age of sixty-five. The circumstances and events of his life are set forth in full detail in Charles Sanford Terry's *Bach: A Biography*, and here may be briefly summarized in the words of Percy A. Scholes, writing in the *Oxford Companion to Music:*

He lived in Protestant north Germany in the days when music there made an important part of the splendour of courts, of municipal dignity, of religious observance, and of the daily happiness of the people, and he occupied successively the posts of choir-boy, violinist in the orchestra of a prince, organist of town churches, chief musician in a court, and cantor of a municipal school with charge of the music of its associated churches. This last position was at Leipzig, with the St. Thomas Church and School of which city his name is chiefly connected, since he remained there for almost the last thirty years of his life, incessantly performing, teaching, training choirs, and composing, in the joy of the exercise of his art and that tribulation which often comes from contact between the clerical outlook and the artistic temperament. He played many instruments, and as clavichordist, harpsichordist, and organist, was supreme in his day. He was twice married and the father of twenty children, of whom several attained a high position in his own profession. Towards the end of his life his eyesight failed and his last months were spent in total darkness. He was of a happy disposition, unworldly, God-fearing and moral, and an indefatigable student of his art, eagerly learning from whatever he could procure of the productions of other nations. His work closes a 'school,' that of the later contrapuntal style, of which the fugue is the most definite expression.

Definitive studies of Bach's art have been written by Philip Spitta and by Albert Schweitzer.‡

THE BRANDENBURG CONCERTOS

Over two centuries ago there lived a young Prussian prince whose hobby it was to collect concertos. This young eccentric was Christian Ludwig, Margraf of Brandenburg (1677-1734). He was a bachelor, living alternately at Berlin and on his estate at Malchow. He not only loved music, but he spent a large part of his income on it, and had acquired a remarkable collection of concertos by famous living composers. He met Johann Sebastian Bach about 1719, and, so the chroniclers report, was 'struck by his musical powers'—which was admirably discerning of him. For his private orchestra he commissioned the promising composer to write some music, and in the spring of 1721 Bach completed and sent to his enlightened friend the set of six works now known to us as the Brandenburg Concertos.

Bach was then living at Cöthen, and he was thirty-six years old. He must have regarded his commission as of special importance, for in the manuscripts of these scores the notes are written with extraordinary and exquisite neatness, and the bar-lines are drawn with the aid of a ruler. He finished the concertos March 24, 1721, and dispatched them to the Margraf with a dedication in French (perhaps written by some courtier at Cöthen, thinks Spitta), in which, being a mere genius addressing a prince, he prostrated himself at the feet of the mighty one and besought him 'very humbly' not to judge the imperfections of the concertos too harshly, but rather to find in them 'by his very kind consideration the profound respect and the very humble allegiance which they seek to convey.'

Today His Royal Highness is remembered only as the man who commissioned half a dozen masterpieces of instrumental music, of which he seems to have thought so little that in the catalogue of his collection (discovered more than a century and a half later in the Royal domestic archives in Berlin) the name of Bach did not appear, though concertos by Vivaldi, Venturini, Brescianello, and others were listed there. It is conjectured that the pieces by Bach were included in a job lot of scores by composers of no particular consequence and offered for sale either among '77 concertos by different masters, and for various instruments,' or among another lot of odds and ends. Each of the Brandenburg Concertos was valued at about the present equivalent of ten cents. After the Margraf's death in 1734 his collection was disposed of. The six Brandenburg Concertos came into the possession (through other hands) of a sister of Frederick the Great, and finally reached the Royal (now the State) Library at Berlin. They were first printed by Peters in 1850.

Although Bach had previously written instrumental pieces of important dimensions—such as the introductions to the Weimar cantatas, *Uns ist ein Kind geboren, Gleich wie der Regen,* and *Der Himmel Lacht*—the Branden-

burg Concertos seem to have been his first essays at absolute instrumental
music constructed on a symphonic scale. He doubtless wanted to show, thinks
Parry, 'that he could make concertos for all the different kinds of solo instruments available in those days, and not restrict himself solely, as usual, to string
soloists.' This considerable feat was accomplished by writing each concerto for
a different group of instruments: the first (in F major) for strings, three oboes,
two horns, bassoon, and, as usual, a harpsichord to fill in the harmony; the
second (likewise in F), for trumpet, flute, oboe, solo violin, and the string band
as tutti; the third (in G major), for three violins, three violas, three 'cellos, and
bass; the fourth (also in G major), for solo violin, two flutes and strings; the
fifth (in D major), for solo harpsichord, violin and flute, with strings; and the
sixth (in B-flat) for two violas, two viole da gamba, 'cello, and harpsichord.

It is perhaps unnecessary to remark that the eighteenth-century 'concerto' was
a very different thing from the variety known to the nineteenth and twentieth
centuries by the same name. Bach, Handel, Vivaldi, Corelli, and their contemporaries wrote their orchestral 'concertos' for a small group of principal instruments called the concertino, assisted by the full orchestra or 'concerto grosso'
(of strings only, or strings and wind, with a harpsichord player, usually the conductor, filling out the harmony). The essential characteristic of these concertos
is the contrast between the small body of solo instruments, the 'concertino,'
and the larger body of instruments, the 'tutti.'

● No. 1, in F major

The first of the Brandenburg Concertos differs from its companions not only
in having a more numerous concertino, but also because there are no special
subjects for each, as was the rule. The concerto is written for strings, three
oboes, two horns, bassoon, and cembalo. Bach's score calls also for a violino
piccolo, or small violin, tuned a minor third higher than the ordinary instrument and having a bright and penetrating tone. Its part is now generally given
to the ordinary violin.

Although Bach in this concerto followed the form as he had helped to
develop it, he made a concession to the taste of his time by adding a fourth
movement in dance rhythms. This is a Minuet with first and second Trios and
a Polacca.

The scheme of this first concerto is as follows: i. Allegro, F major, 'Alla
breve' time; ii. Adagio, D minor, 3-4; iii. Allegro, F major, 6-8; iv. Minuetto,
F major, triple time, with a Trio (in D minor) for two oboes and bassoon,
followed by a Polacca (in F) for the strings without violino piccolo, and concluding with a Trio (in F) for two horns and the three oboes.

The Adagio impressed Spitta as 'one of the most impassioned songs of woe
ever written. The melody gives expression to a piercing grief, often rising to a
shrill cry; the oboe begins in an apparently objectless way on the dominant,
and then the high violin and the bass take it up, one after the other, after
which it is carried on in close canon on the oboe and violin; while below the
quavers on the accompanying instruments keep on in a calm and mournful
manner.'

Bach seems to have been attached to this concerto, for he used its first movement as an Introduction to the solo cantata, *Falsche Welt, dir trau ich nicht* (No. 52).

● No. 2, in F major

The autograph score of the second of the Brandenburg Concertos is entitled: *Concerto 2do à Tromba, 1 Flauto, 1 Hautbois, 1 Violino concertate, 2 Violini, 1 Viola è Violine in Ripieno col Violoncello è Basso per il Cembalo.* ‡The concertino thus comprises trumpet, flute, oboe, and solo violin, opposed to a tutti of strings and harpsichord. There are three movements: an Allegro (in F, 2-2); an Andante (D minor, 3-4); and a final 'Allegro assai' (F, 2-4).‡

Spitta remarks that we have here '. . . a true Concerto Grosso, except that the concertino consists of four, all of high register: namely, one string and three wind [solo violin, one flute, one oboe, one trumpet]; so that a departure is made in every way from the custom which decrees that the concertino shall consist of two violins and a violoncello. . . On account of its crystal-clear and transparent organism this concerto is a greater favorite than the more closely woven First; the feeling, moreover, is throughout of a kind easily entered into. The marvelously beautiful Andante is soft and tenderly simple while the first and last movements rush and riot with all the freshness and vigor of youth.'

Parry is less lyrical, less absorbed, and remarks that the limitations of the trumpet (an instrument which Bach sometimes treated with almost ribald disrespect) gives the subject of the first movement 'rather an Italian air,' because it was 'inevitable to base the passages allotted to it mainly on the component notes of a chord; otherwise that instrument does its best to play the same type of passages as the violins. . . The last movement is a showy one in which the trumpet figures very gaily, and has a part which is almost unplayable in modern times, owing to the extreme altitude to which it is caused to rise.'

This concerto is usually played with modifications of Bach's original scoring. Felix Mottl in his edition divided the formidable trumpet part between two players, using the lower octaves in the extremely high passages; he filled in the continuo for strings, and added parts for clarinets, bassoons, and horns. In the Andante he muted the strings.

In 1909 Richard Strauss conducted a performance of this concerto at a concert of the Royal Orchestra, Berlin. He solved the problem of the high solo passages for the trumpet by giving them to a piccolo-heckelphone, invented by Heckel of Biebrich—an instrument 'with a good deal of oboe character,' though a good equivalent, according to Strauss, for the trumpet.

● No. 3, in G major

‡The briefest, this is also the most frequently performed of the Brandenburg Concertos.‡ In the autograph score there are only two movements; both are in G major, and both marked Allegro. The first movement is in 2-2 time; the second in 12-8 time. There is no slow movement: Bach's original score separates the two Allegros only by a transitional measure, Adagio, 4-4—two forte chords forming a Phrygian cadence, and suspending us for a moment in B major.

Certain conductors have seen fit to introduce at this point, in lieu of the slow movement which they seem to feel that Bach was mistaken in omitting, some kind of substitute. One has interpolated the slow movement from Bach's Concerto for Violin in E major; another has inserted an arrangement of the chorale which concludes the first part of the 'St. Matthew Passion'; another has introduced an arrangement of an Andante from one of the sonatas for solo violin. The majority, however, have been content to let Bach have his own way.

Bach used a version of the first movement of this concerto as the opening instrumental section of his Whitsunday cantata, *Ich liebe den Höchsten von ganzem Gemüthe.*

• No. 4, in G major

The fourth of the Concertos is notable for the conspicuous part played by the solo violin of the concertino. There are three movements: an opening Allegro in G major, 3-8 time; an Andante in E minor, 3-4 time; and a final Presto in G, 2-2 time.

The material of the first movement is given out chiefly by the concertino (the solo violin and the two flutes). The slow movement, 'a beautiful and grave piece, in mournful measure,' seemed to Spitta like music for a funeral procession. The last movement is a Fugue, and its animation, brilliance, wealth of invention, easy solution of technical problems—courted and triumphantly disposed of by this Miracle-Man of music—have persuaded students to place it in the first rank of Bach's achievements in this form.

• No. 5, in D major

The fifth of the Brandenburg Concertos is written for a concertino of clavier (harpsichord), solo violin, and solo flute, with the usual tutti of strings and continuo. In the first movement (Allegro, D major, 2-2), the outstanding feature is the great passage for the clavier, unaccompanied, toward the latter part of the movement—a cadenza of brilliant effectiveness, illustrating, as Parry observes, Bach's extraordinary inventiveness in the line of virtuosity, not for itself, but as a means of expressing musical ideas, and, of course, in this instance, departing from the rule of making all the instruments play similar passages; 'for a great cembalo player like Bach could hardly be contented with setting down anything for it which any other instrument could play.'

The slow movement (Affettuoso, B minor, 4-4) is a lovely and moving trio for the three solo instruments of the concertino, elaborately and tenderly intertwined in melodic figures remarkable for their beauty and plasticity.

The last movement (Allegro, D major, 2-4) was once quite bluntly referred to by that candid truthteller, W. J. Henderson, as an 'Irish jig.' 'Possibly,' he remarked, 'Bach did not know it was Irish; but any of us will be sure of it.' The excellent Spitta ne'er lets the word 'jig' fall from his solemn pen in his comment upon this movement; although the jig (usually spelt 'gigue') was a much commoner thing in the music of the seventeenth and eighteenth centuries than in the music of the nineteenth and twentieth, and Bach wrote a quantity of them. Spitta prefers to tell us that the finale of this concerto is 'in the form which was noticed first in the violin sonatas with harpsichord obbli-gato—for instance, in the second movement of the sonata in A major. The structure is in three sections, after the pattern of the Italian aria; the first, which is completely repeated for the third, is fugal, and the second introduces a subsidiary theme and combines it with the chief subject.'

• No. 6, in B-flat major

The sixth and last of the Brandenburg Concertos was composed for violas, viole da gamba, string basses, and harpsichord. In modern performances, the viola da gamba parts are played by 'cellos.

The viola da gamba, now virtually obsolete, was a predecessor of the violon-cello, and was made in different sizes. J. S. Bach was the last great composer who wrote for the gamba. He composed for it three sonatas (for gamba and clavier), and he used it with incomparable effect in the introduction to his cantata, *Gottes Zeit ist die allerbeste Zeit* (No. 106), as well as in the St. John and St. Matthew Passions. The viola da gamba was exceedingly popular in the sixteenth and seventeenth centuries (it was becoming obsolete in Bach's time). To the amateur of Shakespeare's day it was what the 'cello is in our time. It will be recalled that Sir Toby Belch's highest praise of Sir Andrew Aguecheek was that 'he plays o' the viol-de-gamboy, and speaks three or four languages word for word without book.'

In the first movement (Allegro, B-flat major, 2-2), the opening subject con-sists of a canon for the violas at the distance of a quaver, which persists for sixteen measures above a pulsating bass. 'The whole movement has a strangely mysterious character, such as Bach alone could give it.'

The slow movement is an 'Adagio ma non tanto,' beginning in E-flat major, 3-2 time. The subject is a broad melody treated fugally by the violas, above a *quasi legato* bass part. The movement is developed with a noble gravity that gives it a place apart among the Brandenburg Concertos.

The last movement (Allegro, B-flat major, 12-8), a gigue, is a characteristic example of Bach's zestful and splendidly vital finales.

THE ORCHESTRAL SUITES

It seems probable that Bach composed his four orchestral suites at Cöthen, where he dwelt from 1717 to 1723 as Kapellmeister to Prince Leopold, though there is the possibility to be considered that they were written at a later date at Leipzig, where we know that he performed them before the Telemann Society, which he conducted from 1729 to 1736. Bach designated these works by the title of the first movement common to all of them—'Overture.' They are actually groups of movements in certain of the dance forms of the period, preceded by an introductory movement constructed on the plan of the 'French,' or 'Lullian,' overture—a stately opening section of imposing dignity and breadth, followed by a lively and brilliant one, more or less fugal in tex-ture. ‡See the note above on Johann Christian Bach's Sinfonia in B-flat for further comment on the origins, similarities, and differences between the 'French' and 'Italian' overtures of the period.‡ Parry, in commenting on the 'dance movements, of the liveliest character,' which follow the serious opening, thinks that Bach's genius is here manifested 'in a singular and almost unique phase: for none of the movements, however gay or merry, ever loses the distinction of noble art.' 'However freely they sparkle and play,' Parry continues, 'they are never trivial, but bear even in the lightest moments the impress of a great mind and the essentially sincere character of the composer.' In his turn, Schweitzer remarks that 'in the dance melodies of these suites a fragment of a vanished world of grace and eloquence has been preserved for us. They are the ideal musical picture of the rococo period. Their charm resides in the perfection of their blending of strength and grace.'

Bach's four orchestral suites (they are in the keys of C major, B minor, and —two of them—D major) are, like the Brandenburg Concertos, written for different assortments of instruments. The first, in C, is scored for strings, two oboes, and bassoon; the second, in B minor, is for flute and string; the third, in D, employs two oboes, three trumpets, tympani, and strings; the fourth, also in D, employs three oboes, bassoon, three trumpets, tympani, and strings. In each of the suites the instrumental apparatus was amplified, of course, by the 'continuo' or figured bass, which in Bach's day was elaborated at the harpsichord by the leader, who played and directed at the same time. ‡The suites also vary in the number and character of the movements comprising them, as follows:‡

● No. 1, in C

The seldom-played C major Suite begins, like its companions, with an Overture in the French style: an introductory section, Grave, 4-4, succeeded by a fugal Vivace, and leading back to the opening Grave. Then follow the succession of dances. These comprise a Courante (Allegro, 3-2); two Gavottes ('Allegretto vivace,' 2-2); a Forlane (Allegro, 6-4); a Minuet doubled ('Andante con moto,' 3-4); Bourrées I and II (Allegro, 2-2—the second in C minor, for two oboes and bassoon only); Passepied I and II ('Allegro moderato,' 3-4).

Attention should be called to a charming detail in the Trio of the Gavotte (II). This is properly in three parts only, but the unison violins and violas give out at intervals, pianissimo and staccato, a sort of elfin fanfare—a conceit which Bach had already provided for the horns in the first movement of the First Brandenburg Concerto.

● No. 2, in B minor

In the B minor Suite for flute and strings the opening movement is followed by a Rondo, a Sarabande, a Bourrée in two parts, a Polonaise with variation or 'double,' a Minuet, and a short piece in free style, 2-4 time, called 'Badinerie.' ‡The B minor Suite is easily the most popular of the four; the number of its performances in any given period of time will exceed those of all the others combined.‡

● No. 3, IN D

In this suite the introductory movement (Overture: Grave, D major, 4-4) is
followed by its traditional companion, a contrasting section in lively tempo
(Vivace, same key, same time), in the form of a fugue, with a return of the
slow division. Then comes the celebrated 'Air' (Lento, D major, 4-4), for
strings, known to all music-lovers through Wilhelmj's transcription for solo
violin, in which it is transposed to the key of C major, with the melody
intended to be played on the G string throughout. The third movement is a
Gavotte (D major, 2-2), followed by a second Gavotte, with the first repeated
after it. A Bourée (Allegro, D major, 2-2) and a Gigue ('Allegro vivace,'
D major, 6-8) complete the suite.

● No. 4, IN D

‡The movements of the fourth and last of the Bach suites, like the third in
the key of D major, are five in number: An Overture, Grave, 4-4, leading to a
fugal Allegro, 9-8, and a repetition of the slow opening; Bourrées, a Gavotte,
and Minuetto, and a concluding *Réjouissance*, with the tempo indication
'Allegro vivace,' 3-4.‡

● THE CLAVIER CONCERTOS

Bach as we know was an incorrigible transcriber of his own works. He was so
little a 'purist' that some of his most egregious performances in this field
would give great pain to his more tender-minded commentators if they allowed
themselves to face the full horror of the facts. For Bach did not hesitate to
revamp his music as he saw fit. He transcribed violin music for the clavier
‡a term which in Bach's time was loosely applied to all keyboard instruments,
occasionally even to the organ‡, adapted vocal music for the organ, developed
a chorus from an instrumental Allegro, and thought nothing of taking an oboe
solo from a cantata and making it do duty as the slow movement of a concerto for clavier and strings. The first and second movements of the D minor
Clavier Concerto (No. 1 in the list below) were, for example, used by Bach
in his cantata *Wir müssen durch viel Trübsal in das Reich Gottes eingehen*
(No. 146); and he used the music of the concerto again in his cantata No. 188,
Ich habe meine Zuversicht. In the 146th cantata the Adagio of the D minor
concerto becomes a slow movement for voice and strings and organ, in which
the elegiac mood of the instrumental Adagio admirably suits the words of the
cantata. The opening Allegro of the concerto becomes, in the cantata, an
Overture scored for woodwinds, strings, and organ. ‡Further, it is conjectured
that the form of the music in the clavier concerto is not primary.‡ Certain of
Bach's clavier concertos exist as concertos for violin (see notes, below, on the
violin concertos), and Schweitzer says that the concertos for clavier are 'in
effect, and with one exception only, transcriptions made at Leipzig after 1730,
at a time when Bach saw himself obliged to write concertos for the clavier for
performances at the Telemann Society and for little concerts in his own home.'

‡The extant concertos by Bach for clavier and strings are thirteen in number. There are seven solo concertos, published in Vol. xvii of the *Bach-Gesellschaft* edition, three concertos for two claviers, two for three claviers, and one for four, as follows:

Concerto No. 1, for Solo Clavier and Strings, in D minor. The three movements are, Allegro, D minor, 2-2; Adagio, G minor, 3-4; Allegro, D minor, 3-4. (For use of material from this concerto in various of Bach's cantatas, see above.)

Concerto No. 2, for Solo Clavier and Strings, in E major. No tempo indication is given for the first movement, E major, 4-4 time; the second movement is a Siciliano in C-sharp minor, 12-8; the final movement is an Allegro, 3-8, in the tonic.

Concerto No. 3, for Solo Clavier and Strings, in D major. This concerto is identical with the Violin Concerto in E major. The movements are: an opening fast movement in the tonic in 2-2 time; an Adagio in B minor, 3-4; an Allegro in D major, 3-8.

Concerto No. 4, for Solo Clavier and Strings, in A major. The movements are: Allegro, A major, 2-2; Larghetto, F-sharp minor, 12-8; 'Allegro ma non tanto,' in the tonic, 3-8.

Concerto No. 5, for Solo Clavier and Strings, in F minor. There is no tempo indication for the first movement, in the tonic key and 2-4 time. The second movement, a Largo, 4-4, is popularly known as the Arioso and is frequently heard in transcribed form; Bach employed this movement in one of his cantatas. There is a Presto finale, 3-8.

Concerto No. 6, for Solo Clavier and Strings, in F major. This concerto is a version of the Brandenburg Concerto No. 4. There is no tempo indication for the first movement, in 3-8 time. This is followed by an Andante, D minor, 3-4, and an 'Allegro assai,' F major, 2-2.

Concerto No. 7, for Solo Clavier and Strings, in G minor. This is identical with the Violin Concerto in A minor. The movements are: Allegro, G minor, 2-4; Andante, B-flat major, 4-4; 'Allegro assai,' G minor, 9-8.

Concerto No. 1 for Two Claviers and Strings, in C minor. It is conjectured that the original version of this work was a concerto for oboe and violin, no longer extant. The first movement is an Allegro in common time, the second an Adagio in E-flat major, 12-8, and the Finale an Allegro in the tonic, 2-4.

Concerto No. 2, for Two Claviers and Strings, in C major. This concerto is thought to have come down to us in its original form; the solo parts predominate, and in the beautiful slow movement play without accompaniment. The corner movements, an Allegro in 4-4 time, and a Fugue, are in the tonic key; the intervening 'Adagio ovvero Largo' is in A minor, 6-8.

Concerto No. 3, for Two Claviers and Strings, in C minor. This concerto derives from the Concerto in D minor for Two Violins. The first movement (no tempo indication) is in C minor, 4-4; this is followed by an Andante, 12-8, in E-flat major, and this in turn by an 'Allegro assai' in C minor, 3-4.

Concerto No. 1, for Three Claviers and Strings, in D minor. It is thought that Bach composed his two concertos for three claviers for the instruction of his sons Carl Philipp and Wilhelm Friedemann. The movements of No. 1 are: a fast movement (no tempo mark) in D minor, 3-8; a Siciliano in F major, 6-8, and a final Allegro, 2-4, in the tonic key.

CONCERTO NO. 2, FOR THREE CLAVIERS AND STRINGS, IN C MAJOR. The key of this concerto is uncertain. Bach's autograph score remains undiscovered, and existing manuscript scores are in C and D major. One of these appears to have come down to us from the library of Carl Philipp; it is in the key of C. The movements are: Allegro, 4-4; Adagio, A minor, 4-4; Allegro, 2-2.

CONCERTO FOR FOUR CLAVIERS AND STRINGS, IN A MINOR. This is a transcription by Bach of a string concerto in B minor by Antonio Vivaldi, and included in that composer's third set of concertos, *L'Estro Armonico* (see notes below on Vivaldi). The movements are an Allegro in common time, a Largo, 3-4, and a final Allegro, 6-8.‡ Nothing could be more fascinating for the musician than a comparison of this concerto in its two incarnations: as Vivaldi left it, and as Bach has transformed it. We look over the shoulder of an incomparable master, and watch him edit, amend, evolve, and re-create. We see him give life and plasticity to the polyphonic structure by the crafty addition of a middle voice—as, for example, in the passage beginning at the twentieth measure of the opening Allegro, where he has vitalized the somewhat tentative progress of Vivaldi's counterpoint by a little figure in sixteenth-notes that he has introduced into the left hand of the first cembalo part. Or he gives pith and accent and rhythmic verve to the movement of the bass by some magically simple touch—as in the descending octaves in the same passage. Or he grows impatient, throws Vivaldi's pedestrian bass out of his study window, and invents a new one, lithe and comely and expressive.

In the Largo, for further instance, he shows us what Vivaldi might have done, for he sets a figure from the opening subject in contrary motion against itself, and Vivaldi's thinness becomes full-blooded and expressive. In the Finale he has at times departed widely from Vivaldi's original. He has changed in some instances the intervallic structure of the parts, and has given a new texture and significance to certain measures—as by the addition of long-held notes for the supporting violins and violas above the figuration of the first clavier.

As a whole, he has in this concerto been more faithful to his original than in others of his transcriptions; but such infidelities as he permits himself are priceless.

● THE VIOLIN CONCERTOS

The half-dozen years that Bach spent at Cöthen as Kapellmeister and director of chamber music to Prince Leopold were important for himself and for musical art. It was at Cöthen that he lost a good wife—who had borne him seven children—and married a second, who bore him thirteen more; it was there that he wrote the six Brandenburg Concertos, the first part of the *Wohltemperirte Clavier*, and most of his violin music.

His position at Cöthen promised little that could have seemed to him propitious or rewarding. The Court was Reformed, so there was no church music.

The castle church possessed a small organ of inferior quality; that of the Reformed town church was rather larger. Bach was merely the director of his master's chamber music. But the post offered at least one opportunity: that of exploring the possibilities of instrumental secular music; and Bach turned this opportunity to immortal ends.

There seems to be little doubt that Bach's violin concertos, together with most of his great secular instrumental works, date from the Cöthen period. Of these we possess only half—those left to the composer's son Philipp Emanuel; those inherited by Wilhelm Friedemann have disappeared. The extant concertos comprise two for solo violin and orchestra, in A minor and E major, and the Double Concerto in D minor. Some Bach scholars— Schweitzer, for example—group with these the Fourth of the set of Brandenburg Concertos, in G major, composed for a concertino of one violin and two flutes, with a tutti of strings and continuo (this concerto also exists in the form of a Clavier Concerto in F major). Of the missing violin concertos, Schweitzer believes that at least three—two for solo violin and one for two violins—have come down to us in the form of arrangements for clavier. These are the Clavier Concerto in D minor (No. 1 of the set of seven in Volume XVII of the *Bach-Gesellschaft* edition), corresponding to a lost violin concerto in the same key; the Clavier Concerto in F minor (B.-G. XVII, No. 5), corresponding to a missing violin concerto in G minor; and the Concerto for Two Claviers in C minor (No. 1 of a set of three, B.-G. XXI), which is supposed to represent a vanished concerto for two violins in the same key. But this list, thinks Schweitzer, comprises only a few of the missing works for violin and orchestra.

Furthermore—to add to the excitements in store for the student of Bach— those violin concertos which we actually possess in that form are duplicated in clavier versions: thus the E major Violin Concerto is the D major Concerto for clavier (No. 3 of the seven for solo clavier and orchestra: B.-G. XVII); the A minor Violin Concerto is equivalent to that in G minor for clavier and orchestra (No. 7, B.-G. XVII); and the D minor Concerto for two violins is paralleled by No. 3 of the set of concertos for two claviers and orchestra, transposed to C minor (B.-G. XXI).

It is supposed that, in the case of these duplications, the violin form was primary. That Bach undertook the rearrangement of his violin concertos as works for clavier and orchestra 'merely because he did not care to write new clavier concertos,' is disputed with some heat by Spitta. 'It is an assumption,' he says, 'utterly contrary to Bach's character, and is disproved even by the large number of these rearrangements. No doubt he felt that the style of his violin concertos was so much moulded by his clavier style that their true nature could be fully brought out only in the shape of clavier concertos. It cannot be denied that many details, and notably the cantabile passages, lose in effect in the clavier arrangement; but as a whole we must regard them as new and higher developments, rather than arrangements.'

But Schweitzer is less reverent. Bach, he says, 'needed clavier concertos when he directed the Telemann Society, which he began to conduct at Leipzig in 1729, also for the little family concerts at his own home. . . These transcriptions are of unequal worth. Some were made carefully and with art, while others betray impatience in the accomplishment of an uninteresting task. . . Violin effects to which he could easily have given a pianistic turn are not remodeled at all; later on, he improves them here and there in the score, but leaves them as they are in the clavier part. The reason for this was that he himself played the clavier part, and did as he pleased with the notes before him, making a new part out of them.' Schweitzer wonders how Bach could venture to entrust the two cantabile violin parts in the beautiful Largo of the D minor Double Concerto to the harpsichord, with its abrupt tone. 'Had he not done it himself, we should be protesting in his name today against so un-Bachlike a transcription.'

The A minor Concerto for Violin was described by Bach as *Concerto a violino certato, due violini, una viola, obligati, e basso continuo*. The parts are in the Berlin State Library. The first movement begins in A minor, 2-4 time (there is no tempo mark). The second movement is an Andante in C major, 4-4 time; the Finale is an 'Allegro assai' in A minor, 9-8 time. Joseph Hullmesberger, the elder (1828-93), wrote a cadenza for the violinist in the third movement.

The E major Concerto, as it stands in the *Bach-Gesellschaft* edition, is scored for solo violin, first and second violins, viola, and continuo. Of the first movement (Allegro, 2-2), Spitta remarks that the charm of the working-out is especially remarkable, with the development cast in the three-section form frequently employed in the violin sonatas with harpsichord. The second movement (Adagio, C-sharp minor, 3-4) suggests to Schweitzer the thought of Destiny—just why is not entirely clear. 'The violin,' he says, 'moves about over a "basso ostinato." We involuntarily associate them (the adagio movements of the A minor and E major concertos) with the idea of Fate. The other movements are full of an unconquerable joy of life, that sings its song of triumph in the first movement and the last "Allegro assai," E major, 3-8.'

The autograph score of the D minor Concerto for two violins is no longer in existence, but a set of manuscript parts, copied sometime in the eighteenth century, might at one time have been seen in the State Library at Berlin. The parts for the two solo violins are in Bach's handwriting. The concerto comprises three movements: Vivace, D minor, 2-2; 'Largo ma non tanto,' F major, 12-8; Allegro, D minor, 3-4. The scoring of the accompaniment is for strings and continuo.

• THE MASS IN B MINOR

More than two centuries ago (on July 27, 1733) Johann Sebastian Bach laid before his sovereign, Augustus III, an humble appeal for patronage, accompanied by what he described as a 'trifling example' of his skill as a composer. The 'trifling example' consisted of the first two sections of a work whose greater pages have for over a century been regarded as the ultimate examples of sublimity in musical art—the B minor Mass.

Many questions concerning the Mass that used to perplex even its most learned students have been disposed of by the incredibly patient and exhaustive researches and conclusions of that most clear-minded and authoritative of Bach scholars, Dr. Charles Sanford Terry, the value of whose contributions to the world's knowledge of Bach is beyond estimation. Dr. Terry disposes quite simply, for example, of that question which for so many years has vexed the Bachian commentators—the question whether the B minor Mass is Catholic or Protestant.

One of the many difficulties that beset earlier students of the B minor Mass arose, as Dr. Terry points out, from an incorrect understanding of the Lutheran Mass (or 'Messe') of Bach's day.

The term denoted [he says] the *Kyrie* and *Gloria*, sung at the beginning of the principal service (*Hauptgottesdienst*) on Sundays and festivals. Bach composed four Masses of this kind which, incorrectly distinguished as 'short,' are not Masses at all in the Roman sense. In its first state the Mass in B minor was of this kind: its score bears marks which suggest that, like them, it was used as a Lutheran 'Messe.' It differed from the other four in its larger proportions and in the comparative infrequency of adapted music in its movements.

At Dresden, on July 27, 1733, Bach presented its vocal and instrumental parts to his sovereign, Augustus III, as an 'insignificant example of my skill in *Musique*,' less with a view to its performance, as has been supposed, than as a proof of his competence to fill a post in the royal Kapelle—a favor tardily conferred in 1736. The parts, in Bach's and his wife's autograph, lay neglected in Augustus's Dresden palace. Meanwhile, Bach made additions to them which expanded the Lutheran 'Messe' into a complete Roman 'Missa.' Spitta supposed that he desired to ingratiate himself further with his Roman Catholic sovereign. But the conjecture is uncritical. The proportions of the stupendous work, even its literary text, forbade its use in the Roman ritual; nor, in fact, were its supplementary movements ever forwarded to Dresden to join the *Kyrie* and *Gloria*. Two reasons, themselves complementary, moved Bach to expand his original work. In the first place, the Mass is neither Roman nor Lutheran in intention and outlook, but the expression of a catholic Christianity. In the second place, Bach's genius was Teutonic in its inclination to complete a design. If another reason is sought, it is found in the compulsion to express himself in an art-form which he had studied deeply.

It would be difficult to say when the B minor Mass was 'composed'; for much of the music was borrowed by Bach from others of his works—for the most part, from the rich treasure house of his Church Cantatas. The score of the Mass contains, in round numbers, 2300 measures. Of these, 638, or somewhat less than one-third, are in the movements that Bach drew from his earlier works. But it seems probable that the *construction* of the work, as distinguished from its composition, fell within the years 1733-7 If any should feel disturbed by the fact that the B minor Mass is in large part a compilation, a sane and penetrating comment of Dr. Terry's will supply the fitting reassurance. For it is true, as he says, that 'except in so far as it illuminates the ways of genius, it is of no aesthetic value to discover the proportion of original to borrowed material in the work. The Mass is the design of a superb architect, perfect in proportion and balance. Even in their adaptation, the borrowed movements reveal his creative genius, while a collation of them with their originals exposes the sensitiveness of his judgment and self-criticism.'

Although Bach's text of the liturgy adheres in general to the Ordinary of the Roman Mass, which comprises five sections (*Kyrie—Gloria—Credo—Sanctus*

—*Agnus Dei*), the B minor Mass is unexampled in its immensity. Bach, as Terry points out, treats his text almost clause by clause, alternating choruses with arias and duets; so that each section equals, or exceeds, the dimensions of a cantata. The *Kyrie* is treated in three movements; the *Gloria* in eight; the *Credo* in eight; the *Sanctus* in three; the *Agnus Dei* in two—in all, twenty-four movements.

In the *Kyrie*, Bach deals with the six words of the text (*Kyrie eleison . . .* 'Lord, have mercy upon us'—*Christe eleison . . .* 'Christ, have mercy upon us'—*Kyrie eleison . . .* 'Lord, have mercy upon us') in three extensive and contrasted movements. The first of these movements is a five-part fugue on the first clause of the text (*Kyrie eleison*); the second is a duet for two sopranos on the clause, *Christe eleison*; the third is a four-part fugue on the third clause, *Kyrie eleison.*

In the stupendous first chorus of the *Kyrie*, as Dr. Terry remarks, 'Bach lifts the Mass in its opening four bars to an elevation that no other setting has approached. They are the anguished cry of sin-laden mortality, the passionate supplication of the Church Universal. Thereafter, each part enters the vast assembly on a fugal subject chromatic in structure, the music swelling with increasing urgency, as though the votaries were whipped with taunts of "call Him louder!", until it reaches its tremendous climax eight bars from the end. . . Throughout, the *Kyrie* paints a picture that was evidently very vivid to Bach's imagination. Its opening cry is as dramatic as the despairing "Help, Lord!" of Mendelssohn's *Elijah*, and identical in its significance.'

The second clause, *Christe eleison*, is a serene and confident invocation of the Second Person—'as though the preceding urgency of self-accusation had brought confidence in the divine forgiveness.'

In the third clause, *Kyrie eleison*, the music (again, a massive fugue) has the character of a lament.

In the *Kyrie*, we heard Bach's musical translation of the Church's petition to the Trinity. In the *Gloria*, Bach voices exultantly his homage to the Second Person—'Mediator, Priest, King'—throned above in splendor with the Father and the Holy Spirit. The opening chorus (No. 4) 'breathes the freshness of the first Christmas morn and the joy of the *hymnus angelicus*,' a mood which is carried over into the succeeding aria, *Laudamus te* (No. 5) with its delightful violin obbligato (in Bach's autograph score, the voice part is marked 'soprano 2ndo'). The following chorus, the *Gratias agimus* (No. 6), based on a modal subject, is the first of the borrowed movements: it is derived (as is the last movement of the Mass, the *Dona nobis pacem*) from the opening chorus of Cantata No. 29, *Wir danken dir, Gott*, composed for the inauguration of the Leipzig Town Council in St. Thomas's on August 27, 1731. In both the Cantata and in the Mass, the music is a song of thanksgiving. The remaining movements of the *Gloria* (Nos. 7, 8, 9, 10, 11) apostrophize the atoning sacrifice of Christ, his function as mediator, and his sovereignty.

No. 7, the *Domine Deus*, is a duet for soprano and tenor, with exquisite obbligati for flute and muted strings. The chorus which follows, the *Qui tollis* (No. 8), is one of Bach's supreme pages. It is a vision of Calvary, imagined and expressed with all of Bach's incomparable blend of loftiness and poignancy.

There are moments in this chorus—for example, the marvelous twenty measures beginning at the sixteenth bar—which seem to many students of the Mass
more extraordinary in their searching and unbearable beauty than even the
wonderful *Crucifixus*. The movement was borrowed from Cantata No. 46,
Schauet doch und sehet, a setting of Lamentations 1. 12: 'Behold, and see if
there be any sorrow like unto my sorrow.'

No. 9, *Qui sedes ad dexteram*, is a contralto aria (with oboe d'amore obbligato) and evokes an image of the Saviour pleading for mankind before His
Father. The bass aria that follows, *Quoniam tu solus sanctus*, proclaims the
holiness and supremacy of the Heavenly Father. Bach naïvely provided it
with an obbligato for a hunting horn, appropriate to the princely courts of his
time!

The last chorus of the *Gloria, Cum sancto Spiritu* (No. 11), after an opening
paean, turns into one of Bach's most dazzling and magnificent fugues and
projects an overwhelming vision of the glory of the Deity.

'The Nicene Creed,' remarks Dr. Terry dryly, 'does not lend itself to musical
exposition. Beethoven, Mozart, and Schubert were satisfied to give it a conventionally florid setting. Bach, on the other hand, was urgently drawn to
explore its dogmatic subtleties. The *Credo* of the Mass includes eight movements, all but two of which are choruses. No foundation less solid, Bach felt,
could support the faith it avows. The first movement, a chorus, *Credo in unum
Deum* (No. 12), is built upon an Intonation associated with the *Credo* for
more than fifteen hundred years.

'The text thereafter addresses the Three Persons in order. No. 13, a chorus,
Patrem omnipotentem, pictures God the Father throned amid the seraphic
trumpets. This is another borrowed movement, adapted from the opening
Chorus of Cantata No. 171, composed about 1730. The next four movements
(Nos. 14-17) declare the Church's faith in God the Son. No. 14, *Et in unum
Dominum*, is a duet for soprano and alto. No. 15, a chorus, *Et incarnatus est*,
was an afterthought. Originally its words were set to the music of the second
part of No. 14. Bach, however, felt the obligation to treat the Incarnation by
itself, and the music conveys with extraordinary sensitiveness the mystery the
simple words declare.'

With the next movement (No. 16), the *Crucifixus*, we reach another one of
Bach's incomparable utterances of exalted grief. The form of the movement is
a passacaglia, derived from an old Spanish dance in triple measure whose characteristic feature was a recurring ground bass. The form has been made familiar
to present-day audiences of symphony concerts by Stokowski's orchestral transcription of Bach's great organ work. In the *Crucifixus*, the genius displayed
is still more amazing: for here Bach uses what was originally a popular dance
form as the matrix for a tragic grief. In this case, the ground bass, a descending
chromatic phrase of four bars, thirteen times repeated, underlies the marvelous
structure of the voice parts, each of which enters separately, 'enunciating the
word "crucifixus" in amazed horror before the uplifted Cross and its drooping
burden. The last five bars, one of the greatest passages in all music, are sung
by the chorus alone, save for the throbbing of the basses—the falling voices,
at "sepultus est," seeming to lower the dead Christ into the tomb.' The change

of key at the final chord (from E minor to G major) is of indescribable effect. This, too, is a borrowed movement, derived from the opening chorus of Cantata No. 12, written in 1724 or 1725 for the Third Sunday after Easter.

With the next chorus, *Et resurrexit* (No. 17), we pass from the unutterable gloom and terror of Good Friday into the radiance of Easter Day. This is followed by a bass solo, *Et in Spiritum sanctum* (No. 18), with an accompaniment scored in the autograph for oboi d'amore and continuo. The *Credo* is concluded by a chorus, *Confiteor unum baptisma* (No. 19). 'The ancient Intonation of the "Confiteor" reaffirms the solidarity of the Christian faith.' An unforgettable feature of this chorus is the Adagio passage of twenty-six bars beginning at *Et expecto resurrectionem mortuorum*, a marvelous vision of an unimaginable new world, the Resurrection glimpsed with the incredulous awe of faith and ecstasy. Here, again, is the supreme Bach, the seer of apocalyptic wonders. The second part of the movement (derived from the first chorus of Cantata No. 120, *Gott, man lobet dich in der Stille*, composed about 1730) is a brilliant 'Vivace et Allegro.'

With the opening chorus (No. 20) of the *Sanctus*, we reach one of the towering peaks of music. Of this chorus, Schweitzer did not hesitate to say that 'there is hardly anything else in all music that expresses so perfectly the idea of the sublime.' Bach may well have remembered that passage in Isaiah wherein he read of the choiring seraphim, how 'one cried unto another, and said, "Holy, holy, holy, is the Lord of hosts: the whole earth is full of his glory."' Parry finds in Bach's music 'the suggestion of multitudinous voices singing in adoration, and the rolling of tumultuous harmonies through the infinite spaces of heaven'—an antiphony of the celestial hosts, the first and second sopranos and first altos voicing one angelic choir; the second altos, tenors, and basses the second. In the basses, we hear one of the mightiest of Bach's 'step' motives—a great, striding subject that moves in hugely sweeping octaves, bestriding the limitless firmament.

The brilliant *Osanna* (No. 21), a double chorus, is derived from the opening chorus of the secular *Cantata gratulatoria*, 'Preise dein Glücke,' composed in 1734 to celebrate the accession of Augustus III, on which occasion it greeted Augustus in the market place when he paid an official visit to Leipzig. Yet the music (in the rhythm of a polonaise) is superbly expressive, in the Mass, of the jubilation of Palm Sunday.

The *Benedictus* (No. 22), set as a tenor aria, is in striking contrast to the glories and immensities of the foregoing numbers. The *Osanna* is repeated after the *Benedictus*.

The final section of the Mass consists of two numbers: the alto aria, *Agnus Dei* (No. 23)—founded upon an alto aria in the 'Ascension Oratorio,' Cantata No. 11, composed about 1735—and the chorus, *Dona nobis pacem* (No. 24), set to the music of the *Gratias agimus* in the Gloria.

The B minor Mass, despite the beauty and intimacy of some of the solo writing, is primarily a choral work, and its overwhelming greatness is to be found in those matchless expressions of the genius of Bach which, as one hears them or studies them or remembers them, seem to dwarf, for a while, all other music. There is nothing to be set beside the *Crucifixus*, with its sublimity of pity and of grief; and only Bach could have given us the glory of the *Sanctus*, with its sublimity of adoration, its choiring of the seraphic hosts, 'one crying unto another' in affirmation of the deathlessness of beauty and the holiness of those immortals who are pure in heart.

● THE ST. JOHN PASSION

Of the five settings of the Gospel narrative of the Passion which have at various times been attributed to Bach, two are lost, and one (the 'St. Luke Passion') is of doubtful authenticity. This leaves us with only two which we may confidently ascribe to Johann Sebastian: the 'Passion According to St. Matthew,' and the 'Passion According to St. John.' The more famous and indisputably greater of the two we have often with us, and small wonder. But why the 'St. John' is not more frequently heard would be hard to say, for the music is overflowing with the genius of Bach at its noblest and most profound.

The text of the *Johannespassion* is based chiefly on the eighteenth and nine-teenth chapters of St. John; but portions of it are founded on an egregious text devised by one Brockes, a member of the Town Council of Hamburg, which had previously been set to music by Handel, Keiser, and Mattheson. But Bach used Brockes' text in its original form only in certain arias and in the final chorus, *Ruhet wohl*; elsewhere he made his own adaptation of it, probably assisted by some poetic friend—some 'delicate, unknown poet,' as Schweitzer calls him—who may perhaps have supplied the text for a number of Bach's cantatas. The music of the *Johannespassion* was composed at Cöthen in the winter of 1722-3; it was probably sung at St. Thomas's Church, Leipzig, on Good Friday of 1723 (not 1724, as Spitta thought).

It has been said of the 'St. John Passion' that it is more dramatic, less lyrical and moving, than its better known companion, the 'Passion According to St. Matthew,' and Schweitzer builds up an elaborate argument in support of this view, based upon the special character of the Passion narrative in the Fourth Gospel. The Matthew Gospel, he tells us, yielded a series of short scenes which invited association with lyrical meditations; 'but in the earlier work the text, by reason of its more extended and dramatic character, has few points of repose, and the interpolation of the arias does not always seem inevitable.'

This opinion is not easy to share. The note of tension and agitation and dramatic excitement of which some have spoken is undoubtedly present in the music of the 'St. John Passion'—especially in certain of the choruses. But the brooding tenderness and deep compassion with which Bach describes and meditates upon the incomparable drama are reflected in page after page of gravely poignant beauty—a beauty and tenderness of the most subduing elo-quence. In the words of Jesus; in many passages of the narrative given to the Evangelist; in the famous arioso, *Betrachte, meine Seel'*; in the aria *Es ist vollbracht*—one of Bach's most wonderful inspirations; in the chorales: in these pages Bach is the matchless threnodist, the pitiful singer of the woes of men, the great-hearted celebrant of the immemorial tragedy. And in such moments as the final page of the last chorale, *Ach Herr, lass dein' lieb' Engelein*, he is, as he alone knew how to be, the sublime comforter, the maker of music so transcendent in its divine benignity and tenderness that there are no words with which to speak of it that would not seem impertinent.

It would be idle to pretend that this slighter and earlier work could ever replace its tremendous successor, the *Matthäuspassion*; it would be idle to deny that there are *longueurs* in the score, arid stretches in which Bach is simply formalizing, or following the easier way, or yielding to some moment of creative dejection or disheartenment or fatigue: there are such moments in almost all the great works, even the mighty B minor Mass. The fact is of little consequence. What matters is the incredible height of lofty feeling and inspired utterance that is sustained, the overwhelming pathos and majesty and dramatic power and spiritual greatness that speak from page after page. The 'St. John Passion' is an irreplaceable work, with its own special quality of beauty and expressiveness.

• The St. Matthew Passion

On Good Friday, 1729, there was performed, at the New Church, in Leipzig, a Passion composed by Gottlieb Fröber, who had his eye on the vacant post of cantor at that church. It was an important occasion, the news event of that day, and all the musical quality of Leipzig were there. On the same day, and at the same hour, another Passion was being performed at another Leipzig church, St. Thomas's; but it seems to have attracted little attention. It was a setting of the 'Passion According to St. Matthew,' composed by the cantor of St. Thomas's, Johann Sebastian Bach.

Fröber and his Passion have long since been swallowed by Time's insatiable maw; but today the 'St. Matthew Passion' holds its audiences enthralled and stirred, more than two centuries after Bach first conducted the work at St. Thomas's in Leipzig on that distant Good Friday afternoon, and went home to supper with his considerable family, doubtless reconciled to the fact that his music had fallen flat.

It seems never to have occurred to Bach to wonder whether the congregation that heard his church works understood them. He wrote as well as he could and dedicated the result to heaven. 'Like all music,' he remarked, in setting down the rules and principles of accompaniment that he made for his pupils in 1738, 'the figured bass should have no other end and aim than the glory of God and the re-creation of the soul.'

The 'J. J.' which appears on the upper left corner of the first page of the autograph score of the 'St. Matthew Passion' (the introduction of the chorus *Kommt, ihr Töchter*) meant *Jesu juva*—'Help me, Jesus!'; and, as we listen to that amazing work which has outlasted the drums and tramplings of innumerable conquests—not resting quietly under them, to paraphrase Sir Thomas Browne, but poised unshakable above them—we may easily believe that some tide not wholly terrestrial flowed through the absorbed and worshiping spirit of Bach as he composed those pages of sorrowful, solacing tenderness, with their transported beauty, their touching devoutness, their measureless humanity. Even a pagan of today, as Parry truly observes, can understand, through the power and sincerity of this wonderful music, something of what was in the mind and heart of Bach when he wrote the line that is set down in his *Orgel-büchlein:* 'For the Glory of the Most High, and for the instruction of my neighbor.'

For his instruction, yes: his instruction in the truth that there is continuous vitality in all art that is fervently conceived by a master, even after the conditions that surrounded its conception have passed forever. Bach wrote his church music—his Passions especially—to meet the needs and impulses of a religious outlook far removed from our contemporary sympathies. If our love for his music depended on our response to the characteristic blend of pietism and naïveté which underlies its subject matter, we should feel remote from it indeed. It is a striking and significant fact that one of the most moving pages in the 'St. Matthew Passion,' the soprano aria, *Blute nur, du liebes Herz,* is the expression of an emotional state so incomprehensible to the modern mind that even the apostolic Spitta found himself unable to interpret it. Yet the music, living essentially in a spiritual world independent of the unstable theologies of man, speaks to us with unaltered, unalterable eloquence.

We cannot possibly recover for ourselves the point of view of the worshiper of 1729, listening with emotion to the words of the 'St. Matthew Passion,' no matter how the music may have perplexed him and left him cold. ('Some high officials and well-born ladies in one of the galleries began to sing the first chorale with great devotion from their books. But as the theatrical music proceeded, they were thrown into the greatest wonderment, saying to each other, "What does it all mean?" While one old lady, a widow, exclaimed, "God help us! 'tis surely an opera-comedy!" ') That amorous imagery, for example, in which the Teutonic pietism of Bach's time loved to clothe its religious ecstasies, is for the modern mind a little mawkish and repellent; and though Schweitzer and others insist that Bach was sharply opposed to the pietism of his day, there is no doubt that he was greatly, though perhaps unconsciously, affected by it. Schweitzer admits, indeed, its influence on Bach's Passions and cantatas, which were so direct a product of the religious poetry of the early eighteenth century.

Bach was essentially a Teutonic mystic, and he never became anything else; but by virtue of the unsurpassable vitality and strength and power of his musical imagination, he was able to transmute the weakly sentimental and somewhat morbid religious emotion of certain parts of his texts into a profundity of expression that goes to the roots of mystical subjectivity and releases a timeless spiritual beauty. In a sense that modern psychology thoroughly understands, he truly sublimated the religious impulses of his day.

What does it matter to us, furthermore, that the principal melody in the 'St. Matthew Passion,' that of the great chorale *O Haupt voll Blut und Wunden* (Bach used this melody five times in the Passion, the Christmas Oratorio, and in four of the cantatas) was originally the tune of an old German love song, *Mein G'muth ist mir verwirret von einer Jungfrau zart?* What does it matter that the noble melody of *Was mein Gott will* in the 'St. Matthew Passion' was originally a little French love song of the sixteenth century, one of the *Trente et quatre chansons musicales* published at Paris in 1529 by Pierre Attaignant? Bach used the tune in six of his church cantatas, as well as in the

'St. Matthew Passion,' probably in blissful ignorance of its origin. It served him superbly for the expression of religious faith, and for us it is simply a marvelous piece of music.

How little, too, Bach's naïve tonal symbolism means to us, and how much the beauty of the musical idea itself! The expressive four-note figure on the work *krähen* in that portion of the Evangelist's narrative which tells us how 'Peter remembered the words of Jesus, which said unto him, "Before the cock crow thou shalt deny me thrice," ' was intended by Bach to mimic the crowing of a cock. We know that the audiences of the old Passions awaited with excitement this traditional mimicry of the cock's crowing, and applauded it. Sheibe tells of a certain performance of a Passion in Franconia at which the crowing of the cock was realistically imitated by one of the musicians on his oboe, concealed behind the organ, to the great delight of his hearers.

The music of the 'St. Matthew Passion' is full of such naïve literalism— 'cloud' music, 'thunder' music, music to represent the movement of the sower's arm, and the scourge, and the stumbling feet of Jesus. Bach had a rich supply of more or less standardized musical formulas intended to symbolize all kinds of ideas and emotions and external images. He had 'wave' motives, and 'step' motives, and motives intended to suggest 'angels' and 'grief' and 'terror' and the dropping of tears. But it is exceedingly doubtful if many listeners today will realize that the voice of the Evangelist in his moving narrative of the bitter grief of Peter is imitating the crowing of a cock. It is far more likely that they will simply be touched by the deep pathos of the music, a pathos that survives the centuries.

And so Bach the marvelous tone poet, the master of musical beauty, survives Bach who was merely a man of his time—Bach the pietist, the simple-minded literalist, the cantor of the Thomaskirche, producing, unknown to himself and his generation, imperishable masterworks. We know that in the alto recitative, *Ach Golgotha, unsel'ges Golgotha*, Bach intended to evoke by his familiar representative device of pizzicato strings the distant tolling of funeral bells; but as we listen to this piercing movement we are aware only of the communication of an ageless grief, the grief that is aroused in the tone poet's heart and in our own by contemplation of the dramatized tragedy of human sacrifice and suffering. The negligible words are his librettist's; the musical symbolism is personal to the eighteenth-century mind of Bach; but what is universal and deathless is the implicit humanity of the composer's speech. Hearing it, we are aware of the contents of his brooding spirit, eloquent across the years.

TRANSCRIPTIONS

‡The practice of performing various of Bach's compositions for organ, for clavier, for violin, for the voice, in modern transcriptions for full orchestra is one that has grown in recent years—under the impetus, no doubt, provided by Leopold Stokowski, who during his long tenure as conductor of the Philadelphia Orchestra himself made and frequently performed a great many such transcriptions. Exception is sometimes taken to the practice, though it is

difficult to see in it, especially in relation to Bach's music, any fundamental impiety: Bach himself, as the notes above clearly show (see those on the clavier and violin concertos), was an inveterate transcriber of his own and other men's music. No cries of 'Sacrilege!' greet the performance of a Bach transcription of a Vivaldi concerto, or of a version for clavier, by Bach, of music he originally conceived for the violin. Perhaps the only valid question to be raised in this connection is one of taste—the taste of the transcriber and that of the performer; and in the case of orchestral transcriptions, of the conductor—and questions of taste are notoriously difficult, if not impossible, to answer to the satisfaction of all. It remains a fact that orchestral transcriptions of many of Bach's organ works (especially) have been made in modern times not only by virtuoso conductors but also by composers of unassailable sobriety, not to say severity, of mind, and that through the medium of such transcriptions a vast public has come to a knowledge and love of many of Bach's greatest pages, of which it might otherwise have remained ignorant (for while the opportunity to hear these works in their original form may be said always to exist, it is not likely to be seized upon by the average concertgoer).

The notes below have been selected from many which the annotator wrote on transcriptions of organ works by Bach. The full list is a long one, and it has been thought advisable here to distinguish only those works that are performed with the greatest frequency.‡

• ORGAN FANTASIA AND FUGUE IN G MINOR

The Fantasia in G minor, probably composed at Cöthen about 1720, must be ranked among the most magnificent works in Bach's vast repertoire of masterpieces. Here he is in almost his grandest vein, exulting in one of those quasi-improvisational essays at which he so easily beat Reinken and Buxtehude and others at their own game. Here are those dramatic declamatory recitatives, those tremendous chord progressions with their chains of suspensions, audacious dissonances, and modulations, those mighty scale passages, ascending and descending, 'which rise and fall like the waves of the sea in a storm': music in which Bach, patterning after the style of the Northern School of organists, carried this type of music to a pitch of splendor and expressiveness that makes all other writing for the instrument seem pallid and tentative in comparison.

As for the Fugue (known to organists as the 'Great' G minor), Georg Pölchau over a century ago declared it to be 'the very best pedal piece by Herr Johann Sebastian Bach.' Spitta draws attention to the contrast which it offers to the Fantasia by 'the grand, calm modulations and strict four-part treatment; by the soaring imagination, the lavish and inexhaustible variety of form, the crystal lucidity and modest naturalism, the lofty gravity and deep contentment which strike awe into the hearer, and at the same time tempt him to shout with joy'—a happy summarization!

The wonders of Bach's virtuosity here are the more remarkable because, as Harvey Grace points out in his admirable study of the organ works, Bach handicaps himself with a regular countersubject, for the treble of measures

10-12 often accompanies the subject and countersubject in triple counterpoint.

Griepenkerl, in his introduction to the Peters Edition of Bach's organ works, tells us that in no manuscript were the Fantasia and the Fugue found together. However, on the back of an old copy of the Fantasia was written the subject of the Fugue, with an indication that it should follow the Fantasia. Acting upon this authority, Griepenkerl printed them together for the first time.

● ORGAN FUGUE IN G MINOR (The 'Little' G minor)

This work is known to organists as the 'Little,' or 'Short,' G minor Fugue, to distinguish it from the 'Great' Fugue in the same key (see above). It is one of the compositions of Bach's Weimar period (1708-17). Spitta praises its 'very beautiful theme' and the masterly flow of the writing. One of its prominent features, he says, is 'the counterpoint on the theme, which is always the same, and only in one part, since notes to fill up the harmony, and the doubled sixth (bars 41-42), can scarcely be considered as such. It is only from the fifth bar before the end that it is in three parts.'

● ORGAN PASSACAGLIA AND FUGUE IN C MINOR

Bach composed his Passacaglia and Fugue, in all probability, during the latter part of his Weimar period. The autograph has disappeared, although it is known to have existed up to the middle of the nineteenth century. Bach wrote the work originally for a two-manual clavicembalo with pedals, and afterward arranged it for organ.

A passacaglia (or *passecaille*) was originally an old Spanish or Italian dance in triple time, in which a short bass theme of two, four, or eight bars was incessantly repeated. Musicians understand by the term as applied to instrumental music a piece constructed on a recurring theme. The passacaglia form is closely allied to that of the chaconne (or *ciacona*), though the theorists usually make this distinction between the two: in the chaconne, the theme reappears in the upper and inner parts, whereas in the passacaglia form it is confined to the bass. As Bach in his Passacaglia does not restrict his subject to the bass, the work has been described by some theorists as actually a combination of the two forms.

The eight-bar theme of Bach's Passacaglia is given out at the beginning, in C minor (in the organ form of the piece, it is announced by the pedals alone). On the basis of this theme, Bach constructs twenty variations.

He is assumed to have written this work under the influence of Buxtehude, and to have patterned it after him in consorting the passacaglia with a fugue. But whereas Buxtehude placed his fugue at the beginning, Bach, with his sure sense of climax, places his at the end, linking it with his Passacaglia by partial community of theme. It is a double Fugue, and for one of its subjects, he uses the first half of his Passacaglia theme, while the other is new—a figure in eighth-notes, thrice repeated, the repetitions separated by rests. The work ends with a climax of incomparable grandeur.

● ORGAN PRELUDE AND FUGUE IN E-FLAT MAJOR ('St. Anne')

Here are combined the organ Prelude that begins Part III of Bach's *Clavier-übung* and the Fugue in the same key that stands at the end of the book.

Bach's *Clavierübung* is an extensive work in four parts, containing both organ and clavier music, which appeared between 1731 and 1742. It was probably the first of Bach's works to be engraved. Bach's title for Part III, consisting chiefly of organ music, is as follows:

The Third Part of the Clavier Exercise, containing various Preludes on the Catechism and other Hymns, for the Organ. Composed for amateurs and lovers of such works, and for their recreation, by Johann Sebastian Bach, Composer to the Royal and Electoral Court of Poland-Saxony, Kapellmeister and Director of the Music, Leipsic. Published by the Author.

This third part of the *Clavierübung* begins with a Prelude in E-flat, and ends with a Fugue, also in E-flat—the famous one known as 'St. Anne's,' from the similarity of its opening subject to the hymn tune of that name. Between the Prelude and the final Fugue stands a group of twenty-one movements, founded upon or associated with chorales, and employing hymns which illustrate the Lutheran Catechism.

It is not known whether Bach linked the Prelude with the Fugue in performance. They are, however, joined in the edition of Bach's works published by Griepenkerl and Roitsch.

● ORGAN TOCCATA AND FUGUE IN C MAJOR

Bach's Organ Toccata and Fugue in C major was probably composed during his Weimar period (1708-17). It has been conjectured that it was one of the works written for his recital tours. Pirro thinks that this Toccata may date from the journey which Bach made to Cassel in 1714 to examine a newly restored organ. At least the famous pedal passage in the Prelude recalls that pedal solo executed by Bach before the Hereditary Prince of Hesse with such virtuosity that the Prince drew from his finger a valuable ring and presented it to the embarrassed Johann Sebastian. 'One might have believed,' says Adlung, 'that his feet were winged, with such agility did they move over the keys which caused the powerful basses to respond. If the dexterity of his feet drew from the Prince so rich a present, what should he have given him in recognition of the genius of his hands?'

The work consists of three sections. It opens with a Prelude, which itself is subdivided. There is first an ornate introduction, a bravura passage on the manual closing with a long and remarkable pedal solo, nineteen bars in length. This pedal solo is regarded by organists as one of the finest ever written. It is sometimes compared with the passage with which Franck opens his Finale in B-flat, and with another example in the D minor Symphony of Guilmant. This pedal solo leads into a vigorous Allegro movement, unlike any to be found in Bach's previous organ music. It is possible to detect here the influence of the Italian chamber music with which Bach was occupied in his capacity as Kammermusikus at the Weimar Court. Harvey Grace thinks that Bach tried to adapt the concerto form to the organ by imposing its idiom and construction on the Toccata. The result is a not wholly satisfactory hybrid —a conclusion at which Bach himself may have arrived, for he made no further attempts in the same direction.

This Allegro (built on two subjects derived from the pedal solo) is followed by an Adagio, a grave and beautiful instrumental song of unusual character: for it is sustained by a homophonic accompaniment of a type unparalleled in Bach's music; though the movement recalls in other respects the slow movement of the Italian Concerto (for solo harpsichord). This Adagio suggests also, perhaps even more strikingly, one of the slow movements for violin with cembalo accompaniment which drew from Bach those utterances of rapt lyric meditation so typical of him in his more emotional moods.

The Adagio is separated from the spirited 6-8 Fugue which follows it by a transition through an extraordinary series of suspensions somewhat in the style of Buxtehude, but used by Bach with a power and immensity of effect beyond the power of his predecessor.

• ORGAN TOCCATA AND FUGUE IN D MINOR

Bach's Toccata and Fugue in D minor for organ (not the 'Dorian' Toccata and Fugue in the same key) dates from the early part of Bach's residence at Weimar, where for nine years (1708-17) he was Court Organist and Kammermusikus.

It cannot have been altogether an exhilarating post. At 'Wilhelmsburg,' the palace of Duke Wilhelm Ernst, everyone had to turn in at nine o'clock in summer, eight o'clock in winter. The Duke's favorite indoor activity was theological discussion, and in 1710 (two years after Bach entered his service) he assembled at the Palace a synod of one hundred pastors. Rebuilding seminaries was one of his recreations, and he had an ungovernable passion for numismatics. His face was sharp and meager, with a retreating forehead and a jutting chin.

But despite the synod of one hundred Lutheran pastors and the rigorous bedtime (or perhaps because of them), Bach turned out at Weimar some of his most enlivened and brilliant music. His chief organ works of the concert type belong to these Weimar years.

The word 'toccata' was derived from the Italian *toccare:* to touch, to strike, move, excite, play upon. When the term found its way into the nomenclature of music, it was used at first to describe a composition designed to display the characteristics of music written for keyboard instruments, chiefly the organ, and especially to exhibit the touch and execution of the performer. According to the definition of Michael Praetorious, it meant originally a free prelude, or introduction. In old examples by Andrea Gabrieli (1510-86) and Claudio Merulo (1533-1604), the Toccata begins with full harmonies, followed by running passagework interspersed with brief fugal periods; in which it exhibits the essential character of the toccata as a brilliant showpiece, generally with the flavor of an improvisation.

This D minor Toccata, with its appended Fugue, constitutes one of the most brilliant of Bach's concert works of the virtuoso type; and it is also an extraordinarily dramatic, imaginative, and distinguished piece of music.

The opening Toccata is one of those fiery and rhapsodic movements which Bach handled with such consummate effectiveness. Written under the influence of Buxtehude, it is nevertheless unmistakably Bach: in the freshness and vitality of its invention, in its enormous strength, and especially in those contrasts of dazzling bravura passages and great chordal masses of titanic breadth and power.

The Fugue, 'although very free in appearance,' as Marcel Dupré remarks of it, 'contains the essentials.' It is based on a subject the melodic form of which is outlined through swirling and broken harmonies. At the eighty-fifth measure, Bach begins to work back to the mood of the Toccata, and winds up with a coda of gigantic strength and overwhelming majesty.

• THE CHORALE-PRELUDES

Organ movements based upon chorales were among Bach's earliest attempts at composition. It is probable that his first writing for the organ was a treatment of a chorale melody. He worked intermittently in this field throughout his life, and ended his career, as he had begun it, with an organ piece of a similar kind; for he dictated a chorale-prelude as he lay, nearly blind, on his deathbed.

Bach himself collected almost a hundred of his chorale-preludes into five sets. The first of these includes the forty-six pieces in the *Orgelbüchlein* ('Little Organ Book'), dating from about 1717, when Bach was thirty-two years old. They were composed partly at Weimar (probably while Bach was languishing in jail, where he was imprisoned for a month by the Grand Duke) and were written out later, after his arrival at Cöthen. Twenty-two years later, in 1739, Bach published the third part of the *Clavierübung*, consisting chiefly of organ works, and among these are twenty-one chorale-preludes. Between 1747 and 1749, Schübler, a publisher, issued six of Bach's chorale-preludes, arrangements (made by Bach himself) of three-part chorale arias from the cantatas. The famous set of 'Eighteen Chorale-Preludes' were collected and revised, and perhaps in some cases composed, at Leipzig during the last days of Bach's life. Besides these collections, there are a large number—fifty or so—of miscellaneous chorale-preludes, many of them probably of early date and some of them dull and unrepresentative; and there are others (collected in Vol. xl of the *Bach-Gesellschaft* edition) whose authenticity is doubtful. This makes, all in all, about 140 chorale-preludes which may be attributed to Bach.

It may be said that those who do not know the chorale-preludes are unaware of Bach in almost his profoundest and most intimate phase. Spitta did not exaggerate when he declared that Bach 'went to the utmost limits of absorbed subjectivity' in his chorale-preludes; nor did Parry when he said that in them Bach 'seems to be communing with his own spirit'—that he included in them 'some wonderful innermost human documents of the greatest fascination'; and that his deep love of the national chorales 'made him deal with them as an artist might who had to make a casket for some inestimable treasure which deeply moved his romantic and imaginative faculties and through them brought into play his highest artistic powers.' Nor do we think that Ernest Newman goes a syllable too far when he asserts, in his admirable preface to the collected chorale-preludes, that these organ works are 'the key to the very heart of Bach. If everything else of his were lost, from them we could reconstruct him in all his pathos and almost all his grandeur.'

CHRIST LAG IN TODESBANDEN ('Christ lay in bonds of death'). The chorale melody is drawn from Johann Walther's setting of Luther's Easter hymn of the same name, first published in 1524. Bach's most conspicuous use of the melody is in his chorale cantata, also similarly entitled, composed for Easter Day, 1724. Here the melody is introduced into each movement. The original of the transcription now often heard in the concert room is to be found in the *Orgelbüchlein.*

HERZLICH THUT MICH VERLANGEN ('My heart is filled with longing'). This is one of the most searching and beautiful of Bach's treatments of the hymn tunes of the Lutheran Church. The chorale melody that forms the basis of the prelude was composed by Hans Leo Hassler in 1601 as the setting for a secular love song, 'Mein G'müt ist mir verwirret von einer Jungfrau zart.' Hassler's love ditty was first published in Hassler's *Lustgarten Neuer Teutscher Gesang, Balletti, Galliarden, und Intraden,* issued at Nuremberg in 1601. Like innumerable other sixteenth- and seventeenth-century tunes of slightly frivolous connotation, Hassler's melody was pressed into the service of the Church (which has always been admirably realistic in such matters); and a dozen years after Hassler first published it as a love song, we find the melody, its bright gaze demurely veiled, associated with Christoph Knoll's hymn, 'Herzlich thut mich verlangen' (*Harmoniae sacrae,* 1613). Later, it was used with Schneegass' hymn, 'Ach Herr, mich armer Sünder' (1620), and, still later, with Gerhardt's 'O Haupt voll Blut und Wunden' (1656).

Bach employed the melody, in connection with all three of the hymns, in various works. It is best known through his use of it in the 'St. Matthew Passion,' where it is the predominant chorale melody. It appears there five times, as the theme of the chorales Nos. 21, 23, 53, 63, and 72. Bach used the melody also in the 'Christmas Oratorio,' in four of the cantatas, and in the *Choralgesänge.*

ICH RUF' ZU DIR, HERR JESU CHRIST ('I call on Thee, Lord Jesus'). The original of this transcription is the like-named chorale-prelude in Bach's *Orgelbüchlein,* a collection of short movements based on those chorales which are the mainspring of Bach's art in its religious phase. The autograph of the *Orgelbüchlein,* a small quarto of ninety-two sheets bound in paper boards (at one time in the State Library at Berlin) is thus entitled:

A Little Organ-Book, wherein the beginner may learn to perform chorales of every kind, and also acquire skill in the use of the pedal, which is treated uniformly obbligato throughout.

> To the honor of the Lord Most High
> And that my neighbor may be taught thereby.

Composed by Johann Sebastian Bach, *pro tempore* Kapellmeister to His Serene Highness the Prince of Anhalt Cöthen.

The *Orgelbüchlein* is a fragment, representing a small part of an extensive scheme which Bach never accomplished. Of the ambitious program that he planned, a little more than one-quarter was carried into effect. There are 64 completed movements in the collection, but Bach had projected 164. The Prelude on *Ich ruf' zu dir* is the only completed number in the section 'Christian Life and Experience,' of Part II. The music is brooding and wistful, and touched with that fathomless tenderness wherewith Bach so often turns the heart to water. Bach wove this exquisite little Prelude (it is only sixteen measures long) upon the loom of the anonymous melody which was published with Johannes Agricola's hymn in 1529. Bach used the same tune also in his 177th cantata, of the same title, and in the 185th, *Barmherziges Herze der ewigen Liebe*.

NUN KOMM, DER HEIDEN HEILAND ('Come, Redeemer of our race'). The chorale melody on which Bach's organ prelude is based is associated with Luther's Advent or Christmas hymn, *Nun komm, der Heiden Heiland*, a translation of the *Veni Redemptor gentium* of St. Ambrose, published in 1524 with the melody, a simplification of that of the Latin hymn.

WACHET AUF, RUFT UNS DIE STIMME ('Sleepers, wake! a voice is calling'). This is the first of the set of six chorale-preludes which Bach put together in his later years for issue by Schübler, a publisher of Zelle; the collection appeared not long after Bach's death. The chorale-prelude is Bach's own adaptation of a chorus from the cantata of the same title, No. 140, composed at Leipzig about 1731. The melody is that of Philipp Nicolai's hymn, published in 1599, and Bach's elaboration of it for organ is associated with the second stanza of the hymn [which sets forth the parable of the Wise and Foolish Virgins]. 'Bach's imagination,' remarks Whittaker in his admirable study of the cantatas, 'was brought to a white heat by the imagery of the parable . . . by the vision of the City of Jerusalem aroused in the dead of night with the sudden and enthralling announcement of the coming of the Heavenly Bridegroom, of the mingled confusion, alarm, despair, and joy which would follow such an awakening. . .'

The poetic subject of the music is conjectured to be that of the symbolic bridal procession. The delightful movement which constitutes the chorale-prelude inspired by this dramatic concept 'has the intention of a dance tune . . . Bach may have had in mind the allegorical procession of the Betrothed and the joyous attendance of the Virgins, whose gestures have a wayward grace suggestive of Botticelli.' Parry thinks that the idea of the Virgins of the allegory participating in the welcome of the Heavenly Bridegroom may well have suggested this music to Bach's vividly pictorial imagination.

WIR GLAUBEN ALL' AN EINEN GOTT ('We believe in one God'). The original of this transcription is among the chorale-preludes to be found in Part III of the *Clavierübung*. In Bach's scheme, this chorale-prelude on *Wir glauben all' an einen Gott* (together with a shorter movement in the *Clavierübung*, a fughetta for manuals only, on the same chorale) stands for the Creed among the catechism hymns. Luther's hymn, *Wir glauben all' an einen Gott*, is a free version of the Nicene Creed, and was first published, with the melody, in Johann Walther's Hymn Book, at Wittenberg, in 1524. The hymn was sung at the funeral of Luther's patron, Friedrich the Wise of Saxony, in 1525, and was used as a funeral hymn at a later period. During the Reformation, it was generally sung after the sermon. The tune itself is anonymous, but was probably derived from the plain song of the Creed, and was adapted by Walther. Bach's version of it conforms closely to the original.

Bach's organ prelude on the chorale is a fugue, often known as the 'Giant Fugue' because of the great step-like figure for the pedals that strides upward through the compass of an octave. Professor Terry thinks that these pedal passages symbolize 'the impregnable foundation on which rests the faith of the Church'; and he compares them with the structure of pedal crotchets on which Bach builds the *Credo in unum Deum* and *Confiteor* of the B minor Mass.

Béla Bartók

1881-1945

Béla Bartók's father, director of an agricultural school and a good amateur musician, died when his son was eight, and Bartók's mother was obliged to seek her living as a teacher in elementary schools. She had given her son his first music lessons at the age of six. At nine, he began to compose small piano pieces, and at ten he appeared in public as pianist and composer. Two years later he and his mother settled in Pressburg, the most musically enlightened of the Hungarian cities of that period, and there Bartók heard much music, orchestral, operatic, chamber; steeped himself in the classics and in Brahms, and experimented with music of his own. In 1899, he went to Budapest, where he remained until 1903. During this period he wearied of his former idol, Brahms, and turned for comfort to Liszt and Wagner, found them dust and ashes, and discovered joyfully the art of Richard Strauss. But here, like Zarathustra, Bartók found only delusion and satiety. Shortly after this, his attention was drawn to the study of Hungarian folk music. His researches, in which he had the collaboration of his compatriot Zoltán Kodaly, demonstrated that the genuine traditional folk music of Hungary is a far different thing from the comparatively modern gypsy music exploited by Liszt and by popularizers less admirable than he, and Bartók's own later work was steeped in the somberness and wildness of this ancient, authentic music of the peasantry, which derives largely from the old ecclesiastical modes. As a composer, Bartók passed through various phases, the discontinuity of which was apparent only, not real. There was a time when one might have taken him for one of the gifted gamins of modern music—when he seemed an incorrigible farceur, a comedic revolutionist (though always he was, intermittently, a poet, and a musician of uncommon technical adroitness). Later, he discovered—so it appeared—the potency of a tonal speech stripped of all sensuousness, a new language, harsh, abrupt, austere. Yet to some it was clear, from the beginning, that here was an undoubted master, a musician of dynamic and passionate imagination, ruthlessly logical, a cerebral rhapsodist, a tone poet who was both an uncompromising modernist and a reviver of an ancient past.

● Music for Strings, Percussions, and Celeste

This work was completed at Budapest in the autumn of 1936, and was published in the following year. Bartók does not call his work a 'suite,' but it bears certain obvious resemblances to that highly respectable form. In the first movement, Bartók presents for fugal treatment a subject of anonymous tonality and wayward intervallic design, stated pianissimo by the muted violas ('Andante tranquillo'). There is an incessant change of time signatures—8-8, 12-8, 7-8, 9-8, 10-8, 5-8, 6-8, 11-8. The movement rises to a *fff* climax, and subsides to a *ppp* close. It is scored for divided strings, timpani, cymbals, bass drum, and celesta.

In the second movement, an Allegro, two chief subjects, with their derivatives and subsidiaries, are exploited with astonishing bravura and seemingly inexhaustible dynamic energy. The first of these is the opening subject for a group of the divided strings, pizzicato, and piano; the second is that which follows it immediately, arco, in another string group. The exfoliation of material in this brilliant complex of rhythms and melodic fragments is of dazzling ingenuity and gusto. The movement is scored for strings, piano, celesta, harp, timpani, small drums, bass drum, and xylophone.

The third movement, a brooding and mystical nocturne, elemental and earth-born, opens Adagio, 4-4 time, with a solo for the xylophone. The violas present a subject with a syncopated figure over a timpani roll and a soft tremolo of the string basses. Other strings develop the viola theme. The celesta and two solo violins begin a long-breathed cantilena, accompanied by divided strings and piano. The orchestra becomes a shimmering tissue of glissandi for harp and piano and arpeggios for the celesta, above tremolando passages for the divided strings. There is a stringendo, crescendo; and a new subject for the piano, celesta, and harp in fortissimo octaves brings a short contrasting section, 'Più mosso . . . Allegretto,' 5-4. Then the pace, mood, and material of the Adagio, broadly developed, announce the end, with the final word spoken by the xylophone. Tam-tam (*pp*) and small cymbals are added to the other instruments.

The last movement, of irresistible effectiveness, is an exhilarating 'Allegro molto' based chiefly on a tune of peasant character, a dance melody built on the intervals of the ecclesiastical mode known as the Lydian (corresponding to our modern major scale with a raised fourth), called, by medieval writers, *Modus laetus* (The Joyful Mode). The exuberant subject of Bartók's Finale is introduced at the sixth measure (2-2 time), after prefatory pizzicati chords of the strings. This tune is consorted with another, of more flat-footed character, heard some eighty-five bars further on, in 3-2 time, on the violas and 'cellos. There are subsidiary tunes of folk-like character, and the movement passes through a contrasting phase, 'Molto moderato,' in which material of a more lyric nature is expressively treated, before the concluding return of the original tempo. In the instrumentation of this movement the celesta is replaced in certain passages by a second piano.

● CONCERTO FOR ORCHESTRA

‡Bartók composed no symphony, but his Concerto for Orchestra is a work of symphonic character and dimensions, as earnest of purpose, and as long, as the 'Eroica.' Structurally, no doubt, its affiliations are with the eighteenth-century concerto grosso rather than with the symphony, but our notions of musical forms have become so sophisticated in the past half-century that there is little point in any attempt to find prototypes for modern works in those of the past. Each movement of the Bartók Concerto for Orchestra in effect contrasts a concertino of solo instruments with the orchestral tutti—the brasses in the first movement, the woodwinds in the second, the strings in the Finale— but of this the reader of the score, rather than the casual listener, will be aware. The concerto is in five movements: (1) Introduction, 'Andante non troppo,' leading to the main 'Allegro vivace'; (2) 'Allegretto scherzando'; (3) an Elegy, 'Andante non troppo'; (4) an 'Interrupted Intermezzo,' Allegretto; and (5) a Finale, Presto. It was composed for the Koussevitzky Music Foundation, as a memorial to Natalie Koussevitzky, the wife of the conductor, and was completed in October 1943. The first performance took place a little over a year later—on December 1, 1944—at a concert of the Boston Symphony Orchestra. At that time, Bartók characterized the purpose of the music as 'a gradual transition from the sternness of the first movement and the death-song of the third to the life-assertion of the Finale.'‡

● CONCERTO FOR PIANO AND ORCHESTRA, NO. 1

‡Bartók wrote three concertos for piano and orchestra. The first was completed in 1926 and was first performed in Frankfurt-am-Main, Germany, in July of the following year. During the season of 1927-8, the composer visited the United States, and performances of the concerto, with Bartók playing the solo part, were scheduled by the Philharmonic-Symphony Society of New York and the Philadelphia Orchestra. Both were cancelled—presumably because of the difficulty of the work. Later in the same season, however, it was heard in New York at a concert of the Cincinnati Orchestra, with the composer as soloist, and with Fritz Reiner conducting.‡

Bartók's designation for the work was *Klavierkonzert* in E, and a resolute and sufficiently liberal scrutiny of the score discloses an allegiance to at least the broad principles of tonality. Moreover, the work is erected on a basis of traditional form; it is firmly articulated, logical in plan and procedure. The first movement (in E) opens with a short introductory section ('Allegro moderato,' 2-4). After a dozen preliminary measures for timpani, brass, and piano, the theme of this Introduction is enunciated by four horns, in unison and octaves, above a dissonant chord of the trumpets and trombones. (One uses the word 'dissonant' with full realization that this word has long ceased to have any significance as a term or indication. Broadly speaking, all contemporary music, unless it be deliberately archaic or neo-classic, is a continuous tissue of dissonance—is 'dissonant' consistently and by intention.)

The main movement (Allegro) begins with a fortissimo statement of a new subject, the chief theme—or rather, the first clause of the chief theme, the *protasis*—by the piano in octaves, punctuated by chords of the strings and winds in measures of fluctuating meter—2-4, 3-4, 5-4. This theme suggests the Phrygian Mode, the third of the ecclesiastical modes, whose final is E. (The whole range of the Phrygian Mode in its authentic form extends from E to the octave above—the scale of E without accidentals.) The second and concluding clause of the theme, the *apodosis*, enters soon after, on the piano, illustrating Bartók's addiction to phrases consisting of repeated notes. This subject is briefly enlarged upon; then a trumpet, forte, against a horn in contrary motion, sounds the *Modus Locricus*. The Locrian was the eleventh ecclesiastical mode, which was rejected by musical pietists on account of its illicit tritone; its compass, in the authentic form, ranges from B to the octave above. (The hearer may be reminded that one of the characteristics of the ancient Hungarian folk music unearthed by Bartók is its use of the old church modes.) There are more scale passages, and the orchestra and piano come to a pause, fortissimo, on a chord of E, whose integrity is slightly qualified by the interval of a major second. This ends the first section of the movement.

The second section introduces new thematic material: a subject announced by piano against pizzicato chords of the strings and a counter phrase for the bassoon: and a motive in sixteenth-notes for piano, woodwinds, and strings, pizzicato. The chord of G major, containing the intrusive interval of a major second, is sounded eight times, the former scale passages in contrary motion are heard again in woodwinds and brass, and we reach another phase of the movement, begun by a cadenza for the piano, during which the orchestra is not silent. The principal subject matter is soon recognized as the first theme of the Introduction, rhythmically altered. It is recalled by the piano, alone, and elaborated by both the solo instrument and the orchestra. The pace quickens from allegro to 'allegro molto,' with a variant of the theme for the trumpets. There is an abrupt return to the original tempo. The chief theme of the movement is heard from the oboes, clarinets, and bassoons, and is contrapuntally exploited by orchestra and piano. Material now familiar is passed in review and there is a short coda bringing an abrupt close.

The second movement is an Andante in G-sharp minor, 3-8, scored without strings; only the wind and percussion players accompany the soloist. The movement is in simple song form. The second section of this movement is a sort of interlude in which four different melodies are contrapuntally exhibited in four different keys by the woodwind instruments. The clarinet starts off with a subject in A minor, which is taken up in turn by the English horn and oboe. Eleven measures after the entry of the clarinet, the bassoon introduces a second tune in C-sharp minor. (These tunes, like others in the score, have a decidedly modal character; it would be more exact to say, for example, that the melody for the bassoon is in the Dorian Mode.) The clarinet interjects a third melody, in B-flat, and the English horn a fourth, in C minor. This polytonal complex of woodwind instruments is underlaid by an ostinate accompaniment for the piano and percussion, based on the ground tone C-sharp. The passage rises to a fortissimo climax.

The Finale follows the second movement without pause; it is cast in modified sonata form, and begins, 'Allegro molto,' 2-4, with the piano, fortissimo, propounding the chief theme. This subject is another instance of Bartók's fondness for repeated notes. A second section of the theme is of more lyric outline; the piano sings it above a sustained G-sharp of the strings. Two 'bridge' themes—the first for trombone, with percussion and piano accompaniment, the second for two oboes—and a crescendo drum roll lead to a statement by the piano of the second theme, in B, which is imitated by the strings. There is a return to the opening tempo. The orchestra falls silent and the drums begin an ostinato against which the piano reiterates a fragmentary figure derived from the first theme. The four horns, in unison, marcato, introduce a new theme, with a counter subject for the trombone. This leads to a fugato, which is followed by an elaborate complex of rhythmic and melodic units. The coda is based on the third theme with its attendant counter-theme.

Ludwig van Beethoven

1770-1827

B

‡Whatever may be the position of Beethoven, viewed *sub specie aeternitatis*, among the great composers of the past three centuries, the average man will undoubtedly place him first. Perhaps he belongs there, but the question is not really important. It is possible that Bach or Mozart rose to heights or descended to depths beyond Beethoven's range; that range remains extraordinary, and it seems certain that there are regions of human experience that only he explored in his music. Beethoven, born at Bonn in 1770, was the son and grandson of musicians in the service of the Elector of Cologne. His first teacher was his father; later, in Vienna, to which he was dispatched by the Elector as a youth of promise, he

received some instruction from Mozart and from Haydn. At the age of 21, he settled permanently in Vienna. His quality was soon recognized by persons of consequence, and throughout his life—which he conducted on a plane of extraordinary (for the time) and even arrogant independence— he never lacked the patronage, in the best sense, of highly placed admirers. Money troubles and domestic trials afflicted him almost continuously, but his own resources of courage and enterprise and the aid of devoted friends enabled him to surmount them. His deafness was without doubt his severest burden, his solitary state—he never married—the next in order. But the most adverse circumstances failed to hinder the development of his genius or his amazing productivity. He left an ineffacable imprint upon every department of the musical art. Indeed, the whole subsequent development of Western music can only be understood in the light of his contribution to it; there is even some plausibility in the view that his symphonies, quartets, solo sonatas not merely extended but exhausted the possibilities of sonata form, though it has continued to be the basis of the instrumental music of generations of composers succeeding him. The classic biography of Beethoven is Thayer's, translated into English by H. E. Krehbiel, and two admirable studies of his creative processes may be mentioned here: Newman's *The Unconscious Beethoven*, and Sullivan's *Beethoven: His Spiritual Development.*‡

• SYMPHONY NO. 1, IN C MAJOR, OP. 21

On a certain spring evening in the year 1800, the program of a concert given in Vienna contained some momentous and exciting information; for the greatest sequence of instrumental works ever conceived by the mind of man was about to exhibit its first installment. The Vienna program read as follows:

Today, Wednesday, April 2nd, 1800, Herr Ludwig van Beethoven will have the honor to give a grand concert for his benefit in the Royal Imperial Court Theatre beside the Burg. The pieces which will be performed are the following:

1. A grand symphony by the late Chapelmaster Mozart.

2. An aria from 'The Creation' by the Princely Chapelmaster Herr Haydn, sung by Mlle. Saal.

3. A grand Concerto for the Pianoforte, played and composed by Herr Ludwig van Beethoven.

4. A Septet, most humbly and obediently dedicated to Her Majesty the Empress, and composed by Herr Ludwig van Beethoven for four stringed and three wind-instruments, played by Messrs. Schuppanzigh, Schreiber, Schindlecker, Bär, Nickel, Matauschek and Dietzel.

5. A Duet from Haydn's 'Creation,' sung by M. and Mlle. Saal.

6. Herr Ludwig van Beethoven will improvise on the pianoforte.

7. A new grand symphony with complete orchestra, composed by Herr Ludwig van Beethoven.

Tickets for boxes and stalls are to be had of Herr Beethoven at his lodgings in the Tiefen Graben, No. 241, third story, and of the box-keeper.

Prices of admission are as usual.
The beginning is at half-past six o'clock.

The 'new grand symphony with complete orchestra' was Beethoven's First, in C major. The work was kindly received by a critical correspondent of the *Allegemeine Musikalische Zeitung,* who was present (though he was in no great hurry to review it, for his report did not appear till six months later). He found in the symphony 'much art, novelty, and wealth of ideas'; but he complained because 'there was too much use of the wind-instruments, so that the music sounded more as if written for a military band than an orchestra' (Beethoven scored this symphony for an orchestra of two flutes, two oboes, two clarinets, two bassoons, two horns, two trumpets, timpani, and strings.) A Leipzig critic who heard the symphony in the following year was less amiable. His ears were wounded, his feelings sorely ruffled by Beethoven's music, and he made no bones about saying so. He described the symphony as 'confused explosions of the outrageous effrontery of a young man.'

Thayer doubts if the symphony was composed in the year of its first performance, and thinks it likely that it was 'sketched at an earlier period and worked out in the main by 1799 at the latest.' It was published (in parts) in 1801, and in score nineteen years later. Though it was Beethoven's first completed symphony, it was not the first that he had worked upon. Sketches for the first movement of a symphony in C minor are assigned to 1794 or 1795. But he abandoned that particular project, and turned to other ideas for the new symphony—though a phrase from the sketches for the earlier work is said to resemble the opening phrase of the 'Allegro molto' in the Finale of the C major.

There has been much dispute among the commentators regarding the completeness with which this symphony derives from what Sir George Grove called 'the old order'—the school of Haydn and Mozart. Sir George himself has a good deal to say about the 'audacity' of the opening bars of the slow introduction, which, 'in a composition professing to be in the key of C, begins with a discord in the key of F, and by the third bar lands us in G'—though Sir George recalls that Haydn and Bach had committed equally heinous offenses, and he reminds us that we are not to test the novelty of the procedure by its effect on our own perverted ears. Dr. Riemann insists that this symphony is often original, often truly Beethovenish—as in parts of the Andante, in the Menuetto, in the introduction of the Finale. Sir George Grove does not fail, of course, to extol the originality of the Menuetto. In this movement, he says, Beethoven forsook the spirit of the minuet of his predecessors (although he retained the title), 'increased its speed, broke through its formal and antiquated mould, and out of a mere dance-tune produced a Scherzo, which . . . needs no increase of style or spirit to become the equal of those great move-

ments which form such remarkable features in his later symphonies; though
the change is less obvious, because Beethoven had adhered to the plan and
measure of the old Minuet and Trio. . . When he wrote this part of his
First Symphony he "took a leap into a new world." '

- SYMPHONY No. 2, IN D MAJOR, OP. 36

In Beethoven's Second Symphony we encounter one of the mysteries of the
creative mind: for although the work was written at a time when Beethoven
was in the depths of despair, there is no reflection in the music of his anguish
and bitterness of soul. He composed the greater part of the symphony in the
summer of 1802 at Heiligenstadt, near Vienna. In that year his deafness
oppressed him sorely, and he was disturbed in other ways. His physician, Dr.
Schmidt, had sent him to Heiligenstadt in order to spare his hearing as much
as possible. There Beethoven lived an isolated life, in a house on a hillside
outside the village, visited only by Dr. Schmidt and by his pupil Ries. It was
in the autumn of this year that he wrote the tragically pathetic letter to his
brothers known as 'Beethoven's Will,' in which he laments with affecting
poignancy the affliction that had come upon him, and says that only his art
had kept him from putting an end to his life.

Certain commentators have said that this symphony represents the culminating point of the old world of Haydn and Mozart: that it was the farthest
point to which Beethoven could go before he burst into 'that wonderful new
region which no man had as yet explored, of which no man had even dreamed'
—that world which is disclosed to us for the first time in the 'Eroica' Symphony.

Yet although the Second Symphony seems to us today almost wholly
unperplexing, those listeners of the early nineteenth century who had gladly
accepted its predecessor, the First Symphony, found the Second strange and
unnatural. One of its contemporary reviewers leveled at Beethoven that
favorite charge of the baffled and resentful critic in the presence of art that he
does not understand: he declared that Beethoven's 'anxiety to achieve something novel and surprising was much too evident.' Others condemned the
symphony as too long, too violent, too strange. Yet there were some who perceived in the music fresh ideas, depth of experience, individuality—but these,
of course, were in the minority.

Curious things were found in the music. Lenz discovered in the Allegro
'martial feeling and glittering parade'; in the slow movement (the Larghetto)
he imagined that he heard 'long conversations between Beethoven and a gentle
and beautiful lady friend'; and in the Scherzo and the Finale, he was aware
of 'wanton, wilful, roguish sport.'

It was the Finale which chiefly perplexed the early hearers of this symphony.
What some of them wrote of it is almost incredible. Even the liveliest imagination falters at the task of trying to understand the state of mind into which
a certain Leipzig critic was evidently thrown by this movement when he compared it to 'a repulsive monster, a wounded, tail-lashing serpent, dealing wild
and furious blows as it stiffens into its death agony at the end.'

Berlioz, that consummate program annotator, described the character of the different movements in his pointed way:

I. INTRODUCTION: 'Adagio molto,' D major, 3-4; 'Allegro con brio,' D major, 4-4:—In this symphony, everything is noble, energetic, proud. The Introduction is a masterpiece. The most beautiful effects follow one another without confusion, and always in an unexpected manner. The song is of touching solemnity, and it at once commands respect and puts the hearer in an emotional mood. The rhythm is already bolder, the instrumentation richer, more sonorous, more varied. An 'Allegro con brio' of enchanting dash is joined to this admirable Adagio. The gruppetto (a florid embellishment) which is found in the first measure of the theme, given at first to the violas and violoncellos in unison, is taken up again in an isolated form, to establish either progressions in a crescendo or imitative passages between wind instruments and strings.

II. Larghetto, A major, 3-8:—The [Larghetto] is not treated after the manner of the First Symphony. It is not composed of a theme worked out in canonic imitations, but is a pure and frank song, which at first is sung simply by the strings, and then embroidered with a rare elegance by means of light and fluent figures. Their character is never far removed from the sentiment of tenderness which forms the distinctive character of the principal idea. It is a ravishing picture of innocent pleasure, which is scarcely shadowed by a few melancholy accents.

III. SCHERZO: 'Allegro,' D major, 3-4:—The Scherzo is as frankly gay in its fantastic capriciousness as the second movement has been wholly and serenely happy; for this symphony is smiling throughout; the warlike bursts of the first Allegro are wholly free from violence; there is only the youthful ardor of a noble heart in which the most beautiful illusions of life are preserved untainted. The composer still believes in love, in immortal glory, in devotion. What abandon in his gaiety! What wit! What sallies! Hearing these various instruments disputing over the fragment of a theme which no one of them plays in its complete form, hearing each fragment thus colored with a thousand nuances as it passes from one to the other, it is as though you were watching the fairy sports of Oberon's graceful spirits.

IV. FINALE: 'Allegro molto,' D major, 2-2:—The closing movement is of like nature. It is a second Scherzo, in 2-2 time, and its playfulness has perhaps something still more delicate, more piquant.

● SYMPHONY NO. 3, IN E-FLAT MAJOR, OP. 55 ('Eroica')

One evening at Nussdorf in the summer of 1817, when Beethoven and the poet Kuffner were enjoying a fish dinner together at the tavern 'Zur Rose,' Kuffner made bold to ask the Titan—who happened to be in an amiable mood—which of his symphonies was his favorite (there were then, of course, only eight).

'Eh! eh!' responded Beethoven, in great good humor, 'the "Eroica."'

'I should have guessed the C minor,' remarked his interrogator.

'No,' insisted Beethoven: 'the "Eroica."'

The 'Eroica' was then thirteen years behind him; he had finished the Eighth almost five years before; seven years later he was to complete the Ninth.

With his preference for the 'Eroica' many will find themselves in sympathy. Yet it seemed to some who in 1805 heard the work for the first time that it 'often lost itself in lawlessness'—that it contained much that was 'glaring and bizarre.' A correspondent of the time divided its hearers into three classes:

there were those, 'Beethoven's particular friends,' who kept a tight upper lip and predicted that 'after a thousand years have passed it will not fail of its effect'; another faction saw in it only 'an untamed striving for singularity . . . but genius proclaims itself not in the unusual and fantastic, but in the beautiful and sublime.' A third party, the middle-of-the-roaders, admitted that the symphony contained 'many beauties,' but deplored its 'inordinate length' and feared that 'if Beethoven continues on his present path he and the public will be the sufferers.' Beethoven himself, who conducted the first performance, came in for some blame because of 'discourtesy' toward his hearers: for it appears that 'he did not nod his head in recognition of the applause which came from a portion of the audience.'

It is easy to believe that the effect of the new symphony was exceedingly perturbing. Imagine the impression that must have been made in 1805 not only by such 'wicked whims' (as the horrified Ries called them) as the famous entrance of the horn in the tonic of E-flat major against the dominant B-flat— A-flat of the violins, in the first movement, but by such far more startling things as that passage in the working-out section where the movement achieves its climax in a series of tremendous minor-second chords which evoke the image of a giant fist shaken at the sky; after which the fury of the agonist subsides upon a wholly unexpected minor-ninth chord of the strings, with the oboes calming the fury in the lovely episode that follows it. Well might Sir George Grove exclaim that such passages as this are 'absolute Beethoven'— that there is nothing comparable to their quality in any previous music.

That still seems true—the symphony has lost nothing of its prodigious strength, its towering stature. Only twice again in his symphonies—in the opening Allegros of the Fifth and the Ninth—was Beethoven to achieve this titanic quality, with its implication of vast issues and tragic confrontations.

The vast passions of the 'Eroica' constitute 'such a tornado as would have burst the breast of any but the gigantic hero whom Beethoven believed himself to be portraying, and who was certainly more himself than Bonaparte'—which is Sir George Grove's shrewd and psychologically plausible comment on the celebrated tale that associates the symphony with Napoleon. The tale itself need not, for the thousandth time, be retold in detail—how Ludwig (for whom Napoleon the First Consul was a symbol of human emancipation, a flaming torch thrust in the face of tyranny, an incorruptible enemy of kings) composed the symphony to express his admiration for the great republican, and tore from the score the title page bearing the name 'Bonaparte' in a furious burst of disillusioned rage when he heard that Napoleon had pro-claimed himself Emperor, exclaiming in a bitter fury (according to Ries): 'Then is he, too, only an ordinary human being?' 'The first page,' added Ries, 'was rewritten, and only then did the symphony receive the title *Sinfonia Eroica.*' Beethoven, they say, never again spoke Napoleon's name; but when he heard of his death at St. Helena, seventeen years later, he remarked, 'I have composed the proper music for the catastrophe!' A surviving copy of the score contains on the title page this nearly obliterated note in Beethoven's hand-writing: *Geschrieben auf Bonapart.* The published score he described simply as *composta per festeggiare il sovvenire di un grand'Uomo*—'composed to celebrate the memory of a great man.'

The temporal extent of the 'Eroica' is commensurate with its greatness of substance, but it is without excrescences. It is consistent and valid throughout its prodigious length, a thing of ageless wonder, with the detachment from period and manner that stamps the surpassing masterwork. Nothing in it sounds outworn. And who but Beethoven could have introduced a fugato into a funeral march and charged the formalism of the old device with such plangent lamentation? Listening to this music, with the measureless sorrow of its noble threnody, we may remember the great soul who lives for us in the unforgettable reminiscence of the Baroness von Ertmann. 'She related,' says Mendelssohn, 'that when she lost her last child Beethoven at first did not want to come into the house; at length, he invited her to visit him, and when she came he sat down at the pianoforte and said simply, "We will now talk to each other in tones," and for over an hour played without stopping, and, as she remarked, "he told me everything, and at last brought me comfort."'

● SYMPHONY NO. 4, IN B-FLAT MAJOR, OP. 60

Like Cinderella, the Fourth Symphony of Beethoven is lovely and neglected; but unlike that misused damsel, it is full of gaiety and humor, as well as of tenderness and grace and beauty. Schumann, indeed, likened the Fourth to 'a slender Greek maiden between two Norse giants' (those gentry being, of course, the 'Eroica' and the Fifth). Sir George Grove protests that the simile is not entirely happy, inasmuch as the grace and beauty of the Fourth Symphony are accompanied by humor—'and humor,' he declared, 'is hardly the characteristic of a Greek maiden.' One cannot help wondering what brought Sir George to that surprising conclusion. Had he forgotten Theocritus' Nycheia 'with her April eyes'?—and if 'April eyes' are not those that can laugh as well as weep, the poets have led us wickedly astray. However, whether or not the Fourth is truly 'Greek,' it is certainly, in parts, gay as well as lovely.

Moreover, this music comes to the present generation with credentials of the highest order. 'Believe me,' wrote Berlioz, 'believe me, my dear friend, the being who wrote such a marvel of inspiration as this movement [the Adagio] was not a man. Such must be the song of the Archangel Michael as he contemplates the world's uprising to the threshold of the empyrean.'

Surely Berlioz's raptures were justified. Whether the song proceeded from the throat of an archangel or the imagination of a mere genius, this slow movement is unmatched in Beethoven's scores—not because he wrote nothing more beautiful, but because he wrote nothing like it. Where in Beethoven will you find an analogue for the second theme of this Adagio—that enamoring B-flat song of the clarinet whose opening phrase is heard above an accompanying figure of the climbing strings? Such music remains, indeed, as Berlioz said, a marvel of inspiration, even for Beethoven.

The commentators have certainly done their best to add the charm of human association to the purely musical address of this symphony. The famous author of *Beethoven and his Nine Symphonies* views the outstanding feature of the work—the beautiful Adagio—as a treasury of authentic romance. He invites us to find here not only 'such a height of passion as even Beethoven's fiery nature perhaps never reached elsewhere,' but also the aesthetic record of a definite chapter of passionate experience. He speaks of 'the occasion which inspired the Symphony'; and this is the tale as told by Sir George: 'In May of the year in which Beethoven was occupied over this symphony [1806], he became engaged to the Countess Thérèse, sister of his intimate friend, Franz von Brunswick; and the three famous and incoherent love-letters which were found in his desk after his death, and have been supposed to be addressed to the Countess Giulietta Guicciardi, were really written to that lady [Thérèse von Brunswick]. . . The fact is that music was Beethoven's native language; and, however he may stammer in words, in his most passionate notes [musical notes, Sir George means] there is no incoherence. Though he had often been involved in love affairs, none of them had yet been permanent; certainly he had never before gone so far as an engagement, and when writing the symphony his heart must have been swelling with his new happiness. It is, in fact, the paean which he sings over his first conquest.

'Here, then, we have the secret of the first movement of the C minor [Sir George saw in the first movement of the Fifth Symphony—begun before the Fourth—a reflection of Beethoven's supposed love affair with Thérèse, and 'actual portraits of the two chief actors in the drama'], and an excuse for any height or depth of emotion. . . Beethoven's raptures are here before us, in his music.'

Yet the wise men tell us that though these things may be so, they have not been proved. Thayer speaks of this work as 'the placid and serene Fourth Symphony (the most perfect in form of them all).' It was composed in the summer of 1806. Its successor, the Fifth, had been begun, but was laid aside. 'Nothing more is known of the history of its composition,' says Thayer, 'except what is imparted by the author's inscription on the manuscript: "Sinfonia 4ta, 1806. L. v. Bthvn." '

Finally, there is always Vincent d'Indy to be remembered; for D'Indy declined to recognize the Countess Thérèse von Brunswick as the 'Immortal Beloved,' and, in his brilliant biography of Beethoven, holds a brief for Giulietta Guicciardi. As for the theory that the Fourth Symphony had anything to do with Thérèse, D'Indy is barely polite to it.

All of which does not affect the quality of the work as music, for it is still true, as a Leipzig critic said more than a century ago, that the Fourth Symphony is like the First and Second in being 'highly esteemed, and with good reason.' The gentleman was obviously very brave: for only a year later another critic wrote that Beethoven in this symphony 'is extremely bizarre, and makes himself unintelligible and an object of terror to even cultivated dilettanti.'

● SYMPHONY NO. 5, IN C MINOR, OP. 67

The first performance of Beethoven's C minor Symphony took place in the Theater-an-der-Wien at Vienna on December 22, 1808. The date of the completion of the work is not definitely known—it seems probable that Beethoven put the finishing touches to it at Heiligenstadt in 1807, but his autograph score bears neither date nor number, merely the inscription *Sinfonie da L. v. Beethoven* scrawled on it in red chalk. According to Thayer, 'this wonderous work was no sudden inspiration. Themes for the Allegro, the Andante and Scherzo are found in sketchbooks belonging, at the very latest, to the years 1800 and 1801'—that is to say, to the period between the composition of the First and Second Symphonies. ‡There is similar evidence to show that Beethoven worked on the symphony at intervals between 1804 and 1806, when he was also engaged in the composition of *Fidelio* and the Fourth Piano Concerto.‡

That incurable romanticist, Sir George Grove, was persuaded that Beethoven, in this most famous of all symphonies, concealed an intimate and impassioned chapter of his turbulent career. 'The composition of the C minor,' he says, 'covered the time before the engagement of Beethoven with the Countess Thérèse von Brunswick, the engagement itself, and a part of the period of agitation when the lovers were separated. . . Now, considering the extraordinarily imaginative and disturbed character of the symphony, it is impossible not to believe that the work—the first movement, at any rate—is based on his relations to the Countess, and is more or less a picture of their personalities and association. . . In fact, the first movement seems to contain actual portraits of the two chief actors in the drama. . . At any rate, in this movement, he unbosoms himself as he has never done before . . . we hear the palpitating accents and almost the incoherence of the famous love-letters, but mixed with an amount of fury which is not in them.'

To Sir George's mind, the opening phrase of the symphony 'exactly expresses' Beethoven—'the fierce imperious composer, who knew how to "put his foot down"; while the tender E-flat subject in the violins is the youthful Countess— "the womanly, devoted girl" '—Sir George is referring to the tale of Beethoven's anger during a piano lesson that he was giving to the young Countess Thérèse. Sir George quotes it from *Beethovens Unsterbliche Geliebte*, by Mariam Tenger—a book characterized by Krehbiel, in his edition of Thayer's Life, as 'romantic vaporings.'

But listen to Vincent D'Indy concerning this matter: 'All of those compositions [of Beethoven's Second Period, 1801-15] which tell of or reveal amorous anguish,' he remarks in his book on Beethoven, 'can apparently be traced, chronologically speaking, only to his passion for Giulietta Guicciardi. Neither Theresa Malfatti, nor Amalie Sebald, nor Bettina Brentano, nor the other women whom Beethoven might have noticed, have left any impression on his musical production. . . Still, among the women who were Beethoven's friends, there was one whose name should be mentioned here if only to contradict the newly created legend concerning her. We refer to Countess Thérèse von Brunswick and her mysterious betrothal to Beethoven. . . What artist, what man gifted with the simplest artistic perception, would for a moment admit that the sole work dedicated to Countess von Brunswick, the insipid sonata in F-sharp major, Op. 78, could be addressed to the same person as the passionate love-letters which all the world has read? . . . These two piano pieces in expressionless imitation, without musical interest, could never have been the homage of the Titan Beethoven to his "immortal beloved." '

From 1801 onwards, says D'Indy, we find a new Beethoven: 'heretofore he has written merely music; now it is life whereof he writes. . . He has felt, he has loved, he has suffered. . . In his frenzy he unveils the three loves which fill that soul to overflowing in this second period of his career—the love of Woman, of Nature, of Country.' D'Indy seems to refer the C minor Symphony to the third of these categories, for he speaks of it only to allude to its 'warlike Andante' and its 'absolutely heroic Finale.'

Many things have been found in the Fifth Symphony—the summons of Fate, martial celebrations, the repercussions of a tragic love affair, the note of the yellowhammer heard in country walks. But whatever Beethoven did or did not intend to say to us in this tonal revelation, there is one trait that the C minor Symphony has beyond every other, and that is the quality of epic valor. There is nothing in music quite like the heroic beauty of those first measures of the Finale that burst forth at the end of the indescribable transition from the Scherzo with its swiftly cumulative crescendo, and the overwhelming emergence of the trombones—so cannily held in reserve throughout the foregoing movements. This is music pregnant with the greatness of the indomitable human soul. Listening to it, one knows that the inward ear of Beethoven had almost caught that lost word which, could a man but find it, would make him master of the hosts of Fate and of the circling worlds.

● SYMPHONY No. 6, IN F MAJOR, OP. 68 ('Pastoral')

Beethoven completed his 'Pastoral' Symphony in the summer of 1808, in what were then the wooded environs of Vienna. The first performance was at a concert given by Beethoven at the Theater-an-der-Wien, December 22, 1808. The C minor Symphony (No. 5) was also heard at this concert for the first time.

Berlioz has given us the following delightful exegesis of the 'Pastoral':

FIRST MOVEMENT

['Cheerful impressions awakened by arrival in the country':
'Allegro ma non troppo,' F major, 2-4]

This astonishing landscape seems as if it were the joint work of Poussin and Michaelangelo. The composer of *Fidelio* and of the *Eroica* wishes in this symphony to depict the tranquility of the country and the peaceful life of shepherds. The herdsmen begin to appear in the fields, moving about with their usual nonchalant gait; their pipes are heard afar and near. Ravishing phrases caress one's ears deliciously, like perfumed morning breezes. Flocks of chattering birds fly overhead; and now and then the atmosphere seems laden with vapors; heavy clouds flit across the face of the sun, then suddenly disappear, and its rays flood the fields and woods with torrents of dazzling splendor. These are the images evoked in my mind by hearing this movement; and I fancy that, in spite of the vagueness of instrumental expression, many hearers will receive the same impressions.

SECOND MOVEMENT

['Scene by the Brook': 'Andante molto moto,' B-flat major, 12-8]

Next is a movement devoted to contemplation. Beethoven, without doubt, created this admirable adagio [sic] while reclining on the grass, his eyes uplifted, ears intent, fascinated by the thousand varying hues of light and sound, looking at and listening at the same time to the scintillating ripple of the brook that breaks its waves over the pebbles of its shores. How delicious this music is!

THIRD MOVEMENT

['Merry Gathering of Country-folk': Allegro, F major, 3-4]

In this movement the poet leads us into the midst of a joyous reunion of peasants. We are aware that they dance and laugh, at first with moderation; the oboe plays a gay air, accompanied by a bassoon, which apparently can sound but two notes. Beethoven doubtless intended thus to evoke the picture of some good old German peasant, mounted on a cask, and playing a dilapidated old instrument, from which he can draw only two notes in the key of F, the dominant and the tonic. Every time the oboe strikes up its musette-like tune, fresh and gay as a young girl dressed in her Sunday clothes, the old bassoon comes in puffing his two notes; when the melodic phrase modulates, the bassoon is silent perforce, counting patiently his rests until the return of the original key permits him to come in with his imperturbable F, C, F. This effect, so charmingly grotesque, generally fails to be noticed by the public.

The dance becomes animated, noisy, furious. The rhythm changes; a melody of grosser character, in duple time, announces the arrival of the mountaineers with their heavy *sabots*. The section in triple time returns, still more lively. The dance becomes a medley, a rush; the women's hair begins to fall over their shoulders, for the mountaineers have brought with them a bibulous gayety. There is clapping of hands, shouting; the peasants run, they rush madly . . . when a muttering of thunder in the distance causes a sudden fright in the midst of the dance. Surprise and consternation seize the dancers, and they seek safety in flight.

FOURTH MOVEMENT

['Thunderstorm, tempest': 'Allegro,' F minor, 4-4]

I despair of being able to give an idea of this prodigious movement. It must be heard in order to appreciate the degree of truth and sublimity which descriptive music can attain in the hands of a man like Beethoven. Listen to those gusts of wind, laden with rain; those sepulchral groanings of the basses; those shrill whistles of the piccolo, which announce that a fearful tempest is about to burst. The hurricane approaches, swells; an immense chromatic streak, starting from the highest notes of the orchestra, goes burrowing down into its lowest depths, seizes the basses, carries them along, and ascends again, writhing like a whirlwind, which levels everything in its passage. Then the trombones burst forth; the thunder of the *timpani* redoubles its fury. It is no longer merely a wind and rain storm: it is a frightful cataclysm, the universal deluge, the end of the world. Truly, this produces vertigo, and many persons listening to this storm do not know whether the emotion they experience is pleasure or pain.

FIFTH MOVEMENT

['Shepherd's Song. Glad and grateful feelings after the storm':
Allegretto, F major, 6-8]

The symphony ends with a hymn of gratitude. Everything smiles. The shepherds reappear; they answer each other on the mountain, recalling their scattered flocks; the sky is serene; the torrents soon cease to flow; calmness returns, and with it the rustic songs, whose gentle melodies bring repose to the soul after the consternation produced by the magnificent horror of the previous picture.

For Beethoven, the 'Return to Nature' was no deliberately romantic sophistication. To his devout and passionate spirit, it was a resort as spontaneous and naïve and profound as the inclination of the medieval mystic's soul toward God. He sincerely and piously believed that wisdom broods upon the hills and in the long forest aisles; that sustenance for the heart could be garnered from sunlight and free winds, and spiritual peace drunk from quiet valleys as from a divinely proffered cup. He would have understood that ecstatically confident cry of a Celtic dreamer of today: 'Death will never find us in the heart of the wood!' To his mind, as to Lafcadio Hearn's, had come the thought that illumination of a transcendent kind was yielded 'by the mere common green of the world.'

Beethoven copied from his beloved and much-thumbed volume of Sturm's *Lehr und Erbauungs Buch* this passage: 'One might rightly denominate Nature the school of the heart; she clearly shows us our duties toward God and our neighbor. Hence, I wish to become a disciple of this school and to offer Him my heart. Desirous of instructions, I would seek after that wisdom which no disillusionment can confute; I would gain a knowledge of God, and through this knowledge I shall obtain a foretaste of celestial felicity.' Beethoven himself wrote to the Baroness Droszdick that he was convinced of the fact that 'no one loves country life as I do. It is as if every tree and every bush could understand my mute enquiries and respond to them.' A dozen years before his death he exclaimed: 'Almighty God, in the woods I am blessed. Happy every one in the woods. Every tree speaks through Thee. O God! What glory in the woodland! On the heights is peace—peace to serve Him.' Sir George Grove records a tradition that Beethoven refused to take possession of an engaged lodging because there were no trees near the house. 'How is this? Where are your trees?' 'We have none.'—'Then the house won't do for me. I love a tree more than a man.' Charles Neate, the British musician who knew Beethoven, told Thayer, the master's biographer, that Nature was 'his [Beethoven's] nourishment.'

'When you wander through the mysterious forests of pine,' Beethoven wrote to a friend in Baden nine years after he had composed the 'Pastoral,' 'remember that Beethoven often made poetry there—or, as they say, "composed." ' To the music of the 'Pastoral' Symphony Beethoven transferred his delight in the beauty of the world. Back of its charming and ingenuous picturing of rural scenes and incidents and encounters—its brookside idyls, its merrymaking and thunderstorms and shepherds' hymns; back of the element of profound emotional speech connoted by Beethoven's slightly self-conscious deprecation about his music being 'more an expression of feeling than portraiture'—back of all these more evident aspects rises the image of a poet transfixed by the immortal spectacle, and recording his awe and tenderness in songs that cannot help being canticles of praise.

How endearing the music is at its best! Did Beethoven ever write anything fresher, more captivating, than the themes of the first movement—whether or not they are derivations from Styrian and Carinthian folk tunes? And you will search far in his works before you find anything so simply contrived, yet so delectable, as that modulation from B-flat to D in the 163d measure, with the entrance of the oboe on A above the F-sharp of the first violins.

As you listen to this lucid and lovely music, full of sincerity and candor and sweet gravity, you may recall the folk tale of the old man who could always be found at sunrise looking seaward through the shadow of the woods, with his white locks blowing in the wind that rose out of the dawn; and who, being asked why he was not at his prayers, replied: 'Every morning like this I take off my hat to the beauty of the world.'

• Symphony No. 7, in A major, op. 92

One cannot help wondering what Beethoven would have thought and said about some of the many distinguished commentators who have attempted to 'interpret' the Seventh Symphony. Would he have been pleased by Schumann's discovery, in the second movement, of the marriage ceremony of a village couple? Or by d'Ortigue's pretty fancy that this movement pictures a procession in an old cathedral or in the catacombs? Or by the notion of Dürenberg, 'a more cheerful person,' as Philip Hale has described him, who 'prefers to call it the love-dream of a sumptuous odalisque?'

There have been other and equally discordant readings: Marx discerned in the symphony as a whole a tale of Moorish knighthood, and this notion also seemed plausible to Teetjen, who—though first he says: 'Here the ringing woodland of feudal times is round us, and all the panoply, pride, pomp and circumstance of a royal chase'—afterward gets deeper and deeper into thoughts of chivalry, and is almost tempted to call up pictures of Scott's *Ivanhoe*. Oulibischeff associates with it scenes from a masquerade. Lenz and Seroff, two other Russians, find it full of military pomp. Bischoff, the antagonist of Wagner, to whom we owe the phrase 'music of the future,' treats the work as a sequel to the 'Pastoral' Symphony, and 'conjures up pictures of the autumnal merry-makings of the gleaners and vine-dressers, the tender melancholy of a love-lorn youth, the pious canticle of joy and gratitude for nature's gifts and the final outburst when joy beckons again and the dance melodies float out upon the air and none stands idle.'

We need not wonder, after all, what Beethoven would have said of all this, for we know what he said of an interpreter scarcely more exuberantly imaginative than Schumann or Dürenberg or Marx. More than a century ago, a certain Dr. Carl Iken conceived the idea of helping the public to an understanding of Beethoven's music by devising programmatic expositions of the symphonies. In the Seventh, the keen-eyed Doctor discerned the tone-picture of a political revolution. The 'program' which he invented for it was found by Schindler, with several others, among Beethoven's papers. Here it is, in part:

The sign of revolt is given; there is a rushing and running about of the multitude; an innocent man, or party, is surrounded, overpowered after a struggle and . . . haled before a legal tribunal. Innocency weeps; the judge pronounces a harsh sentence; sympathetic voices mingle in laments and denunciations—they are those of widows; in the second part of the first movement the parties have become equal in numbers and the magistrates are now scarcely able to quiet the wild tumult. The uprising is suppressed, but the people are not quieted; hope smiles cheeringly, and suddenly the voice of the people pronounces the decision in harmonious agreement. . . But now, in the last movement, the classes and the masses mix in a variegated picture of unrestrained revelry. The quality still speak aloofly in the wind instruments. There is a strange bacchantic madness in related chords. We are now on a sunny hill, anon on a flowering meadow where in merry May all the jubilating children of nature sing with joyful voices.

Richly amusing as this precious nonsense may seem to us, one can hardly wonder that it infuriated Beethoven, and that he protested energetically. If expositions were necessary, he held, 'they should be confined to characterization of the composition in general terms, which could easily and correctly be done by any educated musician.'

Philip Hale, remarking that Wagner wrote 'hysterically' about the Seventh Symphony when he saw in it 'the apotheosis of the dance,' recommended the essay of Berlioz as 'the noblest and most poetic appreciation'; but Sir George Grove flings the epithet 'outrageous' at poor Berlioz's head for daring to see in the Vivace of the Seventh Symphony a peasants' dance.

Romain Rolland makes this shrewd comment, apropos of the amazing contemporaneous legend about the symphony having been a product of inebriety: 'The work of an inebriated man indeed it was, but one intoxicated with poetry and genius; one who said to himself, "I am the Bacchus who crushes delicious nectar for mankind. It is I who give the divine frenzy to mankind," '—a comment suggested, of course, by Wagner's observation that he did not know 'whether Beethoven wished to depict a Dionysian orgy in the Finale of his symphony.'

Beethoven's Seventh has been called 'the most beautiful symphony in the world'—a vaulting and delusive phrase. For what does 'beautiful' mean? And what is Beauty? The words are meaningless. Their content is infinite, but infinitely variable. The 'most beautiful symphony'—brave words, with a mirage as the end of their adventuring! More 'beautiful' than the G minor of Mozart, than the Third of Brahms? More 'beautiful' than that last of Beethoven's with its transfigured slow movement? Who shall say? But perhaps even those who shy at the positive use of mighty words will hesitate to dispute the special persuasiveness of the music of this Seventh Symphony. One fancies, listening to it, that George Herbert might have imagined something not unlike it when he wrote: 'My free soul may use her wing.' It has the deathless charm of all motion that is unvexed, spontaneous, perfectly released—the flight of wild swans across an autumn sky, the ripple of windswept corn, a gale through April woods, the running of mountain water. Beethoven patterned after Nature in setting his rhythms to a varying pace. This music is full at times of the ungovernable ecstasy of some pristine and magically recovered spring, the sudden laughter of dryads in immemorial woods, the exquisite gaiety of the vernal earth; or it has at other times the grave pace of some commemorative ritual, evoking an elegiacal and mournful beauty, 'as if veils were dropped, one by one, on a great ceremony.'

• SYMPHONY NO. 8, IN F MAJOR, OP. 93

Early in October 1812, the *Linzer Musikzeitung* thus announced the arrival
of a distinguished visitor to the town of Linz: 'We have had the long wished
for pleasure of having within our metropolis for several days the Orpheus and
greatest musical poet of our time . . . and if Apollo is favorable to us, we
shall also have an opportunity to admire his art and report upon it to the
readers of this journal.'

The Orpheus in question was Ludwig van Beethoven, whose wanderings in
the year 1812 had brought him to Linz (probably from Teplitz via Prague
and Budweis), where he purposed to spend a few weeks with his brother
Johann, the apothecary. Ludwig's fraternal host gave him a large and pleasant
room with a view of the Danube and the lovely country beyond, and there
Beethoven settled down and proceeded to make music and trouble. For it
was then and there that he completed the Eighth Symphony, and (as even
the usually soft-spoken Thayer is forced to put it), took it upon himself to
'meddle in the private concerns of his brother,' which 'he had no more right
to do than any stranger.'

Beethoven appears to have gone to Linz with the firm intention of breaking
up the undiplomatically cordial entente that existed between his brother and
Therese Obermeyer. For Therese, who possessed 'a pleasing, though not
beautiful, face,' had won the affections of Johann van Beethoven. He had
made her his housekeeper—'and [as Thayer so delicately puts it] something
more.' Ludwig was outraged by the situation, and undertook its regulation.
But Johann seems to have entertained the quaintly perverse notion that his
private affairs were none of his brother's business, and he refused the proffered
reformation of his ways. Ludwig, greatly exercised, betook himself to the police
authorities and the bishop, and arranged for the forcible ejection of the
deplorable Miss Obermeyer from the town of Linz; whereupon the amorous
apothecary very inconsiderately checkmated Ludwig's maneuver by hastily
marrying the lady.

It was during this turbulent period that the Eighth Symphony came into
being—it was completed, according to Beethoven's autograph inscription, at
Linz, in October 1812. Sir George Grove thinks that Beethoven's excitement
at the time 'no doubt considerably colored' the music, though he wisely
observes that 'it is exceedingly hazardous to attempt to connect Beethoven's
music with the simultaneous events of his life.' He recalls Tennyson's remark
that 'people in general have no notion of the way in which "we poets" go to
work'; he reminds us that 'the despair of the letter known as Beethoven's Will
was coincident with the satisfied, happy mood depicted in the Second Symphony, of the same date . . .' and that 'the gay strains of the Finale to the
great B-flat Quartet (Op. 130) are actually dated, with his own hand, "November 6" (1826) when he was in the midst of most unpleasant surroundings . . .
In constant contact with the woman whom he hated perhaps more than anyone else in the world.'

The Eighth Symphony compelled from Sir George the epithet 'prodigious.'

And it is he who has most concisely and happily characterized the work, in a paragraph that is a masterpiece of vividly swift projection:

At this time of life (forty-one) his love of fun and practical joking had increased so much on him as to have become a habit; his letters are full of jokes; he bursts into horse-laughs on every occasion; makes the vilest puns, and bestows the most execrable nicknames. . . He had an express term for this state of things: *Aufgeknöpft*—i.e. 'unbuttoned'—was his own word for it. And as what he had in his mind was bound to come out in his music [Was it? See Sir George's own seeming contradiction of this in the quotation above], this comes out in the Eighth Symphony more than anywhere else; indeed, the work might with propriety be called the Humorous Symphony—often terribly humorous; for the atmosphere of broad rough enjoyment which pervades the first and last movements is, in the former, darkened by bursts of unmistakable wrath, while every now and then there is a special stroke—such as the octave figure for bassoon in the first movement, of bassoon and timpani in the last; the bar's rest and staccato notes which usher in the second subject in the first Allegro; the way in which, in the working-out of the same movement, the first subject is persistently *shoved away* each time it appears; the provoking Italian cadence which finishes up the Allegretto just as we want to hear the legitimate repeat; in the Finale the abrupt fortissimo C-sharps; the burst of laughter with which he explodes at the notion of making his coda, according to practice, out of the previous material, and then goes off into entirely fresh subjects and regions; the way in which the brass pull the orchestra back into F-natural when it had got into F-sharp.

Historians have refused to take seriously the legend that the staccato rhythm of the wind instruments in the Allegretto was suggested by the ticking of Maelzel's metronome; but the legend will doubtless outlive the historians who have patiently and circumstantially demolished it.

The first performance of the Eighth Symphony was at a concert given by Beethoven in Vienna on February 27, 1814. The new symphony, according to Czerny, did not please the audience. It followed in the program Beethoven's Seventh Symphony, and some thought that No. 8 suffered by the comparison. Beethoven is said to have been irritated by the listeners' reaction, and protested that the new work was 'much better' than its predecessor.

• Symphony No. 9, in D minor, op. 125

The Ninth Symphony was performed for the first time on May 7, 1824, at the Kärntnerthor Theater in Vienna. 'Herr Ludwig van Beethoven,' said the official announcement of the concert, 'will himself participate in the general direction.' Beethoven had finished the symphony three months before, and the conclusion of the task had cheered his spirits, so that he might once again have been seen on his promenades in Vienna, greeting his friends and acquaintances and 'gazing into the shop-windows through eyeglasses which dangled at the end of a black ribbon.'

Between the completion of the First Symphony and the final scoring of the Ninth, a quarter of a century had elapsed, and Beethoven, having piled masterpieces mountain high in the lap of the nineteenth century, was within three years of that terrible March evening when he shook his clenched fist at the lightning that blazed into his room and died to a thunderous obbligato of cosmic timpani.

The Vienna concert of May 7, 1824, was to begin at seven o'clock, and the *Grand Symphony with Solo and Chorus Voices entering in the Finale on Schiller's Ode to Joy* was the third number. Prices of admission were 'as usual.' The Imperial Family seems to have been laying a cornerstone somewhere else, for the royal box was empty. With this exception, the theater was crowded in every part. Beethoven was present, dressed—so Thalberg told Thayer—'in a black dress-coat, white neckerchief, and waistcoat, black satin small-clothes, black silk stockings, shoes with buckles.' But Thalberg may have been color blind, for Schindler declares that Beethoven wore a green coat ('the theater will be dark and no one will notice').

The music made a profound impression and there were enthusiastic demonstrations by the audience. Michael Umlauf conducted, and Schuppanzigh was the concert master. Beethoven sat in the middle of the orchestra, following the performance with his score. The Conversation Book preserves a report received from Schindler: 'Never in my life did I hear such frenetic yet cordial applause. . . When the *parterre* broke out in applauding cries for the fifth time the Police Commissioner yelled "Silence!" ' Three successive bursts of applause were the rule for the Imperial Family, and Beethoven got five. No wonder the police were annoyed. (Let us hope the memory of this incident brought some consolation to Beethoven two and a half years later, when the King of Prussia palmed off on him a near-diamond ring in return for the Ninth Symphony.)

To all the excitement, Beethoven, deaf and engrossed in his score, was pathetically oblivious. The tale of the incident that followed has become one of the classic Beethoven anecdotes, but it is so touching and dramatic that it bears unlimited repetition. Sir George Grove thus relates it, as it was told to him in 1869 by Fräulein Unger, who had sung the alto part in the quartet: 'The master, though placed in the midst of this confluence of music, heard nothing of it at all, and was not even sensible of the applause of the audience at the end of his great work, but continued standing with his back to the audience and beating the time [‡Thalberg, who was present, told Thayer that the conductor had instructed the orchestra and choir to 'pay no attention whatever to Beethoven's beating of the time, but all to watch him'‡] till Fräulein Unger turned him, or induced him to turn and face the people, who were still clapping their hands and giving way to the greatest demonstrations of pleasure. His turning about, and the sudden conviction thereby forced on everybody that he had not done so before because *he could not hear what was going on* acted like an electric shock on all present, and a volcanic explosion of sympathy and admiration followed.'

According to Schindler, Beethoven fainted when he saw the box office report. But this seems to have been only another of Schindler's romantic embroideries on the blouse of truth. The gross receipts were 2200 florins in the depreciated Viennese currency; the net receipts were only about 420 florins. Beethoven, instead of swooning, was exceedingly wrathy. He invited Schindler, Schuppanzigh, and Umlauf to dine with him at a restaurant in the Prater, and there he exploded with the charge that the management and Schindler had cheated him. Oddly enough, this broke up the party.

Beethoven had finished the entire symphony in sketch form by the end of 1823, and he wrote it out in score the following February. About six and a half years, according to Thayer's reckoning, elapsed between the beginning of the first movement and the completion of the work. Some of the thematic material of the symphony was noted in the sketchbooks as early as 1815, but 'probably with an entirely different purpose in mind.' Beethoven was engaged on other works during this period, and his continuous occupation with the Ninth Symphony did not begin until 1822, after he had finished the *Missa Solemnis*.

But thirty-one years before the completion of the Ninth, Beethoven had had his eye on Schiller's *An die Freude* as a subject for music. While a young man of twenty-three, living at Bonn, he had thought of setting it, at first as a *durchkomponirtes Lied*; and he had recurred more than once to the Ode as a theme for music, planning to use it in various ways. Yet the earlier schemes for the Ninth Symphony did not contemplate the choral finale; an instrumental close was intended for it. Beethoven had in mind two symphonies, and in one of these (it would have been the 'Tenth') he considered introducing a choral part. But the plans for the Ninth and Tenth were merged; the projected instrumental finale of the D minor was displaced by Schiller, whose *An die Freude* yielded, at last, the Finale as we know it—not, however, without hesitancy on Ludwig's part; for even as late as 1823 he seems to have been troubled with doubts concerning the close; and his efforts to establish an organic connection between the three instrumental movements and the vocal setting of the poem were exceedingly laborious.

Was there a poetic scheme in Beethoven's mind, involving the symphony as a whole, which at last persuaded him of the logic and propriety of attaching to the three instrumental movements a choral setting of Schiller's ode? We know that Richard Wagner, who entered more profoundly and lovingly into this music than anyone else who has written of it, found the poetical, or spiritual, contents of the symphony in various phases of man's pursuit of joy. Yet Sir George Grove and other exegetes have taken the disconcerting view that no poetic interrelation need be sought between the first three movements and the ode which inspired its Finale. But the bland assumption indulged by Sir George, and by others like-minded, that 'it is not necessary to reconcile' the several parts of a presumably organic work of art will always strike some as a shocking exhibition of aesthetic irresponsibility. There is still to come, from those who espouse this amazingly frivolous thesis, an explanation that will make it clear how any work of art could possibly be viable if its different parts were irreconcilable as members of a coherent imaginative whole. But this is something which neither Sir George nor those commentators who share his views have bothered to explain.

Some of these commentators have told us that the symphony is integrated, and its unity of design established, by the intervallic similarity of certain of its themes. But this does not dispose of the deeper question of its spiritual and poetical unity. *That* question will not down! Beethoven himself, by his resort

to words and to definite poetic concepts in his choral finale, has compelled us
to ask it, and to remain unsatisfied until we find an answer. We are obliged
to seek extramusical meanings in the symphony as a whole because Beethoven
has plainly invited us to do so; unless we are willing to admit that the work
is a gigantic hybrid, a mixture of species—three-fourths absolute music and
one-fourth cantata, with no unifying spiritual characteristic to give meaning
and integrity to the whole.

One may doubt if it is that. One chooses rather to believe that it is held
together by some unifying poetic principle, some spiritual cord which threads
it, in Shankara's phrase, 'like the string in a chain of pearls.'

The skeptical may wonder if Beethoven's imaginative conception of his
symphony was one that could be put into words. It is quite possible that some
integrating spiritual principle grew into the work without Beethoven's being
consciously aware of it. The processes of musical creation are among the
deeper mysteries of the human will. No musical artist knows quite what he
is saying, or why he is saying it, or from what unfathomable spring his thoughts
have issued. And it is easy to believe that what Wagner's sympathetic penetration discovered in the work as a whole is merely the projection in words of
a mystical conception unrealized by Beethoven himself. If we chose to feel
that in this symphony as a whole, Beethoven, as Noel Sullivan has finely said,
'is not describing to us a spiritual history—he is presenting to us a vision of
life,' we are endowing it with a significance which the music itself profoundly
justifies.

It would seem, then, that there is ground for reassuring ourselves that the
Ninth is really the marvel that we had long suspected it to be, long wanted
it to be. We need not, unless we choose, deny it spiritual and poetic integrity.
We need not feel that it is merely the superb musician who speaks to us from
this score. We are encouraged to believe that Beethoven the musician is doubled
here by Beethoven the dreaming seer, knowing things that we know not,
having a lamp that we have lost, lifting veil after veil beyond the circling
world.

Perhaps only those who approach the mysteries and clarities of Beethoven's
imaginative world with simplicity of spirit, with honesty of purpose, with
affection and with awe, can give us a true sense of the special quality of the
Ninth—its strange blend of fatefulness and transport, wild humor and super-
terrestrial beauty, its mystery and exaltation, its tragical despair and its shouting
among the stars.

● CONCERTO FOR PIANO AND ORCHESTRA, No. 1, IN C MAJOR, OP. 15

This concerto, published as No. 1, is often said to be in reality Beethoven's
Second Concerto for Piano. As a matter of fact, it is neither the first nor is it
the second piano concerto that Beethoven wrote in whole or in part, but the
fourth. There are five piano concertos by Beethoven in the active repertory.
But, actually, Beethoven wrote six concertos for the instrument, and part of
a seventh.

As a lad of fourteen, at Bonn, he composed a concerto for piano and orchestra in the key of E-flat. The manuscript, thirty-two pages, contains the solo part complete, with the orchestral introduction and interludes in piano transcription. There are indications, says Thayer, that the work was scored for small orchestra—strings, flutes, and horns only. This composition was long unknown. Thayer included it in his Catalogue of Beethoven's works published at Berlin in 1865, and quoted the themes. Guido Adler afterward prepared an edition of the music, and this was published in 1888 in the supplement to Breitkopf & Härtel's Complete Edition.

What remains of Beethoven's second Concerto for Piano was unearthed, in copy (solo and orchestra parts), by Adler in 1888. These were found in the possession of Joseph Bezeczny, the head of an educational institution for the blind at Prague. Only the first movement of the concerto survives. It is in the key of D. It was performed at Vienna on April 7, 1889, and was afterward published, as edited by Adler, in the supplement to the Complete Works. Its authenticity was questioned by the vigilant Paumgartner, who thought he had proved his case when he drew attention to the Mozartean characteristics of the music—ignoring, apparently, the fact that for a long time after 1785, especially after Beethoven had met Mozart in Vienna, he was wholly, as Thayer observes, in Mozart's thrall. Thayer thinks it safe to assume that this movement of an uncompleted D major piano concerto was written between Beethoven's eighteenth and twenty-third year, in the period 1788-93—'perhaps before, rather than after 1790.' He conjectures that Beethoven attached little value to it, and laid it aside.

The third piano concerto written in whole or in part by Beethoven (regarding the fragmentary D major as the second) is that in B-flat major, op. 19. It was composed, in Thayer's belief, 'at the latest in March, 1795,' when Beethoven was twenty-five. It was played by the composer at Vienna, as 'an entirely new concerto,' on March 29, 1795, but was not published until 1801, when it was printed by Hoffmeister as Concerto 'No. 2.'

The C major Concerto, op. 15 was published in 1801, as 'No. 1.' It was actually the fourth piano concerto composed by Beethoven in whole or in part. Bekker gives the date of composition as 1797, and the date of the first performance as possibly the Vienna concert of April 2, 1800, at which Beethoven presented for the first time his First Symphony, in the same key.

The last three of the concertos bring us upon familiar ground. They are:

The Concerto in C minor ('No. 3'), op. 37, composed in 1800, performed for the first time, probably, by Beethoven on April 5, 1803; published in 1804.

The Concerto in G major ('No. 4'), op. 58, completed in 1806, performed for the first time in public at Vienna December 22, 1808 (it had been played in private, at Prince Lobkowitz's, in March 1807); published in 1808.

The Concerto in E-flat major ('No. 5,' the 'Emperor'), op. 73, composed in 1809, performed for the first time, probably, at Leipzig, November 28, 1811; published in the same year.

The three movements of the C major Concerto are: (1) 'Allegro con brio,' C major, 4-4; (2) Largo, A-flat major, 4-4; (3) Allegro, C major, 2-2.

One recalls no more apt comment upon this concerto—a comment at once felicitous and concise—than these words of Pitts Sandborn's: 'Although one hesitates, where there is a question of anything by Beethoven, to run counter to the dicta of Paul Bekker [Bekker dismisses this concerto as 'merely interesting through indicating the course of Beethoven's development'], the C major piano concerto—that redoubtable gentleman to the contrary notwithstanding —is a masterpiece in miniature. Vivacious, chic, sparkling, and touched with an harmonic pungency that must have seemed quite astonishing when Beethoven himself played this concerto at the Vienna Burgtheater, the opening and closing Allegros are entirely delightful today. And the intervening Largo is even more. This romanza is touched with a divinity that stems unmistakably from Mozart, breathing forth in its flowering the heavenly aroma of the quartet "Non ti fidar" and the "Mask Trio" in *Don Giovanni.'*

• CONCERTO FOR PIANO AND ORCHESTRA, NO. 2, IN B-FLAT, OP. 19

‡Beethoven's B-flat Concerto, published as No. 2, but actually (see above) of earlier date than the C major Concerto, No. 1, is the weakest of his published works in this form and is seldom performed. Its three movements are: (1) an 'Allegro con brio,' 4-4, in B-flat; (2) an Adagio, 3-4, in E-flat major; and (3) a concluding Rondo, 'Molto allegro,' 6-8, in B-flat.‡

• CONCERTO FOR PIANO AND ORCHESTRA, NO. 3, IN C MINOR, OP. 37

This concerto, composed in 1800, was contemporaneous with Beethoven's First Symphony, the oratorio *Christ on the Mount of Olives*, the Septet, and the first half-dozen of the string quartets.

Beethoven's pupil, Ries, has left us an entertaining account of the first public performance of the C minor Concerto, which occurred, probably, at a remarkable concert given by Beethoven on April 5, 1803, at the Theater-an-der-Wien, the program of which contained not only the new piano concerto, but the First and Second symphonies, *The Mount of Olives*, and some vocal numbers.

The rehearsal [says Ries] began at 8 o'clock in the morning. It was a terrible one, and at half after 2 everybody was exhausted and more or less dissatisfied. Prince Karl Lichnowsky, who attended the rehearsal from the beginning, had sent for bread and butter, cold meat, and wine in large baskets. He pleasantly asked all to help themselves, and this was done with both hands, the result being that good nature was restored again. Then the Prince requested that the oratorio be rehearsed once more from the beginning, so that it might go well in the evening, and Beethoven's first work in this genre be worthily presented.

And so the rehearsal began again.

Ries afterward played the concerto himself—at a concert in the Augarten, Vienna, in July 1804.

Beethoven [he writes] had given me his beautiful Concerto in C minor, op. 37, in manuscript, so that I might make my first public appearance as his pupil with it, and I am the only one who ever appeared as such while Beethoven was alive. . . Beethoven himself conducted, but he only turned the pages and never, perhaps, was a concerto more beautifully accompanied. We had two large rehearsals. I had asked Beethoven to write a cadenza for me, but he refused and told me to write one for myself and he would correct it. Beethoven was satisfied with my composition and made few changes; but there was an extremely brilliant and very difficult passage in it, which, though he liked it, seemed to him too venturesome, wherefore he told me to write another in its place. A week before the concert he wanted to hear the cadenza again. I played it and floundered in the passage; he again, this time a little ill-naturedly, told me to change it. I did so, but the new passage did not satisfy me; I therefore studied the other, and zealously, but was not quite sure of it. When the cadenza was reached in the public concert Beethoven quietly sat down. I could not persuade myself to choose the easier one. When I boldly began the more difficult one, Beethoven violently jerked his chair; but the cadenza went through all right and Beethoven was so delighted that he shouted 'Bravo!' loudly. This electrified the entire audience and at once gave me a standing among the artists. Afterward, while expressing his satisfaction, he added: 'But all the same you are willful! If you had made a slip in the passage I would never have given you another lesson.'

The piano part of the C minor Concerto, according to Ries, was never completely written out in the score: 'Beethoven wrote it down on separate sheets of paper expressly for me.'

Vincent d'Indy insisted upon regarding all of the works composed by Beethoven up to the year 1801 as those of 'a good pupil,' though 'a pupil of genius.' But this rather sweeping generalization should perhaps except the C minor Concerto, in which there are striking and individual pages, memorable touches of power and originality.

- CONCERTO FOR PIANO AND ORCHESTRA, NO. 4, IN G MAJOR, OP. 58

The French army entered Vienna November 13, 1805, and Beethoven's quondam idol, Bonaparte, established himself at Schönbrunn. The Austrian Emperor and the aristocracy had packed their belongings and gone elsewhere, leaving the conquered city to the French. It was in the midst of these somewhat distracting conditions that Beethoven accomplished the task of getting his *Fidelio* produced at Vienna; and it is a striking proof of the fundamental equanimity of the man's soul that, despite this external turmoil, he should have been able to apply himself to creative work upon two of his most consequential scores—the C minor Symphony and the Piano Concerto in G, both of which occupied his mind at about this time. The concerto was finished in 1806. It was played by Beethoven for the first time at a private concert in Prince Lobkowitz's house, Vienna, in March 1807, and was disclosed to the public of Vienna on December 22 of the following year. Beethoven was thirty-six when he completed the score.

A critical historian has spoken of 'the development of the concerto idea in Beethoven's mind from the time when it was still under the influence of Mozart, and the belief that a concerto must be a show-piece for the instrument, up to the complete emancipation of his conviction that the instrument was but a co-agent with the orchestra in the publication of a vast musical project as lofty, aspiring and beautiful as it was vast.' An arresting moment in that growth is the slow movement of the G major Concerto: 'that matchless dialogue between the solo instrument and the orchestra.' ('One of the most original and imaginative things that ever fell from the pen of Beethoven or

any other musician,' Sir George Grove calls it.) Certainly there issues from
this Andante the gaze of the greater Beethoven—that 'large, tender, luminous
eye' of which some have discovered a premonition in the slow movement of
the early concerto in B-flat (op. 19). As for the G major Concerto as a whole,
Huneker declared that it 'outrivals its four companions in poetic meaning,
graciousness of mood, and elfin spirit'; and for him, the Rondo was full of
magic.

Sir George Grove has set down some interesting details about the public
history of this concerto. 'It remained for many years,' he tells us, 'comparatively unknown. Between the less difficult C minor ("No. 3") and the more
imposing E-flat ("No. 5") it was overlooked, and, strange as it may seem, ran
the risk of being forgotten. Its revival was due to Mendelssohn, who seized the
opportunity of his appointment as conductor of the Gewandhaus Concerts at
Leipzig to bring forward this and many another fine composition which had
been unjustly allowed to remain in the shade. Schumann preserved the following little memorandum of the performance, which took place on November 3, 1836:

' "This day Mendelssohn played the G major Concerto of Beethoven with
a power and finish that transported us all. I received a pleasure from it such
as I have never enjoyed, and I sat in my place without moving a muscle or
even breathing—afraid of making the least noise!" '

- CONCERTO FOR PIANO AND ORCHESTRA, NO. 5, IN E-FLAT MAJOR, OP. 73
  ('Emperor')

There are in music certain First Pages, certain exordiums, that subdue the
mind at once by the superb and conquering power of their address—the
opening of the Fifth Symphony, of the *Meistersinger* Prelude, of Brahms'
Symphony in F major, of Strauss's *Thus Spake Zarathustra*, of certain organ
works by Bach. It would be engrossing to attempt a comprehensive list.
Among the first half-dozen that would appear on it would assuredly be the
magnificent page with which Beethoven opens the 'Emperor' Concerto. Those
chords for the orchestra, and the imposing entrance of the piano: this is the
greater Beethoven, the tonal painter who could sweep a mighty brush over
epic canvases.

Yet are these opening pages more to be treasured than the noble simplicity
and elevation of the devotional Adagio; than the captivating Rondo, with its
surprising and exquisite coda?

The concerto was written in 1809, at Vienna. From May till October of
that year Vienna was held by the French. It cannot have been a restful spot.
Beethoven's lodging was 'much exposed to the firing,' says Sir George Grove,
and the noise disturbed him greatly, so that on one occasion at least he took
refuge in the cellar of his brother's house to escape it. 'It is remarkable how
slightly external events interfered with his powers of production,' observes Sir
George; 'as far as quality goes, the piano concerto in E-flat and the string
quartet in the same key (op. 74)—both of which bear the date 1809—are
equal to any in the whole range of his works.' It is more than remarkable: it

is amazing. In this music there is no hint of spiritual confusion or distress. There are, on the contrary, strength and serenity and self-command, and a quality of inspiration that seems at times not only aloof but otherworldly.

● CONCERTO FOR VIOLIN AND ORCHESTRA, IN D MAJOR, OP. 61

‡Beethoven composed only a single concerto for violin. The work is assigned to the year 1806 and is thus contemporaneous with the Fourth Symphony and the three Rasoumovsky quartets. It was first performed, at Vienna, in the Theater-an-der-Wien, by the violinist Franz Clement. Clement played it at sight, without rehearsal (the story goes that Beethoven did not deliver the manuscript to him until the day of the concert), and then exhibited another phase of his artistry by performing a piece of his own composition *holding his instrument upside down.* 'Perhaps it is not astonishing under these circumstances,' writes Morris Hastings, 'that the concerto remained in comparative obscurity until Joachim revived it many years later and disclosed its true magnificence.'‡

The première took place on December 23, 1806. There were some in the audience who were disturbed by Beethoven's 'audacities.' The worthy Johann Nepomuk Möser wrote solemnly in the *Theaterzeitung* that 'it is to be feared that if Beethoven continues upon this path, he and the public will fare badly.' He gave Beethoven a friendly hint: if the composer would only employ 'his indubitable talents' by producing more such works as 'the first symphonies in C and D, the charming septet in E-flat, the ingenious quintet in D major,' he would be more fittingly occupied. Möser complained also that certain passages in the concerto were too much repeated, and that 'the continuity is often broken'; but he granted the work 'many beauties.'

The first movement ('Allegro ma non troppo,' D major, 4-4) exhibits Beethoven the innovator, for it contains the celebrated D-sharp in the first violins (tenth bar) that must have caused many a gasp, even among musical radicals, in the year 1806. The incomparable slow movement, a Larghetto of exalted poetic beauty (G major, 4-4), offered much smoother sailing. The first theme is for the most part in the orchestra, the solo violin embellishing it with exquisite effect. The second theme—a cantilena that only Beethoven could have written—is sung by the solo violin.

The Finale, an exuberant Rondo, has a theme suggestive of a folk dance (Allegro, D major, 6-8).

● TRIPLE CONCERTO FOR PIANO, VIOLIN, 'CELLO, AND ORCHESTRA, IN C MAJOR, OP. 56

Beethoven sketched this work, according to Thayer, 'at the latest, in the spring of 1805'; and he refers to Nottlebohn's researches as showing that all the movements of the concerto were outlined in 1804. The piano part appears to have been written for Beethoven's pupil, the Archduke Rudolph, who was then in his sixteenth year.

I have just now several works [wrote Beethoven to Breitkopf & Härtel from Vienna, August 26, 1804], and because I think of giving them to you, my wish to see them soon published will perhaps be satisfied all the sooner. I therefore tell you straight off what I can give you: my Oratorio [the *Mount of Olives*]; a new Grand Symphony [the 'Eroica']; a Concertante for violin, 'cello, and pianoforte with full orchestra; three new solo sonatas. . . Now if you are willing to take these things, you must kindly tell me exactly the time at which you would be able to deliver them. As I have a strong desire that at least the first three works should appear as soon as possible, we would fix the time by writing, or contract (according to your suggestion); and to this, I tell you quite frankly, I should hold you strictly. The Oratorio has not hitherto been published, because I have added to it an altogether new chorus and several other things; for I wrote the whole Oratorio in a few weeks, and afterwards I was not quite satisfied with it. . . The Symphony is really entitled *Bonaparte*, and in addition to the usual instruments there are, specially, three obbligato horns. I believe it will interest the musical public. . . About the other things I have nothing more to add, although a concertante with three such concerting parts is indeed also something new. If, as I expect, you agree to the *conditions stated* for these works as regards their publication, I would give them to you for a fee of 2000 fl. I assure you, on my honor, that, with regard to certain works—such as, for instance, sonatas—I am a loser, since I get almost 60 ducats for a single solo sonata. Pray do not think that I boast—far be it from me to do anything of the sort—but in order the quicker to arrange for an edition of my works, I am ready to be a loser to some extent. . .

The Triple Concerto was among the few publications of 1807, together with the 'Appassionata' Sonata and the Thirty-two Variations in C minor. It was first performed in public at a summer concert in the Augarten, Vienna, in 1807. After that it was not played again in the composer's lifetime. In 1830 the pianist Bocklet, the violinist Mayseder, and the 'cellist Merk revived it in the Austrian capital. The concerto is interesting, aside from its intrinsic musical quality, as an early nineteenth-century exfoliation of the concerto grosso of the Bach period.

The first movement runs true to the concerto form of its day, with the double exposition, first by the orchestra, then for the solo instruments. The chief theme of the movement (Allegro, C major, 4-4) is exhibited by the 'cellos and basses alone; the second theme (G major) by the first violins against a triplet figure for violas and 'cellos. In the second exposition (for the solo players), the main subject is entrusted to the 'cello. The solo violin enters nine measures later, and soon the piano has its turn at the principal theme, dolce. The development section is extensive, and there is a long coda.

The slow movement is a Largo in A-flat major, 3-8. The solo 'cello begins the tale, 'molto cantabile' (after three introductory measures for the strings, with the violins muted). Then the clarinets and bassoons take it up, while the piano embroiders the melody with flowing arabesques, and the solo strings, following, add their voices. This movement leads directly into the Finale:

'Rondo alla Polacca' (C major, 3-4): The chief theme is played by the 'cello, with string accompaniment, then by the violin. The Polacca rhythm is craftily established, used with fascinating effect, and craftily abandoned. The coda begins in 2-4 time, Allegro; but the first tempo is restored, with a reminiscence of the Polacca.

The orchestral part of the concerto is scored for flute, two oboes, two clarinets, two bassoons, two horns, two trumpets, timpani, and strings.

- OVERTURE TO *Fidelio*, OP. 72
- OVERTURE, *Leonore* NO. 1, OP. 138
- OVERTURE, *Leonore* NO. 2, OP. 72a
- OVERTURE, *Leonore* NO. 3, OP. 72a

The facts (or, more strictly, the conjectures) regarding the various overtures which Beethoven composed for his opera are not yet agreed upon by musicologists. But we may quote here what the late H. E. Krehbiel, admirable editor of the English edition of Thayer's Life of Beethoven, and a magistral authority upon the master and his works, had to say on the subject:

Beethoven wrote four overtures for *Fidelio*, the only opera he ever composed, and there is fragmentary evidence that for a while he contemplated still another. This, as a matter of fact, would have stood as the fourth in the series, but it need not concern us, since the work never proceeded further than a few sketches. Three of the overtures are known as 'Leonore No. 1,' 'Leonore No. 2,' and 'Leonore No. 3'—'Leonore' being the name by which the opera was known during the period, after which the title was changed to 'Fidelio' to avoid association with two settings of the same subject which had been previously made—one in French by Gaveaux, one in Italian by Paër. With the change of title Beethoven never was agreed.

Much confusion long existed in the books (and still exists, for that matter), touching the order in which the overtures were composed. The early biographers were mistaken on that point, and the blunder was perpetuated by the numbering of the works when the overtures were printed. The true first 'Leonore' overture is that known as No. 2. This was the opera's original introduction, and was performed at the first performance in 1805. The story of the production is a sorrowful one. It took place on November 20, at a most unpropitious time. Vienna was occupied by the French troops, Bonaparte was at Schönbrunn, the Austrian Emperor had deserted his capital and most of the nobility and the wealthy patrons of art had followed his example. The performance was a failure, the people who heard it saying that the music was not to their taste, and the opera too long. Repetitions followed on November 21 and 22, but the popular verdict was not reversed. The opera was withdrawn for revision and changes were made, much against Beethoven's will, but in deference to the advice of his friends who met at the house of Prince Lichnowsky for the purpose of saving the work by remedying its defects. In a revised form, the opera was put on the stage a second time on March 29, 1806. The overture had also been revised, and that played at the revival was the one now known as 'Leonore No. 3.' The name of the opera had been changed to 'Fidelio.' In the new form the opera made a better impression, but Beethoven quarrelled with the management and took his work off the boards. It was not heard in Vienna again until 1814. Then it appeared with the introduction now known as the 'Fidelio' Overture.

For performances contemplated when German opera was introduced in Prague in 1807, Beethoven wrote the overture which is now known as 'Leonore No. 1';[1] it was

[1] It should be noted that this so-called 'Leonore No. 1' which Nottebohm, and after him Thayer and Deiters, believe to have been not really No. 1 in a chronological sense, but No. 3, presumably written in 1807, as Krehbiel supposed, for a projected performance at Prague, is now thought by certain German musicologists to be, after all, the veritable first overture written by Beethoven for his opera. The *Leonore* No. 1, op. 138, was described by Schindler as the one that was 'really written by Beethoven as the first overture to his opera, but it was found too light and uncharacteristic when

to be 'easier' of performance. The Prague enterprise fell to the ground, however, and the overture remained unknown till after Beethoven's death.

‡Today, the *Fidelio* overture is used to introduce performances of Beethoven's opera, while the *Leonore* No. 3 serves as an entr'acte preceding the final scene of the work.‡ The *Fidelio* differs from its predecessors in mood and texture. It contains no thematic material from the opera; and its spirit is not somber and exalted, but vivacious and gay. Paul Bekker doubts if Beethoven 'felt any particular inner compulsion' to its composition. 'It has,' he writes, 'the general festal and joyous character of a concert overture. . . It is clear that the work was intended to be a prelude and no more.' ‡The overtures *Leonore* No. 1 and *Leonore* No. 2 are now not commonly associated with performances of the opera, but are performed with some frequency as concert pieces. They derive thematically from the opera and in this respect—and structurally as well—bear certain resemblances to the more celebrated *Leonore* No. 3.‡

Richard Wagner declared that the third *Leonore* Overture is 'less an overture to a music-drama than the music-drama itself'; and certainly this wonderful symphonic projection, a dramatic pattern in tones if ever there was one, does condense and epitomize the substance of the drama in a marvelously concise and vivid way.

Wagner's tribute appears in an essay, 'On the Overture,' published originally in the *Gazette Musicale* of January 10th, 14th, and 17th, 1841. William Ashton Ellis translated it for Vol. vii of his edition of Wagner's Prose Works. Here are some brief excerpts from Wagner's essay:

> Far from giving us a mere musical introduction to the drama, it [the *Leonore* No. 3] sets that drama more completely and more movingly before us than ever happens in the stage action which ensues. This work is no longer an overture, but the mightiest of dramas in itself. . .
>
> In this wondrous tone poem, Beethoven has given us a musical drama, a drama founded on a playwright's piece, and not the mere sketch of one of its main ideas, or even a purely preparatory introduction to the acted play; but a drama, be it said, in the most ideal meaning of the term. . . His object was to condense to its noblest unity the *one* sublime action which the dramatist had weakened and delayed by paltry details in order to spin out the tale; to give it a new, an ideal motion, fed solely by its inmost springs. . .
>
> This is the Leonore Overture, Beethoven's poem. Here all is alive with unceasing dramatic progress, from the first yearning thought to the execution of a vast resolve.

● OVERTURE TO *Coriolanus*, OP. 62

The learned Sir William Smith considered the tale of Coriolanus 'one of the most beautiful of the early Roman legends.' Its hero received the surname 'Coriolanus' because of the valor which he displayed in the capture of the

rehearsed at the home of Prince Lichnowsky, and was discarded.' This formerly disputed assertion of Schindler's has more recently been restored to respectability—see Braunstein's *Beethovens Leonoren-Ouverturen.*

Volscian town of Corioli. But the arrogant attitude of Coriolanus toward the Commons excited their hatred and apprehension, and in 941 B.C. he was impeached and condemned to exile. He took refuge among the Volscians, and promised to help them in war against the Romans. Attius Tullius, King of the Volscians, appointed him general of his army, and Coriolanus took many towns, advancing without resistance until, in 489, he reached the Cluilian dyke near Rome. There he encamped, and the Romans, in panic, sent to him numerous embassies, consisting of the most distinguished men of the state, who sought to placate him. But Coriolanus was obdurate. Then the noblest matrons of Rome, headed by Veturia the mother of Coriolanus, and Volumnia his wife, with his two children, visited him in his tent, and, by dint of warm reproaches and copious weeping (as was even then the practice) turned his will to water. Whereupon he led away his army, and abode innocuously in exile among the Volscians until he died a natural death; though another tradition relates that he was killed by the Volscians upon his return to their country.

The Coriolanus of Beethoven's tonal portrait is not the tragic hero of Shakespeare's version of the ancient and familiar tale, but the hero of a drama by Heinrich Joseph von Collin, a play-writing contemporary of Beethoven. The overture, composed in 1807, was published in the following year.

In their main outlines, the plays of Collin and of Shakespeare are alike, with, however, this difference: the Coriolanus of Shakespeare is slain, while the death of Collin's hero is self-inflicted.

● OVERTURE TO *König Stephen*, OP. 117

To celebrate the opening of the new theater at Budapest in October 1811, Augustus von Kotzebue, the Hungarian dramatist, supplied a Prologue, *König Stephen, Ungarns erster Wohlthäter* ('Hungary's First Benefactor'); a drama, *Belas Flucht*; and an Epilogue, *Die Ruinen von Athen*. For the Prologue and Epilogue, Beethoven was commissioned to write music. He began the task in May 1811, and was done with it before the autumn. But the dedication of the theater was postponed until February 9, 1812, when Beethoven's music finally came to a hearing. It was praised as 'excellent and very original, wholly worthy of the master.'

The overture known as *König Stephen* served as prelude to Kotzebue's play, the chief character of which is Stephen I of Hungary. That potentate lived between 997 (approximately) and 1038. He married Gisela, Princess of Bavaria, with whom he was not happy. He was canonized, and on his Saint's Day, August 20, his memory is solemnly revered.

Beethoven's overture (in E-flat major) begins with a slow introduction, 'Andante con moto,' 2-4, of uncertain tonality. The flute has a gypsy-like tune, and this gypsy character extends also to the first theme of the Presto, stated by wind instruments. The second subject, for flutes and clarinets in thirds, is curiously like the 'Joy' theme of the Ninth Symphony. The overture is exceedingly simple in form. It is scored for woodwind in pairs, with a contrabassoon; four horns, two trumpets, timpani, and strings.

- OVERTURE, *Die Weihe des Hauses,* OP. 124

Beethoven's *Dedication of the House* Overture was composed for the opening of the Josephstadt Theater in Vienna, which took place October 3, 1822. The slow and majestic introduction to the overture enlists the solemn strain of trombones, of which no further use is made. The 'motif' on which the whole of the Allegro is built derives from five notes corresponding to those of the words 'is the king of . . .' in the phrase, 'He is the King of Glory,' in the chorus, 'Lift up your heads,' in Handel's *Messiah.* Beethoven sometimes referred to this work as the 'Overture in Handel's Style.' In one form or another, the thematic bit is repeated over two hundred times. In the hands of a lesser master than Beethoven this would undoubtedly tend toward monotony. In this work, however, there is no such suggestion.

- OVERTURE TO *Die Geschöpfe des Prometheus,* OP. 43

Beethoven in 1800 composed music to a 'heroic and allegorical ballet,' *Die Geschöpfe des Prometheus* ('The Creatures of Prometheus'). The scenario of the ballet was devised by the dancer and choreographer, Salvatore Vigano, who was born in Naples, March 29, 1769, danced his way through Europe from Venice to Hamburg, and died at Milan August 10, 1821. Vigano, wishing to compliment Maria Theresa, the second wife of the Emperor Francis, composed his *Prometheus* Ballet in her honor, while he dwelt in Vienna. Since Beethoven had dedicated his Septet to Maria Theresa in 1800, Vigano had the happy idea of inviting him to compose the music for his ballet. The ballet, together with Beethoven's music—an Overture, an 'Introduction,' and sixteen other numbers—was performed for the first time at the Imperial Court Theater, Vienna, on March 28, 1801. The following description of the action was printed in the program:

The foundation of this allegorical ballet is the fable of Prometheus. The philosophers of Greece allude to Prometheus as a lofty soul who drove the people of his time from ignorance, refined them by means of science and the arts, and gave them manners, customs, and morals. As a result of that conception, two statues that have been brought to life are introduced in this ballet; and these, through the might of harmony, are made sensitive to all the passions of human life. Prometheus leads them to Parnassus, in order that Apollo, the god of the fine arts, may enlighten them. Apollo gives them as teachers Amphion, Arion, and Orpheus to instruct them in music, Melpomene to teach them tragedy, Thalia for comedy, Terpsichore and Pan for the shepherd's dance, and Bacchus for the heroic dance, of which he was the originator.

The ballet was immensely successful in Vienna, and afterward in Italy, but the greater part of the delighted comment which it occasioned was given to the choreography of the balletmaster Vigano, compared with whose pictures and pantomimes the music seemed to the spectators to be of secondary consequence. The book of the ballet is lost, but Beethoven's music for it remains. Two features of the score form interesting subjects for discussion. In a love scene (the fifth number of the score, an Adagio in B-flat) Beethoven used the harp for the first and last time in his career; in the Finale, he used a melody which appears also in the Finale of the 'Eroica' Symphony, and is the theme of a *contretanz* and of the piano variations, op. 35.

The *Prometheus* music as a whole is seldom heard, but the overture survives in the standard concert repertoire. This overture has none of the profundity and power which characterize the greater Beethoven overtures. Some of Beethoven's early commentators were disappointed in it because it seemed to them insufficiently consequential for the ideas suggested by the title—even the devoted Lenz was provoked into referring to it as 'a freckle on Beethoven's youthful cheek' (Beethoven was thirty when he composed it). Yet, as later commentators have pointed out, if it were necessary to justify the style chosen by Beethoven for the overture, this might easily be done by recalling the purpose for which the music was written: *The Creatures of Prometheus* was a ballet, not a drama like *Egmont* or *Coriolanus*.

● OVERTURE AND INCIDENTAL MUSIC TO *Egmont*, OP. 84

Goethe began work upon his *Egmont* at Frankfort in 1775, shortly before his departure for Weimar, as an expedient for distracting his mind from thoughts of Lili Schönemann. He worked at the tragedy spasmodically, remodeling it in the summer of 1787. It was finished in the autumn of that year, and published in 1788.

Goethe, when writing his drama, threw the Muse of History out of the window, thus provoking Schiller's famous strictures. The real Egmont had a wife and nine children; Goethe made him a bachelor. Schiller took him to task for this, and also for exhibiting Egmont as in love. In this respect, observed George Henry Lewes, Goethe 'departed from heroic dignity.' It is hard to see why. May not heroes love? But Goethe knew what he was doing. 'For my purpose,' he said, 'I was obliged to convert [Egmont] into a character possessing qualities which better become a young man than a man in years— an unmarried man better than a man of family—an independent man . . . unrestricted by multiform ties.'

Madame de Staël considered *Egmont* 'the finest of Goethe's tragedies.' Lewes thinks it is 'far, very far, from being a masterpiece. As a tragedy, criticism makes sad work of it; but when all is said, the reader thinks of Egmont and Clärchen, and flings criticism to the dogs.'

It is a sombre and tragic episode in history which is treated in this piece [observes Lewes]. The revolution of the Netherlands was one imperiously commanded by the times; it was the revolt of citizens against exasperating oppression; of conscience against religious tyranny; of the nation against a foreigner. The Duke of Alva, who thought it better that the Emperor should lose the Netherlands than rule over a nation of heretics, but who was by no means willing that the Netherlands should be lost, came to replace the Duchess of Parma in the regency; came to suppress with the sword and scaffold the rebellion of the heretics. The strong contrasts of Spaniard and Hollander, of Catholic and Protestant, of despotism and liberty which this subject furnishes, are all *indicated* by Goethe; but he has not used them as powerful dramatic elements.

Egmont the popular hero—joyous, kind, careless, unsuspicious, a would-be liberator tragically frustrate—is conducted by Goethe to a finale which Schiller thought 'operatic': Egmont asleep in prison, with the disappearing back wall and the vision of Clärchen as the figure of Liberty, resting upon a cloud, extending a laurel wreath to the sleeping hero and hailing him as conqueror; the martyr's awakening, and the entrance of the soldiers, who lead him to execution.

Beethoven in 1809-10 composed music for Goethe's tragedy. This music comprises, in addition to the familiar overture, nine numbers: four entr'actes, two songs sung by Clärchen, and three orchestral movements: 'Clärchen's Death,' 'Melodrama,' and a 'Triumph' Symphony, the latter virtually identical with the coda of the overture. This music was performed for the first time in conjunction with the drama at the Hofburg Theater, Vienna, May 24, 1810. It is program music in the best sense of the term. That Beethoven intended it as such is at once apparent, as various commentators have pointed out, from the heading of several of the movements—e.g. 'Clärchen's Death,' and 'Symphony of Victory'; further, certain passages of the instrumental movements are docketed with such superscriptions as 'She extinguishes the lamp,' 'He goes to sleep as the music continues,' 'Indicating Egmont's death,' 'The victory of freedom gained for his country by Egmont's death,' and 'Freedom draws near, to place the crown on Egmont's head,' et cetera.

In view of Beethoven's expressed intentions regarding certain portions of his incidental music to *Egmont* [wrote Mr. C. A. Barry], it may be asked: are we not justified in extending these to the Overture? Is not this to be viewed as a dramatic tone-picture? Though entering more into generalities than the Overture to *Coriolanus*, which (as Wagner has pointed out) is restricted to a single scene, it is assuredly not less pronouncedly dramatic, or less expressive of the feelings of the principal personages concerned, and of the circumstances surrounding them. Egmont's patriotism and determination seem to be brought before us, in turn with Clärchen's devotion to him. The prevailing key (F minor) serves as an appropriate background to the general gloom of the dramatic picture, but it is occasionally relieved by its relative major (A-flat)—indicative, as it often seems, of Clärchen's loving presence. The Overture concludes with the *Sieges-Symphonie* (Symphony of Victory), which at the close of the drama immediately follows Egmont's last words: 'Fight for your hearths and homes, and die joyfully—after my example—to save that which you hold most dear,' addressed to his comrades as he is led away to execution. This music, occurring in the Overture, seems to indicate prophetically the victory of freedom to be gained by Egmont's death for . his country.

‡Aside from the overture, the four entr'actes, the two songs for Clärchen ('Die Trommel gerühret'—'Let beat the drum'; and 'Freudvoll und leidvoll'— 'Joyful and woeful'), and the final 'Triumph' Symphony, Beethoven's *Egmont* music embraces the following two numbers, occasionally heard in the concert hall:‡

'Clärchen's Death.' This orchestral movement is associated with the episode in the play in which Brackenburg brings to Clärchen the news that Egmont is to die, whereupon Clärchen ends her own life with poison. The music is a Larghetto in D minor, 9-8 time, beginning with repeated pianissimo octaves of the horns, above which the oboe sings a melody of penetrating expressiveness. It is answered by the muted strings, more and more softly, as Clärchen's life flickers out with the dying lamp. The piece is scored for solo oboe, two clarinets, two bassoons, two horns, timpani, and strings.

'Melodrama.' This accompanies the scene in which the doomed Egmont, seated on a couch in his cell, awaiting execution, falls asleep and perceives the vision of Clärchen, which prefigures his own apotheosis. Beethoven's orchestra plays during Egmont's words as he falls asleep and accompanies the projected vision of Clärchen.

● Missa Solemnis, FOR SOLO VOICES, CHORUS, AND ORCHESTRA, IN D MAJOR, OP. 123

Toward the end of August, in the year 1819, Beethoven's devoted friend and biographer, Anton Schindler, went to call upon Ludwig at his country home in Mödling, accompanied by Johann Horsalka. 'It was 4 o'clock in the afternoon,' wrote Schindler in his biography. . . 'In the living room, behind a locked door, we heard the master singing, howling, stamping. After we had been listening a long time to this almost awful scene, and were about to go away, the door opened and Beethoven stood before us with distorted features, calculated to excite fears. . . Never, it may be said, did so great an art work see its creation under more adverse circumstances.'

It was the Missa Solemnis by which Beethoven was thus possessed. We need not wonder at his agitation. For, in addition to his prodigious labors on the Mass, Beethoven was in bad health, he was distraught by personal difficulties of various kinds, and, as though he were not sufficiently occupied by the task of composing the most formidable religious score since the B minor Mass of Bach, he had but lately been making arduous side trips into the difficult uplands of the Ninth Symphony.

It was Beethoven's original intention to compose his setting of the words of the Mass to celebrate the installation as Archbishop of Olmütz of his pupil and patron, the Archduke Rudolph of Austria. The Archbishop's appointment became known about the middle of 1818; and Schindler tells us that 'without bidding, invitation, or summons of any kind, Beethoven resolved to compose a mass for the solemnity; thus turning again, after the lapse of many years, to the branch of his art toward which, after the symphonic form—as he himself often said—he felt himself most drawn. . . I saw the score [continues Schindler] begun late in the autumn of 1818, after the gigantic sonata in B-flat major, Opus 106, had just been finished.'

Beethoven gave himself heart and soul to the composition of the Mass, which was not only dedicated to the Archduke, but had been intended for him from the beginning—a fact which Thayer cites as proof that despite Beethoven's 'petulant outbursts against his exalted pupil, he was, after all, sincerely devoted to him.'

Portions of the Mass, probably the Kyrie and perhaps the Gloria, had been sketched by the end of 1818. The seriousness with which Beethoven applied himself to his task is indicated by his notations in the Tagebuch. For example:

In order to write true church music . . . look through all of the monastic church chorals and also the strophes in the most current translations and perfect prosody in all Christian-Catholic psalms and hymns generally.

Sacrifice again all the pettinesses of social life to your art. God above all things! For it is an eternal providence which directs omnisciently the good and evil fortunes of human men. . . Tranquilly will I submit myself to all vicissitudes and place my sole confidence in Thine unalterable goodness, O God! Be my rock, my light, forever my trust!

Rudolf's installation as Archbishop occurred on March 20, 1820; but Beethoven had long since given up any hope of completing his Mass in time for the event. A Mass by Hummel and an Offertory by Haydn were performed instead, and Beethoven went doggedly on with his score. He placed a manuscript copy of the Mass in the Archduke's hands on March 19, 1823; but he made numerous changes in the score thereafter, and the work did not receive its definitive shape until the middle of 1823.

The first performance anywhere of the Mass was given under the auspices of Beethoven's ardent and generous admirer, Prince Nicholas Galitzin, at St. Petersburg, on April 6, 1824, about a month prior to the performance at Vienna—May 7—of the *Kyrie, Credo,* and *Agnus Dei.* It is often erroneously stated that the performance of the *Kyrie, Credo,* and *Agnus Dei* at Vienna on May 7, 1824 was the first hearing of any portion of the Mass. In one of the standard published scores of the work the date of the St. Petersburg performance is given as 'March 26, 1844' (!)—twenty years after it occurred. Prince Galitzin's remarkable achievement in accomplishing the première of the gigantic work out of his own resources has had curiously little recognition.

If performances of the Mass are infrequent—relative, shall we say, to performances of Bach's Mass or *Matthauspassion*—doubtless the fact may be attributed largely to the cruel difficulty of the music: the parts for the singers are written with Beethoven's usual indifference to the limitations of the human voice. But, aside from this, the work offers many problems of style and interpretation. Beethoven paid scant attention to the rubrics, to institutional traditions and proprieties, to liturgical formulas. The *Missa Solemnis* is far more than a traditional setting of the text of the Mass. For Beethoven, as he proceeded in his treatment of the moving and marvelous words, responded more and more unrestrainedly to their emotional and imaginative suggestions, fixing his attention less on ecclesiastical or ceremonial decorum than on the human implications of the missal text. He remembered the grievous, unconquerable souls of men, suffering, fearing, longing, pleading, hoping, worshiping, praying. And at the thought of the timeless drama of human agony and aspiration, the sanctuary opened before his all-embracing vision and became the peopled earth and all mankind, and above them was a strangely echoing sky, and beyond, the break of day.

Indeed, it could be said of Beethoven in this universal and compassionate music, as it has been said of St. Francis, that his imagination did not falter 'until it held the world.'

Yet Beethoven himself declared that his chief design when writing the Mass 'was to arouse religious emotion in singers and auditors alike, and to render this emotion lasting.' The depth and intensity of Beethoven's piety admit of no dispute, although at no time in his mature life was he an orthodox churchman. 'If order and beauty are reflected in the constitution of the universe, then there is a God,' he wrote in his diary two years before he began the composition of the Mass. And although the cynical might wonder how much weight the initial 'if' in that sentence had in Beethoven's mind, it is impossible to arrive at any true understanding of the fundamentals of Beethoven's character and not realize that his religious beliefs were wholly unquestioning, wholly unaffected by any touch of intellectual subtlety. The Mass had its origin in a period during which Beethoven was oppressed by the melancholy and distress that were caused by his personal difficulties; yet we know from his own record of his thoughts at this time that his simple, unchallenging theism never deserted him. 'Hard is thy situation at present,' he confided touchingly to his journal at this period, 'but He above is, oh, He is! and nothing is without Him. God, my refuge, my rock, Thou seest my heart! Oh hear, Ever Ineffable One, hear me, Thy most unhappy of mortals!'

Beethoven recommended the Mass in D to the King of France as 'l'oeuvre le plus accompli.' He has not been left alone in his favorable opinion of it. Krehbiel once unhesitatingly hailed the work as 'the greatest of all compositions for voice and orchestra,' and Vincent d'Indy declared that in the presence of the Mass we stand before a work with which only the B minor Mass of Bach and the *Parsifal* of Wagner can be compared. These towering superlatives seem not inappropriately altitudinous. This op. 123 of Beethoven is very great music—no wonder that Beethoven raved and agonized as it was born of him, crying out in anguish while it was taking shape in his imagination and on his music paper. Those who were about him at the time say also that he 'seemed transfigured by it.' He had the meaning of the Latin words of the text minutely explained to him, with their proper accentuation. For almost five years he dwelt with them, filled with the anguish of parturition, but also with the ecstasy that must have sustained him as sheet after sheet of the wonderful score passed across his desk; and then one day he set down the last note, and on the manuscript of the *Kyrie* he wrote the simple and characteristic words: 'Von Herzen—möge es wieder zu Herzen gehen!'—'From the heart—may it go to the heart!'

The Beethoven whom we meet in the greater pages of the *Missa Solemnis* —in the *Benedictus* and in the close of the *Agnus Dei*—anticipates the Beethoven of the last phase: the Beethoven who speaks to us in the mystical and otherworldy pages of the last sonatas and quartets; Beethoven the brooding and clairvoyant dreamer, the self-communing seer.

As we sit before the prelude to the *Benedictus*, with its hushed and rapt and fathomless contemplation—in which, as D'Indy said, Beethoven has raised silence into sublimity: as we listen to the ineffable serenity and the superearthly beauty of the *Benedictus*—we know that this is the ultimate and essential Beethoven: that we have plumbed as deeply as we ever shall the mystery of a great spirit. We know that for Beethoven the tragical and passionate dreamer, so simple of heart, so racked by the task of living and by the spectacle of human conflict and frustration, this music of embracing humanity, of boundless tenderness and pity, was a solvent and a miraculous release. We know that, as he set it down, the prophecy of Isaiah must have come true for his turbulent and anguished spirit, and that the eyes of the blind were opened, and the ears of the deaf unstopped.

Alban Berg

1885-1935

B

Alban Berg spent most of his life in Vienna, the city of his birth. His talent for music showed itself early, and he was at first self-taught. But in his nineteenth year he met Arnold Schönberg, who became his only teacher and his friendly adviser. His op. 1, a piano sonata, dating from his twenty-third year, was followed by four songs to texts by Mombert and Hebbel, which 'harmonically,' it has been said, 'are still grounded in *Tristan* chromaticism and also reflect the influence of the whole-tone scale.' ‡ Succeeding works exemplified an ever-greater harmonic boldness, and it was not long before Berg thought and wrote entirely in the atonal idiom of his teacher. ‡ In the celebrated W*ozzeck*, op. 7, Berg is credited with having achieved 'the first extended opera freed from the bonds of tonality.' He died in Vienna in 1935, leaving a second opera, *Lulu,* unfinished.

● LYRIC SUITE, FOR STRING QUARTET (ARRANGED FOR STRING ORCHESTRA)

Four years after the completion of his remarkable opera, W*ozzeck,* Alban Berg composed a Lyric Suite for string quartet. The work, published in 1927, contained six movements: an 'Allegretto gioviale,' an 'Andante amoroso,' an 'Allegro misterioso,' an 'Adagio appassionato,' a 'Presto delirando,' and a 'Largo desolato.' A year later, Berg published three excerpts from the suite scored for string orchestra—first and second violins, violas, 'cellos, and double-basses. These are the second, third, and fourth of the original work: (*a*) 'Andante amoroso'; (*b*) 'Allegro misterioso,' with a 'Trio estatico' for middle portion (this entire movement is scored for muted strings; the double-basses, muted, are used only in the Trio); (c) 'Adagio appassionato.'

'The title,' writes Erwin Stein in a preface to the score of the suite, 'suggests the essentially unsymphonic character of the piece, in contrast to the pronounced symphonic characer of the majority of compositions for string quartet.'

. . . On the whole, the development is not symphonic, but lyrico-dramatic: a matter of atmosphere and expression. The tempo marks of the six parts show this immediately. The joyful, even temper of the 'Allegretto gioviale' is followed by a tender 'Andante amoroso.' After this comes an 'Allegro misterioso' of very pronounced character but of repressed expression, with violent outbreaks in the middle portion, the 'Trio estatico.' The summit of lyric expression is reached in the broad melody of the 'Adagio apassionato'. . .

Much of the music was composed in accordance with Schönberg's technique of the so-called 'composition with twelve inwardly related tones.' A set of twelve different tones gives the rough material of the composition, and the portions which have been treated more freely still adhere more or less to this technique.

The sections are connected with each other in a peculiar manner. For instance, a theme, idea, or passage in one movement always reappears in the next. In this way, certain measures of the 'Allegro misterioso' refer back to measures in the 'Andante amoroso.' The trio of the 'Allegro misterioso' is at the same time the exposition of the 'Adagio appassionato,' though the various forms reappear therein in a different sequence. . .

• CONCERTO FOR VIOLIN AND ORCHESTRA

This last completed work of Alban Berg has a remarkable history. It was written at the suggestion of the Boston violinist, Louis Krasner, a friend of the composer. Krasner desired the celebrated composer of the operas *Wozzeck* and *Lulu* to compose a piece for his use, and he broached the subject to Berg in the spring of 1935. Berg was then engrossed with the unfinished score of *Lulu*, and his interest in the concerto idea seems to have languished.

But in May of that year a personal tragedy stirred profoundly his emotions. A young and talented girl of eighteen named Manon Gropius, daughter of Otto and Alma Maria Gropius (the widow of Gustav Mahler, to whom Berg had dedicated the score of *Wozzeck*), died in Vienna after a long and agonizing illness, which she endured with affecting courage and serenity. Berg was devotedly attached to her, and the effect upon him of her death was at once shattering and imaginatively releasing. He applied himself to the composition of the violin concerto, which he now conceived as a threnody for his young friend. It became in his mind, and in its spirit and its contents, a tribute to the memory of the nature which had seemed to him so lovable and rare.

Shortly after he had completed the instrumentation of the concerto, Berg himself died at Vienna, leaving a memory of gentleness and ardor and sincerity which might well be envied by greater geniuses and lesser men.

The concerto is in two parts, and each of these parts is subdivided: Part One, into a preparatory Andante and a scherzo-like Allegretto; Part Two, into a tragic Allegro followed by the concluding Adagio. Berg is said to have conceived the Allegretto of the first part as a tonal portrait of Manon Gropius. The tortured Allegro holds the precipitation of his anguish and despair. The final Adagio is an elegy. On the manuscript is inscribed the dedication, *Dem Andenken eines Engels* ('To the memory of an Angel').

In the final Adagio, Berg has used a quotation from Bach—the last chorale of the sixtieth Cantata, 'O Ewigkeit, du Donnerwort,' based on a seventeenth-century melody by Johann Rudolphe Ahle of Mülhausen. From the chorale melody, Berg evolves a series of variations.

The instrumentation of the orchestral part is for two flutes, piccolo, two oboes, English horn, three clarinets and bass clarinet, two bassoons and double bassoon, alto saxophone in E-flat, four horns, two trumpets, two trombones and tuba, timpani, bass drum, side drum, tom-tom, gong, cymbals, triangle harp and strings.

The first performance of the work, with Krasner as soloist, was at Barcelona on April 19, 1936, in the course of the Festival of the International Society for Contemporary Music, less than four months after the composer's death.

Herr Willi Reich, of Vienna, spokesman for Berg and also his biographer, wrote for performances of the concerto the following exposition of Berg's constructive principles as applied in the composition of this work:

Free invention within the narrow confines of form is the earmark of Alban Berg's art, and it is the essential characteristic of the Violin Concerto. From the gently surging 'Andante' introduction, there are slowly disengaged mounting melodies, which gradually lapse into the fluctuating motion of the opening. As if rising from the unknown, the 'Allegretto-scherzo' which closes the first part pictures the lamented young woman in two passing trio-like episodes—the one tenderly dreaming, the other a lively folk-tune of native character.

A brief pause, and a turbulent passage introduces the second part, which is conceived as a free, restless, and stormy cadenza for the violin. The music drives its demonic and irresistible course, relieved only by a short and peaceful intermezzo, to the catastrophe. Heavy laments and sharp outcries are heard in the orchestra; then, over a long organ-point, a gradual falling away. At this poignant moment, there is suddenly introduced by the violin solo the grave chorale of J. S. Bach, derived from J. R. Ahle: 'Es ist genug! So nimm, Herr, meinen Geist.' The woodwinds, in an organ-like choir, answer each strophe with the original harmony of the classical prototype. Then there begin artful variations in which the original choral melody always lingers, the 'misterioso' rising from the bass, while the solo violin adds a moving elegy. The death song grows more distinct, the soloist visibly takes the lead of the whole body of violins and violas, drawing them intensely into unison with its voice, then gradually detaching itself. A fleeting recollection of the lovely girl's image, and the chorale, in bitter harmonization, and mingled with a tender melody of the solo violin, brings the tragic work in coda-fashion to its close.

● THREE FRAGMENTS FROM THE OPERA W*ozzeck*, OP. 7

Berg began the composition of his remarkable opera, W*ozzeck*, in 1914, was interrupted during the First World War, and completed the score in 1922 (some say 1920). The opera was first produced at the Staatsoper, Berlin, on December 14, 1925, under the direction of Erich Kleiber. Since then it has become a modern classic; with *Pelléas* and *Elektra* it ranks among the small group of contemporary operas which stand out against the vast mountain chain of the Wagnerian music drama with something like distinctness and saliency. Certainly it is, after *Pelléas*, the most original and seizing thing in the lyrico-dramatic art of the last half-century.

One may not hope to gain a just sense of its quality without bearing in mind the characteristics and prepossessions of the dramatist whose terrible and searing play has patterned the music of Berg—Georg Büchner, a curious and tragic figure, poet, scientist, and early nineteenth-century rebel against the social order, who was born at Goddelau, near Darmstadt, in 1813, and died in Zürich in his twenty-fourth year. Büchner loathed injustice; he fought throughout his brief life against oppression and smug content. He wished, he said, that he might 'hurl his inkwell at the heads of those who are turning into a wilderness the flowering world of the ancients.'

It is in that dark wilderness of cruelty and oppression and malignant irony that the sensitive and wretched Wozzeck, the poor soldier, weak of will and half-cracked, burns his brief candle, tormented and terrified by his visions and his fears, beset by the mysteriousness and the pain of life, abused, insulted, betrayed. We follow him in his swift advance through the fifteen scenes into which Berg has compressed Büchner's loose and fragmentary play. We see him shaving the boorish Captain, playing 'yes man' to his insufferable superior; see him cutting wood in the country beyond the town, where the visionary, semi-lunatic soldier is terrified by inexplicable sights and sounds—horrors that move beneath the ground, conniving with the ominous dusk. We see him as he suffers indignities at the hands of the fanatical Doctor; we see him in the gardens of the inn, anguished and desperate, as he watches Marie and her new lover among the dancers; see him sitting with Marie at dusk beside the pond, trembling, kissing her, thrusting the knife into her provocative throat; see him, later, hunting for the knife on the moonlit path, stumbling over the body of Marie, lying still 'with the new red ribbon around her throat'; flinging the knife into the pond, but not far enough out, for they may find it; wading into the water, which engulfs him—drowning him, he cries, in blood. . . At the end, Marie's child rides his hobbyhorse in the sunlit street before the empty house, then rushes off with his playmates as they cry to him, with joyous savagery, 'Du! dein Mutter ist tod!' while the music comes to its hovering, murmurous close—an end to set beside the wonderful close of *Pelléas*.

Berg has found for his setting of this tragic action an unusual but effective medium. Faced by the problem of expressing the movements and implications of his dramatic subject through music which deliberately renounced coherence of tonal texture, he chose to integrate his score by casting it into certain of the strict forms of absolute music. With rare skill, felicity, and imagination, he has associated the action of each scene with a particular formal pattern. Thus we discover in the first act a Suite (with Prelude, Sarabande, Gigue, Gavotte) and a Passacaglia with twenty-one variations; in the second, the outlines of a five movement symphony; in the third, a series of Inventions (theme with seven variations and a fugue, organ point, 'moto perpetuo,' et cetera).

Through the bars of this elaborately formal structure issues a projective and piercing music, music steeped in the pity, the horror, the grotesquerie, the fantastic pathos and hideousness of the play. Wozzeck, his sun blacked out, his moon demolished, his heaven cracked and empty; Marie, anguished and fearful: these haunting protagonists are set before us with a voraciousness enhanced by the formalism that shapes the music's compassionate and bitter irony.

A German annotator has thus set forth the contents of the three fragments from the score that have been arranged for concert performance:

I.

[From Act 1: Close of Scene 2. Transition to, and beginning of, Scene 3]

Wozzeck, heavily laden with the sticks he has cut for his captain far out from the city, returns to the barracks. The state of visionary exaltation into which he has been thrown by the voices of nature at twilight has given way to profound depression. We hear, at first as from afar, then drawing nearer, the music of the retreat. Marie, the mistress of Wozzeck, holding her child in her arms, scans the passing military-band from her window.

> "Soldiers, Soldiers
> Are handsome fellows!"

Reproached by a woman neighbor for the glowing glances exchanged with the Drum-Major, Marie slams the window with a curse, whereupon the March suddenly breaks off at the reprise. Marie, now alone with the child, turns to it:

'Come, my boy! What do people expect? You may be only a poor harlot's child, yet you give your mother joy with your unhallowed face! (*She rocks the child.*) Hush-a-by, hush . . .

> (*Slumber song*)

'Girl, what are you to do? You have a child but no husband! Why ask? If I should sing the whole night—Hush-a-by, my sweet lad—not a soul would help me.

'Hansel, harness your six white horses, give them their fodder, and give them drink. They'll eat no oats, they'll drink no water: Wine, cool wine it must be!'

(*The child has fallen asleep. Marie is sunk in thought.*)

II.

[From Act III: Scene 1]

(*Marie's room. It is night. Candlelight.*)

Marie, who has become the mistress of the Drum-Major, is seated at the table turning over the leaves of the Bible. She is tormented by pangs of conscience, and has a premonition of her approaching end. Song alternates with speech.

(*Reads:*) 'And there is no guile found in his mouth' . . . Lord! Lord! Look not upon me! (*Turns further:*) 'But the Pharisees brought to him a woman that lived in adultery. Jesus said: I condemn thee not; go and sin no more.' Lord! (*Covers her face with her hands—then observes the child with grief.*) The boy cuts me to the heart. Away! (*Pushes the child from her.*) (*Suddenly, more mildly:*) No, come, come here! (*Draws the child to her.*) Come to me!

(*Narrating:*) 'Once upon a time there was a poor child that had neither father nor mother—both were dead, and there was no one else, and the child was hungry, and wept day and night. And because it had no one in the world' . . . Franz hasn't come; not yesterday, not today. (*Turns hastily to the Bible.*) What is written about the Magdalen? . . . 'And knelt and wept and kissed his feet, moistened them with her tears and anointed them with ointment. . .' (*Beats her breast.*) O Lord, I would anoint them, too! Lord, you had pity on her; have pity on me also! . . .

III.

[From Act III: Close of the 4th scene, to the end of the opera]

Wozzeck, who has slain Marie, has found death in the pond, where he has sought to conceal the traces of his murder. The ripples which break over his body are gradually smoothed. From the now motionless pond, the toads begin their calls. The moon rises. Silence. The succeeding orchestral interlude, a three-part Adagio in D minor, recapitulate the musical substance of the opera. When the curtain is raised for the last time, one sees children playing in the sunlit street before Marie's door. Among them is her boy. Marie lies dead, they shout—'Out on the road, alongside the pond.' They interrupt their play and hasten there to gaze upon her. Marie's child, unsuspecting, rides its hobby-horse—'Hop, hop! Hop, hop! Hop, hop!'

Louis Hector Berlioz
1803-69

B

‡Berlioz was not only a very great composer—the greatest, perhaps, in the history of modern French music—he was also the author of a classic autobiography; and it would be a disservice to the reader to inform him more than sketchily of a life the details of which he may read to such great profit in the words of the man who lived it. Let it suffice, therefore, that, the son of a provincial doctor (he was born at Côte St. André, near Grenoble), he was destined for his father's profession, but forsook it for music; that, after five attempts, he secured the coveted Prix de Rome of the Paris Conservatory; that he projected, but never carried out, a murder; that he married twice, and would have married a third time had the lady been willing; that, after spectacular successes and equally spectacular failures as composer and conductor, he played out the coda of his life in a minor key. But as we listen to his music one fact, of which we are ignorant or neglect the astounding significance, should be borne in mind: only six years separated the completion of Beethoven's Ninth Symphony and the completion of Berlioz's *Fantastique*.‡

● *Symphonie fantastique*, OP. 14a

It is chiefly the image of Berlioz the grandiose young Romanticist that looks out at us with febrile eyes from the pages of the *Symphonie fantastique*—the incandescent rhapsodist of whom Rouget de l'Isle said, in 1830, that his head 'seemed to be a volcano perpetually in eruption.' The older and graver Berlioz of the later works—*L'enfance du Christ, Béatrice et Bénédict, Les Troyens*— was to sing a very different song.

The voice of Berlioz the flamboyant and reckless youth of twenty-six speaks from the pages of this astonishing symphony. It was the product of a grand passion, in the agonies of which Berlioz writhed and burned and composed. The Irish actress whom he afterward married, and who quickly chilled him— the immortal Miss Smithson—had lit a prodigious blaze in his inflammable nerve centers, and Berlioz was wildly miserable. He was obsessed by thoughts of suicide and spectacular revenge; for the affair did not proceed happily for Berlioz, and it was three years after he had emptied the agonies of his 'infernal passion,' as he called it, into the *Symphonie fantastique*, that Miss Smithson considerately lowered his temperature by marrying him. Then Berlioz (as Heine said) cut his rhapsodic hair, while his 'interminable and inextinguishable passion' sank to the normal of an affectionate regard.

Berlioz first saw and succumbed to Henrietta Smithson in 1827 (he was then in his twenty-fourth year). He wrote to his friend Ferrand that if the lady could but realize the wonder of reciprocating his love, she would fly to his arms, even if she died in his embrace. But Henrietta was apparently not ready either to reciprocate or to die, and she kept away from those devouring arms. Scandalous stories concerning her reached the ears of Berlioz. They were afterward shown to be calumnies. But Berlioz was made as one insane by the tales, and he took vengeance upon the unfortunate Miss Smithson in his symphony. For this work he supplied a programmatic explanation, in the original version of which (afterward revised by Berlioz) he permitted his furious resentment toward Miss Smithson to betray him into the ungentlemanly act of symbolizing her as a courtesan worthy only to take part in the orgies of the Witches' Sabbath.

The symphony was completed in 1830, and was performed for the first time on December 5 of that year. Miss Smithson was legally inducted into the arms of the terrible Romanticist on October 3, 1833. She left them seven years later, and lived apart from Berlioz until her death in 1854.

When Berlioz published the score of his symphony, he prefaced it with an elaborate statement of its expressional scheme. Here it is, in the English version of Harry Brett, which is printed, together with the original French of Berlioz, in Breitkopf & Härtel's edition (1900) of the full score:

A young musician of unhealthily sensitive nature and endowed with vivid imagination has poisoned himself with opium in a paroxysm of lovesick despair. The narcotic dose he had taken was too weak to cause death, but it has thrown him into a long sleep accompanied by the most extraordinary visions. In this condition his sensations, his feelings, and his memories find utterance in his sick brain in the form of musical imagery. Even the Beloved One takes the form of a melody in his mind, like a fixed idea which is ever returning and which he hears everywhere. [This recurring melody, or *idée fixe*, which typifies the Beloved One, is first heard in the Allegro, in C major.]

First Movement: Dreams, Passions
(Largo, C minor, 4-4; 'Allegro agitato e appassionato assai,' C major, 4-4)

At first he thinks of the uneasy and nervous condition of his mind, of somber longings, of depression and joyous elation without any recognizable cause, which he experienced before the Beloved One had appeared to him. Then he remembers the ardent love with which she suddenly inspired him; he thinks of his almost insane anxiety of mind, of his raging jealousy, of his reawakening love, of his religious consolation.

Second Movement: A Ball
(Allegro non troppo, A major, 3-8)

In a ballroom, amidst the confusion of a brilliant festival, he finds the Beloved One again.

Third Movement: Scene in the Fields

(Adagio, F major, 6-8)

It is a summer evening. He is in the country, musing, when he hears two shepherd lads who play, in alternation, the *ranz des vaches* (the tune used by the Swiss shepherds to call their flocks). This pastoral duet, the quiet scene, the soft whisperings of the trees stirred by the zephyr-wind, some prospects of hope recently made known to him, all these sensations unite to impart a long unknown repose to his heart and to lend a smiling color to his imagination. And then She appears once more. His heart stops beating, painful forebodings fill his soul. 'Should she prove false to him!' One of the shepherds resumes the melody, but the other answers him no more. . . Sunset . . . distant rolling of thunder . . . loneliness . . . silence. . .

Fourth Movement: March to the Scaffold

('Allegretto non troppo,' G minor and B-flat major, 4-4)

He dreams that he has murdered his Beloved, that he has been condemned to death and is being led to execution. A march that is alternately somber and wild, brilliant and solemn, accompanies the procession. . . The tumultuous outbursts are followed without modulation by measured steps. At last the fixed idea returns, for a moment a last thought of love is revived—which is cut short by the death-blow.

Fifth Movement: Witches' Sabbath

(Larghetto, C major, 4-4; and Allegro, E-flat major, C minor, and C major, 6-8)

He dreams that he is present at a witches' revel, surrounded by horrible spirits, amidst sorcerers and monsters in many fearful forms, who have come together for his funeral. Strange sounds, groans, shrill laughter, distant yells, which other cries seem to answer. The Beloved Melody is heard again, but it has lost its shy and noble character; it has become a vulgar, trivial, grotesque dance tune. She it is who comes to attend the witches' meeting. Riotous howls and shouts greet her arrival. . . She joins the infernal orgy . . . bells toll for the dead . . . a burlesque parody of the *Dies irae* . . . the Witches' round dance. . . The dance and the *Dies irae* are heard together.

● *Harold in Italy*: Symphony in Four Movements with Viola Solo, op. 16

Upon the Romanticists in France—'the heroic boys of 1830,' as Henley called them—the influence of Byron was gripping and profound. To Berlioz in particular, 'greedy of emotion, intolerant of restraint, contemptuous of reticence and sobriety . . . and prepared to welcome, as a return to truth and nature, inventions the most extravagant and imaginings the most fantastic and far-fetched,' Byron, that prince of Romanticists, must have seemed a poet (and a man) after his own heart. Yet, singularly enough, there are in Berlioz's writings comparatively few references to the author of *Manfred* and *Don Juan*.

The manner in which the *Harold* symphony came to be written is related by Berlioz in his Memoirs. The circumstance that this account appears to have little relation to historic fact will disturb only those grubbing literalists who are indifferent to Berlioz's singular talent for romantic fiction. His *Symphonie fantastique* had been played at a concert at the Paris Conservatory (December 22, 1833) with conspicuous success.

And then [says Berlioz], to crown my happiness, after the audience had gone out, a man with a long mane of hair, with piercing eyes, with a strange and haggard face, one possessed by genius, a colossus among giants, whom I had never seen and whose appearance moved me profoundly, was alone and waiting for me in the hall, stopped me to press my hand, overwhelmed me with burning praise, which set fire to my heart and head: *it was Paganini!* . . . Some weeks after this vindicatory concert of which I have spoken, Paganini came to see me. 'I have a marvelous viola,' he said, 'an admirable Stradivarius, and I wish to play it in public. But I have no music *ad hoc*. Will you write a solo piece for the viola? You are the only one I can trust for such a work.' 'Yes, indeed,' I answered, 'your proposition flatters me more than I can tell, but, to make such a virtuoso as you shine in a piece of this nature, it is necessary to play the viola, and I do not play it. You are the only one, it seems to me, who can solve the problem.' 'No, no; I insist,' said Paganini; 'you will succeed; as for me, I am too sick at present to compose; I cannot think of it.'

I tried then to please the illustrious virtuoso by writing a solo piece for the viola, but a solo combined with the orchestra in such a manner that it would not injure the expression of the orchestral mass, for I was sure that Paganini, by his incomparable artistry, would know how to make the viola always the dominating instrument. . .

His proposal seemed new to me, and I soon had developed in my head a very happy idea, and I was eager for the realization. The first movement was hardly completed, when Paganini wished to see it. He looked at the rests for the viola in the Allegro and exclaimed: 'No, it is not that: there are too many rests for me; I must be playing all the time.' 'I told you so,' I answered; 'you want a viola concerto, and you are the only one who can write such a concerto for yourself.' Paganini did not answer; he seemed disappointed, and left me without speaking further about my orchestral sketch. Some days afterwards, suffering already from the affection of the larynx which ultimately killed him, he went to Nice, and returned to Paris only at the end of three years.

Since I then saw that my plan of composition would not suit him, I set myself to work in another way, and without any anxiety concerning the means to make the solo viola conspicuous.

My idea was to write for the orchestra a series of scenes in which the solo viola should figure as a more or less active personage of constantly preserved individuality; I wished to put the viola in the midst of poetic recollections left me by my wanderings in the Abruzzi, and make it a sort of melancholy dreamer, after the manner of Byron's 'Childe Harold.' Hence the title, *Harold en Italie*. As in the *Symphonie fantastique*, a chief theme (the first song of the viola) reappears throughout the work, but there is this difference: the theme of the *Symphonie fantastique*, the 'fixed idea,' interposes itself persistently as an episodic and passionate thought in the midst of scenes which are foreign to it and modifies them; while the song of Harold is added to other songs of the orchestra with which it is contrasted both in movement and character and without any interruption of the development.

According to Adolphe Boschot in his Life of Berlioz (*Un Romantique sous Louis Philippe*), Berlioz's statements about Paganini and the sketch are 'undoubtedly imaginative.' On the other hand, Ernest Newman, in his scrupulously exact and invaluable edition of Berlioz's Memoirs, has this to say:

On January 26, 1834, five weeks after the date on which Berlioz says he met Paganini the *Gazette Musicale* announced that Paganini had just asked Berlioz for 'a new work in the style of the *Symphonie fantastique*' . . . Monsieur Boschot throws doubt on Berlioz's story as told in the Memoirs; he will have it that Berlioz thought what an excellent thing it would be if Paganini were to play the viola in a work of his, and then, or later, invented the rest of the story. It seems hardly likely, however, that with Paganini in Paris at the time, Berlioz and his journalistic friends would have dared to print the account of this 'request' had it been pure invention. Moreover, in a letter of March 19, 1834, to Humbert Ferrand, Berlioz says he is 'finishing the symphony with viola solo requested of me by Paganini.'

Whatever the truth may be, the work itself abides.

The relationship between Berlioz's symphony and Byron's poetic account of the Italian wanderings of his Harold is of the slightest, and any attempt to discover, in Berlioz's program of the moods and incidents of his symphonic hero, definite correspondences with Byron's poem would be more than futile. One who seeks enlightenment concerning the intentions of Berlioz in this symphony must fall back upon the composer's own brief hints as contained in the inscriptions appended to the several movements. The voice of the solo viola, as we know, typifies throughout the 'melancholy dreamer' as conceived by Berlioz—it is Harold undergoing his adventures: in the mountains; encountering a band of devout and simple pilgrims; observing an enamoured mountaineer in the act of serenading his mistress; and, finally, involved in a tumultuous orgy of drunken bandits.

● *Romeo and Juliet:* DRAMATIC SYMPHONY WITH SOLO VOICES AND CHORUS, OP. 17

Berlioz, witnessing at the Odéon in 1827 a performance of Juliet by the Irish actress Harriet Smithson, was overwhelmed by emotion, and resolved then and there to set Shakespeare to music and to marry Miss Smithson. He accomplished the aesthetic project—the composition of his *Romeo and Juliet*—in 1839; he had married the calcfacient Miss Smithson some six years before.

After the gift to Berlioz in 1838 of 20,000 francs (ostensibly from Paganini), the composer, having paid his debts, saw an opportunity, he says, 'to leave off all other work, and write a masterpiece, on a grand new plan—a splendid work, full of passion and imagination, and worthy to be dedicated to the illustrious artist to whom I owe so much. . . At last, after much hesitation, I hit upon the idea of a symphony, with choruses, vocal solos, and choral recitatives, on the sublime and ever novel theme of Shakespeare's *Romeo and Juliet*. I wrote in prose all the text intended for the vocal pieces which come between the instrumental sections. Émil Deschamps set it to verse for me, and I began. No more *feuilletons* now!—or, at least, hardly any. Paganini had given me money that I might write music, and write it I did. I wrote for seven months, not leaving off for more than three or four days out of every thirty. . . To my keen regret, Paganini never either heard or read the work. . . Poor dear friend! Happily for him, he never read the horrible nonsense in many of the Paris newspapers about the plan of the work, the introduction, the Adagio, Queen Mab, and the story of Friar Laurence. One reproached me with the extravagance of having attempted a new form of symphony; another could find nothing in the "Queen Mab" Scherzo but a "little grotesque voice like that of *an ill-greased syringe*." '

Berlioz 'lived ardently' with the spirit of Shakespeare, he tells us, while writing this work. 'How vigorously I struck out in that grand sea of poetry caressed by the playful breeze of fancy, beneath the hot rays of that sun of love which Shakespeare kindled, always confident of my power to reach the marvelous island where stands the temple of true art! Whether I succeeded or not, it is not for me to decide.' Yet, when some pigmy-minded critic asserted that Berlioz 'had not understood Shakespeare,' did Berlioz bow his head? Not conspicuously. 'Toad, swelling with folly!' he retorted. 'If you could prove that to me!' But could the toad conceivably have proved it to his satisfaction?

The first performance of the symphony was in the hall of the Paris Conservatoire, November 24, 1839, with Berlioz conducting. The orchestra comprised 160 players. Among the deadheads was a struggling young composer named Richard Wagner, who had not yet completed his *Rienzi*.

The scheme of the symphony in its entirety is as follows:

INTRODUCTION

Combats.—Tumult.—Intervention of the Prince: Allegro fugato (B minor).
(For Orchestra alone)

PART I

I. Chorus with Contralto Solo: Avec le caractère d'un récitatif, mais à peu près mésuré (B minor).
II. Strophes for Contralto: Andante avec solennité (G major)
III. Scherzetto, 'Queen Mab,' for Tenor Solo and Chorus: Allegro leggiero (F major).

PART II

Romeo alone. Sadness. Concert and Ball. Grand Fête at Capulet's House.
Andante malinconico e sostenuto (F major).
Allegro (F major).
Larghetto espressivo (F major).
Allegro (F major).
(For Orchestra alone)

PART III

Calm Night. Capulet's Garden, Silent and Deserted. The Young Capulets, come from the Fête, pass by, and sing Snatches of the Dance Music.
Male Double Chorus: Allegretto (A major).
Adagio (Orchestra alone) (A major).
Allegro agitato (A major).

PART IV

Queen Mab, or the Dream Fairy

Scherzo: Prestissimo (F major).
Allegretto (D minor).
(For Orchestra alone)

Juliet's Funeral Procession
Fugued March for Chorus and Orchestra: Andante non troppo lento (B minor).
Romeo at the Tomb of the Capulets
Invocation.—Juliet's Awakening.—Delirious Joy, Despair; Last Death Agony of the two Lovers.

Allegro agitato e disperato (E minor).
Invocation: Largo (C-sharp minor).
Allegro vivace ed appassionato assai (A major).
(For Orchestra alone)

FINALE

The Crowd enters the Cemetery.—Fight of Capulets and Montagues.—Recitative and
Air of Friar Laurence. Oath of Reconciliation.
Chorus: Allegro (A minor).
Recitative of Friar Laurence.
Air: Larghetto sostenuto (E-flat major).
Double Chorus: Allegro (B minor).
Oath: Andante un poco maestoso (B major).

'Although voices are frequently employed,' wrote Berlioz in his preface to
the score, 'this is not a concert-opera, or a cantata, but a symphony with
chorus. If song occurs in the beginning, it is for the purpose of preparing the
mind of the hearer for the dramatic scenes, in which sentiments and passions
should be expressed by the orchestra. It is, moreover, to introduce gradually in
the musical development choral masses whose too sudden appearance would
do harm to the unity of the composition. Thus the prologue, in which, after
the example of the prologue by Shakespeare himself, the chorus exposes the
action, is sung by only fourteen voices. Later is heard, behind the scenes, the
male chorus of Capulet; but in the funeral ceremonies women and men take
part. At the beginning of the finale the two choruses of Capulets and Montagues appear with Friar Laurence; and at the end the three choruses are
united.'

‡Performances of *Romeo and Juliet* in its entirety are rare, but Part Two—
Romeo Alone; Sadness; Concert and Ball; Grand Fête at Capulet's House—
and the *Queen Mab* Scherzo from Part Four are frequently heard.‡ The
subject of the Scherzo is, of course, Mercutio's speech in the first act of
Shakespeare's play.

> O, then, I see Queen Mab hath been with you.
> She is the fairies' midwife; and she comes
> In shape no bigger than an agate-stone
> On the fore-finger of an alderman,
> Drawn with a team of little atomies
> Athwart men's noses as they lie asleep. .

● THREE EXCERPTS FROM *The Damnation of Faust* ('Minuet of the Will-o'-
the-Wisps'; 'Dance of Sylphs'; 'Rakoczy March')

‡In 1827 Gerard de Nerval published his French translation of Goethe's *Faust*.
Berlioz read it, was fascinated, and, excerpting certain of the versified portions
of the translation (which was largely in prose), composed eight numbers and
had them printed at his own expense—or rather at that of the pupil from
whom, eventually, he borrowed the money with which to meet the printer's
bill. Berlioz sent his music to Goethe, who approved of de Nerval's translation
of his great work but not of Berlioz's gloss upon it. His acknowledgment (not

over his own signature) of what Berlioz doubtless intended as a tribute was couched in vitriolic terms. Nearly forty years later, Berlioz reverted to the subject and produced his *Damnation of Faust*, a work somewhat difficult to characterize, for it has been variously called, and performed as, an 'oratorio,' a 'cantata,' a 'dramatic symphony,' and an 'opera.' The text of the work was largely of Berlioz's devising, and, when he was criticized for such tampering with Goethe's masterpiece, he was not slow to draw attention to the anomaly in the circumstance that no one had, earlier, upbraided him for paraphrasing Shakespeare's *Romeo and Juliet*. The première of the *Damnation* took place, in concert form, at the Paris Opéra-Comique on December 6, 1846, and was, like many Berlioz premières, a fiasco. The work was first produced in dramatic form at Monte Carlo on February 18, 1903. Three excerpts from the score, the 'Minuet of the Will-o'-the-Wisps,' the 'Dance of Sylphs,' and the 'Rakoczy March,' are staples of the symphonic repertoire.‡

Berlioz's devil—'perhaps the only operatic devil who carries anything like conviction,' as Ernest Newman sagely observed—invokes a serenade by will-o'-the-wisps under Marguerite's window. They flicker and gleam in the woodwind and in sudden flares of the strings (Moderato, D major, 3-4; Presto).

The Ballet of Sylphs is danced in the air after Faust has been lulled to sleep on the banks of the Elbe, at the command of Mephistopheles, by gnomes and sylphs. ('Allegro, tempo di valse,' D major, 3-8. The waltz tune is for violins.) 'The spirits of the air,' says a line in the score, 'hover around Faust in his slumber, then disappear one by one.'

It was during his travels in Austria, Hungary, Bohemia, and Silesia, in 1845-6, that Berlioz began work on his *Damnation of Faust*, which he had conceived seventeen years before. In his autobiography he defends with warmth his ingenious expedient for exploiting further the superb version of the 'Rakoczy March' which he had written to thrill the patriots of Budapest. 'The extraordinary effect it produced at Pesth made me resolve to introduce it into *Faust*,' he says, 'by taking the liberty of placing my hero in Hungary at the opening of the act, and making him present at the march of a Hungarian army across the plain. . . I should not have hesitated in the least to bring him in any other direction if it would have benefited the piece'—or (he might have added) if it had served the excuse for another extraneous number as temptingly effective as the 'Rakoczy March.' 'Moral criticism,' as Newman indulgently remarks, 'would be wasted on one so naked and unashamed as this!'

- OVERTURE TO *Benvenuto Cellini*, OP. 23
- OVERTURE, *Le Carnaval Romain*, OP. 9

Benvenuto Cellini belongs to the period when Berlioz was at the summit of his creative energy. The opera was composed between 1834 and 1837. 'I had been greatly struck with certain episodes in the life of Benvenuto Cellini,' says Berlioz in his Memoirs, 'and was so unlucky as to think they offered an interesting and dramatic subject for an opera. So I begged Léon de Wailly and Auguste Barbier—the terrible poet of *Iambes*—to make me a libretto on the subject.' They were helped by Alfred de Vigny. The result was not impressive. 'To believe even our friends, their libretto did not contain the elements essential to what is called a good play.' Fate, apparently, shared this disdainful view, and treated the work unmercifully. Berlioz, like Mélisande, was not happy. 'Never shall I forget the tortures I endured for the three months devoted to rehearsing the opera' he laments. The musicians were indifferent; the singers refused to take their tasks seriously; Habeneck, the conductor, was in constant ill-humor; there was universal hostility. The singers resented in the text what Berlioz delightfully refers to as 'an abusive term belonging to a vocabulary inconsistent with our present prudishness'; the pure air of the Opera House was contaminated by certain words in a duet of de Wailly's that were thought 'coarse.'

Thus Berlioz, as he says, was 'dragged to execution' at the Paris Opéra on September 10, 1838, when *Benvenuto Cellini* was produced under Habeneck's direction, with Duprez as Cellini. 'The overture,' relates Berlioz, 'received exaggerated applause, but the rest was hissed with admirable energy and unanimity.'

The overture exploits thematic material taken from the opera. After the exuberant opening theme has been put through its paces for twenty measures or so ('Allegro deciso con impeto,' 2-2), we hear, in pizzicato notes for the basses, a reminiscence of the air from the Cardinal's address in the last act, (Larghetto, 3-4), succeeded by the tune of the Harlequin from the Carnival scene, played by the woodwind. The gay opening theme introduces the main movement (again 'Allegro deciso,' 2-2), and after three-score-and-ten measures of energetic development, Romance emerges in the guise of a languishing melody for flutes, oboe, and clarinet, and we hear Cellini the lover sighing for his sweetheart Teresa, for whose sake Cellini (in the opera) stabs his rival Pompeo.

Berlioz wreaks himself upon this and subsidiary material. The tune of the Cardinal's address is apotheosized just before the end, where the orchestra roars out the theme, fortissimo. Berlioz was still an untamed Romantic when he composed this work.

Berlioz's overture, *Le Carnaval Romain*, was originally intended as an introduction to the second act of *Benvenuto Cellini*. The chief theme of the piece is derived from the saltarello that is danced on the Piazza Colonna in Rome in the second act of the opera—a scene of popular festival blended with melodramatic encounters and escapes.

● Overture to *Béatrice et Bénédict*

Berlioz, who would have survived in history as a man of letters had he not been an even greater musician, turned Shakespeare's *Much Ado About Nothing* into a French opera libretto for his own use. Bénazet, manager of the theater at Baden-Baden, had proposed to him an opera on the subject of Shakespeare's play, and Berlioz set to work on the project in 1860. He finished it two years later, February 25, 1862. The opera was produced at Baden on August 9 of that year. Berlioz conducted, though he was suffering tortures from an old complaint, 'intestinal neuralgia,' so-called. There was applause from the audience, but the opera was repeated only once. Berlioz returned to Paris within the next fortnight, depressed in spirits and suffering greatly from pain, so that only opium could relieve him. He had written his last work.

Berlioz borrowed the opening subject for the overture to *Béatrice et Bénédict* from the Duettino sung by the name characters in the last act of the opera. This is heard at the beginning of the overture as the motive played in alternation by strings and wind ('Allegro scherzando,' G major, 3-8). The pace becomes 'Andante un poco maestoso'—horns, with strings pizzicato—and a passage for strings, tremolando and pizzicato, introduces the main movement of the overture, an Allegro in G, 2-2, the chief theme—a derivation from the opening one—being given to the strings. For his second theme, Berlioz proceeds to the relative key of D major and gives his contrasting subject to violins and violas, the woodwinds supporting. The development, which concentrates on the earlier material, is concise and effective.

● ROYAL HUNT AND TEMPEST FROM *Les Troyens*

An untamed Romanticist in his youth, Berlioz in later years turned for inspiration to a master of classic beauty—to Virgil. He had always loved the story of Dido and Aeneas as read to him by his father from Book IV of the *Aeneid*. But it was not until he was in his fifties that he composed his opera, *Les Troyens*, a 'poème lyrique' in two parts: I. *La Prise de Troie*; II. *Les Troyens à Carthage*. The first, *La Prise de Troie*, in three acts, is virtually a prelude to the second and longer work: *Les Troyens à Carthage*, in five acts, the dramatic motive of which is the love affair between Dido and Aeneas. Berlioz wrote both text and music of the two-part opus. The first performance of *Les Troyens à Carthage* was at the Théâtre Lyrique, Paris, November 4, 1863. Berlioz did not live to hear *La Prise de Troie*. The first performance in Paris was at the Opéra, November 15, 1899; but the complete opera had been given at Carlsruhe under Mottl in 1890 (some say 1897).

The 'Royal Hunt and Tempest' was intended by Berlioz as a symphonic interlude in the score of *Les Troyens*, with stage business and a mixed chorus. But Berlioz seems not to have been sure of the viability of this scheme. 'In case the theatre is not large enough,' he wrote on the manuscript, 'to permit of the grand and animated business of this interlude, and if it is impossible to obtain chorus women to run about the stage with dishevelled hair, and chorus men dressed as fauns and satyrs to indulge in grotesque gambols. . . if the firemen are afraid of fire, the machinists afraid of water, the director afraid of everything, this interlude should be wholly suppressed. Furthermore, for a good performance a powerful orchestra is necessary, such as is seldom found in opera houses.'

His fears were only too well founded. At the first performance 'the Interlude of the Chase was wretchedly bungled.' It was omitted from subsequent performances of *Les Troyens*.

Georges Bizet
1838-75

B

‡Had Bizet neglected to write his *Carmen,* it is doubtful whether he would survive to us. The extraordinary and deserved popularity of that work of genius (it is scarcely less) continuously renews curiosity concerning other productions by its author. From time to time this leads to the revival of less distinguished scores; but it is only the aura of *Carmen* that briefly clothes them with interest. The exceptions to be noted are the incidental music to *L'Arlésienne* and the early Symphony in C, 'discovered' and first performed some sixty years after the composer's death. Bizet was essentially a composer in the lighter vein, but his invention and craftsmanship in *Carmen* are of the highest order within this limitation, and the less easily defined flavor of his masterpiece is unique in music. He was the pupil and son-in-law of a more highly regarded but far inferior master, Jacques Halévy (composer of the opera *La Juive*), and a winner of the Prix de Rome of the Paris Conservatory. He died at the early age of thirty-seven—of disappointment, it has been said, over the failure of *Carmen.* But on this, see the notes below.‡

● Symphony in C major

‡Bizet's Symphony in C, an early work (the composer was seventeen when he wrote it) appears not to have been performed during his lifetime. The manuscript reposed unregarded in the library of the Paris Conservatory until, in the mid-thirties of the present century, it was brought to the attention of the conductor Felix Weingartner, under whose direction it was heard, for the first time anywhere, at Basel on February 26, 1935. A note in the published score states that Weingartner's attention was directed to the symphony by D. C. Parker, a 'Glasgow music writer.' (An article in *Le Ménestrel,* on the other hand, attributes the 'discovery' of the symphony to the French musicologist Jean Chantavoine.) The première in Basel was followed by performances in Vienna, under Weingartner; in Paris, under Charles Münch, in London, under Sir Hamilton Harty, and in New York, under John Barbirolli. In the interval since, the symphony has been frequently heard, and it seems probable that it will remain active in the orchestral repertoire for some time to come. According to Martin Cooper, Bizet's biographer, the symphony affords 'amazing proof' of Bizet's early powers. 'It was not profoundly original,' continues

Mr. Cooper, 'but it showed at the worst a great imitative faculty, a most
unusual grasp of design, and an unfailing sense of style, though the style was
often that of his models.' Bizet's models, according to Mr. Cooper, included
Haydn, Mozart, Beethoven, Rossini, and Mendelssohn. Later commentators,
with the advantage over Mr. Cooper of having heard performances of the
symphony, are less patronizing in their judgments of it, and have much
admired the elegance and refinement of the work's design and detail. The four
movements of the symphony are: (1) 'Allegro vivo,' 4-4; (2) Adagio, 9-8, A
minor; (3) Minuetto, 'Allegro vivace,' 3-4, G major; (4) 'Allegro vivace,' 2-2.‡

• INCIDENTAL MUSIC TO *L'Arlésienne*

Bizet was commissioned to write music for the production of Alphonse Daudet's
Provençal drama, *L'Arlésienne*, at the Vaudeville Theater, Paris. The play,
and Bizet's music, were given there on October 1, 1872, but the result was a
lamentable fiasco, and the piece was withdrawn after fifteen performances.
Bizet then chose various numbers out of the twenty-seven he had composed
for the play and arranged them as a concert suite. These include a Prelude, a
Minuetto, an Adagietto, a Danse Provençale, and a Carillon. A second suite
was put together from the score by Guiraud after Bizet's death. This comprises
four numbers, a Pastorale, an Intermezzo, a second Minuetto, and the popular
Farandole.

Daudet's play has no heroine, only a hero: a tragic amorist who goes mad
of love and can find no remedy for his ill but a self-sought and violent death.
This desperate swain—Fréderi, a young farmer of Carmogue—burns for a
maleficent brunette, the Girl of Arles. She is not visible in the play, but she
controls its action, for her influence comes between Fréderi and the impeccable
Vivette, who loves the tormented farmer. He will not be consoled, and at last,
on the night of a festival, he kills himself to the music of peasant merrymaking.

On the occasion of the hundredth performance of *L'Arlésienne* Daudet
wrote the following letter to a friend:

Yes, indeed, I shall be there, my dear Porel—we will attend the centenary of a famous
frost. I cannot forget that one evening, fifteen years ago, Georges Bizet and myself,
standing in the wings, trembling with anxiety, our faces pallid and drawn with that
stupid sense of unrest so prevalent on opening nights, witnessed the downfall of this
very same *L'Arlésienne* as it came to an end on the Vaudeville stage amid public ennui
and indifference. 'They are not listening,' whispered my companion, in heart-broken
tones. But *now* they come, *now* they listen, because Bizet is dead and has become a
classic, because Lamoureux himself has fêted him; perhaps too because my name is
better known than it was fifteen years ago, and the public above all else loves security
in its pleasures.

• *Carmen*

The directors of the Opéra-Comique, Du Locle and De Leuwen, had commissioned Bizet to compose a piece for them. 'Meilhac and Halévy,' wrote Bizet,
'will be my collaborators. They want me to do something gay, which I am to
treat as concisely as possible.'

This 'something gay' became *Carmen*. The score was composed in less than two years and orchestrated in two months, and was first performed at the Opéra-Comique on March 3, 1875. The rehearsals had been hasty; the production was unvitalized. 'At its first performance,' wrote Henri Malherbe, 'this exciting and passionate work of Bizet appeared to be desperately monotonous.'. But the familiar legend that *Carmen* was an absolute failure on this occasion and that Bizet, as a consequence, died of a broken heart seems to hold a considerable measure of exaggeration. The first act was enthusiastically applauded, and such infallibly effective numbers as Escamillo's song in the second act and Micaela's in the third were approvingly received. It is true that the 'modernity' of the score (Bizet, of course, was accused of having sold his soul to Wagner), the alleged 'immorality' of the story, the lack of a happy ending, 'the novel spectacle of women smoking on the stage,' the unrestrained acting of the Carmen, Galli-Marié, were factors that tended to disaffect the Parisian operagoers of 1875. But one of the librettists of *Carmen*, Ludovic Halévy, has written that 'after the vexatious première, the performances went on—and not, as has been alleged, before empty houses. The receipts, on the contrary, were respectable, and generally in excess of those for the other works in the repertoire. Little by little, at each of the performances of *Carmen*, there was an increase in the number of its admirers—at first small. Things went on thus during the months of March, April, and May. Bizet left for the country— sad, but not discouraged.' Three and a half months after its production, by the 18th of June 1875 (Bizet had died a fortnight before), the opera had reached its thirty-seventh performance at the Opéra-Comique. Up to the 15th of February 1876, *Carmen* had been given fifty times. Then it disappeared for a while from the bills of the Comique.

There seems to be no doubt that the critics handled *Carmen* pretty roughly at its first presentation.

The morning after the première [wrote Malherbe in a memorial article published years later in *Figaro*], the critics treated Bizet without mercy. None of his works was attacked with such bitterness. Paul de Saint-Victor in *Le Moniteur*, Oscar Commetant in *Le Siècle*, Arthur Pougin in *Le Ménestrel*, Pierre Véron, all judged him with rancor and without penetration. . . Merimée, Meilhac, and Halévy were none of them spared, but were covered with gross invective.

Among the stupidities published on this occasion was a ridiculous article which reflects accurately the general sentiment. Let us have the charity to forget the author's name, since he is more amusing today than he ever dreamed of being. 'Where,' he wrote, 'is the golden age of *Zampa*, of *Fra Diavola*, those fierce bandits whose innocent carbines never burned powder, even against the birds? Today the brigands of the Opéra-Comique are thorough-going assassins. It is true that the blood they shed merits no pity. Carmen, the heroine of this poem of Messrs. Meilhac and Halévy (two authors often better inspired) is only an ugly creature who, for being borrowed from the story of Prosper Merimée, is no less an evil figure on a stage accustomed to more respect for morality and modesty. What do you think, chaste mothers of families, good fathers relying on the reputation of the past, hoping to entertain your daughters and wives with a pleasant and decent evening—what think you, I say, of an ignoble creature, offering, with a provoking glance, her love to whomever pleased her—and God knows the number of these favored mortals was great!—turning from a mule driver to a dragoon, and from the dragoon to a toreador, and brusquely arrested in her volcanic gallantries by the stiletto of a discarded lover? This evil character, this Célimène of the sidewalks, is acted by Madame Galli-Marié with a realism of provocativeness little calculated to secure pardon for the faults of her singing. The music, frightfully cluttered, is such as was to be expected from Monsieur Georges Bizet.'

But what, asks Malherbe, would 'these miserably virtuous critics' have said if Bizet's librettists had followed more closely the realism of the original story of Merimée?

Carmen had been in the libraries since 1845. The cigarette girl and the soldier were infinitely more reprehensible in Merimée's story. The original Carmen was a girl who robbed the travelers she decoyed, and José was a cynical assassin who expiated on the gallows the crimes with which he was charged. The presumptuous and silly judges of Bizet had neglected, apparently, to read and to re-read the capital text of Merimée. Had they been better informed, they would have complimented, probably, the authors of the lyrical version on their careful taste. Meilhac and Halévy, good opéra-comique writers, were far removed from the harsh realism of Prosper Merimée. In this tale of Carmen and Don José, they introduced with flattering industry the prudent and agreeable figures of Escamillo and Micaela, useful conventionalities of the theatre. In their adaptation, the toreador has replaced the picador Lucas, Don José still most commendably loves his mother and is moved by the angelic Micaela (who recalls the Alice of *Robert le Diable*, but was unknown to Merimée). Garcia, the husband of Carmen, has disappeared, and Carmen herself, between the laborious fancies of such newcomers as Mercedes and Frasquita, is not too offensive, her enterprises being singularly diminished.

It may be suspected that Malherbe did not scruple to indulge his Gallic gift of irony; yet there is something in what he says.

One may doubt, however, if Bizet relished some of the compromises that he was obliged to meet in order to adapt his work, so far as possible, to the assumed requirements of the public taste. He can scarcely have accepted cheerfully the task of writing the duet of Micaela and José in the first act and Micaela's air in the third. Charles Lamoureux has said that the composer of *Carmen* had quite another design for the air of the toreador in the Second Act; but he is known to have remarked, 'Since they want that sort of thing, here it is.' There are some who tell us that if Bizet had lived, he would probably have eliminated from his score those passages which lack his characteristic vitality and color. However, it was precisely these banal pages that saved the piece from disaster at its première.

The more scrupulous and cool-minded among French musical historians take no stock in the romantic fable that Bizet died of grief over the supposed 'failure' of *Carmen*. One of his biographers has pictured him as wandering about the streets all night, heartbroken, after the première. But Ludovic Halévy has told us that on the night of *Carmen's* first performance, Bizet and his two librettists, after listening from a box, returned together to their lodgings in complete calm. Bizet's night of heartbroken wandering is a fable.

Bizet died, not from a broken heart, but as the result of an abscess of the ear on which the surgeons dared not operate. He was much too energetic, too courageous, as Malherbe points out, to be killed by the reception of his opera. On the day that he died, *Carmen* was performed for the thirty-third time. That, surely, must have seemed a heartening fact. And what did Bizet himself write to his teacher Marmontel? 'I have no interest,' he said, 'in a popularity for which are sacrificed talent, integrity and honor.'

‡The music of *Carmen* is heard not only in the opera house, but also in (among a variety of expected and unexpected places) the concert room. Concert suites arranged by other hands from the score of Bizet's masterpiece are numerous and vary greatly. As a rule, they embrace the Prelude to the opera, the three entr'actes, and one or more of the more popular vocal numbers, such as the Habañera, the so-called 'Chanson bohème' (which Carmen sings and dances in Act ii), or Escamillo's famous 'Toreador Song.'‡

Luigi Boccherini

1743-1805

B

Boccherini, who is known to the layman as the composer of a minuet and a 'cello concerto, wrote at least 467 instrumental works. Yet Boccherini was an idler by comparison with, for example, his predecessor Christoph Graupner (c.1683-1760), whose music included more than 1300 church works, not to mention 116 symphonies, 80 overtures, 50 concertos, and other innumerable compositions. Besides such fecundity as this, even Haydn, with his 104 symphonies, seems like a dawdler. ‡Boccherini was born at Lucca, the son of a bass player who early instructed him in the rudiments of musical art and the mastery of the 'cello. In 1757 he was sent to Rome to continue his studies, and there he soon made a name for himself both as a performer and as a composer. Later he toured France, Spain (where eventually he settled), and Germany. He became the rage; publishers vied for his works. He endured many vicissitudes of public and private fortune, and in the end he died nearly forgotten and in want.‡

● CONCERTO FOR 'CELLO AND ORCHESTRA, IN B-FLAT MAJOR, OP. 34

Five concertos for 'cello are ascribed to Boccherini, but the authenticity of certain of them has been questioned. ‡The B-flat Concerto, op. 34, is generally acknowledged to be his work, however, and is the composition by which, today, he is most frequently represented on orchestral programs.‡ It was published in parts (not in score) in 1900, in an edition by Friedrich Grützmacher. It is in three movements: an 'Allegro moderato,' an Adagio, and a final Rondo in rapid tempo.

C. F. Pohl, in his biographical notice of Boccherini, enumerates his virtues

as 'expressive melody, good treatment of ideas, dignified style. . . His originality was great, though only a small proportion of his work is ever heard in the
modern concert-room.' Boccherini and Haydn—they were contemporaries—
are often named together as composers of chamber music, though the Italian
lacked the vigor and variety of the Austrian. Puppo, the violinist, said of him,
'Boccherini is the wife of Haydn'—as, a century later, Massenet was called
by some 'Mlle. Wagner,' which was a bit rough on Wagner.

● MINUET

‡This charming but hackneyed work is in its original form a movement from
a string quintet—the Quintet in E major, op. 13, No. 5. It is one of those
pieces which for reasons beyond the understanding of critics and historians
has caught the fancy of the great public and continues to be disseminated by
amateur and professional musicians in a thousand forms—among them, occasionally, that in which Boccherini cast it.‡

Ernest Bloch

1880-

B

‡Among composers of Jewish heritage prior to the present century were
many of the third and lower grades, one only (Mendelssohn) of the
second, and none at all of the first. It is at least curious that a racial, or
perhaps merely a linguistic and cultural division of the human race that
has displayed such a marked musical gift in the interpretive field should
have made so meager a contribution in the creative. Perhaps this imbalance
will be corrected in our own and future time. Though we cannot set a
final value on the work of our contemporaries, it is a fact that a number
of the salient creative figures in the music of the past half-century have
been or are Jews. Only one of them, however, Ernest Bloch, has avowedly
written any considerable quantity of Jewish music. A European by birth
and training, Bloch has resided in the United States for the past thirty-
five years and has composed a symphony entitled *America*, incorporating
a tune designed to serve as a national anthem. In spite of this, his music
has no discernible American flavor. At its most personal, it is Jewish—that
is to say, Eastern—in profile and coloring; again, it exhibits neo-classic
tendencies. It is, in either phase, music of marked originality and expressiveness, and Bloch must be counted one of the most forceful, as he has
been one of the most productive, composers of his time.‡

● CONCERTO GROSSO, FOR STRING ORCHESTRA WITH PIANO OBBLIGATO

Bloch's Concerto Grosso for String Orchestra with Piano Obbligato was composed between December 1924 and April 1925, while the composer was sojourning at Santa Fé, New Mexico. It is a modernization of the old eighteenth-century form [see notes, above, on the Bach Brandenburg concertos, or below, on the Handel concerti grossi], and comprises a Prelude, a Dirge, a movement entitled 'Pastorale and Rustic Dances,' and a final Fugue.

The Prelude, a movement of drastic energy and condensation, decisively rhythmed, is partly in duple and partly in triple time. It is based on a theme that is stated, after half a dozen bars of heavily accented chords in measures of varying time value, by piano and strings together. The second movement, Dirge ('Andante moderato,' 3-4), begins with a grave and simple theme for strings alone. This is followed by a passage in which strings, doubled by the piano, lament in descending chromatic passages. The time changes to 4-4 and a solo violin, accompanied by divided strings, with arpeggios for the piano, sings a tenderly elegiac melody that is at first in F-sharp major. A noteworthy feature of this section is an example of polytonality in which the 'cellos and basses play a melodic figure in the key of B-flat, against an F-sharp major chord sustained by four solo violins and arpeggios for piano and solo viola. This effect is repeated a few measures further on, with the superimposed keys changed to F- and C-sharp, leading to a misterioso passage with a blending of C-sharp, E and A major. The descending chromatic passage in thirds is heard for the string and piano under a sustained high B of the solo violin, and the Dirge reaches its climax in a return of the opening subject, ending on a pianissimo chord in C-sharp major.

The third movement, 'Pastorale and Rustic Dances' ('assai lento,' 3-4) opens with brief solos for viola and violin, over a double pedal, in the key of F. This eight-bar Prelude leads into an Allegro in 6-8 time with a melody for solo violin. The opening tempo returns; a solo 'cello, then the piano and strings, recall the viola theme of the beginning. The tempo becomes increasingly animated and the instrumental texture richer, ushering in the 'Rustic Dances' ('Allegro giocoso,' 6-8). These are developed at some length. There are reminiscences of the pastoral mood of the opening, and of a motive from the Dirge. The dance tunes recur, and the movement closes, 'molto allargando,' in F major. The Finale is a Fugue, with the subject (Allegro, 4-4) announced marcato, in D minor, by the violas—a movement of striking power and plasticity.

● Schelomo, HEBREW RHAPSODY FOR 'CELLO AND ORCHESTRA

When Schelomo was first performed in New York, at a concert of the Society of the Friends of Music (May 3, 1917), the composer was quoted as declaring that it was not his purpose 'to attempt a "reconstitution" of Jewish music' or to base his work 'on melodies more or less authentic.' 'I am not,' he said, 'an archeologist. . . It is the Jewish soul that interests me, the complex, glowing agitated soul that I feel vibrating throughout the Bible: The freshness and naïveté of the Patriarchs; the violence that is evident in the prophetic books;

the Jew's savage love of justice; the despair of the Preacher in Jerusalem; the sorrow and immensity of the Book of Job; the sensuality of the Song of Songs. All this is in us; all this is in me and it is the better part of me. It is all this that I endeavor to hear in myself and to transcribe in my music: the venerable emotion of the race that slumbers deep down in our soul.'

Schelomo was composed in Geneva, early in 1916, and, together with the *Trois Poèmes Juifs*, the setting of three Psalms, and the symphony *Israel*, constitutes that part of Bloch's work which is avowedly Hebraic in impulse and character.

The texture of the music, and especially the writing for the solo 'cello, is extraordinary in its richness of dramatic, poetical, and pictorial suggestion—an imaginative projection of singular vividness and intensity. The 'cellist and the seconding orchestra are by turns lyricist and tragedian, poet and seer. Schelomo —Solomon, the great King—amid his gorgeousness, reflecting in disillusionment upon his silver and his gold, the treasures of his provinces, the abundance of his gardens and his orchards, the fulfilled desires of his heart and eyes; and the Preacher, somber and mournful in his acrid wisdom as he contemplates the vanishing mist that is all delight—these thoughts are implicit in the imaginings of the tone poet, in the poignant chief subject for the 'cello, with its characteristic figure of a dotted eighth-note, that is heard after the opening five bars of introduction; in the piercing outbursts of despair that invoke the full voicing of the orchestra; in the strange and impressive recitatives for bassoon and other solo voices (ultimately, with mordant power, for two trumpets, fortissimo) which are the somber exhortations of the Preacher; in the intervals of sensuous lyricism and imperial pageantry; in the final descent into the depths, the brooding of the 'cello filling the music with the darkness of shut doors and shadowed windows and resolving dust.

Alexander Borodin

1833-87

B

Borodin, a medical man and a chemist, internationally known as the author of *The Solidification of Aldehydes* and of *Researches upon the Fluoride of Benzol,* was, like a surprising number of the more famous Russian composers of his day, a musician by avocation only and composed under difficulties. An amiable and incredibly patient soul, he gave much of his time to philanthropic and charitable works. Rimsky-Korsakoff tells us of his consecrating himself heart and soul to those works of social regeneration which in Russia were initiated during the latter part of the nineteenth century. When he should have been writing music, this Tol-

stoyan being sat on 'welfare committees' and acted as treasurer of a
benevolent organization. He turned his apartment in the School of Medi-
cine at St. Petersburg into an asylum for those whom he befriended; and
in the summer he lived the life of a peasant in a poorly furnished *izba*—
unselfish, absent-minded, inconsequent. He died at fifty-three—prema-
turely, for he had ideas of genuine power and originality to express. He
influenced, among others, the most individual of the post-Wagnerian
music-makers, Claude Debussy. He left an opera, *Prince Igor*, two symphonies, two string quartets, the orchestral sketch *On the Steppes of
Central Asia*, a few fine songs, and very little else. ‡Borodin was a member
of Balakireff's circle and one of the celebrated 'Five'—Balakireff, Borodin,
Cui, Moussorgsky, and Rimsky-Korsakoff.‡

• SYMPHONY No. 2, IN B MINOR

This symphony was begun in 1871, and the first movement was completed at
the beginning of the winter of 1871-2. Borodin then laid it aside to work
upon *Prince Igor*. He finished the symphony five years later. When the
Russian Musical Society purposed to give the work, it was discovered that the
first movement and the finale were missing, whereupon Borodin, though ill,
was propped up in bed and rescored in pencil the missing pages.

The first performance of the symphony took place on February 2 (14), 1877,
in the Rittersaal, St. Petersburg, under the baton of Napravnik. Borodin afterward revised his score. The symphony was introduced to America at a concert
of the Philharmonic Society of New York on February 5, 1897, under the
direction of Anton Seidl. On this occasion it was observed that the work
'is wholly free from the Teutonism which marks Rubinstein's music, or the
modified Slavicism which gives a barbaric tinge to the wildest of Tchaikovsky's
music. Borodin is all Slav. In the first movement, built almost wholly on a
short phrase, and the last movement, consisting of gorgeously colored and
varied presentations of a Russian dance tune, the national characteristics are
most vividly and convincingly set forth. Only in the slow movement is there
anything like the development of a sustained melody. The work is also characterized by a freakish interchange of rhythms which is also a common element
in Russian folk-song, and gives them a strange restlessness in ears accustomed
to Occidental music.'

Borodin, according to Stassoff, had certain pictures in his mind when he
composed this symphony.

Like Glinka [wrote Stassoff], Borodin is an epic poet. He is not less national than
Glinka, but the oriental element plays with him the part it plays for Glinka, Dargo-
mishsky, Balakireff, Moussorgsky, Rimsky-Korsakoff. He belongs to the composers of
program music. He can say with Glinka: 'For my limitless imagination I must have a
precise and given text.' Of Borodin's two symphonies, the second is the greater work,
and it owes its force to the maturity of the composer's talent, but especially to the
national character with which it is impregnated by the program. The old heroic Russian
form dominates it as it does *Prince Igor*. Let me add that Borodin himself often told

me that in the slow movement he wished to recall the songs of the Slav *bayans* (a kind of troubadour). In the first movement he had in mind the gatherings of ancient Russian princes; in the Finale, the banquets of the heroes to the sound of the *gusli* and the bamboo flute in the midst of the rejoicing crowd. In a word, Borodin was haunted when he wrote this symphony by the picture of feudal Russia, and tried to paint it in his music.

The first movement (Allegro, B minor, 2-2) opens with an energetic theme which serves as a kind of 'motto' (strings in unison, horns and bassoons in alternate measures). The first subject proper is also of strongly marked rhythm, while the second subject ('celli) is flowing and lyrical. The second movement is a Scherzo in F major, Prestissimo, with an Allegretto Trio: (oboe, clarinet, triangle, harp). The third movement (Andante, D-flat major, 4-4, with a song for the horn) is a reminder of the old Slavonic troubadours. The fourth movement, which follows without pause, is in sonata form (Allegro, B major). After an introduction, the chief subject enters forte in the full orchestra, in 5-4 time. The second subject is assigned to the clarinet.

● ORCHESTRAL SKETCH, *On the Steppes of Central Asia*, OP. 7

Borodin composed this tone picture while he was at work upon *Prince Igor*, in 1880. It was written for performance at an exhibition of *tableaux vivants* illustrating episodes in Russian history, devised to celebrate the twenty-fifth anniversary of the reign of Czar Alexander III.

The score contains this program printed in three languages:

In the silence of the arid steppes of Central Asia is heard the refrain of a peaceful Russian song. One hears, too, the melancholy sound of Oriental music, and the approaching steps of horses and camels. A caravan, escorted by Russian soldiers, crosses the immense desert, continuing untroubled on its long way under the protection of the warlike Russian guard.

The caravan moves onward steadily. The songs of the Russians and those of the native Asiatics mingle harmoniously, their refrains dying away little by little in the distance.

The immensity and monotony of the prairie are suggested by the long and persistent violin note that begins at once and is sustained for fifty-three measures ('Allegretto con molto,' 2-4), an inverted pedal on a high E. First a clarinet (cantabile, *p*.), then a horn, sing what Mr. Montagu-Nathan calls 'the Russian theme' beneath the prolonged string tone. The English horn ('cantabile ed espressivo') evokes 'the melancholy sound of the Oriental songs'; though now there is the support of clarinets and horn, and a pizzicato bass. Later, when the two songs are mingled, first and second violins in unison, on the G string, represent the 'Orientals,' while the oboe speaks for Russia. The music dies away on a high A major chord, *pppp*, for eight solo violins, muted, and a flute—'cantabile dolcissimo.'

● OVERTURE AND POLOVETSIAN DANCES FROM *Prince Igor*

Borodin described *Prince Igor* as 'essentially a national opera, interesting only to us Russians, who love to steep our patriotism in the sources of our history, and to see the origins of our nationality again on the stage.' He began work upon the opera in 1870, using a plot furnished to him by his friend Stassoff, who took it from an old national poem, 'The Epic of Igor's Army.' The story deals with a twelfth-century expedition of the Russian Prince Igor against the Polovtsi, a nomadic people, akin to the ancient Turks, who had invaded the Russian principalities. Igor was taken captive; but Khan Kontchak, the magnanimous ruler of the Polovtsi, treated him with the utmost hospitality, giving a banquet in the Prince's honor, and entertaining him afterward with dances of the warriors and their womenfolk.

Borodin prepared his own libretto, and worked intermittently upon the music until he died seventeen years later, leaving it unfinished. The opera was completed by Rimsky-Korsakoff and Glazounoff (the latter wrote out the overture from memory, for he had often heard Borodin play it). The score was published in 1889, and on November 4, 1890, the opera was produced at St. Petersburg. It was given at the Metropolitan Opera House, New York, for the first time in America, on December 30, 1915.

The overture has an introductory Andante (D minor, 2-4 time), leading directly into the main body of the movement (Allegro, D major, 2-4). The chief subject is not heard immediately, but follows a pedal-point and a descending figure in fourths for the string basses. The second subject is for the clarinet. There is a section in B-flat for the full orchestra, fortissimo, with a succeeding horn solo accompanied by the strings—a melody which the violins take up. A brief coda succeeds a modified recapitulation. A statement in Russian, published in the score, ascribes the instrumentation to Glazounoff. It is scored for two flutes and piccolo, two oboes, two clarinets, two bassoons, four horns, two trumpets, three trombones, tuba, timpani, and strings.

The Polovtsian Dances from *Prince Igor* were a feature of Diaghileff's season of ballet and opera at the Châtelet, Paris, in 1909. The choreography was by Fokine. Roerich designed the décor and costumes. Bolm was the chief warrior, with Massine and Woisikovsky appearing in revivals.

Johannes Brahms

1833-97

B

‡Opinions differ respecting the quality and importance of Brahms' contribution to the music of the nineteenth century. While he remains high in the favor of the great public (which, however, only took him to its heart within the rememberable past), there is in intellectual quarters a disposition to reduce this general to the ranks. This 'advanced' view concedes the charm of his minor works—various dances, some of the songs and

shorter piano pieces, the works in variation form—but condemns the larger orchestral, choral and chamber music works as pretentious and ill-wrought. It seems probable that the ultimate verdict on Brahms' music will be less severe, if also less favorable than that conventionally pronounced, which designates him as the greatest of the post-Beethoven symphonists and indeed the most considerable figure in music of the period from Beethoven's death to the present. He was the son of a theater musician of Hamburg, and in early life he supported himself by playing the piano in places of popular resort. Later, he toured with the violinist Reményi as his accompanist. Through this connection he made the acquaintance of several famous musicians of his day—Joachim, Liszt, Schumann—who formed a high opinion of his qualifications, encouraged and aided him. His introduction to Schumann's circle resulted in friendships that endured throughout his life. In the years that followed, he established himself solidly as a pianist, conductor, and composer of the first rank. He was perhaps the first composer to earn during his lifetime any very substantial sum through the publication of his works. He died in Vienna in 1897, a master admired and mourned.‡

THE SYMPHONIES

'You know that your music is as indispensable to our existence as air, light, and heat,' wrote Elisabet von Herzogenberg, that paragon of tact and sympathy, to her friend Brahms in 1882. 'You can't think how glad we are,' she added, 'not to have to give the dead masters *all* our affection and enthusiasm, and how glad that the one to whom we already owe so much still lives and labors, and is, we hope, neither inaccessible nor quite indifferent to us.'

Brahms has neither lived nor labored for over half a century, but in that time how astonishingly he has prevailed!

Elisabet von Herzogenberg was one of a considerable number who recognized the greatness of Brahms while he was still alive; yet a good deal of symphonic water was to pass under the orchestral bridge before his music became for the general concert-going public, as it was for the enthusiastic Elisabet, in any sense 'indispensable.' It was only a while ago that James Huneker (one of the earliest and most sensitive appreciators of the Olympian Johannes) was begging us in his brilliant and compelling way to stop thinking of Brahms as harsh and ascetic and astringent, and insisting that it was really quite possible to learn to love and cherish him—assuring us, with great particularity, that beneath the harsh exterior of Brahms there beat a human and accessible heart. Even H. C. Colles, a perfect Brahmsian if ever there was one, found it necessary in his excellent brochure to take account of what he called 'the difficulty of grasping this music'—and by 'this music' he meant, astonishingly enough, the gravely but transparently beautiful slow movement of the D major Symphony.

When Levi conducted the C minor Symphony at Munich a year after its première, the second movement and the third were hissed; nor was it the Wagnerites, said Levi, who did the hissing, but the 'classicists' so-called. The ineffable John S. Dwight, hearing the symphony in Boston in 1878, brushed it aside as a work not to be mentioned in the same day with any symphony by Mendelssohn: 'It will not be loved,' he declared, 'like the dear master-pieces of genius.'

Alas, for critical prophecy! We no longer hiss the C minor of Brahms; and we most reprehensively do love it. This music has 'the unimaginable touch.' Indisputably great it seems to us today, music infinitely noble and strong and restorative—music akin to that tonic and windswept order of poetry (whether of tones or of words), which, as Elton so finely said of Wordsworth at his rarest, 'disinfects life for us,' and makes it livable and august and rich.

'I miss the melodic flight,' wrote Clara Schumann amazingly in her diary after Brahms had played to her on the piano, in 1876, portions of his First Symphony, including the Finale. Perhaps Brahms, competent and experienced pianist though he was, played his music like a composer—that is to say, inadequately; but it is hardly likely that he failed to bring out the 'melodic flight' that wings that marvelous Finale into the wind and sun of its C major altitudes.

It is doubtless their 'melodic flight,' among other things, that has made these symphonies so widely loved within the last decades. It is a hard thing for the old-fashioned Brahmsian to hear—that old-fashioned Brahmsian who gloried in the master's 'aloofness' and 'difficulty,' as the haughty Meredithians of the 'eighties used to glory in the esoteric and inaccessible quality of *The Egoist*; but the truth can no longer be blinked: Brahms is today as popular as Tchaikovsky.

● No. 1, IN C MINOR, OP. 68

Brahms was middle-aged before this symphony was finished (though it had been maturing for a decade and a half). He completed it in September 1876, when he was in his forty-fourth year. Its ripeness and its confident mastery are evident throughout. If Matthew Arnold had been as responsive to music as to poetry, he would have hailed this symphony as an imposing manifesta-tion of 'the grand style.' It is of course true, as Arnold said, that the presence or absence of the grand style 'can only be spiritually ascertained.' But if it is not in this symphony, it is nowhere in music. The work is what Arnold called 'full-stored.' 'The fulness of thought, imagination, knowledge,' he might have said (as he said of Milton's verse) 'makes it what it is.' The C minor Symphony seems less austere than it did in 1876, when a sapient critic discovered in it 'a sullen asceticism.' It seems, today, abounding in mellowness and humanity.

The elder Henry James (a remarkable man and a writer of genius, strangely neglected) observed that 'Tennyson commanded a style and a music adequate, we may think, for the great poems which he never wrote.' The essential fact to remember and to celebrate about Brahms is that he possessed not only the mechanism of the grand style, but that he was able to exert it as a vehicle for ideas of authentic greatness; and he achieved this miracle with a continence, a sense of balance and proportion, an instinct for the larger contours as well as the finer adjustments of musical design, that were almost unerring.

The momentous opening of the symphony (the beginning of an introduction of thirty-seven measures, 'Un poco sostenuto,' 6-8) is one of the great exordiums of music—a majestic upward sweep of the strings against a phrase in contrary motion for the wind, with the basses and timpani reiterating a somberly persistent C. The following Allegro is among the most powerful of Brahms' symphonic movements.

In the deeply probing slow movement we get the Brahms who is perhaps most to be treasured: the musical poet of long vistas and grave meditations. How richly individual in feeling and expression is the whole of this 'Andante sostenuto'! No one but Brahms could have extracted the precise quality of emotion which issues from the simple and heartfelt theme for the strings, horns, and bassoon in the opening pages; and the lovely complement for the oboe is inimitable—a melodic invention of such enamouring beauty that it has lured an unchallengeably sober commentator into conferring upon it the attribute of 'sublimity.' Though perhaps 'sublimity'—a shy bird, even on Olympus—is to be found not here, but elsewhere in this symphony.

The third movement (the 'Poco allegretto e grazioso' which takes the place of the customary Scherzo) is beguiling in its own special loveliness; but the chief glory of the symphony is the Finale.

Here—if need be—is an appropriate resting place for that diffident eagle among epithets, Sublimity. Here there are space and air and light to tempt its wings. The wonderful C major song of the horn in the slow introduction of this movement ('Più andante,' 4-4), heard through a vaporous tremolo of the muted strings above softly held trombone chords, persuaded William Foster Apthorp that the episode was suggested to Brahms by 'the tones of the Alpine horn, as it awakens the echoes from mountain after mountain on some of the high passes in the Berense Oberland.' This passage is interrupted by a foreshadowing of the majestic choral-like phrase for the trombones and bassoons which later, when it returns at the climax of the movement, takes the breath with its startling grandeur. And then comes the chief theme of the Allegro—that spacious and heartening melody which sweeps us onward to the culminating movement in the Finale: the apocalyptic vision of the chorale in the coda, which may recall to some the exalted prophecy of Jean Paul: 'There will come a time when it shall be light; and when man shall awaken from his lofty dreams, and find his dreams still there, and that nothing has gone save his sleep.'

● No. 2, in D major, op. 73

The D major Symphony was finished only a year after the completion of the First. The C minor Symphony dates from 1876, the D major from 1877. The first performance of the C minor was at Carlsruhe, November 8, 1876; that of the D major at Vienna, December 30, 1877 (Reimann, in his Life of Brahms, gives the date as January 10, 1878; Erb, in his Brahms, gives it as December 24; Kalbeck, Deiters, and Florence May agree on December 20;

contemporaneous music journals—the *Signale,* for example—say December 20).
According to our present view, contemporaneous comment on the two works
seems to have been curiously undiscerning. Half a century ago the C minor
Symphony was regarded as abstruse, austere, forbidding, and the D major
was hailed by many as a grateful relief—as a thing predominantly 'sunny,'
full of happiness and lyric grace. Even the faithful Hanslick said of the C minor
that it affected the hearer 'as though he read a scientific treatise full of deep
philosophical thought.' He found, in the C minor, 'Faust-like conflicts of the
soul,' in the D major 'a vernal earth that laughs and blossoms.' The D major
comforted many who had found the C minor esoteric and severe; on the other
hand, it disappointed hearers who were looking for a repetition of what Miss
Florence May calls 'the sublimities, whether of pain or of joy,' of the C minor;
and these persons made contemptuous remarks about the 'prettiness' of the
D major.

Time, however, has set these two symphonies in rather a different light.
The C minor seems to have borrowed something of the rich tenderness, something of the warmly human quality, that was regarded as the special property
of the D major, and to have conferred upon the latter, in return, something
of its own sobriety and depth of feeling. The C minor appears far less austere
and much more companionable than it evidently did in 1876, and the D major
seems less unqualifiedly a thing merely of 'pure happiness and gently tender
grace'—though Weingartner rather sourly characterized the Allegretto as 'a
graceful trifle almost too insignificant for the other three movements.'

But it is the slow movement, with its somber undertone, that takes the
Second Symphony into a region of musical poetry where it keeps company
with Brahms at his noblest. There cannot be many who are able to listen without emotion to the opening of this 'Adagio non troppo'—in particular, to
that passage where the gravely beautiful melody in eighth-notes for the 'cellos
weaves about the descending trombone phrase in quarters, producing the
bitter-sweetness of those haunting minor and major seconds that dwell in the
ear long after the music has passed on to other moods and other spells, like
Shelly's enamoured wind, 'whispering unimaginable things.' Yet it was this
movement that seemed so baffling to Weingartner when he wrote his study
of *The Symphony since Beethoven.* 'The slow movement,' he said (and his
comment is more astonishing every time one reads it), 'can be satisfactorily
comprehended only after frequent hearing. It is difficult for it to disclose itself
to the musical mind, but it does so thoroughly in the end. If I may be allowed
the comparison, I should like to suggest a Dutch landscape at sunset. The eye
at first sees nothing but the sky over the wide, wide plain; heedlessly and
wearily it lets the glance pass over it. Gradually, a feeling arises, quietly, from
afar, and speaks to us.'

It is doubtful if there are many today, even though they be far less musically
receptive than Felix Weingartner, who find anything difficult of comprehension in this Adagio: music which presents to the imagination not an enigmatic
expanse of landscape and fading sky, but an open window into a poet's
meditative heart.

There are commentators on Brahms who still discuss with solemnity the question whether the D major Symphony is an idyl—'Brahms' "Pastoral" Symphony,' a work essentially eupeptic; or whether the 'undercurrent of tragedy' which some discern in the score takes it definitely out of the class of the innocent, the sunshot, and the 'cheerful' in musical art. Perhaps if we were less eager to put works of art in watertight compartments we should discover that such problems are for the most part imaginary.

Brahms once declared to Clara Schumann that he was 'not at all a sensitive person,' that he was 'absolutely without nerves or sympathy.' But it does not require much psychological penetration into the nature of Brahms the man and the artist to make one realize that the reverse was true. Brahms was, in fact, exceptionally sensitive, his nerves were often on the raw, he was acutely sympathetic. The outward Brahms, he of the curt, abrupt, and boorish exterior, was merely the negligible, the protective Brahms—clad, like Jurgen, in 'the armor of his hurt.'

As an artist it is clear that his sensibility was extreme. He was not only one of those poets who delight in the beauty of the world, who cherish its loveliness in their imagination, but he was also one of that lonelier clan who see in living shapes the vesture of decay.

Brahms the pastoral poet, serene in the presence of the infinite loveliness of the created earth, sings out of the D major canticle of the violins near the opening of the first movement, out of the perhaps too facile 'Allegretto grazioso.' We might say that it is the musing and reminiscent Brahms, haunted by the fleetingness of all belovèd things, who speaks to us in such a passage as that in the coda of the first movement where the solo horn winds its course among the voices of the strings, like 'some grave thought threading a dream.' But it is Brahms the tragic poet, sensible of those evanescent shapes that are as clouding breaths upon the mirror of the world, who is discernible behind the 'Adagio non troppo' of this symphony, that profoundest among his slow movements, with its deep awareness, somberly compassionate, of the pain and mystery of human life.

• No. 3, in F major, op. 90

Wagner died in February 1883, while Brahms was at work on his Third Symphony (completed in that year and published in 1884), and it has been conjectured—Dr. Hugo Riemann ventured the guess—that Brahms may have intended to pay a tribute to the chief citizen of Bayreuth when he recalled in the first movement of this symphony, just before the entrance of the second theme, a phrase from the 'Venusberg' scene in *Tannhäuser*. Without pausing to wonder whether it is likely that Brahms would have paid his tribute in quite that way, involving quite those connotations, it may be recalled that the Sirens of the Venusberg are not the only things that have been found in this inexhaustible symphony.

The final Allegro suggested to Joachim the idea of Hero and Leander (the second subject, in triplet rhythm, for horn and 'cellos, is Leander, according to Joachim). But W. F. Apthorp was reminded—by the first movement of the symphony, at least—of an entirely different person: Shakespeare's Iago.

There is a celebrated cross-relation between the A-flat of the 'motto' (the somber ascending phrase in F minor, F—A-flat—F, in the bass) and the preceding A-natural of the heroic chief subject—the valorous theme that sweeps down in the violins after the introductory chords for the wind; and from this suggestion of conflict Mr. Apthorp deduced, as a possibility, some such underlying dramatic principle as 'the bringing together of two opposing forces: Light and Darkness, Good and Evil, Major and Minor.'

'The first theme,' he continues, 'starts in passionately and joyously, in the exuberance of musical life: the counter-theme comes in darkly and forebodingly, like Iago's.

> . . . O, you are well-tuned now:
> But I'll set down the pegs that make this music,
> As honest as I am.

And so this symphony has recalled, to different ears and minds, images and moods and characters so fantastically assorted that Alice might almost have dreamed of them in Wonderland. You rise from a reading of the commentators with a confused impression that you have been viewing a composite photograph of Iago and Leander, Wagner and the Sirens of the Venusberg. It is less distracting and more profitable to think of the symphony as mere music, unadorned by a 'meaning': as music in which there is a singular blend of heroic beauty and romantic charm: a union of diverse traits exceptional even for Brahms, whose range of expressive speech was so wide.

Perhaps he has not elsewhere—in his symphonies, at least—so influentially united noble directness and puissant breadth, rich tenderness and poetic warmth. The superb opening of the symphony, exposing the great theme that descends with so liberal a gesture through the keys of F major, F minor, and D-flat major, is filled with a sweeping, heroic passion of splendid energy and amplitude. Yet consider, for contrast, the mysterious brooding of that extraordinary passage of antiphonal chords near the end of the Andante, wherein Brahms anticipated by a decade some of the harmonic procedures of Debussy; consider the end of the last movement, with its heart-easing, sunset peace and its murmuring quietude: where in all symphonic literature is there a nobler dying of sunset fires, a lovelier evocation of the peace of evening, than in that brooding, irradiated descent of the tremulous strings through the F major hush of the sustaining horns and wood and trumpets that brings the great work to a close?

The Brahms of this symphony is not the somber, majestic, exultant Brahms of the C minor, with its dangerous skirting of the sublime, nor the warmly idyllic Brahms of the Second, nor the austerer Brahms of the Fourth. In his Third Symphony Brahms is by turns passionate and lyric and heroic, as in its companions; but nowhere else in his symphonies has he spoken quite as he has in the wonderful last movement of the F major. That slow subsidence at the end into a golden twilight peacefulness, mystically contemplative and serene, is the achievement of a mood that he never quite recaptured, and it is among the indescribable things of music.

● No. 4, in E minor, op. 98

'Might I venture to send you a piece of a piece of mine?' wrote Brahms to his devoted friend Elisabet von Herzogenberg on August 29, 1885. 'Should you have time to look at it and tell me what you think of it? The trouble is that, on the whole, my pieces are nicer than myself, and need less setting to rights! But cherries never get ripe in these parts, so do not be afraid to say if you don't like the taste. I am not at all eager to write a bad No. 4.'

The 'piece of a piece of mine' was the first movement of the E minor Symphony.

Brahms had composed his Fourth Symphony during the summers of 1884 and 1885: the first movement and the Andante in 1884, the Scherzo and Finale in the following year. He sent to Frau Herzogenberg the manuscript of the first movement and the beginning of the Andante on September 4, 1885, with a request that 'if the piece should smile' on her at all, he wished it to be 'passed on to Frau Schumann—that is, play it to her. I hope to hear very soon. You will be sure to send me the thing back before you leave?' Elisabet and her husband, he told them, were the first to see any of the new symphony.

Elisabet seems to have absorbed the 'piece' in a few hours. On September 6th we find her writing to Brahms that although the manuscript had reached her only at noon of that day, the music had 'already undergone a fair amount of torture' under her 'clumsy fingers'; for Elisabet appears to have been able to play a MS. orchestral score at sight on the piano (an accomplishment not quite so common among musicians as the trusting layman might suppose). But even the gifted Elisabet encountered some hard going. 'If I had a little more time [she wrote apologetically to Brahms] I should have been pleased and proud to play it to Frau Schumann tomorrow; but as it is, there are certain pages I can hardly make out at all. Unfortunately—and to Heinz's great disgust—I still have difficulty in reading the horn parts, and have to wrestle miserably with those three wicked lines in the score: horns in E, horns in C, and trumpets in E. All the same, I have gained a fair idea of it and some parts come out beautifully and fill me with joy.'

The first performance of the E minor Symphony took place at Meiningen, October 25, 1885; the score was published in the following year. Brahms spoke of the symphony in a letter as 'a choral work without text,' as 'a couple of entr'actes.' He was over fifty when he wrote it, and at the time of its composition he was steeping himself in the tragedies of Sophocles—an unwholesome diet for the middle-aged. Max Kalbeck, who wrote an eight-volume Life of Brahms, sees in the E minor Symphony a reflection of downcast hours induced by the melancholy of antique tragedy. He views this symphony as a commentary upon our sorrowful mundane pageant. The finale moves him to quote from a Chorus in *Oedipus Coloneus*—that woeful Chorus which even the reverent Oxford Translation views with some impatience, beginning: 'Death is the aid (of our troubles) that end with the grave.'

Kalbeck would have thought it appropriate to attach to this symphony some such motto as might have been afforded by that depressing observation of Swinburne's:

Sing while he may, man hath no long delight—

though Kalbeck, we hasten to say, did not quote this disagreeable line. But he does not stop at the suggestion of an association with Sophocles' *Oedipus Coloneus*. The Andante recalls to him a desolate field, perhaps the Roman Campagna, and he discovers in the music an allusion to Brahms' song, *Auf dem Kirchhofe*; although he brightens up when he considers the Scherzo, which reminds him of the Carnival at Milan.

A good deal too much has been made of the presumably tragic contents of this symphony. Its autumnal hue is not pervasive. It is true that Brahms as a composer is often a gravely brooding. commentator on the essentially tragic aspect of human life. Often you fancy that you can hear him asking uneasily that perturbing question, implying a lie that is half truth, a truth that is half lie:

Who dreamed that beauty passes like a dream?

Or he murmurs to himself—

The dead are happy, the dust is in their ears.

Brahms, the social apparition, the outward and visible man—the 'corpulent little gentleman,' with the full beard and 'the very odd mustache, fiery red on one side and grey on the other,' the voice 'unusually high and clear,' and sounding 'as if it were cracked'; Brahms, red-faced and ill at ease in the evening dress which he hated to wear; Brahms, the lover of sauerkraut and Caporal cigarettes (50 pfg. size), the player of pranks, impulsive, boorish, gloriously rude—it is hard to picture this unromantic figure as a kind of musical Senan-cour, if one persists in demanding obvious advertisements of the brooding human soul. But only the incurably naïve, of course, expect to see the artist externalized in the man; and Brahms of the prickly shell was inwardly an artist who felt profoundly and tenderly the tragedy of human pain.

Yet there is small warrant for distorting the frequent gravity and the soberly compassionate melancholy of Brahms the tone poet into a fundamental depression; and to exhibit the Fourth Symphony as an exercise in pessimism is to show it in a misleading light. Dejection is hardly its fundamental note. Much of the first movement sounds (in Reimann's phrase) 'ballad-like'—in the bardic, old-world sense. Those 'cries of pain' which Reimann heard in it are not very piercing to modern ears. In the beautiful Andante, with its haunting coda, there seems to be no emotion more tragic than a dark-hued, romantic melancholy. The Scherzo, with its boisterous vigor and its con-trasting vein of delicately sportive humor and lyric tenderness, is of course anything but somber; and the Finale, with its Gothic sweep and amplitude, seems, despite its passionate earnestness and its occasional solemnity, remote from the mood of Sophoclean tragedy.

This Finale has caused much heart-burning among the analysts. It is described by some commentators as a 'chaconne,' by others as a 'passacaglia.'

Riemann calls it a 'chaconne.' Fuller-Maitland speaks as if the two terms were interchangeable. The theorists are no closer to agreement concerning the Finale of the E minor Symphony than they are when they discuss the great organ Passacaglia of Bach.

The chaconne was originally a dance (in triple time and rather slow movement) consisting essentially of a series of variations on a short theme, usually from two to eight bars in length. It is agreed by all that it closely resembles the passacaglia in form; but the Wise Men are not united as to the characteristics which differentiate the two types. Albert Schweitzer tells us that while the composer of a chaconne is privileged to introduce his recurring theme in any voice, the writer of a passacaglia must—according to the strict rules of the game—confine his theme to the bass, and Spitta agrees with him. Parry, in his admirable study of Bach, defines the distinction between the two forms, and reaches a conclusion precisely the reverse of Schweitzer's; so does Ebenezer Prout; so, also, does the author of the article 'Passacaglia' in *Grove*. And if the student wishes further entertainment, he might consult some of the older theorists on the subject of the two forms.

But, whatever may be the correct designation for the form used by Brahms in the Finale of his Fourth Symphony, there can be no dispute about the magnificence of the thing as music. It is conceived in the grand style, of which Brahms at his best was so assured and complete a master. Broadly speaking, it is a series of transmutations of an eight-bar theme. This theme is heard at once—it is the progression of forte chords for woodwind and brass which opens the movement ('Allegro energico e passionato,' E minor, 4-4). From this subject, Brahms evolves thirty-two variations, in the course of which the theme does not pretend to confine itself to the bass (as, according to Spitta and Schweitzer, every well-trained passacaglia theme should), but conceals itself at times in the upper and middle parts of the tonal structure with most resourceful ingenuity. Yet how overwhelming is the cumulative effect of this towering Finale! 'Who,' asked Elisabet, 'can resist an emotion strong enough to penetrate all that skillful elaboration?'

● Concerto for Piano and Orchestra, No. 1, in D minor, op. 15

This concerto endured many vicissitudes. Its first two movements began life as portions of a symphony upon which Brahms, then in his twenty-first year, worked in 1854. The unfinished symphony became a sonata for two pianos, and that in turn produced the first and second movements of the D minor concerto, which was completed in 1858.

Miss Florence May, in her valuable Life of Brahms, recounts the career of this concerto. 'Schumann's desire that his young protégé should apply his gifts and his skill in the handling of form to the composition of an orchestral work,' she reminds us, 'had not been disregarded by Brahms. He had tried his hand at an overture early in the year [1854], and had worked through the spring and summer at a symphony, making his first attempts at instrumentation with the help of Grimm. . . The symphony was never completed, but the work was thrown into the form of a sonata for two pianos (which Brahms at this period frequently played in private with Frau Schumann or Grimm), of which the first two movements have become known to the world as the first and second of the Piano Concerto in D minor, and the third is immortalized in the wonderful march movement in three-four time, "Behold all Flesh," in the German Requiem.'

Miss May relates that one day, after a performance of the two-piano version of the symphonic movements of 1854, Grimm had urged upon Brahms 'his frequently stated opinion of the inadequacy of this form [the two-piano sonata form] for the expression of the great ideas of the work. Johannes, however, had quite convinced himself that he was not yet ripe for the writing of a symphony, and it occurred to Grimm that the music might be rearranged as a piano concerto. This proposal was entertained by Brahms, who accepted the first and second movements as suitable in essentials for this form. The change of structure involved in the plan, however, proved far from easy of successful accomplishment, and occupied much of the composer's time during two years. The movements were repeatedly sent to Hanover for Joachim's inspection and returned with his suggestions; for his time, sympathy, musicianship, and knowledge of the orchestra were placed, with unfailing generosity, at Brahms' disposal during all the years that led up to the composer's maturity.'

The completed piano concerto was performed for the first time at Hanover on January 22, 1859, with Brahms himself at the piano and Joachim conducting. It was apparently too new, too original, for the reactionaries of those days, and the strength and beauty of its ideas made little impression on the hidebound souls of the Hanoverians and Leipzigers of 1859 (the concerto was performed at a Gewandhaus concert in Leipzig five days after the première, with Brahms again playing the solo part).

Brahms himself wrote to Joachim with grim humor concerning the reception of the work at Leipzig. 'A brilliant and decided failure,' he called it. 'This failure has made no impression at all upon me, and the slight feeling of disappointment and flatness disappeared when I heard Haydn's C minor Symphony and the *Ruins of Athens*. In spite of all this, the concerto will please some day when I have improved its construction. . . I believe it is the best thing that could happen to me; it makes one pull one's thoughts together and raises one's spirit.' A characteristic letter, dogged and brave.

Miss May regards the first movement of the concerto as 'symphonic in *character*, though, as Spitta has pointed out, not in form.'

The desire attributed to the composer [she continues] by Ferdinand Gleich and by many others since, to create a new form, to compose a symphonic work with a pianoforte obbligato, did not exist. Brahms simply wished to use what he had already written, and did not feel that the time had come when he could successfully complete a symphony. He re-wrote his first two movements, therefore, as we have noted, making room in them for a piano solo, put away the third movement, and composed a new finale. How successfully he accomplished his task is today apparent to accustomed ears, for which the first movement, though it contains slight deviations from conventional concerto form, has no moment of obscurity. The imagination of this portion of the work is colossal. It has something Miltonic in its character, and seems to suggest to the mind issues more tremendous and universal than the tragedy of Schumann's fate, with which it must be associated. No one will assert that it contains what are termed 'brilliant piano passages,' the very existence of which is unthinkable in a movement of such exalted poetic grandeur; but that its performance brings due reward to capable interpreters has been proved by the enthusiasm of many a latter-day audience. After all that has been said, the reader will have no difficulty in understanding the fervent intensity of mood which impelled the composition of the slow movement, or in realizing something of the emotions which suggested the motto, *Benedictus qui venit in nomine Domini,* written above it in the original manuscript.

In the Finale, the difficult task of treating something which should relieve the tension of feeling induced by the preceding movements, without impairing the unity of the concerto as a whole, has been well achieved. If it is somewhat more sombre in color than the usually accepted finale in rondo form, it is abundant in vigor and impulse, whilst, on the other hand, though written with a view to the concert-room, it never descends towards the trivialities of mere outward glitter.

● Concerto for Piano and Orchestra, No. 2, in B-flat major, op. 83

This concerto is a monumental work, full-stored and spacious, steeped in loveliness and poetry, overflowing with imaginative life.

Some enthusiasts have unhesitatingly called it the greatest of all piano concertos; but no matter how we may rank it, this is magisterial music—music of heroic scale and exquisite fabrication, an irresistible demonstration of Brahms' creative range and power. It might have been composed to illustrate the esthetic application of the word 'abundance.' Where else in the literature of the piano, as a solo or concerted instrument, is there so conquering a blend of exuberant vitality and a beauty sensitive and fine-textured, yielding us in its rarest moments that gravely contemplative poetry, solacing and restorative, which gives its special quality to the meditations of Brahms?

Brahms conceived this work with the magic of an Italian spring in his blood. In April 1878, he made his first trip to Italy, and there (as he wrote later to a friend) he watched with delight the miracle of a southern spring 'turning to Summer.' His friend Billroth, who accompanied him, records that Brahms was 'charmed with everything.' There is ample reason to give credence to the assertion of his biographer, Kalbeck, that in the music of the B-flat Piano Concerto, which Brahms sketched upon his return in May to Pörtschach, he has mirrored the spectacle that so bewitched him: the vision of an Italian spring shedding its immemorial loveliness over the valleys and groves and hill slopes of the haunted South.

Brahms did not at once develop his sketches for the B-flat Concerto. Three years after his first Italian trip he made another, in 1881, and again he steeped himself in the beauty of the southern spring. He returned to Vienna on his forty-eighth birthday, and by the end of the first week of July he had finished the score.

It is amusing to recall that Brahms himself, with that mastodonic playfulness which must at times have been a bit trying to his friends, belittled the prodigious work. He spoke of it to a friend as 'a tiny, tiny piano concerto with a tiny, tiny wisp of a scherzo'; and to another friend he announced it as 'some small piano pieces.'

The 'small pieces' turned out to be what some critics have called 'a symphony with piano obbligato.' One of them has characterized it, without exaggeration, as 'a work of the amplest proportions and the utmost difficulty.'

The concerto is in four movements, instead of the customary three. The first movement alone fills seventy-nine pages of the Eulenburg edition of the orchestral score; and what Brahms referred to as 'a tiny, tiny wisp of a scherzo' is actually a long and elaborate 'Allegro appassionato,' added to the three other movements because, as Brahms divertingly explained, the opening movement appeared to him 'too simple.' He said that he felt the need of an intervening movement, 'something strongly passionate,' between the first Allegro and the Andante. So he added the opulent, magnificent Scherzo.

James Huneker, whose dicta on Brahms were wickedly persuasive, seemed to like this concerto less well than the first in D minor. In his brilliant and elucidating study of Brahms in *Mezzotints in Modern Music,* he calls the Brahms of the B-flat Concerto 'more of the musician of the world, less of the introspective and contemplative poet.' 'Brilliant,' 'charming,' 'dashing,' 'piquant,' 'less recondite,' 'more popular'—these are some of his epithets for the work. And one might also quote Hermann Deiters, who says that this concerto is 'brighter and more intelligible' than its predecessor; or Miss Florence May, with her incredible recommendation of the Finale as a kind of mid-Victorian musical tea party—'a dainty feast of sound,' she calls it.

To some it will seem that the beauty and power of the B-flat Concerto are not quite adequately recognized in such friendly but disaffecting tributes. These dissenters persist in cherishing the whole of the first movement, with its opening horn-call that is as the voice of 'that vernal gladness which has been man's clarion since Time began'; they rejoice in the music's prodigality and fervor, its evocation of the 'far-swooping, elbowed Earth.' They respond to the rhythmic sorcery of the Scherzo and the Finale.

Above all, they treasure the inestimable slow movement, that Andante upon which a beautiful poetry seems to brood like the quiet-colored end of evening upon some loveliness of the fading hills. That long, sweet, gravely amorous song of the solo 'cello: how conquering it is at the very start (with the striking resemblance in its opening phrase to *Immer leiser wird mein Schlummer*)! And when, toward the end, after the exquisite meditations of the piano, it is heard again, before the music drifts upward into a hovering silence, you will tell yourself, perhaps, that this is surely the Brahms with whom one can live longest and closest—the Brahms of profoundly tender contemplation, of nobly romantic beauty, liquid-toned, large in spirit, lucid and candid, yet recalling to us that woman of whom Conrad writes, 'in whose most precise saying there were enigmatical prolongations that vanished somewhere beyond the reach.'

● CONCERTO FOR VIOLIN AND ORCHESTRA, IN D MAJOR, OP. 77

This concerto was written in 1878, the year after the composition of the Second Symphony. The concerto was composed for Joachim, dedicated to him, and first played by him at a Gewandhaus Concert, Leipzig, on January 1, 1879, under the direction of the composer. (Marcella Sembrich sang at the same concert.)

Brahms remarked to Clara Schumann in 1895 that 'one composes only until one's fiftieth year; then the creative power begins to diminish.' He was within five years of that deadline when he wrote this work; yet it would be rash to say that in it there are indications of impaired creative power. But perhaps Brahms was wrong. The most exuberant of all scores, *Siegfried*, was finished in Wagner's fifty-seventh year; and Wagner was fifty-four when he completed that miracle of creative energy, *Die Meistersinger*. Beethoven's inspiration dwelt on the heights after his fiftieth year. As for Brahms himself, there is the puissant Fourth Symphony to confute him: it belongs to his fifty-second and fifty-third years.

Indeed, Brahms achieved the fullness of his powers in the neighborhood of his fiftieth year. He had accomplished within the previous decade his first, second, and third symphonies, the violin concerto, the second piano concerto, the 'Tragic' and 'Academic Festival' Overtures, the G major sonata for piano and violin, the two superb piano Rhapsodies of op. 79, and the choral setting of Schiller's *Nänie*. He had attained what Miss Florence May cautiously describes as a 'supreme and glorious preëminence in contemporary estimation'; and he had made a decision momentous to any man: he had determined upon the wearing of a permanent beard—that flowing and patriarchal beard which is now inseparable from his imagined image.

This concerto for violin is now over seventy years old. It is still fresh, vivid, companionable—unaged and unaging.

The main theme of the first movement ('Allegro non troppo,' D major, 3-4) is announced at once by 'cellos, violas, bassoons, and horns. This subject, and three contrasting song-like themes, together with an energetic dotted figure, marcato, furnish the thematic material of the first movement. The violin is introduced, after almost a hundred measures for the orchestra alone, in an extended section, chiefly of passage work, as preamble to the exposition of the chief theme. The caressing and delicate weaving of the solo instrument about the melodic outlines of the song themes in the orchestra is peculiarly characteristic of Brahms' concerto.

This feature is even more pronounced in the second movement (Adagio, F major, 2-4), where, after a naïve theme for the oboe, the solo violin, having made its compliments to the opening subject, announces a second theme, which it proceeds to embroider with captivating and tender beauty. Seldom have the possibilities of decorative figuration developed so rich a yield of poetic loveliness as in this concerto. Brahms is here ornamental without vulgarity; florid without excess; these arabesques have the dignity and fervor of pure lyric speech.

The Finale ('Allegro giocoso, ma non troppo vivace,' D major, 2-4) is a virtuoso's paradise. The jocund chief theme, in thirds, is stated at once by the solo violin. There is many a hazard for the soloist: ticklish passage work, double-stopping, arpeggios—the customary *chevaux-de-frise* for the venturesome technician. Also there is much spirited and fascinating music—music of rhythmical charm and gusto.

The concerto was originally planned to comprise a Scherzo, but Brahms discarded it—'for reasons of style,' according to Specht. Kalbeck and others think that this rejected Scherzo found its way into the B-flat Piano Concerto, which was begun in the same year as the Concerto for Violin.

'Possibly the nature of the violin itself, to say nothing of the violinist for whom it was written (Joachim),' remarks H. C. Colles in his admirable book on Brahms, 'is largely responsible for the fact that the work attains to greater clarity of expression than either of the piano concertos. On the piano Brahms expressed his own complex mind, but in writing for the violin, on which the same technical complexities were impossible, and in writing for another to interpret, he rose above himself to that universal expression which is the rare privilege of the greatest alone.'

● DOUBLE CONCERTO, FOR VIOLIN AND 'CELLO AND ORCHESTRA, IN A MINOR, OP. 102

Brahms, in a letter to his friend Elizabet von Herzogenberg sent from Thun, July 20, 1887, wrote thus:

'I can give you nothing worth calling information about the undersigned musician. True, he is now writing down a thing which does not yet figure in his catalogue—but neither does it figure in other people's! I leave you to guess the particular form of idiocy!'

The 'particular form of idiocy' (it was Brahms' style of humor to refer to his music in these terms of mock disparagement) was the Double Concerto for Violin and 'Cello. The work was privately performed at the Baden-Baden Kurhaus, by Joachim and Hausmann, soon after its completion, sometime between July 20th and October 18, 1887. The first public performance was at Cologne, October 18th, with Joachim and Hausmann again playing the solo parts, and Brahms conducting. The concerto was published in the following year, and Brahms, presenting the score to Joachim, inscribed the copy, 'To him for whom it was written.'

It has often been pointed out that in this concerto, Brahms reverts to something not unlike the old concerto grosso form, in which several instruments, as a solo group (the concertino, so-called), were set off against the full orchestra. Brahms' two solo instruments are employed for the most part in this way, and the frequent use of double-stopping on both gives the suggestion of a string quartet alternating with the orchestra.

The old form survived to the time of Beethoven, who in his middle years wrote a triple concerto for violin, 'cello, and piano; and it has been revived in our own day. The form has been blessed with the favor of contemporary composers, and Bloch, Kaminski, and Krenek have recently given us examples of a modern development of the old model.

Brahms has combined the eighteenth-century practice with a modernized view of the possibilities of the form. 'As other concertos combine principles of solo and orchestral music, this one combines those of chamber-music with the orchestra.'

● 'ACADEMIC FESTIVAL' OVERTURE, OP. 80

When Brahms was in his forty-seventh year, the University of Breslau, with a delicate sense of fitness, conferred upon him the degree of Doctor of Philosophy, and Brahms responded handsomely by composing, in 1880, his *Akad-*

emische Festouvertüre, which was proffered to the functionaries of the University and the folk of Breslau on January 4, 1881, with Brahms conducting. It is an ingenious and delightful fantasy on the traditional students' songs of Germany. Brahms uses four of these tunes: 'Wir hatten gebauet ein stattliches Haus' (by the brass, in C major); 'Der Landesvater' (second violins, E major); 'Was kommt dort von der Höh' (bassoons, with violas and 'cellos pizzicato, G major); and finally, by the full orchestra fortissimo, in C major, 'Gaudeamus igitur.'

- 'TRAGIC' OVERTURE, OP. 81

Brahms has left us no elucidation of the meaning of this overture, which was first performed (probably at Vienna) in 1880, and published in the following year. The Vienna critic, Eduard Hanslick, who in all matters pertaining to Brahms spoke as one having authority, has intimated that if the music relates to any definite tragedy, it is to *Hamlet*. But Heinrich Reimann, in his painstaking *Johannes Brahms*, says nothing of *Hamlet*. Brahms has taken, he says, 'no definite, tragical, heroic figure as a basic ideal. It is only the universal, constant, fundamental emotion of tragedy (somewhat in the sense of Aristotle or Lessing) which is reflected. Grandeur, nobility, deep emotional earnestness are the essentials of tragic character. Circumstances, in which a remorseless destiny has involved the hero, fasten the guilt upon him. This guilt is expiated through his tragic downfall, which acts as a purifying agent upon the shaken and sorrow-burdened soul. Terror and pity, which, awakened simultaneously, influence mankind, bring to the hero himself pardon and salvation.'

- VARIATIONS ON A THEME BY HAYDN, OP. 56a

The 'theme by Haydn' (not indisputably original with him) is derived from a set of manuscript *divertimenti* for wind instruments. In Haydn's score the tune is referred to as *Chorale St. Antonii*. The theme, which sounds like a blended hymn tune and folk song (Andante, B-flat major, 2-4), is propounded by oboes and bassoons playing in sixths and thirds, supported by horns, contra-bassoon, and double basses pizzicati.

VARIATION I. ('Poco più animato.') The violins weave an intricately rhythmed tracery above strongly marked phrases in the wind. The likeness to the theme is artfully concealed, as it is elsewhere in the work.

VARIATION II. ('Più vivace,' B-flat minor.) Clarinets and bassoons in sixths elaborate the characteristic rhythm of the theme, against decorative passages for the strings.

VARIATION III. ('Con moto,' B-flat major.) Oboes and bassoons discourse above a passage in double octaves for violas, 'cellos, and double basses. Then the violins enter, dolce, legato, adorned by filigree work in the woodwind.

VARIATION IV. ('Andante con moto,' B-flat minor, 3-8.) Oboe and horn, 'dolce e semplice,' carry the melody, accompanied by the lower strings. Toward the end of the variation the strings play the melody in double octaves, under woodwind embroidery.

Variation V. (Vivace, B-flat major, 6-8.) The strings in unison have an inversion of the initial three-note figure of the theme. The woodwind chatter volubly, paired in thirds, and a piccolo adds its voice. The strings then take over the pattern. The writing is delectably light-handed and fantastic.

Variation VI. (Vivace, B-flat major, 2-4.) Strings outline the theme, pizzicato. A vigorously rhythmed figure is exploited by the wind.

Variation VII. (Grazioso, B-flat major, 6-8.) Flute and violas in octaves play what Fuller-Maitland calls 'a delicious falling theme,' for which the violins and clarinets provide a convenient staircase: a passage descending by the orderly steps of the B-flat major scale. The rhythm is that of a Siciliano.

Variation VIII. ('Presto non troppo,' B-flat minor, 3-4.) The muted strings play 'sempre pianissimo.' Piccolo, clarinet, and bassoon creep stealthily on the scene at the sixth bar. The theme is inverted. The whole variation has a Beethovenish air of soft-footed mystery.

Finale. (Andante, B-flat major, 2-2.) The strings announce a ground bass derived from the first phrase of the Theme. 'The serene opening,' says Fuller-Maitland, 'tells us of what is to come, as surely as Beethoven tells us that matters of great moment are in his mind at the beginning of the last movement of the *Eroica*. The increasing elaboration of the workmanship up to the climax where first the wind instruments and then the strings have a rushing scale, is among the most powerful of musical impressions of any date; and while all the variations are a delight to the ear . . . yet the best is kept to the last.'

Max Kalbeck, in his eight-volume Life of Brahms, declares that Johannes, in writing his Variations on the theme which Haydn entitled *Chorale St. Antonii*, intended to suggest certain phases of St. Anthony's famous adventure in the Egyptian desert. He thought that the charming Seventh Variation, the 'Grazioso' episode in B-flat major in Siciliano rhythm, for flute and violas in octaves, pictures in tone the most atrocious of St. Anthony's ordeals, 'the most atrocious because the sweetest.' He found here the 'quintessence of human voluptuousness.'

One cannot help wondering what the rudely sarcastic Brahms would have said if he had read this amazing tosh. If the music of that gracious Seventh Variation is 'voluptuous' (to say nothing of 'the quintessence of voluptuousness'), then we have all been entertaining lyric wantons unaware for many a year. Perhaps Fuller-Maitland was thinking of Kalbeck's deplorable suggestions when, in analyzing these Variations, he spoke of the melody of this passage as 'a delicious falling theme.'

● A German Requiem, for Solo Voices, Chorus, and Orchestra, op. 45

The full title of this work, in the original, is: *Ein deutsches Requiem, nach Worten der heiligen Schrift, für Soli, Chor, und Orchester (Orgel ad libitum)*. Brahms used the word 'German' in his title to avoid misconception. A 'requiem,' without qualification, is understood as the Roman Catholic requiem mass, a setting of the liturgical Latin text. Brahms' composition is a different matter altogether. There is nothing liturgical about it. The texts consist of excerpts selected by Brahms himself from the German translation of the Scriptures. The texts were culled from various books of the Old and New Testaments and the Apocrypha. They were chosen, without doctrinal purpose, 'as parts of the people's book, of Luther's Bible,' and were so arranged as to present in succession the ascending ideas of sorrow consoled, doubt overcome, death vanquished.

The work has been called 'a series of richly pictured and imaginative reflections upon life this side of the grave and beyond: of the lot of man and the experience of the spirit. The personal, individual note in the Scriptural texts that are connected in it is a significant element that distinguishes this work from those that conform to the utterances of the Catholic liturgy. Resignation, questioning, aspiration, assertion of triumphant certainty, all find their expression in its changing moods.'

Brahms, in other words, forgot both theology and ritual: he remembered the inevitable human lot of mutation and sorrow, death and separation. His meditations twined themselves somberly, tenderly, exaltedly, about the ineffable sorrow and beauty, the ancient solace, of immemorial words: '. . . Behold, all flesh is grass, and the glory of man is as the flower of the field. . . And ye are now sorrowful. . . As one whom his mother comforteth, so will I comfort you. . . Behold, I show you a mystery: we shall not all sleep, but we shall all be changed. . . Blessed are the dead which die in the Lord . . .'

It was generally thought by Brahms' closest friends that he composed the 'German Requiem' as a memorial to his mother. 'We all think he wrote it in her memory,' Frau Schumann said. And Joachim declared, 'Never has a nobler monument been raised to filial love.' Brahms himself said to Deiters, when he played the music to him from manuscript and came to the choral part of the fifth number, that here he had thought of his own mother. Yet some insist that the 'German Requiem' was inspired by Brahms' sorrow over the tragic end of Schumann.

The 'German Requiem' as originally conceived included only six numbers. The soprano solo with chorus No. 5 ('Ye now are sorrowful . . . Yea, I will comfort you, as one whom his own mother comforteth'), was added to the score after the completion and performance of the other numbers. The first performance of the original version took place in the Bremen Cathedral, under Brahms' direction, on Good Friday, April 10, 1868. 'The impression made by the wonderful, splendidly performed work,' wrote Dietrich, 'was quite overpowering, and it immediately became clear to the listeners that the "German Requiem" would live as one of the most exalted creations of musical art.' The entire work as it now stands, with the fifth number included, was performed at the Leipzig Gewandhaus, February 18, 1869, under Reinecke. The score was published in 1868.

The first of the seven movements is a chorus ('Ziemlich langsam und mit Ausdruck,' F major, 4-4) on the Beatitude, 'Blessed are they that mourn, for they shall be comforted.'

The funeral march ('Langsam, marschmässig,' B-flat minor, 3-4) succeeds it. 'The tramp of many feet, the march of all humanity to its end, is present throughout its course.' The orchestra plays a twenty-two bar prelude before the chorus enters. 'Behold, all flesh is as the grass.' There is a contrasting section, 'Now, therefore be patient' ('Etwas bewegter,' G-flat major). The march recurs. There is a superb concluding section, fugally treated ('The redeemed of the Lord shall return again'), with an impressive coda over a double pedal.

In the third movement (D minor, 2-2), the vision alters, is colored again by the hues of mortality. From confidence Brahms relapses into despondency. 'Lord, make me to know mine end,' sings the baritone. Here Brahms utters the cry of the human soul which has attained no releasing height of aspiration, but remembers 'the ceaseless waters of human tears,' and the common end of man. A setting for baritone solo and chorus of the words, 'Now, Lord, what do I wait for?' is succeeded by an accompanied choral fugue set to the words, 'But the righteous souls are in the hand of God'—the famous fugue written over a tonic pedal point.

The fourth number is a chorus, 'How lovely is Thy dwelling-place, O Lord of Hosts!' ('Mässig bewegt,' E-flat, 3-4)—a simple choral song with flowing accompaniment.

The fifth is the soprano solo, with chorus, 'Ye now are sorrowful' (Langsam, G major, 4-4), added after the completion of the rest of the score. It was while writing the choral part of this number that Brahms, as he said to Deiters, remembered his own mother.

The sixth number opens with a choral dirge, 'Here on earth have we no continuing city.' A baritone solo interrupts with the familiar words of Paul: 'Behold I shew you a mystery. . . We shall not all sleep when He cometh, but we shall all be changed. . .' The music is charged with a mysterious agitation, a sense of gathering tremendousness. A crescendo begins, and culminates in a radiant outburst of the chorus and orchestra at the sublime promise of the Resurrection. There is a brief and quiet return of the baritone solo: 'Then what of old was written, the same shall be brought to pass.' The chorus cries forth its jubilant assurance, 'For death shall be swallowed up in victory.' The movement concludes with a magnificent fugue, 'Worthy art Thou to be praised.'

The apocalyptic tale is told, the incredible climax reached. The seventh movement is in the nature of an epilogue—a setting for chorus of the Beatitude, 'Blessed are the dead which lie in the Lord' (Feierlich, F major, 4-4). As one of Brahms' commentators points out, Brahms discloses to us here 'no placid and characterless state: The principal theme is an example of Brahms' vigorous attitude towards the subject: this cry of the angel from Heaven is of triumphant activity.' Nevertheless, the coda is as a benediction, music of majestic serenity and peace.

Max Bruch

1838-1920

B

‡As a composer, Bruch survives almost solely by virtue of works composed for the violin and the 'cello, which are still held in esteem by virtuosos of those instruments. He produced an immense amount of music in other and larger forms, but this today is little regarded, except perhaps in Germany and Austria, where his more ambitious choral works are occasionally performed, and where voices may yet more occasionally be heard to proclaim them masterpieces.‡

● CONCERTO FOR VIOLIN AND ORCHESTRA, NO. 1, IN G MINOR, OP. 26

When this celebrated score was completed, Wagner was working on the first act of *Die Meistersinger*, Richard Strauss was two years old, and Debussy was four. The days of the musical traditionalist were numbered. Even Bruch had begun to dare. Yet he was worried over the 'unconventionality,' the 'constructive freedom' of the first movement of his concerto, and he considered the advisability of calling the work a 'fantasy' rather than a 'concerto.' But Joachim (though he, to be sure, was no wild-eyed iconoclast) reassured him. 'The title "concerto," ' he told the apprehensive Bruch, 'is fully justified . . . the different parts are brought together in beautiful relationship, and yet there is sufficient contrast, which is the chief object.' And he comforted Bruch by reminding him that Spohr 'called his *Gesangsszene* a "concerto." ' But Joachim suggested certain alterations, and Bruch, after the first performance (April 24, 1866), revised the score, publishing it in 1868 with a dedication to his mentor.

The three movements are thus arranged: Prelude, 'Allegro moderato,' G minor, 4-4—leading without pause into the Adagio, E-flat major, 3-8; Finale, 'Allegro energico,' G major, 2-2.

● CONCERTO FOR VIOLIN AND ORCHESTRA, NO. 2, IN D MINOR, OP. 44

This concerto was composed at Bonn in 1887, and was privately played by Sarasate in September of that year. The first public performance was on November 3, 1877, at a Crystal Palace Concert in London. Sarasate again played the solo part, and August Manns conducted. The work, dedicated to Sarasate, was published in 1878.

There are three movements:

(I) 'Adagio ma non troppo,' in D minor, 4-4 time; (II) Recitative, 'Allegro moderato,' in B-flat major, 4-4; (III) Finale: 'Allegro molto,' B-flat major and D major, 3-8.

Bruch was influenced in the composition of this concerto by impressions received from his reading of a narrative of the Carlist Wars, which, he said, awakened in him 'romantic conceptions' that he turned into 'tone-pictures,' as he called them. But he did not say more concerning the nature of those 'romantic conceptions,' or what relation they bore to the different movements of the concerto. The hearer is left to his own devices.

Anton Bruckner

1824-96

B

Bruckner's life spanned almost three-quarters of the nineteenth century. He was born while Beethoven and Schubert were still alive. He was nine years older than Brahms (against whom he was needlessly pitted by his unwise adherents) and eleven years younger than Wagner, whom he adored. He began his First Symphony (really his second: it was preceded by the *Studiensymphonie* in F minor) in the year of the production of *Tristan und Isolde,* and he laid down his pen when Richard Strauss was sketching *Till Eulenspiegel.* Thus his work belongs to the period during which Romanticism attained its noon, and Bruckner's eyes caught something of that meridional light. With the exception of his idol Wagner, he was the best hated composer of the nineteenth century. What was not said of his music by the partisans of Brahms! Elisabet von Herzogenberg called him an 'inflated windbag'; Bülow referred to him as 'the Asiatic Bruckner.' As for the powerful and vindictive Hanslick, he abused Bruckner as if he had been a pickpocket, pursued him and harrassed him with a venom that knew no bounds. But for a few he was, and is, at his most rewardingly characteristic, one who knew the secret of a strangely exalted discourse, grazing at moments the sublime. At his greatest he is both a poet and a seer, looking at us with fathomless, grave eyes, speaking soberly of incredible things, or uttering magnificence like a Hebrew prophet, or rolling up the heavens like a scroll. As a man, he was patient, humble, naïve, sensitive, and pitiable. He dedicated his Second Symphony to Franz Liszt, his Third to 'Master Richard Wagner, in deepest reverence,' his Sixth to his landlord (though he afterward annulled this), his Seventh to the King of Bavaria, his Eighth to the Emperor of Austria, and he intended to dedicate his Ninth to God—at least there is a legend to the effect that he proposed to inscribe it 'To the dear Lord.'

• SYMPHONY NO. 4, IN E-FLAT MAJOR ('Romantic')

This symphony was composed in 1874. Bruckner revised it between 1878 and 1880. The first performance was at a Philharmonic concert in Vienna, under Hans Richter, on February 20, 1881. Anton Seidl introduced the work to America at one of his concerts in Chickering Hall, New York, on March 16, 1888.

If Bruckner, enjoying his Pilsener in an unamended Elysium, remembers his earthly prejudices, he must be haunting some of the analysts who have explored his symphonies. He strongly resented the discovery of poetical, pictorial, or descriptive implications in his music, yet the commentators have repeatedly defied him—not without help, apparently, from Bruckner himself, who, like many other composers, was delightfully inconsistent in this regard. Bruckner made several drafts of his E-flat symphony between 1874 and 1880, and in these autographs there are superscriptions for certain movements and passages.

Walter Niemann in his comments upon this work calls it a 'Waldsymphonie,' and classes it, in poetical intention and substance, with Haydn's *The Seasons*, Beethoven's 'Pastoral,' Weber's *Freischütz*, Wagner's *Siegfried*, and Humperdinck's *Hänsel und Gretel*; but he finds it widely separated in spirit from Raff's *Im Walde*; and certainly there is a depth and gravity of mood in Bruckner's contemplation of nature that is not to be found in the romantic but superficial Raff.

Bruckner as a nature poet was often Wordsworthian. He was an instinctive mystic, and for him the beauty and wonder of the visible earth were an august revelation of the Divine: to him, as to Wordsworth, they were 'the garment of God'—an embodiment of unseen spiritual realities. He might have given Blake's answer to the questioner who asked, 'When the Sun rises do you not see a round disc of fire, something like a guinea?'—'No! I see an innumerable company of the heavenly host, crying "Holy, Holy, Holy is the Lord God Almighty." ' For Bruckner, as for that other devout nature poet in tones who was so different from him in style and method—Vincent d'Indy—the pageant of the universe was a symbol of unutterable and supernal things. The incredible wonder of the dawn, the dark sweep of woods against the sky, shadows in pools, the evening light upon the hills, the peace that falls within the valley —all discoursed to him of the glory and benignity of God.

The first movement of the E-flat symphony ('Ruhig bewegt,' 2-2, E-flat major) establishes at once a deeply contemplative mood. Above string tremolos on the chord of the tonic, a horn pronounces softly the first section of the chief theme. The second section of this theme (violins and flutes) is in the rhythm of which Bruckner was especially fond—two quarter-notes followed by a triplet of quarters—and is not unlike the unforgettable second theme of the first movement of his Eighth Symphony. The violas and first violins divide the lyrical second subject between them; it is in two parts, contrapuntally combined at the start. Walter Niemann perceives in this movement a vision of the nature poet alone in the heart of the wood, his spirit buoyant with songs of praise, of hymns that are almost dithyrambic in their ecstasy.

The Andante (C minor, 4-4) is profoundly melancholy in temper. The chief theme, an expressive canticle for the 'cellos, is heard under an accompaniment of muted violins and violas. There is a choral-like passage for the strings. Woodwind, horns, trumpets, and trombones amplify the solemn lament. This 'funeral music,' so-called, is followed by the second and song-like subject in the violas. At the climax of the movement, the once mournful chief theme becomes a triumphant affirmation, with the brass chanting a variant of the subject in the major mode.

The Scherzo (Bewegt, B-flat major, 2-4) is said to portray a hunt. When the symphony was produced for the first time in America, under Seidl, the hunting-horn fanfares that open the Scherzo and furnish the basis for much of its musical material reminded H. E. Krehbiel of the hunt music in the second act of *Tristan*. He seems to have preferred the latter (New York had heard *Tristan* for the first time more than a year before, in the opera season of 1886-7). Krehbiel, in speaking of this movement, referred to 'its title, "The Hunt." ' This title ('Die Jagd') is printed at the head of the Scherzo in Josef Schalk's arrangement of the symphony for piano solo, though it does not appear in the published orchestral score (Vienna, 1890). But the imaginative content of the music is obvious.

A graceful subsidiary theme (strings and horns) suggests to Niemann what he calls the 'Freia' motive from *Rheingold*. It is not in the least like the 'Freia' motive; but the latter portion of it does suggest the very different motive of the 'Golden Apples' from *Rheingold*. The trio (Gemächlich, G-flat major, 3-4) is fluent and Schubertian. The theme is stated by flute and clarinet. In the MS. of the original partitur of the Scherzo, Bruckner wrote above this passage: 'Tanzweise während der Mahlzeit zur Jagd.'

The opening of the Finale ('Mässig bewegt,' E-flat, 2-2) is curiously impressive. Above an organ-point on the dominant for 'cellos and basses, Bruckner develops an extremely gradual but very powerful crescendo, with the help of a muttering accompaniment figure for the second violins, reminiscences of the hunting call on the horns and trumpets, and premonitory fragments of the chief theme of the movement, which finally bursts forth in a portentous unison passage, fortissimo, for the full orchestra. There is a swift diminuendo, then a second crescendo, and the brass choir proclaims, fortissimo, a variant of the chief theme of the first movement. This outburst, too, is quickly stilled, and finally only the kettledrum is heard, 'rit. e dim.,' followed by a pause. Niemann sees here the suggestion of a gathering, culminating, and subsiding storm. The strings resume the movement, piano, while flute and clarinet in C major announce the more characteristic portion of the second theme.

Bruckner plays resourcefully with his material in this movement, employing his favorite device of inversion; and there is much contrapuntal exercise. Also, material from earlier portions of the symphony is recalled. The close is radiant and triumphant. Apparently, it is bright noon-tide in the woods, and the nature-poet exults. But the MS. of the earlier version of the Finale is said to have borne the superscription, 'Volkfest.' There must, indeed, as Niemann observes, have been a very thoroughgoing alteration of plan on the composer's part to produce so remarkable a metamorphosis.

• SYMPHONY NO. 5, IN B-FLAT MAJOR

Bruckner began the composition of this symphony (sometimes given the appellation 'Tragic') at Vienna in his fifty-first year, in a period of great mental depression. He wrote the slow movement first, in February and March of 1875; the Scherzo followed in April, the Finale in May. The first movement was not begun until March of the following year. On August 9, 1877, the symphony was completed. But Bruckner revised his work in 1878. He never heard the symphony. It was not performed until April 8, 1894, when Bruckner's devoted pupil, Franz Schalk (who succeeded Anton Seidl as conductor of German opera at the Metropolitan in the season of 1898-9), directed the première of the work at Graz. Bruckner, then in his seventieth year, was too ill to attend. The symphony was performed in Vienna, with great success, in 1898—two years after Bruckner's death.

Bruckner's Fifth Symphony has been described as the 'most contrapuntally brilliant' of the nine. That, of course, is a matter of opinion. We are on firmer ground in calling attention to the fact that one of the peculiarities of Bruckner's workmanship, as manifested in this score, is that he seldom introduces a theme without at once consorting a countertheme with it. Frequently this countertheme is an inversion of the original one. Often, the most apparently insignificant motive, so long as it has a distinct and recognizable character, is lifted into importance by the treatment accorded to it.

It should also be pointed out that the movements of this symphony exhibit that community of thematic material which, before Bruckner's time, had appealed to Beethoven and to Schumann as a scheme for enforcing the idea of musical or poetical unity—a device which Tchaikovsky, César Franck, and a host of later composers have adopted.

The symphony has a slow Introduction (Adagio, B-flat, 2-2), which begins with pizzicati scale passages in the string basses, over which an introductory theme appears in the third measure (bassoons and violas). A solemn unison call of the wind and strings is promptly associated with this group, followed by the principal theme of the Introduction, for trombones and bassoons. Scarcely has this theme been announced when it is used in diminution, with a counterpoint above. There is development of this, leading into the first movement proper, the Allegro, in the fifth measure of which, the clarinet, violas, and violoncellos announce the principal theme of the movement, a melody of vague tonality hovering about B-flat minor. A new subject follows (Langsamer), exposed by the strings alone, pizzicato. Later, the first violins, doubled by clarinets and flutes, begin an expressive cantilena which some of Bruckner's Austrian commentators have termed a 'Hymn to holy Love'—a sort of consolatory vision of spiritual felicity glimpsed in the midst of a desperate unhappiness.

The Development section begins with a reference to the slow Introduction, with its characteristic pizzicati.

The second movement (Adagio, D minor, 4-4) discloses a parallel to the Introduction in also beginning with a pizzicato figure in the strings, over which the principal theme is sung by the oboe—the melody in 4-4, the accompaniment in 6-4 time. The second motive of the first phrase of the oboe melody (third measure) is marked by a descending seventh interval (d-e, c-d) which asserts an importance not only in this but also in the succeeding movement, the Scherzo. The opening pizzicato figure of the second movement, transformed from 6-4 to 3-4 time, becomes the foundation of the Scherzo ('Molto vivace,' D minor, D major, 3-4; Trio: Allegretto, B-flat major, 2-4).

In the introduction to the fugued Finale (Adagio, B-flat, 2-2), use is made again of the beginning of the Introduction to the first movement, and also of the principal theme of the symphony's first Allegro, which rings out again in the trumpets at the close of a chorale played by an auxiliary band composed of three trumpets, three trombones, bass tuba, and four horns, which, according to the specifications in the score, are to be stationed on a platform back of the main orchestra.

The symphony is scored for three flutes, two oboes, two clarinets, two bassoons, four horns, three trumpets, three trombones, bass tuba, timpani, and strings. In the Finale, a contrabassoon, cymbals, and triangle are added; and, in the coda, the auxiliary brass choir mentioned above.

• SYMPHONY NO. 7, IN E MAJOR

Bruckner's unaccredited master was Richard Wagner, whom he worshiped this side idolatry; and Bruckner's Seventh Symphony is related in a curious and interesting way to the genius whose mighty shadow overspread the musical world of his time.

Richard Wagner died on February 13, 1883, and Bruckner declared that the Adagio of his Seventh Symphony was conceived as a dirge in Wagner's memory. It is said that Bruckner's annotations on the MS. score in the Imperial Library at Vienna indicate that the Adagio was not completed until April 21, 1883, and so make plausible this statement of Bruckner's. Yet Bruckner's biographer, Rudolf Louis, is authority for the assertion that the Adagio was completed in October 1882, four months before the death of Wagner; and Louis expresses astonishment that Bruckner should have notified conductors of his wish that audiences about to hear this symphony be informed that the news of Wagner's death inspired him to the composition of the Adagio.

The facts in the case are still in dispute. Bruckner afterward explained that he was led to the composition of the Adagio in this symphony by a premonition of Wagner's death. 'One day I came home sad,' he wrote to Felix Mottl; 'I thought to myself that it would be impossible for the Master to live long; and at that time the Adagio in C-sharp minor came into my head.'

Philip Hale has pointedly remarked that letters written by Bruckner to Mottl in 1885, concerning a performance of the symphony at Karlsruhe, show that Bruckner himself was aware that the Adagio 'had not in all respects the character of a dirge.' For Bruckner was at pains to indicate to Mottl the precise point at which the funeral music begins in this movement: 'At letter X in the Adagio—Funeral music for tubas and horns, etc.' And further: 'Please take a very slow and solemn tempo. At the close, in the Dirge (in memory of the death of the Master) think of our Ideal! . . . Kindly do not forget the *fff* at the end of the Dirge.'

The symphony was completed September 5, 1883. It was published in 1885, with a dedication 'To His Majesty, the King, Ludwig II of Bavaria, in deepest reverence'—that same eccentric Ludwig who had befriended Richard Wagner when he was most in need of assistance. The symphony was performed for the first time at Leipzig, under Arthur Nikisch, on December 30, 1884.

The first movement ('Allegro moderato,' E major, 2-2) exposes at once the principal subject: it is stated by the 'cellos and first horn under violin tremolos. There is a *ff* climax, a diminuendo, and then the second theme (which may be recognized by the Wagneresque 'turn' in its second measure) is heard on the oboe and clarinet. Later, this theme is inverted by the violins. The working-out section begins with an inversion of the opening 'cello theme of the movement, now given to clarinets; and this form of the theme is prominent in the development. A climax, *fff*, based on the chief theme in both its aspects, ends the movement.

The second movement (Adagio: 'Sehr feierlich und langsam,' C-sharp minor, 4-4) contains the so-called 'Dirge' in memory of Wagner. It is Bruckner's most celebrated page, and is to be ranked with the slow movement of his Eighth Symphony for depth of feeling and intensity of expression. Bruckner uses in this movement (as in the Finale) the so-called 'Bayreuth tubas' of the *Ring* orchestra; and the principal theme, a solemn and nobly elegiacal melody, is heard at the beginning from the choir of five tubas (two tenor, two bass, and contrabass), doubled by the violas, 'cellos divisi, and basses. The second phrase of the subject is introduced by the strings. At the thirty-seventh measure there is a new section (Moderato, 3-4 time, in F-sharp major) with a second theme given to the violins. There is a return to the opening theme and tempo, with a long crescendo on the first subject. The poignant climax of the movement, *fff*, is built upon the second section of the first theme. It is followed (at letter X, page 47 of the full score) by the funeral music for the five tubas—at first alone, then joined by two horns, culminating swiftly in the *fff* which Bruckner asked Mottl not to forget. The movement closes with a pianissimo reminiscence of the first section of the opening subject, sung by the tubas in the key of C-sharp major. It is continued by the horns, which end the movement very quietly in the major key, above *ppp* pizzicati in the strings. In the music of this elegy, as elsewhere in Bruckner at his most inspired, there is a curious intimation of immortality. These pages are filled with a musing, consolatory tenderness, with a touch of that greatness of style which we sometimes get in the Elizabethans when they speak of death—we might almost fancy that we hear one of the most excellent of them speaking here, telling us that

'We cease to grieve, cease to be fortune's slaves, nay, cease to die, by dying.'

The third movement (Scherzo: 'Sehr schnell,' A minor, 3-4) opens pianissimo, with a decisively rhythmed figure for the strings, above which, at the fifth measure, the trumpet declaims the first and somewhat Beethovenish theme of the movement. This trumpet phrase is, more strictly, only the first section of the chief theme; the second section is presented by the full orchestra. The Trio ('Etwas langsamer,' in F major) is introduced by a pianissimo figure of the kettledrum, with the theme sung by the strings alone. The Scherzo is repeated.

The Finale ('Bewegt, doch nicht schnell,' E major, 2-2 time) is based upon a theme for the violins which is akin to the opening subject of the first movement. The second subject of the movement is a chorale-like melody accompanied by pizzicati of the string basses. The working-out section begins fortissimo in the full orchestra, with much use of Bruckner's favorite device of inversion. After the climax, the recapitulation section is introduced by the chorale-like second subject, instead of with the first theme. The symphony ends in a triumphant vein, with the chief theme of the first movement proclaimed, *fff*, by the brass.

• Symphony No. 8, in C minor

Bruckner began his Eighth Symphony in 1884 (he was then in his sixtieth year), and though he completed it in sketch form at Steyr on August 16, 1885, he did not end his labors upon the colossal task until 1890. The score was published in 1892, and the symphony was performed for the first time at a Vienna Philharmonic concert under Hans Richter, December 18, 1892. Even Hanslick, whose hatred of Bruckner was malignant, admitted that the result was a triumph. The symphony, he wrote, was received 'with boisterous rejoicing, waving of handkerchiefs, innumerable recalls, laurel wreaths.'

The scheme of the four movements of the gigantic work is as follows:

I. 'Allegro moderato,' C minor, 2-2 time.

II. Scherzo: 'Allegro moderato,' 3-4 time; with Trio, in A-flat major, 2-4 time.

III. Adagio: Solemn and slow, but not dragging; D-flat major, 4-4 time.

IV. Finale: Solemn, not fast; C minor-C major, 2-2 time.

It is said that when the symphony was first performed at Vienna, an 'interpretative program' written by a disciple of Bruckner stated that the first theme of the first movement (second measure: violas, 'cellos, double basses, with an upward leap of a sixth) was intended to evoke 'the form of the Aeschylean Prometheus,' and a portion of this movement was characterized as expressing 'the greatest loneliness and silence.' The second and typically Brucknerian theme is exposed by the strings, in G major, beginning at the fifty-first measure.

The Scherzo—which Bruckner, following the example of Beethoven in his Ninth Symphony, places before his slow movement—was intended, according to the aforesaid 'interpretation,' to typify 'the German Michel' (*der deutsche Michel*)—'the plain, honest, docile, long-suffering German.' (Michel, or Cousin Michel, was at one time a humorous personification of the German nation, as John Bull is of the English.) Hanslick asserted that Bruckner himself, in the program of the first performance of the symphony, gave this name, 'the German Michel,' to the Scherzo.

The solemn and marvelous Adagio was said by Bruckner's disciples to convey the thought of 'the all-loving Father of Mankind in his measureless wealth of mercy'; and the Finale was characterized as an utterance of the spirit of 'heroism in the service of the Divine.' In the triumphant C major ending of the Finale, themes from the previous movements are recalled.

Max Auer, in his authoritative study of the composer, calls the Eighth Symphony a *Künstlerdrama,* and declares that it portrays the double nature of the artist, a Promethean struggle which ends with the victorious realizations and affirmations of the Finale.

None of these interpretations is specifically sanctioned by the score itself, which is innocent of mottoes, titles, or superscriptions; and it is wiser to listen to the work as music unadorned by 'interpretations'—as a work extraordinary for largeness and sweep of utterance and depth of feeling. Remarkable as are many pages of the score—pages that have true grandeur and exaltation—the crown of the work is the great Adagio, which some would put at the head of all adagios 'by reason of its solemnity, nobility, and elevated thought': a movement which, from its opening pages, with the deeply expressive song of the first violins heard above throbbing syncopations of the other strings, moves upon the loftiest plane of feeling and aspiration.

● SYMPHONY NO. 9, IN D MINOR

Bruckner began the composition of this symphony—his last, which he never finished—in the summer of 1887, immediately after he had completed his scoring of the colossal No. 8 in C minor. But he suspended work upon the Ninth, and became engrossed in the revision of its predecessor and of No. 1. In February 1891, he resumed work upon the Ninth. On September 4, 1894, Bruckner reached his seventieth birthday. He celebrated the day in bed, at Steyr. He was an ill man, suffering from dropsy and accompanying heart trouble. In the following month he said to a caller: 'I have done my duty on earth. I have accomplished what I could, and my only wish is to be allowed to complete my Ninth Symphony. The Adagio [the third movement] is nearly finished; there remains only the Finale. I trust Death will not deprive me of my pen.'

But Death proved indifferent to Bruckner's hopes. The pen of the aging composer was taken from his hand as he worked on the sketches for the Finale of his symphony, and all that we have of it are the first movement, the Scherzo, and the noble, exalted Adagio—music of an unforgettable solemnity and tenderness, of a beauty transfigured and serene; as if Bruckner's eyes had already been unsealed before the hovering mystery, and had told him that all was finally well with him.

He completed the Adagio on the 31st of October 1894; but he could not fashion the last movement to his satisfaction. He was still busy over the sketches for the Finale on the morning of the day that he died (October 11, 1896); but the sketches that he left give only an imperfect idea of his intentions.

Bruckner is said to have remarked to friends that if the three completed movements were performed after his death, his *Te Deum* (produced at Vienna, with accompaniment arranged for two pianos, in 1885; with orchestra, in 1886) might serve as Finale to the unfinished symphony. This suggestion was adopted when the symphony was performed for the first time at Vienna, on February 11, 1903, under the direction of Ferdinand Löwe, almost seven years after the composer had gone to his grave.

Like the Unfinished Symphony of Schubert, this symphony of Bruckner's seems complete in its incompleteness. It is difficult to think of it with a Finale succeeding the Adagio. The conclusive slow movement and its final measures of seraphic quietude—the elegiacal chant of the tubas about which the violins entwine a fading sunset loveliness—would scarcely brook a following movement. This seems, now, the fitting and perfect close for the symphony—indeed, the only close for it. The thought of an added Finale, conventionally triumphant, pealing, heaven-storming, is insupportable. Would not even the *Te Deum*, despite Bruckner's own recommendation, seem an anticlimax?

A score of the symphony, in an edition by Löwe, was published at Vienna in 1903, when Bruckner had been dead for nearly seven years. It was Löwe's score which represented Bruckner's Ninth Symphony to students and music-lovers for thirty years. Was that score a faithful transcript of the composer's musical ideas? Were the intentions of Bruckner in his last symphony fairly represented by the published score of 1903? It is clear that they were not. The publication of the ninth volume of the complete edition of Bruckner's works, based upon the autograph scores, and edited by Robert Haas and Alfred Orel under the sponsorship of the National Library at Vienna, provided indisputable evidence of the extent to which Löwe tinkered with, misrepresented, and garbled the symphony of Bruckner—doubtless, as in the case of Rimsky-Korsakoff and Moussorgsky's *Boris*, with the best of possible intentions. But Löwe had not Rimsky's skill and genius as his excuse. Musicians need only set the score of the original edition beside that of the familiar edition of 1903 to see for themselves how Bruckner has suffered at the hands of his well-intentioned 'editor.' Löwe's alterations are often of startling audacity. Not only has he altered Bruckner's dynamic scheme in many places, changed his tempo marks, changed his instrumentation, but he has altered Bruckner's harmonic scheme—in one remarkable instance, to the vast detriment of the music's expressive force. Finally, he has had the astonishing temerity to interpolate into the texture of Bruckner's score some measures of his own composition! For two obvious examples of Löwe's operations, the student might compare the score of the original edition, page 180, with Löwe's edition, page 136; and the original, page 41, with Löwe, page 30.

Emmanuel Chabrier

1841-94

C

‡Music was an avocation with Chabrier until, in his thirties, he resigned his post in the French Civil Service to devote himself entirely to art. He greatly admired Wagner and associated, in Paris, with the group of musicians who surrounded César Franck. His own productions—several operas, a few orchestral works, a quantity of piano pieces and songs—were, however, for the most part conceived in a light vein, and today he is chiefly remembered for his orchestral rhapsody *España*, a staple of the popular repertoire.‡

● *España*: RHAPSODY FOR ORCHESTRA

Chabrier visited Spain in 1882, studied the music, the dancing, and the dancers, made elaborate notes, and evolved as one of the results of his investigations the superb rhapsody for orchestra, *España* (written first for piano). When the Lamoureaux Orchestra rehearsed the work for its first performance sixty-odd years ago (November 4, 1883), the players were much disconcerted by its rhythmic novelty and original effects; but they mastered the difficulties of the score so triumphantly that the piece made a huge success.

The rhapsody is based chiefly on two Spanish dances: the *Jota*, fiery and impetuous, a kind of quick waltz, which in Spain is both sung and danced; and the *Malagueña*—languishing, sultry, and heavy-lidded. Like the *Jota*, it is in triple time, but its pace is slower, and it is rhythmically different.

Chabrier wrote vividly of the dances (and the dancers) he saw in Spain, and his letters are uncommonly good reading. He wrote as follows to his friend Edouard Moullé, from Granada in November 1882:

In a month I must leave adorable Spain, and say good-bye to the Spaniards—because (I say this only to you) they are very nice, the little girls! I have not seen a really ugly woman since I have been in Andalusia. I do not speak of the feet, they are so small that I have never seen them; the hands are tiny and well-kept and the arms of an exquisite contour; I speak only of what one can see. Add the arabesques, the side-curls and other ingenuities of the coiffure, the inevitable fan, the flower and the comb in the hair, placed well behind, the shawl of Chinese crepe, with long fringe and embroidered in flowers, knotted around the figure, the arm bare, the eye protected by eyelashes which are long enough to curl, the skin of dull white or orange color, according to the race; all this smiling, gesticulating, dancing, drinking, and careless to the last degree—

That is the Andalusian.

Every evening we go to the café-concerts where the *Malaguenas*, the *Soledas*, the *Sapateados* and the *Peteneras* are sung. Then the dances, absolutely Arab, to speak truth. If you could see them wiggle, unjoint their hips, contortion, I believe you would not try to get away! At Malaga the dancing became so intense that I was compelled to take my wife away; it wasn't even amusing any more. I can't write about it, but I remember it and will describe it to you. I have no need to tell you I have noted down many things; the Tango, a kind of dance in which the women imitate the pitching of a ship, is the only dance in two time; all the others are in 3-4 (Seville) or in 3-8 (Malaga and Cadiz). In the North it is different, there is some music in 5-8, very curious. The 2-4 of the Tango is always like the Habañera. This is the picture: two women dance, two silly men play—it doesn't matter what—on their guitars, and five or six women howl, with excruciating voices and in triplet figure; it is impossible to note down what, because they change the air—every instant, a new scrap of tune. They howl a series of figurations with syllables, words, rising voices, clapping hands which strike the six quavers, emphasizing the third and sixth, cries of *Andá! Andá! La Salud! eso es la Maraquita! gracia, nationidad! Baila, la chiquilla! Andá! Andá! Consuelo! Olé, le Lola, olé la Carmen! que gracia! que elegancia!*—all that to excite the young dancers. It is vertiginous, it is unspeakable! . . . And the more cries, the more the dancer laughs with her mouth wide open, and turns her hips, and is mad with her body.

Ernest Chausson
1855-99

Doubtless the tragic end of Ernest Chausson (he was killed in a bicycle accident in his forty-fourth year), combined with the lovable nature that his friends ascribe to him, accounts in some degree for the singular fervor which characterizes almost all that has been written of him as an aesthetic figure. Jean-Aubry declares that no one wrote music of greater purity and sincerity; Pierre de Bréville says that his heart 'beat only for noble thoughts'; Camille Mauclair was reminded, in contemplating certain artistic principles held by Chausson, of the art of Puvis de Chavannes. Some of this fervor—much of it, perhaps—is to be discounted in any attempt at a cool and just appraisement of Chausson's personality as a man and a music-maker; yet one's conviction persists that the personality was remarkable, and that the artist died too young. ‡He was the pupil of Massenet and came, later, under the influence of Franck. His output, though not large, was of singular evenness of quality, and for a time at least his orchestral works, his chamber music, and his songs seem assured of a place in the repertoire.‡

● Symphony in B-flat major, op. 20

Chausson seems to have been a strange blend of César-Franckian mysticism, Wagnerian passion, and a kind of romanticism which an American might call MacDowellesque. Jean-Aubry has described him as 'a soul from the Round Table, from the time of elves, of water-fays, of rides through legendary forests, of lovelays and attachments devoid of pretense, sustained upon ardor and respect: it was not by accident that Chausson made King Arthur the subject of his only stage work.' (Jean-Aubry is in error here, for in addition to his *Le Roi Arthur,* Chausson composed for the stage a two-act lyric drama, *Hélène,* to a text by Leconte de Lisle.) Others hear in his music the swaying of branches in enchanted woods; they discover the trail that leads to the fairy Brocéliande—'a path through the forests of legend, a new and yet traditional avenue in the French landscape.' This was his Weber-like, Raff-like, Mac-Dowellesque side. The Wagnerian side of him—the ardent, sensuous, *Tristan-esque* vein in his music—emerges in the passionate melancholy of the 'Poème de l'Amour et de la Mer,' and the 'Chanson perpètuelle,' for voice and orchestra, and in other of the songs. The Franckism in his nature—the spiritual, aspiring, mystically rapturous side—is in the symphony, where is also the plangent ghost of Richard of Bayreuth.

The symphony, his only work in the form, was completed and published (with a dedication to the painter Henri Lerolle) in 1890. Like the great symphony of Chausson's master, Franck, this one is in three movements; and in further likeness to its model, it is to some extent cyclic in character, for it employs the device of thematic continuity, material from the first movement reappearing in the Finale. The three movements of the symphony are: (1) an Introduction, Lent, 4-4, of forty-seven measures leading to the main body of the first movement, 'Allegro vivo,' 3-4; (2) the slow movement, 'Tres lent,' D minor, 4-4; a vigorous Finale, Animé, 2-2.

● *Poème* for Violin and Orchestra, op. 25

There is in the music of Chausson something that came straight from the heart and mind of the man himself. It is a truly individual quality—an authentically personal touch: a mood, a spiritual and emotional hue that is unmistakable. This special quality in Chausson's work is a curious thing, for which one can find no precise analogue in music. It is compounded of tenderness, ardor, and complete sincerity. If one could blend something of the elevation and fervor of César Franck, the sensibility of Schumann, the sincerity of Brahms the lyricist, a complex not unlike the musical personality of Chausson would emerge. He seems really to have been what Pierre de Bréville called 'noble.' It takes a truly noble soul to endure that epithet; yet when de Bréville says of Chausson's music that it is 'always affectionate,' that 'it is constantly saying the word *cher*,' you may wince a little in commiseration for the gentle ghost of the dead composer, but you must own that there is a good deal in his music that justifies these ascriptions.

Chausson, says Camille Mauclair, in his *Souvenirs sur Ernest Chausson,* 'impressed one as a man of the world, wholly without ostentation, amiable, cheerful, serene. His life was happy. He had a charming wife and five beautiful children. He was rich; his house was a marvel of taste and a treasury of art; he loved books and pictures, and collected, before they had become fashionable, canvases by Degas, Besnard, Puvis and Carrière.' But the amiable, fortunate, worldly Chausson, the rich composer, was not the essential man or the essential artist. These outward traits masked a painful shyness, modesty, sensitiveness, and depth of feeling. His air of contented well-being, says Mauclair, dissembled *une âme douloureusment émue de la souffrance humaine.* He was devout and a mystic, with a high and clear conception of the necessity of pitying the human soul. He was a compassionate humanitarian, a dreamer, and he had many of those elements which, Lord Dunsany has told us, go to the makings of poetry: 'For what is it to be a poet? It is to see at a glance the glory of the world, to see beauty in all its forms and manifestations, to feel ugliness like a pain, to resent the wrongs of others as bitterly as one's own, to know mankind as others know single men, to know nature as botanists know a flower, to be thought a fool, to hear at moments the clear voice of God.'

A large order. If Chausson had come up to even half of these requirements he would have been a Bach or a Moussorgsky or a Wagner; and he was a long way from being in that class. But he had susceptibility and warmth of temperament and the priceless quality of genuine utterance. These things found a way into his music, into, for example, the wonderful *Poème* for Violin and Orchestra, and speak out of it in beautiful and touching accents.

The *Poème* was composed in 1896, three years before his death, and is nearly the last of the works by which he is remembered today. Ysaye gave it its first performance, at a Colonne concert in Paris on April 4, 1897. It is free in form and employs effectively a contrast of moods between the 'Lento e misterioso' theme, darkly harmonized, with which it opens, and the more ardent subject that is set against it. The orchestral accompaniment is richly scored, for woodwinds in pairs, four horns, two trumpets, three trombones and tuba, tympani, harp, and strings. In recent times, the *Poème* has been choreographed as a ballet, the *Jardin des Lilas* of Anthony Tudor.

Maria Luigi Carlo Zenobia Salvatore Cherubini
1760-1842

‡Cherubini lived long, composed prodigiously, accumulated honors from the crowned heads of Italy (his homeland), England, and France, was regarded by his contemporary Beethoven (of whom his own opinion was less flattering) as one of the very greatest composers of his day, and survives to us chiefly through the overture to one of his minor productions.

Few of the once indisputably great personages of music have suffered so severe a chastisement at the hands of time. But it is possible (if unlikely) that some Mendelssohn of tomorrow may discover, among Cherubini's uncountable masses, oratorios, cantatas, operas, that forgotten work of genius which will restore him to a position of fame and honor.‡

● OVERTURE TO *Anacreon*

The span of Cherubini's life reminds us of the relatively contracted periods of musical history. When Cherubini was born, Bach had been dead for only ten years. When Cherubini died, Tchaikovsky had cut his first teeth.

Cherubini had his day of glory. His *Faniska* was brought out at Vienna in 1806, where it was so successful that when a foolish critic dared to predict that Beethoven's *Fidelio* would one day 'rank as high as Cherubini's *Faniska*,' he was scoffed at. Cherubini dwelt in Vienna from 1805 until 1808, when he returned to Paris after the French occupation.

Two years before he went to Vienna, Cherubini wrote music for an opera ballet, *Anacreon; ou, L'Amour fugitif,* words by Mendouze, choreography by Gardel, founded on one of the odes of Anacreon, the Greek lyric poet who celebrated in his verse with happy impunity the merits of wine and love. The opera ballet was produced October 4, 1803, but the absurd libretto devised by Mendouze was too much even for the public of 1803, and the work fell flat. Of the music, only the overture and one of the airs have survived.

'Cherubini,' said Wagner, 'remained, on the whole, faithful to the traditional type of overture created by Gluck and Mozart. His overtures are poetical sketches of the main idea of the drama, grouped in its broad and general features, and musically reproduced with conciseness, unity, and clearness.' Krehbiel remarked concerning the emotional content of the *Anacreon* Overture that 'it is the antique joyousness of life which has chief expression in Cherubini's music here, though there are shadows which serve to lift the general mood into higher relief.'

● OVERTURE TO *Médée*

Cherubini's *Médée*, lyric tragedy in three acts, words by Hoffmann, was written for the Théâtre Feydeau, Paris, and was performed there for the first time, March 13, 1797.

In the operas given at the Théâtre Feydeau (which was absorbed in the present Opéra-Comique), the dialogue was spoken, and there were no ballets. Franz Lachner (1803-90) afterward turned the dialogue of *Médée* into recitative for performances of the opera in Germany. Scio was the original Médée. The role of the heroine was taken in later years by various eminent singers— among them Tietjens (London, 1865) and Materna (Vienna, 1880).

Medea (whom Thomas Heywood bluntly called a 'Witch'), was, in Greek story, a princess celebrated for her skill in magic. She was the daughter of Aeëtes, King of Colchis. When Jason came to Colchis to fetch the Golden Fleece, Medea fell in love with him, and by her sorcerous arts assisted him in accomplishing his enterprise. Afterward she fled with him to Greece and was for ten years his wife. But Jason forsook her and married Creusa (otherwise Clauce), the youthful daughter of Creon, King of Corinth. Thereupon, Medea took dreadful vengeance: she murdered the children she had had by Jason, and she sent to Creusa an envenomed robe which carried death in its poisoned folds. She then fled to Athens in a chariot drawn by winged dragons, and— still undiscouraged—took another husband in the person of King Aegeus. Jason's end is variously related: according to some, he killed himself from grief; others say that he was crushed by the poop of the ship *Argo*, which fell upon him as he lay under it.

In Cherubini's opera, the action begins with the betrothal of Jason and Creusa (she is called Dirce in the opera), and it ends with the flight of Medea after she has murdered her children and her rival. The culminating point in the third act is a depiction of Medea's inward conflict between her love for her children and her insensate jealousy of the woman who has displaced her; and this has been said to constitute the emotional basis of the Overture.

The heroine has the stage during most of the action—indeed, much of the opera has been called 'virtually a long monody for Medea.' Dirce (Creusa) is an ordinary *seconda donna*. Jason is just a tenor.

Frédéric François Chopin

1810-49

‡Chopin was the archetype of the romantic, ill-starred genius. His precocity as an artist, his great personal charm of appearance and manner, his sensitive, emotional temperament, his celebrated love affair with George Sand, his ill-health, his early death have created a conception of him in the popular mind as remote from reality as that which is held, for similar reasons, of Keats, obscuring the fact that he was one of the greatest composers of the mid-nineteenth century. Though he wrote almost exclusively for the piano and largely confined himself to the smaller forms, he created a music in texture, in color, in style utterly unlike anything known before. Upon models provided by Bellini and Field, he developed a type of melody that all may recognize as characteristic of him, whether encountered in his music or in that of later composers. But his greatest contribution, technically viewed, was his expansion and subtilization of the harmonic apparatus of music, which placed all succeeding composers, notably Liszt and Wagner, in his debt.‡

● Concerto for Piano and Orchestra, No. 1, in E minor, op. 11

Of Chopin's two concertos for piano, the E minor is known as No. 1, for it was published first. But it was the second in order of composition. Chopin completed it in August 1830, and it was published in 1833.

Chopin wrote in March 1830 that he was at work upon 'the first Allegro of my second concerto (the E minor).' Two months later, he was busy with the Rondo—'it is not yet finished because the right inspired mood has always been wanting. If I have only the Allegro and the Adagio completely finished, I shall be without anxiety about the finale. The Adagio is in E major, and of a romantic, calm, and partly melancholy character. It is intended to convey the impression which one receives when the eye rests on a beloved landscape that calls up in one's soul beautiful memories—for instance, on a fine moonlit spring night. I have written for violins with mutes as an accompaniment to it. I wonder if that will have a good effect. Well, time will show.'

The concerto was finished by mid-summer. Chopin seems not to have been completely reassured by the first rehearsal, 'with a quartet.' 'Those who were present at the rehearsal,' he wrote September 18th, 'say that the finale is the most successful movement (probably because it is easily intelligible). How it will sound with the orchestra I cannot tell you until next Wednesday, when I shall play the concerto for the first time in this form.'

Four days later the work was rehearsed with full orchestra (without trumpets or drums, however). The effect appears to have been encouraging. 'I must provide the desks and mutes,' wrote Chopin—'these I had entirely forgotten yesterday. Without the latter [the mutes], the Adagio [Larghetto] would be wholly insignificant and its success doubtful. The Rondo is effective, the first Allegro vigorous. Cursed self-love! And, if it is any one's fault that I am conceited, it is yours, egoist: he who associates with such a person becomes like him.'

The first public performance was in the theater at Warsaw, on October 11, 1830. The arrangement of the program would astonish a twentieth-century audience: for Chopin's concerto was served in two courses separated by an entrée. First came the Allegro of the concerto; then an 'Aria with Chorus,' by Carlo Evasio Soliva, sung by Soliva's pupil, Anna Wolkow; then the rest of Chopin's dismembered concerto—the slow movement and the final Rondo.

This seemingly outrageous dismemberment was an accepted thing a century ago; for, as Hadow reminds us, it was the fashion of the time to give even Beethoven's symphonies piecemeal, and to intersperse the movements with bravura songs and divertimenti for the French horn. 'It seems unlikely,' he remarks, 'that a stage manager would ever present one of Shakespeare's plays with portions of the *School for Scandal* between the acts; but music has always lagged behind the other arts in its appreciation of structure; and if Berlioz, in Paris, could mishandle Beethoven, we need not be surprised at Chopin's tearing his own work to pieces for fear that the audience should suspect it of continuity.'

The concert was a huge success. Chopin, having conquered a bad attack of nerves, played with assurance and extraordinary beauty. The first Allegro went very smoothly, and the audience rewarded him with thundering applause. Of the reception of the Larghetto and the Rondo we know only that in the pause between the first and second parts the connoisseurs and amateurs came on the stage and complimented Chopin in the most flattering terms on his playing. The great success of the evening, however, was his performance of the Fantasia on Polish airs. 'This time I understood myself, the orchestra understood me, and the audience understood us.'

Tausig revised the E minor Concerto, and reorchestrated it, as Klindworth (and after him Richard Burmeister) busied themselves with the F minor.

• CONCERTO FOR PIANO AND ORCHESTRA, NO. 2, IN F MINOR, OP. 21

Would that inflammable dominie, the Reverend Theron Ware, have found it dangerous to listen to the slow movement of Chopin's F minor Concerto? What would its effect have been upon Arnold Bennett's Carlotta Peel if the devastating Diaz had made her play it with him in an arrangement for pianoforte duet? Theoretically, this Larghetto should be ideal campaign material for the polite seductionists of fiction, for it is an avowed love song.

Chopin began the F minor Concerto in the autumn of 1829. He was then nineteen years old, and he was desperately in love with a singer named Constantia Gladkowska, a pupil at the Warsaw Conservatory. Chopin wrote to his friend Woyciechowski on October 3, 1829: 'I have—perhaps to my misfortune—already found my ideal, which I worship faithfully and sincerely. Six months have elapsed, and I have not yet exchanged a syllable with her of whom I dream every night. While my thoughts were with her I composed the Adagio [sic] of my concerto. . .'

It was an abortive and futile passion. Chopin was too timorous to undertake any thoroughgoing explorations in 'the dreadful heart of woman.'

Chopin played the F minor Concerto in Warsaw on March 17, 1830. The work was served in two courses (after the carefree habit of those deplorable times), the first movement being separated from the Larghetto and Finale by a Divertissement for horn by one Görner.

The late James Huneker in his brilliant book on Chopin displays a somewhat platonic attitude toward both the concertos. The first movement of the F minor, he thinks, 'far transcends [that of the E minor] in breadth, passion, and musical feeling. . . The mazurka-like Finale is very graceful and full of pure, sweet melody.' He is cool toward the Larghetto, which for Liszt was 'of an almost ideal perfection,' its expression 'now radiant with light and anon full of tender pathos.'

Ornamental the Larghetto is, no doubt. Yet its adjustments are exquisitely precise. Emil Boutroux, philosopher and Academician, once spoke of Pascal as 'a singular mixture of passion and geometry.' Chopin was often a rhapsodic geometrician, even when, to casual observation, he seemed merely to be abandoning himself to 'the exquisite chromatics of decay.'

Domenico Cimarosa

1749-1801

Cimarosa was born seven years before Mozart and died a little over nine years after him. The Italian's father was a stone mason, his mother a washerwoman. He was sent to a free school maintained for the poor by Franciscan monks, where he studied Latin and music. In 1761 he was admitted to the Conservatorio Santa Maria di Loreto, where the great Piccini taught him the secrets of operatic writing (from Fenaroli he learned harmony and counterpoint, those operatically superfluous arts). In 1772, when he was twenty-three, his first opera was produced at the Teatro de' Fiorentini in Naples. The work was so successful that Cimarosa found himself firmly placed on the musical map, and he proceeded joyously to turn out one opera after another. He traveled widely, and at one time or another held posts as chamber musician to Catherine II of Russia and to the Austrian Emperor, Leopold II. Cimarosa's last years were unfortunate. He manifested sympathy for revolutionary ideas, was imprisoned, and condemned to death, but afterwards restored to liberty on condition that he leave Naples, where he was then in residence. Cimarosa set out for his old stamping-ground, St. Petersburg, but he died on his way there, in Venice, in his fifty-second year.

● OVERTURE TO *Il Matrimonio Segreto*

It was in Vienna that Cimarosa composed his most famous work, *Il Matrimonio Segreto* (*The Secret Marriage*). The opera was given for the first time at the Hoftheater on February 7, 1792. The Emperor, unable to attend the première, was duly on hand for the repetition two days later. Seated conspicuously in his box, he was observed by all to have refrained from applauding throughout the performance—to the consternation of the composer and his friends. But at the close of the opera, His Majesty arose in his place and spoke as follows (his words should be inscribed above the proscenium of every opera house):

'Bravo, Cimarosa! Your opera is admirable, enchanting! I did not applaud, that I might not lose a single note of this masterpiece!'

Thereupon, he ordered refreshments for all concerned, and required that the opera be repeated that very night. 'I must hear it again,' he declared, 'before I go to bed.'

Il Matrimonio Segreto was regarded in its day as incarnating the highest ideal of *opera buffo*. It was the first work of its kind to dispute the previously unquestioned supremacy in that field of Pergolesi's *La Serva Padrona*. The fame of Cimarosa's opera became world-wide, and its popularity knew no bounds. At Naples, in 1793, it had 67 consecutive performances, the composer himself presiding at the cembalo for the first seven. The text, by Giovanni Bertatti, is said to have been derived from a forgotten French operetta, *Sophie, ou le Mariage Caché*, which itself was based on Garrick and Coleman's *Clandestine Marriage* (the origin of the comedy is also traced to Hogarth's *Marriage à la Mode* and Townley's *False Concord*).

The overture to the opera is a masterpiece of vivacity and musical wit. It opens with three humorously portentous, long-held chords in D major, and is then off in a riant 'Allegro molto.' The form is that of a free rondo.

Arcangelo Corelli

1653-1713

Arcangelo Corelli was not only the greatest violin player of his day, but as a composer he advanced materially the art of concerted instrumental writing. The German, Mattheson, hailed him as 'the prince of all musicians.' Giovanni Benvenuti was his master in violin playing, and the papal singer, Matteo Simonelli, taught him counterpoint. In his eighteenth year, Corelli went to Rome, and entered the orchestra of the Capranica Theater. In the course of the next decade he is thought to have sojourned at Munich, Hanover, and Heidelberg. He returned to Rome in 1682, prospered greatly, and was the friend of princes, cardinals, and others among the mighty ones of earth. To one of these friends, Cardinal Ottoboni, in whose palace he had lived, Corelli was able to make a regal gesture from the grave: for his will bequeathed to the Cardinal a sum equivalent to more than a quarter of a million dollars (to say nothing of a collection of paintings)—though it should be noted that the Cardinal very handsomely turned the money over to Corelli's family.

● CONCERTO GROSSO NO. 8, IN G MINOR ('Christmas' CONCERTO)

Corelli completed shortly before his death his most consequential work: a set of twelve Concerti grossi, op. 6. These compositions were written for two violins and 'cello as a solo group (the concertino), with accompanying strings, which might be doubled at pleasure (this orchestral accompaniment was also called, like the form itself, the 'concerto grosso,' as distinguished from the concertino). The player of the cembalo or organ filled out and often elaborated the accompaniment from the *basso continuo*, or figured bass. In Corelli's original score, the 'concerto grosso,' or accompanying orchestra, consisted of first and second violins, viola, bass, and harpsichord (cembalo).

In Dr. Chrysander's Preface to the Augener edition of Corelli's works (London: 188?), the accomplished editor declares that of all the compositions of its kind written at that time, 'this last and greatest opus of Corelli [op. 6, comprising the 12 concerti grossi] is the most solid and instructive.' It appeared in print at Rome in December 1712, in seven books, and, like Corelli's earlier compositions, spread rapidly over Europe through the agency of reprints, 'forming a model for the Grand Concerto of its age.'

This concerto was composed for performance at Christmas, as a superscription on the score ('Fatto per la Notte di Natale') makes clear. There are seven measures of introduction, Vivace, followed by a Grave and an Allegro. The remainder of the Concerto comprises these divisions: (b) Adagio-Allegro-Adagio; (c) Vivace-Allegro; (d) Pastorale: Largo.

In the Pastorale there are clear hints of the picture of the Nativity that must have been in Corelli's mind: the starlit hills, the hushed, mysterious night, the shepherds and their sheep, the sweetness and brooding tenderness of the ancient Mystery.

Rockstro reminds us that in form such works as this Concerto Grosso of Corelli 'bore a close analogy to the ordinary overture and suite peculiar to the middle of the eighteenth century, the movements consisting of a series of Largos, Allegros, and Andantes, intermixed, occasionally, with Minuets, Gavottes, and even Gigues. After the invention of the Sonata-form, the Concerto Grosso died completely out.'

Manuel de Falla

1876-

D

After Albeniz, Manuel de Falla is the most considerable figure in modern Spanish music—modern, that is, in a broad sense. Indeed, he is today even better known to a large public than is his predecessor, thanks to the solid place in the ballet and concert repertoires earned by his *El Amor Brujo* and *El Sombrero de Tres Picos*. His output has not been large, but is almost uniformly distinguished. The native folk and popular songs and dances of Spain are a pervasive influence in his work, which also shows the influence, in its refinement of detail and style, of the French Impressionists—chiefly Debussy and Ravel—with whom he came in contact in Paris during the early years of the century.

- *Nights in the Gardens of Spain:* SYMPHONIC IMPRESSIONS FOR PIANO AND ORCHESTRA

This work is in three parts: 1, 'En el Generalife' ('At the Generalife': 'Allegretto tranquillo e misterioso'); 2, 'Danza lejana' ('Far-off Dance': 'Allegretto giusto'); 3, 'En los Jardins de la Sierra de Cordoba' ('In the Gardens of the Sierra of Cordova': Vivo). The Finale succeeds part two without pause. The music was composed in 1909-16. The first performance was in Madrid, by the Orquesta Sinfonica, in April 1916. Enrique Fernandez-Arbos conducted de Falla's music.

The thematic material of this work is built, as in *La Vida Breve* and in *El Amor Brujo*, on rhythms, modes, cadences, or forms inspired by but never directly borrowed from the Andalusian folk song. 'It is an actual re-creation of the popular soul. In fact, de Falla's intentions (which are wonderfully realized) are more expressive than picturesque or descriptive.'

De Falla, it is said, was not easily satisfied with these Nocturnes. 'Each season,' writes Jean-Aubry, 'we waited in vain [in Paris, where de Falla had lived since 1907] for the first performance. These Nocturnes began to be legendary in the Parisian musical world. . .'

De Falla is much more than a painter of Spain; he is an invoker of Spanish emotion, often the most hidden, the most reserved. Nothing is less brilliant (in the vulgar meaning of virtuosity that is attributed musically to this epithet) than these Nocturnes; but nothing is more strongly colored by the play of lights and shadows skillfully contrived. The force and the simplicity of the effects are remarkable; the *Far-off Dance* based on a tango rhythm swells by a simple augmentation to an astonishing intensity.

The piano part has nowhere a tendency to remind one of an ordinary concerto. . . It is always heard as part of the symphonic structure, or by way of adornment or sonorous embroidery of the orchestral background.

The score was published in 1923.

- CONCERT SUITE FROM *El Amor Brujo*

El Amor Brujo (*Love, the Magician*), a ballet with voices and orchestra, in one act and two scenes, on a libretto by Gregorio Martinez Sierra, derived from an Andalusian gypsy tale, was produced at the Teatro de Lara, Madrid, April 15, 1915, with the Señora Pastora Imperio assisting. Later, according to G. Jean-Aubry, the composer's biographer, de Falla 'drew from the music certain symphonic excerpts, in which he suppressed the spoken or sung parts and enlarged the instrumentation. . . But this did not alter the essential character of the work, which is to be found in its particular color, or the semi-Arabian style of its idioms.' A concert version, presumably the one referred to by Jean-Aubry, was performed at Madrid in the season of 1915-16 at a concert of the Sociedad Nacional de Musica, under the direction of E. Fernandez-Arbos.

In an authorized statement, issued at the time of the première of the work, it was said that 'the composer, whose feeling for and command of his country's folk-music are well-known, saw that it would be impossible to write true gypsy music by restricting himself to instrumental dances alone, and without resorting to the gypsies' most characteristic feature: their songs. But he has by no means used actual folk-melodies; every song is his own invention, and it is his particular glory that he has succeeded in making it almost impossible to believe that they are not actual popular material.'

The following synopsis of the action of the ballet is published as a preface to the score:

Candelas is a young, beautiful and passionate woman, who has loved a wicked, jealous, dissolute, but fascinating and cajoling gypsy. Although her life with him had been a very unhappy one, she has loved him intensely, and mourned his loss. She is unable to forget him; her memory of him is like some hypnotic dream—a morbid, gruesome, and maddening spell. She is terrified by the thought that the dead man may not be entirely gone, that he may return, that he continues to love her in his fierce, shadowy, faithless, caressing way. She lets herself become a prey to her thoughts of the past, as if under the influence of a spectre. Yet she is young, strong and vivacious.

Spring returns, and with it a new lover in the shape of Carmelo. Carmelo, a handsome youth, enamoured and gallant, courts her ardently. She, not unwilling to be won, almost unconsciously returns his love, but the obsession of her past weighs against her present inclination. When Carmelo approaches her and endeavors to make her share in his passion, the Spectre returns, and terrifies Candelas, separating her from her lover. They cannot exchange the kiss of perfect love.

Carmelo being gone, Candelas languishes and droops; she feels as if bewitched, and memories of her past love flit about her like malevolent and foreboding bats. Carmelo is determined to break this evil spell, and he believes he has found a remedy. He was once the comrade of the dead lover, whom he knew as a typically faithless and jealous Andalusian gallant. Since he appears to retain, even after death, his fancy for beautiful women, he must be taken on his weak side and diverted by means of a decoy, Lucia, a young and enchantingly pretty girl.

Lucia, out of friendship for Candelas and from feminine curiosity, would flirt even with a spectre, and anyway the dead man was so mirthful in life! So eventually the Spectre appears and makes love to Lucia, whose coquetry almost brings him to despair. In the meantime, Carmelo succeeds in convincing Candelas of his love and good faith, and life triumphs over death and over the past. The lovers at last exchange the kiss that defeats the evil influence of the Spectre, who perishes, definitely conquered by love.

● THREE DANCES FROM *El Sombrero de Tres Picos*

De Falla's ballet, *The Three-Cornered Hat*, performed for the first time by the Russian Ballet at the Alhambra, London, July 23, 1919, was written for a scenario devised by Martinez Sierra. Pablo Picasso designed the settings and costumes for the London production. The principal roles were danced by Massine, Karsavina, and Woisikovsky. Ernest Ansermet conducted. The subject for the ballet was derived from the novel, *El Sombrero de Tres Picos*, by Don Pedro Antonio de Alarcón (1833-91). The story was originally entitled *El Corregidor y la Molinera* ('The Corregidor and the Miller's Wife'). The novel by de Alarcón suggested to Hugo Wolf the character and plot of his opera, *Der Corregidor*.

The action of the ballet was outlined as follows at the time of the London première:

Over the whole brisk action is the spirit of frivolous comedy of a kind by no means common only to Spain of the eighteenth century. A young miller and his wife were the protagonists, and if their existence be idyllic in theory, it is extraordinarily strenuous in practice—choreographically. But that is only another way of saying that M. Massine and Madame Karsavina, who enact the couple, are hardly ever off the stage, and that both of them work with an energy and exuberance that almost leave one breathless at moments. The miller and his wife between them, however, would scarcely suffice even for a slender ballet plot. So we have as well an amorous Corregidor, or Governor (he wears a three-cornered hat as badge of office), who orders the miller's arrest so that the way may be cleared for a pleasant little flirtation—if nothing more serious—with the captivating wife. Behold the latter fooling him with a seductive dance, and then evading her admirer with such agility that, in his pursuit of her, he tumbles over a bridge into the mill-stream. But, as this is comedy, and not melodrama, the would-be lover experiences nothing worse than a wetting, and the laugh, which is turned against him, is renewed when, having taken off some of his clothes to dry them, and gone to rest on the miller's bed, his presence is discovered by the miller himself, who, in revenge, goes off in the intruder's garments after scratching a message on the wall to the effect that 'Your wife is no less beautiful than mine!' Thereafter a 'gallimaufry of gambols' and—curtain!

Claude Achille Debussy

1862-1918

‡Debussy was a Parisian, a *boulevardier*, an opportunist who deserted one woman who had only love to offer him for another who had money as well. He was also a brave man who for nearly ten years endured with fortitude the painful sickness which eventually killed him. And finally, he was a great composer, and a technical innovator whose discovery and exploitation of novel musical resources placed him, in his own century, in the company of Beethoven, Chopin, and Wagner. Musicologists may amuse themselves and exasperate their lay readers by tracing Debussy's harmonic 'system' to Oriental or modal music, or to passages in Moussorgsky (to whose influence he is said to have responded) which in fact exemplify no deliberate daring on the part of that erratic and ill-schooled genius, but only the uneliminated residuum of his natural crudity and primitivism. But Debussy's music was cut from whole cloth—cloth, moreover, of his own fabrication, unique in texture and dye. It is as useless to seek precedents for the first page of *Pelléas* as it is to seek them for the

Chopin Preludes or the first page of *Tristan:* they are not to be found. All one can say and still make sense is that this expressive potential existed in the resources of music from the remotest time, but was first seen and seized upon and exploited by Debussy. This was his service to music in general. His service to French music was to enrich its emotional substance and extend its imaginative awareness.‡ He found the musical art of France beginning to shake itself free from a long bondage to the inferiority into which it had lapsed after the death of Berlioz. It was, for the most part, an empty and paltry thing, emotionally shallow and imaginatively thin, oscillating between theatricalism, unabashed sentimentality, and second-hand classicism: an art often externally refined and adroit, but inwardly meager and unrewarding. Debussy left it deepened and sensitized. He gave it sincerity and intensity of feeling, subtlety, imaginative reach; and he endowed it with an authentically original voice, with a style of rare and high distinction. He found it speaking mediocre rhetoric; he left it speaking poetry. He was at once the least French and the most French of composers; for while he had none of the typical faults of French music, he had all its transcendent virtues, besides others that he himself was the first to confer upon it.

● PRELUDE TO *The Afternoon of a Faun*

Before Debussy thought of writing music for *L'Après-midi d'un Faune,* he had sat at the feet of Mallarmé among that famous company of experimentalists in new kinds of beauty, new conceptions of style and form—Verlaine, Gustave Kahn, Pierre Louys, Stuart Merril, De Regnier—who gathered about 'the Poet of Poets,' as he was so indulgently called in the dim and yeasty 'nineties. Debussy consorted, in Mallarmé's circle, with poets, painters, musicians, critics. And the musicians, for a wonder, were treated with respect by their confrères—were treated almost as if they had been artists on the same plane of intellectual dignity as poets and novelists and critics. As Louis Laloy remarks somewhat caustically in his admirable study of Debussy, it was the first time for many years that men of letters had displayed any interest in music or any disposition to view it seriously. 'One recalls the superb contempt in which it was held by the Romantics: Lamartine, Hugo, Balzac, Théophile Gautier, faithful to the classic tradition of Corneille, Saint-Evremont, Boileau, and Voltaire.' Verlaine even dared to stand for the precept: 'De la musique avant toute chose.' It was Richard Wagner whom they worshiped—he was only seven years dead (though Debussy afterward turned against him, and said catty things about the creator of Wotan). Some of the most distinguished of the group—Mallarmé, Huysmans, Catulle Mendès, Villiers de l'Isle-Adam, and others—were collaborators in the production of the *Revue Wagnérienne.*

Debussy had taken fire from these bright flames of the other arts, and had set poems by Baudelaire and Verlaine. In 1892 he turned into exquisite orchestral sound the *Après-midi d'un Faune* of Stéphane Mallarmé, written in 1876 for Coquelin *aîné*, and published in the same year, with illustrations by Manet. Debussy's Prelude was performed for the first time at a concert of the Société Nationale in Paris, December 23, 1894.

Mallarmé's poem may be, as it has been called, a 'famous miracle of un-intelligibility'—and certainly it does not belong among the bedside books. Yet the almost equally famous digest contrived by that master of English prose, Edmund Gosse, is as lucid and unperplexing as if Mallarmé's original had never provoked the indisposing epithet 'cryptic.' Here is what Gosse said he got out of the poem:

A faun—a simple, sensuous, passionate being—wakens in the forest at daybreak and tries to recall his experience of the previous afternoon. Was he the fortunate recipient of an actual visit from nymphs, white and golden goddesses, divinely tender and indul-gent? Or is the memory he seems to retain nothing but the shadow of a vision, no more substantial than the 'arid rain' of notes from his own flute? He cannot tell. Yet surely there was, surely there is, an animal whiteness among the brown reeds of the lake that shines out yonder. Were they, are they, swans? No! But Naiads plunging? Perhaps! Vaguer and vaguer grows the impression of this delicious experience. He would resign his woodland godship to retain it. A garden of lilies, golden-headed, white-stalked, behind the trellis of red roses? Ah! the effort is too great for his poor brain. Perhaps if he selects one lily from the garth of lilies, one benign and beneficent yielder of her cup to thirsty lips, the memory, the ever-receding memory, may be forced back. So when he has glutted upon a bunch of grapes, he is wont to toss the empty skins into the air and blow them out in a visionary greediness. But no, the delicious hour grows vaguer; experience or dream, he will never know which it was. The sun is warm, the grasses yielding; and he curls himself up again, after worshipping the efficacious star of wine, that he may pursue the dubious ecstasy into the more hopeful boskages of sleep.

Debussy has told us what he aimed to do in his treatment of the poem:

'The music of this prelude,' he wrote, 'is a very free illustration of the beauti-ful poem of Stéphane Mallarmé. It makes no pretensions whatever to being a synthesis of the poem. It projects, rather, a changing background for the dreams and desires of the Faun in the heat of that summer afternoon, as, weary from pursuing the frightened Nymphs and Naiads, he falls into a wine-drugged sleep, free at last to enjoy every bounty that he had craved of Nature.'

The mood of languorous reverie is fixed by a meditative flute, singing, unaccompanied, the chief theme—a drowsily voluptuous phrase ('doux et expressif') that falls and rises indolently between C-sharp and G-natural, as if undecided whether to stay in the key of E or wander into C major. In the fourth measure, Debussy waves his conjurer's wand, and we are reminded of that warning uttered by another wonder-working poet—

> Enter these enchanted woods,
> You who dare . . .

for Debussy, by a single instrumental gesture—a chord of the woodwind, a shimmering of harp tones, and a brief dialogue for the horns—has laid his spell upon us, and has opened a path into that incredible world of his where the familiar and the magical are inverted. There is a short crescendo on a motive that Debussy afterward made use of in the fourth act of *Pelléas*. The chief theme returns in the flute, and then, for ten measures, we get an unclouded golden stream of pure Arcadian loveliness.

The sky darkens. The clarinet plays a whole-tone scale; the muted horns are vaguely sinister; the serenity of the scene is briefly ruffled—but only briefly; for a flute trill introduces a new theme for the oboe that has us back again in the warm sun among the yielding grasses, with the lake-water shining through the reeds.

The orchestra grows more and more animated ('Was he the fortunate recipient of an actual visit from nymphs, white and golden goddesses, divinely tender and indulgent?'). There is a diminuendo; and then, in the key of D-flat, a new and lingeringly ecstatic theme (woodwind and horns), leads to the climax, with the rapturous melody delivered by the strings in unison under a triplet figure for woodwind and horns. A solo violin broods upon this theme. The first subject, in augmentation, returns, first for the flute and afterward for the oboe, interrupted by a fluttering of the horns and an agitated staccato descent of the woodwind.

The end is neared through an exquisite passage: over tremolos in the strings, flutes recall the main theme; above them two solo violins in octaves play a counterpoint of ravishing and pensive beauty, and there are gleams of silver light from the antique cymbals ('the delicious hour grows vaguer; experience or dream, he will never know which it was'). The theme is repeated by flute and solo 'cello, through a drifting harmonic mist—a delectable interchange of seventh-chords between the keys of F-sharp and E-flat. A pair of muted horns, and some of the violins (also muted), play a wraith-like version of the main theme harmonized in major and minor triads. The music dissolves in a pianissimo chord of the flutes, with a final glint from the cymbals.

• THREE NOCTURNES FOR ORCHESTRA

Debussy's three Nocturnes—*Nuages* ('Clouds'), *Fêtes* ('Festivals'), and *Sirènes* ('Sirens')—were composed in 1897-9 and performed for the first time at a Lamoureux concert in Paris on December 6, 1900. The third of the set, *Sirènes*, is written for orchestra and women's voices, without words.

Debussy is said to have made the following rather cryptic comment upon these pieces at the time of their first performance, though the published score is innocent of any explanatory note:

'The title *Nocturnes* is to be understood in a wider sense than that usually given to it, and should be regarded as conveying a decorative meaning. The form of the nocturne has not entered into consideration, and the term should be viewed as signifying all that is associated with diversified impressions and special lights.'

In *Nuages* ('Clouds'), Debussy thought, he says, of 'the unchanging aspect of the sky, with the slow and melancholy passage of the clouds dissolving in a gray vagueness tinged with white.'

In *Fêtes* ('Festivals'), he imagined 'the restless, dancing rhythms of the atmosphere, interspersed with abrupt scintillations. There is also an incidental procession—a wholly visionary pageant—passing through and blended with the argent revelry; but the background of uninterrupted festival persists: luminous dust participating in the universal rhythm.'

Debussy has not attempted to give us tonal impressions of clouds, of festivals, of the ocean's alluring choristers: the music represents an effort to evoke, by indirectness of suggestion, the spiritual counterparts of these things—their reflection in the supersensuous consciousness. For this singular tone poet, the world has scarcely more than a penumbral existence. It is only upon the borderland of the spirit that he finds what others know as the reality of imaginative experience. In his eager search for all loveliness that is fugitive and interior and evanescent he reminds one of the Irishman Yeats—for Debussy is often more Gaelic than Gallic. He is like Yeats in his disdain of those indicative gestures that are merely traditional and immediately significant, in his longing to fix in rhythm and cadence the uncapturable music that haunted his imagination, and the wonder of the world that was his recurrent dream.

The exquisite reticence of this music, its Mozartean economy of means, should be remarked. With the two clarinets and two bassoons that move across the orchestral canvas at the opening of *Nuages*, and the brief, melancholy plaint of the English horn, Debussy starts the imagination, fills the spiritual eye. In the superb *Fêtes*, with its quivering, iridescent effects of light and color, the most wonderful of its moments is the most simply accomplished: the sudden pianissimo in the middle of the piece at the suggestion of the distant rumor of the advancing procession, with the soft throbbing of the harps, timpani, and low strings pizzicato, and the three muted trumpets. The gradual approach of the phantom pageant, the dazzling moment of its arrival, and the vanishing of the chimerical revellers in the distance are among the unforgettable achievements of the musical imagination.

The strange power and unique intensity of Debussy's art proceed from a clairvoyant intuition of hidden processes—the invisible life of the soul, the dream within the dream, the secret voices of woods and skies and waters. Like Tristan, he hears the voice of the light. His is a world where, 'even in the swaying of a hand or the dropping of unbound hair, there is less suggestion of individual action than of a divinity living within.' He is forever remembering some distant country of the spirit, some shadowy margin of a vanished world—

> . . . The grass beyond the door
> The sweet keen smell
> The sighing sound, the lights around the shore.

His music is full of those swift, silent intimations that transcend the spoken word. It bridges the gulf of human separateness, and, hearing it with sensibility, we have communion with the souls of the living, and, like the visionary of the *Phaedo*, we 'see the moon and stars as they really are.'

● *Images* FOR ORCHESTRA. NO. 1: *Gigues*

Debussy, always the rider of dreams and the pursuer of visions, was fond of the word 'Images' as a titular noun. There are two sets of *Images* for piano—three in each set—and there is a series of three for orchestra. Of the latter,

Ibéria (No. 2) and *Rondes de Printemps* (No. 3) are fairly well known in American concert rooms. The first of the set, *Gigues* (or *Gigue Triste*, as it was originally called) is less familiar—chiefly, no doubt, because, though it now heads the series, it was the last to be completed and published. Finished in 1912, it was begun, according to the conscientious Daniel Chennevière, much earlier.

The chief subject of the piece is first heard as an unaccompanied solo for the oboe d'amore, after twenty measures of introduction. Later, the bassoons give out a theme which suggested to Felix Borowski, when *Gigues* was played in Chicago, November 13, 1914, the Scotch tune, 'Weel may the keel row.' Philip Hale thought the resemblance slight, and one is inclined to agree with him. This is certainly a very remote and attenuated double. In rhythmic and intervallic structure the tunes are not within shouting distance of each other. But the inquisitive may judge for themselves by turning to No. xxix of *The Songs, Airs, and Legends of the Adherents to the House of Stuart*, collected by the illustrious James Hogg, author of *The Queen's Wake*, et cetera, where the tune and the words of the old song are to be found. One must leave the specialists in thematic origins to settle the matter of Debussy's indebtedness to Scotland.

• *Images* FOR ORCHESTRA. No. 2: *Ibéria*

Manuel de Falla was a close personal friend of Debussy's. He has said that the author of *Ibéria* wrote Spanish music 'without knowing intimately Spanish territory; though he was acquainted with Spain through books, through pictures, through songs and dances sung and danced by genuine Spaniards.'

Penetrated as he was [writes de Falla] by the musical language of Spain, Debussy created spontaneously, I might even say unconsciously, such Spanish music as might be envied him—who did not really know Spain—by many others who knew her only too well. Once only he had crossed the frontier, in order to spend a few hours at San Sebastian and to see a bull fight. It was little enough, but he nevertheless preserved a lasting remembrance of the impression made on him by that peculiar light of a 'Plaza de Toros': the striking contrast between the part flooded by sunlight and that covered by shadow. 'The Morning of a Fête Day,' in *Ibéria*, might perhaps be accepted as an evocation of that afternoon spent on the threshold of Spain.

But it must be said that this was not his Spain. His dreams took him farther afield, for it was particularly the entrancing Andalusia that his thoughts preferred to linger over. The first two movements of *Ibéria*, 'In the Streets and Byways' and 'Odors of the Night,' testify to this preference.

When *Ibéria* was first performed, Debussy was quoted as saying that he had no intention of writing Spanish music, but wished rather to interpret musically the impressions which Spain awoke in him. Manuel de Falla credits him with having been singularly happy in the realization of this aim: 'The echoes from the villages, a kind of *sevillana* (in the first movement)—the generic theme of the work—which seems to float in a clear atmosphere of scintillating light; the intoxicating spell of Andalusian nights, the festive gaiety of a people dancing to the joyous strains of a *banda* or *guitars* and *bandurrias* . . . all this whirls in the air, approaches and recedes, and our imagination is continually kept awake and dazzled by the power of an intensely expressive and richly varied music.'

The first movement, 'In the Streets and Byways' ('Assez animé, dans un rhythme alerte mais precis,' 3-8), opens with a joyous burst of instrumental color—reiterated chords in the woodwind, the triplet rhythm punctuated by castanets; consecutive fifths, pizzicato, in the strings, and the chief theme of the movement—a jaunty and slightly insolent melody in sixteenth notes for two clarinets, accompanied by oboes and bassoons, the tambourine marking the rhythm of the persistent triplet figure. Clarinet and bassoon in unison have an expressive theme; violins, 'cellos, and English horn contribute another and more song-like one, and these are alternated and combined—this score is far more polyphonic than Debussy's earlier orchestral writing. There is a crescendo, and the violins and piccolo repeat, fortissimo, the main theme.

A curious episode follows: the second violins, on the dominant-seventh chord of A, play an accompaniment—colored by tambourine, castanets, and harps—to a delicately dissonant melody ('piano et doux') in G-flat, traced in harmonics by the first violins, doubled by the piccolo. This is twice repeated, the second time against the chief theme as a counterpoint on the clarinets, and with a new theme added to the polyphonic web: a melody, sung with meditative tenderness by oboe and solo viola, which will be heard again in the succeeding movement.

The tempo changes (Modéré) and the four horns in unison proclaim an emphatic march-like theme (12-16), which is taken up by the violas and continued by the woodwind. Horns and 'cellos, then trombones and woodwind, contribute sentimental counter-themes. There is a return to the first tempo and to the chief subject (oboes). The music dissolves, melts into silence.

In the second movement, 'Odors of the Night' ('Lent et rêveur,' 2-4), Whitman's 'mystic and amorous night' breathes from an enchanted orchestra. One thinks of shadowy gardens dark against the darker trees, under a benignant sky, with the rumor of fountains spreading a silver coolness in the conniving dusk.

Muted strings and flute sustain an ethereal G, while the oboe murmurs a short motif, reflective and hesitant; there are argent gleams from the celesta; tambourine and xylophone sound faintly. The violins play soft glissandi, and there are delicate chromatic runs in the woodwind. Then, above rich-hued chords for divided violas and 'cellos, the oboe begins a song of penetrating sweetness—that which was foreshadowed in the first movement. The higher strings (still muted and divided) join the lovely choiring of syncopated seventh-chords, and the oboe resumes its song. A solo horn responds with a melancholy phrase in triplet rhythm; there is a passionately urgent theme for the violins, which alternates with the quieter horn motif, now played ('lointain et expressif') by a bassoon and solo violin. Muted trumpets, in three-part harmony, together with flutes, piccolo, violins, and 'cellos, recall the chief theme of the first movement.

The music becomes increasingly ardent. The violins re-utter their urgent cry ('avec une grande intensité dans l'expression'). There is a climax on this theme for the full orchestra, then a rapid diminuendo. The seventh-chords recur in the divided lower strings; horns and violins play a new melody; the oboe reminisces. Muted trombones accompany the melancholy horn tune, now voiced by flute, bassoon, and solo violin. Bells sound in the distance.

Without pause begins the third movement, 'The Morning of a Fête-Day' ('dans un rhythme de marche lointaine, alerte et joyeuse,' 4-4). Low strings and tambourines outline the rhythm; the bells sound on; gradually all the voices of the orchestra join in. Themes from the preceding movements are recalled. Woodwind instruments parody the tender song of the slow movement —romance is unfeelingly burlesqued. The strings, pizzicato, 'quasi guitara,' begin a 'mouvement de marche, joyeuse et alerte.' The festival is under way.

● *Images* FOR ORCHESTRA. No. 3: *Rondes de Printemps*

Rondes de Printemps was completed in 1909. The first performance was in Paris, March 2, 1910, at a concert of music organized by Debussy's publisher, Durand. Debussy conducted.

The score has no avowed program, except that which is hinted by the motto printed on the first page of the score—

> Vive le Mai, bienvenu soit le Mai
> Avec son gonfalon sauvage—
> *(La Maggiolata)*

and by another hint contained in the music: for the chief theme of the piece, foreshadowed in the melody first sung by the oboe in the twenty-sixth measure, 'gracefully and gaily,' is derived from an old French children's song, 'Nous n'irons plus au bois'—a 'round' of which the text and music are given in Weckerlin's *Chansons populaires du pays de France*. Debussy uses both the air and the refrain—the latter may be heard in the A major passage with which the strings burst forth exuberantly soon after the oboe has finished its solo. Debussy's music is an orchestral dance of spring, pervaded, as Louis Laloy has pointed out, 'by one idea unceasingly varied, from which it flowers as from a supple branch.'

Debussy might well have had in his mind, while composing this delectable spring song, the last four of those wonderful lines from Shelley's *Ode to the West Wind*:

> . . . O thou,
> Who chariotest to their dark wintry bed
> The wingèd seeds, where they lie cold and low,
> Each like a corpse within its grave, until
> Thine azure sister of the spring shall blow
> Her clarion o'er the dreaming earth, and fill
> (Driving sweet buds like flocks to feed in air)
> With living hues and odours plain and hill.

● *La Mer*: THREE SYMPHONIC SKETCHES

Debussy completed *La Mer: Trois Esquisses Symphoniques* in 1905. He began it in 1903, the year following the production of *Pelléas et Mélisande*. Thus it stands between his masterpiece, that unique achievement of the post-Wagnerian lyric-drama (1893-1902), and the three *Images* for orchestra: *Gigues, Ibéria,* and *Rondes de Printemps,* which date from 1907-12.

La Mer and the three *Images* were the final symphonic expression of Debussy the master. The genius died; the man survived—Debussy lived for six years longer. The music that he produced during those last years of his life was only intermittently distinguished and characteristic. There were brief revivals of the sinking flame, but, for the most part, the music of that closing chapter is tragically inferior to the work of his great period—the period that, beginning in 1892 and ending about 1912, brought forth a succession of masterworks: *L'Après-midi d'un Faune,* the string quartet, the *Nocturnes, Pelléas et Mélisande, La Mer, Ibéria, Rondes de Printemps,* among the larger scores; besides such songs and piano pieces as the *Proses lyriques,* the *Chansons de Bilitis, L'Isle joyeuse, Cloches à travers les feuilles,* and certain of the Preludes.

Thereafter the quality of his writing began to decline. It became formularized, arid, banal. It is painful to look through the 'cello and violin sonatas, the *Noël des enfants qui n'ont plus de maisons,* the *Berceuse héroïque*—painful to look through these, and to recall the tone poet of *La Mer* and *L'Isle joyeuse.*

La Mer is therefore to be classed among those of Debussy's works which sprang from his imagination at a time when it was fertile and distinguished, when his command of beautiful speech was easy and triumphant, when his art was most nearly flawless. *La Mer* stands with *L'Après-midi d'un Faune, Ibéria,* and *Rondes de Printemps* as one of that small but incomparable group of orchestral tone poems in which Debussy said new and enchanting things in an unforgettable way.

La Mer is without a program, argument, preface, motto, or other aid to the fancy except the mighty words that designate the piece as a whole, and the subtitles of the different movements: I. 'De l'aube à midi sur la mer' ('From Dawn till Noon on the Sea'); II. 'Jeux dc vagues' ('Sport of the Waves'); III. 'Dialogue du vent et de la mer' ('Dialogue of the Wind and the Sea').

The three divisions of the work are bound together, musically, by partial community of theme. The characteristic portion of the chief subject of the first part—the phrase declaimed by muted trumpet and English horn in the twelfth measure, after the vague and mysterious opening—recurs in the last movement; and the solemn and nobly beautiful theme for the brass that seems to lift the sun into the blue just before the dazzling close of 'De l'aube à midi sur la mer,' is heard again in the magnificent finale.

This music is a sustained incantation, of rare subtlety and magic; a tonal rendering of colors and odors, of mysterious calls, echoes, visions, imagined or perceived; a recapturing and transcription, through the medium of a necromatic art, of 'the most fantastical sports of light and of fluid whirlwinds'—but of lights, shadows, sounds, colors, that have been subtly altered by the creative processes of the tone poet.

Debussy had what Sir Thomas Browne would have called 'a solitary and retired imagination.' So, when he essays to depict in his music such things as dawn and noon at sea, sport of the waves, gales and surges and far horizons, he is less the poet and painter than the spiritual mystic. It is not chiefly of those aspects of winds and waters that he is telling us, but of the changing phases of a sea of dreams, a chimerical sea, a thing of strange visions and stranger voices, of fantastic colors and incalculable winds—a phantasmagoria of the spirit, rife with evanescent shapes and presences that are at times full of bodement and dim terror, at times lovely and capricious, at times sunlit and dazzling. It is a spectacle perceived as in a trance, vaguely yet rhapsodically. This is a sea which has its shifting and lucent surfaces, which even shimmers and traditionally mocks. But it is a sea that is shut away from too curious an inspection, to whose murmurs or imperious commands not many have wished or needed to pay heed.

Yet, beneath these elusive and mysterious overtones, the reality of the living sea persists: the immemorial fascination lures and enthralls and terrifies; so that we are almost tempted to fancy that the two are, after all, identical—the ocean that seems an actuality of wet winds and tossing spray and inexorable depths and reaches, and that uncharted and haunted and incredible sea which opens before the magic casements of the dreaming mind.

Like all of Debussy's works that truly represent him, *La Mer* exemplifies his ability to rouse the inward vision, to express that which is inexpressible. He might have echoed that warning uttered by the character in Maeterlinck's play, *Intérieur*—'Take care! We do not know how far the soul extends beyond man.' The strange power and unique intensity of Debussy's art proceed from an acute awareness of the world beyond the senses—the inner life of the imagination, the secret voices of woods and clouds and waters. For Debussy, in his most characteristic expressions, was concerned not with what Maeterlinck contemptuously called 'the famous "real life," the outward life, the life we see and hear,' but with 'that other life which lies at the bottom of men's hearts and in the privacy of their consciences and in the unknown mysteries of the world . . . that life which is silent to our ears but not to our sympathies.'

Debussy's most individual achievement is to have given us, for the first time in music, a sense of those twilight domains of consciousness, those secret regions of the spirit which, as William James has told us, are parted from our normal, waking, rational consciousness by screens of gossamer thinness, but which most men become aware of only through dreams and glimpses. Debussy, having the piercing vision of the mystic, found nothing obscuring in those tenuous screens. His imagination passed into and dwelt at ease in that world beyond the senses; and throughout his life as a creative artist he continued to bring back to us from across the border circumstantial tales of an unknown country—tales of enchanted landscapes and unexplored skies, of fabulous shores where the noise of the sunfire on the waves at daybreak is audible for those who have ears to hear.

No one had done this before in music; no one had stood at so far-flung an outpost of the perceptive mind and reported these mysteriously burdened winds, these tides so incalculably rhythmed, these fantastic and dream-colored landscapes, these murmuring voices of desire, the passionate, grave gestures of these enigmatic beings of some unknowable and hidden land. This was Debussy's special contribution to creative music. He enlarged the boundaries of its imaginative world, the extent of its awareness, the scope of its expression.

He taught it to speak, with unexampled fidelity and beauty and profundity, of things for which there are no words.

● *La Damoiselle Élue*, Lyric Poem for Women's Voices and Orchestra

La Damoiselle Élue is a very early work indeed. Debussy was twenty-six when he completed it. The *Nocturnes* were still ten years ahead of him, *Ibéria* twenty. When *La Damoiselle Élue* was written, Wagner had been dead for only five years, Brahms and Tchaikovsky were still alive, and Stravinsky, a boy of six, was presumably riding his velocipede in the suburbs of St. Petersburg.

Debussy, as a student at Rome in his early twenties, came upon Dante Gabriel Rossetti's celebrated poem, *The Blessed Damozel*, in a French translation by Sarrazin, and was captivated by its delicate loveliness and depth of feeling. He finished his music for it in 1888, after his return to Paris. It was his third *envoi*. The Academy approved the work, with modified rapture. But the first performance did not take place until April 8, 1893, at a Société National concert.

Dante Gabriel Rossetti, the English poet-painter, whose ancestry was three-fourths Italian, was called by an eminent critic the most variously gifted artist since William Blake. But his pre-Raphaelite affiliations obscured for years, and still obscure, his essential nature. For years he was misunderstood by those who could not see Rossetti the great and original poet because of the pre-Raphaelite cult from which he had long before emerged. The real Rossetti was not the pre-Raphaelite painter. The real Rossetti was not a painter at all. The real Rossetti was one of the major poets in the English language. He died nearly three-quarters of a century ago, while Browning and Tennyson and Ruskin were alive. Yet his finest poetry is still poetry of the future. Probably no one today, save students and critics, reads *The House of Life*—as no one today reads or knows that other great poetic sequence, Meredith's *Modern Love*, which belongs to about the same period as Rossetti's masterpiece. Both are demodé at present. Apparently, they are 'cast down deep below the rolling tides of time.' Actually, they ride serenely through an unchanging upper sky, obscured, for a while, by low-lying clouds.

The latter part of Rossetti's life was deeply tragic and pitiful, filled with bitter remorse and haunted memories and illness and delusions and a torturing sensibility that would not let him rest. But in his early years, before his genius and his life took on their more darkly passionate tone, Rossetti, as a youth of nineteen, wrote in 1847 that unique poem which was to become one of the most famous, and most ridiculed, in English literature, *The Blessed Damozel* —poetry that has nothing of the depth and passion and greatness of style that were to mark *The House of Life*, yet poetry of singular tenderness and delicacy of touch: lyric poetry that is partly narrative, partly revery and dream and vision.

Rossetti told Hall Caine that he got the idea of his poem from Poe's *The Raven*. 'I realized,' said Rossetti, 'that Poe had done the utmost it was possible to do with the grief of the lover on earth; so I determined to reverse the conditions and give utterance to the yearning of the loved one in heaven.'

He has handled with exquisite tact this difficult and perilous conception of the beloved woman who has died in all the loveliness and security and pride of youth, and who awaits in heaven the coming of her lover, who still dwells, disconsolate, on earth.

Debussy's setting of Rossetti's poem divides the narrative portions of the text between a chorus of women's voices and the solo alto voice of a Narrator. The Blessed Damozel herself is a soprano soloist. Debussy omitted ten entire stanzas of the original text, among them the two finest lines in the poem— which is perhaps just as well: for at that stage of his musical development he could scarcely have set them adequately. Also, he omitted the parenthetical and moving verses in which the lover speaks. He did not conceive the poem in quite the dramatic way that Rossetti did, and so the lover on earth is shut out from the angelic communion of the Blessed Damozel, except as he is reflected to us in her longings and her prayers.

In the music we encounter a score that is relatively simple and direct. Occasionally it is trite, insipid. The lethal hand of Massenet at times lies heavily upon it. Yet *La Damoiselle Élue* remains an astonishing work, beautiful and affecting at its best, with many premonitions of the later Debussy. Behind the brooding and pitiful and prayerful voice of the Blessed Damozel we hear, again and again, the utterance of Mélisande, and on almost every page there are signs that announce the arrival of a new and original genius.

Frederick Delius

1862-1934

D

Frederick Delius, one of the most distinguished and fine-grained spirits that have expressed themselves in modern music, was born on English soil of German parents domiciled in Yorkshire (for many years he called himself Fritz Delius). His father was unsympathetic with the musical aspirations of his son, and young Delius was not permitted to follow music as a profession. In his twentieth year he came to America, settled in Florida, grew oranges, and slyly courted Euterpe, far from the stern parental eye, devoting as much of his time as he could spare to the study and practice of music. He took lessons while in Florida of Thomas F. Ward, organist of a Brooklyn church, who had been ordered South for his health. In 1886 he returned to Europe, and studied at the Leipzig Conservatory under Reinecke, Sitt, and Jadassohn. In 1888, he settled in Paris, and from 1899 until his death he lived at Grez-sur-Loing, near Fontainebleu (a favorite haunt of Robert Louis Stevenson in the seventies). His art is of rich and

exquisite fabrication, and the spiritual nature that it bespeaks is like no
other in music. His characteristic vein is one of ecstatic contemplation and
impassioned tenderness, charged with nostalgic poignancy. Whenever his
music is most typical, it is full of that sense of spiritual exile which is the
burden of his remarkable opera, A *Village Romeo and Juliet*. Through all
his music, as through that score, blows fitfully this wind as from a far
country, and on it we hear the words of the Boatmen in the singular and
haunting music-drama of Delius, 'Heigho, travellers we a-passing by'—
words that are charged with the immemorial sadness of men in the presence of all that is transitory and evanescent and beloved. Delius is always
reminding us, as Mr. Cardus has finely said, that 'beauty is born by contemplation after the event, not while it is growing and taking shape before
us. . . For beauty is what is left for us when the show of life has passed
on.'

● *Appalachia:* Variations on an Old Slave Song, for Orchestra and
Chorus

In March 1884, Delius, a music-loving Britisher then in his twenty-third year,
determined to become a composer in defiance of the wishes of his bigoted
and tyrannical father, a wool merchant of Bradford, Yorkshire, who had no
sympathy with his son's aesthetic inclinations. Young Delius saw no way of
escaping a commercial career save by a desperate expedient. He therefore
announced to his despotic parent that he was going to Florida to become an
orange planter. After some difficult scenes, he finally obtained a reluctant consent and the necessary financial backing. In March 1884, he set sail on the
Cunard liner *Gallia* for the New World.

His destination was an orange plantation named Solano Grove. His father,
hoping to save young Delius from that fate worse than death (as he thought),
the career of a musician, had rented the property for him, with an option
for purchase. It was an old Spanish plantation, on the banks of the St. John's
River, which was at that point several miles wide. 'All about it were acres
and acres of semi-tropical vegetation. The river and the barrier of forests shut
him off from the world outside. It was an ideal situation for Fred,' remarks
his sister, Clare Delius (who is also his biographer), 'who wanted time to
dream and think, but it was quite unsuited to the object which my father
had at heart of making of his son a prosperous business man, who might, in
the orange trade, win those spurs which he had allowed to grow so deplorably
rusty in the business of bartering wool.'

The illusion that he might make something of orange planting soon faded.
Delius was now having, for the first time in his life, that peace and seclusion
in which his musical genius could blossom. Here there was no distraction; here
he could forget everything except his pursuit of an imagined beauty of captur-
able sound. For months he saw no white man, so that, as he said afterward.

his first contact with anybody of his own color was an almost uncanny experience.

Before the autumn of that year his interest in oranges had vanished completely. He had found an old Negro, a quondam slave, with his wife, to relieve him of the burden of running the bungalow. A few other Negroes and an overseer attended to the oranges. Fred (or Fritz, as his sister sometimes calls him, referring to his boyhood name) dreamed and played music. The only instrument he had in his house was his violin, and on this he was fond of playing tunes from *Carmen*. There was no piano on the premises, and without a piano he felt that his wings as a composer were clipped. He determined suddenly that a piano he must have. The nearest town where he could have bought one was Jacksonville, three days' journey away on the St. John's River. Fred determined to make the journey. On arriving there he visited the chief store, and began to try the various pianos offered for sale. A local musician, Thomas F. Ward, who was the organist at the principal church, attracted by the astonishing harmonies that proceeded from the store, entered the premises to discover who was responsible. Thus began a close and remarkable friendship. Delius often said in after years that he had learned more from Ward than he ever learned from anybody else.

It was at this time that Delius conceived the idea for that remarkable composition which he completed many years later, in 1902, long after he had abandoned Florida and returned to Europe. This work, unusual in content and form, was eventually entitled *Appalachia: Variations on an Old Slave Song, for Orchestra and Chorus*. In some reminiscences by 'A Fellow Student'—as he signed himself—published at the time of the first London performance of the work in 1907, this associate of Delius recalled that the 'old slave song' which forms the basis of the composition was sung nightly outside the shanty where Delius, the potential orange-planter, dwelt in Florida. The singer was a former slave; and in the variations which Delius afterward evolved from the song, he depicts, according to his 'fellow student,' 'his impressions of the vast virgin forests of the country traversed by the Mississippi, the miles on miles of untouched forest; and the old Negro himself plays spiritually an important part in them.'

Another friend of Delius who has left us his reminiscences, the young British musician Eric Fenby, companion and amanuensis of the blind composer in his last years, has told us of Delius's delight in phonograph records of Negro music—long after he had returned from Florida and had made his home in France on the little river at Grez-sur-Loing. 'They gave him great pleasure,' writes Fenby, 'for the singing was reminiscent of the way his Negroes used to sing in Florida, when as a young orange-planter he had often sat up far into the night, smoking cigar after cigar, and listening to their subtle improvisations in harmony. "They showed a truly wonderful sense of musicianship and harmonic resource in the instinctive way in which they treated a melody," Delius used to say, "and, hearing their singing in such romantic surroundings, it was then and there that I first felt the impulse to express myself in music." '

Concerning *Appalachia*, however, it is Delius's earlier biographer and friend, the exceptionally sensitive and clairvoyant Philip Heseltine, who has written most enlighteningly. He quotes the note prefixed by Delius to his score: '*Appalachia* is the old Indian name for North America. This composition mirrors the moods of tropical Nature in the great swamps bordering on the Mississippi River which is so intimately associated with the life of the old Negro slave population. Longing melancholy, an intense love for Nature, childlike humor, and an innate delight in dancing and singing are still the most characteristic qualities of this race.'

'Here,' remarks Heseltine, 'the deep impression made on Delius by his life in Florida, which colors many of his earlier works, finds its mature utterance. The work consists of a lengthy introduction, fifteen variations on an old Negro folksong (curiously reminiscent of the first theme of the quartet in the last act of *Rigoletto*), and a choral epilogue which ends with an echo of the introduction.'

The voices, however, are heard before the close. The tenors and basses enter at the end of certain variations, reiterating the vocables 'la-la-la.' 'These little choral doxologies that round off the variations,' observes Heseltine, 'are so full of mysterious and haunting suggestiveness that the work would lose much of its unique charm by their omission. The voices at these points enter pianissimo, and the effect is almost as though the spirits of the forces of Nature invoked by the music became suddenly articulate to acknowledge the master who had called them forth.'

- *On Hearing the First Cuckoo in Spring*
- *Summer Night on the River*

These are two compositions for small orchestra written by Delius in 1911 and 1912. The first performance of the two pieces was by the Gewandhaus Orchestra at Leipzig, on October 2, 1913.

Philip Heseltine, in his book on Delius, classes the two pieces among the composer's 'orchestral impressions of the seasons.' He regards them as 'certainly the finest achievements of Delius in purely orchestral music. To anyone quite unacquainted with his music, *The First Cuckoo* might be presented as an epitome of the whole of Delius's life work. It is based upon a twofold melody; the first part is Delius's own, a sequence of phrases that echo each other like distant cuckoo calls; the second is derived from a Norwegian folksong.'

The piece begins Langsam, C major, 6-4 time. The Norwegian folksong enters on the last beat of the third measure ('with easy, flowing movement,' mezzo-forte) in the strings. The piece is scored for flute, oboe, two clarinets, two bassoons, two horns, and strings. The violins, violas, and 'cellos are divided throughout.

Percy Grainger, a close friend of the composer, has said that *Summer Night on the River* is 'a night-impression of the river Loing near the composer's home at Grez-sur-Loing, near Paris, and some croaky notes on the bassoons towards the close were inspired by a chorus of frogs that abound in a marsh near by. The music is mostly of impressionistic character, with curious chromatic harmony; the only melodic material is the fragment of tune given out by a solo violoncello, and continued by solo violin and viola. At the very end is an exceedingly original tonal suggestion of the silence and coolness of the night scene: violins and violas in open fifths, the second violins, divisi and pizzicati, and woodwind coming in with elusive harmonies after the beat. The final chord is for low (muted) strings, with vague sad notes hesitating in bassoon and low flute.'

The instrumentation is for flutes, oboes, clarinets, bassoons, and horns, in pairs, and the usual strings.

• *Paris: A Nocturne (The Song of a Great City)*

The full title of this work, as printed (in a mixture of German and English) in the score is: *Paris, Ein Nachtstück (The Song of a Great City), für grosses Orchester.* The music was composed in 1899, a year before Delius began work on his opera, *A Village Romeo and Juliet.* The first performance of *Paris* was at Elberfeld, under the direction of Dr. Hans Haym, in 1901.

The score contains no 'program,' no guide whatever to the expressional significance of the work, except that which the title suggests. Philip Heseltine, in his book on Delius, seems to take a malicious glee in the fact that Delius, after the manner of Strauss in certain of his tone-poems, gives the hearer so much guessing to do. 'There is no program to the work,' says Mr. Heseltine, 'nor is there any portrayal—scarcely, indeed, more than a suggestion—of external things. Paris, for Delius, is not so much the capital city of France as a corner of his own soul, a chapter of his own memories.'

Yet the late R. A. Streatfeild, a friend of the composer, presumably spoke with authority when he declared that '*Paris* is a musical picture of the composer's impressions of a great city, by night. It is no mere exercise in musical realism, though it displays a keen sense of pictorial effect. Rather is it a personal record of the feelings engendered by the contemplation of the sleeping city. It is a study of effects rather than of causes, and in this it is a peculiarly characteristic example of Delius's attitude toward music, and of his employment of its resources.'

The music contains many alterations of mood and pace. The beginning is Adagio, D major, 6-8, with a song of the oboe heard above a pedal D on the timpani and basses, introduced by a phrase for the bass clarinet (with chords for the divided 'celli). It is succeeded by a festive Vivace section in the same key and meter; an 'Adagio con espressione' in C major, 4-4, begun by the strings; an 'Allegretto grazioso,' 6-8; a 'Tempo di marcia' in G-flat major, the subject given to harps and glockenspiel with a counter-theme in the violas and 'celli. Other changes of character and tempo follow—'Adagio molto' (solo violin, oboe, flute), 'Vivace grazioso,' 'Allegretto grazioso,' Prestissimo, with a *fff* climax. But the close is tranquil, with the oboe theme of the introduction rounding off the work, which ends on a long-held chord, diminuendo, for the full orchestra.

• INTERMEZZO: 'The Walk to Paradise Garden' (FROM A *Village Romeo and Juliet*)

Delius's opera, A *Village Romeo and Juliet*, was composed in 1900-1901. The composer supplied his own text (originally in German), basing it on a tale by Gottfried Keller, *Romeo und Julia auf dem Dorfe*, and it was under this title that the opera was first performed, at the Komische Oper, Berlin, under the direction of Fritz Cassirer, February 21, 1907. Three years later, it was produced in England, in an English version, with the title A *Village Romeo and Juliet*.

‡Keller's celebrated *novella* and Delius's opera recount the story of Sali and Vrenchen, between whose fathers, farmers of the village of Seldwyla, in Switzerland, a breach has widened. The childhood friendship of the young people ripens into love, but they are separated by the enmity of their parents, and tragedy overtakes them. Determined to wrest happiness from fate, they flee together, but malice besets them on every side. Death is the only refuge for their illusions and their love, and they seek it together. They board a hay-barge moored to the river bank, cast it adrift, and as it moves downstream, Sali removes a plug from the bottom of the boat and tosses it into the water. In the distance the voice of a boatman is heard: 'Heigh-ho, travellers, we a-passing by!'‡

The intermezzo occurs between the fifth and sixth scenes, or 'pictures,' as Delius calls them.

'I know another place not very far from here,' says Sali at the close of the fifth scene, 'where we'll be quite unknown. In the Paradise Garden we will dance the night away. . . Come! Let us go!' The curtain falls. The music subsides in a decrescendo from *ff* to *p* (E-flat major, 'Più tranquillo,' 3-4). The succeeding Intermezzo is an Andante of intense and sustained expressiveness, full of Delius's characteristic mood of ecstatic contemplation and impassioned tenderness. 'It is in itself an epitome of the drama,' remarks Heseltine.

The score of the opera is published in two versions, which differ materially. The first, without date, is a manuscript facsimile, 'propriété de l'Auteur,' containing only the original German text and styling the work 'musikdrama in einem Prolog und drei Akten.' In that version the Intermezzo is only sixty-one measures long. The second version was published in 1910. In this version the opera becomes a 'Musikalisch lyrisches Drama in sechs Bildern.' The text is given in German and English. Evidently Delius revised the music sometime between 1901 and 1910; for in the later version the Intermezzo has been greatly extended, and now fills 148 measures, counting from the beginning of the E-flat major section, 'Più tranquillo,' to the B major chord, *pppp*, just before the beginning of Scene VI.

Vincent d'Indy
1851-1931

D

Vincent d'Indy was almost the last of the *grands seigneurs* of music. He belonged to another age than this. A man of noble and ancient lineage, he was unpretentious and single-minded in his life, an aristocrat in his art: a creator whose purity of style and loftiness of aim caused the hasty to think of him unjustly as 'austere.' It is true that his attitude toward the art which he practiced so devotedly was almost priestly; yet D'Indy the music-maker was often a poet and a rhapsodist, in love with the loveliness of the earth, exerting, when he chose, a passionate and far-sweeping eloquence. In an age that has made a virtue of its skepticism, D'Indy believed in many things—in Bach, in Beethoven, in Wagner, in good counterpoint, in God. He was born between the death of Spontini and the composition of Wagner's *Rheingold*; he heard himself denounced as an aesthetic radical, and lived to find acceptance, and to die at last in the odor of musical sanctity and conservatism. He had the many-sidedness, the energy, the rich interests of the artists of the Renaissance. He was scholar, composer, conductor, teacher, pianist, editor, historian. For many years he occupied a position of unchallenged pre-eminence in the musical art of France, and he was honored wherever the sense of a noble and plastic tradition of artistic excellence is abiding and influential. As a tone poet, he will be remembered longest, perhaps, for his celebration of the natural world. Like Beethoven, he was an incorrigible pantheist. The magic and exhilaration, the delight and wonder of the created earth —the long sigh of the pine-woods, 'Summer's honey breath,' the horn-call of autumn noons: these for him were but the signals of divinity. He would have found no undue exaltation in that question of Walt Whitman's: 'What subtle tie is this between one's soul and the break of day?' D'Indy knew what the tie is.

● SYMPHONY FOR PIANO AND ORCHESTRA, *On a French Mountain Song*, OP. 25

Philip Hale, reviewing in the Boston *Herald* a performance of this work years ago at Symphony Hall, warned those who were unfamiliar with D'Indy's composition that they must not regard it 'as a thinly disguised concerto: it is

nothing of the kind: the piano is an instrument in ensemble . . . no more a
soloist than the oboist or the English horn player. . . . The fact that a pianist
is seen at work excites the attention of those interested in a soloist rather than
in a conventionally scored symphonic work, and their name is legion.' True
talk, which should be kept standing at the head of all annotations on this
symphony of D'Indy's. Nevertheless, D'Indy himself has chosen to feature
the piano part in his symphony by the form of his title, which is: *Symphonie
pour orchestre et piano sur un chant montagnard français*—reasonably enough,
of course, since a piano is not normally a member of the orchestral household.
But if D'Indy had really wanted to insinuate the piano into his orchestra,
trusting that it would snuggle among the other instruments as shyly as the
bass tuba or the English horn, he had a precedent that he might have followed
in the example of Saint-Saëns's Symphony in C minor, which is scored for
orchestra and piano, and requires not one, but two pianists, as the part is
written sometimes for two hands, sometimes for four: yet Saint-Saëns entitled
this work simply: *Troisiéme symphonie en ut mineur par Camille Saint-Saëns,
op.* 78—the pianists are ignored on the title page as completely as if they
were mere mortals, like oboists or 'cellists or trumpeters. But D'Indy would
doubtless remind us that in Saint-Saëns's symphony, the piano has a far less
important part than it has in his own score (the two works were composed in
the same year—1886, but Saint-Saëns's was performed first, at a London Philharmonic concert, May 19, 1886. The first performance of D'Indy's symphony
was at a Lamoureux concert, Paris, almost a year later: March 20, 1887). In
Saint-Saëns's symphony, the piano part is, indeed, almost negligible. The symphony of D'Indy, on the other hand, while it is certainly not 'a thinly disguised concerto,' nevertheless has a piano part of much importance, and the
composer was fully justified in the form of his title.

The *chant montagnard français* which is the pervading theme of the symphony is the melody that is sung by the English horn, with accompaniment
of muted strings, beginning at the second measure of the short introduction
to the work ('Assez lent,' G major, 9-8). This melody is a folk tune pertaining
to the mountains of the Cévennes, where D'Indy spent many of his summers.
Julien Tiersot quotes the tune in his *Histoire de la Chanson Populaire en
France,* and he says apropos of its kind:

The high mountains give to melodies that become acclimated to their altitude something of the purity of their atmosphere. It seems as though there were in these mountain songs—they are generally songs of shepherds—something fluid, ethereal, a gentleness that is not found in folk-songs of the plains. . . It is the same melodic essence
that, in spite of diversities of form, still flavors Alpine songs, of which the Swiss *Ranz
des Vaches* are types known to everyone. It is the same spirit that distinguishes that
air of the Cévennes which M. Vincent d'Indy took for the theme of a symphonic work.

The three movements of D'Indy's symphony are based on this 'mountain
song.' In the main part of the first movement ('Modérément animé,' 3-4), the
folk tune is metamorphosed into the lively chief theme (for the bassoon and
strings). This is developed conjointly with a second theme in B major (flute,
horn, and harp).

The piano begins the second movement ('Assez modéré, mais sans lenteur,' B-flat, 3-4, 2-4), with a variant of the mountain song, which later becomes a horn fanfare above a drum-roll and a tremolo for the violas, and then is heard on a stopped horn, with suggestions of a funeral-like rhythm in the basses. A tranquilizing song of the clarinet, accompanied by the piano and chords of the wind and strings, ends the movement.

The piano and harp, which in this score are often consorted, open the third movement (Animé, G major, 2-4) with still another transformation of the mountain song. Except for an episode that recalls the graver mood of the second movement, the Finale is immensely vigorous and high-spirited. D'Indy himself (to whom the present annotator is indebted for this condensed analysis) has said that the last movement expresses 'l'allégresse de la montagne.' The work ends with a final return of the mountain song, fortissimo, for the trumpets and piano.

- *Summer Day on a Mountain:* SYMPHONIC PICTURES, OP. 61

Jour d'Été à la Montagne, which is in three movements, has been variously described as a 'symphonic suite,' 'a program symphony,' and 'a triptych of tone poems.' It was characterized by the composer himself as 'symphonic pictures' (*tableaux symphoniques*)—though this designation does not appear in the published score, which bears simply the title of the work and the sub-titles of the three movements—I. 'Aurore' ('Dawn'); II. 'Jour: Après-midi, sous les pins' ('Day: Afternoon, under the Pines'); III. 'Soir' ('Evening').

The music was suggested by Roger de Pampellone's *Les Heures de la Montagne—Poèmes en Prose,* and D'Indy's score is prefaced by extracts from that work, which are subjoined in an English version:

D'Indy's composition is more than a mere concatenation of tone poems. The work is formally integrated. The three movements are structurally unified by the Franckian device (though it is also, of course, a Schumannesque device and a Beethovenian device) of thematic community. Furthermore, the opening of the first movement is almost literally repeated in the last, with a felicitous variation: for whereas, in the first ('Dawn'), the somber tonality of C minor is resolved, as the day breaks, into a luminous B major, in the final movement ('Evening') this process is reversed, and the music fades from B major into the dusk of C minor.

'Dawn': Muted and divided strings sustain, pianissimo, a long orchestral stillness ('Très modéré,' C minor, 4-4). The music reminds us of what Thoreau calls 'the auroral hour.' D'Indy's music evokes its solitude, its cool hush, the lifting vapors and paling stars, the indescribable freshness and fragrance, the slow gilding of the fir-tops, the larks arising out of the dew of the ravine. There is a 'Waldweben'-like murmuring—flutes, bassoons, clarinets, violas, trumpet, horn—with bird-songs in the higher woodwind. The trombone proclaims a theme that will recur, with various modifications, in the other movements. The pace becomes increasingly brisk; there is a spreading radiance in the orchestra, and the chief theme sounds majestically in B major from the trumpets through the shimmering and sparkling of harp and string arpeggios; later, from all the strings in unison and octaves, and finally, in diminution from the horns, trumpets, and woodwind. The strings have a joyous counter-subject, and the movement ends radiantly.

'Day' (Afternoon, under the Pines): The mountain-top is lapped by the slow tides of the summer afternoon. In the hot, windless silence the lordly clouds drift sleepily. The music is full of drowsy murmurings. First violins, without mutes, accompanied by the other strings muted, have the indolent chief subject of this movement ('Très modéré,' E major, 6-4). In the tenth measure, a solo violin recalls the binding motif of the work—the trombone theme of 'Dawn'—followed in the strings and woodwind by a variant of the jubilant concluding theme of the preceding movement. The music sinks to a pianissimo, and there is a pause. Then begins a scherzo-like middle section ('Très vif,' 3-8). A snatch of peasant dance-music is borne upward toward the valley. The clarinet sings a rustic tune, and this is taken up by the violas, woodwind, trumpet, and violins, until almost the whole orchestra has sported humorously with it. The tranquil earlier mood returns; but the distant merry-making, now more insistent, is heard again from the valley, and there is the suggestion of a summer storm (the ghost of the 'Pastoral' Symphony hovers over this movement). Gradually the intrusive sounds subside. The trombone theme recurs in the brass; and, very faintly from the clarinet, we hear a reminiscence of the peasant's dance-tune. The poet is once more at peace upon his hilltop, companioned only by 'the lush and pompous day.'

'Evening': The last movement begins exultantly ('Très animé et joyeux,' B major, 4-4), with a theme derived from the triumphant phrase given to the violins at the close of the dawn music, while the main theme of the work is treated canonically in the basses, horns, and woodwind. The elation of the music subsides. The mood grows more and more tranquil, becomes charged with the suggestion of declining light and spreading shadows and an enwrapping peace. The strings ('Très lent,' 3-4, muted and *ppp*) play a meditative variant of the opening theme of the movement: a passage of serenely poetic beauty, rich in twilight tenderness. The opening of the first movement—the music of the breaking day—is recalled (C minor, 4-4). The dusk of sunrise becomes the dusk of night.

The orderly and genteel Addison declared in 1705 that the Alps as viewed from the Lake of Geneva formed 'one of the most irregular and misshapen scenes in the world.' How profound an amazement would have filled his neatly clipped soul if he could have known that two centuries later a maker of music would assemble an army of instruments for the purpose of celebrating in tone the beauty and majesty of the heights! Yet it was long before Addison's day that Petrarch, climbing Mount Ventoux in 1335, said that his soul 'rose to lofty contemplations' upon the summit. Vincent d'Indy would have sided with Petrarch.

D'Indy's approach to the immemorial pageant of what Henry More called 'the Outworld' was a blend of poetic rapture, grave tenderness, and an almost priestly elevation of spirit. He did not, like the unparalleled Debussy, see in it a pageant of evanescent and anonymous visions: the amorously pensive Faun of the *Après-midi* would have been as ill at ease on D'Indy's mountain-top as a dryad in a cathedral. For D'Indy, even when he was not a worshiping pantheist, betrayed an imagination from which the quality of sensuous suggestion was almost wholly absent.

The Nature worship of D'Indy is predominantly religious. It is celebrated in rapturous songs that are devotional canticles, offerings of praise. The *Jour d'Été à la Montagne* is in essence an ecstatic hymn in praise of the eternal miracle of the created earth.

● *Istar*: SYMPHONIC VARIATIONS, OP. 42

D'Indy's work illustrates a French version of an ancient and enigmatic Babylonian poem, 'Ishtar's Descent into Hades,' the original of which is believed to have been in the Library of Sardanapalus. Verses from the French translation are printed as a preface to the score.

The story of the Babylonian poem is as follows: Ishtar [Istar] arrives before the gates of the Land of No-Return. There are seven gates, and at each gate the porter strips her of some ornament (for Ishtar's clothing seems to have consisted almost entirely of jewelry). At the seventh gate, the porter removes the last covering from her body. Ishtar is then brought naked and helpless before Allatu, the queen of the nether-world, who commands that she be smitten with plagues in all parts of her body—with diseases 'of the eyes, hips, feet, heart,' et cetera.

Ishtar, the chief deity of the Babylonians and Assyrians, was regarded as the personification of fertility (both of the soil and of human and animal life). Therefore, after she had descended to the Land of No-Return, a dreadful calamity befell the upper world. The absence of Ishtar caused all procreation to cease upon the earth, and there was no new life.

But Queen Allatu relented. Ishtar was sprinkled with the waters of life, and was sent upward through the seven gates; and at each gate the ornament or garment of which she had been stripped was restored to her.

When D'Indy's work was first performed at a Boston Symphony Concert in Boston, under Gericke, February 18, 1899, the late William Foster Apthorp, then the brilliant editor of the Boston Symphony Orchestra's program-book, printed the following English translation of the French version of the Babylonian original which is published as a preface to the score:

Towards the immutable land, Istar, daughter of Sin, bent her steps, towards the abode of the dead, towards the seven-gated abode where He entered, towards the abode whence there is no return.

At the first gate, the warder stripped her; he took the high tiara from her head.

At the second gate, the warder stripped her; he took the pendants from her ears.

At the third gate, the warder stripped her; he took off the precious stones that adorn her neck.

At the fourth gate, the warder stripped her; he took off the jewels that adorn her breast.

At the fifth gate, the warder stripped her; he took off the girdle that encompasses her waist.

At the sixth gate, the warder stripped her; he took the rings from her feet, the rings from her hands.

At the seventh gate, the warder stripped her; he took off the last veil that covers her body.

Istar, daughter of Sin, went into the immutable land, she took and received the Waters of Life. She gave the sublime Waters, and thus, in the presence of all, delivered the Son of Life, her young lover.

The last paragraph of the French version is apparently a coda invented by the Gallic translator. The words have no equivalent in the original Babylonian poem. Nor does the French translator specifically remove Ishtar from Hades, though his allegorical last paragraph is doubtless an attempt to sum up the conclusion of the Babylonian poem in a few well-chosen metaphors. Moreover, the French version is credited in D'Indy's preface to the Gilgamesh epic (the Assyrio-Babylonian epic of which Izdubar, or Gilgamesh, is the hero), with which the story of Ishtar's descent into Hades has nothing to do.

Apthorp thus set forth the peculiarity of D'Indy's tone poem: 'The theme is not given out simply at the beginning ['très lent,' F minor, 4-4], neither is it heard in its entirety until the last variation, in which it is sung by various groups of instruments in unison and octaves, and worked up later in full harmony. Each one of the variations represents one of the seven stages of Istar's being disrobed at the gates of the "immutable land," until in the last she stands forth in the full splendor of nudity. . . By following the poem, and noting the garment or ornament taken off, the listener can appreciate the composer's poetic or picturesque suggestiveness in his music.' Another commentator has observed that D'Indy has here 'reversed the customary process. . . He unfolds by degrees, from initial complexity, the simple idea which was wrapped up therein, and which appears only at the close, like Istar unveiled.'

Paul Dukas

1865-1935

‡Dukas was a lesser contemporary of D'Indy, Debussy, and Ravel. He was a product of the Paris Conservatory, and in his turn he taught there. It will always be impossible to form a just estimate of his abilities, since he ceased publishing his works some twenty-five years before he died, and himself consigned his unpublished manuscripts to the flames.‡

● *The Sorcerer's Apprentice:* SCHERZO FOR ORCHESTRA

Dukas's amusing and delightful 'scherzo' (as he calls it) was composed in 1897. It is a tonal anecdote based on Goethe's poem, *Der Zauberlehrling,* which was derived from a dialogue in Lucian's *The Lie-Fancier;* thus the story is at least 1800 years old.

Here is a condensation of Goethe's verses, in the form of a 'dramatic monologue' written by R. A. Barnet:

They call him 'the Great Magician!' 'Great?' Bah!
I, too, am great—as great as he, for I, too, can call up imps and sprites to do whate'er
    I bid!
Now will I call some uncanny sprite to fetch me water from the pool.
The broom! Come, broom! thou worn-out battered thing—
Be a sprite! Stand up! 'Tis well! Two elfin legs now I give thee!
Good! What's more, a head! There! Now, broom!
Take thou a pail and fetch me water from the pool!
Go quickly and draw water for me, for me, your Master!
Bravo! Thou faithful broom! Thou bustling broom!
What? Back again? And—again?
And—yet *again?* Stop!
This pailful completes thy work; the bath is filled!
You impish broom, stop!
Stop, Stop! I say. I *Command!*
Thou diabolic damned thing, stop!
Be a broom once more! What? Wilt not obey?
O thou cub of hell!
Then, will I with my hatchet cut thee in two!
There! . . .
Ye demons! Now thou art *two* and double thy hellish work!
The flood increases—the water engulfs me—Master!
Master of Masters! Come! I am a poor helpless creature, the sprite I called will not obey!
The master came and said:
'Broom! To thy corner as of old!
See! I make sprites do as they are told!'

Dukas's music begins with a mysterious introductory section, 'Assez lent,' 9-8. The first theme (it has been called the theme of the Apprentice) is heard at the second measure, in the muted violins, above harmonics sustained by violas and 'cellos. The important second theme (this has been called the theme of the Broom) is foreshadowed immediately in the woodwind (at first in the clarinet). The Apprentice utters the magic formula, and there is music of powerful command from a muted trumpet, fortissimo, and horns—the theme of the Sorcerer. Then follows a long and portentous silence. It is broken (Vif, 3-8) by a soft, curious, clucking chord of the bass clarinet, contra-bassoon, and horns in their sub-cellar registers. Another pause, of five measures, then other clucking chords of the wind—an irresistibly droll effect. A rhythmic pattern is then outlined by the clucking chords, and this is filled in by the second theme played in its complete form by three bassoons in unison, over the hopping rhythm maintained by the pizzicato strings. The first theme recurs in the violins and violas.

Magic is abroad, and the uncanny business proceeds. The dreadful plight of the apprentice—the appearance of the second sprite—the engulfing flood—the mounting panic of the amateur wizard are depicted in the music with irresistible humor and vividness. Finally the Sorcerer's return is announced by furious blasts of his motive in the fortissimo brass, under trills of the woodwind and tremolos of the violins. The master speaks his disenchanting formula. The quiet mood of the introduction is re-established ('Assez vif,' 3-8). A brusque command (Vif, fortissimo), in the final bar, sends the Broom to its corner.

Antonin Dvořák

1841-1904

‡Dvořák began his life in poverty and obscurity, as the son of a butcher, and ended it in affluence and fame as one of the most celebrated composers of his day. The transition was of his own working, and was accomplished against formidable odds. Brahms had a hand in it, but it is not quite true that he 'discovered' Dvořák, who already was the recipient of a small pension from the *Cultusministerium* in Vienna when Brahms, in 1877, was appointed to the examining board of that institution and thus had his attention drawn to Dvořák's music. But it was at Brahms' suggestion that the publisher Simrock commissioned Dvořák to compose a set of Slavonic dances for piano duet, and it was these dances, published in 1878, that gave a European and even wider extension to Dvořák's hitherto parochial reputation. During the last twenty-five years of his life he was internationally known and honored. His work assimilates the folk music of his native Bohemia to the music of the mid- and late-nineteenth century German romantic composers. It is honest and accomplished and effective, without being distinguished by high originality of method or profundity of content.‡

THE SYMPHONIES

The list of Dvořák's works, published and unpublished, includes nine in the symphonic form. The Symphony in D major, op. 60, composed in 1880, was the first to be published. The Symphony in D minor, op. 70, written for the Philharmonic Society of London, was composed in 1884-5, published in 1885; the symphony in F major, composed in 1875 as 'op. 24,' was published in 1888 as 'op. 76'; the G major, op. 88, was composed in 1889 and published by Novello of London in 1892; the E minor, op. 95 (an old friend sometimes disguised under the title *Z nového světa*), was composed in 1893, and published in the following year. Two other symphonies, both relatively early works, were published without opus numbers after Dvořák's death: one in E-flat, composed in 1873; and a second in D minor, composed in 1874. A still earlier symphony, in C minor, entitled *The Bells of Zlonice* (described by Dr. Hoffmeister as Dvořák's first), and his second, in B-flat major, both dating from 1865, are still, we believe, unpublished.

In the notes below, the numbers of the symphonies are those usually assigned to them.

● No. 1, in D major, op. 60

This work is variously numbered among Dvořák's essays in the symphonic form: sometimes as 'Symphony No. 1,' sometimes as 'Symphony No. 3.' The score published by Simrock in 1882 bears no number. The title page reads: *Symphonie (D dur) für grosses Orchester, von Anton Dvořák: op. 60.* When the symphony was introduced to the repertoire of the Philharmonic Society by Theodore Thomas on January 5, 1883 (this was probably the first performance in America), it appeared on the program as 'Symphony in D, op. 60 (new).' Nor, obviously, was the symphony 'composed in 1884,' a statement made in a well-known concert guide. According to Dvořák's biographer, Dr. Karel Hoffmeister (professor of piano in the 'Master School' of the Prague Conservatory of Music, and a student there under Dvořák's administration), 'this symphony, which had been slowly maturing in Dvořák's mind, was completed in the Autumn of 1880.' It is dedicated to Hans Richter, in recognition of Richter's services to the composer. According to Dr. Hoffmeister, the symphony was performed at one of the Slavonic Concerts in Zofin under the conductorship of Adolf Cech. (Dr. Hoffmeister does not give the date of this performance.) 'No sooner was it published than it made its way abroad to Leipzig, Rostock, Graz, Cologne, Frankfort, New York, and Boston, finally attracting even the reserved public of England.'

Dr. Ottakar Sourak speaks of the work as 'this joyous symphony, full of the fragrance and melody of the Bohemian fields and forests, full of light and of cheerful courage, with the Furiant in the Scherzo—a work of striking originality.' For this symphony is one of the many works in which Dvořák steeped his imagination in the rich sources of the national music that he loved —principally the dances of the folk. After remarking that 'the most eloquent things in Dvořák's cyclical works are the slow movements,' Dr. Sourak pays tribute to the 'highly characteristic' scherzi, 'in which Dvořák idealizes certain typical Czech or Slavonic dances, which break forth in a bubbling stream of rhythmic verve.'

The Furiant which constitutes the Scherzo of the Symphony in D major is a rapid Bohemian dance of a fiery and impulsive character, marked by alternating rhythms and irregular accentuation. Dvořák has built upon it the most salient movement of his D major Symphony. This Scherzo begins Presto, D minor, 3-4, with four introductory measures for the strings, crescendo. After that, the music is off on its mad dance (full orchestra for nineteen bars, repeated). Then follows a contrasting theme, for the violins in octaves, clarinets, bassoons, and violas (F major, *p*, dolce). The excitement of the opening

section returns, and mounts to a 'fortissimo grandioso.' The whole of the foregoing is then repeated, and a connecting passage (a reiterated diminuendo
chord of the wind and strings) leads to the Trio: 'Poco meno mosso,' D major,
3-4, with a melody given to the oboe, flute, and piccolo. The return of the
Presto brings a tumultuous close, 'poco a poco accelerando.'

The two preceding movements of the symphony are an opening 'Allegro
non tanto,' D major, 3-4, with the chief theme, after a few bars of quiet preluding, heard from the violins and woodwind, and the ingratiating second
subject from the divided 'cellos doubled by two horns, against an accompaniment figure of the violins; and a romantic Adagio in B-flat, 2-4, with the
chief theme (a 'broad lyrical folk song,' Dr. Hoffmeister calls it) given to the
strings, after four introductory measures for the wind. There is a coda in which
the persuasions of the 'cello section are not forgotten.

The Finale ('Allegro con spirito,' D major, 2-4) is based upon two chief
subjects redolent of the Bohemian countryside and 'overflowing with capricious
humor': the opening theme, for the strings, and an engaging A major tune in
faster tempo for the clarinet, accompanied at first by violas, 'cellos, oboes,
bassoon, and horn.

The symphony is scored for woodwind and trumpets in pairs, four horns,
three trombones and tuba, timpani, and strings.

• No. 4, IN G MAJOR, OP. 88

This symphony, sometimes called the 'English Symphony,' was composed in
1889 and was first performed in the following year, by the London Philharmonic Society, under Dvořák's direction. It was published in 1892. On
March 11 of that year, the Philharmonic Society of New York performed the
symphony at the Metropolitan Opera House, under the direction of Anton
Seidl. Arthur Mees, then the annotator of the Society's programs, introduced
it as follows:

It is a striking peculiarity of Dvořák that he succeeds at the very outset in communi-
cating to the impressible listener the mood in which his composition has been conceived. In the present symphony, the introduction to the first movement serves this
purpose. It is one of the most beautiful melodies in the whole work. A quiet dignity
and seriousness pervade it, which cannot but affect the themes which are subsequently
proclaimed. This introduction is in the minor mode, and only its last chord suddenly
announces the major key in which the symphony stands. The flute at once follows with
a bright, delicate theme, like the chirping of a bird, after which a cadenza leads up to
the first principal subject in the 'cellos. The first part of the second subject is soon
heard in the strings, and is carried on by the flutes and clarinets. After this has been
disposed of, a lovely episode is introduced pianissimo by the woodwind instruments,
and taken up fortissimo by the full orchestra. With a repetition of the first theme
gradually dying out while the oboes and flutes seem to suggest the tinkling of bells, the
exposition of the subject-matter of the first movement comes to an end.

The second part is ushered in by the quiet introduction above mentioned, which
subsequently recurs once more, but forte, in brilliant trumpet tones. Then the composer proceeds to build up his structure with the chosen musical ideas. In this Dvořák
is a master of masters. His inventiveness in presenting melodies and parts of melodies
in ever new forms and combinations, with fascinating rhythmic and harmonic changes

and ever varying tone colors, seems inexhaustible. At times it appears as if it were with great difficulty that he restrains his impetuosity so as to satisfy the requirements of the form and character of the symphony. These abrupt changes in mood constitute one of Dvořák's pronounced traits. The utmost impulsiveness and calm repose stand side by side. Outbursts of violent energy alternate in bewildering rapidity with moments of tranquility.

The second movement opens with a somber introduction for the strings, consisting of a phrase three times repeated, which furnishes the principal melodic and rhythmic elements of its first part. This the clarinets take up in that strange admixture of minor and major of which the composer is so fond. The second part is a melody in major which is accompanied by a staccato figure alternately in the string and wind instruments. The latter becomes useful in leading up to an impressive climax. Both parts are repeated, with modifications in harmony, after which the movement comes to a close with a short coda.

The third movement is in slow waltz time. The principal subject is rhythmically peculiar in that it covers ten measures. In the accompaniment, the figure in the flutes and clarinets which Dvořák often introduces, repeatedly appears. The melody of the second part, which takes the place of the Trio, in its charming simplicity cannot but call to mind similar passages in Schubert's compositions. The movement closes, after a repetition of the first part, with a coda in double time, which, with rapid staccato chords in the oboes and bassoons and counter-themes in the strings in conflicting accents, sounds thoroughly comical.

The last movement is ushered in by an odd theme for the trumpets which seems to announce one of those unrestrained, wild dance tunes in which the Bohemian composer often indulges his fancy. Instead of this, a pompous subject peculiarly archaic in form is announced in the strings. Its two clear-cut periods of eight measures each, with repeats, conventional modulation, simple rhythm with 'imitations' in the bass and middle voices, sound as if transplanted from the last century into the present. After a number of variations on this subject, two new themes appear. The first one of these, a solo for the flute, is in the same vein as the opening theme. The second, a duet for the clarinets accompanied by a grotesquely rumbling figure in the bass, is full of droll humor. Soon the first subject reappears, the tempo becomes more rapid, the instrumentation more sonorous; and, as the final climax approaches, reminiscences of the first movement of the symphony are introduced.

● No. 5, IN E MINOR (*From the New World*), OP. 95

When the 'New World' Symphony was performed for the first time, at a Philharmonic Concert in New York under Anton Seidl, December 15, 1893, the program book published this announcement, on the authority of the composer:

In order to facilitate the understanding of the work and of the spirit in which it was conceived, as well as of the theory on which it is constructed, Dr. Dvořák has kindly given the following explanation: On his arrival in America the composer was deeply impressed by the conditions peculiar to this country and the spirit of which they were the outward manifestations. In continuing his activity he found that the works which he created here were essentially different from those which had sprung into existence in his native country. They were clearly influenced by the new surroundings and by the new life of which these were the material evidence. Dr. Dvořák made a study of Indian and Negro melodies and found them possessed of characteristics peculiarly their own. He identified himself with their spirit, made their essential contents—not their formal, external traits—his own. As Liszt, Brahms, and particularly Schubert reproduced the spirit of Hungarian music in their works, as Dvořák had done in regard to Bohemian music in his Slavonic Dances, so he strove in the present symphony to reproduce the fundamental characteristics of the melodies which he had found here, by means of the specifically musical resources which his inspiration furnished. In doing this he acted according to conviction, according to the theory to which he has given much thought, not with a view to displaying his ingenuity or masterly skill of composition.

While the contents of the symphony have been suggested by Negro and Indian melodies, the symphonic form has been carefully observed. The composer has created a work in accordance with the laws of the highest type of music, but in the spirit and moods to which these melodies gave rise. The second and third movements were written under the influence of Longfellow's *The Song of Hiawatha*, for which the composer has a profound admiration. In the second movement and in the Finale reminiscences of the themes of the first movement will be found. . .

Let us hear another witness. Henry E. Krehbiel, who was an intimate friend of Dvořák, occupied a peculiarly close relation to the 'New World' Symphony in its formative period. The score of the work was in his hands before it was published—when, indeed, it was still in sketch form; and Dvořák in conversation with him frequently discussed its character. Krehbiel succinctly set forth as follows the composer's intention: 'Dr. Dvořák held it to be the duty of composers to reflect in their music the spirit of the folk-tunes of the people to whom they belonged, not by using those tunes baldly as themes, but by studying their characteristics and composing in their vein. When he came to New York he put his precepts into practice. He studied the tunes which seemed to him to hit the popular taste, and some of the slave songs of the South. Having grasped what he conceived to be their feeling and noted their structural peculiarities, he embodied his conception in this symphony and published the fact in the descriptive title which he gave it, namely: *From the New World*.'

Dvořák himself was quoted as saying, in a statement made in advance of the performance of the symphony, that he was 'satisfied that the future music of this country must be founded upon what are called the Negro melodies. These can be the foundation of a serious and original school of composition, to be developed in the United States. When first I came here, I was impressed with the idea, and it has developed into a settled conviction. These beautiful and varied themes are the product of the soil. They are American. They are the folk-songs of America, and our composers must turn to them. . . Only in this way can a musician express the true sentiment of a people. . . In the Negro melodies of America, I discover all that is needed for a great and noble school of music. They are pathetic, tender, passionate, melancholy, solemn, religious, bold, merry, gay, gracious, or what you will. . . There is nothing in the whole range of composition that cannot find a thematic source there.'

When the E minor Symphony was performed in Berlin in 1900, Dvořák is said to have written to the conductor, Oskar Nedbal: 'I send you Kretzschmar's analysis of the symphony, but omit that nonsense about my having made use of "Indian" and "American" motives—that is a lie. I tried to write only *in the spirit* of those national American melodies.'

There is, finally, the symphony itself, which it is now possible to view solely as music, rather than as a source of polemics. Thirty years ago, a commentator remarked that 'it has created a greater stir in the musical world than any instrumental piece composed within the last decade or more, except, possibly, Tschaikowsky's *Symphonie Pathétique.*' Dvořák's symphony is received a good deal more quietly now—as is the 'Pathétique'; yet for many hearers the rhythmic and melodic charm of the music, its gusto and spontaneity, its freshness and saliency and sweetness, survive and fascinate.

- OVERTURE, *In der Natur*, OP. 91
- OVERTURE, *Carnaval*, OP. 92
- OVERTURE, *Othello*, OP. 93

When Dvořák came to America in the autumn of 1892, to assume his post as Director of Mrs. Thurber's National Conservatory, he was exhibited to the natives at a 'Grand Concert' (as the announcements proclaimed it) in Carnegie Hall. It was indeed an occasion. Colonel Thomas Wentworth Higginson made a speech about 'the New World of Columbus' (which, by a happy accident, had been discovered just 400 years before) and 'the New World of Music'— not the celebrated E minor Symphony of Dr. Dvořák, as yet unwritten, but the new tonal continent about to be explored by the eminent Bohemian. There was a great audience; *America* was sung by a chorus of 300; Anton Seidl conducted Liszt's *Tasso;* the incomparable Emil Fischer and Mme de Vere-Sapio appeared as soloists; and Dvořák himself conducted a *Te Deum* written especially for the occasion, and a tripartite work for orchestra announced as *Triple Overture: Nature, Life, Love.*

This trio of overtures was later dissociated and its component parts published separately with different titles, 'Nature' being represented by *In der Natur* (op. 91), 'Life' by the *Carnaval* Overture (op. 92), and 'Love' by *Othello* (op. 93). But when Dvořák composed the pieces in 1891 he intended them to be played together; and a program note circulated at the New York concert conveyed to the audience what was understood to be an authorized interpretation, by the composer, of his poetic scheme:

This composition [declared the annotator] is a musical expression of emotions awakened in Dr. Dvořák by certain aspects of the three great creative forces of the Universe— Nature, Life, and Love. It was conceived nearly a year ago, while the composer lived in Bohemia. The constituent parts of the triple overture are linked together by a certain underlying melodic theme. This theme recurs with the insistence of the inevitable personal note marking the human individual, who observes and is moved by the manifold signs of the unchangeable laws of the Universe.

NATURE [IN DER NATUR]

As a typical expression of his fondness for nature and of the blissful and occasionally reverent feelings which it stirs in him, the composer chose to present the emotions produced by a solitary walk through the meadows and woods on a quiet summer afternoon, when the shadows grow longer and longer till they lose themselves in the dusk and gradually turn into the early dark of night. Unlike Beethoven in his *Pastoral* Symphony, the unconscious summer music of drowsy crickets [sic] and birds is not actually represented by musical equivalents. The predominating suggestions are peace and quietude with little interruptions here and there, such as are occasioned by the sudden rustling of tree tops in the forest or by the subdued exclamations of a garrulous little brook. Finally, when darkness has set in, there are only the sounds of night. The pervading mood of the composer becomes similar to that of Milton's *Il Penseroso*, when night overtakes him while he listens to the evening song of the nightingale and hears

> The far-off curfew sound
> Over some wide-watered shore
> Swinging slow with sullen roar.

LIFE ['CARNAVAL']

If the first Overture suggested *Il Penseroso*, the second, with its sudden revulsion to wild mirth, cannot but call up the same poet's *L'Allegro*, with its lines to 'jest and youthful jollity.' The dreamer of the afternoon and evening has returned to scenes of human life, and finds himself drawn into 'the busy hum of men,'

> When the merry bells ring round
> And the jocund rebecks sound
> To many a youth and many a maid

dancing in spirited Slavonic measures. Anon the wild mirth dies away. Violin and flute in a dialogue seem to suggest the conversation of a pair of lovers who have stolen away from the throng. Their voices vanish in the distance. Again the band of merry maskers bursts in. The stirring Slavonic theme of the introduction reappears and the three themes of the second overture, the humorous, the pathetic, and the pastoral, are merged into one, with the humorous in the ascendant till a revulsion changes the order. The whole ends in the gay major key with which it began.

LOVE ['OTHELLO']

If the first two parts represented the impressions of Nature and Life as gay and stirring in general, the third overture [*Othello*] lets Love appear as a serious and burning passion. The composer has tried to express some of the emotions engendered in him by the final scenes of *Othello* as an embodiment of both the gentlest and the fiercest expressions of love. The composition is by no means a faithful musical interpretation of the Shakespearean drama, but rather the after-revery of a man whose imagination has been kindled by the theme of the play. The main part begins with a choral-like melody, the prayer of Desdemona before retiring. While she is still praying, weird [sic] sounds in the orchestra suddenly announce the approach of the murderer. This is but an effect of the imagination, however, for presently the prayer of Desdemona continues till she falls asleep. Once more the orchestra announces the approach of Othello. He pauses at the threshold. He enters the room, looks long at Desdemona, and kisses her. The theme [sic] changes to an allegro. Desdemona awakes, and then follows the cruel, pathetic scene between Desdemona and the Moor. Gradually the imaginary conversation becomes tinged with a note of melancholy, and a regretful love scene ensues, according to the composer, till the Moor's jealousy and mad revenge gain the upper hand again. The scene of anguish follows. Desdemona throws herself at his feet.

> Desd.: 'Kill me tomorrow, let me live tonight!' . . .
> 'But while I say one prayer!'
> Othello: 'It is too late.' [Smothers her.]

Othello rises from the deed, and looks wildly about him. Then comes the remorseful consciousness that he has been deceived. The prayer motif of Desdemona surges up from the overlying themes, this time in the deep tones of Othello. It is his turn to make his last prayer.

● CONCERTO FOR VIOLIN AND ORCHESTRA, IN A MINOR, OP. 53

Dvořák completed a first version of this concerto in 1879, revised it in the following year, and then sent it to Joachim (first aid to various composers for the violin at that period) for expert criticism. 'Joachim,' wrote Dvořák in 1882, was so kind as to make over the solo part.' And then Dvořák, still unsatisfied, did some further tinkering with his score. The concerto, properly enough, is dedicated 'to the great Master, Joseph Joachim, with deepest respect.'

The concerto has been described as follows:

There are the customary three movements, though the first and second are closely connected. The principal subject meets us at once in the first movement ('Allegro ma non troppo,' A minor, 4-4). It has two parts, the first of which is heard in the orchestra; the second, with a supplemental cadenza, in the solo voice. The second subject enters in an orchestral tutti built on the second part of the first theme; it is accompanied by a flowing counterpoint in the middle voice, which soon exchanges place with the melody and is then freely brought into notice. The violin then returns to the first motive, and carries it on at length. An episode soon makes its appearance in the shape of a lovely flowing melody for the solo instrument, which by means of an accompanied cadenza, leads back into the two principal subjects. A new and undulating melody is introduced. With a crescendo, it rises higher and higher in the scale, suddenly to return, in a charmingly graceful variation, Scherzando. These are the principal contents of the first movement.

The second movement follows without pause. The transition to this 'Adagio ma non troppo' (F major, 3-8) is formed by means of the principal subject. The movement is simple in construction. A long melody ushers it in, accompanied by counter-themes in the orchestra. Then follows a forceful, recitative-like second section, in which the violin and the orchestra are alternately prominent.

The Finale ('Allegro giocoso, ma non troppo,' A major, 3-8) consists of a series of dance tunes, national in character. Here again the composer exhibits his inexhaustible fund of melodies. Of these there are four which can be easily traced, as each one is of a pronounced individuality. There are many episodes which give to the solo performer opportunity to display digital skill. With all its contrasts, the movement is as bright and cheeful as possible, full of life and juvenile vigor, and replete with humor.

● CONCERTO FOR 'CELLO AND ORCHESTRA, IN B MINOR, OP. 104

Dvořák composed his 'cello concerto while he was sojourning in America—it dates from 1895, and was one of the last works that he wrote in this country. It was played for the first time at a London Philharmonic concert on March 19, 1896, when Dvořák conducted the orchestra and Leo Stern was the solo 'cellist.

Dvořák is said to have been helped in contriving certain of the bravura passages by the late Alwin Schroeder, the accomplished American 'cellist; and it was Schroeder who played the concerto for the first time in the United States, at a Boston Symphony concert on December 19, 1896. But it is also asserted that for some of the solo writing Hans Wihan (founder of the Bohemian String Quartet and teacher of the 'cello at the Conservatory of

Prague) was responsible. Dvořák dedicated the score to Wihan, but he seems to have been a bit anxious lest his friend should impose too many of his own ideas on the work, and he wrote to his publishers as follows:

> . . . I give you my work only if you will promise me that no one—not even my friend Wihan—shall make any alteration in it without my knowledge and permission; also that there be no cadenza such as Wihan has made in the last movement; and that its form shall be as I have felt it and thought it out. The cadenza in the last movement is not to exist either in the orchestral or the piano score; I informed Wihan, when he showed it to me, that it is impossible so to insert one. The finale closes gradually diminuendo—like a breath—with reminiscences of the first and second movements; the solo dies away to a pianissimo, then there is a crescendo, and the last measures are taken up by the orchestra, ending stormily. That was my idea, and from it I cannot recede.

The three movements are constituted as follows: I. Allegro, B minor, 4-4; II. 'Adagio ma non troppo,' G major, 3-4; III. 'Allegro moderato,' B minor, 2-4.

Edward Elgar
1857-1934

‡To say that Elgar is the most consequential creative figure in English music of the period from the death of Purcell (1695) to the present is to imply not his equality with that seventeenth-century master, but a startling and altogether inexplicable fact concerning the musical history of the English people. Ever in the vanguard of nations in recognizing and rewarding the great composers of Germany and Austria, of Russia and France, England has, in over two and a half centuries, produced none of her own. In relation to music, the English people have exhibited a highly developed faculty of appreciation, but their creativeness has been channeled into other arts. For over two hundred and fifty years, there has been no English composer of the first or even of the second grade. Even Elgar was a very minor master, though his countrymen did their best to convince him and themselves otherwise. Every honor at their disposal accrued to him during the last thirty years of his life, and he died a baronet. His music expresses a typically English sensibility in the idiom of late Central-European Romanticism; it has all the attractions that sincerity and expert craftsmanship, unallied to genius, could give it.‡

- Variations on an Original Theme (*Enigma*), op. 36

Elgar himself explained the scheme of these Variations at the time of their production in England. 'In this music,' he said, 'I have sketched, for their amusement and mine, the idiosyncrasies of fourteen of my friends. . .' The Variations are musical portraits of those friends. Strictly speaking, there are only thirteen, for the fourteenth Variation, the Finale, is a portrait of the composer himself.

Elgar never made a full and public confession of the identity of the friends whom he chose for his subjects. In the course of time, however, some of the truth leaked out, and the identity of certain of the originals has long been known to those concert-goers who read program notes. But only since Elgar's death in 1934 has this entire musical portrait gallery been opened to the public, with the correct names affixed to the tonal likenesses of the sitters. The facts were made known through the London *Musical Times* by one of Elgar's closest and oldest friends, the British musician Sir Ivor Atkins, long the organist of the cathedral at Worcester, Elgar's own city.

The first Variation, with its passionate tenderness and depth of feeling, is a portrait of the composer's wife; and those who knew the late Alice Elgar are at one in assuring us that the music of this Variation is a fitting tribute to the woman who was the mainstay and inspiration of her husband's life.

The initials at the head of the second Variation are those of H. D. Stuart Powell, a pianist whose trick of exercising his fingers before he got to work on the keyboard is idealized in the opening measures of Elgar's tonal description.

The third Variation pictures an amateur actor named Richard Baxter Townshend, who was remarkably clever at changing his deep voice into a realistic falsetto when he impersonated an old man. Elgar turns this trick to humorous account in his playful use of the woodwind in this Variation.

The fourth Variation brings before us, in its headlong impetuosity and its rather terrifying energy, an English country squire, Mr. William M. Baker, whose strenuous activities are amusingly reflected in Elgar's turbulent music.

The fifth Variation pictures Richard Arnold, son of the great English critic and poet, Matthew Arnold. Elgar's music makes clear to us the blend of dreaminess and vivacity which has been ascribed to its subject.

The sixth Variation is entitled 'Ysobel' in the score. It appears that the original 'Ysobel' is an amateur viola player, Miss Isabel Fitton, and Elgar has made the viola, that instrument of veiled and melancholy beauty, the heroine of this gravely lovely variation.

The seventh Variation, a Presto of furious energy, is devoted to another one of Elgar's excitable friends, Mr. Arthur Troyte Griffith, who liked to argue stormily with the composer.

Variation number eight is the picture of one of Elgar's closest friends, Miss Winifred Norbury, a patrician lady of the older generation who lived in a charming eighteenth-century house in the country outside Worcester. The gracious distinction and the light-hearted, blithe exquisiteness of Elgar's music suggest a miniature on tonal ivory.

The noble Adagio in E-flat major which constitutes the ninth Variation—the most profoundly felt and deeply expressive of the set—is a tribute to Elgar's music-loving friend, the late August Jaeger. Of this Variation, Elgar himself has said: 'It is a record of a long summer evening talk, when my friend Jaeger grew nobly eloquent—as only he could—on the grandeur of Beethoven, and especially of his slow movements.' In this Variation we seem to hear reflections of the mood, if not of the incomparable voice, of the Beethoven of certain slow movements; though the accent of this music is also exceptionally characteristic of Elgar's style, with its elevation and amplitude of speech, and is actually an unconscious tribute to the warmth and idealism of his own nature.

In the tenth Variation, the dance-like Intermezzo headed 'Dorabella,' we encounter Miss Penny, a lady whose conversation was marked by a pretty hesitation of speech, which Elgar's woodwind tactfully indicates in his portrait.

Miss Penny's delicate hesitancies are broken in upon by another one of those headlong Variations, number eleven, in which Elgar seemed to find so much amusement. This one, initialed 'G. R. S.,' has long been supposed to stand for Dr. George Robertson Sinclair, organist of Hereford Cathedral. But according to unimpeachable authority, this Variation is a composite portrait, and is actually devoted in large part not to Dr. Sinclair, but to Dr. Sinclair's bulldog, Dan. In order that the skeptical may be convinced, let us quote what Elgar's friend and associate, Sir Ivor Atkins, says about this eleventh Variation: 'Though this Variation,' he writes, 'bears the familiar initials of George Robertson Sinclair, the music is as much, perhaps a good deal more, a picture of Sinclair's bulldog, Dan. The Variation opens with a rushing, tumbling figure in the strings which shows us Dan hurling himself down the bank of the river. At bar 2 he is paddling against the current. At bar 5, Dan lands on the other side with a bark of fierce joy. The abrupt entry of the theme, fortissimo, on the brass, marks the appearance of his master on the scene, and the portrait at once recalls Sinclair's exuberant energy and buoyant spirit . . .' 'Thereafter,' concludes Sir Ivor, 'Dan becomes more and more active and engrossing.'

Well, why should not Elgar be allowed his musical bulldog? Dan is not the first canine to find a welcome in music's hospitable halls; and he has inspired Elgar to one of the most exhilarating pages in this score.

In the succeeding Variation, the twelfth, Elgar becomes again the poet that he usually is. The subject here is Basil Nevinson, a 'cellist, who used to take part in trios with Elgar and another friend; and this section is for the most part a solo for the 'cello, serving as a felicitous bridge to the most imaginative of all the Variations, number thirteen, entitled 'Romanza.' Elgar was thinking here of his friend Lady Mary Lygon, who, when the music was written, had embarked upon a voyage to Australia. Elgar himself said of this Variation: 'The soft tremor of the drums suggests the distant throb of the engines of a liner, over which the clarinet quotes a phrase from Mendelssohn's Overture, "Calm Sea and Prosperous Voyage," while the quiet undulations of the violas suggest the peaceful motion of the waters.'

The Finale of the Variations (number fourteen) is the composer's self-portrait. It has been said that this Finale portrays his own struggles and ideals; and the Variations end with music in which it is permissible to hear an utterance of the faith and fortitude of a truly valorous and heroic spirit, a great artist, and a noble mind.

- OVERTURE, *Cockaigne* ('In London Town'), OP. 40

This overture, published in 1901, was first performed at a concert of the London Philharmonic Society, at Queen's Hall, June 20, 1901, under the baton of the composer. The score is dedicated 'To My Many Friends, the Members of British Orchestras.'

There is no 'program' or argument printed in the score; but the music has been described as presenting a series of pictures of London life, by turns tender and humorous, reflective and boisterous. There is a nobilmente theme 'representing the stronger side of the London character'; there are 'easy-going' Londoners strolling through St. James's Park; there are street urchins, and a Salvation Army band that plays excruciatingly out of time; and there is what an analyst reassuringly called 'a love theme proper.'

The scoring is for two flutes (the second interchangeable with a piccolo), two oboes, two clarinets, two bassoons, double-bassoon, four horns, two trumpets, two cornets, three trombones, tuba, three kettledrums, bass drum, cymbals, triangle, side drum, bells, tambourine, organ, and strings.

- INTRODUCTION AND ALLEGRO FOR STRINGS, OP. 47

This work was published in 1905, performed for the first time anywhere at Queen's Hall, London, March 8, 1905, by the London Symphony Orchestra, and for the first time in America by the Chicago Symphony Orchestra, under Frederick Stock, March 23-24, 1906.

The composition follows in general the classic pattern of the concerto grosso form, in which a group of solo instruments is combined and contrasted with the orchestral tutti. In this instance the solo group, or concertino (as it would have been called in the eighteenth century), consists of a solo string quartet, with the main body of strings (all divided) as the supporting and contrasting tutti.

The composer is said to have told Ernest Newman, the English musical critic and essayist, that this work had its origin in Wales, 'when he was impressed by the sound of distant singing, in which the cadence of a falling third caught his fancy. From the train of thought thus generated sprang the main theme of the work—the pseudo-Welsh tune. Later on, a song heard in the valley of the Wye reinforced the Welsh impressions, and led to the completion of the work.'

The work opens fortissimo with a vigorous subject given to both groups of strings (Moderato, G minor, 4-4). At the sixteenth measure, the 'Welsh tune,' with its 'falling third,' is heard on the solo viola. The Introduction terminates with a pause. The Allegro is begun by the orchestra, with the chief subject announced, *pp*, by the first violins. A second theme is presented, staccato, by the quartet. Later, the second violins initiate a fugato. In the recapitulation section, the Welsh tune, now heard in G major, is played by the combined strings, fortissimo and 'molto sostenuto.'

The score is dedicated to Elgar's friend, the late Professor S. S. Sanford of Yale University. It was in the year of the composition of this work that Elgar paid his first visit to the United States. On June 28, 1905, Yale conferred upon him the degree of Doctor of Music.

• SERENADE FOR STRING ORCHESTRA, OP. 20

This work was published in 1893, in Elgar's thirty-sixth year. Colles in his biography of the composer assigns Elgar's music of the early 'nineties to 'the beginning of his public career,' which was inaugurated by the production of the *Froissart* Overture (op. 19) in 1890. Yet it was only half a dozen years after the appearance of the Serenade for String Orchestra (op. 20) in 1893 that Elgar put forth one of his most vital and characteristic works, the 'Enigma' Variations, first played under Richter at St. James's Hall on June 19, 1899.

Elgar himself thought well of the Serenade. He remarked, more than ten years later, after he had added to his products such mature scores as *The Dream of Gerontius*, the *Cockaigne* Overture, and *The Apostles*: 'I like it as well as anything I have done.'

The Serenade is in three movements, transparently simple in structure, yet composed with that richness and subtlety of texture which Elgar had already learned how to achieve.

The first movement ('Allegro piacevole,' E minor, 6-8) introduces at the third measure the chief theme, a subject making expressive use of rising and falling phrases for the violins, with a middle section in E major.

The second movement is a Larghetto in C major, 2-4 time, with a typically Elgarian melody leading off in the first violins, in which again we hear the rising and falling phrases. This characteristic, which might almost be called the melodic hallmark of the composer's thought in this score, appears once more in the design of the phrases from which the final Allegretto springs—an engaging movement in 12-8 time beginning in G major and ending in E major. In the closing section, the second part of the first movement is recalled.

César Auguste Franck

1822-90

F

‡'The life of Franck,' Percy Scholes reminds us, 'was that of a saint—but of a "cheerful saint," as a friend records of him, "always crackling with wit and repartee." He rose early, lived simply, and set aside a period every day for quiet meditation.' He was the son of a Belgian banker who, oddly

enough, did not oppose but countenanced and encouraged the musical
inclinations of his two sons, César and his brother Joseph. He received
his training as an organist and composer at the Paris Conservatory, and
later he taught there; for forty years he served as organist at the Church
of Ste. Clothilde, in Paris. He composed prodigiously, but much of his
early music is of a triviality and banality passing description; there is in
it scarcely a hint of the latent capacity that, in the last decade of his life,
was to produce the Symphony in D minor, the Symphonic Variations for
Piano and Orchestra, and that small handful of chamber and piano music
upon which today his fame securely rests. It is not surprising that recognition as a composer was long denied him, and that when at last it was
given, it was given grudgingly and sparingly. His consolations, while he
lived, were his faith in God, his modesty, and the devotion of his pupils.‡

● SYMPHONY IN D MINOR

'I shall go on with them as soon as I get better,' said César Franck on his
deathbed, thinking of the uncompleted versicles of his *Magnificat*—'or else,'
he added in a lower tone, 'perhaps God will let me finish them in His eternity
to come.'

In another man, the remark might have been the semi-mechanical repetition
of a pious formula; but for César Franck the words unquestionably corresponded to a deep and intense conviction of the spirit. Romain Rolland, who
knew him well—'well enough to love him,' as he says, 'and to catch a glimpse
of the beauty and serenity of his soul'—has told us how remarkable was the
completeness and assurance of Franck's religious faith: a faith which knew
no doubts, which was the mainspring of his life. The purity, the otherworldli-
ness, the exalted mysticism of César Franck the man, are reflected in much
of his music—in the *Beatitudes*; in the *Redemption*, in portions of the symphony. Through this music—to the imagination of his pupil, Vincent d'Indy
(himself a man of faith and aspiration, a medieval Christian)—stream 'troops
of angels as purely imagined as Filippo Lippi's or Fra Angelico's.'

It is easy for the sympathetic to perceive in this often spiritualized and
touching music those luminous beings that brightened the shadows of the
organ loft where the devout and humble Franck mused and played and mused
again. One imagines him as he sat there for so many years, alone, but not
alone, companioned by ineffable presences, absorbed above his keyboard,
'singing forth in a low voice,' like that old mystic of so different a type, Jona-
than Edwards, his 'contemplations of the Creator'; for to César Franck all
life and all nature discoursed of divine and immortal things.

Yet Rolland thinks that perhaps there was more trouble in the depths of
Franck's heart than the valiant serenity of his exterior would lead one to
believe, and he warns us particularly in the case of the Symphony to beware
of seeking in it only the expression of a transfigured and rapturous exaltation.
'I ask those who love this music because they find some of their own sadness

reflected there,' says Rolland, 'whether they have not felt the secret tragedies that some of his passages unfold—those phrases that seem to rise in suppli- cation to God and often fall back in sadness and in tears. It is not all light in that soul; but the light that is there does not affect us less because it shines from afar.'

Vincent d'Indy, in his admirable Life of César Franck, describes the cir- cumstances of the first performance of this symphony. The première was at a Conservatoire concert in Paris, February 17, 1889. (Franck had completed the score in August of the previous year.)

The performance [writes D'Indy] was against the wish of most members of the famous orchestra, and was accomplished only through the benevolent obstinacy of the conductor, Jules Garcin. The subscribers could make neither head nor tail of the symphony, and the musical authorities were in much the same position. I inquired of one of them—a professor at the Conservatoire, and a kind of factotum on the Com- mittee—what he thought of the work. 'That a symphony!' he replied in contemptuous tones. 'But, my dear sir, who ever heard of writing for the English horn in a symphony? Just mention a single symphony by Haydn or Beethoven introducing the English horn. There, well, you see—your Franck's music may be whatever you please, but it will certainly never be a symphony!' This was the attitude of the Conservatoire in the year of grace, 1889.

At another door of the concert hall, the composer of *Faust*, escorted by a train of adulators, male and female, fulminated a kind of papal decree to the effect that this symphony was the affirmation of incompetence pushed to dogmatic lengths. For sin- cerity and disinterestedness we must turn to the composer himself when, on his return from the concert, his whole family surrounded him, asking eagerly for news. 'Well, were you satisfied with the effect on the public? Was there plenty of applause?' To which 'Father' Franck, thinking only of his work, replied with a beaming countenance: 'Oh, it sounded well, just as I thought it would!'

In one of Flaubert's letters to Madame X, he complains somewhat petu- lantly that 'the French mind has such a rage for amusement that it is neces- sary for it always to be seeing things!' Is there something in the French mind, some passion for externalization and objectivity, that, on its musical side, has seemed to disincline it toward the essential inwardness of the symphony—that type of symphony which is an exposition of spiritual history; not the dramatiz- ing, pictorializing symphony of Berlioz? 'In France,' said Henri Duparc, pupil of César Franck, 'we have too great a love for dramatic music. Dramatic music is an . . . inferior species, which does not allow the artist to express himself directly.'

Certainly it is a significant commentary upon the trend of the French musi- cal mind that a symphony which was composed only six years after the aging necromancer of Bayreuth had added the last touches to the score of *Parsifal*, should remain, more than half a century later, in unchallenged pre-eminence as the crown of symphonic art in France; and this symphony was written by a composer born in Belgium.

There are, of course, other and variously admirable French symphonies besides the outstanding one that was composed by a Belgian—among those of our time, there are the symphonies of Saint-Saëns, Chausson, D'Indy, Dukas, Roussel—to name but a few. Yet the fact remains that, speaking with rough truth, there is still, for the contemporary concert world, but one French symphony that is sufficiently compensating to reward inexhaustibly, year after year, the attention of performers and listeners; and that is the D minor Symphony of Franck.

'Majestic, plastic, perfectly beautiful,' are D'Indy's characterizing words for his master's score. But one can think of other symphonies that are majestic and plastic and perfect in beauty. It is less, one fancies, because of the quality of its musical tissue, than because of that which the music conveys to us, that one returns to Franck's symphony again and again without satiety.

'All our age,' said Mallarmé, 'is full of the trembling of the veil of the temple.' Sometimes, as for César Franck in this symphony, the veil is withdrawn, and we become suddenly aware that we are listening to one who has received unspeakable intimations—we hear the echo of immortal promises and confirmations. 'These are they which came out of great tribulation. . . They shall hunger no more, neither thirst any more. . . And they sung as it were a new song before the throne. . .'

● SYMPHONIC VARIATIONS, FOR PIANO AND ORCHESTRA

Vincent d'Indy, a pupil of César Franck, expresses the opinion in his admirable study of the Belgian master that the *Variations symphoniques* for piano and orchestra are 'a continuation of the amplification of this form which Beethoven began with such a master hand.' The work was composed in 1885, and belongs to the great 'Third Period' of Franck's creative activity, which extended from 1872 to his death. It stands in order of composition between the *Prelude, Chorale and Fugue* for piano (1884), and the *Prelude, Aria and Finale* (1886-7), both of them milestones in the history of piano music. The work was performed for the first time at the Salle Pleyel, Paris, on May 1, 1886, by Louis Diémer. The music was published in a two-piano arrangement shortly after its composition; but the full score did not appear until 1894.

One of Diémer's most eminent pupils, Alfred Cortot, has thus introduced the *Variations symphoniques:*

The *Variations symphoniques*, though not involving so potent an ideal as the *Prelude, Chorale and Fugue*, the Quartet, or the first movement of the Symphony, is assuredly, with the Sonata for pianoforte and violin, the most perfect—not the most beautiful, but the most lucid and finished—of Franck's artistic realizations. Here both balance and proportion are ideal. The role of the pianoforte in relation to the orchestra shows an understanding of its resources and an unusual regard for its limitations. Both union and contrast of tone-color are so spontaneous that as the work proceeds one feels that the music has found, in the combination of soloist and orchestra, not only its most fortunate, but its sole means of expression.

From the outset of the *Variations symphoniques*, as a kind of introduction, Franck shows the conflict between the two elements of his theme: the vehement and almost aggressive rhythm of the strings, and the answering melodic supplication of the pianoforte. Immediately there is created the general tendency of the work, which is to appeal rather to the heart than to the brain.

We are thus led up to a dramatic development in which we see these two elements in turn clashing or uniting, opposing or blending with each other, without loss of individuality.

• SYMPHONIC POEM, *Le Chasseur maudit*

Le Chasseur maudit, composed in 1883, tells the story of Bürger's ballad, *Der wilde Jäger*. The following argument is prefaced to the score of Franck's symphonic poem:

'Twas a Sunday morning; far away resounded the joyous sound of bells and the joyous chants of the crowd. . . Sacrilege! The savage Count of the Rhine is winding his horn.
Hallo! Hallo! The chase rushes over corn-fields, moors, and meadows.—'Stop, Count, I entreat you; hear the pious chants!'—'No!' Hallo! Hallo!
'Stop, Count, I implore you; take care!'—'No!' and the riders rush on like a whirl-wind.
Suddenly the Count is alone; his horse refuses to go further; the Count would wind his horn, but the horn no longer sounds. . . A dreadful, implacable voice pronounces a curse [according to César Franck, the bass tuba is the chosen instrument of Satan]: 'Sacrilegious man,' it cries, 'be forever hunted by Hell!'
Then flames flash all around him. . . The Count, terror-stricken, flees faster and even faster, pursued by a pack of demons . . . by day across abysses, by night through the air.

In the music there is first the portrayal of the serene Sabbath landscape, the chanting chorus; there is pealing of bells, and the sacred song rises to a climax.

Then follows the entry of the sacrilegious huntsmen, led by the Count; the chase is portrayed, and we hear the appeals of the frightened peasants.

The Count, suddenly left alone, attempts in vain to wind his horn; then, in uncanny and terrifying tones, the curse is pronounced.

The Infernal Chase begins, there are wild horn calls; the pace grows more and more precipitate until the close.

• SYMPHONIC POEM, *Les Eolides*

Les Eolides, composed in 1876, was Franck's first venture into orchestral music. It had its earliest hearing on May 13, 1877, at a concert of the Société Nationale in Paris. In 1882 Lamoureux produced it at one of his concerts, and he performed it again in 1894.

Georges Servières is authority for the statement that Franck employed as a program for his *Eolides* the 'exquisite lines of Leconte de Lisle.' But the score does not claim this. Nor can it be said that the music conforms in details to the poem.

In his note on *Les Eolides*, as published in the program of the Philharmonic Society on February 21, 1918, Mr. Humiston called attention to the fact that 'Aeolus (a Greek word meaning rapidly turning or moving) was the god of the winds,' and that 'he had six sons and six daughters,' although De Lisle's poem refers only to the latter.

W. F. Apthorp, at one time the brilliant annotator of the Boston Symphony Orchestra's programs, made a prose translation of De Lisle's lines. A few excerpts may serve to give an impression of the verses that inspired Franck:

Skimming over the crystal waters like a swift flock of swallows, do ye return to the green reed-grass of Eurotas, faithful Virgins?

The air where murmurs your flight is filled with aroma and harmony; do ye return from Ionia, where is the green Hymettus and honey of gold?

Hail Aeolidae! Cool messengers, it is ye, indeed, who sang over the cradles of the Gods; and the clear Ilyssos has bathed the down of your light wings in a melodious wave.

Under the plane-tree where one is sheltered from the fiery darts of day, ye sighed of love upon the lips of Theocritus.

Ye who once floated to the lips of genius, breezes of the divine months, visit us once more; pour out to us as ye pass, from your golden urns, repose and love, grace and harmony!

Michael Ivanovich Glinka

1803-57

G

‡Glinka's importance in the history of Russian music greatly exceeds the value of his personal contribution to it. He was almost literally the father of Russian music as we know it, for in the history of the development of the art in his country no name survives of earlier date than his, and it would be difficult to overestimate the influence he personally exerted on the generation of Russian composers who immediately succeeded him, and whom he knew and proselytized as young men. There had been music in Russia before him; but it had been largely Italian music, French music, German music. Glinka was almost the first to whom it occurred to graft this exotic art on native stock. Balakireff, and through him Rimsky and Borodin, Tchaikovsky and Moussorgsky, were all clearly conscious of their enormous debt to Glinka: as well they may have been, for it was he who established the conditions that made possible their development as essentially Russian musicians.‡

- *Kamarinskaya*: Fantasia for Orchestra

'Kamarinskaya' is the name of a Russian dance, which is accompanied by sung words that inquisitive translators have been advised to leave in the original tongue. Glinka's fantasy, composed in 1848, is built upon two Russian folk tunes: a wedding-song, 'Over the Hills, the High Hills,' and the dance-song, the 'Kamarinskaya.' There are subsidiary themes.

The piece begins 'Moderato, ma energico,' in D minor, 3-4 time, with a few introductory bars; then the wedding-song is heard from the strings, afterward by the woodwind. There is development ('Allegro moderato,' D major, 2-4), and then, after brief preluding, the dance-song is begun by the first

violins. The melody of the Kamarinskaya song is akin to the Russian air used
by Beethoven in his piano variations published in 1797, a tune actually derived
by Beethoven from Wranitzky's ballet, *Das Waldmädchen*, given at Vienna,
September 28, 1796.

Glinka in his Autobiography says that he was guided in composing this
work exclusively by 'his inner musical feelings, with never a thought of what
goes on at rustic weddings, nor to the revels of our orthodox people, nor to
the belated drunkards who go knocking at the doors of huts to be let in.
Nevertheless, a critic assures me that at the rehearsal of *Kamarinskaya*, the
Czar [who was present] told him that in the last section of the work, where
the first horn holds a pedal on F-sharp, and then the trumpet on C, there was
intended a realistic representation of the tipsy peasants, hammering on their
cottage doors. This idea seemed to me vastly amusing, as it would never have
occurred to me in my life.'

Tchaikovsky confided to his diary in 1888 the conviction that '*Kamarinskaya*
is a work of remarkable inspiration. Without intending to compose anything
beyond a simple, humorous trifle, Glinka has left us a little masterpiece, every
measure of which is the outcome of immense creative power.'

- OVERTURE TO A *Life for the Czar*
- OVERTURE TO *Russlan and Ludmilla*

Riemann (not altogether happily, perhaps) called Glinka the 'Berlioz of the
Russians.' The generous Rubinstein classed him with Bach, Beethoven, and
Schubert. Tchaikovsky declared him—more moderately—to be 'a true creative
genius,' though the 'Slavsia' (the great national chorus in A *Life for the
Czar*) he ranked with 'the work of the greatest geniuses.' Glinka, he wrote in
a letter to his patroness, Mme von Meck [see the notes below, on Tchaikovsky,
for the history of the relations of these two], 'is quite an unusual phenomenon!
Reading his Memoirs, which reveal a nice, amiable, but commonplace man,
we can hardly realize that the same mind created the wonderful "Slavsia"! . . .
Glinka was a gifted Russian aristocrat of his time, and had the faults of his
type: petty vanity, limited culture, intolerance, ostentatiousness, and a morbid
sensibility to and impatience with criticism. . . Yet he composed the "Slavsia." '

But Tchaikovsky wrote in another letter to Mme von
Meck, 'in spite of their astonishing and original beauty, suffer from glaring
irregularities of style. Side by side with touches of genius and passages of
imperishable beauty, we find childish and weak numbers. What might not
Glinka have accomplished had he lived amid different surroundings, had he
worked like an artist who, fully alive to his power and duty, develops his
gifts to the ultimate limit of perfection, rather than as an amateur who makes
music his pastime!'

But Tchaikovsky seems to have wavered a good deal in his opinion of
Glinka. At one moment he dismisses him as an 'average amateur,' and at the
next, he is on his knees before him. 'A dilettante who played the violin and
the piano a little'—he remarks impatiently; 'who concocted a few insipid
quadrilles and fantasies on Italian airs; who tried his hand at more serious

musical forms, but accomplished nothing which rose superior to the jejune taste of the 'thirties; suddenly, in his thirty-fourth year, he creates an opera [A *Life for the Czar*] which, for inspiration, originality, and irreproachable technique, is worthy to stand beside all that is loftiest and most profound in musical art.' A dozen years later, Tchaikovsky remarked to the Grand Duke Constantine Constantinovich that 'if Glinka had been a cobbler, rather than a gentleman, he would have given us, besides his two very beautiful operas, perhaps fifteen others, and ten fine symphonies into the bargain.' Can there, then, be no gentlemanly genius? It seems a cruel verdict.

Glinka's first opera, A *Life for the Czar*, produced before the Imperial family at St. Petersburg in December 1836, was an immediate success—though some 'aristocrats' (as Newmarch calls them), 'sneering at the national coloring of the work, spoke of it as "the music of coachmen"'; but it was generally felt that the opera marked a new aesthetic departure—the birth of an authentic school of Russian music. Then Glinka set to work upon *Russlan and Ludmilla*, which was completed slowly and in the midst of many difficulties. Glinka used a libretto based upon Pushkin's like-named poem. The poet himself had given his help in the construction of the book of the opera, but he was killed in a duel before his task was ended, and the libretto, a thing of shreds and patches, was laboriously completed with the help of various Russian men of letters (Koukolnik, Gedeonoff, and others, besides Glinka himself). The opera was produced December 10, 1842.

The opera tells the story of Ludmilla, the lovely daughter of Prince Svietozar of Kiev. Among Ludmilla's three suitors, Russlan was her favorite; but their union was prevented by the abduction of Ludmilla, who had fallen into the hands of the magician Chernomor. The three knightly suitors were dispatched by Ludmilla's father in search of her, with the promise of her hand as their reward. Russlan was the fortunate rescuer of the lady, but as he was homeward bound with her, they were intercepted by one of the unsuccessful suitors, who left Russlan asleep under a magic spell, bore home the maiden, and demanded his reward. But Russlan awoke in time to foil the plot, and the outcome was precisely what it should have been.

In the overture, use is made of thematic material from the finale of the opera, and of an air sung by Russlan in the second act. One of its most interesting features is the employment (in the coda) of the whole-tone scale, wherewith Glinka anticipated Dargomyshky's use of the device in *The Stone Guest* by twenty years, and Debussy's much more celebrated employment of it by half a century.

Christoph Willibald von Gluck

1714-87

G

‡Apparently the seed of corruption was implanted in opera in the earliest times, for it has always exhibited a tendency to descend from the plane of lofty art to that of trivial entertainment. Strong-minded reformers have been needed to keep it in line, and Gluck was one of these. But he did not begin as one. The first operas of this German-born 'French' composer were in the popular Italian manner of his day. He was nearly fifty when he saw the light and produced, in *Orfeo ed Euridice*, the first of a series of masterpieces that were to restore dignity and serious purpose to a degraded art form. The nature of the reforms instituted by Gluck is discussed below. It is necessary to add here only that he was not merely a theoretician of great influence, he was also a composer of genius. If today *Orfeo* and the two *Iphigénies*, *Armide, and Alceste* still hold the stage, it is not because of their form and style, which have only a historical importance, but because of the magnificent (a word here used with some apprehension of its true meaning) music that they incorporate.‡

• *Orfeo ed Euridice*

It was almost two centuries ago that Gluck, impatient with the inanities of Italian opera, perceived that the first step in the reform which seemed to him imperative was the choice of a libretto capable of interesting a reasonably adult mind. At Vienna, shortly after 1762, he might well have paralleled the remark of Grétry about the opera in Rome: 'When anybody went there, it was to hear this or that singer; but when the latter was no longer on the stage, everyone retired to his box to play cards and eat ices, while the pit yawned.' Years earlier, Marcello had written his scarifying satire upon the intellectual degradation of the Italian stage.

But Gluck, from the first, had had vague leanings toward the ideal of making opera a more dramatic and reasonable thing than it was in his time. Even in his first opera, *Artaserse* (1741), he dared to be dramatic in a rudimentary way. It was long, however, before he succeeded in working out a definite and viable formula; his innovations were essentially evolutionary. Yet what he did in his works prior to *Orfeo*, as W. F. Apthorp has pointed out, 'was new enough to scare the critics, who, as academic policemen, guarded nothing more carefully than the inviolability of traditional forms.'

Gluck in his middle years was an earnest student of art and literature. His associates in Vienna were men of cultivated tastes and habits. It was inevitable that Gluck, with his vigorous and challenging mind, should have come to realize, by the time he had reached his forty-ninth year, that the libretto of the Italian opera of that day, with its extreme intellectual economy and its general and incurable idiocy, would be of no use to him in the operatic reforms which he projected. He met, about 1760, the Italian man of letters, Raniero de' Calzabigi, who, born in Livorno in 1715, and having dwelt for a time in Paris, where he edited Metastasio's works, went to Vienna in 1761. Calzabigi had made some name for himself as a critic and poet. He had edited Dante and had expounded his notions of dramatic consistency in a two-hundred-word preface to a collection of his poems.

Obviously, he was Gluck's man. Together they worked upon the text of *Orfeo ed Euridice,* a labor to which Gluck now assiduously applied himself. Gluck's share in the preparation of the libretto is not definitely known. It was in all likelihood a supervisory one. Doubtless he saw to it that fatuous clichés and sham sentiment were excluded; that the recitatives were made as faithful to dramatic truth as possible; that the arias became expressive and the choruses at least as vital as those of Rameau, whose *Castor et Pollux* was probably not far from Gluck's thoughts when he set out to compose *Orfeo.*

The completed work, *Orfeo ed Euridice,* was brought out at the Vienna Burgtheater on October 5, 1762. The performance has been described as 'the first cannon-shot of the new operatic Revolution.' The première, as might have been expected, aroused some opposition, and opened very wide the eyes of the Viennese. But the antagonism subsided, and by the time the work reached its fifth performance, its place was definitely assured. It conquered the public even in Italy, and (as Desnoiresterres records) 'at Parma itself, Traetta, one of the greatest masters of that time, was unable to have his *Armide* performed; the public wished only to hear *Orfeo.*'

Ernest Newman, in his admirable study of Gluck, points out that the composer was impeded in the carrying out of his musico-dramatic reforms by various compromises and contradictions resulting from his acceptance of a poorly constructed libretto, and his irresolute attitude toward certain conventions of his time. Yet the music of *Orfeo* prevails and persuades after nearly two centuries, overcoming us by its beauty and power and truth of dramatic utterance. The score from which Gluck conducted the first Vienna performance bears the title, *Orfeo, Dramma per Musica.* . . That is a truthful description. The drama has been caught up into the music, translated into eloquent and exalting tone, so that, granting the premises of their period, their style, and their intention, the drama *is* the music, and the music the drama—the two are fused and identical.

‡The action of *Orfeo* is extremely simple. In the first act, Orpheus (contralto) mourns at the grave of his beloved Eurydice (soprano), and receives the permission of the gods to seek her in Hades and restore her to earth on condition that he does not look at her during the journey. In the second act, overcoming the menaces of the Furies, he passes through Hades, finds Eurydice in Elysium, and begins the return journey to earth. In the third, Eurydice, on

the return journey, implores Orpheus to look at her, to speak to her. Orpheus cannot resist; he turns to her, and she expires. Orpheus, in despair, would kill himself and follow her. But the gods relent, Eurydice is restored to life and reunited with Orpheus.

The opera is interspersed with ballets, and these are often excerpted for concert performance; the most famous is the 'Dance of the Blessed Spirits,' which occurs in the scene in the Elysian fields. Concert performances of the opera in its entirety are not infrequent.‡

● Overture to *Alceste*

One of Gluck's friends, the printer Corancez, sought out the composer in the wings of the theater after the failure of *Alceste* upon its performance in Paris, April 23, 1776. Corancez desired to condole with the unfortunate author, but he found Gluck in an argumentative and expository mood, and not particularly cast down.

Gluck discussed with Corancez the fate of his opera. 'The failure of such a piece is very odd,' he said, 'and will be an epoch in the history of your country's taste. I can imagine a piece composed in some particular musical style succeeding or not succeeding—it would be a matter of the audience's variable taste. I can also imagine a piece of that kind having an enormous success at first, and then quickly falling out of favor in the presence, so to speak, and with the consent, of its first admirers. But I admit I am bothered to know why a piece should fail when it is stamped with the truth of nature, and when all the passions have their true expression.' '*Alceste*'—he added proudly—'is not the kind of work to give momentary pleasure or to please because it is new. Time does not exist for it, and I claim that it will give equal pleasure two hundred years hence, if the French language does not change. My reason is that the piece is founded upon nature and has nothing whatever to do with fashion.'

Alceste had followed five years after *Orfeo*. Calzabigi supplied the text. When the work was given in 1776 in Paris, Gluck altered the libretto in some respects, particularly at the end, 'where Calzabigi's conclusion is dispensed with and a new character, Hercules, is introduced as *deus ex machina*,' the words being supplied by Du Roullet.

The Overture to *Alceste* was characterized by Ernest Newman, in his penetrating study of Gluck, as 'a notable triumph of dramatic expression, and is all the more remarkable by its complete contrast with the aimless futility of the overture to *Orfeo*. Gluck's hold upon dramatic feeling is admirable at all times, and nowhere, perhaps, has he maintained this hold with such consummate power as in the Overture to *Alceste*.'

● Overture to *Iphigénie en Aulide*

'The famous Gluck, who is celebrated throughout all Europe,' wrote the accomplished Du Roullet in August 1772 to Dauvergne, the Director of the Académie Royale de Musique, 'has written a French opera, which he earnestly desires to have brought out in Paris . . . after having written more than forty

Italian operas, which have had the greatest success in every theater where that language is admitted.' The opera was *Iphigénie en Aulide,* the text adapted by Du Roullet from the tragedy of Racine, which in its turn was derived from Euripides. It was performed at the Opéra, Paris, on April 19th, 1774.

Racine perverted the play of Euripides to some extent, especially in his alteration of the dénouement, which supplies a happily domestic finish for Iphigenia through her marriage with Achilles, and provides a new character, Eriphile, to fill the place of Euripides' hind. Du Roullet, in amending Racine's drama, dropped Eriphile out of the action. It is made known that the gods have received enough attention; Iphigenia is restored to the family circle, and the opera ends cheerfully with ballets and a chorus.

Gluck had his troubles in producing the work. Orchestra, singers, ballet, were grossly inefficient; disorder and abuse reigned throughout the establishment, without protest; and the actors and actresses 'pushed indecency to such a point as to appear outside the scenes, the actresses in white camisoles with *une culotte d'argent,* the actors in a simple dressing-gown.' The orchestra was like 'an old coach drawn by consumptive horses, and led by one deaf from his birth.' The singers roared and yelped and shrieked, behaving as if in the throes of convulsions. Vestris wanted to introduce a chaconne at the end of the opera. 'A chaconne!' exclaimed Gluck, 'whenever did the Greeks dance a chaconne?' 'Did they not?' replied Vestris commiseratingly; 'then so much the worse for them!' But the production, when it was at length effected, added greatly to the fame of Gluck. The opera became the vogue, and the ladies of Paris adopted a coiffure which is thus described by Gustave Desnoiresterres: 'A headdress in the form of a coronet of black flowers surmounted by the crescent of Diana, whence escaped a kind of veil that covered the back of the head; it was called *à l'Iphigénie.'*

Richard Wagner considered the Overture to *Iphigenia in Aulis* 'Gluck's most perfect instrumental piece.' The original overture has no conclusion, but leads without pause into Agamemnon's opening recitative and air, 'Pitiless Diana, in vain dost thou command this fearful sacrifice.' A conclusion for the overture was written in 1854 by Wagner (a finale of thirty-three measures). Wagner also expatiated, at considerable length, upon the emotional, dramatic, and musical significance of the overture. Among other things, he observed that 'the whole content of Gluck's overture appeared [to him] as follows:

(1) A motive of Appeal, from out a gnawing anguish of the heart.
(2) A motive of Power, of imperious, overbearing demand.
(3) A motive of Grace, of maidenly tenderness.
(4) A motive of Sorrowing, of agonizing pity.
The whole compass of the overture is filled by nothing but the constant interchange of these motives, linked together by a few subsidiary themes derived from them.'

● BALLET SUITE (*Arranged by Felix Mottl*)

The movements of this suite were put together by Felix Mottl from operas by Gluck. The score of the suite was published in 1900. The first movement combines two contrasting passages ('Air gai' and a Lento) from *Iphigénie en*

Aulide (1774), with an introductory passage taken from Gluck's ballet-opera, *Don Juan, oder das steinerne Gastmahl* (words by Angiolini), produced at Vienna in 1761, portions of which were afterward utilized by Gluck in his *Armide* and *Iphigénie en Aulide*.

The second excerpt is the famous 'Dance of the Blessed Spirits' from the second act of *Orfeo ed Euridice* (1762), arranged by Mottl for strings, two horns, two flutes and English horn. The following number is the 'Musette' from *Armide* (1777), scored for strings, woodwind, horns, and trumpets. The concluding number is an 'Air gai,' again from *Iphigénie en Aulide*, coupled with a Sicilienne from *Armide*.

Edvard Hagerup Grieg

1843-1907

‡No one will dispute Grieg's pre-eminence among Norwegian composers. Sinding scarcely measures beside him, and who else is there? However, it is not to lack of competition only that Grieg owes his position. His quality is undeniable. He had an incxhaustible fund of melody (for he drew much less than is generally supposed on folk music for his themes), an original harmonic sense, and the intelligence to work for the most part in the small forms that were best suited to the sort of communication he had to make. He was recognized and admired by Liszt and others of the great of his day, and he achieved without effort an enormous popularity with the public at large. None of Grieg's compositions is in the class of great masterpieces, but a number are deservedly among the most popular ever penned.‡

● CONCERTO FOR PIANO AND ORCHESTRA, IN A MINOR, OP. 16

Grieg's only concerto for piano belongs to his twenty-fifth year (he lived to be sixty-four). It was composed in 1868, during a vacation spent in the Danish village of Sölleröd. Henry T. Finck in his book on Grieg remarks upon its 'juvenile freshness of invention combined with mature technical skill. . . It is a model in the way it avoids both of the common defects of being either a symphony with piano accompaniment, or a show-piece for the soloist with orchestral accompaniment. . . The first movement is replete with beautiful, haunting melody, and nothing could be more lovely than the orchestral introduction to the slow movement—one of the saddest preludes ever written: a prelude illustrating Grieg's gift of creating an emotional atmosphere with the simplest means.' Finck thinks that this concerto 'has perhaps done more even than the *Peer Gynt* Suites to establish the fame of its composer.'

Franz Liszt wrote warmly to Grieg in 1868 concerning his Sonata in F for Piano and Violin, op. 8, and this praise from the mighty Franz (wholly unsolicited by Grieg) was instrumental in procuring from the Norwegian Government a grant of money which made it possible for Grieg to travel abroad. He was thus enabled to accept the invitation of Liszt to visit him, and in the following year he met Liszt in Rome. In a letter written to his parents, Grieg described as follows his experiences [the translation is from Finck's entertaining and valuable book]:

I had fortunately just received the manuscript of my pianoforte concerto from Leipzig, and I took it with me. Besides myself there were present Winding, Sgambati and a German Lisztite, whose name I do not know, but who goes so far in the aping of his idol that he even wears the gown of an abbe; add to these a Chevalier de Concilium, and some young ladies of the kind that would like to eat Liszt, skin, hair and all; their adulation is simply comical. . . Winding and I were very anxious to see if he would really play my concerto at sight. I, for my part, considered it impossible; not so Liszt. 'Will you play?' he asked, and I made haste to reply: 'No, I cannot' (you know I have never practised it). Then Liszt took the manuscript, went to the piano, and said to the assembled guests, with his characteristic smile, 'Very well, then, I will show you that I also cannot.' With that he began. I admit that he took the first part of the concerto too fast, and the beginning sounded helter-skelter but later on, when I had a chance to indicate the tempo, he played as only he can play. It is significant that he played the cadenza, the most difficult part, best of all. His demeanor is worth any price to see. Not content with playing, he, at the same time, converses and makes comments, addressing a bright remark now to one, now to another of the assembled guests, nodding significantly to the right or left, particularly when something pleases him. In the Adagio, and still more in the Finale, he reached a climax, both as to his playing and the praise he had to bestow.

A really divine episode I must not forget. Toward the end of the Finale the second theme is, as you may remember, repeated in a mighty fortissimo. In the very last measures, when in the first triplets the first tone is changed in the orchestra from G-sharp to G, while the piano part, in a mighty scale passage, rushes wildly through the whole reach of the keyboard, he suddenly stopped, rose up to his full height, left the piano, and with big, theatric strides and arms uplifted walked across the large cloister hall, at the same time literally roaring the theme. When he got to the G in question he stretched out his arms imperiously and exclaimed 'G, G, not G-sharp! Splendid! . . .' In conclusion, he handed me the manuscript, and said in a peculiarly cordial tone: 'Keep steadily on; I tell you, you have the capability, and—do not let them intimidate you.'

This final admonition was of tremendous importance to me; there was something in it that seemed to give it an air of sanctification. At times, when disappointment and bitterness are in store for me, I shall recall his words, and the remembrance of that hour will have a wonderful power to uphold me in days of adversity.

● Two Elegiac Melodies for String Orchestra, op. 34

These miniature tone poems are arrangements for string orchestra of two of Grieg's most moving songs, 'The Wounded Heart' and 'Springtide'—settings of texts by Aasmund Olafsen Vinje, Norway's 'peasant poet' (1818-80). Grieg's transcriptions of the songs for string orchestra are published without any exhibition of their verses as programmatic guides; but Grieg, to supply this deficiency, altered his original titles somewhat in order to make them more indicative of the character of the music. He changed 'The Wounded Heart' to 'Heart Wounds' (*Herzwunden*—or *Hjertesar*, for those who know Norwegian); and 'Springtide' to 'The Last Spring' (*Letzter Frühling*, or *Vären*). But the pieces tell with clear eloquence their own emotional tales.

In the first—'Heart Wounds' ('Allegretto espressivo,' 4-4, C minor; C major) —we hear the immemorial lament of a sorrowful heart confronted by the tragically contrasted spectacle of the vernal earth. In the second—'The Last Spring' (Andante, G major, 4-4)—the mood is that expressed in two of the closing lines of Vinje's poem:

> But flowers will bloom on the scars that close,
> For so in Spring on the earth it goes. . .

● INCIDENTAL MUSIC TO *Peer Gynt*

‡ When in 1867 Hendrik Ibsen completed his *Peer Gynt* he was entering his fortieth year and the true nature of his extraordinary genius was as yet unguessed by the world. He had written a number of plays of a romantic and poetic cast on themes supplied by history and legend, but another decade was to pass before he produced, in *Pillars of Society* (which soon was followed by *A Doll's House* and *Ghosts*), the first of that series of naturalistic dramas in which he subjected the inequities, hypocrisies, and vices of the society of his time to a furious and revealing scrutiny. ‡

Grieg told his biographer, Henry T. Finck, that he composed his music to Ibsen's *Peer Gynt* between the summer of 1873 and the summer of 1875. It was first heard at a performance of the play on February 24, 1876, at the Christiania Theater. Afterwards, Grieg put together four numbers from the score in the form of a suite, op. 46, published in 1888, and these pieces are known to all the world. A second suite, less popular, was later assembled by Grieg from his music to the drama; this second suite was published in 1893 and bears the opus number 55.

The story of Ibsen's *Peer Gynt*, has been told as follows:

Peer Gynt is a rough Norwegian peasant lad who drives his mother, Aase, to distraction by his fantastic talk and ruffianly actions. His dream is to become emperor of the world. Everyone dreads and avoids him. He hears that the beautiful Ingrid is to be married, goes uninvited to the wedding, and carries off the bride into the mountain wilderness. The next day, deaf to her laments, he deserts her, after taunting her with not having the golden locks or meekness of the tender-hearted Solvejg, who at the wedding loved him at first sight, notwithstanding his appearance and behavior.

After various adventures, Peer finds himself in the Hall of the Mountain King, where he is tortured by elves and gnomes. He is rescued at the last moment by the sound of bells in the distance, which causes the collapse of the hall of the goblins. Then he builds a hut in the forest and Solvejg comes to him on her snowshoes of her own free will. Weeping, she tells him she has left her parents and her sister to share his hut and be his wife. Happiness seems to be his at last, but he is haunted by the gnomes, who threaten to torment him every minute of his life, whereat, without saying a word to his bride, he leaves her and returns to his mother.

Aase is on her deathbed and soon expires in his arms. Later, Peer turns up in Africa, where he has divers adventures. Having succeeded in stealing from robbers a horse and a royal garment, he goes among the Arabs and plays the role of a prophet. He makes love to the beautiful Anitra, daughter of a Bedouin chief, and elopes with her on horseback; but she, after cajoling all his stolen jewels from him, suddenly turns her horse and gallops back home.

In the last act, Peer Gynt, after suffering shipwreck on the Norwegian coast, returns to the hut he had built in the forest. There he finds Solvejg faithfully awaiting his return.

The four movements of Grieg's *Peer Gynt* Suite No. 1 are entitled: (1) 'Morning Mood'; (2) 'Aase's Death'; (3) 'Anitra's Dance'; (4) 'In the Hall of the Mountain King.'

I. 'Morning Mood' ('Allegro pastorale,' E major, 6-8): This movement of the suite is the Prelude to the fourth act. It was originally intended as an introduction to the fifth scene of the same act, and was entitled 'Early Morning'— 'there is a faint sound in the air as of distant chimes . . . it is Sunday morning on the sunlit fjord.'

II. 'Aase's Death' ('Andante doloroso,' B minor, 4-4): This exquisitely poignant music, one of Grieg's surest claims on the affection of posterity, is a lament over the death of Peer Gynt's mother, and was intended as prelude to the episode in Aase's room. Later, it is played softly behind the scenes.

III. 'Anitra's Dance' ('Tempo di Mazurka,' A minor, 3-4): This music accompanies the scene in the fourth act where Peer Gynt, in Africa, luxuriates in a cozy-corner, smoking a long pipe and enjoying a demi-tasse, while Anitra and her aphrodisian companions dance for him.

IV. 'In the Hall of the Mountain King' ('Alla Marcia e molto Marcato,' B minor, 4-4): This is the immensely characteristic, clumsily baroque dance of the dwarfs in the cave of the 'Troll-Princess' (Act II). Peer Gynt, having refused to marry the unlovely daughter of the Mountain King, is pursued by a troop of malignant gnomes. 'They lead him a chase which grows wilder and wilder, and the climax comes at the end in a crash representing the collapse of the hall at the sound of distant church-bells.' In the stage version, there is a chorus of imps crying 'Slay him!'

The movements of the Suite No. 2 are the following: (1) 'Ingrid's Lament'; (2) 'Arabian Dance'; (3) 'Return of Peer Gynt'; (4) 'Solvejg's Song.'

George Frideric Handel
1685-1759

‡Handel has been called the greatest of English composers, and such, except for the accident of his German birth and training, he was. He first visited London in 1710 (he was then a young man of twenty-five), and he settled there permanently the following year. Thenceforth, the environment which England provided, the influences which it brought to bear, shaped the development of his art. He was for many years primarily an operatic composer, but when the caprice of fashion threatened his supremacy in this field, he turned his attention to the larger choral forms and produced a line of oratorios of unexampled grandeur of conception and nobility and power of execution. The *Messiah*, *Judas Maccabeus*, and *Saul* are rivaled in their field only by the Passions of Johann Sebastian Bach. Handel's output of purely instrumental music was also considerable, and here too he achieved the heights, for the twelve concerti grossi of op. 6 are prodigies of invention and skill. Handel and Bach were born in the same year—1685—and the temptation to draw a parallel between them is great. But while Handel was one of the very greatest composers who ever lived, he is a phenomenon comprehensible—as are Mozart and Beethoven—in a way in which Bach is not, in known terms of human intellectual capacity and spiritual range.‡

● TWELVE CONCERTI GROSSI FOR STRINGS, OP. 6

‡Handel composed his 'Twelve Grand Concertos' (as he called them) in the space of a month and a day (between September 29 and October 30, 1739), thus averaging a concerto every two and a half days. Surely this is one of the great creative feats of musical history; for there is more music in the twelve concertos than in the score of *Don Giovanni* or *Die Zauberflöte*, and the level of inspiration and craftsmanship that Handel sustained in them was never far below his highest. Various, masterful, and fascinating as are the Brandenburg Concertos, they remain second-rate Bach; but the Twelve Concerti Grossi are first-rate Handel. Shortly after he had completed them, he undertook to have them published, by subscription, and 'with His Majesty's Royal License and Protection.' They were issued by Walsh in 1740.‡

The essential characteristics of these eighteenth-century concertos—so different from what the twentieth century understands by the term concerto—is the contrasting use of a small group of solo instruments, called the concertino, and the full body of strings, with an accompanying clavier, against which the solo group is set off. [See the notes, above and below, on Bach's Brandenburg Concertos, the 'Christmas' Concerto of Corelli, and Vivaldi's *The Four Seasons*.] In all twelve of Handel's concerti grossi, the concertino consists of two violins and a 'cello, the concerto grosso of first and second violins, violas, 'cellos, basses, and clavier. Romain Rolland, in his book on Handel, calls attention to an old picture in the British Museum which gives a clear idea of the arrangement of the Handelian orchestra: 'The picture shows Handel in the midst of his musicians, seated at the clavier. . . At his right are two violins, 'cello and two flutes, comprising the concertino—directly under his eye. The rest of the instrumentalists are behind him, out of sight. . . Thus his directions and his glances would control the concertino, who would transmit in their turn (his) wishes to the concerto grosso. . . The different bodies of the Handelian orchestra governed one another with elasticity, and it was the incisive rhythms of the little cembalo which put the whole mass in motion.' The picture thus described shows the seating of the Handelian orchestra for the performance of an oratorio, but doubtless much the same disposal of forces was made for performances of the concerti grossi.

‡ Handel's concertos vary greatly in the number and character of the movements which comprise them. Of the twelve, six are in five movements, five are in four, and one is in six, but in many cases the conventional introductory slow movement, though distinguished from the succeeding fast movement, in effect combines with it to approximate a single movement having the character of the so-called 'French overture' (see the notes, above, on J. C. Bach's Sinfonia in B-flat). Fugal movements are to be found in all but one of the concertos; dance movements are employed more sparingly. In general, Handel alternates movements in contrasting tempi; but there are instances in the concertos where two slow movements or two fast movements occur in succession. The structure of the single movements, of whatever character, exhibits the greatest variety, and since it will be impractical in these notes to analyze the concertos in detail, the interested reader is urged to study them in score and thus to acquaint himself at first hand with the many marvels of Handel's tonal architecture. In the brief notes below, the movements of a given concerto are, unless otherwise indicated, in the tonic key.

No. 1, in G major. Five movements. (1) 'A tempo giusto,' 4-4; (2) Allegro, 4-4; (3) Adagio, E minor, 3-4; (4) a fugal Allegro, 4-4; (5) Allegro, 6-8.

No. 2, in F major. Four movements. (1) 'Andante larghetto,' 4-4; (2) Allegro, D minor, 4-4; (3) Largo, 3-4; (4) 'Allegro ma non troppo,' 3-4.

No. 3, in E minor. Five movements. (1) Larghetto, 3-2; (2) Andante, 12-8, a slow fugato; (3) Allegro, 4-4; (4) a Polonaise, Andante, 3-4, in G major; (5) 'Allegro ma non troppo,' 6-8.

No. 4, in A minor. Four movements. (1) 'Larghetto affetuoso,' 4-4; (2) a fugal Allegro, 4-4; (3) Largo, F major, 3-2; (4) Allegro, 3-4.

No. 5, in D major. Five movements. (1) A French overture, consisting of a slow introduction (3-4) followed by a fugue, Allegro, in common time; (2)

Presto, 3-8; (3) Largo, B minor, 3-2; (4) Allegro, 4-4; (5) a slow Minuet, 'un poco larghetto,' 3-4.

No. 6, IN G MINOR. Five movements. (1) 'Largo affetuoso,' 3-2; (2) 'A tempo giusto,' 4-4, fugal in character; (3) a Musette, Largo, in E-flat major and triple time (with a contrasting middle section in a faster tempo); (4) Allegro, 4-4; (5) Allegro, 3-8.

No. 7, IN B-FLAT MAJOR. Four movements. (1) An introduction, Largo, succeeded by a fugue, Allegro, in common time; (2) 'Largo e piano,' in G minor, triple time; (3) Andante, 4-4; (4) a Hornpipe, 3-2 (the Hornpipe was a lively dance, popular in Handel's day, with the accent falling characteristically on the second or weak beat of the measure).

No. 8, IN C MINOR. Six movements. (1) An Allemande, andante, in common time; (2) Grave, F minor, 4-4; (3), 'Andante allegro,' 4-4; (4) Adagio, 3-4; (5) a Siciliano, andante, 12-8; (6) Allegro, 3-4.

No. 9, IN F MAJOR. (1) Largo, 3-4, followed by an Allegro, 4-4; (2) Larghetto, D minor, 6-8; (3) a fugal Allegro, in common time; (4) a Minuet in F minor— F major; (5) a Gigue, 12-8.

No. 10, IN D MINOR. Five movements. (1) An overture consisting of a slow movement (4-4) followed by a rapid fugue in 6-8 time; (2) Air, Lento, 3-2; (3) Allegro, 4-4; (4) Allegro, 3-4; (5) 'Allegro moderato,' D major, common time. It may be noted that three of the movements in this concerto have a fugal character.

No. 11, IN A MAJOR. Four movements. (1) 'Andante larghetto, e staccato,' 4-4; (2) a fugal Allegro, in common time; (3) Andante, 3-4; (4) Allegro, 4-4.

No. 12, IN B MINOR. Five movements. (1) Largo, 4-4; (2) Allegro, 4-4; (3) Aria, 'larghetto e piano,' in E major, 3-4 time, with variations; (4) Largo, 4-4; (5) a fugal Allegro, in common time.‡

● THE WATER MUSIC

The origin of this music of Handel's has been the subject of endless discussion among historians. Let us first recall the story of the 'Water Music' as legend enshrined it for many years.

The tale was first told by Mainwaring in his *Memoirs of the Life of the Late George Frederic Handel*, published anonymously in 1760, the year after Handel's death. Handel in 1712 was living in Hanover as Kapellmeister to the Elector, who was so soon (and so inconveniently for Handel) to be transformed into George I, King of England. The composer obtained leave from the Elector to pay a second visit to England, where he had sojourned a while before (1710-11), 'on condition that he engaged to return within a reasonable time.' But Handel forgot or ignored his promise, and he tarried in England— whether, as Mainwaring says, 'he was afraid of repassing the sea, or whether he had contracted an affection for the diet of the land he was in, so it was that the promise he had given at his coming away had somehow slipped out of his memory.'

This Rinaldo 'lingered dangerously in the enchanted gardens of Armida,' as Streatfeild puts it. Not only was he playing truant in the most unwarrantable fashion, but he was spending his time in the manner of all others most calculated to displease the Elector: for he was accepting favors from Queen Anne, who lost no opportunity of showing her dislike of everything connected with Hanover. Handel (and this was the head and front of his offending) wrote not only an ode in celebration of the Queen's birthday, but a festival *Te Deum* and *Jubilate* to commemorate the Peace of Utrecht (they were performed at St. Paul's in 1713).

It was not quite tactful of Queen Anne to die at just this juncture, without sufficient warning to the truant Handel; and when the Elector whom Handel had trifled with ascended the English throne in 1714, as his Britannic Majesty George I, Handel found himself in an embarrassing position. He kept away, naturally, from St. James's Palace, and retired to the seclusion of Burlington House to see which way the royal cat would jump. He soon discovered that he was exiled from Court. The King was willing to hear Handel's *Rinaldo* and *Amadigi*, for he liked going to the opera. But he would have nothing to do with the composer.

At about this time a certain Baron Kilmannsegge conceived a happy thought. This Baron was, in Mainwaring's phrase, 'a noble friend' of Handel's. He had been a rather shady adherent of the King when that gentleman was Elector of Hanover, and had followed George to England. His wife, the Baroness, who was no better than she should have been, enjoyed an *entente cordiale* with the King; and this enabled Kilmannsegge, who was now the King's Master of the Horse, to put into effect a canny scheme suggested by Lord Burlington for the reconciliation of Handel and his former friend.

The river Thames in the early eighteenth century was far more of a London highway than it is now, and on a summer's day one could stand on any pier between Blackfriars and Putney and signal one of the fleet of passenger boats as one would hail a taxi today on Piccadilly. Besides these river taxis, there were private barges, luxuriously equipped. King George enjoyed the river, and liked to journey on the royal barge from Whitehall, when the Court was there, up 'the silver Thames' to Richmond or to Hampton Court, accompanied by an attendant boat bearing his musicians, who soothed his troubled soul with aquatic serenades, 'elegantly performed by the best masters and instruments.'

Now the clever scheme of Kilmannsegge and Burlington worked out as follows (we are still adhering to the tale as related by Mainwaring in his narrative of 1760):

The King was persuaded to form a party on the water. Handel was apprised of the design, and advised to prepare some music for that occasion. It was performed and conducted by himself, unknown to His Majesty, whose pleasure on hearing it was equal to his surprise. He was impatient to know whose it was. . . The Baron then produced the delinquent, and asked leave to present him to His Majesty as one who was too conscious of his fault to attempt an excuse for it. . . This intercession was accepted without any difficulty. Handel was restored to favor.

Mainwaring gave no date, but this water party has been identified as that of August 22, 1715; for on that day, a history of the time informs us, 'the King, Prince, and Princess of Wales, and a large party of nobility, went in barges with music from Whitehall to Limehouse.'

But alas for the romantic patness of legend! Clio, frowning with cold severity, insists that the 'Water Music' was composed not for the royal barge party of 1715, but for one that contemporaneous history records as having taken place two years later (July 17, 1717), and that when this occurred, the King and Handel were already the best of friends.

In 1717, the envoy from the Duchy of Brandenburg to the English Court was Frederic Bonnet. A report written by Bonnet and dated July 17-30 was eventually discovered in the State Archives at Berlin. It appears from this report that Kilmannsegge, on a hint from the King, arranged the July 17 river concert 'at his own expense' (it cost him £150, without reckoning in the 'splendid supper at the pleasure house of the late Lord Ranelagh' which his wife supplied). Bonnet's report states unequivocally that 'Ce concert avait été composé exprès par le fameux Handel.'

This report of Bonnet's has generally been viewed as a revelation—Newman Flower, for instance, in his exhaustive life of Handel, seems to regard it as a disclosure of something not previously known. As a matter of fact, the royal water party of July 17, 1717 and Handel's connection with it were described in the London *Daily Courant* of July 19, 1717, substantially as in the report of Bonnet.

It is true that the authorities differ, and that some still cling to the original tale. But W. Barclay Squire, the eminent British musicologist, believed that the water party for which Handel composed his music took place, in all likelihood, in 1717. There is, of course, the difficulty of accounting for Mainwaring's circumstantial account of the reconciliation between King and composer, which he definitely attributes to the composition of the 'Water Music' in 1715. But Squire suggests, as a possible solution, the theory that the estrangement lasted for three years, and not one, and that Handel really did win his way back into favor with the King in 1717 by his 'Water Music.'

The 'Water Music' is a serenade in the form of a suite of dance tunes, airs, and other movements, introduced by an overture. Rockstro points out that the style of the instrumentation (the work is scored, in Arnold's edition, for flutes, piccolos, oboes, bassoons, horns, trumpets, and strings) was undoubtedly influenced by the fact that the music was designed for performance on the water. 'The parts for the wind instruments—especially for the horns—are so arranged as to produce the loveliest effects when heard across the water.' In modern performances the 'Water Music' is seldom heard in its entirety (Bonnet reported that the performance consumed an hour); the form in which it is most familiar to us today is that given it by Sir Hamilton Harty, and comprises six movements: Allegro, Air, Bourrée, Hornpipe, Andante, and 'Allegro deciso.'

● THE FIREWORKS MUSIC

If you had happened to be walking in Mayfair, London, on an April day in the year 1749, it is quite possible that you would have been struck by the sight of a burly and rather elderly gentleman shuffling down Brook Street, going heavily and bent, with the aid of a huge walking-stick, and talking to himself. He would have been dressed carefully, though not extravagantly, in a gold lace coat, ruffles, a three-cornered hat. You would have noticed that he stopped at times, looking at nothing, and that he muttered constantly to himself. You might have heard wild scraps of monologue. One day he was heard to exclaim, 'He is ein damn scoundrel, and good for nothing!' after the manner of a man who, though he spoke English, could not conceal the fact that he was born a German.

This would have been no less a personage than the redoubtable Mr. George Frideric (yes, that is the way he spelled it) Handel, walking from his home in Brook Street, near Hanover Square, upon his lawful occasions. Shortly before the time of our imagined encounter with him, he had produced his oratorios *Susanna* and *Solomon*. Neither was successful; but Handel, then in his sixty-fifth year, was making money from revivals of earlier works. The season of 1748-9 had been a fortunate one for him. The signing of the peace of Aix-la-Chapelle in October 1748 had raised the spirits of the English, and public entertainments prospered. There was widespread rejoicing, and in these re-joicings Handel was bidden to take part. The King planned a mighty celebration of the concluded peace. Handel was sent for by the Court, and commissioned to prepare music for what His Majesty had determined would be the greatest thing of the kind in the nation's history.

The feature of the occasion was to be an imposing display of fireworks, for which a 'machine' (as they called it) was designed in the form of a Doric temple erected in the Green Park. It was built by the celebrated Chevalier Servandoni, who was famous both as an architect and as a showman (he designed the façade of St. Sulpice in Paris, and had accomplished prodigies of spectacular effect in the mounting of an opera at Stuttgart). Handel was instructed to write *al fresco* music for the festivity, to precede and accompany the display of fireworks. Perhaps it was of this that he was thinking on that spring day when we might have encountered him on Brook Street, stumping along, muttering, staring at nothing.

The 'machine' in the Green Park was an enormous wooden building, an unsightly affair over a hundred feet high, with two wings extending north and south. There was a huge musician's gallery, topped by 'a crude figure of Peace attended by Neptune and Mars—or so the crowd was left to surmise from the atrocities in wood which leered down from aloft,' writes Newman Flower, with a chilling lack of enthusiasm. 'Greatest triumph of all,' he adds, 'they crowned the whole contraption with an immense bas-relief showing King George handing out peace to Britannia. At the summit of that was a towering pole uplifting a vast sun, which, on the night of celebration, burst suddenly into flame and blazed with such power that the whole park was lit by the light of day.'

The beginning of the fête was set for the 27th of April. The public furor surpassed all bounds. Enormous crowds jammed their way into the Park. Even the King could not contain himself. His excitement was intense. He changed his uniform twice in the first two hours. One moment he was beaming on the crowd, another moment inspecting restlessly the Chevalier Servandoni's Temple of Peace, or distributing purses of money among the workmen, or reviewing the

Guards from the garden wall. As night fell, the crowds grew denser. Coaches struggled through the packed and narrow side streets, and were brusquely turned back. Thieves plundered as they chose. London was on the loose.

Handel spread himself lavishly upon his musical fireworks. His band included 40 trumpets, 20 horns, 16 oboes, 16 bassoons and a contra-bassoon, 8 pairs of kettle-drums, 12 side-drums, and flutes and fifes. To this considerable aggregation of instruments Handel added strings.

Handel's music in its original shape consisted of the overture, to be played before the fireworks display, and five short movements, intended to accompany and illustrate certain of the allegorical set pieces. The most substantial part of the score is the overture, 'a sort of stately march in D major,' Romain Rolland calls it, and he compares it to Beethoven's *Ritterballet*—'like that work, it is joyful, equestrian, and very sonorous.' Handel derived the overture from material contained in the two orchestral concertos in F major and D major which are to be found in volume XLVII of the *Deutsche Händel Gesellschaft*, where they are published as 'Concerto A,' and 'Concerto B.' The overture, as used by Handel for the 'Fireworks Music,' begins with a section which in the autograph has no tempo mark; but it corresponds to the Largo opening, in 4-4 time, of the concerto upon which it is founded. The succeeding Allegro is in 3-4 time (opening with a subject not unlike the beginning of the 'Cudgel' motive in *Die Meistersinger*). The overture was scored by Handel for all the instruments.

The succeeding movements comprise a Bourrée in D minor, 2-2 time (scored for oboes, bassoons, and strings); a 'Largo alla Siciliana' entitled 'La Paix'— ('music of a beautiful heroic grace, which lulls itself to sleep')—D major, 12-8 time, scored in the original for oboes, horns, bassoons, trumpets, and strings; a sprightly Allegro in D, 4-4 time, entitled 'La Rejouissance,' for the full band; and two Minuets: the first in D minor, scored for strings and oboes; the second in D, with a different scoring used for each of its repetitions.

● OVERTURE IN D MINOR

While Handel was living with the Duke of Chandos at Cannons, England, in 1718-20, he composed a series of anthems which contain some of his noblest music. For one of them, 'In the Lord Put I My Trust,' a setting of passages from the ninth, eleventh, twelfth, and thirteenth Psalms, Handel composed a superb introductory movement in D minor for strings and oboe, consisting of an opening slow movement followed by a fugued allegro. It is sovereign writing, in Handel's lordliest vein. From it is derived the Overture in D minor.

Handel used some of the same material for the fifth of his Concerti Grossi for orchestra, op. 3. These are the six concertos known as the 'oboe concertos,' published by Walsh of London, in three editions, between the years 1729(?) and 1734. Samuel Arnold, who printed them in score in 1797, described them as 'chiefly composed at Cannons, in the year 1720.' Hawkins referred them to the occasion of the marriage of the Princess Anne with the Prince of Orange in 1733. Chrysander thinks that some of them, at least, were composed much earlier—at Hanover in 1711-12.

The first and second movements of the fifth 'Oboe Concerto' are closely related to the substance of the Introduction to the Chandos Anthem, which stands as No. 2 in the Complete Edition of the German Handel Society.

The Overture begins with an opening maestoso section, a sort of free prelude in 3-4 time upon the motive in triplets which is announced at the beginning. This is followed by the fugued allegro, a brilliant movement in common time. The end is a return of the opening maestoso.

As an instance of Handel's thrift in making the same musical ideas serve more than a single purpose, it may be said that the material of the fugued allegro which forms the second section of the introduction to the Chandos Anthem and the second movement of the fifth 'Oboe Concerto,' was used by him in the third movement of his F-sharp minor harpsichord suite (the first set of *Lessons for the Harpsichord*).

• SUITE FROM *Alcina*

Handel's *Alcina*, opera in three acts, with a libretto by Antonio Marchi, was completed, according to a note on the manuscript, April 8, 1735. It was produced at Covent Garden Theatre, London, on the sixteenth of that month. The cast was as follows: Alcina, Signorina Strada; Ruggiero, Signor Carestini; Morgana, Mrs. Young; Bradamante, Signorina Maria Negri; Oronte, Mr. Beard; Oberto, 'Young Mr. Savage' (he is called 'the Boy' in Handel's score). The part of Melisso was taken by the delightfully named Mr. Waltz, Handel's cook.

A week before Christmas of the year 1734, Handel removed his activities to Covent Garden Theatre, then newly built. Here, besides reviving many of his earlier works, he produced, within the space of less than three years, six new operas: *Ariodante, Alcina, Atalanta, Arminio, Giustino,* and *Berenice.* In *Ariodante* and in *Alcina*, the principal man's part was sung by Carestini, who made himself famous by provoking an immortal outburst of Handel's. Carestini had grown restive under the dictatorship of the great autocrat, and had refused to sing the lovely air in Act II of *Alcina*, 'Verdi prati,' which had been especially composed to show off the beauty of his voice. He sent back the song to Handel as 'unworthy for him to sing.' Handel, though he could ill afford to quarrel with Carestini, was not intimidated. He called a carriage, drove to Carestini's rooms, and furiously accosted the singer. 'You dog!' he cried, 'don't I know better as yourself what is good for you to sing? If you will not sing all the songs what I give you, I will not pay you ein stiver!'

The sight of the furious composer storming up and down his room appears to have daunted the rebellious Carestini. He sang the song at the performance of the opera, and with it scored one of his most brilliant triumphs; but he never forgave Handel, and left the company at the end of the season, much to Handel's embarrassment.

With *Alcina*, Handel achieved one of the great successes of his career, though the delightful ballet music, for which Mlle Sallé and her troupe appear to have been the provocation, was not well received, and Sallé, according to Prévost, was hissed.

Handel's devoted friend, Mrs. Delany (the former Mary Granville, who as a child first met Handel in 1710), wrote of *Alcina* with enthusiasm: 'Yesterday morning my sister and I went to Mr. Handel's house to hear the first rehearsal of the new opera *Alcina*. I think it is the best he ever made, but I have thought so of so many, that I will not say positively 'tis the finest, but 'tis so fine I have not words to describe it. Strada has a whole scene of charming recitative—there are a thousand beauties. Whilst Mr. Handel was playing his part, I could not help thinking him a necromancer in the midst of his own enchantments.'

The libretto of *Alcina*, which was derived from Ariosto, has features in common with the books of *Rinaldo* and *Amadigi*. Ruggiero, a Christian knight, has fallen into the amorous clutches of Alcina, a Circe-like enchantress, who has so bewildered his mind with her spells that when Bradamante, his plighted bride, appears on the scene to rescue him, he shows a marked disinclination to leave his voluptuous bondage. He is brought to his senses by means of a magic ring, and he and Bradamante make their escape after breaking the urn on which Alcina's power depends, reducing the palace and the enchanted gardens to a dreary wilderness.

Music from *Alcina* has been arranged for concert performance by several hands. Usually included in such concert suites are the Overture, the Dream Music ('Entry of the Agreeable Dreams,' 'Entry of the Menacing Dreams,' 'Combat of the Dreams,' et cetera), and a variety of short movements in eighteenth-century dance forms.

● CONCERTO FOR VIOLA AND ORCHESTRA, IN B MINOR

The authorship of this concerto is (to understate the case) a matter of some question. The score was published in 1925 and exhibits the following inscription on the title page: *G. F. Handel: Concerto en Si mineur, pour Alto, avec Accompagnement d'Orchestre; Réalization de la Basse et Orchestration par Henri Casadesus*. According to information given by Casadesus to the violist Samuel Lifschey, who first played the concerto in the United States, Casadesus 'discovered' the manuscript of the work in the British Museum. But later researches failed to locate it there or elsewhere. Nor are there references to it, or to any other viola concerto by Handel, in the exhaustive and authoritative publications of the Handel Gesellschaft. Nor is the thematic material of the concerto traceable to any authenticated or disputed work by Handel.

The first movement is a vigorous 'Allegro moderato' in 4-4 time. The viola enters after a half-dozen measures of introduction for the accompanying orchestra. The slow movement ('Andante ma non troppo,' B minor, 3-4) is a gravely beautiful meditation in which Casadesus represents Handel as using some strikingly romantic harmonization, as in the lovely passage for solo flute and strings near the end of the movement, which might almost have been written by Beethoven. The final movement is a vigorous gigue ('Allegro molto,' 6-8), the solo viola leading off at once with the exhilarating tune, against an accompaniment of pizzicato chords. The instrumentation is for two flutes, two bassoons, and strings.

- MESSIAH

It was on August 22, in the year 1741, that 'Mr. George Frideric Handel' sat at his desk in the little front room of the house in Brook Street, London, and began to put notes on paper with astonishing speed. He must have written like lightning; and we know that he was completely absorbed in his task. He did not leave the house. His manservant brought him food, and often returned to the room an hour or so later and found the food untouched and his master either staring vacantly out the window, or bent over his music paper, writing furiously.

Twenty-three days later (the date was September 14), the magnificent Mr. Handel shut his manuscript in his drawer, snuffed his candle, and went to bed. He had completed *Messiah*. All of it was original work, except four of the choruses, which were adapted from a set of Italian duets that he had composed earlier in the same year. Later, Handel spent much time and thought over his score, and left different versions of certain pages. (Handel's oratorio, by the way, is almost invariably referred to as *The Messiah*. But that is not quite correct. Handel in his autograph score styles it *Messiah*, and both Handel and Charles Jennens, compiler of the text, referred to it as such in their correspondence. Only twice was Handel known to speak of it as 'The' *Messiah*.)

It has long been thought remarkable that Handel should have taken only twenty-three days to compose *Messiah*. But some have conjectured that the scores that Handel turned out with such extraordinary speed had been composed *da mente*, or that he made sketches, which he afterward destroyed. Mendelssohn, himself a prolific and at times a rapid writer of music, evidently did not believe that Handel composed as he wrote, for, in his preface to his edition of *Israel in Egypt*, he refers to 'the great haste with which Handel used *to write down* his works.' Dr. Burney, speaking of Handel from personal recollection, tells us that he spent 'so studious and sedentary a life as seldom allowed him to mix in society, or partake of public amusements.' If Handel spent such a life, what was it that occupied him during the relatively long intervals between his various compositions? The suggestion that he worked them out in sketch form, and that the subsequent process was chiefly one of 'writing down,' as Mendelssohn conjectured, is reasonable.

The composition of *Messiah* was a task which had deeply moved him. One day his servant found him at his desk with tears streaming from his eyes. He had just finished the Hallelujah Chorus. 'I did think,' he remarked brokenly to his man, 'I did see all heaven before me, and the great God Himself.' It is clear that Handel was stimulated by the words of *Messiah*, and therefore due credit should go to the man who selected and arranged the English text. This man, Charles Jennens, would have seemed to the casual observer a singularly unpromising person to accomplish such a labor. He was a rich aristocrat, a pompous and foolish fop, a conceited ass, and at best an amateur poet. When he took his proofs from his house in Bloomsbury to his printers in Red Lion Court—a very short distance—he drove there in a coach and four, attended by lackeys. Alighting at the entrance court, he directed that a servant precede him to remove any rubbish that might be in his path. He was absurd enough to write this to a friend: 'I shall show you a collection I gave Handel, called *Messiah*, which I value highly, and he has made a fine entertainment out of it, though not near so good as he might and ought to have done. I have with great difficulty made him correct some of the grossest faults in the composition.' Yet Jennens must have had likable qualities, for Handel—who did not suffer fools gladly—remained his friend, and left him two pictures in his will. It should be added that according to some (Newman Flower, for example), the real work of compiling the text of *Messiah* was done by Jennens' secretary, a clergyman named Popley.

Handel had at first no idea of a production of *Messiah*. The score of the oratorio remained in his desk for seven weeks. London had turned against him, and he was sick at heart. He might have shaken the English dust from his buckled shoes and returned to his native Germany if an invitation had not come to him from the Lord Lieutenant of Ireland to visit Dublin and give some benefit concerts for certain charities. So Handel, disgusted with his faithless English public, packed his music and set out for Ireland.

He reached Dublin in November, and there, as he wrote in his quaint spelling to his collaborator Jennens, he passed his time 'with Hounour, profit and pleasure.' He remained for the winter in Ireland, and on Tuesday, the 13th of April 1742, 'Mr. Handel's new Grand Oratorio, called the *Messiah* [in the words of the newspapers], was performed for the first time at the Musick Hall in Fishamble Street, for the benefit of the Prisoners in the several Gaols, and for the support of Mercer's Hospital, and of the Charitable Infirmary on the Inn's Quay.' The 'Gentlemen of the Chorus of both Cathedrals' assisted, 'with some Concertos on the Organ by Mr. Handel.'

Books of words were sold for sixpence each. The Dublin papers had printed a notice requesting 'the Favour of the ladies not to come with hoops this day to the Musick Hall in Fishamble Street. The gentlemen are desired to come without their swords.' It is said that the capacity of the hall was increased by 100 by these noble sacrifices (for the request was graciously heeded), and that 700 persons were thus permitted to hear the performance. Hundreds more waited in the street.

It was a highly successful occasion. There was 'a most Grand, Polite and Crowded Audience.' And the music 'was allowed by the greatest judges to be the finest composition of Musick that was ever heard.' 'Words are wanting to express the exquisite Delight it afforded to the admiring Crowded Audience,' wrote *Faulkner's Journal* the next day. Two of the principal singers had come from London. These were Mrs. Cibber and Signora Avoglio. The tenor and bass solos were sung by men from the Dublin Cathedral chorus. Handel wrote to Jennens that 'the chorus singers by my direction do exceedingly well. As for the instruments, they are really excellent, Mr. Dubourgh being at the head of them, and the music sounds delightfully in the charming room, which puts one in such spirits, and my health being so good, that I exert myself on my organ with more than usual success.'

The Mrs. Cibber who sang in the performance was that famous sloe-eyed beauty who had been Susanne Arne. This was the woman of whom George II complained indignantly that 'she would hush the King!' She prepared her seductions with consummate deliberation, and boasted that it always took her three hours to do her hair. Handel's friendship with her had begun in 1738. We are assured by the biographers that it was 'a great and clean friendship,' and no doubt it was; yet Mrs. Cibber was not without her frailties; and she understood, we are told, the meaning of certain passages in *Messiah* with a singular completeness. So poignant was her singing of 'He was despised' that Dr. Delaney, sitting in the audience, was moved to exclaim, 'Woman! for this be all thy sins forgiven thee!' And Handel himself was so impressed that for long afterward he wrote all his contralto songs for her.

Handel returned to London four months later. On March 23, 1743, he produced *Messiah* for the first time in England, at Covent Garden, and repeated it twice in the same season. One performance was attended by the King, who, as everyone knows, was so moved by the exalted splendor of the Hallelujah Chorus that he rose to his feet and remained standing until the end of the number. Still, *Messiah* was not at first a success in England. Handel had prudently entitled it 'A Sacred Oratorio'—they had told him it would be fatal to call it *Messiah*. Even so, the Church was outraged and viewed the work as sacrilege. The clergy tried to close the theater. Their argument was that 'any work about the Omnipotent should never be performed in a playhouse.' But Handel revived the work from time to time. He gave it twice in 1745, and then not again until 1749. Between 1750 and 1759 he produced it every year in the chapel of the Foundling Society for the benefit of that charity. He conducted it for the last time on April 6, 1759, eight days before his death.

The great work is still marvelous in its blend of strength and tenderness, in its elevation of style, in its beauty and sweep of line. Music has learned much since Handel's day—has learned things that would make the superb George Frederic's eyes pop and stare. Stravinsky has even written an imposing oratorio in the style of Handel (or so he says); but no one has duplicated *Messiah*. Handel, hurrying at his task, enslaved by time, was unaware that he had built for endlessness. In this music immemorial words, immortal words, 'become flesh and walk among us.'

Franz Josef Haydn

1732-1809

John Runciman said of Haydn, during the time that he was on the payroll of Prince Esterházy, that 'every morning he rose with the lark, dressed himself with a degree of neatness that astonished even that neat-dressing age, and sat down to compose music'—which suggests the reflection that

Haydn has too long been the butt of many who still perversely choose to think of him as good 'Papa Haydn,' the cheery, rather naïve chap who did his bit to help along the education of the Heavenly Maid, but who cannot speak very urgently or pointedly to the taste of the twentieth century. To be sure, we are very fine fellows these days (as Stevenson remarked) and a Haydn symphony is not intimate and vivid to our imaginative world as is music by Bartók or Schönberg or Stravinsky, or by others who speak the tonal language of our time. Yet Haydn was far more than the simple-minded prank player of the 'Surprise' Symphony, or the naïve pictorialist of *The Creation*, or the abstract Historic Figure whom we respect and are grateful to because he assisted in putting Euterpe through college. It is astonishing that even so shrewd a critic as Berlioz could say of Haydn's music that 'it belongs to the kind of naïvely good and gay music that recalls the innocent joys of the fireside and the *pot-au-feu*. It goes and comes, never brusquely; noiselessly, in morning négligée, clean and comfortable; at 9 o'clock it puts on a night-cap, says a prayer, and sleeps in the peace of the Lord.' The Haydn of the nightcap and the cheerful *pot-au-feu* existed, of course; but there was another Haydn —the fine, essential, sensitive, memorable Haydn, with a supply of musical ideas under his periwig that should have made the strutting tonal barn-stormer of the *Symphonie fantastique* think twice before he sneered at him. Music was a trade at which Haydn worked with indefatigable industry; it was also an art, a means of expression and communication, of which he was one of the greatest masters.

THE SYMPHONIES

‡Haydn has frequently been called the 'father of the symphony,' the term symphony being understood to define an orchestral sonata in several movements, of which one or more are constructed in so-called sonata form. Haydn was not the inventor of the symphony thus defined, but it did assume under his hands characteristics which for two hundred years have continued to distinguish it. Sammartini, Stamitz, and Philipp Emanuel Bach, among others, wrote symphonies, and Haydn's early essays in the form were imitations of the work of these predecessors, exhibiting the sonata form in a rudimentary state of development, and seldom aspiring to any seriousness or force of expression. In the later symphonies, by which Haydn is chiefly remembered today, a developed sonata form is employed in the opening movements and elsewhere, and this increased complexity of structure is paralleled by an increased seriousness of content. (Sonata form, as exemplified in the works of Haydn and later composers, is a tripartite form, A1—B—A2; in which A1 consists of the exposition, B of the development, and A2 of the recapitulation of A1, usually in a more or less modified form. The classic formula calls for two themes, con-

trasted in character and tonality, in A1; the development, B, subjects one or both of these themes to a free analysis or 'working-out.')

Haydn composed over a hundred symphonies. These are now usually identified by the numbers assigned to them in the Breitkopf & Härtel Complete Critical Edition of Haydn's works, publication of which was begun in 1907 and still continues.‡

• SYMPHONY IN D MAJOR, B. & H. NO. 13

It is regrettable, though undoubtedly necessary, that this symphony should be published as No. 13 in the Critical Edition, since that is the number long given in earlier editions and in concert programs to a later and quite different symphony of Haydn's, composed in 1786 for the society known in Paris as the *Concert de la Loge Olympique,* and now listed, in the Critical Edition, as No. 88. Thus may confusion arise in the minds of the unwary.

This symphony was composed two years after Haydn had been called into the service of the Esterházy family in 1761. He was then thirty-two years old. His first symphony was only two years behind him. This symphony has a minuet. Four of the twelve symphonies that preceded it have none. Even twenty-five years later, as Brenet points out, the minuet appeared to be so entirely a mere accessory in the architecture of a symphony that orchestras felt themselves under no obligation to play those which composers included in their works. The autograph manuscript of a symphony (*La Poule*) which Haydn sent to London in 1786, twenty-five years after he composed No. 13, bears the following notice in an unknown hand: 'Minuets to be left out' ('Minuets' —that is to say, the Minuet with its trio or alternativo).

This symphony has no slow introduction. The main movement begins at once, 'Allegro molto,' D major, 4-4, with a lively theme, forte, for the unison violins, which at first is scarcely more than a sort of bugle-call for the bowed instruments. The plan which Haydn adhered to in these early symphonies, and which he gradually extended and developed, involved at first the use of a single theme, surrounded only by accessory formulas. Sandberger, in his *Zur Geschichte des Haydns Quartetts,* finds rudimentary beginnings of thematic development in only nine of his first thirty-two; and there is little more in the corresponding symphonies, which, as Brenet remarks, 'owe their charm mainly to the easy, cheerful style which issues from the fertile imagination of youth.'

In this symphony the slow movement is the most remarkable. It is an 'Adagio cantabile' in G major, 2-2, consisting of an extended and ornately embroidered 'cello solo, accompanied only by the other strings. The Minuet is in D major, 3-4, with a captivating G major trio for solo flute and strings. The Finale ('Allegro molto,' D major, 2-4) is based chiefly upon a theme which foreshadows the subject of the Finale of Mozart's 'Jupiter' Symphony. It is propounded in unison by the first and second violin, *p*, and is afterward heard in both the wind and stringed instruments, brilliantly set off against opposing material in the other voices.

The instrumentation of the symphony is for two flutes, two oboes, four horns, timpani, and strings.

● SYMPHONY IN D MAJOR ('With the Horn Call'), B. & H. No. 31

Haydn, at the time of the composition of this symphony, had been for four years in the service of the Esterházy family at Eisenstadt as second Kapellmeister. Although Haydn's superior, the aging Werner, did not think much of his assistant (he called him 'a mere fop' and 'a scribbler of songs'), Haydn had nevertheless built up for himself a very pretty reputation as a composer. His symphonies, quartets, trios, cassations were available in print or MS. in Leipzig, Paris, Amsterdam, London; and the official gazette, *Wiener Diarium*, referred to him the following year (1766) as 'our national idol.' Yet 'our national idol,' in accordance with the agreement signed in 1761 by His Serene Highness Paul Anton, Prince of the Holy Roman Empire, of Esterházy and Galantha, et cetera, and by Josef Haydn, was required to eat with the domestic staff, or take his half-gulden per day and find his own food. The assistant Kapellmeister wore, according to instructions, white stockings, white linen, his wig powdered and worn either in a net or with a pigtail, and a livery of dark red cloth braided with gold (later the family changed their colors, and Haydn wore a pale blue coat with silver embroidery and buttons). Haydn preferred the pigtail to the net and wore one to the end of his life.

In the castle at Eisenstadt, the musical performances during Haydn's first five years there took place, except during meals, either in a large hall equipped as a theater, or in a drawing room. The new palace erected near the southern end of the Neusiedler-See by the extravagant Prince Nikolaus Esterházy after his accession, was not ready for occupancy until 1766. It was built in the Italian style, and contained, besides apartments of state, 126 chambers filled with curios, pictures, treasures from China, and many books. It 'astonished all visitors by its magnificence' (the Prince had visited Paris and Versailles and had developed delusions of grandeur; his diamond-covered uniform was famous). But at Esterház the musicians dwelt in the servants' quarters—there were no luxurious surroundings, no pictures or Chinese curios or books for Haydn, who was only a genius.

Haydn's orchestra, during his first years at Eisenstadt, comprised fourteen players; the musical staff, in addition, included an organist and six singers. Later, under Prince Nikolaus, the orchestra at Haydn's disposal was increased to thirty players. Having a variety of instrumentalists under his orders to play virtually nothing save his own works, Haydn, as he himself has told us, was able to experiment as he chose with combinations of tone. When composing, he did not consider merely the general resources of an instrument, but what could be got out of it as played by such and such a performer, personally known to him. Preoccupation with color effects played a large part in his calculations when writing for an orchestra, although he does not appear to have introduced a single unusual instrument.

The Symphony No. 31 has striking features. The score requires four horns; and this was probably the first instance in which four horns were used in a symphony. In the slow movement there are solos for violin and for 'cello. In the Finale, a theme with variations, there are solo passages for flute and for violin.

As relaxation from his arduous labors, Haydn was fond of hunting and fishing on the Esterházy estate. He was proud of his skill in shooting. It has been said that the music of the 'Symphony with the Horn Call' has 'the joy of the chase.' The symphony opens (Allegro, D major, 3-4) with the horn call —four horns in unison, forte, accompanied by a figure of the strings, *p*. At the ninth measure, a solo horn, *p*, suggests a distant answering call. The movement is in sonata form, and is scored for flute, two oboes, the four horns, and strings.

In the second movement (Adagio, G major, 6-8), only the horns and strings are used. A solo violin presents an ornate melody, accompanied by pizzicati chords of the other strings. The music becomes a dialogue between the solo violin and two horns; a solo 'cello adds its voice, and the string quartet is heard. The melodic material, and the accompaniment, suggest the rhythm of the Siciliano. The horns are in two keys, D and G.

The Minuet (D major, 3-4) is scored for all the instruments—flute, two oboes, horns, and strings. In the trio, the woodwind and horns are set off against the strings.

The Finale ('Moderato molto'—Presto, D major, 2-4) is a theme with variations, remarkable for its ingenious use of solo instruments and solo groups. The strings alone announce the simple theme. There are seven variations:

Var. 1. For two oboes and two horns, with accompanying strings.

Var. 2. 'Cello solo, with accompanying strings.

Var. 3. Flute solo, with strings accompanying.

Var. 4. The horn quartet (with taxing high notes for the first horn), accompanied, pianissimo, by the strings.

Var. 5. Violin solo, the other strings accompanying.

Var. 6. For all the instruments (playing *p* throughout).

Var. 7. 'Cello solo, with supporting strings. The tempo changes to Presto (3-4). A new subject is briefly heard, forte, under a sustained A of two horns and the first violins, and is repeated, *p*, as an echo. The opening theme of the symphony's first movement brings a lusty conclusion.

• SYMPHONY IN D MAJOR, B. & H. No. 86

This symphony, composed in 1786, is the fifth in a set which Haydn was commissioned to write for the society known as the *Concert de la Loge Olympique*. He began the series at Esterház in 1784 and finished the job five years later.

The *Concerts spirituels* for which these symphonies were composed attracted audiences of the highest distinction to the Salle des Gardes in the Tuileries from 1786 to the year when the fall of the Bastille disturbed the ordered elegance of Parisian days and nights. Marie Antoinette was often seen there, with others of the court, in full regalia. The orchestral players fiddled and blew in ruffles and embroidery, and wore pretty shining swords, and the lace on their cuffs often interfered with the bowing of the fiddlers, unless they were unusually deft.

The notable feature of the Symphony No. 86 is the second movement, which, following the opening 'Allegro spiritoso,' is entitled 'Capriccio' and consists of a fantasy of extravagantly ornate description, Largo, G. major, 3-4. The Finale, a sonata form 'Allegro con spirito,' is rich in Haydn's characteristic humor.

● SYMPHONY IN G MAJOR, B. & H. No. 88

When this symphony was written, the United States had not yet elected its first President. It was the year in which Philadelphia was stirred by the doings of the Constitutional Convention—the year in which for the first time (as John Adams remarked) 'the thirteen clocks all struck together.' In Europe, the French revolution was still two years off, and the *Concerts spirituels* were still attracting their notable audience to the halls of the Tuileries.

This symphony is therefore one year older than the three great ones of Mozart—the E-flat, G minor, and C major of 1788. Haydn himself was fifty-five when he wrote it; his contemporary Mozart was thirty-one; and the first performance of the First Symphony of Beethoven was not to occur until thirteen years later. Yet so wayward and incalculable a thing is the musical imagination that it is possible to find in this score—although it is now well over a century and a half old—passages that are astonishing in their modernity; a modernity that, if it is hardly Schönbergian, has at least a Wagnerian hue. Consider, for example, that charming passage in the first movement from which the face of Eva Pogner looks out with sweet archness—many years before Wagner dreamed her into being in the linen-scented streets of Nuremberg; although in the symphony she has less of tremulous anxiety because of the cheerier pace of Haydn's Allegro.

But set this surprising passage beside Wagner's (composed eighty years later), and note that Haydn's harmony in this passage is even more 'modern' than Wagner's. The comparison is with the form assumed by Eva's 'Anxiety' motive (so-called) in the form given to it five bars after its first appearance in the fourth scene of Act III of *Die Meistersinger*, where it accompanies Eva's words to Sachs: '. . . wer sieht dann, wo's mir beschwerlich. . .' Haydn's anticipation of it is almost identical in melodic and rhythmic contour and in harmonization; but this amusing detail should be remarked: the fifth note of Wagner's melodic pattern is harmonized with a simple major triad (used in that place, of course, because it was just what he wanted there). But the daringly futuristic Haydn employs for the harmonic color of the corresponding note of *his* melody a chord of the 'minor ninth'; and when it is remembered that minor ninths in Haydn's day (though he and his predecessors had used them confidently) were more or less under surveillance by the plain-clothes men of the academic tradition, the intrepidity of the daredevil Haydn will be better appreciated.

● SYMPHONY IN G MAJOR, B. & H. No. 92 ('Oxford')

This symphony derives its name from the circumstance that it was performed at the second of three concerts given at Oxford, England, while Haydn was there for the purpose of receiving his degree of Mus. Doc. from the University.

The concert in question took place July 7, 1791. Although the symphony, which opened the second part of the program, was announced as 'expressly intended for this concert,' those pernickety persons, the musicologists, have taken leave to doubt the statement. But though they think it probable that Haydn did *not* intend the work expressly for that occasion, they believe it possible that it had not been heard before—though Leopold Schmidt, in his book on Haydn, declares that the symphony had been played, and that Haydn merely added drums and trumpets to the score. Some historians assert that the symphony was composed at least three years before Haydn went to Oxford.

Whatever the truth may be, it appears certain that this symphony was played at Oxford July 7, 1791, and that Haydn conducted. The music was much admired. The *Morning Chronicle* said that 'a more wonderful composition never was heard. The applause given to Haydn was enthusiastic; but the merit of the work, in the opinion of all the musicians present, exceeded all praise.'

The symphony opens with an Adagio introduction, 3-4, in G major. The main movement is begun, 'Allegro spiritoso,' by a theme given to the strings, which also propose, after transitional material, the second subject. The second movement is an Adagio in the dominant key, and in 2-4 time, written in three-part form. It opens with a theme for the violins. The second section of the movement is in D minor, followed by a return of the major tonality.

The third movement (Allegretto, G major, 3-4), is a Menuetto of traditional style and form. The trio is in the tonic. The strings begin the Finale (Presto, G major, 2-4 time), in form a rondo on two dance themes.

• SYMPHONY IN D MAJOR, B. & H. No. 93

‡The last twelve 'authentic' symphonies listed in the thematic index which prefaces Volume 1 of the Breitkopf & Härtel Critical Edition, under the numbers 93-104, are those Haydn composed at the behest of the London impresario, Johann Peter Salomon, between 1791 and 1794.‡

Haydn left Vienna on December 15, 1790, bound for England in company with Salomon. They crossed the Channel on New Year's Day 1791 (the crossing then took nine hours), and from Dover proceeded straight to London. The first of Salomon's concerts took place March 11, in the Hanover Square Rooms. The orchestra, led by Salomon (on later occasions Haydn himself conducted), consisted of between thirty-five and forty players. On this first visit, Haydn remained in London until the end of June 1792, when he returned to Vienna. During this period the first set of six so-called Salomon symphonies were written.

In the eighteenth century, symphonies grew almost as painlessly as beards; so it is doubtful if the deft and experienced Haydn turned a hair when Salomon later invited him to add six new symphonies to those he had already written for the London manager. He went again to London in the winter of 1793-4, and when he departed, in August of 1795, he left behind him a loving widow [Mrs. Schroeter—see notes on Symphony No. 100, below], but took with him the sum of twelve hundred pounds, earned on this visit alone. He had also written his last symphonies—the six of the second Salomon set.

The Symphony No. 93 is listed as No. 2 of the Salomon symphonies in the catalogue of the London Philharmonic Society. It opens with a slow introduction of twenty measures, thematically unrelated to what follows. The chief theme of the succeeding main movement, 'Allegro assai,' D major, 3-4, is given out at once by the strings, *p*. To the strings is allotted also the proposal of the second theme, a graceful subject in the dominant key, introduced by a staccato ascending scale of the first violins. The development section is devoted principally to an exploitation of a figure derived from the second theme, worked out contrapuntally with some new material. When the first theme, in the strings, begins the recapitulation section (after a fermata), it will be observed that the continuation of the subject is transferred to the second fiddles, the first playing a contrapuntal figuration in eighth-notes against it. There is a short coda.

The slow movement ('Largo cantabile,' G major, 4-4) is in form suggestive of a rondo. It consists of the development of the opening subject, in alternation with a subsidiary theme in triplets.

The Menuetto begins as an Allegretto, 3-4, in the tonic key of the symphony. The Trio presents one of Haydn's harmonic subtleties. It is announced by a reiterated octave and unison D, forte, sounded by the wind and timpani, after which the strings enter in the key of B minor. The reiterated D's return, and the strings again follow them, but this time in G major. This procedure is in part repeated in the second section of the Trio, with the note of the repeated wind and timpani changed to A, which becomes, at the entry of the strings, the mediant of F major.

The Finale ('Presto ma non troppo,' D major, 2-4) is a jocund Rondo on two themes.

● SYMPHONY IN G MAJOR, B. & H. No. 94 ('Surprise')

This symphony, known as the 'Surprise' Symphony, and, in Germany, as the 'Symphony with the drum-stroke,' is No. 3 of the Salomon set. Adalbert Gyrowetz in his autobiography tells us that he visited Haydn while the composer was at work on this symphony. Haydn had just completed the Andante and was so delighted with it, says Gyrowetz, that he played it for his caller on the piano, and when he reached the first of the crashings which break in on the quietly preceding tune, he remarked mischievously, 'That's sure to make the ladies jump!' These sudden orchestral outbursts occasioned the subtitle by which the symphony became famous. Yet Haydn himself repudiated the idea that the chords were devised for the purpose of making the audience sit up. The symphony was performed for the first time at the sixth of the Salomon concerts in London, March 23, 1792, and a contemporary reviewer was reminded by the crashing chords in the Andante of a sleeping shepherdess startled out of her repose by the firing of a musket.

The symphony has a slow introduction, 'Adagio cantabile,' 3-4, of sixteen measures. The main body of the first movement is begun by the violins, 'Vivace assai,' 6-8. In the succeeding slow movement, Andante, C major, 2-4, Haydn springs his little joke, the first of his 'surprises,' at the sixteenth bar—a fortissimo chord of the strings, woodwind, horns, trumpets, and kettledrums. The movement consists of a theme with variations. Haydn later used the theme in his oratorio *The Seasons*.

The third movement, Menuetto ('Allegro molto,' 3-4) begins forte, with the theme given out by flutes, bassoons, and first violins. Bassoons and first violins begin the trio, in the key of the movement (G major) with a flowing theme. The Finale is a Rondo on two chief themes, 'Allegro di molto,' 2-4.

● SYMPHONY IN C MINOR, B. & H. No. 95

This symphony, composed in the year of Mozart's death, is not without traces of his influence. The first movement ('Allegro moderato,' 4-4) is energetic and comparatively brief. The second (Andante, E-flat major, 6-8) has in general the form of a theme with variations. The familiar Minuet (C minor) has a trio in the tonic major. In the Finale (Vivace, C major, 2-2) Haydn exhibits himself as a contrapuntalist, though without undue severity.

● SYMPHONY IN D MAJOR, B. & H. No. 96

‡The four movements of this, the sixth of the Salomon symphonies, are: 'Adagio-Allegro,' 3-4; Andante, in G, 6-8; a Menuetto, Allegretto; a Finale, Vivace, 2-4.‡

● SYMPHONY IN C MAJOR, B. & H. No. 97

‡This symphony is listed as No. 1 in the London Philharmonic Society's catalogue of the Salomon symphonies. It is in the usual four movements: 'Adagio-Allegro,' 3-4; Adagio, in F major, 4-4; a Menuetto, Allegretto; a Finale, 'Presto assai,' 2-4.‡

● SYMPHONY IN B-FLAT MAJOR, B. & H. No. 98

This, No. 4 of the Salomon set, is one of the less familiar of Haydn's symphonies. Its first performance was at the third concert in Salomon's series at the Hanover Square Rooms, March 25, 1791. Haydn conducted at the clavier, and Salomon, an accomplished violinist as well as a manager, was the concertmaster. Haydn in his diary recorded that 'the first and last Allegros were encort' (*sic*). The symphony was repeated a year later, and on that occasion the critic of the *Morning Chronicle* spoke thus of the composition: 'Every instrument is respected by his [Haydn's] muse, and he gives to each its due proportion of efficacy. He does not elevate one, and make all the rest contributory as a mere accompaniment; but the subject is taken up by turns, with masterly art, and every performer has the means of displaying his talent.'

The first movement is preceded by a slow Introduction (Adagio, B-flat minor, 4-4), scored for the strings alone. The main body of the Allegro (B-flat major, 2-2) presents as its chief theme the subject of the Introduction, now in the major mode, announced by the strings.

The student's attention should be drawn at this point to an interesting detail: Haydn's use in this symphony of the then uncommon chord of the dominant major ninth (fiftieth bar of the Allegro, strings and bassoon); which may be noted as a corrective of the astonishing statement made by Alfredo Casella, in his book *The Evolution of Music,* that in Schubert's 'Walzer per pianoforte, Op. 90' (*sic*), 'we have the first appearance of that chord of the dominant major ninth which is without any doubt the greatest harmonic discovery of the nineteenth century.' It was not only Haydn who anticipated this 'greatest harmonic discovery of the nineteenth century'; for the dominant major ninth chord was used as early as 1611 by Carlo Gesualdo in one of his madrigals. But indeed this symphony of Haydn's is full of interest for the student who may not be fully awake to the fact that Haydn was often a subtle and adventurous experimentalist in musical invention.

The slow movement is an 'Adagio cantabile' in F major, 3-4 time, of singular charm and expressiveness—and this movement, too, is not without its harmonic surprises.

The Menuetto (Allegro, B-flat major, 3-4) has a trio in the same key, on a subject for the first violins and bassoon in octaves.

The Finale (Presto, B-flat major, 6-8) is remarkable for the violin solo in the development section, which devotes itself to a working out of the second theme of the movement.

The symphony is scored for flute, two oboes, two bassoons, two horns, two trumpets, timpani, and strings.

● SYMPHONY IN E-FLAT MAJOR, B. & H. No. 99

This symphony opens with a slow introduction (Adagio, E-flat, 4-4). A fortissimo chord of the tonic is followed by a brief cantabile phrase, *p*, for the first violins, accompanied by bassoon, clarinet, and the other strings. A forte chord of the dominant for the whole orchestra interrupts brusquely. This alternation of lyric amiability and intrusive roughness, which suggests the fondness of Beethoven for such dynamic contrasts, is brought to a close by a fermata on a dominant seventh chord. The main movement begins ('Vivace assai,' E-flat, 4-4) with a lively theme announced piano by the first violins, accompanied by the other strings, and repeated forte by the full orchestra. The second theme, in B-flat, is for first violins and clarinet, with, at first, a string accompaniment.

The second movement is one of those deeply felt Adagios which we find not infrequently in Haydn's symphonies—movements which foreshadow the symphonic Beethoven. This Adagio (G major, 3-4) is developed chiefly from two subjects: the opening cantabile theme for the violins, in the key of the movement, and that in the dominant key for first violins, oboe, and bassoon (the melody in unison and octaves, the other strings and wind accompanying). There is a middle section in D minor. The movement is remarkable for its beautiful and expressive harmonization, its grave lyricism, and its dramatic intensity.

The third movement (Allegretto, E-flat major, 3-4) is a minuet of traditional character. The trio is in C major.

The Finale (Vivace, E-flat major, 2-4) is in rondo form.

The instrumentation is for flutes, oboes, clarinets, bassoons, horns, and trumpets, in pairs; timpani, and strings.

• SYMPHONY IN G MAJOR, B. & H. No. 100 ('Military')

The so-called 'Military' Symphony is one of the second half-dozen of the Salomon symphonies, and had its première during Haydn's second visit to London, on May 2, 1794, at the Hanover Square Rooms. Haydn had started from Vienna on January 19 of that year, reaching London sixteen days later. He took lodgings at No. 1 Bury Street, St. James—'probably to be near Mrs. Schroeter,' as Ferdinand Pohl conjectured. This Mrs. Schroeter, the widow of John Samuel Schroeter, the Queen's music master, was Haydn's dearest friend in London. She was his pupil and became greatly attached to him— but Haydn, unhappily for her, was already supplied with a consort. Haydn afterwards described her, with a slight lapse from gallantry, as 'an English widow who fell in love with me.' 'She was,' he remarked, 'a very handsome woman, though over sixty; and, had I been free, I should certainly have married her.' Not being free, the best he found it possible to do for the enamored lady was to dedicate three clavier trios to her.

Those were the days of courtly amenities among musicians, and the Viennese master was doubtless not at all surprised when he was told that the famous Italian violinist and composer Giardini, when urged to call upon Haydn, remarked, 'I don't want to see the German dog.' To which Haydn retorted (silently) by writing in his diary, after hearing the Italian play, 'Giardini played like a pig.'

The G major Symphony, No. 100, was dubbed the 'Military' Symphony because, presumably, of the bass drum, cymbals, and triangle that are required in the second movement (an Allegretto, in C, 2-2) and in the Presto Finale. The other movements are more conventionally scored for flute, two oboes, two bassoons, two horns, kettledrums, and strings, and comprise an opening Allegro in 2-2 time (preceded by the usual brief Adagio introduction), and a Menuetto, Moderato.

• SYMPHONY IN D MAJOR, B. & H. No. 101 ('Clock')

This symphony is sometimes known as the 'Clock' Symphony because of the 'tick-tock' effects in the slow movement. The first movement has a slow introduction of twenty-three measures (Adagio, D minor, 3-4). The main section (Presto, D major, 6-8) presents at once the vivacious chief theme, opening with an ascending staccato scale for the first violins—it is heard later, as a counter-subject, with the scale reversed in the upper voice (first violins), against the original ascending form for the second violins and violas in thirds. The first violins are entrusted also with the statement of the second theme, which they propose alone (A major, bar 59 of the Presto). There is ingenious contrapuntal elaboration in the development.

The slow movement, save for the G minor episode in the middle, is chiefly a fantasia upon the naïve opening theme (Andante, G major, 2-4) for the first violins, accompanied by pizzicati of the second violins and basses, and bassoons in thirds. Here is heard the ticking of Haydn's eighteenth-century clock.

In the Minuet the jovial chief theme (Allegro, D major, 3-4) is announced by the whole orchestra, forte, with a soft answer by the strings and flute. The trio has long perplexed the pundits—why did Haydn, they have asked, maintain that tonic D major triad for the strings through the first ten bars, against the second and third measures of the melody for the flute, where the tune, at the four reiterated E's, undoubtedly calls loudly for a change to the dominant harmony? The passage does not seem very startling today, having obviously the character of a drone-bass. At its repetition, Haydn does change the supporting harmony to the dominant (though the basses grimly hang on to the tonic D as pedal-point). Yet these things are in accordance with Haydn's manuscript.

The Finale (Vivace, D major, 2-2) opens with a chorale-like subject for the strings, which later in the movement tempts Haydn to a spirited fugue, at first for the string section alone, but finally, as climax and conclusion, for the entire band.

The symphony is scored for flutes, oboes, clarinets, bassoons, horns, and trumpets (all in pairs), timpani, and strings.

● SYMPHONY IN B-FLAT, B. & H. No. 102

This symphony, No. 9 of the Salomon set, is in four movements: 1—Largo, 4-4; 'Allegro vivace,' 2-2; 2—Adagio, F major, 3-4; 3—Menuetto, Allegro, 3-4; 4—Finale, Presto, B-flat, 2-4. The most remarkable of the movements is the Adagio, in which the elaborate ornamentation of the melodies is consorted with an expressiveness typical of Haydn at his best.

In the violin phrase of the Largo introduction to the first movement (after the hold on the keynote), the pattern of the initial curve of the melody reflects a characteristic of the Slavonic folk songs to which Haydn so often resorted for his tunes—in this case, the pattern may be found in the ballad, 'Na placi sem stal': the first phrase of the song and of Haydn's subject are identical.

In the theme which opens the Finale of this symphony we find Haydn resorting again to his beloved folk tunes, this time to a Croatian march which is commonly played in Turopol at rustic weddings.

The instrumentation is for flutes, oboes, bassoons, horns, and trumpets—all in pairs, timpani, and strings.

● SYMPHONY IN E-FLAT MAJOR, B. & H. No. 103

This is the 'Symphonie mit den Paukenwirbel'—the 'symphony with the drum-roll.' It begins with an Adagio introduction (E-flat, 3-4). The feature which gave the work its name is the kettle-drum roll heard in the opening measure (and again in the first of the twelve Adagio measures that precede the coda of the first movement). The dynamics of this celebrated drum-roll have long been a subject of dispute. The old Breitkopf edition of the score called for a fortissimo; and 'inasmuch,' says the editor of the Philharmonia edition, 'as the ff sign stands not only in the score but on the cover, which gives the opening bars of the symphony, a misprint or an error seems out of the question.' Nevertheless, the Philharmonia score has not adopted the ff ('as it is entirely contradictory to the custom practised at performances of this symphony'), but marks the drum-roll thus: 'p< >.' The latest Breitkopf & Härtel edition prefers an opening pianissimo, with crescendo and diminuendo.

The string basses and bassoons announce a subject which is taken up by the first violins. This subject is influential in the structure of the main movement. The 'Allegro con spirito' begins with the chief theme announced by the strings, pianissimo (6-8), in the first violins. The second chief theme (B-flat major) is stated by the oboe and first violins in unison. An allusion to the theme of the introductory Adagio may be detected in the violas and 'cellos at the nineteenth measure of the working-out section, following a fermata. The reminiscence of the opening Adagio just before the short coda is noteworthy; and the coda itself is begun by the theme of the introduction, with altered rhythm.

The slow movement is a two-part theme with variations. The violins in unison announce, *p*, the first section (Andante, C minor, 2-4); the second section, in C major, is begun, forte, by oboes, horns, bassoons, and strings. In this movement Haydn introduces a violin solo, as he does elsewhere in his symphonies.

The Menuetto is in E-flat major, with a trio in the same key, introduced by the first violins alone.

The Finale ('Allegro con spirito,' E-flat major, 2-2), presents the chief theme of the movement in dismembered form. We hear first the harmonic support of the tune—on the horns; then, after a fermata, the rest of its musical body, the tune itself, in the first violins, with the legs in their proper place. A secondary motive springs from this theme.

According to the learned and industrious Dr. Kuhac (in his *South-Slavonic Popular Songs*), the opening theme of the first Allegro of this symphony, and the C minor–C major tunes of the Andante, are derived from Croatian folk songs of the Oedenburg district; and the chief theme of the Finale is that of the song 'Divojcica potok gazi,' which was common among the Croats of Haydn's district.

The symphony is scored for two flutes, two oboes, two clarinets (in the first and last movements), two bassoons, two horns, two trumpets, timpani, and strings. There was also, of course, the usual harpsichord part, elaborated at the keyboard by (as a rule) the leader.

● SYMPHONY IN D MAJOR, B. & H. NO. 104

The program of the London concert at which this symphony was first performed—that of May 4, 1795—was, for those times, a rather skimpy one, containing only two symphonies (both by Haydn), two concertos, and a few odds and ends—duets, songs, et cetera. Certain of the symphonic movements were separated by interpolated numbers, as was then the custom. The Symphony in D was announced as a 'New Overture' by Haydn; the other symphony was the 'Military.' In spite of what must have been a long evening, Haydn recorded in his diary that the concert was highly successful: 'The hall was filled with a picked audience. The whole company was delighted, and so was I. I took in this evening four thousand gulden. One can make as much as this only in England.'

When Haydn left England three months later, he had earned by his second London visit the very pretty sum of twelve hundred pounds. Many friends (Clementi and Tattersall among them) gave him parting gifts—one was a talking parrot, which brought 1400 florins at Haydn's death; and so warmly was the memory of Haydn's visit cherished in England that nine years after he departed from the British Isles he received from Gardiner of Leicester six pairs of cotton stockings, into which were worked favorite themes from his music. No wonder he thought well of England.

This last of Haydn's symphonies opens with an Allegro in the tonic key, prefaced by an Adagio introduction in D minor. The slow movement (Andante, G major, 2-4) is a theme with variations. The Mcnuetto (Allegro) is in D, with a trio in B-flat. The Finale is an 'Allegro spiritoso' in 2-2 time.

Some have detected suggestions of Mozart's *Don Giovanni* and *Nozze di Figaro* in the first movement of the symphony. But more remarkable features of the vivid and charming score are such unusual details as the wide intervallic leaps, whole-measure rests, crescendo drum-rolls, and trills of the strings and wind in the Menuetto; and the pedal-point with a drone effect that begins the Finale. The chief theme of this Finale (announced at the third measure by the first violins over a pedal D) is derived from a Croatian folk tune, that of the ballad, 'Oj Jelena,' belonging to the district of Kolnov, near Oedenburg. It was commonly sung in the region where Haydn dwelt with the Esterházy family.

● CONCERTO FOR 'CELLO AND ORCHESTRA, IN D MAJOR, OP. 101

Anton Kraft, born in 1752 near Pilsen, was fortunate in his paternal parent, for the elder Kraft was both a music-lover and a brewer. Young Anton was encouraged to study the 'cello. He went to Vienna, and eventually wound up in Prince Esterházy's orchestra, for which Haydn engaged him as solo 'cellist. Kraft remained in the orchestra for twelve years—from New Year's Day 1778 until the disbanding of the orchestra in 1790. Haydn became attached to him, and taught him composition. Also he wrote a 'cello concerto for him. It is in D major, and was composed between 1781 and 1784—there is a disagreement as to the year.

Haydn scored the orchestral accompaniment of this concerto for strings, two oboes, and two horns; but when the insatiable Gevaert revised the concerto he amplified the score by supplying additional wind parts—two flutes, two clarinets, and two bassoons; and he also wrote cadenzas.

The first movement ('Allegro moderato,' D major, 4-4) begins, in the original version, with an orchestral exposition of the two chief themes. The 'cello then presents the first theme, and, after intervening passage-work, the second, in A major.

The slow movement is an Adagio in A, 2-4 time. The 'cello begins the proceedings with a subject of expressive character. There are contrasting themes, and the movement passes through the keys of E and C major.

The Finale, one of Haydn's neat and vivacious rondos, is derived from two themes, with an effective coda.

A score of this concerto in its original form has been published with a preface in which it is asserted that Dr. Hans Volkmann has proved (to his own satisfaction, at least) that the concerto was really composed by Kraft, and not by Haydn. It is said that the demonstration of this alleged fact 'is not complete.'

Paul Hindemith

1895-

‡A quarter of a century ago Hindemith was rated as an ultramodernist, and to remind ourselves of the fact, when we listen to his music, is to bring an ancient phenomenon sharply into focus. What today seems wayward and arbitrary in the technique of an art is quite likely tomorrow to be accepted as conventional and entirely reasonable procedure. Our receptivity, apparently, is infinitely educable. Yet this lesson, which every generation is taught by both history and experience, is really learned by none. Richard Strauss, himself a *Kulturbolshevik* of an earlier time, once remarked to Hindemith, 'Why do you write atonally, since you have talent?' Hindemith might have replied succinctly, 'Because I have.' But in fact, even twenty-five years ago, Hindemith was an atonalist but north-northwest; when the wind blew from the proper quarter, he knew a triad from a chord of superimposed fourths. He had good masters, and he absorbed from them all they could teach, and there was always an irreducible core of classicism in even his more experimental works. His position in Germany was already established by the end of the 'twenties; he occupied an important teaching post, his latest works were awaited with interest and heard with approbation (though there were, of course, dissenting voices); and it was probably his association with artists of revolutionary political views and 'impure' racial heritage that led the Hitler Government to condemn his music, rather than the qualities of that music as such. He left Germany in the early 'thirties, and since then has resided in the United States.‡

● SYMPHONY, *Mathis der Maler*

This work is a symphonic integration of three instrumental excerpts from Hindemith's opera, *Mathis der Maler* ('Matthias the Painter'), based on the life of the sixteenth-century master, Matthias Grünewald. The three movements of the symphony—(1) 'Angelic Concert'; (2) 'Entombment'; (3) 'Temptation of St. Anthony'—were inspired by the great triptych painted by Grünewald for the Isenheim altar at Colmar, in Alsace. Hindemith's symphony was performed for the first time anywhere at a Berlin Philharmonic concert, under the direction of Wilhelm Furtwängler, on March 12, 1934.

Grünewald—his real name was Mathis Neithart Gothart—was the chief Rhenish painter at the beginning of the sixteenth century. An artist of extraordinary power and emotional force, a religious mystic whose imagination was both passionate and exalted, he has been called 'the last and greatest representative of the German Gothic.' The Isenheim altarpiece at Colmar is a triptych with a double course of painted shutters. At the sides of a carved centerpiece are the Temptations of St. Anthony, and the Hermits Anthony and Paul. The first pair of wings, when closed, display the Virgin and Child between the Annunciation and the Resurrection. The second pair of wings discloses the Crucifixion. Richard Muther, in his *History of Painting*, declares that Grünewald's famous altarpiece is 'the most astonishing work produced by German art during the sixteenth century'—which, considering that the great Dürer lived in Germany in that same century, is high praise indeed. Grünewald, remarks Professor Muther, traversed the whole scale of human emotion, from tragical despair to joyful ecstasy. In his picture representing the Temptation of St. Anthony (reflected by Hindemith in the last movement of his symphony), a Witches' Sabbath is let loose. Then there is a change of scene, and cherubim descend and flowers arise, as if by magic, from the landscape. In the other wings of the altar, a wild cry of pain afflicts us. The sufferings of the Saviour are over, the arms of the cross bend under the burden of His lifeless body; the wounds made by the scourge still bleed, the fingers are cramped, the toes stretched, the head sinks heavily to one side. Magdalen cries aloud, and Mary sinks to the earth in deathlike rigidity.

These images of a religious art that was at once naïve and tremendous and profound seem to have stirred deeply the imagination of Hindemith. He has given us, in the first movement of his symphony, music inspired by Grünewald's painting of the Nativity, in which the old German song, 'Es sungen drei Engel,' is used with delicate and poetic skill. The second movement is a poignant reflection of that picture which delineates the Saviour's entombment —a musical lament of somber power and expressiveness. In the third movement, Hindemith remembers the scene of St. Anthony's temptation, and his final glorified vision, with a hymn of praise ('Lauda Sion Salvatorem') sung by the woodwind, and the brass choir chanting a resplendent Hallelujah at the end.

● *Noblissima Visione:* CONCERT SUITE FROM THE BALLET, *St. Francis*

This is music from the ballet *Saint Francis: Choreographic Legend in One Act and Five Scenes,* music by Hindemith, choreography by Massine, composed especially for the Ballet Russe de Monte Carlo 'in close collaboration with the choreographer.' The first performance of *St. Francis* was at the Drury Lane

Theatre, London, on July 21, 1938. The score of Hindemith's music was published by B. Schotts Söhne in 1938, under the title *Noblissima Visione*. The instrumentation is for one flute, one oboe, one bassoon, two clarinets, two horns, two trumpets, one trombone, timpani, glockenspiel, percussion, and strings.

Hindemith has described his music as follows:

The suite, *Noblissima Visione*, consists of three movements: (1) Introduction and Rondo; (2) March and Pastorale; (3) Passacaglia.

The Introduction consists of that part of the original music (for the ballet) during which the hero of the action, Franziskus, is sunk in deep meditation. The Rondo corresponds to the music in the stage score for the mystic union of the Saint to Mistress Poverty, the scene having been inspired by an old Tuscan legend. The music reflects the blessed peace and unworldly cheer with which the guests at the wedding participate in the wedding feast—dry bread and water only.

The second movement pictures the march of a troop of medieval soldiers. First heard but distantly, their gradual approach is observed. The middle portion of this movement suggests the brutality with which these mercenaries set upon a traveling burgher and rob him. The pastoral section of the second movement pictures the sleeping St. Francis. In his inspired dream he visions the appearance of three symbolic female figures: Obedience, Chastity, and Poverty. The short closing section of this movement intimates a scene, often on paintings of Sassetta and other early masters of the Florentine School. These artists picture the sleeping St. Francis. Poverty, her eyes fastened upon him, is his constant companion.

The third and closing movement, Passacaglia, corresponds to that portion of the ballet score representing the dance: Hymn to the Sun. Here all the symbolic personifications of heavenly and earthly existence mingle in the course of the different Variations through which the six-measure-long theme of the Passacaglia is transformed. In the ballet this closing piece bears a special title borrowed from a chapter-heading in an old version of the *Cantique du Soleil*, which reads: 'Incipiunt laudes creaturarum.'

Gustav Theodore Holst

1874-1934

The ancestors of Holst were of Swedish blood; but the Holst family came to England from Russia, where they had long been settled, more than a century ago. On his mother's side, Holst was pure English. His father, Adolf Holst, who had made Cheltenham his home, was known there as a pianist and organist. It was his hope that his son would be a painter, but Gustav was bent upon becoming a musician. He entered the Royal College of Music, London, where he studied composition with Villiers Stanford, though he was obliged by neuritis to give up the study of keyboard instruments. Instead, he took a course in choir training and trombone playing. Later, he played trombone in the orchestra of the Carl Rosa Opera Company. He gave up orchestral playing to become musical director and teacher of composition at Morley College, and principal teacher at St. Paul's School, London. He journeyed to the Orient, and during the War he served with the Salonika Expeditionary Force. Holst wrote an enormous quantity of music—stage works, choral works, orchestral pieces, chamber·music, songs. He was one of the most vital and energizing influences in twentieth-century English music.

● *The Planets*, OP. 32

Holst gave to the seven movements of his work the following titles: (I) 'Mars; the Bringer of War.' (II) 'Venus; the Bringer of Peace.' (III) 'Mercury; the Winged Messenger.' (IV) 'Jupiter; the Bringer of Jollity.' (V) 'Saturn; the Bringer of Old Age.' (VI) 'Uranus; the Magician.' (VII) 'Neptune; the Mystic.'

Five of the movements were performed in London at a concert of the Royal Philharmonic Society on February 27, 1919, under the direction of Adrian C. Boult. The work was not heard in its entirety until November 15, 1920, at a performance in Queen's Hall under Albert Coates.

At the time of the first London performance of *The Planets* in 1920, Holst explained them as follows:

'These pieces were suggested by the astrological significance of the planets. There is no program-music in them, neither have they any connection with the deities of classical mythology bearing the same names. If any guide to the music is required, the subtitle to each piece will be found sufficient, especially if it be used in a broad sense. For instance, Jupiter brings jollity in the ordinary sense, and also the more ceremonial kind of rejoicing associated with religious or national festivities. Saturn brings not only physical decay, but also a vision of fulfilment. Mercury is the symbol of mind.'

This explanation was elaborated by Edward Evans (no doubt upon the authority of the composer). 'The generally accepted astrological associations of the planets are in themselves a sufficient clue to the imagination,' he wrote in the London *Musical Times*. 'One may be skeptical concerning horoscopes, but one will nevertheless be carried away with the aggressive rhythm of "Mars," the "Bringer of War"; and any schoolboy pictures Mercury as the "Winged Messenger." The very word "joviality" connotes Jupiter, and the sand-glass and scythe connect Saturn with old age. It may be new to some of us to regard Venus as the "Bringer of Peace"—as she is, astrologically speaking— for many have held her responsible for strife in worldly affairs. It is also unfamiliar to hail Neptune, the sea god, as a mystic, and Uranus as a magician; but once these relations are established in the titles, it is easy to fall into the mood of the respective movements.'

Gustav Holst had achieved, some time before his death, an indisputable place among the leaders of creative thought in contemporary English music. He stood in the pre-eminent group that included Elgar, Delius, Vaughan Williams, Bax, and—of the younger men—Lambert and Walton.

Fifty years ago, before Byrd and Purcell and the other great masters of English music in the sixteenth and seventeenth centuries had been rediscovered and made popular, English music, as then generally known to the world, was scarcely one of the Lively Arts. When English composers of the late Victorian Age turned to the writing of symphonic or choral works, especially of a sacred or semi-sacred character, they were haunted, as a rule, by the pious ghost of Mendelssohn, or they attempted to draw the bow of the mighty Handel; or they remembered Gounod. Then, near the turn of the century, Elgar came with his *Enigma Variations* and his *Dream of Gerontius*; Delius appeared upon the tonal scene with his fine-textured and sensitive scores; Holst and others of that generation began to be heard from; and British music was suddenly and surprisingly reborn.

He was a gifted artist, a gifted teacher; a man of flexible and capacious imagination, a wit, a poet, a mystic (though he would not have liked to be called so). He was on familiar terms with the cosmos, and could paint for us imposing tonal portraits of Mars and Venus, Mercury and Jupiter and Saturn, as easily and brilliantly as he could toss off a satirical opera (libretto and score) or a suite for a school orchestra. He was learned in the Wisdom of the East, was attracted by the noble simplicity of the *Rig Veda* hymns, and, not liking the standard translations, set to work and mastered Sanskrit so that he could make his own English versions. This he did, and some of his choral settings of the hymns are music of exalted and piercing beauty.

Engelbert Humperdinck

1854-1921

‡Humperdinck in his late twenties was a friend and disciple of Wagner, frequented the Wagner circle at Bayreuth, and assisted the master in preparing the première of *Parsifal*. But the work by which he survives to us today, the charming fairy-tale opera, *Hänsel und Gretel*, owes much more to the influence of German folk music than to that of the *Ring*. With every occasion and inducement to model himself upon his idol, Humperdinck had sufficient intelligence and modesty and strength to realize that his native gifts limited his range.‡

● OVERTURE AND DREAM PANTOMIME FROM *Hänsel und Gretel*

Hänsel und Gretel was not originally composed for public performance, but grew out of a project for the amusement of Humperdinck's children. His sister, Frau Adelheid Wette, conceived the idea of producing a children's play at family gatherings. She asked her brother to compose a tune for certain words, and Humperdinck wrote the melody of what is now the song, 'Brother, Come and Dance With Me,' which Gretel sings in Act I of *Hänsel und Gretel*. Frau Wette was captivated by this, and proposed to her brother that they work up together a little opera for domestic use on the subject of one of Grimm's Fairy Tales, *Hänsel und Gretel*, combined with a bit from another tale, *Brüderchen und Schwesterchen* ('Little Brother and Little Sister'). Humperdinck became fascinated with the theme, and the ultimate result was the opera as we know it. The Humperdinck children were deprived of their home-made amusement, but the world became richly the gainer.

The opera was completed in 1892, and Humperdinck offered it to the theater at Gotha, whose director, with the enlightenment characteristic of his kind, rejected it as 'unsuitable for the stage.' The piece came to the attention of the famous conductor, Hermann Levi (the first conductor of Wagner's *Parsifal*). Levi was delighted with the opera, and planned a production of it at Munich. But Richard Strauss forestalled him by producing it at Weimar, under his own direction. It was a success both there and at Munich (where Levi gave it a week later), and it soon became immensely popular throughout Germany.

In the opera, as finally developed by Frau Wette and Humperdinck from Grimm's story, the action proceeds as follows: The rising curtain discloses a room in the cottage of Peter, a poor broom-maker (he is a wood-cutter in Grimm's tale), on the edge of a forest. The two children of the family, Hänsel and Gretel, have been left alone in the house. They soon tire of their tasks, and Gretel volunteers to teach her brother how to dance. In the middle of their play, Gertrude, their mother, comes in, and angrily sends them off into the woods to pick strawberries. Then, tired and faint, she sinks into a chair, bewailing the lot of a poor peasant's wife, with empty cupboards and with hungry mouths to feed. Peter's voice is heard singing in the distance. He has made a satisfactory sale of his brooms, and he returns laden with good cheer. But his high spirits are dashed by the absence of Hänsel and Gretel; and when he learns that they are out alone in the forest, he alarms his wife with the story of the witch of Ilsenstein, who is in the habit of eating little children. They both hasten off to find Hänsel and Gretel and bring them home.

In the next act, we find ourselves in the heart of the legendary German forest. Hänsel and Gretel have been amusing themselves by picking strawberries and making flower garlands, until the approach of night, when they realize that they have lost their way. Terrified, they search vainly for the path, and at last, completely worn out, sink down upon the moss beneath a spreading tree.

The Sandman, a little gray man with a sack on his back, appears and throws sand into their weary eyes, singing his captivating song ('I Shut the Children's Peepers—Shhh!'). Together the children sing their evening hymn, and drop off to sleep locked in each other's arms. Then the heavens open, and down a luminous staircase come fourteen shining angels, who group themselves round the sleeping children, there to guard them until the break of day.

Hänsel and Gretel are aroused by the Dew-man, or Dawn Fairy, who sprinkles dewdrops from a bluebell over them and drives the sleep from their eyes. They tell each other of the marvelous and radiant dream which came to both of them; and then, looking round for the first time, they discover, quite near them, a beautiful little house made of ginger-bread and pastry, with a roof of cake. This is the home of the Witch of the forest, who bakes little children into ginger-bread in her great oven, and eats them up. While the children are delightedly engaged in nibbling bits of the fascinating house, they are caught by the Witch, who very nearly succeeds in her atrocious scheme; but the children, with admirable presence of mind, outwit her by pushing her into her own oven. They then proceed to bring to life the other children who have been turned into ginger-bread by the Witch's magic spell. Peter and Gertrude arrive in time to join in a hymn of thanksgiving.

The Overture to *Hänsel und Gretel* (a potpourri of tunes from the opera) and the Dream Music from the end of the second act, are often heard in the concert room.

Edouard Lalo

1823-92

‡Fifteen years older than Bizet, whom he outlived, Lalo was a composer of comparable gifts (though he wrote no *Carmen*). That is to say, he was a facile and original melodist, and a skilful painter of orchestral canvas. He was trained in the conservatory of Lille, the city of his birth, and lived the greater part of his life in Paris. His successes as a composer for both the concert hall and the theater were numerous, and an admiring and grateful government bestowed upon him, in 1880, the ribbon of the Légion d'Honneur.‡

● *Symphonie Espagnole*, FOR VIOLIN AND ORCHESTRA, OP. 21

Spring was late in smiling upon the neighborhood of Clarens, Switzerland, in 1878; and Peter Ilich Tchaikovsky, kept indoors by the storms of March, had nothing to do but occupy himself with music—not only his own music (the Fourth Symphony, completed in January, had just been performed for the first time), but other men's.

Today [he wrote Mrs. von Meck on the 15th of March] I played nearly all day with Kotek. Do you know the *Symphonie espagnole*, by the French composer, Lalo? The piece has been recently brought out by the very modern violinist, Sarasate. It is for solo violin and orchestra, and consists of five independent movements, based upon Spanish idioms. The work has given me great enjoyment. It is so fresh and light, and contains piquant rhythms and melodies which are beautifully harmonized. It resembles many other works of the modern French school with which I am acquainted. Like Léo

Delibes and Bizet, Lalo is careful to avoid all that is *routinier*, seeks new forms without trying to be profound, and is more concerned with musical beauty than with tradition, as are the Germans. The young generation of French composers is really very promising.

Sarasate, to whom the work is dedicated, played the *Spanish Symphony* for the first time at a Colonne concert in Paris on February 7, 1875. Lalo was then over fifty; yet it was only a year earlier that the production of his violin concerto, op. 20 (also dedicated to and first played by Sarasate) had made him famous. Indeed, Lalo's early neglect by the public caused him such depression of spirits that, a decade before, he had given up composition and turned for precarious solace to matrimony with a contralto.

The *Symphonie espagnole* added to his renown; but he had to wait more than a dozen years longer before the production in 1888 of his best-known work, the opera *Le Roi d'Ys*, placed him securely among the foremost composers of his day.

● CONCERTO FOR 'CELLO AND ORCHESTRA, IN D MINOR

Lalo wrote this concerto for 'cello two years after Sarasate's performance of his violin concerto at a Chatelet concert in 1874 had made him famous, and one year after the *Symphonie espagnole* for violin and orchestra in 1875 had made him more so. It was played for the first time by Adolphe Fischer, the Belgian virtuoso (1847-91), at the Cirque d'Hiver, Paris, December 9, 1877. The first movement (Prelude) begins with a twenty-bar Introduction (Lento), followed by an 'Allegro maestoso,' D minor, 12-8. The second movement is an Intermezzo, derived from two themes: 'Andante con moto,' G minor, 9-8; Allegro, G major, 6-8. The Finale (Rondo), 'Allegro vivace,' D minor, 6-8, is introduced by a brief Andante.

● OVERTURE TO *Le Roi d'Ys*

Lalo began work on the score of his opera in the seventies of the last century and finished his sketch in 1881, revising and completing the music in 1886-7. The opera was given at the Opéra-Comique, Paris, on May 7, 1888. Lalo's libretto, by Edouard Blau, is based upon an ancient Breton legend—the tale of the engulfing of the old Amorican city of Ys. The plot of the opera, which deals rather cavalierly with the legend, has been outlined as follows:

King Karnac loves Margaret, daughter of the King of d'Ys, though he is her father's enemy. He agrees to conclude a peace with Ys on condition that Margaret become his bride. But Margaret is in love with Mylio, and refuses King Karnac's hand on the day appointed for their marriage. Karnac swears vengeance, and the wars are renewed. In the ensuing battle, Karnac is defeated. But Margaret now learns that Mylio loves not her but her sister Rozenn. Now it is her turn to seek revenge, and aided by Karnac, she opens the dikes which protect the city of Ys from the sea. The King of Ys, Margaret, Rozenn, and Mylio and other fugitives seek safety on a high hill, whence Margaret, stricken with remorse, casts herself sacrificially into the rising flood. The apparition of St. Corentin appears and like King Canute (but more effectively) commands the waters to recede.

Franz Liszt

1811-86

L

‡When Liszt was born, Beethoven had still sixteen years to live; when he died, Richard Strauss was a young man of twenty-two. The drama of his life thus unfolded upon a stage crowded with brilliant figures—Berlioz, Mendelssohn, Schumann, Chopin, Wagner, Brahms, Meyerbeer, Verdi, Gounod, Bizet, Balakireff, Tchaikovsky. Yet even at this remove in time he dominates that noontime pageant of Romanticism. He was the greatest piano virtuoso of record; he was a creative artist of revolutionary originality (and sadly deficient taste); he commanded and was accorded the honors paid to the kings of the earth. He was a voluptuary and a peacock; he was also a man of infinite kindness and generosity of mind and heart and hand. He taught all who came to him with talent, and took no fees. He amassed a fortune, and distributed it freely to friends and strangers alike. His immense prestige and influence were ever at the service of those whom he might well have regarded as dangerous rivals for the priceless favor of posterity. He was a sovereign personality. One hopes that he is shielded from the knowledge that, with the passage of the years, less and less of saliency and worth is found in the music he wrote by those who find more and more to admire and respect in the man he was.‡

● A *Faust Symphony*

Liszt described his *Faust Symphony* as 'Three Character Pieces After Goethe: 1—Faust; 2—Gretchen; 3—Mephistopheles,' with a final chorus for men's voices with solo tenor, singing the Chorus Mysticus ('Alles Vergängliche / Ist nur ein Gleichniss') with which Goethe's great drama ends. He worked upon his score during the period in which Wagner composed the music of his *Rheingold*—1853-4. But Liszt revised and amplified the symphony in '57 (it was then that he added the final chorus). The score was published in 1861. Liszt had already composed or sketched out most of his symphonic poems and his 'Dante' Symphony (begun in 1847-8, completed in 1855). But the *Faust Symphony*, according to Lina Ramann, Liszt's voluminous biographer, has a longer background than these dates would indicate. She says that Liszt conceived the idea of his *Faust Symphony* in the 'forties, inspired by the *Damnation of Faust* of Berlioz (to whom the score is dedicated). But he does not appear to have put any of it on paper until a decade later.

Huneker in his book on Liszt declares roundly that the work 'is not a symphony'; though he inserts a parenthetical query: 'What is the symphonic archetype?' and hastens on without answering his own question. The *Faust Symphony* he calls 'a congeries of symphonic moods, structurally united by emotional intimacy and occasional thematic concourse.' William Apthorp, long before, had perhaps more happily termed it 'a concatenation of three symphonic poems, rather than a symphony, properly so-called. . . Yet there are, nevertheless, some symphonic characteristics discoverable in the first movement.'

The general plan of the symphony—its dramatic and musico-poetic framework—may be described as an attempt to develop a philosophical and poetical idea by giving musical delineation to what the composer conceived to be the fundamental moods of the three principal characters in Goethe's tragedy, in themselves and their relationship to one another. This purpose is suggested in the title. The names of the three characters (Faust, Gretchen, Mephistopheles) are put as superscriptions over the three movements which make up the symphony. Briefly stated, the plan is as follows: By means of musical treatment given to four motives, or themes, in the first movement, the idea of Faust is presented—a type of humanity harassed with doubt, rage, despair, loneliness (the first theme, Lento); his strivings and hopes (second theme, 'Allegro agitato'); his ideals and longings (third theme, Andante); his pride and energy (fourth theme, Grandioso).

The subject of the second movement is Goethe's heroine. There is a brief prelude for flutes and clarinets, which introduces a melody obviously designed to give expression to the gentle grace of Gretchen's character (Andante); then a motive borrowed from the beginning of the first theme of the first movement suggests the entrance of Faust into Gretchen's mind; it is followed by the second extended melody, which delineates the feeling of love after it has taken complete possession of her imagination. This gives way in turn to the third theme of the first movement, in which the composer has given voice to the longings of Faust, and which, in its development, shows the clarifying influence of association with the Gretchen music.

In the third movement, Mephistopheles appears in his character as the spirit of negation (*der Geist der stets verneint*). The music consists of mimicries and parodies of the themes of the first movement, especially the third (Faust's ideals and longings), which, remarked Krehbiel, 'is made the special subject of the Evil One's sport, because it enables him to get nearest to Gretchen, whose goodness protects her from his wiles.' By these means, Liszt develops a conflict which finds its solution in the epilogue sung by male chorus and solo tenor: 'Alles Vergängliche ist nur ein Gleichniss'—all passing things are but resemblances.

For many students of Liszt's symphony, this choral setting of the close of Goethe's drama is the most remarkable and engrossing thing in the score. What, one might have conjectured, could this singular and enigmatic Finale, with its unplumbed depths of philosophic wisdom and its supersensual ecstasies, mean to Liszt—to Liszt the showman, the virtuoso, the sensationalist, crossed with that other Liszt who was poet and path-breaker; to Liszt the playactor and the penitent, the charlatan and the saint. One had thought, it may be, of Liszt the tinseled Titan, the darling of the footlights, the boudoir god, the fashionable male modiste of tones; but also one had remembered Liszt the prophet of musical tomorrows, Liszt the generous and kindly human being; and one had doubtless speculated upon the music that such a flawed, unintegrated spirit would press from that incomparable Epilogue in which the transfigured apparitions of the poet's vision 'are made to pass before us as in a glass, and the divine wisdom is unfolded in a divine ascent.' For in this unique scene, Goethe, as he himself remarked of Filippo Neri, received the gift of ecstasy, that standing outside oneself in freedom, and became the Pater Ecstaticus of his own enraptured vision.

It would be idle to pretend that Liszt has given us in his setting of Goethe's Chorus Mysticus an equivalent, or anything like it, of the spiritual and imaginative values of the poem. Liszt, after all, despite his authentic genius, was no Bach, no Beethoven, no Wagner. Yet Liszt, the everlasting anomaly among creative artists, has disclosed himself here, for a few extraordinary pages, as a visionary, a master of lofty and tender beauty. There are luminous, revelatory moments in these last hundred measures of the *Faust Symphony*—music in which the imagination of the tone poet, like that of the dramatic poet himself, suggests, in Goethe's words, 'a hovering of the spirit above the earth.'

• SYMPHONIC POEM, *Les Preludes*

The imagination of Liszt was quickened by a passage from the *Méditations poétiques* of Alphonse Lamartine, and he embodied the thoughts and emotions that inspired him in the following paraphrase, printed as a preface to his score:

> What is life but a series of preludes to that unknown song whose initial solemn note is tolled by death? The enchanted dawn of every life is love; but where is the destiny on whose first delicious joys some storm does not break?—a storm whose deadly blast disperses youth's illusions, whose fatal bolt consumes its altar. And what soul thus cruelly bruised, when the tempest rolls away, seeks not to rest its memories in the calm of rural life? Yet man allows himself not long to taste the kindly quiet which first attracted him to Nature's lap; but when the trumpet gives the signal he hastens to danger's post, whatever be the fight which draws him to its lists; that in the strife he may once more regain full knowledge of himself and all his strength.

The music was composed at Weimar, where the first performance took place on February 23, 1854, with Liszt conducting from manuscript. The score was published two years later.

The commentators have divided Liszt's tone poem into a succession of contrasted but of course connected movements, marked by significant variations of tempo and mood. This division into sections which correspond in general to the programmatic scheme suggested by the thoughts attributed to Lamartine may be indicated as follows (the designations are those evolved by the musicologist and critic of Leipzig, Alfred Heuss, for Breitkopf & Härtel's analytical guide):

First, the Introduction (Andante, C major, 4-4, strings), with the solemn theme that afterward found its way into César Franck's symphony. Heuss entitles this 'Man, a Mortal Being.' Second part: 'Happiness in Love' (E major, the sensuous and flowing theme for horn quartet, strings, and harp). Third part: 'The Storms of Life' ('Allegro ma non troppo,' 2-2). Fourth part: 'The Return to Nature' ('Allegretto pastorale,' A major, 6-8, a charmingly rustic tune for horn, oboe, clarinet). Fifth part: 'To the Combat as Volunteer' ('Allegro marziale animato,' C major, 2-2—heroic passages for the brass with piccolo and drums; here the militant spirit of the music transforms the character of even the love theme). There is a triumphant coda ('Andante maestoso,' 12-8), an apotheosis of great power and imposing sonority.

● SYMPHONIC POEM, *Mazeppa*

Mazeppa, a Cossack chief (born, they say, 1644, died 1709), was, in his youth a page at the court of Jan Casimir, King of Poland. In Warsaw he exchanged glances with the Lady Theresa (Byron's name for her), who suffered the ill-fortune of being thirty years the junior of her husband, the proud Count Palatine. She had what Byron, in his celebrated poem, makes Mazeppa refer to in his old age as 'the Asiatic eye.' Instead of reading together romantic fiction, like Paola and Francesca in their tender meetings, the youth and the unhappy Countess played some game which Mazeppa, recalling the incident many years later, does not identify—

> A frivolous and foolish play,
> Wherewith we wile away the day;
> It was—I have forgot the name.

It was probably some early form of Russian Bank. At any rate, they played on 'for hours,' caring not if either won or lost, until finally Mazeppa could no longer endure alone the burden of his amorous pain, and declared his state. Thereafter, there was no more Russian Bank:

> We met in secret, and the hour
> Which led me to that lady's bower
> Was fiery Expectation's dower. . .

Quite naturally, the bower was raided, and, as Byron cautiously puts it, 'the Count was something more than wroth.' Voltaire in his *History of Charles XII* briefly recounts the distressing sequel: 'Le mari le fit lier tout nu sur un cheval farouche, et le laissa aller en cet état. Le cheval, qui était du pays de l'Ukraine, y retourna, et y porta Mazeppa, demi-mort de fatigue et de faim. . .' Mazeppa, after his dreadful ride, was nursed back to health, became eventually a Ukrainian prince, and fought against Russia at Pultowa. But he died in wretchedness, as a fugitive, ending his life by poison.

Liszt, moved by Victor Hugo's poem *Mazeppa*, rather than by Byron's, wrote as a young man a piano piece to which he gave the same title. Later he developed this into a symphonic poem, and it was published in that form in 1856, having been performed for the first time at Weimar two years before. In its final shape, as in the earlier piano version, the music is an illustration of the verses in Hugo's *Les Orientales* which tell, with allegorical trimmings,

Mazeppa's story from the point where the ride begins. Hugo's lines, in French and in German, preface the score.

● SYMPHONIC POEM, *Orpheus*

Even Grand Duchesses have their uses. Or, at all events, they had once; for in our progressively democratic days we like to pretend that, as Mark Twain said about acrobats who have lost their legs, 'those parties cease to draw.' But in 1854, at least, Grand Duchesses had not yet ceased to draw, and their birthdays were occasions for public festival and song. It is to the birthday celebration of a Grand Duchess that the world owes Liszt's fourth (the number is in dispute) symphonic poem. This fact, to some recalcitrant souls, may seem an additional reason for going after what remains of the scalps of the aristocracy; for there are still those who are made unhappy by the music of Liszt, and criticism has not yet decided whether in his case it is to be thumbs down or a bungalow on Parnassus.

The Grand Duchess who acted, in a way, as *accoucheuse* for Liszt's *Orpheus* was Maria Paulowna of Saxe-Weimar. The lady had a birthday in February 1854, and in celebration of that occasion there was to be held at the Weimar Theater a performance of the *Orpheus* of Gluck, under Liszt's direction. Now if the Grand Duchess had chosen to keep quiet about her birthday, and there had been no celebration, Liszt might not have been set to dreaming over the Orpheus myth, and might not have been moved to compose his commentary upon the legend. But all these things did happen in due course and sequence, and *Orpheus*, composed by Liszt in a fortnight's time, and played as an orchestral prelude to the performance of Gluck's opera at the birthday celebration, survives to us today as one of his several symphonic poems.

The music begins ('Andante moderato') with a long-sustained G for the horns, softly held through a shower of harp tones. There are seventeen measures of contemplative and lovely preluding, with modulations through E-flat and D major to F, and then the chief theme—the song of Orpheus—is heard from the horn and 'cellos in C major. The oboes repeat it an octave higher, and then comes a phrase, for horns, harp, and strings, wherein those who wish may detect the germ of the second half of the 'Wanderer' motif in Wagner's *Siegfried*. Wagner heard a performance of Liszt's *Orpheus* in November 1856, while he was working upon the music of *Siegfried*. He liked *Orpheus*—'a unique masterwork of the highest perfection,' he called it. The persuasive Huneker thinks he annexed some of it for *Tristan* (which he began the following year); but to our mind the foreshadowing of *Siegfried* in this score is more striking. What does it matter, though? Liszt makes little of that particular theme. Wagner molds it into a thing of superb majesty and beauty.

After this passage in *Orpheus* we get a page that is sheer undivided Liszt: a rhapsodic song for the English horn in E major over harp arpeggios. This is followed by a wistful melody for solo violin, which has been interpreted as a call to Eurydice. Later, there is a return of the *Siegfried* embryo, and a swiftly reached climax on the theme of Orpheus' song. A persistent growling figure in the basses has suggested to some the sinister menacing of Erebus, or, symbolically considered, the dark forces that oppose the civilizing ministrations of Art. The full orchestra attains a second climax on the Orpheus theme; the English horn sings ('espressivo dolente') the 'Eurydice!' call; and there is a serenely luminous close in C major.

● SYMPHONIC POEM, *Tasso: Lament and Triumph*

For the celebration at Weimar in 1849 of the centenary of Goethe's birth, Liszt developed from an earlier piano piece (composed at Venice in 1840) a symphonic prelude to Goethe's drama *Tasso*. This in turn was revised, and in 1856 was published as the second of the symphonic poems. In a preface to the score Liszt sets forth his purposes as follows:

In 1849 all Germany celebrated brilliantly the centenary of Goethe's birth. At Weimar, where I then happened to live, the programme of the festival included a performance of his drama *Tasso*, appointed for the evening of August 28th. The sad fate of the most unfortunate of poets has stimulated the imagination of the greatest poetic geniuses of our time—Goethe and Byron. Goethe, whose career was one of dazzling prosperity; Byron, whose sufferings outweighed the advantages of his birth and fortune. I shall not conceal the fact that, when in 1849 I was commissioned to write an overture for Goethe's drama, I was inspired more by the reverent compassion of Byron for the memory of the great man whom he invoked than by the work of the German poet. Nevertheless, although Byron conveyed to us the groans of Tasso in his prison, he did not add to the recollection of the sorrows so nobly and eloquently expressed in his *Lament* the conception of the triumph that awaited, by an act of belated yet striking justice, the chivalric author of *Jerusalem Delivered*.

I wanted to define in the title of my work this contrast, and it was my aim to depict in music this grand antithesis of genius: ill-used and misunderstood in life, but in death surrounded with a halo of glory whose rays should penetrate to the hearts of his persecutors. Tasso loved and suffered in Ferrara, was avenged in Rome, and lives to this day in the popular songs of Venice. These three viewpoints are inseparably connected with his immortal renown. To express them musically, I first invoked his mighty shadow, as he wanders by the Venetian lagoons, proud and sorrowful in countenance, or watching the feasts at Ferrara, where his masterpieces were created. I followed him to Rome, the Eternal City, which bestowed upon him the crown of glory, and canonized in him the martyr and the poet.

Lament and Triumph—these are the contrasts in the fate of those poets of whom it was said that, although a curse might rest upon their lives, a blessing could not be wanting from their graves. In order to give to my idea not only the authority but the brilliance of living fact, I borrowed the form of my tone-picture from reality, and chose for its theme a melody to which, three centuries after the poet's death, I have heard Venetian gondoliers sing the first strophes of his *Jerusalem:*

> *Canto l'armi pietose e'l Capitano,*
> *Che'l gran Sepolcro liberò di Cristo!*

The motif itself has a slow, plaintive movement, a spirit of monotonous mourning; the gondoliers, however, by drawling certain notes, give it a peculiar coloring, and the mournfully drawn-out tones, heard at a distance, produce an effect not dissimilar to the reflection of long stripes of fading light upon a mirror of water. This song once made a profound impression on me, and when I attempted to illustrate Tasso musically, it recurred to me with such imperative force that I made it the text of my discourse. . .

The Venetian melody is so charged with inconsolable mourning, with bitter sorrow, that it suffices to portray Tasso's soul; and again it yields to the brilliant deceits of the world, to the illusive, smooth coquetry of those smiles whose slow poison brought on the dreadful catastrophe, for which there seemed to be no earthly recompense, but which was eventually clothed in a mantle of more shining purple than that of Alphonse.

● MEPHISTO WALTZ

Liszt composed in 1858-60 two orchestral works based on episodes from the *Faust* of Nicolaus Lenau: 'Der nächtliche Zug' ('The Nocturnal Procession') and 'Der Tanz in der Dorfschenke' ('The Dance in the Village Tavern'). Liszt intended these two pieces to be played in sequence. There was, he admitted, 'no thematic connection between the two; but, nevertheless, they *belong together*, owing to the contrast of ideas.' In spite of Liszt's wish, however, the two pieces are not often heard together. The first, indeed, is scarcely known, though the second—generally called the 'Mephisto Waltz'—is a familiar number on contemporary concert programs.

In order that Liszt's conception may be understood in its totality, let us glance at both pieces. Frederick Niecks has thus presented the programmatic gist of the first episode, 'The Nocturnal Procession':

> Heavy, dark clouds, profound night, sweet spring feeling in the wood, a warm, soulful rustling in the foliage, fragrant air, carolling of the nightingale. Faust rides alone in sombre mood; the farther he advances the greater the silence. He dismounts. What can be the approaching light illuminating bush and sky? A procession, with torches, of white-dressed children carrying wreaths of flowers in the celebration of St. John's Eve, followed by virgins in demure nuns' veils, and old priests in dark habits and with crosses. When they have passed by and the last glimpses of the lights have disappeared, Faust buries his face in his horse's mane and sheds tears more bitter than ever he shed before.

Niecks characterizes the second piece, the 'Mephisto Waltz,' as 'an episode of a very different nature. The "Dance in the Village Inn," or "Mephisto Waltz," is, he says, 'the *ne plus ultra* of weirdness and unbridled sensuality in the whole domain of music, and one of the most remarkable *tours de force* of imagination, combination, and instrumentation.' Here is a condensed paraphrase of the lines from Lenau's poem that are printed (in German) in the score:

> There is a wedding feast in progress in the village inn, with music, dancing, carousing. Mephistopheles and Faust pass by, and Mephistopheles induces Faust to enter and take part in the festivities. Mephistopheles snatches the instrument from the hands of the lethargic fiddler, and draws from it indescribably seductive and intoxicating strains. The amorous Faust whirls about with a full-blooded village beauty in a wild dance: they waltz in mad abandonment, out of the room, into the open, away to the wood. . . The sounds of the fiddle grow softer and softer, and the nightingale warbles his love-laden song.

● CONCERTO FOR PIANO AND ORCHESTRA, NO. 1, IN E-FLAT

This brilliant and vital score (its age already exceeds the span of years allotted to man by Scriptural decree) is the work to which Hanslick gave an undetachable tag when he dubbed it 'the triangle concerto.' That was at Vienna, in the season of 1856-7, when Dionys Pruckner played the concerto there. Hanslick, that ferocious aesthetic Comstock of nineteenth-century criticism, attended the concert, heard the triangle in the Scherzo, and was scandalized. The fact that good Papa Haydn had used a triangle (likewise cymbals and a bass drum) in his G major Symphony (B. & H. No. 100), and that Beethoven and Schumann also used the triangle symphonically seems not to have appealed to the implacable Hanslick as constituting sufficiently respectable precedents. So he drew aside the skirts of his unsullied dressing-gown and turned this erring concerto out into the snowy night.

In Vienna the opposition of the orthodox to Liszt's concerto placed it under the ban for a dozen years. But in 1869 Sophie Menter braved the wrath of the embattled purists and announced that she intended to play it. Her friends went to her in dismay. Rubinstein warned her excitedly: 'You are mad to attempt this concerto! No one has succeeded with it in Vienna.' Bösendorfer, representing the Philharmonic, added his admonition. But the intrepid Sophie was undeterred. 'If I can't play it,' she replied, with imperturbable serenity, 'I won't play at all. I don't *have* to play in Vienna.' And play it she did—with emphatic success.

This concerto, as the pundits have carefully noted, is in free form. The four movements, or sections, are continuous. 'It is constructed,' says Huneker in his book on Liszt, 'along the general lines of the symphonic poem. . . The score embraces four sections arranged like the four movements of a symphony, although their internal development is of so free a nature, and they are merged one into another in such a way, as to give to the work as a whole the character of one long movement developed from several fundamental themes and sundry subsidiaries derived therefrom.'

Liszt himself expatiated upon the concerto in an interesting letter to his relative, Eduard Liszt (the younger half-brother of Franz's father), written from Weimar in the spring of 1857, shortly before the publication of the score:

> The fourth section of the Concerto [he wrote], from the 'Allegro marziale' on, corresponds with the second section, the Adagio. It is only an urgent recapitulation of the earlier subject-matter with quickened, livelier rhythm, and contains no new motive, as will be clear to you by a glance at the score. This kind of *binding* together and rounding off a whole piece at its close is somewhat my own, but it is quite maintained and justified from the standpoint of musical form. The trombones and basses take up the second part of the motive of the Adagio (B major). The pianoforte figure which follows is no other than the reproduction of the motive which was given in the Adagio by flute and clarinet, just as the concluding passage is a Variante and working up in the major of the motive of the Scherzo, until finally the first motive on the dominant pedal B-flat, with a shake-accompaniment, comes in and concludes the whole.
>
> The scherzo in E-flat minor, from the point where the triangle begins, I employed for the effect of contrast.

● CONCERTO FOR PIANO AND ORCHESTRA, NO. 2, IN A MAJOR

Liszt made sketches for this concerto in 1839. The music was completed and scored ten years later. It was played for the first time from manuscript, on

January 7, 1857, at a pension-fund concert given in Weimar for the benefit of the local orchestra. The pianist was Hans von Bronsart (Hans Bronsart von Schellendorf, 1830-1913). The manuscript bears the title, *Concert symphonique*, and it has been suggested that the concerto might justifiably be regarded as a symphonic poem for piano and orchestra.

It is in one movement, and the chief subject ('Adagio sostenuto assai,' A major, 3-4) integrates the work. This subject is set forth at the start by the woodwind—a lamenting and melancholy theme, to which the solo instrument, after a dozen bars, adds its voice. The horn contributes a poetic meditation, and the oboe and a solo 'cello are heard, followed by a cadenza for the piano, introducing a new theme in D minor. A crescendo leads to a change of mood and tempo, 'Allegro agitato assai,' B-flat minor, 6-8, and later, after another cadenza, to 'Allegro moderato,' E major, 4-4. A solo 'cello speaks again, followed by a third cadenza, and an 'Allegro deciso,' with development, and then the orchestra and solo instrument restate, *ff*, 'Marziale un poco meno allegro,' the chief theme, followed by a coda.

- FANTASIA ON HUNGARIAN FOLK MELODIES, FOR PIANO AND ORCHESTRA
- HUNGARIAN RHAPSODIES

Liszt's *Fantasie über Ungarische Volksmelodien, für Pianoforte und Orchester (für Hans von Bülow komponiert)*, was performed for the first time on June 1, 1853, at the Hungarian National Theater, Pesth. The piano part was played from manuscript by Bülow; Franz Erkel conducted the orchestra. Bülow played the work at different times under various titles—*Hungarian Rhapsody for Piano and Orchestra*, or *Magyar Rhapsody*, or *Hungarian Fantasia*. The score was published in 1864.

The musical material contained in the work exists in three different embodiments. The original form of it is the Fourteenth Hungarian Rhapsody for piano, composed at Weimar, for von Bülow, in 1852. Two decades later, the weariless Franz, aided and abetted by Franz Doppler, scored for orchestra alone half a dozen of the Hungarian Rhapsodies, including the Fourteenth, and they were published in that guise in 1875. The orchestral versions are numbered differently from their keyboard prototypes, and four of them are transposed to other keys. The one corresponding to No. 14 for piano is No. 1 of the orchestral set.

Liszt based his Hungarian Rhapsodies upon the folk songs of the Magyars, and in making use of that material, he attempted to reproduce the traits of the performances which the folk music received at the hands of the gypsies from whom he learned it. Because of this fact, and because of Liszt's own opinions as expressed in his book, *Des Bohemiens et de leur musique en Hongrie*, the impression gained currency for many years that the Magyar melodies are of gypsy origin. But the investigations of students of folk song have shown that this is not so. The gypsies were for years the musical practitioners of Hungary, but they were not the composers of the music of the Magyars, in spite of the fact that they imposed upon those melodies certain characteristic traits.

The true Hungarian folk songs are representative of the national characteristics of the Magyars, and many of them are centuries old. The Magyars are Orientals, and several of the peculiarities of their music are characteristic of Oriental music—for example, the use of a minor scale containing one or even two superfluous seconds; and their songs have also a rhythmical peculiarity which, as has been pointed out by students, is a direct product of the Magyar language. This peculiarity consists of 'a figure in which the emphasis is shifted from the strong to the weak part, by making the first only a fraction of the second.'

There is an indubitably Oriental relic in the profuse embellishments with which the gypsies adorn the Hungarian melodies when playing them; but, as H. E. Krehbiel shrewdly observed, the gypsies impose the same embellishments upon Spanish and Russian music; in fact, upon all the music that they play: thus indicating plainly enough that the impulse to do so is native to them, and has nothing to do with the national taste of the countries for which they provide music.

Liszt's purpose in writing his Hungarian Rhapsodies was to create what he called 'Gypsy epics.' He had gathered a large number of the melodies without a definite purpose, and was wondering what to do with them, when it occurred to him that 'these fragmentary, scattered melodies were the wandering, floating, nebulous part of a great whole; that they fully answered the conditions for the production of a harmonious unity which would comprehend the very flower of their essential properties, their unique beauties.' He thought that they might be united 'in one homogeneous body, a complete work, its divisions to be so arranged that each song would form at once a whole and a part, which might be severed from the rest and be examined and enjoyed by and for itself; but which would, none the less, belong to the whole through the close affinity of subject-matter, the similarity of inner nature and unity in development.' The basis of Liszt's Rhapsodies being thus distinctively national, he has in a manner imitated in their character and tempo the dual character of the Hungarian national dance, the Czardas, which consists of two movements, a Lassu or slow movement, followed by a Friss, or lively one. These alternate at the will of the dancer, who gives a sign to the band when he wishes to change from one to the other.

● *Totentanz* ('Dance of Death'), FOR PIANO AND ORCHESTRA

Liszt as a young man saw at Pisa during his first stay in Italy (1837-40) the grisly and sinister fresco in the Campo Santo entitled 'The Triumph of Death,' attributed to Andrea Orcagna. Liszt, who was irresistibly drawn to the macabre and the grotesque, perceived in Orcagna's fresco an ideal subject for his musical imagination to wreak itself upon, and he sketched at Pisa in 1839 his *Danse macabre,* or *Totentanz,* for piano and orchestra. He worked at it in Weimar in 1849-50 and again in 1853, revised and completed it in 1859—twenty years after its inception. Hans von Bülow played it with orchestra at The Hague in 1865. The score and an edition for two pianos were published in the same year.

Orcagna's fresco is an amazing fantasy on the theme of Death as the malevolent interrupter of human joys, the scourger of human hearts, in contrast with the sweet ways and illusive security of Life, with its mirage-like gardens and meadows, its deceitful songs, the ghastly irony of its loveliness and gaiety and peace, the mockery of its dawns. And the figure of Death in Orcagna's fresco is a woman—malign, bat-winged, demonic.

Liszt's piece is a free paraphrase, in the form of variations for piano and orchestra, of the plainsong *Dies Irae*, appointed in the Roman Missal to be sung in masses for the dead. Tradition ascribes the poetry of the medieval hymn to Thomas de Celano, disciple and biographer of St. Francis of Assisi, and Rockstro supposes him to have written the tune as well. The *Dies Irae* has appealed to many composers, aside from its ecclesiastical treatments, as an effective and extremely moving device whereby the thought of death, or any of the somber or threatening connotations of mortality, might be suggested or evoked. Composers as modern as Loeffler and Rachmaninoff have employed its ominous intervals. In Liszt's piece, the somber chant is begun by trombones, tuba, bassoons, clarinets, and low strings, above an accompaniment-figure for the piano and drums. There is a cadenza for the piano, and a forbidding utterance of the plainsong by the full orchestra. Then the piano gives the *Dies Irae* as theme for the variations that follow.

Charles Martin Loeffler

1861-1935

L

‡An Alsatian by birth, an American by adoption, Loeffler had a distinct creative personality. Though we may detect the strong influence of German Romanticism and French Impressionism on his music, hearing in it now Wagner, now Debussy, in the end its originality confounds and drowns these echoes. The faculty of self-criticism was highly developed in him, and as a consequence he permitted only a small part of his relatively large output of orchestral and choral and chamber music to be printed. Nearly all of this is marked by the greatest refinement of invention and execution; but the orchestral piece A *Pagan Poem* is undoubtedly Loeffler's masterpiece, and perhaps the most distinguished contribution to date, in its field, to American music.‡

• A *Pagan Poem* (*After Virgil*), OP. 14

A *Pagan Poem*, composed originally, in 1901, as chamber music, was remodeled for orchestra in 1905-6. The first performance of the work in its present form was by the Boston Symphony Orchestra under Karl Muck, at Symphony Hall, Boston, November 22, 1907. The full score was published in 1909.

Loeffler has not avowed in his published score the particular subject of this work. The title page reads simply: 'A Pagan Poem (after Virgil). Composed for orchestra, with piano, English horn, and three trumpets obbligati. Op. 14'— only that and nothing more. You are left to wander without guide or compass through the *Georgics*, the *Eclogues*, and the *Aeneid* in search of the special chapter and verse that suggested the music; unless you happen to know (it was afterward divulged) that the object on which the composer had his eye was the love poem allotted to Alphesiboeus in the Eclogue called *The Sorceress*. 'The pretext for this piece,' wrote Loeffler to the present annotator, 'was the second love incantation of the Eighth Eclogue. The subject is the pagan incantation of a Thessalian girl, who by the aid of sorcerous spells draws back to her cottage her truant lover, Daphnis. Whether I have created musically the mood which lies in the poem, and without following it word for word, is for [others] to say. . . The three trumpets (*très lointain*) intone the refrain: "Ducite ab urbe domum, mea carmina, ducite Daphnim." ' (In Dryden's translation of this Eclogue, given as *Pastoral VIII*, this refrain is rendered thus: '. . . Restore, my charms, My lingering Daphnis to my longing arms.')

Loeffler's score enlarges upon the significant connotations—poetic, dramatic, emotional—of its Virgilian original. Such of its hearers as are responsive to imaginative suggestion will perceive in the music whatever the Eclogue could impart to it of movement and atmosphere and event. In and through its dark brooding and its far-sweeping ardors, the co-operative listener will be made aware of the music's responsiveness to the essentials of the poet's tale—the echo of magic incantations, the rumor of pagan rites and conjurations, and, always and pervadingly, the thought of the desirous and forsaken woman, the sorceress sick with love, chanting her urgent songs.

The work opens ('Adagio, misterioso,' 2-2) with a motive six measures long, a somber and brooding phrase for the low strings, bassoons, and harp, of which, with its inversion, subsequent use is made. The dark-hued and dolorous chief theme (which pays its respects to diabolism in the use of the traditionally unholy 'tritone' for its characteristic interval) is then announced. It is in three parts: the first section, for three flutes and muted solo viola in unison, is in B-flat minor, ascending to its relative major; the second section (trumpet, flutes, clarinets, viola) is a descending four-note phrase in whole tones; the third (viola, English horn and flutes in octaves) is a sighing plaint that chromatically mounts and falls. A score of measures after the entrance of the piano (in an inversion of the introductory motive), the violins make their first melodic appearance with one of those eloquent subsidiary themes that Loeffler so prodigally devotes to subordinate uses in his compositions. This expressive theme, a cantilena first heard in the dominant of D-flat, occurs only twice again: in the piano part, repeated by the violins, soon after its first appearance; and at the rapturous climax shortly before the end of the work.

The repetition of this melody by the strings leads to an anticipation of the second theme, given out by the piano in G minor, against part of the chief theme as a counterpoint on the trumpets. It is heard in its complete form in the succeeding Allegro. A cadenza for the piano introduces, much further on (ninety measures), a mournful third theme ('Lento assai,' 6-4), for the English horn. And then comes the feature of the work: the refrain of the three distant trumpets behind the scenes, suggesting the burden of the Sorceress: 'Draw from the city, my songs, draw Daphnis home'—a strange and unforgettable phrase, in which the once-accursed consecutive fifths are full of magic and allurement. 'Cellos and violas in unison, accompanied by arpeggios for the piano, give out a new subject, repeated with passionate insistence by the full orchestra fortissimo.

There is elaborate development of this material—a development richly polyphonic and fertile in melodic output. An agitated motif for four horns in unison, violins, and violas ('più vivo') is succeeded by a long-breathed melody sung by the piano, 'molto tranquillo' (it is derived from the plaint of the English horn). This is repeated by the strings, horn, and bassoon. The refrain of the trumpets is heard for the second time, but still distantly. The dolorous English horn theme recurs, now transferred to the violins and afterward developed by the piano and the full orchestra; there is increasing tension and excitement. For the third time the refrain is heard from the trumpets, still behind the scenes, but drawing gradually nearer, while the concurrent lament of the English horn is slowly overborne. As the trumpets are heard on the stage, the orchestra voices the triumph of the Sorceress in an outburst of exultant passion. Trombones and horns shout forth the once melancholy chief theme against a wildly jubilant fanfare of the trumpets.

Gustav Mahler

1860-1911

M

‡Mahler enjoyed a brilliantly successful, if stormy, career as a conductor of opera and symphony. For many years his rule over the Vienna Opera was absolute. He exacted the utmost from singers and instrumentalists, but he achieved a standard of performance which raised the institution he served to a place of now legendary pre-eminence among the opera houses of the world. Later he associated himself with the Metropolitan Opera House in New York, and was for some seasons conductor of Philharmonic Orchestra in that city. There his unconventional procedures made him the target of the Bourbons and obscurantists among the critics, and his last years were embittered by their attacks. Meanwhile, between 1883 and 1911, the year of his death, he composed that series of ten massive symphonies, the last unfinished, in which he has communicated

the experiences of a unique sensibility and the speculations of a wide-ranging intellect. It is still impossible to assess his contribution with confidence, but the belief grows that he was one of the giants. His highly individual methods of organizing his musical materials, and his extraordinarily subtle and inventive scoring, have profoundly influenced later composers.‡

• Symphony No. 1, in D major

Mahler detested the ascription of illustrative purposes to his music. The story goes that once, at a supper party following a performance of his C minor Symphony (the Second), he rose to his feet to denounce all annotators in no uncertain terms. 'Away with program notes!' he cried, according to one version of the incident. 'Away with program notes, which only beget false ideas! Let the listener have his own thoughts about the work performed!' Yet with the exasperating inconsistency of the artist-mind, Mahler seems to have based most of his symphonies upon programmatic schemes of the most detailed and elaborate sort. Nor was he always himself guiltless of interfering with the listener's innocence of approach to his music. Something is known, for example, of Mahler's expressional intentions in the D major Symphony. According to a synopsis supplied by Mahler for one of the early performances of this work, but afterward withdrawn, his intention in it was to portray, successively, spring; the awakening of nature at dawn; a 'chaplet of flowers'; something 'under full sail'; a grotesque funeral march in the manner of Callot, suggested by the burlesque picture of a hunter's funeral procession in an old German fairy-tale book; and, finally, in the last movement, a transition 'from Hell to Heaven.' When the symphony was produced at Budapest in 1889, under the composer's direction, the program described it as 'a symphonic poem in two parts.' At Weimar, in 1894, it was called the 'Titan' Symphony, after the romance by Jean Paul Richter, and the motto 'From the Days of Youth' was given to the first part, while the second bore the tag 'Commedia umana.' Yet not a hint of any of this is conveyed by the published score, which is innocent of any printed 'argument,' of any literary superscriptions whatsoever.

Paul Stefan, in his pious study of Mahler, published while the composer was still alive, discusses the First Symphony with apparent authority. He finds the introduction to the first movement suggestive of 'the melancholy of the Moravian plains.' Then comes 'the up-striving fanfare of the clarinets, a cuckoo-call in the woodwind, a lovely song in the horns; then, over the pedal A, a gradual rolling movement . . . like the reawakening of the earth after a clear summer night.' The main body of the movement begins, 'Allegro ma non troppo,' with a theme quoted from the second of Mahler's *Lieder eines fahrenden Gesellen* (*Songs of a Wayfarer*): 'As I walked abroad this morn / Dew was sparkling on the grass.'

Stefan describes the second movement as 'a merry, dancing Scherzo, an Austrian *Ländler*, like those of Bruckner and Schubert, exquisitely harmonized and scored. A horn leads into the oldtime trio. The *fahrender Gesell* has discovered a hidden village where people are happy as of yore. But precisely this merry-making recalls his own sad flight from love.' The third movement emboldens Stefan to remember the suppressed scenario by Mahler to which reference was made above. It suggests 'a grotesque funeral march.' A solo double-bass, muted, gives out the subject, derived from the old French round, *Frère Jacques.* Later, 'an oboe bleats and squeaks in the upper register; the shrill E-flat clarinet quacks; over a quiet counterpoint in the trumpets, the oboes are tootling a vulgar street-song.' There are other parodistic effects, followed by an episode in which much use is made of another theme borrowed from the *Songs of a Wayfarer*—this time from the fourth of them, *Die zwei blaue Augen* ('Two Blue Eyes'): 'Deliverance—"Then knew I not how life may be, and all again was well with me." But the barrel-organ canon straightway starts up again, dies away finally, and leads after a short pause into the last movement. Raging, a chromatic triplet rushes downward . . . everything ferments and fumes. . . Then an even louder climax, where seven horns must be heard above everything, even the trumpets. They sound like a chorale from Paradise after the turbulence of Hell. Saved!' And Stefan adds, with delectable naïveté, 'A "programme" is unnecessary.' But the composer at one time, and his disciple at another, seem to have thought differently.

As a texture of sound, the score is often delightful. Its great quality is its sincerity. In the first movement, especially, there is much that beguiles by reason of its naïveté and freshness and simplicity, its candor and sweetness that suggest at times the thought of Schubert, yet are indisputably Mahler's own, original and self-sprung, stamped with his signature and image. The childlike and ingenuous directness, the lyric charm of many pages are irresistible. The homely tenderness, the folk-like humor, the long, nostalgic reveries, the poignant brooding of the music at its best—these qualities are not easily to be forgotten. But Mahler could not resist the temptation to associate the childlike with the metaphysical. We sigh a little when he turns from the things of his dear Bohemian countryside, whose secret speech he knew exquisitely, and wraps himself in the mantle of the apocalyptic and the grandiose, storming Paradise to the tune of seven horns, 'semper fortissimo.' If only he could have been content with the little moment that is mercifully given, and the morning fires on the bough, and 'the largeness of the evening earth'!

● SYMPHONY NO. 2, IN C MINOR

Mahler began his Second Symphony at Leipzig in the late 'eighties and finished it at Steinbach, on the Attersee, in June 1894. The following March, Richard Strauss conducted the three instrumental movements (the symphony is in five, of which the last two employ voices) at a Berlin Philharmonic concert. On December 13 of the same year—1895—Mahler himself conducted the entire symphony in Berlin.

Mahler has given us a clue to the significance of this symphony, not only in the words which are sung by the solo voices and chorus in the fourth and fifth movements, but in his exegetical comments. 'When I conceive a great musical picture,' he wrote, 'I always arrive at the point where I must employ the "word" as the bearer of my musical idea. . . My experience with the last movement of my Second Symphony was such that I literally ransacked literature up to the Bible to find the redeeming "word." ' He found it, finally, in his favorite source-book, *Des Knaben Wunderhorn,* and in a hymn by Klopstock, which he heard at Bülow's funeral, and to which he added lines of his own. The voice is first heard (contralto solo) in the fourth movement of the symphony, to which Mahler has given the title *Urlicht* ('Primal Light'); here the text, a lament on mortality, is taken from *Des Knaben Wunderhorn* (a famous anthology of German folk poetry). The words sung by the chorus and solo voices in the Finale—to which Mahler has given the superscription *Der grosse Appell* ('The Great Summons')—are partly from Klopstock and partly by Mahler. 'The verses are a summons to faith; nothing is in vain; loving, struggling, suffering are not in vain; on pinions gained through life's feverish struggle the soul will soar to Light that no eye has ever beheld. In the long preluding to this movement, brass instruments sound the Great Summons.'

The symphony has been called (with good reason, apparently) the 'Resurrection' Symphony; but this title was displeasing to Ernest Otto Nodnagel, who wrote at length about Mahler's works in his *Jenseits von Wagner und Liszt.* Nodnagel preferred to see in the first Allegro 'the funeral music of a great man,' with hints at episodes in his life; in the idyllic second movement he perceived 'a reference to an episode of sunny happiness'; in the 'demoniacal' Scherzo, a 'portrayal of the doubt and despair of a racked soul'; and in the fourth, 'comfort'; while the fifth brings 'the longed-for deliverance, not as a "resurrection," a confession of religious belief, but "in the sense of our modern biological views." ' Nodnagel explains the bird's trillings in the last movement, which have puzzled many commentators, as being 'a symbol of the last expiring vestige of life on earth.'

• SYMPHONY NO. 3, IN D MINOR

Following his usual habit, Mahler issued this work (published in 1902) without programmatic indications of any kind. The score contains no title, motto, preface, or other concession to the extra-musical mind except the hints as to its imaginative content which may be gleaned from the poetic texts that form the basis of two of its six movements—for this symphony, like Mahler's Second, Fourth, and Eighth, is partly vocal. The fourth movement is a setting for contralto voice and orchestra of the 'Song of the Night Wanderer' from Nietzsche's *Zarathustra* (or 'The Drunken Song,' as Nietzsche afterwards called it)—that strange and haunting meditation which Zarathustra spoke at midnight into the ears of the 'higher men,' as 'the old, deep, deep midnight bell' tolled through the cool and thoughtful night; while even the dancing ass (who, it will be recalled, had been filled with sweet wine) stood quiet in the moonlight and hearkened. The fifth movement of the symphony employs a chorus of women's voices, and a boy choir, in addition to the alto soloist. They sing words from *Des Knaben Wunderhorn.* Mahler resorted frequently to these naïve medieval verses, and they supplied him with texts for many of his songs as well as for the voice parts which he liked to introduce into his symphonies.

But the words that are set to music in this symphony are not the only source of information which we possess as to its poetic significance. The symphony was originally entitled A *Summer Morning's Dream*, and when it was first performed, under Mahler's direction, the following titles for the various movements were printed in the program: Introduction: Awakening of Pan. (1) Summer enters. Procession of Bacchus. (2) Minuet—What the flowers of the meadow tell me. (3) Scherzo—What the animals in the forest tell me. (4) Contralto solo—What man tells me. (5) Women's Chorus, Boy Choir, Contralto—What the angels tell me. (6) Adagio—What love tells me.' The program annotator of the Concertgebouw Orchestra in Amsterdam once said that in the first part of this symphony we were to find 'an expression of the emotion of earthly fellowship, which attains its highest organized form in human society. Toward the end, Mahler unites us with the loftier fellowship —that of the spirit, of belief, of love.'

This is an interpretation of Mahler's scheme which is in harmony with his known intentions. Mahler never publicly divulged the real program of this symphony. He had many antagonists during the latter part of his life and he feared misrepresentation, or, at the best, imperfect comprehension. The legends about the 'Awakening of Pan,' the 'Entrance of Summer,' the 'Procession of Bacchus,' et cetera, which he saw fit to attach to the symphony, seem to have been devised as a sort of programmatic red-herring. They told no more than Mahler was willing to tell at the time, yet indicated by their poetic symbolism many of the essential moods of the music. But the true significance of the work is something a good deal larger and graver and nobler than the rather vacuously romantic titles on the program of the first performance would lead one to suspect. Mahler often discussed the meaning of the music with his friend Willem Mengelberg, and Mengelberg in turn made known to the present annotator the substance of Mahler's programmatic scheme.

This music, in brief, is an expression of Mahler's ideal of universal brother-hood. While he conceived it, he sat humbly at the feet of the Beethoven of the Ninth Symphony; and he desired to fill his music with something akin to the poetic and emotional content of the Ninth, as seen in relation to the spiritual problems of our own time. Mahler had a profound conviction of human solidarity. He had come to realize that our only hope of abiding happiness lies in our privilege of seeing it through other men's eyes, and in the sense of comradeship. He knew that Destiny is little to be trusted as a dispenser of enduring personal delight. He knew that the wind on the heath can bring an unutterable sadness upon the spirit, and that on any evening, coming home across the fields, one might find that the Dark Hour had fallen on one's household. He remembered, with Pindar, that 'man is a dream about a shadow'; but that 'when some God-given splendor falls, a glory of light comes over him, and his life is sweet.' In this radiant peace he perceived a reflection of that 'jubilation of joy' which Wagner recognized in Beethoven's Ninth as signifying the triumphant end of man's pursuit of happiness—when 'we clasp the whole world to our breast in an outpouring of universal love.'

Mahler aimed, then, at a kind of musical parable of the uneasy and joy-seeking heart of man in relation to its environment—human, natural, and spiritual: an emotional history of the efforts of the soul to orient itself in the plan of the visible and invisible worlds. Which is merely another way of saying that Mahler in this Third Symphony has had the instinctive wisdom to expound a theme as old as human art and as poignantly engrossing as human destiny—a subject that, in the words of Santayana, 'covers the whole field from which poetry may be fetched, and to which poetry may be applied, from the innermost recesses of the heart to the outward bounds of nature and of destiny.' It is a theme of the profoundest fascination, and the artist who seeks to turn it into symbols of beauty and eloquence and power—even if his attempt remains but an attempt—cannot meet us with wholly empty hands. God, said St. Bernard, is never sought in vain, even when we do not find him.

● SYMPHONY NO. 4, IN G MAJOR

Mahler in this symphony revels in that atmosphere of elaborately contrived artlessness which he loved so dearly. For Mahler was only a little less happy when he was approximating the style of a folk song than when he was trying to parallel one of the Brobdingnagian musical 'jubilees' of the fabulous Patrick Sarsfield Gilmore, with their choruses of 20,000 and their 2000 instruments reinforced by cannon shots and anvils. Mahler's imagination aspired to the grandiose and the apocalyptic with unterrified audacity. He believed that he could speak at will with the artlessness of the Bohemian countryside or in accents weighty with mystical revelation. One can imagine him fancying himself at his ease among those illuminated beings described by Plato in the *Phaedo*: 'They hear the voices and oracles of the gods, and see them in visions, and have intercourse with them face to face; and they see the moon and the stars as they really are.' You perceive him in one of his comfortable strolls across the evening landscape, telling himself, with Jasper Petulengro, that 'life is very sweet, brother; who would wish to die?'—and then suddenly remembering that he is a Symphonist with a Revelation, calling out, as one divinely chosen, 'Bring me my bow of burning gold, Bring me my arrows of desire'—like an inconceivably solemn Blake.

'The solemn is safe,' said Browning; but he was not thinking of the solemn in art. It is unnecessary to attempt an appraisal of the worth of Mahler's dallyings with the apocryphal, or to guess at the real value of his immense portentousness. It is enough to note here that it constitutes one extreme of his astonishing imaginative gamut—this quality which his spokesmen call his 'heroic sublimity.' The other extreme is seen in his passion for the naïve, for peasant humor and simplicity, the homely ingenuousness of the folk spirit. Mahler in this vein is undeniably engaging and persuasive, even touching; and this is the vein of the Fourth Symphony.

The apparatus required by Mahler in this opus is a relatively moderate one (the symphony is scored without trombones), but a soprano soloist is essential to the Finale, and the words that are sung in this movement are thought by some to indicate the programmatic basis of the entire work. They are the words of an old Bavarian folk song, 'Der Himmel hängt voll Geigen,' drawn from *Des Knaben Wunderhorn*. The poem describes with inimitable gusto and naïveté a perfect peasant paradise of the Middle Ages: a delectably literal and materialistic heaven where the suppressed desires of the medieval folk achieve a glorious consummation—a paradisiacal home life, filled with merriment and ease and gastronomic satisfactions, where game, fish, vegetables, wine, and fruit may be had for the asking, where hares and deer run invitingly about the streets, and bread is baked by angels. St. John brings forth his lamb, St. Luke his ox. Herod is the butcher, and St. Martha the cook. Cologne's eleven thousand virgins dance without teasing, while Cecilia and her relations make an excellent court orchestra, and St. Ursula smiles benignly upon the revels.

● SYMPHONY No. 5

According to Paul Stefan, Mahler's biographer, the Fifth Symphony was composed in 1901-2, 'in the quiet of a cottage near Maiernegg on the Wörthersee,' and was contemporaneous with the fourth and fifth of the *Kindertotenlieder*. The first performance was at a Gürzenich concert in Cologne, October 18, 1904. The symphony is in two parts. Part One contains the first and second movements; Part Two, the third, fourth, and fifth.

To the opening movement, Mahler himself gives in his score the title *Trauermusik*—'Funeral Music.' This is in C-sharp minor, 2-2 time. The score bears this direction: *In gemessenem Schritt. Streng. Wie ein Kondukt* ('With measured tread. Austerely. Like a funeral train'). The second movement has this direction: *Stürmisch bewegt. Mit grosster Vehemenz* ('Stormily agitated. With the utmost vehemence'). It is in A minor, with the time signature 4-4. The third movement, a Scherzo in D major, has this direction at the beginning: *Kräftig, nicht zu schnell* ('Vigorously, but not too fast'). The fourth movement is an Adagietto in F major, 4-4, scored for strings and harp. The fifth and last movement is entitled in the score 'Rondo-Finale' (D major, 2-2). The opening tempo mark is Allegro. The symphony is for the usual large Mahlerian orchestra, but no voice parts are introduced, as they are in the Second, Third, Fourth and Eighth symphonies.

This symphony has at least one episode of extraordinary power. It is that passage in B-flat minor in which the music, grown suddenly and passionately vehement, breaks in upon the measured tread of the 'Funeral Music' like an uncontrollable outburst of shattering, maniacal, wild-visaged grief. Above an ostinato of the double-basses and bassoons, a trumpet shrieks its heaven-storming woe, against the chromatic wailing of the strings. The plangent, tumultuous despair of this passage is like nothing else in music that one can recall. Tchaikovsky's is restrained and decorous beside it. Mahler has here imagined an elemental and universal human emotion with sensibility and with justice and has turned it into direct and vivid and irresistible musical speech. It is said, with what degree of accuracy one does not know, that when Mahler wrote this symphony he was sorrowing over the death of his child. The artist, to be sure, is in no need of personal verification of universal themes; but it is easy to believe that this music is an intimate declaration, a personal souvenir of exceptional authenticity. Whether it is or not, it is music that comes close to greatness.

• SYMPHONY NO. 7

The first performance of Mahler's Seventh Symphony took place two years
after the production of the Sixth and two years before that of the Eighth. It
was played for the first time in Prague, September 19, 1908. The score was
published the following year. It carries no programmatic guide to the music—
indeed, Mahler has not even given his symphony a key designation. Its title is
austerely plain: *Siebente Sinfonie von Gustav Mahler*—nothing more. As to
its proper key designation, the historians and commentators are not in agreement: some say 'in E minor'; others say, 'in B minor.' Stefan, playing no
favorites, describes the symphony on one page as being in B minor, on
another as in E minor. An examination of the score discloses the fact that the
slow introduction begins in B minor, while the main movement opens in
E minor and ends in E major. The second movement is in C major, the third
in D minor, the fourth in F major, the fifth in C major.

The five movements are curiously assorted. The first, 'Allegro con fuoco,'
2-2 (which has an introduction, Adagio) is followed by a movement called
Nachtmusik ('Allegro moderato'; 'Andante molto moderato,' 4-4); then comes
a Scherzo with the direction *Schattenhaft* ('Shadow-like') *Fiessend: aber nicht
schnell* ('Flowing, but not fast'); then a second piece of *Nachtmusik* ('Andante
amoroso,' 2-4) and a Rondo-Finale (Allegro, 4-4).

Mahler is reported to have said that the first of the two movements called
Nachtmusik (nocturne, or serenade) was inspired by Rembrandt's painting
'The Night Watch.' And Richard Specht declares that Mahler said of the
first subject in the introduction to the first movement, 'Hier röhrt die Natur.'
It is altogether likely that Mahler composed his Seventh Symphony to some
kind of program—poetic, philosophic, dramatic, or what not. There are indications of this in the music itself; and what we know of the history of his
other symphonies supports this conjecture. But it is not the privilege of an
annotator to ascribe a meaning outside itself to even so apparently programmatic a work as this, unless the composer's intentions have been made reasonably clear.

• SYMPHONY NO. 8 ('Symphony of a Thousand')

The Eighth Symphony, according to Richard Specht, was for Mahler 'the
complete expression in tones of his inner vision. He regarded his preceding
works as preludes to this great "Hymn of Love." ' It was not quite his last
work. Mahler completed the Eighth Symphony in 1909, and in that year he
composed his Ninth and sketched his Tenth. The poignant *Lied von der
Erde* was written while he was still at work upon the Eighth Symphony.

The Eighth Symphony is austere and remote in subject: it is an expression,
conceived on the loftiest plane, of a supremely exalted theme. For Mahler here
has essayed nothing less than a musical projection of the final scene of Goethe's
Faust, prefaced by an elaborate setting of the Latin hymn, 'Veni Creator
Spiritus.' The composer sought to link his setting of the ancient hymn of
Hrabanus Maurus—which Mahler conceived as 'a song of yearning, of raptur-

ous devotion, in invocation of the creative spirit, the love that moves the worlds'—with the concluding scene of *Faust*, which he viewed as the invocation's answer, issuing from one of those transfigured apparitions wherein the poet's visions 'are made to pass before us in a glass and heavenly wisdom is unfolded in a divine ascent.' For Mahler's inner life was a perpetual and agonized interrogation of the *magnum mysterium*: it was his impassioned aim to achieve those states of transported reverie and mystical apprehension wherein the consciousness is disengaged and enfranchised.

It could never be said of Mahler, as someone once amazingly said of Schumann—apparently in praise—that he, in his *Faust* music, 'does not attempt to compete with the poet, to convince the world that the musician can be a "thinker." ' Mahler had no such contempt of intellectual activity. It seemed to him not impossible that a musician, no less than a poet, could be a thinker without doing irreparable injury to his work. He was not impressed by the singular theory that music may be benefited by purging it of ideas. Indeed, it is precisely its width of reference, its contact with the great intellectual and spiritual currents of the nineteenth century, that gives Mahler's art its prime distinction and interest as a contribution to the music of his time, whatever one may think of the outcome of his attempt—in Rossetti's phrase—to 'mix his colors with brains.'

It is no affair of the critic's, so far as his function as a suggester of values is concerned, what means an artist elects to use in embodying his conceptions. A good deal of witless comment has been provoked because Mahler in this choral 'Symphony of a Thousand' (or dramatic cantata, if you choose) asks for extraordinary forces—for two mixed choruses, a boys' chorus, eight solo voices, and a huge orchestra, comprising a piano, an organ and—a mandolin: in all, about one thousand performers. The fact is interesting but irrelevant. The point, since one is discussing not a circus but a work of art, is rather: What has Mahler succeeded in doing with his multitudinous choristers and his eight soloists and his immense orchestra—and his mandolin?

Well, it is indisputable that he has handled them like a master, with a constructive technique that takes the breath by its surety, its address, its resourcefulness, its imposing command of mass and its fertility in detail. Here is a superb piece of tonal architecture, majestic and harmonious in plan, noble in its amplitude and sweep of line. And as for the stuff within, the spiritual and poetic content of the score, the character of its musical inspiration—it must be evident to any sympathetic student or listener that Mahler has been sensitive to the spiritual greatness of Goethe's conception, and that its quality is reflected in many pages of his score. This music, in its best moments, has caught something of the unique ecstasy, the mystical passion, the other-worldliness, the ineffable serenity and tenderness, the rapturous exaltation, of the original. Such moments are the speech of Pater Ecstaticus; the line 'Wenn du hehr gebietest,' in the speech of Doctor Marianus, with the succeeding interlude and choral passage; and the lines beginning 'Neige, neige,' of Una Poenitentium—especially the music, of exceeding loveliness, to the ecstatic 'Er kommt zurück!' And in the non-Goethian first part of the symphony, the setting of 'Veni Creator Spiritus,' one does not easily forget the overwhelming tonal plangency of the *Gloria Patri*.

That the texture of this music is not throughout of this rich and glowing quality is scarcely remarkable. Mahler undertook a venture that would have taxed the genius of a Wagner—the one musician who was fully qualified not only to apprehend but to complement the universal mind of Goethe.

• SYMPHONY No. 9

It was Mahler's conviction, apparently, that no symphony could be too long, provided he was the composer. He believed that when one of his symphonies was played, it should fill the entire program, without aid, comfort, contrast, or alleviation from competitive music-makers. Doubtless he would have said of himself, quite sincerely and simply, as Beethoven is supposed to have said concerning his 'Eroica,' 'If I write a symphony an hour long, it will be found short enough'—though as a matter of fact, there are few Mahler symphonies, there is in fact only one, the First, that pre-empts so meager a measure of time for its performance.

But length in music is, after all, a relative thing. *Die Meistersinger* is almost twice as long as *Thaïs*; but not everyone would believe it without a stopwatch. And so it makes no difference at all whether Mahler's Ninth is traversible in an hour (which it most decidedly is not) or in twenty minutes: let us, as Emerson said, 'leave hurry to slaves.' We are reasonable as aesthetic appraisers only when we ask ourselves, in this case, How absorbing is Mahler's discourse? Does it seize and engross us, or does it bore and weary us? This, to be sure, is altogether a personal matter; but so is every sort of critical reaction—to a necktie, or a goulash, or a climate, or a symphony, or a woman's face.

Well, what is certain is that Mahler's Ninth Symphony is a remarkable score. It is not consistently fine and distinguished in musical thought; none of Mahler's symphonies is that, for Mahler had no inward censor: he never knew when he was saying something memorable and choice, and when he was delivering himself of platitudes and banalities. Yet the genuineness of his feeling, his burning and indubitable sincerity as an artist, give even his most portentous futilities at times a kind of impressiveness, and soften one's resentment of their triteness.

Mahler, they say, was obsessed by premonitory thoughts of death when he composed this music. One of his apostles, Richard Specht, has called it 'a symphonic grave-song.' Paul Stefan sees in its concluding Adagio a farewell to earth, a 'farewell without bitterness,' as sequel to earlier pages in which the composer storms and weeps and mocks, savagely deriding the life that men are given here to lead. In the final Adagio, music that at last is murmurous with peace, Mahler is said to have found music for the ultimate act of reconciliation.

Yet what of this alleged serenity, this deep and final reconciliation, in the face of Mahler's later symphonic utterance, his last and uncompleted symphony, the Tenth? Those who have seen a facsimile of the score tell us that the MS. is annotated as by one in an agony of terror and foreboding, scribbled over with exclamations, appeals, imprecations, in which the composer cries to God and to the fiends of that tormenting hell with which his own sick mind companioned him. For Mahler was usually either scaling the heights of his apocalyptic visions or groveling miserably in the depths.

The truth appears to be that Mahler the artist never in all his tragic inner life outran his fears and his morbidities. With him, as with Tchaikovsky, spiritual valor was a thing glimpsed rather than achieved. He might have regarded as his own the fate decreed by the incomparable Sonneteer—'So shalt thou feed on Death.' Mahler the artist fed, he banqueted, on death. His terrible despair cries out to us again and again in his music—a vehement, cataclysmal thing, tearing at the keyless iron door with bleeding fingers, as did Ygraine in the dreadful play of Maeterlinck. His utterance of this obsessing mood is not so extraordinary in the Ninth Symphony as in the Fifth; yet those pages in the Ninth in which he speaks his fears and woes and lamentations are, musically, the most memorable in the score. They occur in certain pages of the first movement, but they are most moving in the final Adagio.

Mahler has erected this Adagio with admirable skill upon the conventional 'turn,' that 'gruppetto' which for so many years has served composers chiefly as an ornament; though sometimes it has been put to profoundly expressive use, as by Bach in a chorale-prelude ('Nun komm, der Heiden Heiland') and by Wagner in *Tristan* and *Götterdämmerung*. Bach made it the voice of devotional reverie; Wagner, the voice of ecstasy and love. And Mahler, in this Adagio, has made it the voice both of grieving and of peace. From the opening of the movement, when the unison violins stab us with the intensity of sorrow that it conveys, to the last serene and acquiescent pages in which the muted violas sing it quietly in augmentation, this ancient device is made to carry the diminishing burden of a poet's grief, until that burden is lifted, for a time at least, from his spirit, and the music becomes tranquil and gentle and assuaging, as if it were folding the hands of the poor agonist, telling him that 'nothing is here for tears, nothing to wail . . . nothing but well and fair. . .'

● *Das Lied von der Erde* ('The Song of the Earth')

Mahler on the title page of his score describes this work as 'a symphony for tenor and contralto (or baritone) and orchestra.' Some have preferred to view the work rather as a song cycle for two solo voices and orchestra. 'But the instrumental part is infinitely more than an accompaniment, and the vocal part is frequently less (or more) than a lyric: for at times the voice part is a truly lyric utterance, which the orchestra underlines and amplifies and adorns, and at other times the orchestra becomes the lyricist, and the voice takes the role of an expounder. But invariably the music goes for its moods and its pictorialism to the poems of which it is a vivid and intense expression.'

The words are derived from old Chinese poems translated (or rather paraphrased) by the German poet Hans Bethge, who published his versions in a collection which he entitled *Die Chinesische Flöte* ('The Chinese Flute'). The poems chosen by Mahler were altered, amplified, or epitomized by him 'so that they should express one predominating idea—withdrawal from the world.'

The poems, laden with Oriental symbolism, expound a philosophy of existence—Mahler's philosophy, the philosophy of a musical Senancour. We hear at times almost the very voice of Senancour: 'Sensibility which no words can express! charm and torment of our vain years! Deep awareness of a Nature everywhere greater than we are, and everywhere impenetrable!' Mahler might almost have said, in Goethe's words, that he had consecrated himself to the worship of sorrow: for in *Das Lied von der Erde*, this unconquerable melancholy, these passionate protestations against the mystery and the fleetingness and the pain of life, cry out of the music irrepressibly.

This music is full of the poignant nostalgia and regret of those who have lost a spiritual home—who have watched the fading of a civilization that had yielded a beauty personal and intimate and dear, a beauty shaped to the patterns and textures of a world that died before their eyes. Listening to the final measures of *Das Lied von der Erde*, with the contralto voice murmuring its reiterated 'Ewig! Ewig!' while the flute and oboe sustain the A of that unresolved suspension which is the fitting musical comment upon Mahler's life, we remember the epitaph that Senancour desired for himself: 'Eternité, deviens mon asile.'

It is easy to believe that Mahler would have found that thought a sympathetic one. Indeed, his intimate disciple, Paul Stefan, tells us almost as much: that in *Das Lied von der Erde* he took bitter and prophetic leave of a world which his nature estopped him from viewing as a friendly dwelling-place, and turned his vision elsewhere—toward some mysterious sanctuary of the dreaming mind. Certainly the strangely tragic peace, the mood of sorrowful assuagement, that broods upon the dying close of *Das Lied von der Erde*, speak to us of the essential Mahler, that maimed spirit—again, like Senancour, 'profoundly incomplete, profoundly touching.'

The Chinese poems paraphrased by Hans Bethge and adapted for his own purposes by Mahler deal less with aspects of nature than with that view of life and human destiny which was so deeply influential on the composer's art. The first poem, 'Das Trinklied von Jammer der Erde' ('The Drinking Song of Earthly Woe') is Epicurean—the world is full of woe, the skies are eternal, the earth will long endure, while man's life is but a span; look down, an ape crouches on the graves of the dead. Now bring me wine, and my lute, now it is time to drain the goblets! Dark is life, dark is death! The second poem, 'Der Einsame im Herbst' ('The Lonely One in Autumn'), describes nature in the pall of autumnal mists—cold winds bend the stalks, scatter the blossoms, send the withered blooms of the lotus scudding across the lake. 'My heart is weary, my little lamp sputters out, Oh, give me the refreshment of rest! Will the sun of love never again shine on me, to dry my tears?' The third song, 'Von der Jugend' ('Of Youth'), evokes a happier but still nostalgic mood. Its imagery is authentically Chinese—the picture of a bridge across a pond, a gay pavilion, people making merry, and all reflected upside down in the watery mirror. The fourth, 'Von der Schönheit' ('Of Beauty'), describes a scene of lovers wandering through an enchanted landscape, picking flowers, and bestowing languishing glances on one another. But the pessimistic mood returns, and in the fifth poem, 'Der Trunkene in Frühling' ('The Drunkard in Spring'), life again appears a burdensome dream of woe: so, therefore, wine again: let us sleep the sleep of forgetfulness.

Finally, in the sixth and last poem, 'Der Abschied' ('The Farewell'), two poems are united. Long calls of the oboe and flute resound in the approaching night. The wind blows gently, everything breathes sleep. The weary ones are homeward bound, to seek in sleep forgotten fortune, youth. In the darkness a man awaits his friend, to say farewell. The friend comes and goes again, solitary, into the mountains, never to return. And over all and forever, the luminous blue of space—forever, forever.

Mahler gave the completed manuscript of *Das Lied von der Erde* to his friend Bruno Walter for his opinion. When Walter brought it back to him, almost unable to utter a word, Mahler turned the pages to the final movement, the lacerating *Abschied*, and asked: 'What do you think? Is this to be endured at all? Will not people make away with themselves after hearing it?' The degree to which one may find endurable the closing pages of this work will depend, of course, upon one's willingness and ability to project one's self into another mental world than one's own, to see life and human destiny from a standpoint that may be fundamentally alien to everything that one knows and has experienced and believes in. This music, with its passionate introspection, its disclosure of a lofty and susceptible nature wrought upon by the inscrutable mystery and cruelty of existence, is the voice of an essentially solitary spirit, lonely and introvert and unabsolved. An ill man, Mahler became mindful of his end. Like the wounded Prince Andre in Tolstoy's *War and Peace*, he began to dissociate himself from life, and his *Lied von der Erde*, in Spinoza's phrase, is a creation *sub specie mortis*. Mahler saw the things of the world falling behind him, losing their contour and relevance. But though he still stretched forth his hands to hold them, nevertheless the Farewell of the closing movement is music touched with a fathomless tranquillity, so that we remember the enigmatical saying of Thoreau: 'Only the convalescent raises the veil of Nature . . . There is more day to dawn.'

● *Lieder eines fahrenden Gesellen* ('Songs of a Wayfarer')

Mahler, while occupying the post of second conductor at the opera house in Kassel (1883-5), composed a cycle of songs, to words of his own, resembling in form and spirit those folk songs which so deeply influenced his imagination as an artist. The songs were composed in December 1883, but they remained in manuscript until 1897, when four of the original group of six were published for voice and orchestra (and in an arrangement with piano accompaniment) as *Lieder eines fahrenden Gesellen*.

Mahler, during his sojourn at Kassel, fell deeply in love with one of the singers at the opera house, the blue-eyed, golden-tressed Johanne Richter. Johanne deemed it best that they should not marry, and they agreed to part. The episode was a tragic one for Mahler; he regarded himself 'as one compelled to exile.' Under the emotional compulsion of this experience, he composed the verses and music of the *Lieder eines fahrenden Gesellen*. 'I have written a song cycle,' he said at the time, 'dedicated to her. She does not know the songs.

But they can tell her only what she already knows. Their burden is this: a man who has found only sadness in love goes forth into the world a wanderer.'

In his First Symphony, begun at this time, Mahler used themes from two of the songs—the second and fourth. The text of the five may be briefly paraphrased as follows:

‡1. 'Wenn mein Schatz Hochzeit macht': On the day when my sweetheart is married to another, the saddest day of all for me, I will go to my darkened room and weep. . . Do not fade, sweet flowers; sing on, sweet bird, for the world is fair . . . But spring passes, the song ceases, the blossoms wither, and I go to rest, my heart heavy with my sorrow.

2. 'Ging heut Morgen über's Feld': As I crossed the fields this morning dew was on the grass and a bird greeted me merrily, and the flowers too asked, Is the world not fair to see? And I thought, Perhaps a time of happiness has come for me, too. But no! that time will never come.

3. 'Ich hab' ein glühend Messer': I bear a burning, tearing knife in my breast, and have no peace by night or day—for everything reminds me of my love. If only I were dead, my eyes closed forever!

4. 'Die zwei Blaue Augen': It is my love's blue eyes that have sent me forth into the world, without a word of farewell from anyone, with only grief and love for company. . . But I found rest under a linden, which shed its blossoms on me, and I forgot what life does to one, and all again seemed well to me.‡

● *Kindertotenlieder*

There is no satisfactory English equivalent for the German title of this work. When it was introduced to America—on January 26, 1910, at a concert of the Philharmonic Society of New York conducted by Mahler, with Ludwig Wüllner as the singer—the program translated the title as *Five Children's Death Songs* (which is at least an improvement upon the 'official' English version in the score—*Five Songs on the Death of Infants*).

The songs are settings of poems by Friedrich Rückert (1788-1866). The poet's verses have been described as 'natural and tender reflections called up in the mind of a German poet of exquisite sensibility by the death of two of his children.' Mahler's settings were prompted by a similar emotion, prophetically experienced. The composer was married to Alma Maria Schindler in March 1902 and at the end of that year their first child, Maria Anna, was born. It was then that Mahler composed the *Kindertotenlieder*. Four years later, when Maria Anna died of scarlet fever, Mahler is reported to have exclaimed, in the deepest grief: 'Under the agony of fear that this was destined to occur, I wrote the *Kindertotenlieder*.'

The five songs of the cycle are:

‡1. 'Nun will die Sonn' so Hell aufgehn': Now the sun rises again, as if nothing had happened. Only to me did misfortune come in the night, when my little lamp was darkened.

2. 'Nun seh' ich wohl, warum so dunkle Flammen': Now I understand the meaning which your loving, childlike glances strove to convey to me: I would

gladly stay with you, but Fate will not allow it. Look into these eyes—soon they will be but stars in the night sky.

3. 'Wenn dein Mütterlein': When your mother comes to the door and I turn to look at her, I look first at the place where you should be, dear child; and when, with the candle, she enters the room, I think I hear your footsteps following her, as in the past.

4. 'Oft denk' ich, sie sind nur ausgegangen': I often think to myself, They have only gone for a short time, they will soon be back—the day is fine, they have taken the path to yonder height. . . Yes, they have taken the path to yonder height, but there they will remain, in the sunlight of Eternity.

5. 'In diesem Wetter': In such weather I would never have let the children out to play. But they were taken from me, and there was nothing I could say, and now they sleep as safely as at home, where no storm can reach them, in God's care.‡

Felix Mendelssohn-Bartholdy

1809-47

M

‡The greatest composers rarely command as men the respect we extend them as artists. Mendelssohn is one of the exceptions. He was an affectionate and dutiful son (he had reason to be; he had model parents); he was a loving husband and father, a devoted and ever-helpful friend. He had all the social virtues—modesty, gentleness, kindness, generosity, and a sense of humor. He had his reward, for though his life was brief, it was lived in sunlight to the end. His talents matured early—the Octet for Strings and the *Midsummer Night's Dream* Overture were the work of his sixteenth and seventeenth years—and he embarked upon a brilliantly successful career as pianist, conductor, and composer almost as involuntarily and effortlessly as Aladdin possessed himself of the genie's treasure. And what of his music? It has the characteristics of the man who wrote it: sweetness and light, and to require more from it—a profundity and range beyond Mendelssohn's aspiration as beyond his capacity—would be ungenerous folly.‡

• SYMPHONY NO. 3, IN A MINOR, OP. 56 ('Scotch')

Perhaps the first things that should be remarked of this symphony are that the designation 'Scotch' was originally no part of its official title, and that it is not really Mendelssohn's third symphony.

History records that when someone told him that a certain passage in his *Meeresstille* Overture suggested 'the tones of love entranced at approaching nearer the goal of its desires,' Mendelssohn replied that his idea was quite different: that he had pictured 'some good-natured old man sitting in the stern of the vessel, and blowing vigorously into the sails, so as to contribute his part to the prosperous voyage.' This, it has been said, was a jocular evasion; for Mendelssohn was irritated by attempts to 'explain' his music too confidently.

At all events, he did not place the title 'Scotch' on the score of his A minor Symphony. Yet it was while he was evolving the plan of this work that he wrote in a letter to Frau von Pereira that 'notes have as definite a meaning as words, perhaps even a more definite one'; and elsewhere he elaborates his belief that music is not too indefinite to be put into words, but too definite; that words are susceptible of a variety of meanings, while music has only one.

Although Mendelssohn did not place the title on his score, he spoke of the work repeatedly in his letters as the 'Scotch' Symphony. Its genesis may be traced to his visit to Scotland in the summer of 1829. In a letter dated July 30 of that year, he wrote from Edinburgh: 'We went, in the deep twilight, to the Palace of Holyrood, where Queen Mary lived and loved. There is a little room to be seen there, with a winding staircase leading up to it. This the murderers ascended, and, finding Rizzio . . . drew him out; about three chambers away is a small corner where they killed him. The chapel is roofless, grass and ivy grow abundantly in it; and before the altar, now in ruins, Mary was crowned Queen of Scotland. Everything around is broken and mouldering, and the bright sky shines in. I believe I found today in that old chapel the beginning of my Scotch symphony.'

Yet the symphony was not completed until 1842—thirteen years later.

George Hogarth, who was with Mendelssohn in Scotland, wrote that 'in this symphony he embodied some of his reminiscences of a period to which he always looked back with pleasure. The delightful manner in which he has reproduced some of the most characteristic features of the national music— solemn, pathetic, gay, and warlike—is familiar to every amateur.' Philip Hale has said that though there was no thought of a direct attempt at musical portraiture in Mendelssohn's mind, he 'no doubt remembered the haunted room, the chapel, the sky, the spirit of the pipers—all that he saw and heard in that romantic country; and his recollections colored the music of the 'Scotch' Symphony. . . That Mendelssohn in this symphony is a musical landscapist, there is no doubt; but he makes the impression, he does not elaborate detail.'

It remains to be added that although the 'Scotch' is numbered the third in Mendelssohn's symphonic series, it was, in order of composition, the fifth. The 'Italian,' composed in 1833, was really the third of the symphonies.

Mendelssohn intended that the movements of the 'Scotch' should be played consecutively, without pause.

● SYMPHONY NO. 4, IN A MAJOR, OP. 90 ('Italian')

This symphony was the musical issue of Mendelssohn's Italian sojourn in 1830-31. The work was begun at Rome in 1831, but it was not completed until March 13, 1833, in Berlin. The first performance, from manuscript, took place two months later, at a concert of the London Philharmonic Society on May 13, during Mendelssohn's third visit to London. He himself conducted. He also played the D minor Piano Concerto of Mozart in the first part of the concert, enrapturing the audience with the brilliancy of his cadenzas.

The name 'Italian' was applied to the symphony by Mendelssohn himself. In his letters written from Italy, he alludes repeatedly to the work under that title. Writing from Rome on February 22, 1831, after he had been there four months, he tells his sisters that 'the Italian Symphony is making great progress. It will be the most mature thing I have ever done. The last movement, Presto, will be the gayest. For the slow movement I have not yet found anything exactly right, and I think I must put it off for Naples.' A week later he is of the same mind; and, lamenting how fast the time flies, and upbraiding himself for not making the best use of it, he continues, 'If I could do but one of my two symphonies here! but the Italian one I will and must put off till I have seen Naples, which must play a part in it.'

The first movement of the symphony ('Allegro vivace,' A major, 6-8) is a lucid and charming piece of writing constructed on traditional lines. The second movement ('Andante con moto,' D minor, 4-4), has been called, without any warrant, 'the Pilgrims' March.' The third movement ('con moto moderato,' A major, 3-4) derives its character from the older minuet rather than from the scherzo. There is a trio in E major. The concluding Saltarello (Presto, A minor, 4-4) is derived from three themes, each of them based on a figure in triplets—the first two (flutes in thirds; violins) of a skipping character, the third a smoothly rhythmed figure for the strings suggestive of a tarantella.

● SYMPHONY NO. 5, IN D MINOR, OP. 107 ('Reformation')

Mendelssohn, touring Great Britain in the summer and early autumn of 1829, meditated various compositions. 'His head,' remarks the apostolic Sir George Grove, 'was at this time full of music—the string quartet, op. 12; an organ piece for the wedding of his sister Fanny; the "Reformation" Symphony, the "Scotch" Symphony, the *Hebrides* Overture, as well as vocal music.' The 'Scotch' Symphony was not completed until thirteen years later. The 'Reformation' Symphony was completed less than a year after Mendelssohn planned it: he finished it at Berlin in April 1830. It was performed for the first time, from manuscript, on November 15, 1932, at the Singakademie, Berlin, under Mendelssohn's direction; but the score and parts were not published until March 1868—almost twenty-one years after Mendelssohn's death.

Mendelssohn was of several minds concerning a title for this symphony; but he finally decided upon that which appeared upon the program of the first performance, and which is published on the title page of the score: *Symphony for the Festival of the Reformation of the Church.*

The most noteworthy feature of the work is its employment of music possessing religious associations. In the first movement, Mendelssohn utilizes the Amen formula of the Saxon Lutheran Church—the so-called 'Dresden Amen,' with the rising sixths, of which Wagner afterward made such impressive use in the 'Grail' motive of *Parsifal*. It has been said that Mendelssohn originally intended this symphony for the Tercentenary of the Augsburg Confession, June 25, 1830 (one of the titles which he thought of for the work was *Confession Symphony*); and commentators have discovered in the first movement a representation of 'the reformers' joy in combat, their firmness of belief and trust in God.' Some difficulty was encountered in deciding exactly what the second movement, the 'Allegro vivace' (which corresponds to a Scherzo), had to do with the Reformation; but the association is fully justified in the 'Andante con moto,' in which Mendelssohn makes use of the Lutheran chorale, 'Ein' feste Burg ist unser Gott.'

The symphony comprises these movements: (1) Andante, D major, 4-4; 'Allegro con fuoco,' D minor, 2-2; (II) 'Allegro vivace,' B-flat major, 3-4; (III) Andante, G minor, 2-4; Chorale: 'Ein' feste Burg ist unser Gott': 'Andante con moto,' G major, 4-4; 'Allegro vivace,' G major, 6-8—'Allegro maestoso,' D major, 4-4.

The 'Dresden Amen' exists in two different versions. Neither form was followed exactly by Mendelssohn or Wagner, except in respect to the ascending progression of sixths which ends the better-known version of the *Amen*. When *Parsifal* appeared, Wagner's adversaries accused him of borrowing from Mendelssohn's 'Reformation' Symphony. The charge of plagiarism was easily disposed of by Wilhelm Tappert, the Berlin scholar, who pointed out the liturgical origin of the theme, and advanced the obvious explanation that Mendelssohn and Wagner, both of whom lived in Dresden for a time, were doubtless impressed by the beauty of the formula, and noted it down for future use, each in his own way.

Richard Heuberger, the Viennese musicologist, has suggested that the formula of the 'Dresden Amen' might have been composed by an Italian musician, Giuseppe Antonio Silvani, maestro di cappella of St. Stephen's in Bologna in the first quarter of the eighteenth century, and a composer of church music. Some of Silvani's compositions were sung in former days in the Court Church at Dresden. Silvani's works, which comprise a large number of *Responsoria*, were probably, thinks Heuberger, brought to Dresden by one of the choirmasters of the Kings of Saxony. Most of these choir-masters were Italians, or had been educated in Italian schools of music.

● Concerto for Piano and Orchestra, No. 1, in G minor, op. 25

Mendelssohn was twenty-one when he sketched this concerto (at Rome in November 1830). He finished it about a year later, in October 1831, at Munich. He himself was the pianist at the first performance of the work in the month of its completion, in the large hall of the Odeon, at Munich. He does not seem to have regarded that task as sufficient for one evening, since he conducted at the same concert his C minor Symphony (op. 11), and his Overture to *A Midsummer Night's Dream*, and improvised on the melody of *Non più andrai*, proposed by the King.

At the public performance the concerto was greatly liked. 'I was received,' wrote Mendelssohn, 'with loud and long applause . . . but I was modest and would not appear. Between the parts the King sent for me and praised me highly, asking all sorts of questions, and whether I was related to the Bartholdy in Rome, to whose house he was in the habit of going, because it was the cradle of modern art, etc.'

The concerto is in three movements. The first (G minor, 4-4 time, 'Molto allegro con fuoco') is developed from the customary two themes—both given out by the solo instrument. The second movement (which follows without pause), is a romanza-like Andante—in E major, 3-4 time. The last movement is preceded by a Presto introduction. The main body of the movement is a 'Molto allegro e vivace' in G major, 4-4 time. Toward the close, there are reminiscences of the thematic material of the first movement.

● Concerto for Violin and Orchestra, in E minor, op. 64

The completion and first performance of this superlatively famous concerto were among the later achievements of Mendelssohn's brilliant and compact existence. The work occupied his thoughts at intervals between 1838 (when he was twenty-nine years old), and 1844 (three years before his death). The first performance was by Ferdinand David at a Gewandhaus concert in Leipzig, March 13, 1845.

The three movements of the concerto are linked together. The first movement, 'Allegro molto appassionato' (E minor, 2-2), begins after an introductory measure with the first subject stated by the solo violin. This is developed at length by the solo instrument, which then proceeds with cadenza-like passage work. The theme is repeated and developed as a tutti by the full orchestra. The second subject is given out in G major, pianissimo, by clarinets and flutes, over an organ-point held by the solo violin. The brilliant cadenza ends with a series of arpeggios, which continue on through the repetition of the chief theme by the orchestral strings and wind. The concluding section is in regular form.

The Andante (C major, 6-8) consists at first of a development of the song-like theme begun by the solo violin. The middle section of the movement is concerned with the development of the second theme, a somewhat agitated melody. The third part is a repetition of the first, with the melody in the solo violin, but with a different accompaniment.

The Finale opens with an introductory section, 'Allegretto non troppo' (E minor, 4-4). The main body of the Finale, 'Allegro molto vivace' (E major, 4-4), begins with fortissimo wind chords, answered by arpeggios of the solo violin and a figure in the orchestral strings. The chief theme of the rondo is announced by the solo instrument and woodwind. There is a second theme, in B major, proposed *ff* by the orchestra.

● Music for A *Midsummer Night's Dream*

Sir George Grove, in a moment of absent-minded generosity, said of Mendelssohn that in the Overture to A *Midsummer Night's Dream* he 'brought the fairies into the orchestra and fixed them there.' Of course that is not strictly true of Mendelssohn, for Weber had turned the trick shortly before him. It would be more truthful to say that Mendelssohn was one of those who brought Shakespeare into the orchestra. The reading of A *Midsummer Night's Dream*, said Hazlitt, 'is like wandering in a grove by moonlight; the descriptions breathe a sweetness like odors thrown from beds of flowers.' It would be needlessly Draconian to test Mendelssohn's incidental music to the play by the touchstone of that characterization—to expect it to give us the musical equivalent of such poetry as

> By paved fountain or by rushy brook,
> Or in the beached margent of the sea. . .

Yet Mendelssohn nevertheless succeeded in bringing something authentically Shakespearean into the orchestra—something of the charm and gaiety of the play, and something of its romantic sweetness, when, as a youth of seventeen, he wrote the Overture to the *Dream*, extemporizing it (as he told Hiller) on the piano of a beautiful lady who lived close by the Mendelssohn dwelling in Berlin.

His sister Fanny and himself were then deep in translations of Shakespeare. Mendelssohn, indeed, was steeped from childhood in A *Midsummer Night's Dream*. The play, wrote his sister Fanny in 1843, 'has occupied an important part in our household. We had all at different ages gone through the parts from Peasblossom to Hermia and Helena. . . Felix especially had made it his own.' Mendelssohn was commissioned by the King of Prussia in 1843 to write music for the *Dream*, and he composed it early in that year. His music for the play comprises twelve numbers, in addition to the overture which he had composed seventeen years before—in 1826.

In the thrice-familiar overture, he gives us fairy music (near the beginning, played by strings). Later, he suggests the dance of the rustic clowns, the hunting-horn of Theseus, and the bray of the ineffable Bottom.

The exquisite Nocturne ('Andante tranquillo,' E major, 3-4) was intended to be played between Acts III and IV of the play, and recalls the picture of the sleeping lovers in the wood.

The Scherzo ('Allegro vivace,' G minor, 3-8) comes between Acts I and II, following the delectable episode in Quince's house where the Pyramus and Thisbe project is discussed. But the music is delicate and jocund, and avoids the broad comedy of Shakespeare's scene.

Of the Wedding March it would doubtless be impertinent to speak.

● OVERTURE, *Fingal's Cave*, OP. 26 (*Hebrides* Overture)

The miniature island of Staffa, only one and one-half miles in circumference, belongs to the Hebrides group, and lies about ten miles to the west of Mull. It is famous for its basaltic cavern, 'Fingal's Cave,' thirty-three feet wide and about twice as high, and penetrable for a distance of several hundred feet. Mendelssohn visited Scotland in 1829, as a young man of twenty, and in August he and his companion Klingemann made an expedition to the cave. Klingemann wrote of their adventure as follows, in a letter dated August 10:

'Staffa, with its strange basalt pillars and caverns, is in all picture-books.

We were put out in boats, and climbed—the hissing sea close beside us—
over the pillar stumps to the celebrated Fingal's Cave. A greener roar of waters
surely never rushed into a stranger cavern—comparable, on account of the
many pillars, to the inside of an immense organ, black and resounding, lying
there absolutely purposeless in the utter loneliness, the wide gray sea within
and without.'

Two days before, Mendelssohn had written to his sister: 'In order to make
you understand how extraordinarily the Hebrides affected me, the following
came into my mind there'; and he quoted the opening measures of the overture. Mendelssohn completed the first version of the overture December 16,
1830, in Rome. But more than a year later—in January 1832—he wrote that
he could not 'bring *The Hebrides* to a hearing' because he did not consider
it finished as he originally wrote it—'the whole so-called "development" smacks
more of counterpoint than of blubber, sea-gulls, and salt-cod.' By the spring
of the same year he had dissembled the counterpoint and heightened the
pungency of the salt-cod to his satisfaction, and on May 14 the overture was
performed at a Philharmonic concert in London, creating 'a great sensation.'
It was then entitled *The Isles of Fingal*. Mendelssohn in his letters refers to
it variously as *The Hebrides* and *The Solitary Isle (Einsame Insel)*. The score
as first published bore the title, *Die Fingals Höhle*, but the orchestral parts
were entitled *Die Hebriden*. In Breitkopf & Härtel's edition of Mendelssohn's
overtures the score is entitled: *Ouverture zu den Hebriden (Fingals-Höhle)*—
which seems to cover the case.

Richard Wagner—who may be conceded to have known good tone poetry
from bad—greatly admired this overture. 'I hold it,' he wrote in his essay
On Poetry and Composition, 'for one of the most beautiful musical works
that we possess'; and to Edward Dannreuther he wrote: 'Wonderful imagination and delicate feeling are here presented with consummate art. Note the
extraordinary beauty of the passage where the oboes rise above the other
instruments with a plaintive wail, like seawinds over the sea.'

● Overture to *Ruy Blas*, op. 95

Victor Hugo in his play *Ruy Blas* intended to offer a picture of the Court of
Charles II of Spain. The veracity of this portrayal has been disputed by
historical specialists. Nor did the plausibility of the action convince all those
who attended the première of the play in Paris. A dubious critic remarked to
Hugo that it was not easy to accept as possible, 'under the given conditions,'
the intrigue between the Queen of Spain and a valet. 'My dear Merle,' replied
Hugo, in his loftiest manner, 'I intended my drama to contain things beyond
the range of your vision, and I see that I have succeeded.'

Hugo, in his elaborate preface to *Ruy Blas*, goes at length into the historical
and human symbolism of his play, its philosophy and its motivation. 'The
philosophical motive of *Ruy Blas*,' he explains, 'is a people aspiring to a higher
state; the human subject is a man who loves a woman; the dramatic interest
is a lackey who loves a queen.' Humanly considered, Don Salluste de Bazan
'would be the personification of absolute egotism, anxiety without rest; Don

Caesar, his opposite in all respects, would be regarded as the type of generosity and thoughtful carelessness; Ruy Blas would express the spirit and passion of the community; the Queen would exemplify virtue undermined by wearing monotony. . .'

Mendelssohn composed his Overture to *Ruy Blas* as an act of bravado. He tells the story in a letter written to his mother on March 18, 1839:

> Six or eight weeks since, an application was made to me in favor of a representation to be given for the Theatrical Pension Fund (an excellent benevolent institution here [Leipzig] for the benefit of which *Ruy Blas* was to be given). I was requested to compose an overture for it, and the music of the romance in the piece, for it was thought the receipts would be better if my name appeared on the bills. I read the piece, which is detestable, and more utterly beneath contempt than you could believe, and said that I had no leisure to write an overture; but I composed the romance for them. The performance was to take place last Monday week; on the previous Tuesday the people came to thank me politely for the romance, and said it was such a pity I had not also written an overture, but they were perfectly aware that time was indispensable for such a work. In the ensuing year, if I would permit them, they would give me longer previous notice. This put me on my mettle. I reflected on the matter the same evening. On Wednesday there was a concert rehearsal, which occupied the whole forenoon; Thursday, the concert itself; yet the overture was in the hands of the copyist early on Friday; played three times on Monday in the concert room, tried over once in the theater, and given in the evening as an introduction to the odious play. Few of my works have caused me more amusing excitement.

A portentous phrase for the brass and woodwind (Lento, 2-2), followed by an impetuous subject ('Allegro molto') for the first and second violins in unison, begins the introduction. These contrasting passages are twice repeated; and then the chief theme, evolved from the spirited string figure of the introduction, is stated by the first violins and flutes, above a syncopated accompaniment. The second theme is given out staccato by the strings, pianissimo. A buoyant melody for the first violins and bassoon in octaves enters a little further on, and is made much of at the climax of the piece.

It was Mendelssohn himself who remarked that he intended to call this work 'not the Overture to *Ruy Blas*, but to the Theatrical Pension Fund.'

● Scherzo for Orchestra (from the Octet for Strings, op. 20)

Mendelssohn completed in 1825, when he was in his seventeenth year, an Octet for Strings—four violins, two violas, and two 'cellos. The Octet has four movements: an opening 'Allegro moderato ma con fuoco,' in E-flat, 4-4 time; a meditative Andante, richly embroidered; a Scherzo in 2-4 time, G minor, 'Allegro leggierissimo' (the original of the movement we are considering); and a Finale, E-flat major, opening with a Presto fugue.

Four years after its composition, Mendelssohn arranged the Scherzo of the Octet for orchestra for use at a concert given by the London Philharmonic Society on May 25, 1829, under his own direction. His Symphony in C minor was a feature of the program. On that occasion, he introduced the orchestrated Scherzo from the Octet into the symphony (composed in 1824) in place of the original Minuet.

The Scherzo in its orchestral form is scored for two flutes, two oboes, two clarinets, two bassoons, two horns, trumpet, timpani, and strings. This phantasmal, aerial music, which is played pianissimo and staccato almost throughout, has much the character of the famous Scherzo from the *Midsummer Night's Dream* music. It is easy to credit the assertion that Mendelssohn, composing this music, was inspired by the famous lines from *Faust* beginning:

Wolkenflug und Nebelflor. . .

Modest Patrovich Moussorgsky

1839-81

‡It is often said that Moussorgsky was the greatest of nineteenth-century Russian composers. But some qualification of this statement seems desirable. The opera *Boris Godounoff* and some of the songs are masterpieces, but in their pages strength runs parallel to weakness, and subtlety to crudity, which are too readily overlooked. Most probably the conventional estimate of Moussorgsky's music is influenced by pity for the man. He lived and died wretchedly, in need, dissipated and diseased. Yet the circumstances which are supposed to have ruined him were circumstances to which many other Russian musicians and literary men of his day rose superior. He was a flawed man—and, not surprisingly, a flawed artist, and the recognition of this fact sets his qualities, and the qualities of his music, in their proper context.‡

● *Pictures at an Exhibition*

The eminent Russian architect and painter, Victor Hartmann, died in 1873, at the age of thirty-nine. Shortly after his death, an exhibition of his watercolors and drawings was held at the Academy of Arts, St. Petersburg. Moussorgsky, who had been an intimate of Hartmann, visited the exhibition, and, desirous of paying a tribute to his friend, set about translating certain of the pictures into terms of music. He composed a set of ten piano pieces, *Pictures at an Exhibition*, each one descriptive of a picture in the show. The manuscript is dated June 22, 1874, but the work was not published until twelve years later.

The original piano edition of Moussorgsky's suite contains the following explanatory analysis:

The Introduction is entitled *Promenade* [Stassoff, to whom the Suite is dedicated, remarked of the *Promenade*, which reappears several times as an interlude between the pieces: 'The composer here portrays himself walking now right, now left, now as an

idle person, now urged to go near a picture; at times his joyous appearance is damp-
ened, he thinks in sadness of his dead friend. . .'

'One can imagine nothing more subtle, more elastic, more evocative than the music
of these *Promenades*,' declares Calvocoressi in his Life of Moussorgsky—'so ingeniously
rhythmed, sustained, persisting without monotony, thanks to the diversity of nuances'].

I. 'Gnomus.' A drawing representing a gnome, dragging himself along with clumsy
steps by his little twisted legs.

II. 'The Old Castle.' A castle of the Middle Ages, before which a troubadour is
singing.

III. 'Tuileries.' Children disputing after their play. An alley in the Tuileries gardens
with a swarm of nurses and children.

IV. 'Bydlo.' A Polish wagon with enormous wheels drawn by oxen.

V. 'Ballet of Chickens in Their Shells.' A drawing made by Hartmann for the
staging of a scene in the ballet 'Trilby.'

VI. 'Samuel Goldenberg and Schmuyle.' Two Polish Jews, the one rich, the other
poor.

[Pierre d'Alheim in his *Moussorgsky* (Paris, 1896) remarks: 'Two Jewish melodies,
one replying to the other. One of them is grave, imposing, decisively marked; the other
is lively, skipping, supplicating. One cannot be deceived in the two persons: one of
them, the portly one, walks square-toed, like a dog with a pedigree; the other, the thin
one, hurries along, dwarfs himself, twists about, like a puppy. He revolves in a funny
way, courts a look from the other, begs. There is no doubt about them, one sees them—
and the barking of the fat one who frees himself, in two triplets, from the bore, proves
that Moussorgsky could draw from the pianoforte, as from the voice, as from the
orchestra, comical effects.']

VII. 'Limoges: The Market-place.' Market women wrangle furiously.

VIII. 'Catacombs.' In this drawing Hartmann portrayed himself, examining the
interior of the Catacombs in Paris by the light of a lantern. [In the original manuscript,
Moussorgsky wrote above the Andante in B minor: 'The creative spirit of the dead
Hartmann leads me towards skulls, apostrophizes them—the skulls are illuminated
gently in the interior.' ' "The Catacombs," with the subtitle "Sepulchrum romanum," '
writes Calvocoressi, 'are invoked by a series of sustained chords, now pp, now ff. Then
comes under the title "Con mortuis in lingua mortua" (*sic*) a de-rhythmed transformation of the "Promenade" theme.']

IX. 'The Hut on Fowls' Legs.' The drawing showed a clock in the form of the
hut of Baba-Yaga, the fantastical witch, standing on the legs of fowls. Moussorgsky
added the witch rushing on her way seated on her mortar.

X. 'The Great Gate at Kieff.' Hartmann's design for the construction of an
entrance gate for the city of Kieff, conceived in the massive, old Russian style, had a
cupola shaped like a Slav helmet.

In the early twenties of the present century Maurice Ravel made an
orchestral transcription of Moussorgsky's piano pieces. This transcription was
first performed in Paris, at a Koussevitzky concert, May 3, 1923. There are
other orchestral versions of Moussorgsky's suite. Eight of the piano pieces
were scored by M. Touschmaloff and performed at St. Petersburg in 1891.
An orchestral arrangement of the suite made by Leonidas Leonardi, a pianist
and composer in Paris, at the request of the publisher Bessel (holder of the
rights of Moussorgsky's compositions), was performed at a concert of Russian
music at the Salle Gaveau, Paris, by the Lamoureux Orchestra, conducted by
Leonardi, in June 1924. Sir Henry Wood also scored the pieces for perform-

ance at his concerts in London. In addition, there are versions by Lucien Caillet and by Leopold Stokowski.

• *A Night on Bald Mountain*

M. D. Calvocoressi, in his able and authoritative Life of Moussorgsky, calls this 'the most developed' of Moussorgsky's instrumental compositions. The phrase might easily be read as slyly jocose, were not Calvocoressi an incorruptibly serious person: for this music underwent a remarkable series of transformations.

The origins of the work are obscure, and the historians, as usual, do not agree on the matter. Vladimir Stassoff, to whom the score is dedicated, says that the material for *A Night on Bald Mountain* was derived from Moussorgsky's uncompleted opera *Salammbo*, which he began in 1863, using a libretto of his own based upon Flaubert's novel. Other portions of the *Salammbo* music, according to Stassoff, were used in *Boris Goudonoff*. Rimsky-Korsakoff in his autobiography says that *A Night on Bald Mountain* was originally a youthful composition entitled *St. John's Eve*, for piano and orchestra, written in 1867 under the influence of Liszt's *Todtentanz* and Berlioz's 'Witches' Sabbath.' But it was 'severely criticized' by Balakireff, and Moussorgsky laid it aside. Later he returned to it, and revamped it for the opera-ballet *Mlada*, which Moussorgsky, Rimsky-Korsakoff, Borodin, and Cui planned to write in collaboration (this was three or four years later). Moussorgsky adapted his piece for use in the composite opera as music for the revels of Chernobog, the Black God, and he introduced voice parts. But the *Mlada* project fell through. Moussorgsky then purposed to introduce the much-modified composition into his opera *The Fair at Sorochintzy*, which he began in 1877 to a libretto after Gogol, but did not finish.

In its final and most familiar incarnation, the piece exists as a 'fantasy for orchestra,' which is partly the work of Rimsky-Korsakoff and which he introduced at St. Petersburg, in the course of a concert of the Russian Symphony Society in October 1886, some five years after Moussorgsky's death.

The score is prefaced by the following argument:

Subterranean sounds of unearthly voices. Appearance of the Spirits of Darkness, followed by that of the god Chernobog. Glorification of Chernobog, and celebration of the Black Mass. Witches' Sabbath. At the height of the orgies, the bell of the little village church is heard from afar. The Spirits of Darkness are dispersed. Daybreak.

Bald Mountain, near Kieff, in Southern Russia, was the legendary scene of the Slavic Walpurgisnacht, and there the witches, sorcerers, demons and unclean spirits foregathered for their Sabbath revels. On that night the peasants bolted their doors and shuddered within their cottages, after placing nettles in their windows as a protective charm against the Powers of Darkness.

Calvocoressi points out that the form of this work is clear and simple: a symphonic Allegro running into a short Andante. Assuming that the original version of the piece was not materially different from this final one, he pronounces *A Night on Bald Mountain* 'a significant creation.' At that time, as he reminds us, the Russian school of music-makers had scarcely begun the series of picturesque symphonic poems with which we are familiar. Rimsky's *Sadko* (afterward revised) was composed in 1867; Balakireff's *Thamar* was begun in 1867, completed in 1882. Tchaikovsky, then twenty-seven, composed his first symphonic poem, *Fatum* ('Destiny'), in 1868; *Romeo and Juliet* was begun in 1869. Moussorgsky, thinks Calvocoressi, deserves, therefore, to be counted amongst the innovators. A *Night on Bald Mountain*, he remarks, differs from the 'Witches' Sabbath' in Berlioz's *Fantastic Symphony* in this respect; its picturesqueness arises from 'the quality of the themes and the tonal and rhythmic atmosphere—as with all Russian symphonic poems—and not from mere picturesqueness of arrangement, as in Berlioz.' This distinction, though perhaps a little obscure (one is not quite sure what Calvocoressi means by 'picturesqueness of arrangement'), is nevertheless worth pondering. He admits handsomely that Berlioz's work 'furnished the Russians with a precedent, if not a model'—which is fairly obvious, since the *Symphonie fantastique* preceded by thirty-seven years the earliest of the Russian works mentioned by Calvocoressi.

● PRELUDE, ENTR'ACTE AND DANCES FROM *Khovantchina*

Moussorgsky worked intermittently upon his last opera, *Khovantchina*, between 1872 and the year of his death; but he did not finish it. The score was completed by Rimsky-Korsakoff and published in 1882.

As in the case of *Boris*, Moussorgsky (who wrote his own libretto) went for his subject to Russian history, and, prompted by Stassoff, chose the most troubled period in this country's past, the end of the seventeenth century, when religious and political schisms divided the nation into opposing camps. To the resultant series of conflicts, in which Prince Khovantsky played a leading part, Czar Peter gave the appellation *Khovantchina*.

Moussorgsky's libretto concerns the fortunes of the saintly young Lutheran, Emma, who is amorously pursued by the dissolute Prince Andrew Khovantsky; the mystical and passionate Martha, betrayed by Prince Andrew; Dositheus ('Docithé,' in the French text), leader of the Raskolniky or 'Old Believers'; Prince Ivan Khovantsky, the fanatical and half-barbarous conservative, chief of the ferocious Archers-of-the-Guard (the 'Streltsky'), and Prince Galitsin, the semi-liberalized aristocrat to whom a new Russia is not inconceivable. Galitsin is visited by the clairvoyant Martha, who reads his future in a silver bowl filled with water, and predicts his downfall and banishment. Nor is Prince Khovantsky without his troubles: for while he is in retirement at his country-place, diverted by feasting, songs, and Persian dancers, he is assassinated on his own threshold.

This event occurs at the close of the first scene of Act IV. The second scene of the act passes in a public square in Moscow, in front of the Church of Vassily Blajeny. Galitsin, fulfilling the prophecy of Martha, is seen on his way to exile, escorted by a troop of cavalry. Dositheus joins the watching throng in the square, and learns that the Old Believers have been sentenced to death by Peter; but he determines that this death shall be self-inflicted.

Young Prince Andrew Khovantsky, unaware of his father's fate, enters, seeking his Lutheran Emma; he hears from Martha that Emma has married, and, in a rage, summons the Streltsky to seize her—this clairvoyant who tells him unpleasant truths. His bugle-blast brings his soldiers upon the scene—but they are under guard, and on the way to their own execution; which at the last moment is prevented by the clemency of Peter. The Old Believers, however, prefer death to apostasy, and, exalted by Dositheus, immolate themselves on a pyre in the midst of a wood, singing an exultant canticle from the heart of the flames, while Prince Andrew mounts upon the pyre beside them. The Old Russia was passing—or so it seemed, at least, in 1682.

The Prelude to the opera depicts the coming of the cold northern daybreak above the Kremlin in Moscow. 'Nothing in Russian music,' says Rosa Newmarch in her book, *The Russian Opera*, 'is more intensely or touchingly national in feeling. The curtain opens upon the Red Square in the Kremlin, just as the rising sun catches the domes of the churches, and the bells ring for early matins.'

The entr'acte comprises the music played by the orchestra at the beginning of the second scene of the fourth act, as the banished Galitsin, guarded by a troop of cavalry, crosses the public square on his way to exile, with the bells of the Church of Vassily Blajeny tolling mournfully as if in lamentation. In the opera, the passing of the cortege across the square is accompanied by the comments of the chorus. The passage opens (Adagio, E-flat minor, 4-4) with a dirgelike figure in the basses, under chords of the wind. Then we hear the dolorous melody sung by the clairvoyant Martha in the scene of her 'Divination by Water' in the second act, in which she foretold to Galitsin his downfall ('in shame and disgrace I behold thee, in exile alone in a distant land'). Not only the somber and fateful theme sung by the orchestra but the ostinato accompaniment figure are derived from Martha's prophetic song in the earlier act.

The Persian dances occur in Act IV, in the scene at Prince Ivan Khovantsky's palace.

Wolfgang Amadeus Mozart

1756-91

M

‡Few will deny that Mozart was one of the most astonishing geniuses of record, unsurpassed in natural musical aptitude, and unequaled in acquired proficiency. From the earliest age, music poured from his mind and hand in a ceaseless stream; and his inspiration kept pace with his fabulous facility. Masterpieces by Mozart are to be found among the very greatest works in every category of music, and not a page exists, authenti-

cated as his, which does not bear in some detail the stamp of genius. It is of course not true that all recognition was withheld from him. But his occasional brilliant successes only emphasized the indifference that was his portion at other times. The patronage so essential to the musician in his day was sparingly and grudgingly accorded him; he never enjoyed the prestige and security that were Haydn's; and when he died, there was none to do him honor.‡

● SYMPHONY IN E-FLAT, K. 16

Leopold Mozart and his two astonishing children, Wolfgang and Nannerl, left Paris for London on April 10, 1764. In London they took lodgings with Mr. Williamson in Frith Street, Soho. Shortly after their arrival the children appeared at Court before the King and Queen, receiving for their services (as Papa Leopold somewhat discontentedly noted in his account) 'only 24 guineas.' But the next day, their Majesties were pleased to bow from their carriage to the Mozart family in St. James's Park, and that was more than sufficient compensation. The children reappeared at Court soon after, when the eight-year-old Wolfgang, sitting stiffly upright at the clavier, in his embroidered clothes, powdered hair, and diminutive buckled shoes, played at sight pieces by Handel, Johann Christian Bach, Abel, and Wagenseil, accompanied Queen Charlotte in an aria and a flautist in a solo, and improvised a melody upon the bass-part of a Handel air. He also played on the palace organ. On June 5, the children gave their first concert in London at the Great Room in Spring Garden. Their canny father had chosen the King's birthday as the date for the occasion, and consequently felt certain of a crowded London in holiday mood. He announced the concert in the *Public Advertiser* as follows:

For the benefit of Miss Mozart, of eleven, and Master Mozart, of seven years [*sic*] of age, Prodigies of Nature . . . [a phrase is missing from the advertisement at this point]. This method is therefore taken to show to the Public the greatest Prodigy that Europe or that even Human Nature can boast of. Everybody will be struck with Admiration to hear them, and particularly to hear a young boy of Seven Years of Age play on the Harpsichord with such dexterity and perfection. It surpasses all Understanding and all Imagination; and it is hard to say whether his Execution upon the Harpsichord and his playing at Sight, or his own compositions, are the most astonishing. His Father brought him to England not doubting but that he must meet with success in a Kingdom where his countryman Handel received during his lifetime such particular protection.

Tickets at Half a Guinea each, to be had of Mr. Mozart, at Mr. Cousin's, Hair-cutter, in Cecil Court, St. Martin's Lane.

The concert was a huge success; the receipts were 'as much as 100 guineas.' Even Leopold, that prince of press agents, was astonished.

The Mozarts had intended to stay in England for only three months; but Leopold caught cold on the way home from a musical party at Lord Thanet's, and developed a severe attack of quinsy. Shortly after, the family moved to Chelsea (then a neighboring village), where they remained for seven weeks while Leopold convalesced. At this time, Wolfgang, unwilling to disturb his father by playing the clavier, occupied himself with composition—among other works, with a symphony in B-flat major (K. 17). This symphony Mozart left unfinished. The next to which he set his hand is the one in E-flat (K. 16). It was the first that he completed. Mozart wrote it after the family had returned from Chelsea to London. The precise date of its composition, as we noted above, is not known. It was finished in the winter of 1764-5, within a few weeks of the boy's ninth birthday.

The autograph score bears the inscription: *Sinfonia di Sig. Wolfgang Mozart à London*. There are many corrections in the score. It was the belief of Jahn that these corrections were made by Wolfgang himself, 'partly to improve the instrumentation.' But modern scholars have expressed the conviction that these amendments, and others in Mozart's works of this period, were, in all probability, made by the elder Mozart. Leopold remarked that in one of these compositions, some consecutive-fifths had been overlooked; and he viewed this contretemps philosophically, because, he said, it would 'prove to the public that the work was really Wolfgang's own composition.'

But whatever the extent of the elder Mozart's contributions to the facture of the score, there are many signs in Wolfgang's compositions of this period—despite their tentative character and their obvious dependence upon Abel and Johann Christian Bach—that he was developing, with incredible rapidity, from a mere *Wunderkind* to an authentic master ('doubled,' as Wyzewa remarks, 'by a poet').

The E-flat Symphony (K. 16) is in three movements: 'Allegro molto'—Andante—Presto. It is scored for two oboes, two horns, and strings. Both in form and in manner the astonishing little work derives from Mozart's model, Johann Christian Bach. The influence of that admirable master is evident in Mozart's employment of the 'galant' style; in the frequent alternation of piano and forte; in the repetition of phrases; in the differentiation of the two subjects of the first Allegro—the one markedly rhythmic in character, the other, contrastingly melodic; in the shaping of the Finale as a diminutive rondo, fluent and brilliant.

• SYMPHONY IN C MAJOR, K. 200

Although musicologists do not agree in dating this symphony, it belongs unquestionably to either Mozart's eighteenth or nineteenth year. The date on the autograph score has been effaced. Jahn and Köchel ascribe the composition of the work to the year 1774; but later and more exhaustive research (see the admirable study of T. de Wyzewa and G. de Saint-Foix: *W. A. Mozart: Sa vie musicale et son oeuvre de l'enfance à la pleine maturité*) makes it seem probable that the symphony was written, at least in part, in 1773, at Vienna, during Mozart's sojourn there with his father from July to October.

That brief visit to Vienna, undertaken in the hope that something profitable might turn up, was not rewarding in a pecuniary sense, for either the father or for his prodigious son. Leopold Mozart wrote to his wife that his body was 'growing fat in proportion as his purse grew thin.' But he was not disheartened. 'Things must and will mend—take courage: God will help us!'

Providence failed to oblige as expected; yet Wolfgang profited as a creative artist from his stay in Vienna. He came to know then the quartets of Haydn; and from them he learned much; his musical thinking became bolder, of stronger flight. The developmental sections of his quartet and symphonic writing became ampler, more adventurous. The sonata form was applied to finales; and Mozart learned from Haydn various details of workmanship—as the device of the so-called 'false entrance,' occurring in the Finale of this symphony.

The first movement is an 'Allegro spiritoso,' C major, in 3-4 time. There is due contrast between the first theme, with its energetic opening figure, descending in unison and octaves, forte, for the strings and wind, and the gracious second subject in G major. This is announced, piano, by the strings, with a decorative figure in sixths for the oboes. At its repetition, this relationship is instrumentally reversed, the oboes (doubled by the violas an octave lower) giving the melody in thirds, the violins embroidering.

The slow movement (Andante, F major, 2-4) begins with a simple theme for the strings (the violins 'con sordino'), with a subsidiary section which is rhythmically striking.

The Minuet (Allegretto, C major) has a Trio scored for the strings alone. This Minuet has been praised as 'worthy of being considered a sort of first sketch for the Minuet of the "Jupiter" Symphony. . . It is to be ranked the highest in all the instrumental writing of the young composer up to the time of his definite departure from Salzburg.'

The Finale is a brilliant Presto in 2-2 time. It begins with a theme on a trilling figure, exposed in a sportive and delightful passage, p, for the violins alone, which is interrupted, with almost Beethovenish abruptness, by two forte bars for the full orchestra. The strings alone have the more lyrical theme in the dominant key.

The symphony is scored for two oboes, two horns, two trumpets, and strings. There are no kettledrums in the autograph score or in the first published edition of the symphony; but an autograph part for them was discovered among the manuscripts in the possession of André of Frankfort.

● SYMPHONY IN A MAJOR, K. 201

This symphony was composed, in all probability, at Salzburg in 1774, when Mozart was eighteen. There is no date on the autograph score; but it is almost certainly one of that series of four symphonies (K. 200, 183, 201, 202) which Mozart wrote in 1773-4 after his return to Salzburg from Vienna in October 1773. A memorandum in the catalogue published by André of Offenbach, who bought Mozart's papers, records that this work belonged to 'the symphonies which Mozart was in the habit of carrying with him on his travels for purposes of performance.'

The four symphonies composed by Mozart at this period (they are in the keys of C major, G minor, A major, and D major) are considered by modern investigators of Mozart's aesthetic history to represent the most significant expression of his creative activity in the symphonic field prior to the works of his maturity. Of this group, the Symphony in G minor (K. 183)—composed some fourteen years before its famous successor in the same key—and that in A are the most remarkable. Dyneley Hussey, in his thoughtful study of Mozart's artistic development, finds in this symphony, and in its companion work in G minor (K. 183), a 'tragic nobility.' Hussey finds also some repercussion of that romantic impulse which was making itself felt in Germany through such manifestations as Bürger's *Lenore* and Goethe's *Werther*.

Otto Jahn, who was not always responsive to the gravity of implication in Mozart's music, would doubtless have been amazed at Hussey's discovery in the A major Symphony of emotional seriousness; for to Jahn the music is 'full from beginning to end of cheerful humor.' But regarding the difficulty of placing ourselves in a true relation to the emotional and spiritual contents of the music of Mozart's period, Ernest Newman has shrewdly remarked that we do not always hear this and other old music as the composer and his contemporaries heard it, 'because we have lost, owing to the huge development of musical language since then, the true sense of a hundred niceties of vocabulary and distinctions of formula that were of the utmost significance to them. . . In what seems to us the seemingly unruffled flow of much of Mozart's music, there are, I am convinced, disturbing elements that stood out for him and his contemporaries in a way that they do not do for us.'

The work has four movements: I. 'Allegro moderato,' A major, 'Alla breve' time (in Breitkopf & Härtel's edition of the full score the time signature of the first movement is 4-4). II. Andante, D major, 2-4 time (in this movement the violins are muted throughout, except in the last five measures of the coda). III. Minuet, A major, 3-4 time. IV. 'Allegro con spirito,' A major, 6-8 time. The instrumentation is for two oboes, two horns, and strings.

● SYMPHONY IN D MAJOR, K. 297 ('Paris')

Mozart composed this symphony, known as the 'Paris' Symphony, and sometimes as the 'symphony without minuet' (though other of the Mozart symphonies lack minuets) at Paris in 1778. He was then twenty-two years old; in search of his fortune he had, with his mother, undertaken a tour which led him from Salzburg through Munich and Augsburg to Mannheim and Paris. In Mannheim he met a young singer, Aloysia Weber, and out of love and pity (she was attractive, gifted, and poor) would in all probability have married her had his father not objected strenuously and urged him on to Paris. (Four years later, Mozart married not Aloysia, but her younger sister Constanze.) The Symphony in D was one of a number of works written during a six-month stay in the French capital. Of simple construction, it begins 'Allegro assai,' 4-4, with a vigorous forte chord, all the strings attacking together, and initiating the chief theme, which is proposed by the violins. The second movement is an Andante in G, 6-8, developing a long cantilena in various instruments—actually, a tripartite theme. The third movement, an Allegro in the tonic key, 4-4, is in sonata form. The symphony is remarkable for the fidelity with which it adheres to the keys of the tonic and the dominant. It is scored for flutes, oboes, clarinets, bassoons, horns and trumpets in pairs, strings, and timpani.

• SYMPHONY IN B-FLAT, K. 319

This symphony was composed in July 1779, after Mozart's return from Munich to Salzburg in January of that year. The symphony was composed originally in three movements, without minuet. The minuet was written later, probably for a performance in Vienna, and was inserted on a separate leaf in the manuscript of the score. The instrumentation of this symphony is for oboes, bassoons, and horns, and the customary strings. The structure of the work is transparently simple. The full orchestra presents at once the principal thematic material of the opening movement ('Allegro assai,' B-flat major, 3-4), a curious feature of which is the appearance in the working-out section (at first in the violins, in the dominant key) of the subject of the great fugue in the 'Jupiter' Symphony—an old church tune of which Mozart was fond, for he used it in the *Credo* of his Mass in F (1774), in the *Sanctus* of the Mass in C major (1776), and in the first movement of the E-flat Sonata for Piano and Violin (1785).

The slow movement, an 'Andante moderato' in E-flat major (2-4), opens with a melody for the violins, accompanied at first only by the other strings. A second subject, of more poignant expressiveness, follows it at the nineteenth measure, also for the strings alone. There is yet another melody, begun by the first violins alone.

The vigorous Minuetto (no tempo mark, B-flat, 3-4 time) has a Trio in the tonic key, based on a deliciously flowing tune for the violins, doubled afterward by the oboes in thirds.

The Finale ('Allegro assai,' B-flat major, 2-4), the most remarkable of the four movements, presents at once, forte-piano, the first theme, an energetic subject for the strings based on a reiterated figure in triplets. Later, the strings alone (in F major) have a captivating subject of flowing grace and humor; and there is another, lustier but almost equally engaging, for the oboes and bassoons, staccato, playing in doubled thirds and octaves adorned with trills. After the double bar, the violins introduce a more expressive subject, in which Mozart gives us a reminder, by his use of the minor ninth, of his mastery of harmonic poignance. The passage reaches a forte in a striking unison passage for the woodwind and strings, after which the buoyant triplet figure is resumed. The end is unqualifiedly merry.

• SYMPHONY IN C MAJOR, K. 338

Mozart composed at least eight symphonies in the key of C major (one of them is fragmentary). The symphony on this program was composed at Salzburg in 1780—the date on the score is August 29. Mozart was then twenty-four years old. The symphony lacks a minuet. The three movements are an 'Allegro vivace,' an 'Andante di molto,' and the Finale, 'Allegro vivace.' Mozart at first intended to include a minuet, but he completed only the first part, and crossed it out in the score.

This symphony is probably the one referred to by Mozart in a letter written from Vienna, April 11, 1781. 'I have forgotten to tell you,' he says, 'that the symphony (conducted by the old Kapellmeister Bono) went *magnifique,* and had a great success.'

Otto Jahn found this symphony 'grander in conception and more serious in tone than the earlier one in B-flat major, composed the summer before (K. 319). This is particularly noticeable in the first movement, where a constant propensity to fall into the minor key blends strength and decision with an expression not so much of melancholy as of consolation. In perfect harmony of conception, the simple and fervent "Andante di molto" combines exceeding tenderness with a quiet depth of feeling.'

The opening movement ('Allegro vivace,' C major, 4-4) introduces at once the chief theme, for the full orchestra. Another section of this theme is heard from the strings and bassoons, piano. The second theme is a vivacious subject in G major. The 'Andante di molto' which constitutes the second movement is in F major, 2-4 time, scored for strings and bassoon with two independent viola parts. The Finale is an 'Allegro vivace,' C major, 6-8, in rondo form.

The symphony is scored for two oboes, two bassoons, two horns, two trumpets, timpani, and strings.

• SYMPHONY IN D MAJOR, K. 385 ('Haffner')

This work, the so-called 'Haffner' Symphony, was composed in a hurry, even according to eighteenth-century conceptions of the time which should be devoted to so trifling a thing as a symphony. Mozart wrote it at Vienna in less than a fortnight, in the summer of 1782, to oblige the Haffner family of Salzburg.

Some years before, Fräulein Elise Haffner, daughter of 'the worthy merchant and burgomaster, Sigmund Haffner of Salzburg,' had elected to marry a young man named Späth, and Mozart was asked to contribute music for the nuptial festivities. Accordingly he wrote in July 1776, in his twenty-first year, the work known as the 'Haffner' Serenade (D major, K. 250); and he also supplied a march in the same key.

Six years later, Mozart was asked by his father to contrive more festal strains for the Haffner family. Wolfgang was deeply engrossed at the time in more exciting matters. He was, in the first place, distressingly in love with Constanze Weber. Mozart had described her half a year before as 'not ugly, though far from beautiful,' and 'not clever'; but she was, he said, 'neat and clean,' and had a good heart. It does not sound precisely ecstatic; yet one suspects that Constanze was absorbing enough to get in the way of Mozart's music at that time.

'Infamous lies' had been spread concerning Mozart and Constanze; chiefly, he believed, by the malicious Peter Winter—who, despite the fact that he dwelt in the sobering neighborhood of a bassoonist, appears to have been a person of deplorably gaudy morals. He had said to Mozart: 'You will be foolish to marry; you can earn enough—why should you not keep a mistress?'

But Constanze and calumny were not the only things that distracted Mozart at this time. He was busily occupied in arranging music from his opera, *Die Entführung aus dem Serail,* for wind instruments—a troublesome and not too pleasurable task; and he was at work on his Serenade in C minor (K. 388).

'I have certainly enough to do,' he wrote to his father (July 20, 1782), 'for by Sunday a week my opera must be arranged for wind instruments, or else someone will get the start of me, and reap the profits! and now I have to write a new work! I hardly see how it will be possible. . . You shall certainly receive something every post-day, and I will work as rapidly as I can, and as well as I can, compatibly with such haste.'

A week later he writes: 'You will make a wry face when you receive only the first allegro; but it could not be helped, for I was called on in such great haste. . . On Wednesday the 31st I will send the two minuets, the andante, and the last movement. If I can, I will send a march also.' The march followed a week after.

At first the work had the form of a serenade, with a march as the introductory movement; and there were two minuets. But the serenade became a symphony, and the march and one minuet were dropped. Six months after the score was completed, Mozart had so far forgotten the contents of the score that when his father, at Wolfgang's request, sent the manuscript back to him in February 1783, this incredibly casual genius wrote: 'The new "Haffner" Symphony has quite astonished me, for I did not remember a note of it. It must be very effective.'

The symphony was performed at a concert given by Mozart in Vienna a month later (March 22, 1783), before the Emperor, who was so gracious as to express his satisfaction with the new work. The scheme of the symphony comprises an 'Allegro con spirito' in D major, 2-2 (the working-out is short, and the opening section is unrepeated); a G major Andante, 2-4; a Menuetto in D, 3-4 (with the A major Trio recalling an aria from *La Finta Giardiniera*, which Mozart had written for the Munich Carnival of 1775); and a final Rondo (Presto, D major, 4-4).

● SYMPHONY IN C MAJOR, K. 425 ('Linz')

This symphony was completed at Linz in November 1783. It betrays something of Haydn's influence, both in form and in thematic structure. As to form, note the slow introduction to the first movement—an Adagio in 3-4 time 'such as Mozart had heard in Haydn's symphonies, with which his sojourn in Vienna had better acquainted him,' remarks Brenet. Yet Mozart's style is unmistakable throughout.

Paumgartner thinks that Mozart strove in this symphony 'for brilliancy and festive splendor—trumpets in the slow movement! But true to Mozart's characteristic style, the exuberant gaiety of the music is frequently relieved by an impassioned cantabile.' In the development sections of the first and last movements, as well as in the slow movement, secondary thematic material assumes unusual prominence; this feature struck the observant Paumgartner as the most remarkable of the symphony.

The Adagio Introduction (C major, 3-4, for full orchestra, forte) with its bold and high-headed opening, leads at the twentieth measure (after a fermata), into the main movement, 'Allegro spiritoso,' C major, 4-4, with the theme given to the strings alone. The second subject is in G major.

The slow movement ('Poco adagio,' 6-8) begins quietly in the strings (F major), but the brass, wood, and timpani enter *fp* at the fifth measure. The C major—C minor passage a dozen bars later, with its beautiful cantilena for the violins, is Mozart at his most persuasive (note the exquisite effect of such a detail as the chromatic descent of the oboes from G sharp to F natural against the ascending phrase of the violins).

The third movement, Menuetto, is in C major, with a Trio in the same key (the latter is begun by the oboe and first violins in octaves).

The Finale (Presto, C major, 2-4) is somewhat unusual in form. W. F. Apthorp said of the first part of the movement, presenting two subjects in C major and others in G, that 'some of these themes might be taken as subsidiary to others by those anxious to preserve the symphonic nomenclature; but it is nearer to the fact to call this first part of the movement—like that of the first movement in Beethoven's Ninth Symphony—a mere succession of several different themes, each of which has its own character, but reflecting little of the usual relations of first, second, and conclusion theme.'

The instrumentation of the symphony is for oboes, bassoons, horns and trumpets in pairs, timpani, and strings.

• SYMPHONY IN D MAJOR, K. 504 ('Prague')

The month of December 1786 was a relatively slack one for Mozart. Between the 4th and the 27th of that month he composed only one symphony, one piano concerto, and a song with obbligato piano solo which he wrote for Storace, the original Susanna in *Figaro*.

The D major Symphony of 1786 was performed for the first time on January 19, 1787, at Prague. The Bohemian city was at that time Mozart-mad —or rather *Figaro*-mad. The citizens of Prague had gone wild with enthusiasm over the opera. When Mozart on the night of his arrival at Prague (January 11, 1787), was taken by Count Canal to the Breitfeld Ball, he was delighted to find, as he wrote his friend Gottfried von Jacquin, that 'the flower of the Prague beauties were whirling about to the music of my *Figaro* turned into waltzes and country dances: for nothing is talked of here but *Figaro*, no opera is cared for but *Figaro*, nothing is played, sung, or whistled but *Figaro*—everlastingly *Figaro!* Truly a great honor for me.'

At the concert of January 19, the new symphony was acclaimed with such enthusiasm that Mozart, to appease the audience, improvised on the piano for half an hour. But that did not satisfy them, so he returned to the instrument and began to improvise some more. A voice shouted the word 'Figaro!' and Mozart, stopping midway in the phrase that he had commenced, began to play variations on 'Non più andrai,' that air which Prague had taken to its heart. This, it appears, brought down the house.

The D major Symphony, which preceded by a year and a half the great final trio of symphonies that Mozart composed in the summer of 1788 (the E-flat, the G minor, and the 'Jupiter'), contains only an Allegro, Andante, and Finale. The first movement is noteworthy for its possession of a slow introduction—frequently to be found in the symphonies of Haydn, but present in only four of Mozart's. The slow introduction to the D major symphony (Adagio, 4-4) begins with a figure that is strikingly like the opening subject of the 'Jupiter' Symphony. The chief theme of the main movement (Allegro, D major, 4-4) has suggested to some commentators the first theme of the Overture to *Don Giovanni*, though the resemblance is not very marked.

- SYMPHONY IN E-FLAT, K. 543
- SYMPHONY IN G MINOR, K. 550
- SYMPHONY IN C MAJOR, K. 551 ('Jupiter')

Mozart composed his three greatest symphonies—those in E-flat, in G minor, and C major—within the space of two months. The year was 1788. The E-flat Symphony is dated June 26; the G minor, July 25, and the C major, August 10.

It was a bad time for Mozart. He was desperately hard-up and his creditors were wearing out his door with their knuckles. Dismal thoughts, he wrote, often came to him—and no wonder. Puchberg lent him two hundred florins, but that was only a stop-gap. The day after he completed the E-flat Symphony he wrote to Puchberg saying that unless he could obtain help he should lose both his honor and his credit. Yet Jahn found in this symphony the expression of 'perfect happiness . . . unalloyed happiness and joy in living.' It was, he said, 'a veritable triumph of euphony,' and if 'some shadows' fall across the pages of the Andante, they only 'serve to throw into stronger relief the serenity of a mind that communes with itself and rejoices in the peace which fills it.'

A month after the completion of the E-flat Symphony, some hint of Mozart's distress had begun to find its way into his music, for Jahn, no longer so complacent, tells us that in the G minor Symphony 'joy and gladness' have yielded to 'sorrow and complaint.' He declares that this utterance of melancholy in the music begins at once. He hears 'a piercing cry of anguish later in this movement, but strive and struggle as it will,' he continues, 'the strength of resistance sinks again into the murmur with which the movement closes. The Andante, on the contrary, is consolatory in tone; not reposing on the consciousness of an inner peace, but striving after it with an earnest composure which even attempts to be cheerful.'

Why the third of this trilogy of masterpieces, the great C major, is called the 'Jupiter' Symphony, and who christened it, is not known. Some have conjectured that the brusque triplets in the opening measures may have suggested to naïve minds the thunderbolts of Jove. But this seems unlikely. The man who wrote the Statue scene in *Don Giovanni* could have extemporized more terrifying thunderbolts than these, even in the estimation of the most innocent. Cramer—J. B. Cramer, pianist and pedagogue—has been credited with inventing the appellation, as an utterance of his enthusiastic appreciation of the height, breadth, and noble fervor of the symphony. Jahn thought that it was doubtless thus called ('I do not know when or by whom') 'more to indicate its majesty and splendor than with a view to any deeper symbolism'; and he enlarged upon the 'dignity and solemnity' of the score, 'manifested in the brilliant pomp of the first movement, with its evident delight in splendid sound effects.' Jahn contrasts this symphony with its predecessor, the G minor. He thinks that the 'Jupiter' is not 'so full of passion' as the G minor, though 'in more than one respect it is the greatest and best. . . It has no passionate excitement, but its tender grace is heightened by a serenity which shines forth most unmistakably in the subject already alluded to' (Jahn here refers to Mozart's adaptation of the air which he had written, three months previously, for Albertarelli, a bass singer who was displeased with his part in Anfossi's opera, *Le Gelosie Fortunate*).

The four-note theme which opens the Fugue-Finale had been repeatedly used by Mozart. It is based on an old church tune that Mozart had employed in the *Credo* of his Mass in F major (1774), in the *Sanctus* of another one of his Masses (C major, F. 257), in the B-flat symphony of 1779 (K. 319), and elsewhere. Other composers have dealt with it, literally or derivatively— Bach, Handel, Schubert, Mendelssohn, Richard Strauss. It can even be found in that least ecclesiastical of scores, *Tristan und Isolde*, though its appearance there in the passionate disguise which Wagner's imagination gave it was no doubt fortuitous. Mozart's exploitation of the subject, and of the other thematic material in this superb piece of polyphonic bravura, is one of the transcendent things of music.

The order of movements in the three symphonies is as follows:

K. 543, IN E-FLAT: (1) An Introduction, Adagio, 2-2, leading to an Allegro in triple time; (2) an 'Andante con moto,' 2-4, in A-flat; (3) the well-known Minuet, Allegro; (4) a sonata-form Allegro, 2-4, in the tonic key.

•K. 550, IN G MINOR: (1) 'Allegro molto,' 2-2; (2) Andante, E-flat, 6-8; (3) Minuet, Allegretto; (4) 'Allegro assai,' 2-2.

K. 551, IN C MAJOR: (1) 'Allegro vivace,' 4-4; (2) 'Andante cantabile,' F major, 3-4; (3) Minuet, Allegretto; (4) 'Molto allegro,' 2-2.

● *Eine kleine Nachtmusik*

The year 1787 was an important one for Mozart. It was the year in which he composed *Don Giovanni* and two of the greatest of his string quintets. He was then thirty-one years old, and was within four years of the end of his life. On the 10th of August he wrote the famous and lovely work which is thus referred to in his autograph catalogue of his works: '*Eine kleine Nachtmusik*, consisting of an Allegro, Minuet and Trio, Romance, Minuet and Trio, and Finale. 2 Violine, Viola e Bassi.' The double entry of the Minuet and Trio was presumably due to a slip of the pen, for in the autograph score of the music there is only one Minuet and Trio, and the number of movements is four.

Köchel in his catalogue of Mozart's works classifies the work as a string quartet; but Jahn remarks that 'it does not belong to quartet-music proper. The direction for contrabass as well as violoncello points to a fuller setting, which is confirmed by the whole arrangement, especially in the treatment of the middle parts.'

The movements are as follows: (1) Allegro, G major, 4-4; (2) Romanza, Andante, C major, 2-2; (3) Menuetto, Allegretto, G major, 3-4 (Trio, D major); (4) Rondo; Allegro, G major, 2-2.

- CONCERTO FOR PIANO AND ORCHESTRA, IN E-FLAT, K. 449
- CONCERTO FOR PIANO AND ORCHESTRA, IN B-FLAT, K. 450
- CONCERTO FOR PIANO AND ORCHESTRA, IN D MAJOR, K. 451
- CONCERTO FOR PIANO AND ORCHESTRA, IN G MAJOR, K. 453

Early in the winter of 1784, the newly married Mozart began to keep an account of his receipts and expenditures (one cannot help wondering how many pages of priceless music that time-wasting and idiotic habit deprived us of). Otto Jahn is inclined to blame Constanze for the lack of thrift and efficiency in the management of Mozart's household affairs. 'Without wishing to reproach her,' he begins—and then reproaches her, 'we may say at least that had Constanze been as good a housekeeper as Mozart was a composer, things would have gone well with him.' Perhaps. But if Constanze had been 'as good a housekeeper as Mozart was a composer,' there would have been no living with her.

Mozart entered his receipts—from lessons, concerts, et cetera—on a long sheet of paper; his expenditures, confessed with painful exactitude, were listed in a small notebook. On a certain page he made these entries:

> May 1, 1784..... Two lillies of the valley = 1 kreutzer.
> May 27, 1784..... A starling = 34 kreutzers.

Following this are four bars of musical notation, recording a tune in the key of G major, 'alla breve' time, with the remark: 'Das war schön!' The tune is a parody of the first subject of the Finale of the Piano Concerto in G major (K. 453), which Mozart had composed in the previous month. 'The pleasure he felt on hearing this tune piped with so comic an alteration,' says Jahn, 'induced him to buy the bird. He grew very much attached to his "Vogel Stahrl"—as indeed he was to all animals, especially birds—and when it died he erected a gravestone to its memory in his garden, with an epitaph in verse.'

The G major Concerto, K. 453, was the second of two that Mozart composed between February and April of 1784 for one of his pupils, Barbara Ployer, the daughter of Councillor Ployer, a representative in Vienna of the Salzburg court. The first was the E-flat Concerto, K. 449. The intervening concertos in B-flat and D were doubtless written for Mozart's own use, for he was at this time at the height of his fame in Vienna as a performer on the clavier, and gave numerous concerts, both private and public. All four concertos were produced with apparently effortless facility in a space of less than eight weeks.

The E-flat Concerto—for which, Mozart confided to his father, 'Fräulein Ployer paid me handsomely'—was apparently first played in public by the master, not the pupil. The three movements are an 'Allegro vivace' in triple time, an Andantino, 2-4, and a Rondo-Finale, 'Allegro ma non troppo,' 4-4. It is the first of Mozart's masterpieces in the form, and not the least of them. Fräulein Ployer may have paid the composer handsomely, but he acquitted himself of his commission more handsomely still. The theory that the special qualities of this work were fortuitous—that Mozart was unaware of the fact that it was a work of different character and quality entirely from his earlier concertos for clavier (different, too, from the B-flat and D major concertos which immediately succeeded it) and that genius was here producing a master-piece blindfolded—will not hold up. Those who will be blind to the evidence in the music that the composer had his wits about him when he set this wonderful work on paper cannot gainsay the evidence offered by his letters. 'The E-flat concerto,' he wrote to his father, in the course of comments on its successors, 'is a concerto of quite a peculiar kind.' It is scored for oboes and horns in pairs, and the usual strings.

The B-flat Concerto, K. 450, and the D major Concerto, K. 451, revert to a more conventional type of virtuoso concerto. In K. 449, solo instrument and orchestra are equal partners; in K. 450 and K. 451 the solo instrument lords it throughout. The first movement of the B-flat is an Allegro in common time, the second movement an Andante in E-flat, 3-8, the third a Rondo, Allegro, 6-8. To instrumental forces consisting of strings, and oboes, bassoons, and horns in pairs. Mozart in the last movement adds a flute. The D major Concerto opens, 'Allegro assai,' 4-4, progresses through an Andante, in G major, also in common time, to a Finale 'Allegro di molto,' 2-4. Trumpets and drums are added to the usual woodwinds and strings of the tutti.

But if the B-flat and D major concertos, coming after the E-flat, are rela-tively uninteresting, the fourth of the group, in G, K. 453, is again a master-piece. Like the E-flat Concerto, it was written for Miss Ployer, who seems to have had the faculty of inspiring Mozart to his best efforts. A fortnight after he had blown in 34 kreutzers for his starling, Wolfgang wrote to his father: 'Tomorrow there is to be a concert at Herr Ployer's country-house in Döbling. Fräulein Babette is to play the new concerto in G, and I shall play the quintet [for piano, oboe, clarinet, bassoon, and horn, K. 452]. Then both of us will perform the grand sonata for two pianos [in D, K. 448, also written for Miss Ployer]. I am to take Paisiello, who has been here since May on his return from St. Petersburg, in order that he may hear my compositions and my pupils.'

The G major Concerto is scored for an orchestra of one flute, two oboes, two bassoons, two horns, and strings (there are no trumpets, drums, or clari-nets). The autograph bears the inscription: *Di Wolfgango Amadeo Mozart Vienna li 12 d'Aprile 1784 per la Sgra. Barbara Ployer.*

This concerto, one of Mozart's most rewarding and characteristic, is remark-able especially for its deeply expressive and subtly textured slow movement, the Andante in C major, 3-4, and for its Finale, which is one of the few move-ments in Mozart's concertos composed in the variation form. The five varia-tions which Mozart evolved from the theme of the last movement of the G major Concerto (that which the starling parodied) are among his most imaginative and masterly examples of transmutation. The last of them brings in its train an irresistible Presto conclusion in which new thematic material is introduced by the prodigal Amadeus.

Mozart composed for this concerto two different sets of cadenzas.

● CONCERTO FOR PIANO AND ORCHESTRA, IN B-FLAT, K. 456

There is evidence that Mozart wrote this concerto for the remarkable Marie Therese von Paradis, the daughter of a court official, and goddaughter of the Empress Marie Therese. Blind almost from birth, she early exhibited musical leanings and was instructed in clavier, organ, and voice by outstanding masters of the day. As the goddaughter of the Empress, she was naturally a favorite with the aristocracy, but her own gifts must have been quite exceptional, for she was in demand everywhere, playing before the French court at the Paris *Concerts spirituels* [see notes above, on the Haydn symphonies] and in London at Salomon's concerts. Later she settled in Vienna and devoted herself to composition, producing a profusion of works of every description, many of which enjoyed considerable popularity at the time. In 1784 she set forth on a progress through the capitals of Europe, and it may have been with this in mind that she equipped herself with a concerto by Mozart.

The B-flat Concerto, K. 456, was composed during the late summer of 1884. It is remarkable chiefly for its slow movement, an Andante, in G minor, 2-4, in variation form, of an affectingly melancholy cast. This is one of the most beautiful and touching of Mozart's slow movements, and if its companions in the concerto approached it in the quality of their content, this B-flat Concerto would doubtless be one of those most often heard, instead of a relative stranger to concert programs. The concerto opens with an 'Allegro vivace' in 4-4 time, and concludes with an 'Allegro vivace,' 6-8, in which there is a brief and surprising throwback to the mood of the Andante.

● CONCERTO FOR PIANO AND ORCHESTRA, IN F MAJOR, K. 459

Mozart composed six concertos for clavier in 1784; of these, the Concerto in F is the last. It was doubtless intended for his own use, for his concertizing during this year reached an extraordinary pitch: During the six weeks from February 26 to April 3, for example, he played in public on twenty-two occasions. The F major Concerto, a work of limpid and sunny charm, comprises three movements: Allegro, 4-4; Allegretto, 6-8 in C major; Allegro, 2-4.

● CONCERTO FOR PIANO AND ORCHESTRA, IN D MINOR, K. 466

Mozart composed this concerto with his customary speed and his breathtaking certainty of skill and genius. He performed it himself at its first hearing in Vienna, and when his father called on him the day before the concert, he found Wolfgang so busy looking over the work of the copyist that he had not yet taken time to run through the difficult concluding Rondo even once. Yet we know that on the following day, February 11, 1785, when he presented the new work to his Vienna public, he played it with his usual brilliancy and charm.

The concerto was introduced to the world under distinguished auspices. Leopold Mozart wrote on January 22, 1785, to the composer's sister, as follows: 'I have just received a line from your brother, saying that his concerts begin on February 11th, and are to continue every Friday.' This was a series of concerts undertaken by Mozart in Vienna with a subscription list of more than 150, at three ducats each. Mozart, the amazing virtuoso, played for a public of quality. He drew, says Ferdinand Pohl in hushed tones, 'the cream of the nobility.' In the list of subscribers for his concerts in 1784 were eight princes, one duke, two counts, one countess, one baroness, and others of the exalted who are unkindly summarized by history as 'etc.'

To the casual eye, this D minor Concerto of Mozart's, so limpid, so crystalline, so apparently effortless in conception, may not seem to offer very difficult problems to the interpreter. Any such impression would be decidedly misleading. This music is deceptive to the superficial view. To give a full account of it, to convey all that it holds of incomparable patrician grace and gaiety and meditative loveliness, is a task not only for a virtuoso of the highest skill, but for an artist of the rarest sensibility and taste. It requires a player who is first a master of his craft, secondly a poet, and thirdly a magician—for he must summon out of the past, must recapture for us, that peculiar spiritual essence which was the creative mind of Mozart. Even the matter of playing the Rondo Finale with the requisite speed and clarity and finesse is something to daunt almost any pianist—although the newer edition of the published score has changed the terrifying Prestissimo of the earlier editions to a more merciful 'Allegro assai' (the autograph score gives no tempo mark whatever for this movement, or for the second movement, the 'Romanza').

This most frequently played and best known of Mozart's concertos for solo clavier comprises three movements: (1) Allegro, D minor, 4-4; (2) Romanza, B-flat major, 4-4; (3) Rondo, D minor–D major, 2-2. They are singularly lucid in design, singularly Mozartean in expression. The orchestra employed requires a flute, two oboes, two bassoons, two horns, two trumpets, timpani, and strings.

Both Beethoven and Hummel wrote cadenzas for this concerto.

How did Mozart perform his own music? What were the characteristics of his style as a pianist? Fortunately, these questions are not unanswerable, for we have a description of the master's pianism left us by Franz Niemetschek. Mozart detested, says Niemetschek, all exaggeration, all 'effects,' all 'fireworks.' His playing was stamped with a 'simplicité adorable, une expression émouvante et profonde.' His hands moved so quietly and naturally over the keys that the eye as well as the ear was pleased. He had an astounding facility, due to his close study of the works of Ph. E. Bach, from which he had worked out his system of fingering. He demanded of the pianist a light and accurate and steady hand, so light, so flexible, that the music would 'flow like oil,' as he said.

These qualities of lightness and precision and fluidity were, with him, at the service of an inimitable poetry and distinction; they were mated to the qualities of such works as the choicest of the concertos, 'ces oeuvres nobles, fines, et tendres.' They were evidently the ideal voicing of this music with its delicately swelling line, the fervent and lovely patterns that move with the candid grace of winged, uncapturable creatures: music so exquisite in its blend of spontaneity and craft that you cannot listen to it without incurring something of that nostalgia of the spirit which attends the contemplation of all art that has compassed its moment of perfection.

- Concerto for Piano and Orchestra, in E-flat, K. 482
- Concerto for Piano and Orchestra, in A major, K. 488
- Concerto for Piano and Orchestra, in C minor, K. 491

Mozart began work on his *Marriage of Figaro* in the autumn of 1785. On November 11, his father wrote to Mozart's sister Marianne that Wolfgang was 'over head and ears at work on the opera. He has put off his pupils to the afternoon, so that he may have his mornings free. . . Having procrastinated and let the time slip, after his usual fashion, he is obliged now to set to work in earnest.'

One might suppose that life would have been a bit easier for Mozart at this time if he had abstained from composing anything else. But a mere opera did not suffice him. In his thematic catalogue for the period between November 5, 1785, and the end of the following April, we find that he worked during that time upon the following compositions: three piano concertos; a sonata for piano and violin; a quartet and terzet for Bianchi's *Villanella Rapita*; the *Schauspieldirektor*; duet and air for the private performance of *Idomeneo*; a rondo for piano; and the *Marriage of Figaro*. In addition to all this, he was busy with his Lenten concerts—for which, by the way, he succeeded in mustering up 120 subscribers.

The three concertos which occupied him at this time were written for these three Lenten subscription concerts. The first of these concertos, that in E-flat, K. 482, was completed December 16, 1785; the A major Concerto was completed on March 2, 1786, and the C minor on March 24.

Mozart composed three solo clavier concertos in the key of E-flat, and all are remarkable works. The first, K. 271, was composed in 1777, and is the last of the solo concertos in the Salzburg group, and the earliest of the Mozart concertos still to be heard with any frequency in the concert room. The second E-flat Concerto is K. 449 [see notes above]; the third is K. 482. It is by far the most complex and impressive in design of the three; the first movement, an Allegro in 4-4 time, is among the most elaborate to be found in the Mozart concertos, and is followed by an Andante in C minor in variation form which reveals unique structural features. The concluding Rondo, in 6-8 time, is marked Allegro.

The A major Concerto, K. 488, followed close upon the heels of the E-flat. The scheme of the A major Concerto comprises an Allegro in 4-4 time, an Andante (in some editions marked *Adagio*) in F-sharp minor, which is one of Mozart's loveliest slow movements, and a Rondo-Finale, Presto, in 2-2 time. The orchestral part is scored for flute, two clarinets (which are employed in all three concertos in this group, but not in any other concertos by Mozart), two bassoons, two horns, and strings.

The third and last of the 1786 Lenten concertos is the great C minor, the most dramatic and impassioned of all of Mozart's works in the form. The first movement, with its long orchestral introduction, its wealth of material, its great complexity of organization, is symphonic in conception and effect, and the Finale, an Allegretto in variation form, is its fitting companion piece. The intervening Larghetto suffers somewhat from the proximity of these two masterly creations, but perhaps the attention of the hearer needs those moments of relaxation which it provides.

● CONCERTO FOR PIANO AND ORCHESTRA, IN D MAJOR ('Coronation' Concerto), K. 537

Mozart completed this concerto at Vienna, after his return from Prague, on February 24, 1788. It was the last but one of his concertos for clavier. It belongs to the same year as the three great symphonies in E-flat, G minor, and C major ('Jupiter'). This work is known as the *Kronungsconcert* ('Coronation' Concerto), because of the circumstance that Mozart performed it at Frankfort during the festivities attending the coronation of Leopold II.

Leopold was crowned at Frankfort, October 9, 1790. Mozart was not included among the musicians who were sent to Frankfort with the Emperor's retinue. Wolfgang had determined upon a professional tour, and Frankfort seemed a favorable place to begin it. He set out in the company of his brother-in-law, the violinist Hofer. They arrived at Frankfort September 23, and on the 14th of October, in Coronation Week, Mozart gave in the Stadttheater a concert devoted to his own compositions. He played the D major Concerto and the Concerto in F (K. 459). But Mozart had played the 'Coronation' Concerto a year and a half before—at Dresden, on April 14, 1789, when he was summoned to perform at Court. This was 'an unusual honor,' says Jahn, and was followed by a present of 100 ducats.

The first movement is an Allegro, D major, 4-4; the second a Larghetto in A, 2-2; the third an Allegretto in D, 2-4. The orchestral part is scored for one flute, two oboes, two bassoons, two horns, two trumpets, timpani, and strings.

● CONCERTO FOR PIANO AND ORCHESTRA, IN B-FLAT MAJOR, K. 595

This beautiful and richly expressive work, the last of Mozart's piano concertos, was finished at Vienna January 5, 1791, in the final year of the composer's life (he died just eleven months later). It was probably intended for a Lenten concert. Mozart had given no concerts in Vienna for several years. He is said to have developed a 'strong repugnance' to Vienna because he so heartily disliked the 'frivolous audiences' of that city. But his debts and other financial stringencies left him small choice.

Mozart drove himself cruelly in the last year of his life. For the carnival he composed, during January and February, no fewer than thirty-five minuets and other dances of full orchestral parts, among them the waltzes which were danced to at the balls. He composed also, during that year, his Fantasia in F minor for Mechanical Organ, his last quintet for strings (in E-flat), a final chorus for Sarti's *Le Gelosie Villane*; the motet, *Ave verum corpus*; his last two operas, *Die Zauberflöte* and *La Clemenza di Tito*; the Clarinet Concerto in A; the Masonic cantata, *Laut verkünde unsre Freude* (November 15—the last work catalogued by himself); and, finally, whatever part of the fantastically circumstanced *Requiem* the tonal anatomists may decide upon as his.

During the last week of November, Mozart, a dying man, took to his bed. To the end he could speak rationally of music, 'could follow in imagination

the performances of *The Magic Flute,* noting by his watch the passage of the
scenes; and could add to the *Requiem* a touch here and there until the
unfinished *Lacrimosa* became blurred by his own tears.' He died early in the
morning of December 5, and the following day his body was hurried into a
pauper's grave in St. Mark's Churchyard.

The B-flat Concerto is among the most ingratiating of Mozart's works in
this form. For some of its material, Mozart seems to have drawn, unconsciously
or not, upon ideas in certain of his earlier scores. Thus the subject for the
first violins which, beginning at the second bar, opens the first movement
(Allegro, B-flat major, 4-4), bears an unmistakable likeness to the opening
subject of the Romanza of the D minor Concerto, composed six years earlier.
The two melodies are not, of course, in their entirety, identical; but the second
bar of the violin melody of the B-flat Allegro contains a phrase of half a dozen
notes which is virtually the same as a phrase in the famous melody of the
earlier Romanza—though the difference between the tempi of the two movements tends to disguise the resemblance. There is also a likeness, less marked,
between the first measure of the theme for the piano which begins the
Larghetto of the B-flat concerto and the opening subject of the Andante of
the E-flat Symphony composed three years before. But a more striking resemblance is that between the ascending chromatic phrase which forms the fourth
measure of the opening theme of the Larghetto and the ascending chromatic
phrase that is so memorable a feature of the Andante of the 'Prague' Symphony
(K. 504, composed in 1786). The two phrases are most nearly alike in the
fourth bar of the Larghetto of the concerto and the seventh bar of the
Andante of the symphony. In both cases, this phrase is an important element
in the melodic texture of the respective movements.

The opening theme of the first Allegro of the concerto—a theme noteworthy for its romantic lyricism—is enunciated by the strings alone. It is soon
broken in upon by an energetic motive for the wind (flute, oboes, bassoons,
and horns), which intrudes at the fifth bar upon the quiet flow of the strings.

After this material has been developed for seventy-three measures, the piano
enters with a solo based upon the chief theme, but exquisitely adorned with
a gruppetto. Four bars later, the orchestra enters with an accompaniment figure
based on the formerly energetic wind motive, now uttered quietly by the strings.
In the *Durchführung,* the chief subject achieves a warmly lyrical expansiveness
that is rare even for Mozart. (One of the remarkable features of this development section is the appearance of the chief theme in the irrubrically distant
tonality of B minor!)

The Larghetto (E-flat major, 4-4) opens with an eight-bar solo for the piano,
introducing the theme alluded to above. The orchestra takes it up, in a forte;
the piano is again heard in a longer solo; and then the strings and wind bring
forward a more vigorous theme.

The final movement is a captivating Rondo (B-flat major, 6-8 time), begun
by the piano alone, and evolved with brilliant and exhilarating vitality and
resourcefulness. In the middle section we encounter, surprisingly enough, what
seems to be a reminiscence of the ascending chromatic phrase from the Larghetto, extended and intensified.

The instrumentation of the concerto is for flute, two oboes, two bassoons, two horns, and strings.

● CONCERTO FOR TWO PIANOS AND ORCHESTRA, IN E-FLAT, K. 365

'Free and cheerful' is Jahn's summing up of the character of this concerto. It dates from 1780. In design and treatment, it is essentially similar to the earlier Triple Concerto (K. 242) composed at Salzburg for three deserving Countesses —Antonie, Luise, and Josepha Lodron—in February 1776.

Mozart played the concerto in Vienna on November 24, 1781, with Fräulein Josephine Aurnhammer, the unfortunate young woman whom Wolfgang described concisely, in a letter to his father, as 'a horror.' Josephine annoyed Mozart by making love to him and by spreading abroad the report that they were to be married, and his railings against her were something less than gentlemanly. She was, he said, 'an amorous fool,' 'as fat as a peasant girl'; one sight of her face ('which would have served a painter as a model for the Evil One') was enough, wrote Mozart, 'to make one wretched the whole day.' Nevertheless, he spent a good deal of time with Josephine, visiting her, at the height of his displeasure with her, at least every other day.

To the original accompaniment of the concerto—oboes, bassoons and horns in pairs, and strings—Mozart added for the November 24 performance two clarinets, an instrument he had learned to value at Mannheim three years before. 'Oh, if we only had clarinets,' he wrote from Mannheim in December 1778. 'You cannot think what a splendid effect a symphony makes with flutes, oboes, and clarinets!'

The three movements of the two-piano concerto are an Allegro, an Andante, and a Rondo-Finale marked Allegro.

● THE VIOLIN CONCERTOS

In 1775, at Salzburg, Mozart wrote five violin concertos—probably for his own use; for he was a violinist of uncommon ability, though he seems to have had small real liking for the instrument (in later years, if he had to take part in the performance of a quartet or other concerted piece for strings, he preferred, like Bach, to play the viola). These five concertos were composed as follows: the Concerto in B-flat major, K. 207, in April; the first of the two in D major, K. 211, in June; the G major, K. 219, in September; the second in D, K. 218, in October; the A major, K. 219, in December. A sixth concerto, that in E-flat major, K. 268, is believed to be only in part the work of Mozart.

There are, in addition, two further Mozart concertos for violin:

In 1907, a manuscript copy of a violin concerto attributed to Mozart was discovered in the Royal Library at Berlin by the eminent musicologist Dr. Albert Kopfermann. The manuscript bore this inscription: *Concerto per il Violino di Wolfgango Amadeo Mozart. Salisburgo, li 16 di Luglio,* 1777. The score was published in 1907 by Breitkopf & Härtel, with a preface by Dr. Kopfermann in which the circumstances of his discovery and alleged authentication of the concerto (which is in D major) are related. It should be said that there is not complete agreement among scholars as to the authenticity of this

seventh Concerto. But Donald Tovey in his admirable article on Mozart in
the *Encyclopaedia Britannica* asserts his belief in Mozart's authorship of the
work.

Finally, there is the 'Adelaide' Concerto, composed by Mozart in his eleventh
year, presumably in Paris, and dedicated to the Princess Adelaide, the eldest
daughter of Louis XV of France. For many years the manuscript of this
concerto reposed in a private collection in France. Though its existence was
known to scholars, there seemed little disposition to track it down, and none
to publish it, which was just as well, for Mozart had written it on two staves
only, and had completed it neither in harmonic structure nor instrumentation.
However, in the early thirties of the present century, it came into the hands
of Marius Casadesus, who filled in the sketch and supplied the scoring, 'using
Mozart's later concertos as models.' The concerto was performed in public
for the first time at a Courtland-Sargent concert in London, November 13,
1932, by the violinist Yelly d'Aranyi.

Of the general characteristics of Mozart's violin concertos, Jahn writes as
follows: 'Usually the first movement, the most elaborate, is even more suggestive of the aria than is the corresponding movement of the symphonies.
There is the same fixed alternation between solo and tutti passages, the same
adornment of the solo part with passages and cadenzas, and indeed the whole
movement is a reminiscence of the serious aria. . . On the other hand, the
structure is more condensed and more animated. . . The second movement
is generally simple, and rests essentially on the delivery of the *cantilena*;
embellishments are not excluded, but they are kept in the background. . .
The tone is that of a romance. . . The last movement is, as a rule, in the
form of a rondo, in which the solo part moves more freely, especially in the
connecting middle passages.'

● OVERTURE TO *The Marriage of Figaro*

'Never was anything more complete than the triumph of Mozart and his
Nozze di Figaro,' wrote Michael Kelly, in his Reminiscences, of the first performance of Mozart's opera at Vienna on May 1, 1786. Kelly was the original
Don Basilio and Don Curzio of the opera. Born at Dublin in 1762, he was
at various times a singer, a musical shopkeeper, a composer, and a wine merchant—'a composer of wines and an importer of music,' as Sheridan said of
him. He died in 1826.

Kelly wrote with memorable gusto of the rehearsals and first performance
of *Figaro* (an incomparable one, he insisted). 'It was allowed,' he says, 'that
never was opera more strongly cast. I have seen it performed at different
periods in other countries—and well, too—but no more to compare with its
original performance than light is to darkness. All the original performers had
the advantage of the instruction of the composer, who transfused into their
minds his inspired meaning. I never shall forget his little animated countenance
when lighted up with the glowing rays of genius; it is as impossible to describe
as it would be to paint sunbeams. I remember at the first rehearsal of the full
band Mozart was on the stage with his crimson pelisse and gold-laced cocked

hat, giving the time of the music to the orchestra. Figaro's song, "Non più andrai," Benucci gave with the greatest animation and power of voice. I was standing close to Mozart, who, *sotto voce*, was repeating: "Bravo! bravo, Benucci!" and when Benucci came to the fine passage, "Cherubino, alla vittoria, alla gloria militar!" which he gave out with stentorian lungs, the effect was electricity itself . . . the performers and those in the orchestra vociferated: "Bravo! bravo, maestro! viva, viva, grande Mozart!" Those in the orchestra I thought would never cease applauding, by beating the bows of their violins against the music-desks. The little man acknowledged his thanks by repeated obeisances.'

Otto Jahn in his Life of Mozart wonders how the composer of *Figaro* could have chosen so 'depraved' a subject for his opera as Beaumarchais' 'representation of immorality in all its nakedness,' and he regards with sorrowful disapprobation the fact that Mozart, who 'willingly allowed himself to glide along the pleasant stream of life in Vienna,' and whose 'merrier moods were often productive of free or even coarse jests,' failed to be repelled by what he delicately alludes to as 'the frivolous element' in Beaumarchais' comedy.

However, it is reassuring to bear in mind that no taint of this corrupting subject matter affects the *Nozze di Figaro* Overture, which sounds, to the sharpest ear, quite blithely unequivocal. Krehbiel, in a charming passage in his *Book of Operas*, calls it 'the merriest of opera overtures . . . putting the listener at once into a frolicsome mood.'

• Overture to *Don Giovanni*

In September 1787, Mozart went from Vienna to Prague and took lodgings near the theater; but it is probable that he spent a good part of his time at the Villa Bertramka, a little house in the suburb of Smichow, on the west bank of the Moldau. This pleasant villa was the property of a singer named Josefa Duschek, of whom Mozart saw a good deal at the period to which *Don Giovanni* belongs. Mozart had met her at Salzburg in the summer of 1777, and, as one of his biographers observes, 'the merry young people soon became very fond of each other.' The villa at Smichow, which later served as Mozart's 'Asyl,' had, in all likelihood, been purchased by Josefa with funds generously placed at her disposal by an admiring Bohemian nobleman who rejoiced in the name of Count Christian Clam.

It was at the Villa Bertramka that Wolfgang completed *Don Giovanni*. In the garden of the villa there still stands (or did until recently) the little summer-house in which Mozart worked; and some have maintained that the Villa Bertramka, rather than his birthplace in Salzburg or his dwelling-place in Vienna, should be known as 'the Mozart House.'

Jahn refers grudgingly to 'the received tradition that represents Mozart as bringing the unfinished opera to Prague in September 1787, and completing it, incited by contact with the intended performers and the stimulating society of his enthusiastic friends and admirers'; but he alludes with indignation to Rau's *Mozart*, a 'kulturhistorischer Roman,' as 'an appalling calumny on Mozart's moral and artistic character.'

Legend doubtless encrusts rather thickly the facts of *Don Giovanni's* completion—especially as regards the composition of the overture. The most familiar of the tales concerning this event (Jahn relates it as fact in his Life of Mozart) is that for which the composer's widow, Constanze, is alleged to have been the authority:

On the day before the performance, when the dress rehearsal was over, Mozart said in the evening to his wife that he should write the overture that night; that she should brew punch and stay by him to keep him cheerful. She did this, and told him stories about Aladdin's Lamp, Cinderella, and like tales, which made him laugh until the tears came to his eyes. The punch made him so sleepy that he nodded whenever she stopped and worked only while she told the tales. But the intense application, the sleepiness and the frequent nodding made the work too hard for him. His wife advised him to lie down on the sofa and promised to wake him in an hour. He slept so soundly that she could not bear to disturb him, and she let him sleep two hours. It was then five o'clock. The copyist had been engaged at seven, and at seven o'clock the overture was ready.

Later and more realistic historians have branded this naïve tale, which may have been put into shape by that romantic journalist Friedrich Rochlitz, as incredible. Merely to score the 292 measures of the Overture to *Don Giovanni* overnight would have been no trifling task. That Mozart composed and orchestrated the music in eight or nine hours is improbable, even when we take into account his prodigious facility. It is more likely that he had worked out in his head most of the details of the overture, and that, trusting to his astounding memory, the only thing which remained was to set down the notes on paper—a sufficiently formidable task in itself under the circumstances.

Il Dissoluto Punito; ossia, Il Don Giovanni. Dramma giocoso in due atti. La Poesia è dell' Sign. Abbate da Ponte, Poeta de' Teatri Imperiali. La Musica è del Sig. Wolfgango Mozart, Maestro di Cap., was produced at Prague October 29, 1787, with Mozart conducting.

Berlioz says that when he visited the theater in 1845 (he heard music and conducted some of his own works there), 'it was dark, small, dirty, and of wretched acoustic properties. Since then it has been restored. The personnel of the orchestra and chorus were in exact relationship with the scanty dimensions of the hall, and seemed to accuse the manager of stinginess.' The orchestra of the National Theater at Prague in 1787 consisted of twenty-six players: four first violins, four seconds, two violas, one 'cello, two double-basses, two flutes, two oboes, two clarinets, two bassoons, two horns, two trumpets, and timpani. Trombones were specially engaged when required.

The Overture to *Don Giovanni* is scored for flutes, oboes, clarinets, bassoons, horns and trumpets in pairs, timpani and strings. The opening Andante (D minor, 2-2) derives from the catastrophe of the opera, in which the contumacious libertine meets his doom—the scene which begins with the entrance of the Statue and his speech, 'Don Giovanni, a cenar teco m' invitasti.' The Allegro of the overture ('Molto allegro,' D major, 2-2) is based upon fresh material.

• Overture to *Così fan tutte*

Mozart's *Così fan tutte*, opera buffa in two acts, libretto by Lorenzo da Ponte, was produced on January 26, 1790, at the Burgtheater, Vienna. The outline of the plot of the piece is said to have been suggested by the Emperor, Joseph II, who had founded the tale, according to rumor, upon an actual incident. The late Vernon Blackburn, defending Da Ponte's text, which has been foolishly described as 'immoral' and 'cynical,' remarked that 'the book is an agreeable charade; it is the mere amplification of a catch word to which Shakespeare was not ashamed to subscribe when he identified woman with frailty.'
The plot has been thus described:

A cynical old bachelor, Don Alfonso, has made a wager with two young Neapolitan officers—Ferrando and Gugliemo—that the fidelity of their respective fiancées, Fiordiligi and Dorabella, is an uncertain quantity. To provide the necessary test, the two officers declare that they have been called away from Naples on duty, but they return the same afternoon disguised as Albanian noblemen. The pretended strangers make violent love to the two girls, and finally the latter succumb and consent to marry their new wooers. The wedding contracts are brought by the notary, when suddenly drums are heard and Don Alfonso announces the return of the soldiers. The Albanians hastily vanish, but reappear as Ferrando and Gugliemo to reproach their respective sweethearts for their fickleness. The mystery is made clear to the women, and Don Alfonso, pocketing the wager which he has won, reconciles them with their lovers.

• Overture to *The Magic Flute*

In March of 1891, nine months before his death, Mozart, his fortunes at their lowest ebb, was persuaded by the impresario Schikaneder, himself hard-up, to set to music a libretto he had written, in which much Masonic symbolism was incorporated in a fairy tale of patent absurdity. With less thought to his own need than to Schikaneder's, Mozart agreed, and set to work. The result was *Die Zauberflöte* (*The Magic Flute*), the noblest and most remarkable of his operas. It was produced for the first time at Schikaneder's little theater in the Viennese suburb of Wieden in September of that year, under Mozart's personal direction. A little over two months later, Mozart was dead.

It is a curious fact that the two outstanding features of this thrice-famous overture ('this inimitable masterpiece of German instrumental music,' as Jahn called it) seem not to have been wholly of Mozart's own conception. Speaking of the much-discussed 'Masonic' chords for the full orchestra, which are heard at the beginning and in the middle of the overture, and again in the temple scene, Krehbiel in his study of Mozart's opera tells us that this device—in which symbol-hunting analysts have chosen to see an allusion to the Masonic signals given by knocking at the door of the lodge room—was not unique when Mozart applied it. 'I have found it used,' he says, 'in an almost identical manner in the overture to *Günther von Schwarzburg*, by Ignaz Holzbauer, a German opera produced in Mannheim fifteen years before *Die Zauberflöte* saw the light of the stage lamps.'

As for the theme of the fugued Allegro, even the reverent Jahn took due note of the resemblance between it and the theme in the first movement of

Clementi's B-flat major Sonata, which Mozart heard Clementi play before the Emperor Joseph when the two music-makers met at court in December 1781, for their trial of skill at playing and improvising (on which occasion, it will be remembered, Clementi mistook the incomparable Wolfgang for 'an imperial valet-de-chambre' because of his 'elegant attire'). Clementi thought it advisable on the republication of his sonata to assert his claim to priority, which he did as follows: 'Cette sonate, avec la toccata qui la suit, a été jouée par l'auteur devant Sa M. J. Joseph II., en 1781, Mozart étant présent.' There can be no doubt, says Jahn, 'that Mozart was conscious of the reminiscence.'

But, as Krehbiel sensibly points out, in the eighteenth century such likenesses were 'frank borrowings in which there was no moral obliquity; for originality then lay as much in treatment as in thematic invention, if not more.' In Mozart's time, he remarks, they did not bother to account for these resemblances as being the products of 'unconscious cerebration.'

Francis Poulenc

1899-

P

Francis Poulenc achieved fame shortly after the First World War as one of the members of the group of advanced young French composers known as 'The Six,' consisting, besides himself, of Milhaud, Honegger, Durey, Auric, and Germaine Tailleferre. The group, as a group, has long since faded into oblivion, but Poulenc, Milhaud, and Honegger, at least, have remained in the public eye and ear, and continue to accumulate honors. Poulenc received a classical education, but his study of music was interrupted by the war, in which he served as a soldier in the French army. After the war, he came under Satie's influence. He has written music in various forms, much of it in a style that seeks to capture a neo-classic transparency and delicacy of texture. His numerous songs are highly regarded.

● Concerto for Two Pianos and Orchestra

The Concerto for Two Pianos and Orchestra was composed in 1932, and was performed for the first time on September 5th of that year at the International Music Festival in Venice. The pianists were the composer and Jacques Fevrier. The orchestra was that of La Scala, Milan, under the direction of Désiré Defauw.

There are three movements. The first, 'Allegro ma non troppo,' D minor, 4-4, is initiated by two *sforzando* chords of all the instruments and a brilliant passage for the first piano based on a figure in sixteenth-notes, which is soon handed over to the second piano. A descending chromatic passage for the first player prefaces the first subject, a staccato four-note phrase in eighths, first heard in the string basses and in the bass of the second piano, then exchanged between the upper and lower strings and the two solo instruments, with the later addition of the wind. After twenty-four measures of this, the woodwind and horn bring forward a new and lively theme in the manner of a popular song, recalling Poulenc's fondness for borrowing certain of his themes from what has been called the 'Parisian folk-lore'—refrains from popular song hits of a former day, from almost forgotten street tunes, from music of the *café-concerts*, and so forth. Examples of this propensity of Poulenc's are to be found in the Sonata for piano duet and the *Cocardes* for voice and small orchestra. The gay tune in the first movement of the concerto generates others of similar verve, which are engagingly displayed. Then the pace slows, the tunes become more sentimental. There is a brief cadenza for the two pianos, a return to the first tempo, and the first subject is heard in augmentation, with the rhythm altered, in the brass and lower strings, fortissimo. Some of the merry tunes of the middle section are heard in contrapuntal combination, and there is a fermata. In the key of B-flat major, 'très calme,' the first piano begins the coda, with a close full of quiet and meditative sentiment.

The second movement, Larghetto, is a development of two melodic subjects of unusual simplicity and charm, together with subsidiary material. The first, an exceptionally ingenuous theme in B-flat major, 2-2 time, is begun by the first piano without accompaniment. At the ninth measure, the second piano takes up the song and continues it, to the accompaniment of the first. After the solo instruments and the orchestra have elaborated this material for half a hundred bars, there is a change to a faster pace and to the key of A-flat, and the two pianos together, at first unaccompanied, introduce a new melodic subject, which is worked up to a fortissimo climax with the orchestra. The first theme and first tempo are resumed, and bring the movement to an end.

The Finale, a movement uncommonly fertile in melodic ideas, begins with a few forte measures of introduction by the orchestra ('Allegro molto,' 2-2, 3-4) and toccata-like solos for the two pianos in succession and combination; after which the solo players and the violins present the first subject, a march-like tune with a dotted-eighth rhythm, which is developed to a fortissimo climax. The mood of the music becomes quieter, and the pianos and orchestra, at first separately, then in combination, bring forward a group of song-like themes closely related in melodic contour and expressiveness. The march theme recurs, and sweeps the music, agité, through a crescendo to a fortissimo climax. This is calmed by the return of a variant of one of the song themes, an engaging melody for the second piano, the first accompanying, which is worked up to another and concluding fortissimo, with a brilliant close.

Sergei Prokofieff

1891-

P

‡In his twenties and thirties a stranger to the land of his birth, Prokofieff chose in his forties to return there and make his peace with the
powers that be. Since 1936, he has not emerged, nor does it seem likely
that he ever will. But the products of his industry as a servant of the
Soviet State are often exported, and we learn from them that he continues to assert a strong, almost wayward, individuality where it is both
unfashionable and hazardous to do so. He is by far the most variously
and richly endowed of the Soviet composers. But Western praise will
almost certainly be an embarrassment, and conceivably may be a danger
to him.‡

● CLASSICAL SYMPHONY, IN D MAJOR, OP. 25

This symphony was sketched in Russia in 1916 and completed the following
year. It was first heard in this country in December 1918 at a concert by the
Russian Symphony Society in Carnegie Hall, New York City. When it was
played in Paris by Sergei Koussevitzky in 1923, it was said, apparently with
authority, that 'the composer's intention was to write a work in the style of
the classic symphony.' The scoring calls for a Mozartean orchestra of flutes,
oboes, bassoons, clarinets, horns and trumpets in pairs, with timpani and
strings. But the work is essentially a *jeu d'esprit*, a deft and witty parody
rather than a copy of its ideal prototype. There are four movements: an
Allegro in D major, 4-4, in sonata form; a Larghetto in A major, 2-2; a
Gavotte (replacing the Minuet of the typical eighteenth-century symphony),
'Non troppo allegro,' D major, 4-4; and a Rondo-Finale, 'Molto vivace,'
D major.

● CONCERTO FOR PIANO AND ORCHESTRA, NO. 3, IN C MAJOR, OP. 26

The themes of this concerto were sketched at Petrograd in 1917; but the composition of the work was interrupted by the composer's first visit to America.
The score was completed at St. Brevin, France, in October 1921. The work
was performed for the first time anywhere at a concert of the Chicago Symphony Orchestra on December 16, 1921, with the composer as pianist.

The following analysis was supplied by the composer:

1. The first movement opens quietly with a short introduction, Andante, 4-4. The
theme is announced by an unaccompanied clarinet, and is continued by the violins for

a few bars. Soon the tempo changes to Allegro, the strings having a passage in semi-quavers which leads to the statement of the principal subject by the piano. Discussion of this theme is carried on in a lively manner, both the piano and the orchestra having a good deal to say on the matter. A passage in chords for the piano alone leads to the more expressive second subject, heard in the oboe with a pizzicato accompaniment. This is taken up by the piano and developed at some length, eventually giving way to a bravura passage in triplets. At the climax of this section, the tempo reverts to Andante, and the orchestra gives out the first theme, *ff*. The piano joins in, and the theme is subjected to impressively broad treatment. On resuming the Allegro, the chief theme and the second subject are developed with increased brilliance, and the movement ends with an exciting crescendo.

II. The second movement consists of a theme with five variations. The theme is announced by the orchestra alone, Andantino.

In the first variation, the piano treats the opening of the theme in quasi-sentimental fashion, and resolves into a chain of trills as the orchestra repeats the closing phrase. The tempo changes to Allegro for the second and the third variations, and the piano has brilliant figures, while snatches of the theme are introduced here and there in the orchestra. In Variation Four, the tempo is once again Andante, and the piano and orchestra discourse on the theme in a quiet and meditative fashion. Variation Five is energetic ('Allegro giusto'). It leads without pause into a restatement of the theme by the orchestra, with delicate chordal embroidery in the piano.

III. The Finale begins ('Allegro ma non troppo,' 3-4) with a staccato theme for bassoons and pizzicato strings, which is interrupted by the blustering entry of the piano. The orchestra holds its own with the opening theme, however, and there is a good deal of argument, with frequent differences of opinion as regards key. Eventually the piano takes up the first theme. and develops it to a climax.

With a reduction of tone and slackening of tempo, an alternative theme is introduced in the woodwind. The piano replies with a theme that is more in keeping with the caustic humor of the work. This material is developed, and there is a brilliant coda.

● *Scythian Suite* (Ala and Lolli), OP. 20

The Scythians were an ancient nomadic people who dwelt along the north shore of the Black Sea. Their race is doubtful—probably Aryan, with an admixture of Mongol blood. They disappeared from history about 100 B.C. What is thought to have been the first mention of them was made by the Greek poet Hesiod, eight centuries before Christ. Herodotus has left us a detailed description of them. These nomadic barbarians seem not to have been charming people. They were fat and flabby, lived on boiled flesh and mare's milk, and rejoiced in a form of government that was chiefly a despotism tempered by assassination. Certain of their habits were reprehensible. They had, of course, their gods—a sun god, a health god, a heaven god, an evil god, and others. The sun was their supreme deity, and was named Veles. The daughter of the sun was called Ala. One of their heroes was Lolli. The subject of Prokofieff's suite deals with the great harm to which Ala came at the hands of the Evil God, and her rescue by the hero, Lolli.

It is said that Prokofieff, impressed by the legends, rites, and tribal customs of the ancient Scythians, determined to use them as the subject of a ballet or mimodrama; but that he altered his original purpose, and wrote instead a concert suite to which he gave the title *Scythian*. He composed it in 1914, and conducted it at the Imperial Maryinsky Theater, in Petrograd, January 29, 1916. The suite is in four movements, and has the following program:

I. 'INVOCATION TO VELES AND ALA.' ('Allegro feroce,' 4-4 time.) The music describes an invocation to Veles, the sun-god of the Scythians. This invocation is followed by the sacrifice to the well-beloved idol, Ala, daughter of Veles.

II. 'THE EVIL GOD AND THE DANCE OF THE PAGAN MONSTERS.' ('Allegro sostenuto,' 4-4 time.) The evil god summons the seven pagan monsters from their subterranean realms, and, surrounded by them, dances a frenzied round.

III. 'NIGHT.' (Andantino, 4-4 time.) The evil god comes to Ala in the darkness, and great harm befalls her. The moon rays fall upon Ala, and the moon maidens descend to bring her consolation.

IV. 'THE GLORIOUS DEPARTURE OF LOLLI AND THE CORTÈGE OF THE SUN.' ('Tempestoso,' 4-4 time.) Lolli, a Scythian hero, goes forth to save Ala, and he fights the evil god. In the uneven battle, Lolli would have perished, but Veles, bright lord of the heavens, rises with the vanishing of the night and smites the evil god. With the description of that conquering sunrise the suite comes to its end.

This Finale of the *Scythian Suite* limns for us a pagan dawn as seen through the savagely ecstatic eyes and frenzied brains of sun-worshipping barbarians. The piercing, exultant, hieratical trumpets, the cumulative radiance of the whole orchestra as the wild men chant their hymn to the dazzling god and the world takes fire, are like nothing else in the literature of music.

Henry Purcell

1658(?)-95

P

Henry Purcell, whom John Runciman somewhat impolitely called 'the last great English composer,' lived an uneventful but enormously productive life, and died before he was forty (the year of his birth has not been established, but it was either 1658 or 1659). He was the second son of Henry Purcell, a gentleman of the Chapel Royal, Master of the Choristers of Westminster Abbey, and a member of the King's Band, who died in 1664. Young Purcell entered the Chapel Royal as a chorister soon after the death of his father, and he studied music under Cooke, Humfrey, and Blow. In 1680 he was appointed organist of Westminster Abbey, and held that post until his death fifteen years later, at the age of thirty-six or thirty-seven—for Purcell, like Mozart and Schubert and Shelley, was one of those masters of beauty whom an improvident destiny saw fit to cut off in their prime.

If English music was ever greater than in Tudor days, that time came three-quarters of a century after the death of Queen Elizabeth, when Henry Purcell, still under twenty, issued in 1676 what was probably his first published work, a song in Book I of Playford's *Choice Ayres, Songs and Dialogues.* Thereafter, until he died in 1695, English music, by virtue of his composing, was aflame with the genius of a master who left his countrymen a deathless heritage of inspired and characteristic work: music which, in spite of the Italian and other influences that molded it, is as English as a hawthorn tree—which at its best, indeed, is Shakespearean in magic and felicity of style. Purcell in the finest of his works is an artist of consummate craft and subtlety and power, commanding a beauty and expressiveness that leave us breathless with amazement and delight.

● *Dido and Aeneas*

One day toward the end of the seventeenth century, when Oliver Cromwell had been safely dead for a generation, and Johann Sebastian Bach was a little boy of four, and the French and Indians were fighting the English colonists in America, Henry Purcell, Composer in Ordinary to His Majesty the King of England, put the final touches to his opera, *Dido and Aeneas*, snuffed his candle, and went unconcernedly to bed, apparently unaware that he had composed one of the masterpieces of the world's music.

Purcell wrote the work for performance by the young gentlewomen of Josias Priest's boarding-school at Chelsea, to a text by the famous Nahum Tate, who based his libretto on the familiar story in Virgil's *Aeneid.* Josias Priest's boarding-school cannot have offered a very spacious concert room, and it is easy to understand why Purcell scored his music for a little chamber orchestra of two violins, viola, bass, and harpsichord, as accompaniment to the solo and choral parts which Mr. Priest's young gentlewomen were to sing (the alto, tenor, and bass parts of the choruses, it is conjectured, were sung by male singers from a theater). It is not unlikely that Purcell himself presided at the harpsichord to supply the filling-in and elaboration of the accompaniment.

The date of the little affair at Mr. Priest's school is highly important for the reason that when Purcell so casually turned out this score he achieved the first English opera that has survived until our own time with undiminished vitality and effectiveness. It is not a fact, however, as historians long supposed, that *Dido and Aeneas* was the first English opera to be composed. The first English opera was *The Siege of Rhodes*, music by Matthew Lock, with contributions by four other composers, to a libretto by Davenant, produced in 1656, thirty-three years before *Dido and Aeneas.* But not a measure of the score of *The Siege of Rhodes* remains.

Dido and Aeneas was formerly assigned by historians to Purcell's youth. But the researches of modern scholars have established the fact that the opera dates from about 1689—not from 1675 or 1677 or 1680, as had been thought

—and that it is, therefore, a product of Purcell's maturity. *Dido and Aeneas* remained in manuscript for a century and a half, when the score (the complete libretto had not then come to light) was published in 1841 by the Musical Antiquarian Society. A vocal score with text appeared in 1870, but it was not until 1889 that the excellent and indispensable Purcell Society issued the work in full score, 'as left by the composer.'

Dido and Aeneas is a complete and veritable opera, without spoken dialogue. There are recitatives, airs, duets, choruses, descriptive instrumental movements. Several of the many plays and masques for which Purcell wrote music—sometimes only songs, dances, and 'curtain tunes'—were called 'operas' on the title page and were once regarded as such, but *Dido and Aeneas* is his only real opera. The text is short and is scarcely extraordinary as literature. Purcell's librettist, Tate, was hardly a poet of blazing genius. He added trimmings of his own to Virgil—a chorus of witches and a sorceress, which gave Purcell an excuse for a captivating choir of laughing devils and a charming 'echo' chorus, 'In Our Deep Vaulted Cell'—evidently performed originally by two groups of singers, one behind the scenes which echoed the words and notes of the singers on the stage.

But the play is of no consequence. The music's the thing. Purcell's score is, in the first place, extraordinary for its dramatic life, its variety, its expressiveness, its mastery of characterization. Here Dido lives and moves, individual and distinct; and how vividly actual are Purcell's witches and sailors, heroes and courtiers! The work is compact of genius. The rollicking tunes and dances, with the influence of English folk music strong upon them; the superb choruses, the beautiful songs, with their fervor and grace of line; the declamation—that 'lyrical recitative' which is handled with such perfect art and such amazing eloquence: these things are beyond praise.

But above everything else the music takes the breath by its modernity. Remember that when Purcell composed it, Bach was a child, and Debussy was not to be born for almost two centuries. Now examine the chord which begins the thirty-third measure of Dido's Farewell (counting from the beginning of the voice part). This chord is identical with one of the favorite suspensions used by Debussy in *Pelléas et Mélisande* two hundred years after Purcell died. You will rub your eyes, but there it is. And you will rub them again and again as you go through or listen to the score of *Dido*.

Such things are mysteries.

‡Music from *Dido and Aeneas* has been arranged for concert performance by various hands (the suites edited by John Barbirolli and Lucien Cailliet may be cited); in a majority of these arrangements, parts for wind instruments and percussion have been added—they are, in effect, transcriptions of Purcell's music.‡

● TRUMPET VOLUNTARY

Purcell wrote freely for the trumpet. There are numerous 'Trumpet Tunes' among his scores, and ornate display pieces used for obbligati. Purcell liked especially to write obbligati parts to be played by John Shore, the most eminent trumpeter in the England of his day. Shore lived to be almost ninety, but he split his lip in playing his instrument and was professionally incapacitated some time before his end.

The Trumpet Voluntary frequently heard at orchestral concerts and ascribed to Purcell is an arrangement by Sir Henry Wood of one of Purcell's many trumpet tunes; Sir Henry has scored it for a trumpet in C, two additional trumpets, three trombones, organ, timpani, and side-drum. The piece is in D major, 'alla breve' time, 'Allegro maestoso.' It opens, forte, with the superb tune heard on the solo trumpet, accompanied at first by the organ alone. At the ninth measure the rest of the brass choir, with the timpani, join in. Later, the tune and the accompaniment are given to the organ, with the timpani added to the brass. At the climax, all the instruments are heard together.

The word 'Voluntary' is associated today with set pieces or improvisations for the organ played in connection with church services. But other meanings have been conveyed by the term. It was not always or necessarily applied to music played during a church service. Dr. Johnson, in 1785, defined it as 'a piece of music played at will, without any settled rule.'

The word in its musical meaning is found at least as early as 1450, when it appeared in T. Mulliner's *Virginal Book*.

Sergei Rachmaninoff

1873-1943

R

‡As a composer, Rachmaninoff enjoyed a popular rather than a critical success. That is to say, professional musicians—composers, theoreticians, critics—found little to interest them, and not much more to admire, in works which employed conventional means to express a conventional sensibility. But the sensibility was bona fide: what Rachmaninoff communicated was honestly and deeply experienced, and affectingly conveyed, and a large and happily unsophisticated public took him to its heart. It has with justice been said that he left music exactly where he found it —but so, after all, did Tchaikovsky, the master he so greatly admired. Significant innovations are found in the works of relatively few of even the greatest artists. The possibility must be allowed that the C minor and D minor Concertos, the Paganini Variations, the E minor Symphony, the shorter piano pieces, and the songs have already meant more to more people (a criterion not to be despised) than the music of, say, Stravinsky, will have meant at the end of time.‡

● SYMPHONY No. 2, IN E MINOR, OP. 27

This symphony received the Glinka award of 1000 rubles in December 1908—
the prize founded by a bequest of the munificent Russian publisher Belaïeff.
In spite of this millstone around its neck, however, the symphony has had a
most prosperous career, for it has been greatly liked and frequently played.
The work was composed in 1906-7 at Dresden, and performed at Moscow,
for the first time anywhere, in the season of 1908-9, under the composer's
direction.

The symphony (dedicated to Sergei Ivanovitch Taneieff) is in four movements, constructed to some extent upon the principle of thematic community
made fashionable by César Franck and Tchaikovsky—although Schumann and
even Beethoven had set the fashion much earlier. The first movement opens
with a long Introduction (Largo, 4-4) in which the violins foreshadow the
principal theme of the symphony. The main movement begins ('Allegro
moderato,' E minor, 2-2) with the chief subject in the violins, after four
measures of preparation. The second theme, in G major, is shared by the wind
and strings. A solo violin begins the development section. There is a long
crescendo, with brass fanfares, and a perturbed coda.

The second movement ('Allegro molto,' A minor, 2-2) begins, after several
introductory bars, with a first theme decisively affirmed by the horns, and
continued by the violins. After four-score measures given to the elaboration
of this material, a more lyric theme in C major (moderato, 'molto cantabile'),
is sung by the violins. There is a trio ('meno mosso') introduced by a marcato
figure in the second violins. Near the close, the opening of the Largo introduction to the first movement is recalled.

The Adagio (A major, 4-4) opens with a cantabile subject of Tchaikovskian
flavor in the first violins. The clarinet, then the violins and oboe, contribute
other sections, and material from the Introduction to the first movement is
again recalled.

The Finale is an 'Allegro vivace' in E major, 2-2. Four preliminary measures
for the full orchestra introduce the chief theme. After a fortissimo development, a diminuendo brings a subject of march-like character for the wind.
The second theme is in D major, allotted to the strings in octaves. Again in
this movement there are reminiscences of themes from the earlier movements.
The triplet figure of the main subject of the Finale forms the basis of the coda.

● SYMPHONY No. 3, IN A MINOR, OP. 44

An interval of nearly thirty years elapsed between the completion of Rachmaninoff's Second Symphony and the completion of his Third. The latter work
was begun in the spring of 1935, and finished in August of the following
year, at the composer's summer home on Lake of Lucerne, Switzerland. It is
characterized by a profusion of those sweeping cantabile phrases, darkened by
moods of melancholy brooding and impassioned stress, which are typical of
Rachmaninoff's works. Somber, lyrical, defiant, it is a work wholly representative of the Slavic genius and of Rachmaninoff in particular, by reason of
certain unmistakable turns of phrase and of orchestral diction.

The symphony is in three divisions. The first is an 'Allegro moderato,' begun by a slow introduction of four bars, *Lento*. The second is unusual in form—an 'Adagio non troppo,' linked with a long section in fast tempo, 'Allegro vivace,' and closing with a return of the Adagio mood and pace. In the Finale, almost half the middle section is devoted to fugal treatment of a subject derived from the first theme of the movement.

The first movement is introduced by four measures (Lento, common time) in which a melancholy tune is sung in unison by a muted solo 'cello, horn, and two clarinets, without accompaniment. There is a fermata; and an upward rush of strings and woodwind above emphatic chords of the brass and percussion, 'Allegro moderato,' begins the main movement, with the first theme (A minor, 'dolce e espressivo'), exposed by oboes and bassoons in thirds, above a swaying accompaniment figure of the second violins, which has prominence in the development. Strings continue this theme, with a subsidiary based on a triplet figure in imitation. The second theme is heard from the 'cellos, in E major, 'dolce cantabile,' with a woodwind accompaniment of syncopated chords. This cantilena is enlarged expressively by the unison and octave strings. There is a subsidiary cantilena in F for the strings. In the development section the theme of the movement's slow introduction is recalled, and it is heard in the coda, on the brass.

The second movement opens with an introductory horn theme, a romantic melody ('Adagio ma non troppo,' 3-4 time) supported by harp chords. At the tenth measure, the first chief theme (C-sharp major) is heard as a violin solo against a background of sustained chords of the woodwind and horns. All the violins, in unison, take this up and carry it to a forte. There is a second subject, begun by solo flute above an accompaniment of divided strings, which sounds like an offshoot of the E-major 'cello theme of the first movement—but doubtless the resemblance is fortuitous. There is an impassioned crescendo, and a fortissimo; then the music sinks to a pianissimo, as the solo flute recalls the first chief theme of the movement. The strings again speak ardently in their favorite lyric vein. There is a 'poco accelerando,' on an agitated figure begun by the violins. The Adagio becomes an 'Allegro vivace,' in 3-4 time, initiated by a subject for strings and wood, in which prominent use is made of a springing triplet figure heard first on the strings and afterward exchanged among the wind instruments, together with an exuberant motif for the strings introduced by an ascending run of sixteenth notes. The climax of this 'Allegro vivace' section occurs in the form of a complex of ascending and descending chromatic passages, fortissimo. The harp chords of the slow introduction return, with a long-held C sharp of a horn against tremolos of the muted violins. The slower tempo of the beginning is gradually re-established; the lyric, meditative mood returns; and the movement ends Adagio.

The Finale begins, Allegro, with an impetuous upward-rushing figure of the violins and woodwind, introducing at once, fortissimo, the chief theme (violins and violas in unison, A major, 4-4 time). Another of those cantabile string subjects with which the symphony abounds is heard in the tonic key, and the tempo slows to 'Andante con moto.' But it is soon whipped up to an Allegro, then to 'Allegro vivace': Rachmaninoff the impassioned lyrist turns contrapuntal and energetic, and for almost half the movement, the music occupies itself with an extremely spirited fugal treatment of material derived from a subject based on the chief theme of the movement. The lyric mood returns before the end, but the close is 'Allegro vivace,' full voiced and emphatic.

• SYMPHONIC POEM, *The Isle of the Dead*, OP. 29

The subtitle of this tone poem reads: 'To the Picture by A. Böcklin.' The picture referred to must be known to all frequenters of printshops. Böcklin might have taken for the motto of his most celebrated canvas the opening lines of the sonnet by Thomas Hood:

> There is a silence where hath been no sound;
> There is a silence where no sound may be.

Indeed, Böcklin is said to have remarked of his picture that 'it must produce such an effect of stillness that anyone would be frightened to hear a knock on the door.' The lonely, sunless island, awful in its solitude, with its frowning cliffs and mournful cypress trees, rising out of a windless sea; the boat that is slowly nearing the harbor with its mysterious cargo, the garlanded coffin and the white-robed, anonymous figure; the utter lifelessness and isolation, the unending, unbreakable silence of this desolate kingdom of shadows—what music-maker of imagination, attracted by Böcklin's somber fantasy, could fail to be moved to eloquent or at least sympathetic utterance?

Rachmaninoff projects for us the unruffled sea, the solemn approach of the barge with its quiet passengers, the forbidding and timeless haven which it nears—the monotonous wave-like figure in 5-8 time for harp and muted 'celli, divisi, which continues so persistently throughout the opening section of the tone poem, exerts a strange and oppressive power. But he has not been content with evoking unearthly and disquieting apparitions; he has given us the emotional implications, the human background, of the picture. He discerns its mortal complement. He remembers the grief, the lamentation, the loneliness, of those who are still of this world—who have not yet taken passage upon that uncharted sea with that unhastening ferryman: he remembers 'the measureless waters of human tears.' And in that passage where the *Dies Irae* is suggested by the 'cellos under a descending chromatic wail in the violins, he achieves not only a faithful commentary upon the picture, but an amplification of its idea. He has enlarged upon its text, though he has told us nothing which was not contained in it. He has said more than Böcklin has said, but nothing that Böcklin did not imply. His subject gave him neither opportunity nor excuse for saying anything in a different key. Böcklin's vision is a fundamentally despondent, a fundamentally unillumined one. The musician could not justifiably impose a different hue upon it. There is no elevation in the music; but there is none in the picture.

Here there can be no thought of that solacing figure of Whitman's imagination, the 'Dark Mother always gliding near with soft feet'; nor of the strangely similar though sublimer Mother of the Katha Upanishad—the Great Mother, 'full of divinity, who comes forth, through life, standing hid in secret.' In this picture, in this music, mournfully submissive eyes are bent upon the River of

Forgetfulness, or gaze despairingly toward that destination 'where neither ground is for the feet nor any path to follow . . . no map there, nor guide, nor voice sounding, nor touch of human hand . . . nor lips, nor eyes, are in that land . . .' but only

The wind of death's imperishable wing.

CONCERTOS FOR PIANO AND ORCHESTRA

Rachmaninoff's four concertos for piano represent a creative span of thirty-five years. The First Concerto, in F-sharp minor, op. 1, was written in his student days at Moscow, and the composer first played it there, when he was eighteen years old, under the direction of Safonoff. He revised it in 1917, before he left Russia. No new thematic material was introduced, but the original subject matter was freshly developed, and the instrumentation recast. The score is dedicated to Rachmaninoff's distinguished compatriot and cousin, Alexander Siloti.

The Second Concerto (the best known of the group), in C minor, op. 18, was composed in 1900, published in 1901, and performed for the first time, with the composer as pianist, at a concert of the Moscow Philharmonic Society, October 14, 1901. Siloti played the work in St. Petersburg in April of the following year. This concerto had won for the composer, in the previous year, the Glinka Prize of 500 roubles, founded by Belaïeff, the plutocratic and incredibly generous publisher who helped so many of the younger Russian music-makers.

The Third Concerto dates from 1909.

The Fourth Concerto, in G minor, op. 40, was completed in the summer of 1926. It was performed for the first time anywhere, from manuscript, by the composer and the Philadelphia Orchestra in Philadelphia, March 18, 1927.

• No. 1, in F-sharp minor, op. 1

The first movement begins (Vivace, 4-4) with a reiterated F-sharp, fortissimo, for clarinets, bassoons, and horns and an impetuous descending passage in octaves for the piano. A brief cadenza for the solo instrument introduces the chief subject, a song-like theme for the first and second violins in unison (Moderato, espressivo), which students of American music will readily identify because of the amusing resemblance of its opening phrase to Edward Mac-Dowell's *Folksong* (op. 47, No. 3), which he composed in Boston at about the same time that the youthful Rachmaninoff was writing his concerto in Moscow. The cadenza is distinguished by an episode (Lent—'Allegro moderato') in which harmonic bittersweet from a Cornish garden blossoms shyly—a lyric moment of progressive intensity that culminates in a fortissimo assertion (Maestoso) of the chief theme.

In the Andante (D major, 4-4) a phrase for the horn, answered by strings, woodwind, and trombones, and a short cadenza for the piano, introduce a meditative song for the solo instrument. This is unaccompanied until the eighteenth measure, when a solo bassoon, with an air of somewhat bashful uneasiness, intrudes upon the piano's cloistral contemplation; but it withdraws after four measures with its finger on its lips, and the piano is again alone in its luxuriously romantic solitude. The strings are bolder, but even they dare enter only on tiptoe, *ppp*. Philip Hale once remarked of the orchestral accompaniment in the original version of this movement that it was 'exceedingly discreet.' In the revised version it is still discreet, and the piano part remains, as Henry James might have said, 'beautifully dominant.'

The Finale (beginning 'Allegro vivace,' 9-8) is capricious in mood, restless and complex in its rhythmical transformations. A contrasting middle section ('Andante ma non troppo,' 3-4) proffers a sentimental interlude, wherein the strings, adorned by the piano, soon give place to the solo instrument, which, left to itself, becomes for a time the mouthpiece of the poet's lyric fervor. The resumption of the first tempo leads to a tumultuous close.

• No. 2, in C minor, op. 18

Between September 1897 and the latter part of 1899—a period of more than two years—Rachmaninoff's activity as a composer was somewhat relaxed. He had already written his one-act 'gold-medal' opera *Aleko*, his first piano concerto, his symphonic tone-picture, *The Cliff*; his 'Elegiac' Trio for piano, violin, and 'cello, in memory of Tchaikovsky; his *Gypsy Caprice* for orchestra; his first symphony, some choruses, songs, and smaller pieces for piano (including the most famous of all modern preludes for that instrument—adequately indicated by James Huncker as 'It'). The *première* of the First Symphony at St. Petersburg in September 1897, had been a fiasco. Though the performance had clearly misrepresented the work, the critics were unsparing in their attacks, and Rachmaninoff began to doubt his powers. Though in the two years that followed he produced a few songs and a few piano pieces, he was unable to bring any larger project to completion. Early in 1900, he was persuaded to consult a Dr. Dahl about his difficulties, and to submit to treatment by hypnosis and suggestion. The result was a restoration of self-confidence, and a fresh impetus to creative work, which had its issue in the Second Concerto, which the composer dedicated to Dr. Dahl.

The three movements of the C minor Concerto are: (1) Moderato, C minor, 2-2; (2) 'Adagio sostenuto,' E major, 4-4; (3) 'Allegro scherzando,' C minor, 4-4. The orchestral portion of the work is scored for woodwind and trumpets in pairs, four horns, three trombones and bass tuba, a set of three kettledrums, bass drum, cymbals, and strings.

• No. 3, in D minor, op. 30

The Third Concerto, as Dr. Otto Kinkeldey pointed out in an admirable exposition of the work, is

Russian throughout—Russian in its melodic conception, in its rhythms, and in the robust, virile qualities even of its gentler passages. In several passages we may clearly discern the composer's place in the lineage of Tchaikovsky.

In form [he continued] the concerto is more or less conventional, with lengthy working out of episodic material and free use of remodeled motives or melodies to secure unity throughout the whole work. The first theme of the first movement, a typical Slavic chant, is played very simply by the piano to a rhythmic accompaniment of muted strings and pizzicato basses. Horns and violas repeat the theme. The whole section has a subdued character which has something mysterious in it. The second theme, which is anticipated by horns and trumpets before it really appears in its full form after the first orchestra forte, is short and has a throbbing rhythm, played pianissimo and staccato by the strings and answered by the piano. From it is derived a beautifully warm and expressive episode for the solo instrument. Reminiscences of this theme and this episode will be heard in the second movement and will play a large part in the development of the last.

The second movement begins with another typical Russian theme, tender and melancholy, and yet not tearful. It is relieved by a section in 3-8 time, with a pizzicato waltz accompaniment in the strings, to which the reeds sing sweetly a melody, which is nothing but the first theme of the concerto in another guise.

The last movement ('alla breve') follows the second without interruption. Its general character is that of ceaseless, driving activity. The first theme at times takes on a martial sound. Several subsidiary themes are heard. One of them appears first as a long succession of syncopated chords in the piano, followed immediately by a smooth flowing statement of the same melody, also by the piano. A Scherzando, 4-4, and a Lento are based largely upon reminiscences of themes in the first movement. After the Lento the restless 'alla breve' is resumed.

• No. 4, IN G MINOR, OP. 40

This concerto was finished in the summer of 1926, and was performed for the first time anywhere by the composer and the Philadelphia Orchestra at Philadelphia, March 18, 1927.

The first movement begins, 'Allegro vivace,' 4-4, with six measures of introduction for the orchestra, after which the piano enters with the chief theme—a typically Rachmaninovian subject of broad arch and spacious melodic design, which sweeps upward through an octave and a half, and downward through two octaves, accompanied by reiterated wind chords and accented by sforzandi of the strings. The introductory phrases of the orchestra recur, and the piano repeats its commanding theme. There are subsidiary themes for the wind, against passage-work for the solo instrument. The tempo changes to Moderato and the piano, unaccompanied at first, exposes the cantabile second theme, in B-flat major. Beneath its extension (a development of one of its phrases in triple rhythm) the strings, 'dolce espressivo,' sing a chromatic counterpoint. The Allegro tempo returns. A variant of the chief theme is heard from the strings. The piano introduces a subject (A-flat minor) against an upward-striding figure for horns and tuba. There is an acceleration of pace. The piano soars upward through a modified form of the first subject to a *fff* outburst, and the strings take over the melody. Now it is the turn of the second theme, and we hear it in E-flat as a flute solo against piano arpeggios, then on the oboe. The first theme and its derivations return. Against piano arpeggios over a chord of the ninth on F, the first violins sing, tranquillo, the chief theme, doubled at the octave by a clarinet. A brief, plaintive solo for English horn arouses the slumbering orchestra to a brief and energetic coda.

The slow movement is a Largo of dolorous expressiveness, written in com-

mon time. After five introductory measures by piano alone, the strings utter
the melancholy chief theme, but immediately hand it over to the piano which
develops it without assistance for nine measures. After that, the strings and
woodwind, with horns, sing it in a kind of brooding antiphon. There is a
brief agitato section, followed by a new subject, 'cantabile e tranquillo,' for
the piano, accompanied by clarinets and English horn. But the more somber
theme returns. The 'cellos, joined by a horn, sing a long-breathed melody
against a background of arabesques for the piano. The sorrowful chief theme
returns ('cellos and bassoons, first violins) and the movement ends with a
'quasi glissando' and trills for piano, above mutterings of the theme in the
basses and a vague threatening of stopped horns. The third movement follows
immediately. This is a long and brilliant Finale, varied in mood and elaborate
in structure. There are reminiscences of thematic material previously heard,
and opportunity for a cadenza is provided. There is an irresistible coda, 'Vivace-
presto,' and a close in G major.

● Rhapsody on a Theme of Paganini, for Piano and Orchestra, op. 43

This work was begun on July 3, 1934, at Rachmaninoff's summer home on
the Lake of Lucerne (opposite Triebschen, Richard Wagner's dwelling-place
from 1866 until 1872). The score was completed on August 24. The first
performance was at Baltimore, November 7, 1934, by the Philadelphia
Orchestra under Leopold Stokowski and with the composer as soloist.

The Rhapsody is in form a series of variations on a theme of Paganini's,
and the manuscript score originally bore the title, *Rhapsodie (en forme de
Variations) sur un Thème de Paganini.* Rachmaninoff afterward struck out the
parenthetical phrase.

The Paganini theme chosen by Rachmaninoff for beneficent exploitation is
that of the last of the *Ventiquattro Capricci per Violino Solo*, op. 1, for which
Paganini himself composed eleven variations and a finale. The theme is known
to all musicians and most music-lovers as that employed by Brahms in his
famous Variations for Piano, op. 35.

The Rhapsody begins with an Introduction of nine measures ('Allegro
vivace,' 2-4, A minor), in which the theme is foreshadowed. Then comes a
sort of musical analogue of the singular court procedure in *Alice in Wonderland*, as announced by the Queen: 'Sentence first, verdict afterwards!' For
we hear, first, Variation I, in which the orchestra toys with fragments of the
theme, before we hear the formal statement of the theme itself, which follows,
instead of preceding, 'Variation I.' It is stated in A minor, 2-4 time, by the
first violins, rhythmically punctuated by the piano, 'poco marcato.' This is
followed by Variation II ('L'istesso tempo'), for the piano, accompanied at
first by brass and wood, then by the strings.

There are twenty-four variations, all of them musically resourceful and
ingenious; but certain among the two dozen should be called especially to
the listener's attention. In Variation VII ('Meno mosso, a tempo moderato'),
the piano expatiates on a melody derived from that of the *Dies Irae* (of which
Rachmaninoff makes such beautiful and moving use in his tone poem, *The*

Isle of the Dead), while the 'cellos and bassoon concern themselves with the Paganini theme in augmentation. In Variation x, the sinister tones of the *Dies Irae* are heard again, at first in double octaves for the piano, against the Paganini theme in the second violins and a counter-subject for clarinets. The variation rises to a *ff* climax.

In Variation xv, the orchestra is silent for twenty-seven measures, while the piano alone ('Più vivo scherzando,' 3-4) executes a florid interlude. Later, the strings and woodwind enter.

Variation xviii ('Andante cantabile,' 3-4, D-flat major) is distinguished by an expressive cantilena for the solo instrument (developed from an inversion of the characteristic sixteenth-note figure of the theme). Later, the first violins and 'cellos take up the melody, the piano and woodwind accompanying.

In the Finale, the intervals and rhythm of the theme are heard in the piano and woodwind against an ominous recurrence of the *Dies Irae* proclaimed, pesante, *ff*, by the brass and strings. But the piano has the last word, with a concluding assertion of a fragment of the theme.

The work is scored for piccolo, two flutes, two oboes, English horn, two clarinets, two bassoons, four horns, two trumpets in C, three trombones and tuba, timpani, percussion, bells, harp, and strings.

Maurice Ravel

1875-1937

R

When a French critic, many years ago, sought to explain the meaning of Ravel's piano piece, *Alborada del Gracioso*, he implied that the Spanish word 'gracioso,' difficult to translate, evoked a tonal portrait of Ravel himself—'a jester with finesse, alert, ironic, a sort of Figaro. For him it is ever the hour of aubade, always the hour of smiles and delicacy. He is skillful in mockery and loath to vociferate. He enjoys the sweetness of living, and is not unaware of its reflections.' There is much of Ravel in that portrait, but not all of him; and what is omitted is important. Ravel was more than a delicate and witty jester. He was a poet and an exquisite artist. He could say inimitable and lovely things with the utmost economy of means, yet with astonishing completeness of effect. He could spin a web of gossamer and tender beauty, saved by his Gallic gift of irony from the offense of prettiness or whimsicality. He has been called 'a little master.' Doubtless he was not a great one. He belonged, perhaps, to a category somewhere between the two. The tone poet who gave us such music as *La Valse* and *Daphnis et Chloé* is secure from the disparagement of stupid epithets. Let us be content to say that he was a master.

● *Alborada del Gracioso*

This, in its orchestral form, is a transcription, made by Ravel himself, of one of the pieces in *Miroirs*, written for piano solo. The five numbers of *Miroirs* were composed in 1905; they stand in chronological order among Ravel's piano works between *Jeux d'Eau* (1901) and *Gaspard de la Nuit*.

Alborada del Gracioso is to be grouped among those works of Ravel in which the Spanish influence is prominent. It may be associated from this point of view with the *Habanera* for violin, with the *Rhapsodie espagnole* and the *Bolero*, and with the delectable comic opera, *L'Heure espagnole*.

Alborada means an aubade, or morning serenade. Rimsky-Korsakoff also used the term as title for the first and third movements of his *Spanish Caprice*. Ravel's music is of extraordinary rhythmic vitality, and drenched in Spanish color. It is scored for an orchestra of woodwinds in pairs, with piccolo, English horn and contra-bassoon, four horns, three trumpets, three trombones, tuba, timpani, percussion, two harps, and strings.

● *Bolero*

Ravel's ballet, *Bolero*, was produced at the Opéra, Paris, in November 1928, by Ida Rubinstein and her company of mimes, with Walter Straram conducting. Alexander Benois contrived the settings and costumes, which recalled a painting by Goya. 'On a platform like that for the Andalusian *baile*, the dancer executed a stylized interpretation of the bolero, amid the growing excitement of a crowd of spectators, encouraging her with their applause and their pounding heels. At the moment when the music took a dramatic turn, we saw a brawl. Everything seemed to be swept along by the music, a most beautiful spectacle.'

Henry Prunières unhesitatingly pronounced Ravel's *Bolero* the work of 'a supreme artist.' Perhaps. But let us content ourselves for the moment with saying that this daring, ingenious, and craftily effective treatment of a rhythmical pattern—that of the dance we know as the Bolero—consorted with a single theme, incessantly repeated, without modification of any sort, except in the instrumentation, is the work of a most resourceful and audacious craftsman. Ravel has turned out, in his brilliant and fluent way, an astonishing piece of bravura. The insolent disdain of monotony's dire peril; the wit (insolent, too) of the manner in which the saxophones in the orchestra are employed; the long and insidious crescendo; the effect of the modulation to E major, six measures before the close—these things are irresistible demonstrations of Ravel's assured and necromantic art.

● *Daphnis et Chloé*: SUITES NOS. 1 AND 2

Ravel's ballet, *Daphnis et Chloé*, a 'choreographic symphony' in three parts, was composed in 1910, to a scenario by Fokine. It was produced by Diaghileff's

Ballet Russe at the Châtelet, Paris, in June 1912. The part of Daphnis was mimed by Nijinski, that of Chloe by Karsavina. Pierre Monteux conducted. Ravel afterward extracted two concert suites from the score of the ballet.

The scenario devised by Fokine for the ballet was based upon the familiar pastoral romance of the fourth-century Greek Sophist, Longus. The tale of the youthful lovers, Daphnis and Chloe, has served as the model for various romantic chronicles, from Tasso's *Aminta* to St. Pierre's *Paul and Virginia* and Allan Ramsay's *The Gentle Shepherd*. The action of Fokine's adaptation of the romance has been set forth as follows:

In front of the altar of the nymphs a crowd of young girls bearing garlands prostrate themselves. Daphnis and Chloe are among these devotees. The ceremony resolves itself into a religious dance. Daphnis has not awakened to the fact that he loves Chloe, and she in turn fears that he is not master of his own heart, but jealousy lays bare their mutual regard. Chloe suffers at seeing the maidens embrace Daphnis in their dances, and Daphnis resents the presence of the young men about Chloe. In innocence Chloe draws into the dance the clownish herdsman, Dorco. Whereupon the company propose a contest between the herdsman and Daphnis. A kiss from Chloe shall reward the victor. Dorco dances a grotesque figure; Daphnis follows with steps light and gracious. Daphnis and Chloe fall into mutual embrace while the crowd admire their beauty. Chloe runs away, while Daphnis lapses into dreaming languor, not responding to the wiles of Lyceion.

Presently is heard the shout of voices in alarm, and a group of women pursued by brigands cross the scene. Daphnis flies to the aid of Chloe, whose life is perhaps in danger. An instant later Chloe reappears, distracted, and throws herself before the altar of the nymphs, but the brigands seize her and carry her off. Daphnis, returning, finds a sandal lost by a young girl in the melée. He curses the gods, and falls inanimate. Light grows dim, and the statues of the nymphs one by one become endowed with life, and, leaving their pedestals, descend to console Daphnis. They invoke the god Pan, who emerges from a rock.

The scene changes to the camp of the brigands, where Chloe is a prisoner. She performs a dance of supplication. Briaxis, the pirate chief, woos her, when suddenly the atmosphere changes, and strange gleams light up the night. Pan appears in a cloud and enfolds Chloe.

The limpid serenity of the first scene is again resumed. Search is made for Daphnis and Chloe, and when their companions bring them back and Daphnis beholds his beloved, he knows that his dream was prophetic and that Pan has really intervened in his behalf.

Then Lammon, the old countryman, tells to all that Pan has graciously acted in memory of his ancient love for the nymph Syrinx. Whereupon the assembled company join in a dance of celebration of this old love-tale, and end in joyous applause of the betrothal of Daphnis and Chloe.

Each of the two *Daphnis et Chloé* suites comprises three movements. In Suite No. 1 these are entitled 'Nocturne,' 'Interlude,' and 'Danse guerrière'; in Suite No. 2 (the more frequently performed), they are 'Lever du Jour' ('Daybreak,'), 'Pantomime,' and 'Danse général.'

- *La Valse:* CHOREOGRAPHIC POEM FOR ORCHESTRA

When this *poème choréographique* was given in London at a concert of the Queen's Hall Orchestra, under Sir Henry Wood, on May 3, 1921, Edwin Evans introduced it with some instructive observations. He bade his hearers remember, for example, that Ravel is 'fond of looking at a style or a period, as it were, with his head on one side, and speculating what is to be done with it.' It was due to this solicitous preoccupation of Ravel's that we had his *Valses nobles et sentimentales,* his *Tombeau de Couperin,* his *L'Heure espagnole.* Eventually his roving and speculative eye fell upon what Evans indicates as 'the Vienna that acknowledged the sway of the "Waltz King," before merry widows came into fashion.' Ravel, like most musicians, has a warm regard for the genius of the Strauss who antedated Richard; and according to Evans, he has essayed here an apotheosis of the Viennese waltz 'as it was in the Golden Age'; but it is obvious, as we shall find, that this troubling and haunted music is much more than a mere glorification of the dance complex of the 'fifties.

The score contains the following preface:

At first the scene is dimmed by a kind of swirling mist, through which one discerns, vaguely and intermittently, the waltzing couples. Little by little the vapors disperse, the illumination grows brighter, revealing an immense ballroom filled with dancers; the blaze of the chandeliers comes to full splendor. An Imperial Court about 1855.

The fancy and virtuosity which Ravel has expended upon his metamorphosis are as dazzling as the images he evokes. He has achieved a reincarnation of the old Viennese idioms of Strauss and Lanner remarkable for its invention, its gusto, its imaginative and poetic transmutation of material whose original charm he has neither forgotten nor obscured. But this is only half his achievement. *La Valse,* despite its surface charm and scintillation, is essentially a work of tragic irony. It is as perturbing and ominous as a mobilization order. Raymond Schwab, the French critic, indicated the sinister undertone of the music when he called attention to 'a certain threatening in this bacchanale, a drunkenness, as it were, warning itself of its decay.' He noted its 'implied anguish, with some Prud'homme exclaiming: "We dance on a volcano." '

In the beginning, the themes are foreshadowed as unrelated fragments of dance tunes, dance rhythms, inchoate and amorphous—shadowy, formless specters of dead waltzes, drifting through gray mists. Little by little, in the course of the progressive clarification, these fragments become organized and integrated, and assume their logical relation to the whole.

- *Ma Mère l'Oye* (Mother Goose)

Ravel's *Mother Goose* derives from Charles Perrault of seventeenth-century France (and certain of his imitators), rather than from Perrault's Massachusetts contemporary, the illustrious Mrs. Goose of Boston. The *Cinq pièces enfantines* were conceived originally as four-hand piano pieces for the amusement of two children, Mimie and Jean Godebski (to whom they are dedicated). Ravel afterward scored them for orchestra. The piano pieces date from 1908. The orchestral score was published four years later.

I. 'PAVANE OF THE SLEEPING BEAUTY.' The Sleeping Beauty is, of course, the famous and fortunate lady who enjoyed a hundred-year sleep in a castle where she was sequestered by an impenetrable wood that sprang up and enclosed her, until she was disenchanted by the valorous prince who woke and wedded her.

The grave and stately movement of the pavane is initiated by the flute, against a counterpoint of the muted horn and muted violas, pizzicato (Lent, 4-4). The Princess, probably weakened by her century of sleep, does not dance long; the piece ends at the twentieth measure.

II. 'HOP-O'-MY-THUMB.' At the head of this section of his score Ravel quotes a passage from Perrault's tale: 'He believed that he would have no difficulty in finding his way by means of the bread-crumbs which he had strewn wherever he had passed; but he was greatly surprised when he could not find a single crumb; the birds had come and eaten them all.' After three introductory measures for muted violins ('très modéré,' 2-4, 3-4, 4-4), the oboe sings the pensive theme, the violins accompanying it in thirds.

III. 'LAIDERONNETTE, EMPRESS OF THE PAGODES.' In the Countess d'Aulnoy's fairy tale, *Serpentin Vert*, the Princess Laideronnette was condemned by the curse of a depraved witch to endure from her cradle the burden of an atrocious ugliness; and so it was only natural that Laideronnette, when she became of age, determined to seclude herself in a distant castle where she would never be stared at. She encountered in the adjacent forest a gigantic green serpent, who boasted to her of an earlier condition of pulchritude, and with whom Laideronnette made a sea voyage in a frail craft that was wrecked on the shore of a country where dwelt the luxurious race of Pagodes—apparently the profiteers of Fairyland: diminutive creatures with bodies made of jewels, crystal, porcelain, and other expensive substances. Their mysterious king was really, as you will have guessed, the Green Snake, who, like Laideronnette, had been bewitched by the wicked fairy. Of course they were both, in due time, restored to their true forms, with an entangling alliance in prospect.

This movement is in march rhythm (2-4). The piccolo, in the ninth measure, announces a theme in sixteenth and eighth notes. There is a second subject, for the oboe, which is a kind of rhythmic and melodic inversion of the first, and a third subject for horns, woodwind, celesta, and harp, in unison and octaves. The movement ends on an iridescent chord for the full orchestra in which all the notes of the pentatonic scale in F-sharp major are sounded together, fortissimo.

IV. 'CONVERSATIONS OF BEAUTY AND THE BEAST.' 'Mouvement de Valse, modéré' (3-4). A clarinet impersonates Beauty (second measure); the double-bassoon (half a hundred measures further on) enacts the Beast. You hear them joined—apparently, both are talking at once. There is a climax, a pause, a harp glissando, and the transformed Beast appears in delicately magical harmonics for a solo violin; after which, the Prince makes love on his 'cello, while Beauty responds on her harp, in company with a discreetly chaperoning piccolo.

For the Finale of his suite, 'The Fairy Garden,' Ravel offers us no clues beyond his title. We can only listen with innocent ears and remember a line from Poe: 'Ah, bear in mind *this* garden is enchanted!' The movement begins softly, in slow tempo, triple time, for strings alone. The close is radiant and jubilant—you might almost think you were in that marvelous garden opened by Tyltyl's magic key, with a thousand million bluebirds flying in the moonlight among the jeweled boughs.

• *Rhapsodie Espagnole*

This four-movement suite dates from 1907. It still constitutes, with Debussy's *Iberia* and Chabrier's much older *España*, an unequaled trio of symphonic scores derived from a Spanish inspiration—and not one of them was composed by a Spaniard.

I. 'PRÉLUDE À LA NUIT' ('Très modéré,' 3-4). The mood is voluptuously drowsy and ecstatic. Violins and violas, muted, *ppp*, reiterate a descending phrase of four notes. Clarinets in octaves sing a counter-theme. There is a passionate phrase for the strings. Clarinets play a cadenza in two-part harmony. This is imitated after an interval by a pair of brotherly bassoons, heard above a sustained chord of the 'cellos and double-basses, which is veiled by a curious effect of arpeggiated harmonics for a solo violin, with trills for three other fiddles. A vaporous pianissimo chord for divided 'cellos and basses, in harmonics, leads into the succeeding movement.

II. 'MALAGUEÑA' ('Assez vif,' 3-4). The Malagueña is a dance of southern Spain, and is grouped with the Fandango and Rodeña. It is usually in 3-8 time, 'slow and sensuous,' and is accompanied by guitar and castanets. In Ravel's piece, the Malagueña is introduced by a persistent figure in the double-basses, repeated through a score of measures. A muted trumpet, with tambourine accompaniment, contributes the salient theme of the movement; there is a recitative ('Assez lent') for the English horn, and the descending figure of the *Prélude à la Nuit* is recalled (violin, viola, 'cello, celesta).

III. 'HABANERA' ('Assez lent,' 2-4). The Habanera has been described as 'a Spanish song and dance, of an older origin than its name implies, having been introduced into Cuba from Africa by the Negroes, whence it was very naturally imported into Spain. A "Habanera" usually consists of a short introduction and two parts of eight or sixteen bars, of which the second, should the first be in a minor key, will be in the major, and will answer the purpose of a refrain; but these rules are by no means strictly adhered to. . .'

The 'Habanera' of Ravel's suite has an eight-measure introduction (muted strings, and a syncopated figure for clarinets). Oboe, English horn, clarinets, and later solo viola, exhibit the chief theme. The music was revamped from an early piece of Ravel's—a 'Habanera' for two pianos, composed in 1895.

IV. 'FERIA' ('Assez animé,' 6-8). This is a musical Fair, and Ravel empties his box of paints into the orchestra to depict it. This fourth movement occupies more than half the total extent of the suite. It is a brilliantly fantastic hurly-burly, a medley of gorgeous and delicate hues, grotesque humors, ingenious and enchanting arabesques. A two-bar subject for the flute, a joyously raucous tune for muted trumpets in three-part harmony, accented by the tambourine, and a sentimental solo for the English horn ('très modéré,' 3-4) are the chief thematic features. There is a tumultuous conclusion.

● SUITE, *Le Tombeau de Couperin*

A month before the 1914-18 War began, Ravel started work upon a suite for piano to be entitled *Le Tombeau de Couperin* ('Couperin's Tomb'). Interrupted by the shattering years that followed, Ravel did not complete the suite until late in 1917. It was published in 1918, with dedications to the memory of certain friends of the composer who had fallen in the war. The original piano suite contained six movements, written for the most part in old dance forms—those which would have been familiar ground to François Couperin, that incomparable master of the clavecin. Later, Ravel chose four of the six movements of the piano suite—the Prelude, Forlane, Menuet, and Rigaudon—and scored them for orchestra. In this form, the work was heard for the first time at a Pasdeloup concert in Paris, under the direction of Rhené-Baton, on February 28, 1920.

The published orchestral score contains no dedication or inscription of any kind, and there is no reference to the dead comrades of Ravel or to the war. Only Couperin is memorialized upon the printed page. Thus Ravel 'returned to a favored period, and to the expression of admiration for a French master'; for these pieces, delicately archaic in manner, though artfully modernized, constitute a tribute to Ravel's great predecessor of the eighteenth century—tonal wreaths, not too somber nor too profuse, laid with tenderness upon an unforgotten tomb.

The suite is scored for an orchestra of modest dimensions: flutes, oboes, clarinets, bassoons, and horns, in pairs; English horn, trumpet, harp, and strings.

The Prélude is in E minor, Vif, 12-16 time; the Forlane (the 'Forlano' of the Italians, deriving from the Venetian gondoliers), is an Allegretto in 6-8 time; the Menuet is an 'Allegro moderato,' 3-4, ending on an unresolved dissonance; the final Rigaudon (an animated dance traceable to Provence and Languedoc) is marked 'Assez vif,' 2-4.

François Couperin ('Couperin Le Grand'), the greatest clavecinist of his time, was born at Paris in 1668 and died there in 1733. Thus he preceded Bach's arrival in this world by seventeen years and his departure hence by the same length of time. Both men lived to be sixty-five. Not only Bach, but Scarlatti and Handel and others learned a good many excellent tricks from Couperin. Bach was especially sedulous: he even copied some of Couperin's faults.

Couperin the Great was a personage in the France of his time. He was clavecinist to the King, a pet of the great ladies of Paris, the most fashionable teacher of the harpsichord. Almost any Sunday evening might have found him playing the clavecin at Court, or in the smart salons of Paris—affable, a little pompous, benignly cynical, his face plump and ruddy beneath his wig, his laces and brocades always in perfect trim; or giving a lesson to one of his aristocratic pupils, whom he had flattered or piqued by the prettily mysterious title of some one of his descriptive pieces. 'They are, in a way, portraits,' he confessed, 'bestowed on the charming originals whom I wished to portray.'

For Couperin, according to the fashion of his day, turned a good many of these clavecin pieces into a naïve kind of program music. Together with the pieces that bore merely the names of the various dances that he included in his suites, or *ordres,* were others bearing such fanciful and descriptive titles as we have alluded to above. 'I have always,' he wrote in his dedication of the First Book, 'had an object in composing these pieces, inspired by various events; the title corresponds to the ideas I had in my mind; I need not explain them, but as some of the titles may seem to be flattering me, it is perhaps as well to mention that the pieces bearing them are likenesses which have some-times been considered very characteristic when I played them.'

Can one not imagine the flutter over these pieces called 'Mimi' or 'Fleurie ou la tendre Nanette,' or those that were apparently attempts at delineation of character, as 'The Voluptuous Woman,' 'The Chatterbox,' 'A Troubled Soul'? There were still odder and slyer titles: 'Slight Mourning, or the Three Widows,' 'Dodo, or Love in the Cradle,' and the 'Folies Françaises ou les Dominoes,' with their remarkable captions—'Hope in Green,' 'Ardour in Red,' 'Perseverance in Gray,' 'Silent Jealousy in Purple-Gray,' 'Virginity in a Color Which Is Invisible' (for Couperin was not without the treasurous gift of malice). The 'Folies Françaises' have impressed some students as a premonition of Schumann's *Carnaval;* indeed certain scholars have even asserted that Couperin—who seems really to have aimed at a kind of psychological portrayal —was 'a forerunner of Schumann.'

His life appears to have been uneventful, although it was brilliantly success-ful and conspicuous. For more than a generation he was clavecinist to the King and organist of the Royal Chapel, and he taught music to the royal children. He sailed smoothly and magnificently down the shining streams of his existence, and there is little to chronicle concerning him, except that he was a darling of the gods and an exquisite artist. He published in 1717 what appears to have been the first book of instruction specifically devoted to the playing of the harpsichord, the famous *Art de Toucher le Clavecin.*

• *Pavane pour une Infante Défunte*

This work was composed by Ravel as a piano piece in 1899, when he was twenty-four. It was first heard in public at a Société Nationale concert on April 5, 1902, played by Ricardo Viñés. Ravel orchestrated the piece in 1910.

The precise significance of the music has long been a subject of dispute. Apparently the 'Infante défunte' refers to an Infanta of Spain (or Portugal). But whatever Ravel may have had in mind when he composed it, the mood of the music is unmistakable. It is deeply and tenderly elegiacal, steeped in a sense of the pathos of early death.

The pavane (pavan, or pavin), a slow and solemn dance, popular in the six-teenth and seventeenth centuries, is appropriate to the noble and dolorous sentiment of such an imaginative theme as Ravel may have conceived. In old masquerades, pavans were played as processional music, and were even used at religious ceremonies. Like most early dances, the pavan was sung as well as danced. Morley, in his *Plaine and Easie Introduction to Practicall Musicke*

(1597), spoke of it as 'a kind of staide musicke, ordained for graue dauncing, and most commonlie made of three straines, whereof eurie straine is plaid or sung twice. . . After euery pauan we vsually set a Galliard.'

Ravel's *Pavane* is classical in form, and is built on the principle of the rondo. It begins with a modal melody, gravely wistful, harmonized with wan chords from which the third is often absent. A solo horn has the opening and melancholy tune, against sustained notes in the bassoons and broken chords in plucked and muted strings. There is a duet for oboe and bassoon, repeated by the strings, and the flute has a solo. After a climax, the original theme returns in flutes and violins. The scoring is for small orchestra—two flutes, oboe, two clarinets, two bassoons, two horns, harp, and strings.

● CONCERTO FOR PIANO AND ORCHESTRA

Ravel was engaged on this concerto for more than two years at his country house in Montfort l'Amaury—'refusing all invitations, and working ten and twelve hours a day.' It was completed only in time for performance at the Ravel festival given in the Salle Pleyel, Paris, January 14, 1932, with the co-operation of the Lamoureux Orchestra.

The concerto is in three movements: (1) Allegramente (G major), 2-2; (2) 'Adagio assai,' E major, 3-4; (3) Presto, G major, 2-4. The work is light in vein, and the Finale is distinguished by what Henry Prunières referred to as 'discreet allusions to jazz.' The solo part is tricky stuff, with many pitfalls for the clumsy and the timorous and the inexpert. It must be played, if it is to make its effect, with wit and tact and elan, with a subtle touch of parody, an almost continuous sly malice, and a taste that is sufficiently acute to guide the artist to the secret of Ravel's droll and captivating blend of delicate travesty and poetic charm. For there are passages in this apparently quite frivolous piece where Ravel, the lover of loveliness, conquers the farceur and the slick showman and the aesthetic trimmer and trifler that Ravel was ever in danger of becoming.

Ottorino Respighi

1879-1936

R

Ottorino Respighi studied music at first with his father. Later, he entered the Liceo Musicale at Bologna, the city of his birth, and there his masters were Martucci and Sarti. He was graduated from the Liceo in 1907, and visited Russia, studying with Rimsky-Korsakoff, and Germany, studying with Max Bruch. Returning to Italy, he filled successively a number of important pedagogical posts, conducted, played the piano, and composed.

His works are very numerous and include operas, ballets, cantatas, symphonies, tone poems, chamber music, songs, et cetera.

● SYMPHONIC POEM, *The Fountains of Rome*

Respighi composed this most famous of his orchestral works in 1916. The first performance was under the bâton of Arturo Toscanini, on February 10, 1918, at one of a series of concerts given in Rome for the benefit of artists disabled in the war.

The score of Respighi's *Fontane di Roma* contains this explanation of the music (the four sections of which are played without pause):

> The Fountain of Valle Giulia at dawn
> The Triton Fountain in the morning
> The Fountain of Trevi at mid-day
> The Villa Medici Fountain at sunset

In this symphonic poem the composer has endeavored to give expression to the sentiments and visions suggested to him by four of Rome's fountains, contemplated at the hour in which their character is most in harmony with the surrounding landscape, or in which their beauty appears most impressive to the observer: The Fountain of Valle Giulia at dawn; the Triton Fountain at morn; the Fountain of Trevi at mid-day; the Villa Medici Fountain at sunset.

The first part of the poem, inspired by the Fountain of Valle Giulia, depicts a pastoral landscape; droves of cattle pass and disappear in the fresh, damp mists of a Roman dawn.

A sudden loud and insistent blast of horns above the trills of the whole orchestra introduces the second part, the Triton Fountain. It is like a joyous call, summoning troops of naiads and tritons, who come running up, pursuing each other and mingling in a frenzied dance between the jets of water.

Next there appears a solemn theme, borne on the undulations of the orchestra. It is the Fountain of Trevi at mid-day. The solemn theme, passing from the wood to the brass instruments, assumes a triumphal character. Trumpets peal; across the radiant surface of the water there passes Neptune's chariot, drawn by sea horses and followed by a train of sirens and tritons. The procession then vanishes, while faint trumpet blasts resound in the distance.

The fourth part, the Villa Medici Fountain, is announced by a sad theme, which rises above a subdued warbling. It is the nostalgic hour of sunset. The air is full of the sound of tolling bells, birds twittering, leaves rustling. Then all dies peacefully into the silence of the night.

● SYMPHONIC POEM, *The Pines of Rome*

Shortly after the composition of *Pini di Roma*, Respighi wrote to the present annotator as follows concerning the work, which he intended as a companion-piece to his celebrated *Fontana di Roma*:

> The symphonic poem, *The Pines of Rome*, was composed in 1924, and performed for the first time at the Augusteo, Rome, in the season of 1924-5. While in his preceding work, *The Fountains of Rome*, the composer sought to reproduce by means of tone an impression of Nature, in *The Pines of Rome* he uses Nature as a point of departure in order to recall memories and visions. The century-old trees which dominate

so characteristically the Roman landscape become testimony for the principal events in Roman life.

Pini di Roma, which is in four connected sections, is based upon this program, printed as preface to the score:

1. 'THE PINES OF THE VILLA BORGHESE' ['Allegretto vivace,' 2-8]. Children are at play in the pine-grove of the Villa Borghese, dancing the Italian equivalent of 'Ring-Around-a-Rosy'; mimicking marching soldiers and battles; twittering and shrieking like swallows at evening; and they disappear. Suddenly the scene changes to—
2. 'THE PINES NEAR A CATACOMB' [Lento, 4-4; beginning with muted and divided strings, muted horns, *p.*; later, trumpet behind the scenes]. We see the shadows of the pines which overhang the entrance to a catacomb; from the depths rises a chant which re-echoes solemnly, sonorously, like a hymn, and is then mysteriously silenced [the hymn begins, *p*, in the low strings and wind—a melody of Gregorian character: it is in the Aeolian mode, the fifth of the 'Authentic' modes. The opening theme for the horn, and a phrase from the trumpet solo, are heard as counterpoints].
3. 'THE PINES OF THE JANICULUM' [Lento, 4-4; piano cadenza; clarinet solo]. There is a rustling in the air. The full moon reveals the profile of the pines on the hill. A nightingale sings.
4. 'THE PINES OF THE APPIAN WAY' ['Tempo di marcia']. Misty dawn on the Appian Way. The tragic country is guarded by solitary pines. Indistinctly, incessantly, the rhythm of innumerable steps. To the poet's phantasy appears a vision of past glories; trumpets blare, and the army of the consul advances brilliantly in the grandeur of a newly-risen sun toward the sacred way, mounting in triumph the Capitoline Hill.

The feature of this score is its use of a gramophone record—the first instance of the sort in symphonic music. The reader will have noted the last sentence in that paragraph of the foregoing synopsis which describes the third section of the work, 'The Pines of the Janiculum': 'A nightingale sings.' The 'nightingale' is represented in the score by 'No. R. 6105 of the Concert Record Gramophone: The Song of a Nightingale.' The bird's song occurs at the end of the movement. It is introduced by the clarinet melody first heard at the beginning of the section. The gramophone song is accompanied by trills of the muted violins, *ppp*, harp notes, and a chord of the 'cellos and violas.

The huge crescendo that ends the last section of the work, 'The Pines of the Appian Way,' is probably the mightiest effect of cumulative sonority in the orchestral repertoire.

• SYMPHONIC POEM, *Roman Festivals*

In this symphonic poem Respighi completed the cycle of Roman impressions begun with *Fontane di Roma* (1917) and continued with *Pini di Roma* (1924). In the first he 'sought to reproduce, by means of tone, impressions of certain natural aspects of the Eternal City'; in the second, he 'resorted to Nature as a point of departure in order to recall memories and visions'; in the third, *Feste Romane*, he gives us 'visions and evocations of Roman fêtes.'

This work was completed in 1928. It was performed for the first time anywhere by the Philharmonic-Symphony Society, under Arturo Toscanini, at Carnegie Hall, February 21, 1929.

The composer has elucidated as follows the programmatic basis of this series of Roman impressions:

'The Circus Maximus.' A threatening sky over the Circus Maximus, but the people are celebrating: Hail Nero! The iron gates open, and the air is filled with a religious chant and the roaring of savage beasts. The mob undulates and rages: Serenely, the song of the martyrs spreads, dominates, and finally is drowned in the tumult.

'The Jubilee.' Weary, in pain, the pilgrims drag themselves through the long streets, praying. At last, from the summit of Mount Mario, is seen the holy city: Rome! Rome! And the hymn of jubilation is answered by the clangor of multitudinous church-bells.

'The October Excursions.' Fetes of October, in the castles engarlanded with vine-leaves—echoes of the hunt—tinklings of horse-bells—songs of love. Then, in the balmy evening, the sound of a romantic serenade.

'Epiphany.' The eve of Epiphany in Piazza Navona: a characteristic rhythm of bugles dominates the frantic clamor: on the tide of noise float now and again rustic songs, the lilt of saltarellos, the sounds of the mechanical organ in some booth, the call of the showman, hoarse and drunken cries, and the stornello in which the spirit of the populace finds expression: 'Lassátece passá, semo Romani' ('Let us pass, we are Romans').

Nicholas Rimsky-Korsakoff

1844-1908

‡Nicholas Rimsky-Korsakoff's parents were well-to-do members of the small Russian aristocracy. Though quite able and willing to recognize their son's musical gift and to encourage its development as a social asset, they were not prepared to countenance his adoption of a musical career. Accordingly, Nicholas became an officer in the Navy of His Imperial Majesty, the Czar of all the Russias, and wasted valuable years seeing the world—even that remote and barbarous region which lay west across the Atlantic from the continent of Europe. But in the end, he had his way. He had made the acquaintance of Balakireff and Cui and Moussorgsky and corresponded with them; in the leisure that his duties allowed him, he attempted composition. One of the early fruits was a symphony—the first by a Russian composer—which Balakireff brought to performance at Petersburg in 1865 (Rimsky was then twenty-one). A few years later, he was appointed professor of composition at the Petersburg Conservatory, though he knew scarcely more about his subject than did his pupils, and resigned his commission. The interested reader may consult his auto-biography (*My Musical Life*) for further details—it is an interesting document, extroverted, realistic, gossipy, a perfect expression of its cheerful,

competent, self-confident author, who viewed art and life from an eminently practical point of view and made, inevitably, a success of both.
If these remarks seem to belittle Rimsky, that is not the intention with
which they are written. He was a greatly gifted man—but his music is
entertainment music and nothing more, the music of a tale-spinner and
fantasist, and a virtuose craftsman. No purpose is served by pretending
otherwise.‡

● SYMPHONIC SUITE, *Antar*, OP. 9

This work was composed in 1868 and was first performed on March 22 of the
following year at a concert of the Russian Musical Society in St. Petersburg.
On that occasion it was designated as the composer's Second Symphony. Later,
Rimsky re-titled it. 'I was wrong,' he recorded in his autobiography, 'in calling
Antar a symphony. [It] was a poem, suite, fairy-tale, story, or anything you
like, but not a symphony.'

Antar was a famous Arabian warrior-poet of pre-Mohammedan times. He
lived in the sixth century, and his inspiration and eloquence as a poet were so
revered that one of his poems, inscribed upon deerskin, was hung up among
the idols in the Kaaba, the sacred shrine of the Islamites at Mecca, said by
tradition to have been created by God out of cloud and mist at the beginning
of the world. Rimsky-Korsakoff's suite is based on a tale by Sennkovsky, of
which Antar is the hero. It is in four movements, which unfold the following
programmatic scheme:

1. Largo—'Allegro giocoso'—'Allegretto vivace.' Antar, hating mankind,
which has returned him evil for good, dwells in solitude among the ruins of
Palmyra, in the desert of Sham. He rescues a gazelle from an attacking giant
bird, and in sleep is transported to the abode of the fairy Gul-nazar. It was
she he rescued in the likeness of the gazelle, and in gratitude she offers him
the three great joys of life. He accepts, and awakens to find himself again
among the ruins.

2. Allegro. A representation of the first joy granted by the fairy Gul-nazar:
the joy of vengeance.

3. 'Allegro risoluto alla marcia.' The second joy: that of power.

4. 'Allegretto vivace'—'Andante amoroso.' The third joy: that of love, by
which Antar, at his own wish, is consumed.

The grave theme for violas and woodwind which is heard in the opening
Largo, and which recurs throughout the symphony, has been called the 'Antar'
motive; while the graceful motive for flute and accompanying horns in the
succeeding Allegro section has been said to characterize the transformed gazelle
—the miraculously potent fairy queen through whose love Antar finally meets
his end.

● SYMPHONIC SUITE, *Schéhérazade*, OP. 35

The score of this most famous of Rimsky's works is prefaced by a note which
recalls the tale of the Sultan Schahriar and the Sultana Schéhérazade, to which

tradition assigns the origin of that collection of Arabian myths, legends, and folk tales known as *The Thousand and One Nights*. Convinced of the wantonness of women, the Sultan Schahriar put each of his wives to death after the first night. But the daughter of his vizier, the Sultana Schéhérazade, averted her doom for a thousand and one nights by entertaining her lord with a succession of tales of wonder and romance and humor, which she cunningly left unfinished at the break of day. In the end the Sultan, convinced of Schéhérazade's fidelity, and instructed by her tales, renounced his bloody vow entirely.

There are no further annotations in the published score of 1889. But when the suite was first performed, under Rimsky-Korsakoff's direction, the four movements were supplied with these titles: (1) 'The Sea and Sindbad's Ship'; (2) 'The Story of the Kalendar Prince'; (3) 'The Young Prince and the Young Princess'; (4) 'Festival at Bagdad'—'The Sea'—'The Ship Goes to Pieces on a Rock Surmounted by the Bronze Statue of a Warrior'—'Conclusion.'

I. 'THE SEA AND SINDBAD'S SHIP.' The chief theme of this movement, the unison phrase for trombones, tuba, strings, and low woodwind, heard fortissimo at the opening ('Largo e maestoso,' E minor, 2-2), is that which Rimsky-Korsakoff refers to as 'depicting Schéhérazade's stern spouse'—the Sultan. Thereafter we hear (solo violin, with harp chords) the motive of Schéhérazade the Narrator. Then begins the main movement ('Allegro non troppo,' E major, 6-4). An undulating arpeggio figure has been called the Wave motive, and a theme first sung by the flute, above arpeggios on a solo 'cello, that of the Ship. The Sultan's motive brings a climax for the full orchestra, followed by a placid close.

II. 'THE STORY OF THE KALENDAR-PRINCE.' There is a brief introductory passage (Lento, 4-4), and we hear Schéhérazade's theme on the solo violin, with harp accompaniment. Then (Andantino, B minor, 3-8) the bassoon comes prominently upon the orchestral scene with a theme that ranges in expression from lumbering burlesque and a kind of mock heroism to a gravity that is almost pathos. The tempo quickens. The scene brightens, takes on color and movement. There are fanfares from the brass, evolving a new motive, of an aggressive and brilliant incisiveness, for trombone and trumpet. The development of this material is long and elaborate.

III. 'THE YOUNG PRINCE AND THE YOUNG PRINCESS.' This is a romantic idyl, played in the twilight of an Oriental garden to the sound of fountains, 'like flutes far away'—on terraces above dark pools, against a background of minaret and dome, while behind them 'a carven moon, without faintest aureole, a voluptuous moon, mysteriously marked, holds her hand upon the circle of her breast; and all around is subdued color, embroidered stuffs, bronze lamps traced with inscrutable designs, and scent burning in silver dishes.' But the lovers themselves are simple and naïve, and speak in accents as freshly candid as those of a folk song.

The music is derived from two lyrical themes of singular charm and character. The Prince (it is doubtless he) enters at once, with the delightful song of the violins ('Andantino quasi allegretto, G major, 6-8). The Princess enters accompanied in the orchestra by a clarinet ('Pochissimo più mosso,' B-flat major, 6-8), later by snare drum, tambourine, cymbals, and triangle. Schéhérazade and her violin, you are reminded, are not yet silenced.

IV. 'Festival at Bagdad—The Sea—The Ship Goes to Pieces on a Rock Surmounted by the Bronze Statue of a Warrior—Conclusion.' The motive of the Sultan thunders forebodingly at the beginning of the last movement, and the talkative Sultana is heard. Then begins the Festival in Bagdad ('Allegro molto e frenetico,' E minor, 6-8; later, Vivo). The music is riotous with the clamor of crowds and the shrilling of Eastern instruments, rank with strong perfumes and with the grosser odors of the bazaars and streets, ablaze with the color and radiance of Asiatic noons. Then, abruptly and mysteriously, as in a fantastic dream, we find ourselves no longer among the Bagdad revellers, but on shipboard, fatefully headed for the magnetic rock. The theme of the Sultan—which has now, apparently, become the motive of the Sea—is menacingly proclaimed by the trombones, in a gigantic augmentation. The surges rise and fall with cumulative power, and shatter the vessel with its merrily oblivious company against the cliff. The tumult and the shouting dies, and in the silence Schéhérazade's appeasing fiddle is heard for the last time as she comes to the end of her tale-spinning, indomitable and triumphant.

• Suite from Le Coq d'Or

Le Coq d'Or ('The Golden Cockerel') was Rimsky-Korsakoff's last opera. It was begun in the summer of 1906 and completed in 1907. A performance had been planned for that year, but the Government censor was unfavorably impressed by the vivacity with which Rimsky-Korsakoff had apparently satirized monarchial institutions, and he forbade the production. Rimsky-Korsakoff's death in 1908 was thought by some to have been hastened by the censor's prohibition of his opera. The ban was lifted in 1909, and on September 24 of that year the opera was performed for the first time at the Solodovnikoff Theater, Moscow. In the following year it was performed at St. Petersburg.

In 1912, Michel Fokine adapted the work as an opera-pantomime, despite the protest of Rimsky-Korsakoff's family. It was in that arrangement, as a ballet-opera, that the work became familiar in America through performances at the Metropolitan Opera House, New York, where it was first given on March 6, 1918.

The opera tells, in terms of fantasy and wit, the story of King Dodon, to whom an Astrologer presents a magic bird, the Golden Cockerel, whose crowing will warn the King when dangers threaten. The King in return pledges himself to grant the Astrologer's dearest wish, but he expresses none. Presently, the cock crows, warning of peril, and the King's sons, and finally the King himself, go off to the wars. The princes are killed, and the King falls victim to the charms of the mysterious and beautiful Queen of Shemakha and carries her back to his capitol as his bride. Now the Astrologer reappears and demands his reward: the Queen. The King refuses, and is attacked and killed by the magic bird. Amid thunder and lightning, the Astrologer and the Queen vanish. The tale is framed in a prologue and epilogue of enigmatic character, spoken—or rather, sung—by the Astrologer.

Rimsky-Korsakoff's librettist, Vladimir Bielsky, based his text on the celebrated tale by Pushkin. Bielsky observes in his preface: 'The purely human
nature of Pushkin's *Golden Cockerel*—that instructive tragi-comedy of the
unhappy consequences following upon mortal passions and weaknesses—permits us to place the plot in any region and in any period.' Some have thought
this a rather feeble attempt to fool the censor.

Excerpts from the opera were arranged as a concert suite 'in accordance [so
says a note in the score] with the composer's intentions, carried out by Alexander Glazounoff and Maximilian Steinberg.'

● SUITE FROM *The Tale of Czar Saltan*, OP. 57

This suite was put together by Rimsky-Korsakoff from the music of his opera,
The Tale of Czar Saltan. The opera, to a libretto by Bielsky, after Pushkin's
fairy-tale in verse, was composed in 1899-1900 and produced by the Private
Opera Company of Moscow in December 1900. The suite, in three movements, was performed at St. Petersburg shortly before the production of the
opera.

The events of Pushkin's fairy-tale took place in that magical era when it
was unsafe to express a wish, because it might come true. In those days there
lived in Russia a malefactor of great wealth who had three daughters. Now
each of these daughters nourished in her heart a desire to marry the Czar
Saltan, who was young and good to look upon; and so the sisters, talking among
themselves, uttered each her wish, and told what she would do to compensate
her royal spouse if she should win him. The first declared that she would
bake for him bread made from flour of priceless quality. The second swore that
she would weave for him such linen as had never issued from the loom; the
third—who seems to have possessed only those routine abilities conferred on
her by Nature—promised to bear her lord such offspring as would bring glory
to the royal line.

It so happened that Czar Saltan was an earnest sociologist and a doer of
public welfare work. It was the Czar's amiable habit to go secretly among his
people after nightfall in order that he might learn their problems and their
needs; and, so doing, he overheard the confidences of the three sisters. Being
supplied, apparently, with a satisfactory chef as well as sufficient tablecloths
and nighties, he 'plumped' for the youngest sister—she who had dedicated
herself to the holy task of maintaining the supply of Czars; and within no
time at all they were One.

But alas, the royal honeymoon was brusquely interrupted. A war was raging,
and duty summoned the bridegroom to the front. In order that his bride might
not lack companionship in his absence, Saltan arranged that the two elder
sisters should come to live with her. It was a fatal move, for thereby he took
into his household two vipers—spinster vipers, at that. And now the troubles
of the royal family began. The envious sisters contrived a plot. They sent to
the Czar a false and disconcerting message to the effect that the Czarina in
his absence had given birth not to a proper heir, according to contract, but to,
instead, 'a beasty strange and dwarfish.' And so it befell that the unfortunate

Czarina and her young son were condemned to banishment and cast upon the waters in a barrel.

But the destiny which in those times watched over the fate of Czars was benign and devoted, and the barrel drifted upon an island—the magic island of Buyan. Here the Czarevich waxed and flourished, and good fortune lay across his path. Saving a swan from a pursuing pike, he was rewarded with mighty powers. Upon the island's cliffs and deserts there rose at his command a wondrous city, where gardens blossomed overnight, and palaces flaunted their gleaming turrets against the dawn, and happiness was to be had for the asking. And this island was called the Island of the Three Wonders, because of the trio of miracles revealed to those who dwelt upon it.

There was first the Wonder of the Squirrel that gathered nuts of gold and emerald, the while it merrily whistled Russian folk songs. Secondly, there was the Wonder of the Three and Thirty Warriors, who, full-armed and helmeted in gold, were cast upon the Island's shore by thunderous seas. Thirdly, there was the Wonder of the ineffable Princess, garlanded with stars, the moonlight tangled in her braids, who, like Isolde, loved the night and was fearful of the day. She it was, as you may have guessed, whom the Czarevich had really saved in rescuing the Swan; for then the Princess resumed her proper human form, and most indulgently agreed to share the royal throne.

It was not long before Czar Saltan, returning from the wars and learning of all that had happened in his absence, hastened to the enchanted isle, where, beyond a doubt, the marvelously resourceful squirrel had prepared for him a welcoming nut-sundae, frosted (somewhat indigestibly, you might think) with gold, while the Swan-Queen held hands with the Czarevich under the banquet board and blushed beneath her diadem of stars, and the Czarina happily dispensed the emerald tarts.

Rimsky gave to his suite the title, 'Musical Pictures'; and each of the tonal 'pictures' is prefixed in the orchestral score by lines from Pushkin's charming fairy-tale. The first 'picture' is headed by a verse telling of Czar Saltan's departure for the wars, and his parting admonition to his bride. There are eight introductory measures (Allegro, 2-4) consisting of a trumpet fanfare; and these fanfares preface each of the other 'pictures' (they brought down upon Rimsky-Korsakoff's head the horrid charge that he betrayed therein 'an undue reverence for the ceremonial of Bayreuth'). The main theme ('Allegretto alla marcia') is a gallant tune given first to two flutes and two clarinets, with the tambourine marking beats. Martial rhythms are suggested almost throughout by the trumpets or the instruments of percussion.

The second 'picture' is prefaced by the lines from Pushkin's poem that tell of the barrel and its human prisoners adrift on the sea. This movement is a lament. After the introductory fanfare, 'cellos and violas begin a persistent wave-like figure above long-sustained chords for bassoons, horns, trumpets, trombones and tuba, forte, with a roll of the timpani (Maestoso, 3-2). The flute complains in a sighing chromatic phrase colored mournfully by diminished-seventh harmonies in the horns and woodwind. The arpeggio figure returns in the lower strings, accompanying a dolorous melody for flutes and clarinets. There is an outburst of the full orchestra, fortissimo, on a sobbing chromatic figure for the violins and woodwind. This despairing outburst is repeated, and the first complaining sigh of the flute is heard, now transferred to violins and violas harmonized in thirds. There is a quiet close. The cask drifts on under the stars.

The third and last movement of Rimsky's suite is prefaced in the score by a long description of the miraculous isle. Here Rimsky-Korsakoff is in his element as a tone painter of the marvelous and the fantastic. No one has quite his touch as a spinner of orchestral fairy-tales, as a wizard of the incredible. Like Maeterlinck's Tyltyl, he has only to turn the jewel in his magic cap and we are transported to the world at the back of the heavens, where wonders and enchantments are as daily bread, and only the commonplace is strange.

The familiar trumpet call is heard, and it is repeated frequently in the course of this movement. The rhythm of the trumpet call, Presto, brings a jubilant conclusion.

The familiar concert number entitled 'The Flight of the Bumble-Bee' is derived from the first scene of the second act of the opera. Rimsky did not include it in the score of his suite.

● *Sadko: A Tone Picture*, OP. 5

Rimsky-Korsakoff, who as a young man served as an officer in the Russian Navy, disclosed in his music a striking power of delineating the moods and aspects of the sea. His *Sadko: Tableau symphonique*, op. 5, composed in 1867, when Rimsky was twenty-three, has often been called 'the first Russian symphonic poem,' though Balakireff's *Russia* was composed in 1862. Rimsky revised his tone poem in 1891.

The score contains this preface:

The vessel of Sadko, a famous *gusli* player of Novgorod, is becalmed at sea. Sadko, marked by Fate, is thrown overboard with his *gusli* as a propitiatory offering to the Sea King, while the vessel pursues its course.

Sadko, in the ocean depths, is received by the Sea King, and finds himself in the midst of a great festival: for the King is celebrating the marriage of his daughter to the Ocean. He compels Sadko to play upon his *gusli*. The King and all his Court begin to dance to Sadko's music. The dance grows wilder and wilder, the sea becomes stormier and stormier. Sadko breaks the strings of his *gusli*, the merriment and the dancing come to an end, and once more the sea is calm and the depths are dark and still.

The work is scored for two flutes and piccolo, two oboes, two clarinets, two bassoons, four horns, two trumpets, three trombones, tuba, timpani, bass drum, cymbals, tam-tam, harp, and strings. It is dedicated to Balakireff.

Rimsky-Korsakoff returned to the legend of *Sadko* in another and far more ambitious work, his opera, *Sadko: A Musical Legend*, completed in 1896. The opera contains material drawn from the tone poem. It was produced at Moscow in December 1897.

● OVERTURE, *La Grande Pâque Russe* (*The Russian Easter*), OP. 36

Rimsky-Korsakoff composed his *Russian Easter* Overture in the same year as *Schéhérazade* (1888). In it, he used thematic material drawn from the music

of the Russian Church, and he prefaced the score with the following program
—a mixture of quotations from the Old and New Testaments and sentences
of his own authorship:

Let God arise, let His enemies be scattered: let them also that hate Him flee before
Him.

As smoke is driven away, so drive them away; as wax melteth before the fire, so let
the wicked perish at the presence of God. (Psalm LXVIII. 1-2.)

And when the Sabbath was past, Mary Magdalene and Mary, the Mother of James,
and Salome, had bought sweet spices, that they might come and anoint Him. And very
early in the morning, the first day of the week, they came unto the sepulchre at the
rising of the sun. And they said among themselves, Who shall roll us away the stone
from the door of the sepulchre? And when they looked, they saw that the stone was
rolled away: for it was very great.

And entering into the sepulchre, they saw a young man sitting on the right side,
clothed in a long, white garment: and they were affrighted. And he saith unto them,
Be not affrighted: ye seek Jesus of Nazareth, which was crucified: He is risen. (Mark
XVI. 1-6.)

And the joyful tidings were spread abroad all over the world, and they who hated
Him fled before Him, vanishing like smoke.

'Resurrexit!' sing the chorus of Angels in heaven to the sound of the Archangels'
trumpets and the fluttering of the wings of the Seraphim. 'Resurrexit!' sing the priests
in the temples, in the midst of clouds of incense, by the light of innumerable candles,
to the chiming of triumphant bells.

It was Rimsky's opinion that to appreciate his overture, the hearer must
have attended the Easter morning service of the Russian Church—'at least
once,' he added cautiously. As it has turned out, greater confidence on his part
in the power of his music to evoke the hieretic splendors of the service would
have been fully justified.

● Capriccio Espagnol, OP. 34

Rimsky-Korsakoff in his autobiography tells us much that is interesting concerning his *Spanish Caprice*. He had intended to write 'a virtuoso violin fantasy' (as he refers to it) on Spanish themes; but he composed the *Spanish
Caprice* instead from the sketches that he had made for the violin piece.
'According to my plans,' he says, 'the "Capriccio" was to glitter with dazzling
orchestral color, and, manifestly, I had not been wrong.' The first performance
of the work was at a Russian symphony concert in Petrograd, October 31, 1887.

There are five movements in the suite, intended by the composer to be
played without pause.

I. 'ALBORADA' ('Vivo e strepitoso,' A major, 2-4). This is a kind of morning
serenade, or, more strictly, an aubade. The movement is derived from the energetic opening theme.

II. VARIATIONS ('Andante con moto,' F major, 3-8 time). The five variations
that constitute this movement are evolved from the horn theme that is heard
at first over a string accompaniment.

III. 'ALBORADA' ('Vivo e strepitoso,' B-flat major, 2-4 time). This is virtually
a repetition of the first movement, with the key changed from A major to
B-flat major, and with different scoring.

IV. 'Scene and Gypsy Song' (Allegretto, D minor, 6-8 time). The first part of this movement consists of a chain of cadenzas: the first for horns and trumpets, the second for solo violin, the third for flute, the fourth for clarinet, the fifth for harp. A glissando introduces the 'Gypsy Song,' which is begun by the first violins over chords for the trombones and tuba, punctuated by the cymbals. The tempo grows more and more animated, and at the height of its impetuosity it passes into the finale.

V. 'Fandango of the Asturias' (A major, 3-4 time). The fandango is an Andalusian dance, a variety of the Seguidilla, traditionally with guitar and castanet accompaniment. The tune of Rimsky's fandango in this number is announced at the start by the trombones, with accompaniment of the full orchestra. The Alborada of the first movement recurs as a coda, vivo.

Tchaikovsky greatly admired the *Capriccio Espagnol*. He wrote to Rimsky-Korsakoff in November 1886: 'I must add that your "Spanish Caprice" is a *colossal masterpiece of instrumentation* [Tchaikovsky's italics], and you may regard yourself as the greatest master of the present day.'

Gioachino Antonio Rossini

1792-1868

R

‡Rossini composed his first opera at the age of eighteen, and his thirty-sixth and last some nineteen years later. Though he lived for nearly forty years following the completion of his *William Tell*, he never again wrote for the theater. Various theories have been advanced to account for this wholly voluntary inactivity, of which the least flattering are probably also the least true. Circumstances imposed a temporary silence on Rossini; still other circumstances led to extensions of the sentence; and thus were forged the chains of sloth from which, later, he neither was able nor wished to free himself. His successes as a young man had been spectacular and had earned him a fortune which now enabled him to live elaborately without giving thought to the morrow; his works held the stages of the world, and honors continued to accrue to him, like interest on gilt-edged securities, without effort on his part. It would have required deeper and more urgent drives than any he had ever felt to force him, thus situated, to resume an activity which could bring him no material advantages he did not already possess in abundance. If it is argued that as a genius he had responsibilities beyond those of ordinary men, it may be answered that he discharged them: for *The Barber of Seville, Semiramide, William*

Tell and half a dozen other of his operas are among the treasures of the literature.‡

- OVERTURE TO *The Barber of Seville*

Rossini's opera, originally entitled *Almaviva, ossia l'inutile Precauzione,* was produced at Rome on February 5, 1816; in London on March 10, 1818; at Paris on October 26, 1819. But five months before, New York had scored a beat on Paris, at least: for the opera was given at the old Park Theater (then in Chambers Street, east of Broadway), in English, on May 17, 1819, with the quaintly named Miss Leesugg as Rosina.

Rossini had composed his opera in thirteen days—some say fifteen. Incredulous ones, hearing the report that he had done so, asked Donizetti if he believed that Rossini had really written the score in thirteen days. 'It is quite possible,' answered Donizetti; 'he is so lazy!'

Because of the partisanship of the Romans for Paisiello, who had treated the same subject in his famous *Barber* (composed twenty-six years before), Rossini's opera was a fiasco on its first production at Rome; but within a week it had conquered opposition, and was a howling success.

Rossini lived for half a century after *Il Barbiere di Siviglia* had made its triumphal way through the world, but he never put himself to the trouble of replacing the original overture to the work, which had been lost soon after the first production. The overture which leads us into the opera nowadays was borrowed from Rossini's earlier opera *Elisabetta, Regina d'Inghilterra*—to which, in turn, it had been adapted from the overture to the still earlier *Aureliano in Palmira.* 'Persons with fantastic imaginations,' remarks Krehbiel frostily, 'have rhapsodized on its appositeness, and professed to hear in it the whispered plottings of the lovers and the merry raillery of Rosina . . . but when Rossini composed this music, its mission was to introduce an adventure of the Emperor Aurelian in Palmyra in the third century of the Christian era. . . Truly, the verities of time and place sat lightly on the Italian opera composers of a hundred years ago.'

- OVERTURE TO *Cenerentola*

Rossini, probably the laziest of composers ('Next to doing nothing,' he said to Blaze de Bury, 'I know no more delightful occupation than eating'), nevertheless wrote twenty operas within a certain eight-year period: 1815-23. One of them was *Cenerentola, ossia la bontà in trionfo* ('Cinderella, or Virtue Triumphant'). The subject was suggested to him by the manager of the Teatro Valle at Rome. But the stage equipment of the smaller Italian theaters at that time was so inadequate that Rossini had the good sense to stipulate that he would accept the subject proposed to him only upon condition that the supernatural elements be completely omitted. A libretto conforming to this requirement was written by Ferretti, and Rossini set it to music. The opera was produced during the Carnival of 1817 with emphatic success.

Gustave Chouquet, in his biography of Rossini, insists that in the profusion and charm of its ideas 'this delicious work is probably equal to *Il Barbiere di*

Siviglia, but it is inferior in unity and style. No doubt this is partly owing to the fact that many of the pieces were originally composed to other words. The duet, "Un soave non so chè," the drinking chorus, and the mock proclamation of the Baron, are all borrowed from *La Pietra del Paragone* [Milan, 1812]. The air, "Miei rampolli," is from *La Gazzetta* [Naples, 1816]; other passages are derived from *Turco in Italia.*'

The overture has an introduction, maestoso, which leads to the main portion of the work, 'Allegro vivace,' begun by a subject for the strings. A modulation to the minor has suggested to a commentator the thought of Cinderella weeping; 'but soon we are back in the sunshine.'

- Overture to *La Gazza Ladra*

Rossini's opera, *La Gazza Ladra* ('The Thieving Magpie'), in two acts, Italian libretto by Tommaso Gherardi del Testa (founded on the French play, *La Pie voleuse; ou, La Servante de Palaiseau*, by Louis Charles Caigniez and Jean Marie Théodore Baudouin) was produced at La Scala, Milan, May 31, 1817, when Rossini was in his twenty-sixth year.

The story of *La Gazza Ladra* tells the half-comic, half-melodramatic tale. of a little servant girl, who, on circumstantial evidence (which cannot be rebutted owing to the necessity of shielding her father from arrest as a deserter) is condemned to death for the theft of a silver spoon which has in reality been hidden by a pet magpie. The plot is complicated by the fact that the servant girl and her mistress's son are secretly engaged, much to the mother's disgust, and that the ruling official of the town, in whose hands her fate lies, is animated by intentions toward her that are strictly dishonorable. Everything, however, ends happily, but not before the audience has been pleasantly stirred.

Rossini had planned his opera shrewdly, for the Milanese took it to their hearts at the première. Stendahl, who was present, summed up the evening as the most successful first night he had ever attended. The audience, he reported, was so excited after the overture that, contrary to custom, everybody began talking to his neighbor, and Rossini was acclaimed. The opera remained the most popular item in the repertoire throughout the season.

Toye goes so far as to call the Overture to *La Gazza Ladra* 'possibly, after *William Tell*, the best of all Rossini's overtures.' Apart, he says, 'from the fact that the themes are in themselves excellent, it is characterized by a directness which was at that time quite new. Moreover, it possesses some links with the opera as a whole. The orchestration, too, even some of the harmonic schemes, must have seemed very bold to the opera's first audiences.'

The opera, though it had a long life—especially in France—seems now to be almost, if not quite, dead.

- Overture to *L'Italiana in Algeri*

Rossini's opera buffa in two acts, *L'Italiana in Algeri* ('The Italian Woman in Algiers') was produced at Venice May 22, 1813, with immense success. Rossini was a young man of twenty-one, with his masterpiece, *Il Barbiere di Siviglia*, still three years ahead of him.

The overture is one of those typically Rossinian ones composed, remarks Lionel Dauriac, in his Life of Rossini, 'in a manner of a symphonic Allegro: at first, for exordium, an Andante (3-4). Then the main movement (Allegro, 4-4). This is followed by a development with a repeat; to nourish this development, two themes, the second of which appears at first in the relative key of the overture. When the first theme returns, it brings the second in its train, and all ends, as in a symphony by Haydn, in the opening key. And the crescendo—the famous Rossinian crescendo?—the crescendo holds its place: it ends the first repeat, and returns in the peroration.'

● OVERTURE TO *Semiramide*

Rossini's opera, *Semiramide*, was composed for the Carnival of Venice, and was produced at the Venice Theater, February 3, 1823. Rossini declared that he wrote it at his leisure—'My contract allowed me forty days, but I was not forty days in composing it.' Rossini had demanded as payment 5000 francs, hoping that he would be refused.

The text of *Semiramide* is based on Voltaire's tragedy *Semiramis*. Philip Hale has told us that there are more than thirty operas with Semiramis as heroine Myth identifies her as the wife of Ninus, and co-founder with him of Nineveh. She succeeded her husband on the throne (some say she murdered him with this end in view), and reigned for over forty years. According to the indispensable Dr. William Smith, 'She built numerous cities and erected many wonderful buildings . . . she built the city of Babylon, with all its wonders; and she constructed the hanging gardens in Media, of which later writers give us such strange accounts.'

The overture to Rossini's opera opens with a long timpani roll on D, and a sotto voce figure for the violas and 'cellos ('Allegro vivace,' D major, 6-8). A crescendo draws in the full orchestra, and after three *ff* chords there is a fermata. An Andantino section follows (it is introduced by the horns in four-part harmony). The thematic material of this section derives from the Quintet and the Finale of Act I. The Allegro begins in the strings, sotto voce (D major, 4-4 time). The subject matter recalls a chorus in Act II of the opera.

● OVERTURE TO *Il Signor Bruschino*

Rossini's *Il Signor Bruschino, ossia Il Figlio per Azzardo*, 'farsa giocosa' in one act, the libretto by Giuseppe Foppa, was produced late in January 1813, during the Carnival, at the Teatro Giustiniani (San Moise), Venice. The year 1813 was that of *Tancredi* and *L'Italiana in Algeri*; Rossini was just under twenty-one. According to most of his biographers, he composed his farce in revenge for an ugly joke that the manager of the San Moise theater tried to play on him. Having a grudge against Rossini, this individual is reported to have compelled him to fulfill an earlier agreement to compose an opera for the San Moise theater, and to have supplied him for the purpose with an impossible libretto which, had Rossini treated it seriously, would have spelled disaster. But the ready-witted Rossini easily turned the situation to his advantage, burlesquing the libretto in his musical treatment of it, introducing into his score all sorts of outrageous pranks.

But according to the monumental and authoritative Life of Rossini published in three volumes, between 1927 and 1929, by Giuseppe Radiciotti, this story has little basis in fact. It is Radiciotti's belief that Rossini's earlier biographers did not take the trouble to examine either the libretto or the score of *Il Signor Bruschino*. Of the various alleged jocosities that most writers ascribe to the work, there are actually only two to be found in it. One of these jests is that which occurs in the overture, where the second violin players are directed to strike with their bows the tin shades of their desk lamps at certain points in the score and for a few consecutive bars (the first place occurs at the thirty-second measure). 'I admit,' says Radiciotti, 'that the libretto is a silly piece of buffoonery. But it is hardly worse than other librettos that pleased the Italian public of the day. As to the music, I have verified the fact that it is not at all mediocre.'

The opera failed at Venice in 1813 and was unperformed until June 1844, when it was sung at the Carcano Theater, Milan. In Paris, thirteen years later, the librettist Desforges made an adaptation of the original Italian text, and Rossini's music was fitted to this in an arrangement by Offenbach. The result was performed at the Bouffes Parisiens, December 29, 1857, under the title *Bruschino*. It was received with acclaim. Rossini, though he was at that time in Paris, refused to hear his youthful work thus revamped. He was invited to attend a rehearsal but declined firmly. 'I give you permission,' he said, 'to do what you have done. But I refuse absolutely to become an accomplice.'

● OVERTURE TO *William Tell*

Let those who may be inclined to view the Overture to *William Tell* as what our French friends call 'old hat,' take note of the fact that the genius of Rossini bulks large in the modern critical view. Rossini has become fashionable again. Alfredo Casella has bid us pause and consider the transcendent merits of the old Italian. He confessed (under the title: 'Some Reasons Why a Futurist May Admire Rossini') that he 'adores' the composer of *William Tell*. There is none among his operas that does not seem to Casella to 'bear the stamp of genius.' 'The imagination is inexhaustible, the verve infinite, the rhythmic power perpetually alert, the harmony often cunning, the orchestration astoundingly novel and even audacious for the period, and the melody incomparably fresh and full of grace and taste.' 'Incomparably,' to be sure, is a brave word; although Casella rightly insists upon the admirable taste of Rossini at his best. 'If time,' he observes, 'has wrinkled his art, the original nobility of its features remains visible, and the "pure breed" of this or that page, though remote today, remains undefiled.'

William Tell was produced at the Paris Opéra August 3, 1829; and with this work Rossini downed his tools as an opera-maker and never again wrote for the stage—though he was only thirty-seven, was dazzlingly successful, in perfect health and excellent spirits, and lived thirty-nine years longer. Apthorp thinks he was too lazy to produce further operas of the caliber of *Tell*, and too proud to revert to his earlier Italian manner: 'he preferred not writing at all to not writing easily.'

We all know the traditional poetic and dramatic contents of the famous overture—its opening suggestion of the mountain sunrise, the gathering Alpine storm, the clearing, the shepherds' song of thanks and the 'Ranz des Vaches' of the English horn; the summoning trumpet calls and the march of the Swiss soldiers—these things are still potent, dramatically and tonally vivid.

Camille Saint-Saëns

1835-1921

When Camille Saint-Saëns died at Algiers on December 10, 1921, he was full of years and full of honors, a salient and ironic figure who summed up in his brilliant and chameleonic personality many tendencies, many styles. He had absorbed innumerable influences—almost all that were available, indeed, save the influence of the heterodox, whom he abhorred. His was an astonishing career, a career dazzling in its record of varied and successful accomplishment, of popularity won and retained. Applauded by the sophisticated for his scholarship and technical mastery, Saint-Saëns knew how to make those traits palatable to the ingenuous. ‡A famous musician, asked to identify a work by Saint-Saëns that was played to him anonymously answered without hesitation, 'Saint-Saëns!' And when he was asked how he had known, he replied, 'The first movement sounded like Schumann, the second like Mendelssohn, and the third like Franck—but neither Schumann nor Mendelssohn nor Franck wrote for the music-hall.' Saint-Saëns was rightly praised for his 'skill in the adaptation of means to an end': the end he never lost sight of was popularity, and the means that never failed him was imitation of his betters. A surprising number of his works survive, such is the charm of adroit and complacent vulgarity.‡

• SYMPHONY NO. 3, IN C MINOR, OP. 78

Saint-Saëns composed this symphony for the London Philharmonic Society, and he himself conducted its first performance at a concert of that venerable organization in London on May 19, 1886. Less than a year later, Theodore Thomas, who let no symphonic grass grow under his feet without promptly making hay of it for the American market, displayed the new symphony of

Saint-Saëns at a concert of the Philharmonic Society of New York on February 19, 1887.

When the symphony was first performed in London, it was explained that the two divisions of the work were equivalent to the conventional four: 'The first [movement], checked in development, serves as an introduction to the Adagio; and the Scherzo is connected, after the same manner, with the Finale.' Thus, it was explained, had the composer 'sought to shun in a certain measure the interminable repetitions which are more and more disappearing from instrumental music.' The symphony is scored for large orchestra, with the addition of organ and piano (two players are required at the latter instrument), and it was noted in this connection that 'the composer thinks that the time has come for the symphony to benefit by the progress of modern instrumentation.' In the symphony, the Lisztian principle of the 'metamorphosis of themes' is extensively employed, and the principal theme of the first 'Allegro moderato' (which is preceded by a few measures of introduction, Adagio) recurs in one form or another throughout the work.

The fact that the published score of this symphony is dedicated 'To the Memory of Franz Liszt' has made trouble for incautious commentators. An eminent musical educator, for example, once published the discovery that 'the program of this, the composer's greatest symphonic work, is contained in the dedication. All his life, Saint-Saëns was a devoted admirer and friend of Liszt, and into this work he seems to have poured all the emotions which the memory of the great master stirred in him. The first part of the first movement is a Lamentoso in which the strings, in a gentle murmur, or river of tears . . . accompany the main theme, which seems to express eloquently the grief of the composer at the death of his great friend.'

If Saint-Saëns when he composed this symphony was expressing grief at the death of Liszt, he was in rather an unseemly hurry over the matter, for Liszt was still alive when the symphony was composed. He died July 31, 1886, more than two months after its first performance. The placing of his name upon the score was evidently an afterthought. If it is necessary to discover a 'river of tears' in Saint-Saëns' symphony, it would be more in accord with the facts of musical history if we could manage to trace it to some other source than the composer's 'grief' over the death of a friend who was still conspicuously alive.

• SYMPHONIC POEM, *Le Rouet d'Omphale*, OP. 31

Le Rouet d'Omphale ('Omphale's Spinning-Wheel') was the first of Saint-Saëns' symphonic poems. It dates from 1871, and was originally a piano piece. These sentences, in French, introduce the score:

> The subject of this symphonic poem is feminine seductiveness, the triumphant contest of weakness against strength. The spinning-wheel is merely a pretext; it is chosen simply for the sake of its rhythmical suggestion and from the viewpoint of the general form of the piece.

The note conveys the further and slightly ironical information that 'those who are interested in the study of details will see, at letter J [page 19 of the score] Hercules groaning in the bonds which he cannot break [a labouring phrase in the 'cellos, double-basses, bassoons, double-bassoon, and trombone, repeated with cumulative expression], and at letter L [page 32 of the score] Omphale deriding the hero's futile efforts'—a theme sung by the oboe, in 6-8 time, C major, above a reiterated major-second in the clarinets, introduced by a soft stroke of the triangle. Nor is it unreasonable to hear in the music of the opening pages (though Saint-Saëns said nothing about this) a suggestion of the spinning-wheel performing its accustomed function.

The symphonic poem has been interpreted as falling naturally into the three following sections: '(1) the power of feminine allurement. Triumphant struggle of weakness against strength; in fact, Omphale's fascination of Hercules. (2) Hercules in bondage; or, as the author has it, "Hercules groaning in the bonds which he cannot break." (3) Omphale deriding the vain efforts of the hero.'

● Symphonic Poem, *Phaëton*, op. 39

This, the second in order of composition of Saint-Saëns' symphonic poems, was written in 1873 and published two years later. The score has this preface:

Phaëton has obtained permission to drive across the heavens the chariot of the Sun, his father. But his unskillful hands lead the coursers astray. The blazing chariot, swerving from its path, approaches the terrestrial region. The entire universe is endangered by the flames, when Jupiter strikes with his thunderbolts the presumptuous Phaëton.

Phaethon, says the priceless Dr. Smith, means in Greek 'the shining,' and is used as an 'epithet or surname of Helios (the Sun), but is more commonly known as the name of a son of Helios by Clymene.' Zeus, in the legend, disposed of the trouble-making Phaethon by killing him with a flash of lightning and hurling him down into the river Eridanus. His sisters (the Heliadae or Phaethontiades), 'who yoked the horses to the chariot, were metamorphosed into poplars, and their tears into amber.'

After four introductory measures, the memorable drive begins in the orchestra, the gallop of the horses suggested by a repeated figure in the strings, then in the woodwind and horns. The chief theme is proclaimed by trumpets and trombones in unison. The suave and noble theme that is heard later for the horns in four-part harmony has been thought by some to suggest celestial visions glimpsed by the charioteer in the course of his flight. It has also been said to represent 'nymphs bemoaning Phaëton's danger, and, at last, his death.' The furious rhythm of the drive is heard again, but is cut short by the Jovian thunderbolt (kettledrums, bass drum, cymbals, tam-tam, *fff*). Then, as the crash of the catastrophe dies away, we hear again the august harmonies of the second theme. There is a reminiscence of the main theme, and a pianissimo close.

● Symphonic Poem, *Danse Macabre*, op. 40

The third and most famous of Saint-Saëns' symphonic poems, *Danse Macabre* ('Dance of Death' is a loose but serviceable English paraphrase), was composed in 1874. It illustrates the type of gaily mortuary poetry which Rossetti once referred to as 'lively little ballads of the tomb.' The verses were written by the Frenchman Henri Cazalis, and are quoted on a fly-leaf of Saint-Saëns' score. Here is an English version of them (by an unknown translator):

> Zig, zig, zig, Death in cadence,
> Striking with his heel a tomb,
> Death at midnight plays a dance-tune,
> Zig, zig, zig, on his violin.
> The winter wind blows and the night is dark;
> Moans are heard in the linden-trees.
> Through the gloom, white skeletons pass,
> Running and leaping in their shrouds.
> Zig, zig, zig, each one is frisking,
> The bones of the dancers are heard to crack—
> But hist! of a sudden they quit the round,
> They push forward, they fly; the cock has crowed.

Midnight strikes in the orchestra. Death begins his fiddling, and the clattering of the dancers' bones is suggested by the xylophone. The grisly merriment grows wilder and wilder, but it is suddenly cut short as the first streak of daylight brightens in the horns, while the oboe crows cheerily. The skeletons vanish, the Supreme Concertmaster grins ironically as he packs his fiddle, and again—for a little while—the birds sing heedlessly in the orchard and the living forget their doom.

● *Le Carnaval des animaux: Grande Fantasie zoölogique*

'The Carnival of the Animals,' a 'grand zoological fantasia,' was composed by Saint-Saëns in his thirty-second or thirty-third year (the historians are not agreed as to the date, but it was either 1886 or 1887). Saint-Saëns lived for a generation longer; but he permitted only a few performances of the work, under special conditions, and the music was not published until after his death —although one inhabitant of this tonal zoo, the *Swan*, escaped through the bars and defied recapture.

Probably Walter Damrosch, in his comments on this work at his performance of it for the first time in New York (October 29, 1922), guessed right: he conjectured that Saint-Saëns withheld the work from complete publicity because he distrusted the sense of humor of the average musical audience. No doubt Saint-Saëns shuddered over the certainty that pious academic souls would rebuke him solemnly for 'diverting music from its proper sphere'; no doubt he was bored by the anticipated necessity of reminding them that a good jest, tersely and pointedly told, is a welcome thing even in the haunts of the Ninth Symphony and the *Liebestod*. So he probably smiled sourly to himself, boarded up his Zoo, and hid the key. Two months after his death, the animals disported themselves in full publicity at a Colonne concert in Paris conducted by Gabriel Pierné, February 25, 1922.

The *Carnaval* is a suite in fourteen movements for two pianos, two violins, viola, 'cello, double-bass, flute, clarinet, celesta, and xylophone. The participants in Saint-Saëns' tonal circus may thus be briefly introduced:

I. 'INTRODUCTION AND ROYAL MARCH OF THE LION' ('Andante maestoso,' 4-4; 'Allegro non troppo'): After the slow introduction, the roaring of the jungle's lord may be heard in the chromatic scale passages for the pianos and low strings.

II. 'HENS AND ROOSTERS' ('Allegro moderato,' 4-4): The two pianos, clarinet, and strings crow and cackle irresistibly.

III. 'WILD ASSES' ('Presto furioso'): These 'animaux véloces,' as Saint-Saëns characterizes them, race madly up and down the pianists' keyboards.

IV. 'TORTOISES' ('Andante maestoso,' 4-4): The strings and first piano play in absurdly sluggish tempo two famous tunes from the dance music of Offenbach's *Orphée aux Enfers*.

V. 'THE ELEPHANT' ('Allegretto pomposo,' 3-8): Our long-nosed friend gambols with the careless grace of a frolicsome stone-crusher to a double-bass tune which recalls measures from the 'Dance of Sylphs' out of Berlioz's *Damnation of Faust*, and there is a hint of Mendelssohn's *Midsummer Night's Dream* music.

VI. 'KANGAROOS' (Moderato, 4-4): The delineation of the grotesque hopping and skipping of these astonishing beasts has been entrusted by Saint-Saëns to the two pianos alone.

VII. 'AQUARIUM' (Andantino, 4-4): The celesta, flute, and muted strings, with liquid-toned piano arpeggios, paint the moving and shimmering of the waters with their darting iridescent swimmers.

VIII. 'PERSONS WITH LONG EARS' (Tempo *ad lib.*, 3-4): These parties (as Mark Twain would have called them) bray alternately in the first and second violins.

IX. 'THE CUCKOO IN THE HEART OF THE WOODS' (Andante, 3-4): This is one of the poetical interludes of the suite—for the *Carnival* is not remorselessly jocose. Meditative piano chords summon the mood of forest solitude, while from afar is heard the call of the cuckoo (played off-stage, with exquisite effect, by the clarinet).

X. 'THE AVIARY' ('Moderato grazioso,' 3-4): With the twittering of flute, strings, and pianos, the orchestra becomes a bird-house—here, again, humor is subdued by charm.

XI. 'PIANISTS' ('Allegro moderato,' 4-4): What these almost-human creatures are doing in a Grand Zoological Fantasy is not explained by the composer. Ernest La Prade, in his charming program notes for Damrosch's performance of the *Carnival*, wondered if Saint-Saëns 'meant to imply that pianists—beginners, at least—are dangerous beasts that ought to be kept behind bars; or does he suggest that they would be better seen than heard? The hearer may decide after listening to this delightful parody of a Czerny exercise (piano and strings).'

XII. 'FOSSILS' ('Allegro ridicolo,' 2-2): Here Saint-Saëns most amiably burlesques himself: for he parodies his own *Danse Macabre* as well as certain tunes which apparently had become to him a weariness of the flesh—three old French songs ('J'ai du bon tabac,' 'Ah! vous dirai-je maman,' 'Partant pour la Syrie'), and one of Rosina's airs from *The Barber of Seville*. This section enlists the xylophone, clarinet, strings, and pianos.

XIII. 'The Swan' ('Andantino grazioso,' 6-4): This thrice-familiar piece (it was published thirty-six years ago in a version for 'cello solo with piano accompaniment) needs no introduction. The song of the 'cello is supported here by both pianos.

XIV. Finale ('Molto allegro,' 4-4): In this concluding section, for all the instruments, most of the animals reappear for a final roar, cackle, twitter, dance, or bray.

● Concerto for Piano and Orchestra, No. 2, in G minor, op. 22

Saint-Saëns' G minor Concerto, was composed and first publically performed (by Saint-Saëns) in 1868. It has been remarked that the 'form of this concerto is defective, like that of Beethoven's Sonata in C-sharp minor, op. 27, No. 2,' because 'what would be technically the first movement is omitted by the composer.' The first movement of the G minor Concerto is in reality the slow movement of the work. It opens, 'Andante sostenuto,' 4-4, with a free contrapuntal cadenza for the solo instrument, ending with a chromatic progression which particularly aroused the admiration of Liszt. The chief theme is presented by the piano after an eight-measure irruption of the orchestra. There is a great deal of exuberant passage-work for the piano, and the soloist's modesty is not encouraged.

The 'Allegretto scherzando' (6-8) that follows assumes the first-movement form. A kettledrum figure introduces the fleet and graceful chief theme in E-flat (piano). 'Cellos and basses have the second theme, which is heard against a strikingly rhythmical effect for the piano. Later, the soloist plays fondly with this subject.

In the third movement (Presto, 2-2), triplet figures in the bass—first for the piano, then for the orchestra—prepare the way for the principal theme (G minor), given to the solo instrument. The assertive second subject enters in A on the piano, rather brazenly adorned with trills. A feature of this movement is the chorale-like passage for orchestra, projected against the irrepressible exuberance of the soloist.

● Concerto for Piano and Orchestra, No. 4, in C minor, op. 44

The C minor Piano Concerto belongs to that period in Saint-Saëns career as a composer during which he created the 'definitive models' (in Octave Séré's phrase) of a genre new to French music: his symphonic poems. The C minor Concerto, written in 1875, stands between the third and fourth of these poems—La Danse Macabre and Jeunesse d'Hercule. It was performed for the first time, with Saint-Saëns himself as soloist, at a Châtelet concert in Paris on October 31, 1875. The work was then played from manuscript; it was not published until 1877.

This concerto illustrates the paradoxical fondness of Saint-Saëns (who was temperamentally a conservative) for taking liberties in his concertos with the traditional requirements of the form—liberties so unsettling that the perplexed analysts have not known quite how to view them. Thus in the C minor Piano Concerto there is first—according to one distinguished commentator—

'a species of introduction' ('Allegro moderato,' C minor, 4-4); but others regard this so-called 'free prelude' as a movement in itself. It is chiefly, in effect, a dialogue between piano and orchestra. This leads without a break to an Andante (A-flat major, 4-4), which exploits a subject of earnest character, exposed by the woodwind, then taken over by the piano. Then follows, after a pause, an 'Allegro vivace' (C minor, 2-4, 6-8), at first of scherzo-like character, succeeded by an Andante section in the same key, 4-4 time. In this movement there are reminiscences of the earlier portions of the work. The Finale (Allegro, C major), which follows without a pause, has somewhat the character of a rondo.

In its qualities as music, this concerto bears out the interpretation of Saint-Saëns' intellectual and artistic character arrived at by Vauzanges, 'an expert who has specialized in the graphology of musicians.' This enquiring graphologist analyzed the handwriting of Saint-Saëns, and declared that it indicated these characteristics of the man and of the artist: 'an intelligence of the first order, one very lucid, very open . . . a clean-cut, vivid and impulsive spirit, remarkably active, one which . . . assimilates with ease, at once creative and practical. . . The writer's taste is very fine, very delicate; his character good, his soul upright; his will-power is gentle, regular, and doubled by tenacity.' If Vauzanges had been a critic instead of a graphologist, he could scarcely have done better.

● Concerto for Piano and Orchestra, No. 5, in F major, op. 103

Early in the year 1896, the versatile and accomplished Monsieur Saint-Saëns found himself in Egypt. What could be more appropriate than to contrive on the banks of the Nile an allegory as memorable as Mrs. Malaprop's? It was no sooner thought of than done, and the issue was the F major Concerto for Piano and Orchestra, in the second movement of which (the Andante) the composer has permitted us to discover, if not quite a musical allegory, at least a tonal symbolization of the Orient in some of its most seizing phases. Since it is not a *Carnaval des Animaux*, no alligators, allegorical or otherwise, need be sought in it; but the Nile is there beyond peradventure. In a communication to a friend, Saint-Saëns explained that the second movement of this concerto (Andante, D minor, 3-4) is 'a sort of musical journey in the East, which, in the F-sharp major episode ('poco più mosso'), goes to the Far East. The section in G major ('allegretto tranquillo quasi andantino') is a Nubian love song which I heard sung by boatmen on the Nile when I went down the river in a dahabeeyah' (the piano has the melody, under an arpeggio figure, with sustained harmonics in the violins).

Neither in the preceding movement ('Allegro animato,' F major, 3-4), nor in the Finale ('Molto allegro,' F major, 2-4), however, are we warranted in seeking any moods, emotions, or tonal memoirs of any kind. They appear to be merely music.

Saint-Saëns himself played this concerto for the first time in Paris on June 2, 1896, at a concert given to celebrate the fiftieth anniversary of his own début in 1846, when, at the age of ten years and seven months, he played the piano for the first time in public.

• Concerto for Violin and Orchestra, No. 1, in A major, op. 20

This early work of Saint-Saëns dates from 1859. It was published in 1868, with a dedication to Sarasate. It is in three connected movements, an Allegro, an 'Andante espressivo,' and a final Allegro. The material of the last movement is related to that of the first, and the concerto therefore exhibits something of the cyclic character to which César Franck's symphony gave popularity and vogue a generation later, and which Saint-Saëns himself exemplified in subsequent works.

The opening Allegro, in A major, 6-4 time, begins, after a chord of the orchestra, with the energetic chief theme for the solo violin. Later, the soloist is allowed to relax in a subsidiary melody of song-like character. This material is embellished in various ways, with plenty of double-stopping and florid passages for the soloist. A cadenza with a long concluding trill leads to the slow movement ('Andante espressivo,' D major, 2-4). The melody is given to the solo violin, 'molto cantabile,' above a 'cello counter-theme, with the muted orchestral strings accompanying.

The Finale, like the slow movement, is introduced by a long trill of the solo violin. The tempo is that of the first Allegro (6-4), and the opening subject is the second theme of the first movement, followed by a return of other familiar material from that movement.

• Introduction and Rondo Capriccioso, for Violin and Orchestra, op. 28

This composition, one of the golden apples of Saint-Saëns' tonal garden which has nourished his fame for well over half a century, dates from his twenty-eighth year. It was composed in 1863, dedicated to Sarasate, was first played by him in Paris, and is (to change our metaphorical key) the most famous of Saint-Saëns' lighter dallyings with the Muse whom he so long and so variously wooed. It is the ideal equivalent in tones of that phenomenon which Dr. Middleton characterized as 'a fantastical planguncula.'

There is a thirty-six measure Introduction. The rest is piquancy almost unalloyed.

• Concerto for 'Cello and Orchestra, No. 1, in A minor, op. 33

This is the first and more frequently played of Saint-Saëns' two concertos for 'cello. The second, in D minor, op. 119, was composed in 1902 (thirty years after the first).

This concerto was written in Saint-Saëns' thirty-eighth year, and August Tolbecque—musician, antiquarian, collector, and man of letters—played it in Paris in January 1873; oddly enough, the concerto turned out to be dedicated to him. This work stands, in order of composition, between the two symphonic poems, Le Rouet d'Omphale (1871) and Phaëton (1873). Saint-Saëns had already composed the first three of his concertos for piano and the first two for violin. Samson et Dalila was five years ahead of him; and he had almost half a century more in which to live and to express his curiously multiform personality.

The three movements of this concerto are continuous, with a pervasive main theme. The work begins 'Allegro non troppo' (A minor, 2-2), and proceeds to an 'Allegretto con moto' (B-flat major, 3-4), in which muted strings and dance tunes make glad the heart; then follows a recurrence of earlier material (as before, 'Allegro non troppo,' 2-2), with a close in A major.

Arnold Schönberg

1874-

S

‡There seems no reason to doubt that Schönberg, now in his late seventies, is one of the two most important figures in the musical history of the twentieth century. The other is, of course, Stravinsky. Virtually all music that employs post-Romantic means to the attainment of post-Romantic ends owes something—owes, often, everything—to the influence of one or the other of these two great innovators. If for the time being the influence of Stravinsky appears dominant, that of Schönberg may well prove the more enduring. For the principles and practices of Schönberg's atonal system (a system which divorces music from tonality, however conceived) are profoundly revolutionary, and at the same time self-consistent and, within the given frame of reference, supremely logical. But while Schönberg's position and authority are everywhere and readily acknowledged by professional musicians and informed and sober-minded observers of the musical scene, his works, aside from the early and immature *Verklärte Nacht*, are all but unknown to the musical public at large, and it would seem that the time had come to rectify an inequity that is said to have caused Schönberg some bitterness.‡

● *Verklärte Nacht*, OP. 4

For those who are unfamiliar with this work, it should be explained that *Verklärte Nacht* represents not the later Schönberg, but the Schönberg who was still a neo-Romantic, haunted by *Tristan und Isolde*. This is not the revolutionary Schönberg of *Pierrot Lunaire*, of the celebrated Five Pieces for Orchestra, of the enigmatic and forbidding little piano studies of op. 11 and op. 19, of *Die Glückliche Hand*, of the orchestral variations. *Verklärte Nacht* belongs to the days of Schönberg's young manhood; he was twenty-five when he wrote it. It was composed in 1899 as a sextet for strings (two violins, two violas, two 'cellos) and was published in that form in 1905.

In 1917, Schönberg published an arrangement of *Verklärte Nacht* for string orchestra—first and second violins, first and second violas, first and second 'cellos, double-basses. The piece is now virtually a symphonic poem for an orchestra of strings, as before it was a symphonic poem for string sextet.

The title page of the original version of *Verklärte Nacht* acknowledges as the source of its inspiration a poem from Richard Dehmel's *Weib und Welt*, and this poem is printed in the score of the sextet, and in the score of the later version for string orchestra. It is a poem uncommonly rich in impassioned imagery; and when the Kneisels played Schönberg's sextet in 1915, there was some scandalized whispering over certain passages in Dehmel's text, which would doubtless seem to the present lost generation as erotically exciting as *The Courtship of Miles Standish.*

The following paraphrase of Dehmel's poem was written by H. E. Krehbiel, and published in his *Tribune* review of the Kneisels' performance of *Verklärte Nacht* in 1915. This synopsis benignly tempered the heated winds of Dehmel's imagination to the shorn lambs of the Comstockian era:

Two mortals walk through a cold, barren grove. The moon sails over the tall oaks, which send their scrawny branches up through the unclouded moonlight. A woman speaks. She confesses a sin to the man at her side. She is with child, and he is not its father. She had lost belief in happiness, and, longing for life's fullness, for motherhood and mother's duty, she had surrendered herself, shuddering, to the embraces of a man she knew not. She had thought herself blessed, but now life had avenged itself upon her by giving her the love of him she walked with.

A man speaks. Let her not burden her soul with thoughts of guilt. See, the moon's sheen enwraps the universe! Together they are driving over chill waters, but a flame from each warms the other. It, too, will transfigure the child, which she will bear to him. For she has inspired the brilliant glow within him and made him, too, a child. They sink into each other's arms. Their breaths meet in kisses in the air. . . Two mortals wander through the wondrous moonlight.

Schönberg when he composed this work was steeped in the romantic mysticism of the 'nineties. The Wagnerian throne had scarcely begun to totter, though Richard II was creating an ominous hubbub in the courtyard. The Schönberg of those days wrote obviously under the influence of the immense enchantment of *Tristan*, and he had listened to Richard Strauss. Yet his accent was his own; his eloquence had a novel tang, a definitely personal sentiment, an individual hue.

● *Gurrelieder*, FOR SOLO VOICES, CHORUS, AND ORCHESTRA

This work, virtually a cantata, set to a text by the Danish poet Jens Peter Jacobsen, was composed in 1900-1901. The music represents the younger Schönberg, the twenty-six-year-old Romanticist who was still abiding in the shadow of that great rock which men call Wagner—though he was not unaware of Bruckner, and he anticipated the lyric Titanism of the later Mahler of the 'Symphony of a Thousand.' In the huge score of the *Gurrelieder*, with its five soloists, speaker, three male choruses and a mixed chorus, its twenty-five woodwind parts, twenty-nine-voiced brass section, and strings in proportion, we encounter one of the last and most grandiose manifestations of nineteenth-century musical Romanticism—'a vast monument,' as Arthur Bliss has called it, 'to the romantic tradition.' In the story of the love of King Waldemar for Tove, and in those portions of the work which are portrayals and evocations of the world of external nature, we have a reflection, hugely magnified and definitely intensified, of the literary attitude of Tieck and Novalis. The later Schönberg, the drastic atonalist, the arch-modernist, was still hidden in the mists of a relatively distant and perhaps debatably radiant dawn.

The score of the *Gurrelieder* bears no opus number. The work stands between the string sextet, *Verklärte Nacht*, op. 4 (1899), and the symphonic poem, *Pelleas und Melisande*, op. 5 (1902-3). Only the two songs of op. 1 (1898), the songs of op. 2 and op. 3 (1898-1900), together with the sextet for strings, precede it in the history of Schönberg's published works. Schönberg began the scoring of the *Gurrelieder* in the summer of 1901, but—hard pressed by the exactions of pot-boiling—his progress with the instrumentation was interrupted, and he did not complete it until 1911. The score was published in 1912. The first performance of the work took place in Vienna, under Franz Schreker, February 23, 1913. The public reception was enthusiastic, and this success was repeated at subsequent performances in Leipzig and Berlin under Nikisch and Schönberg.

The work is written for five solo singers, three four-part male choruses, one eight-part mixed chorus, and a *Sprecher*, who delivers a kind of *Sprechgesang* that is akin to the device used by Schönberg in his *Pierrot Lunaire* and *Die glückliche Hand*—the reciter is given the task of speaking on notes without singing them, and these notes are all carefully written out in the score. The solo parts represent the voices of Waldemar (tenor), Tove (soprano), the Wood-Dove (mezzo-soprano or alto), the Peasant (bass), and Klaus the Fool (tenor).

The instrumentation is for four flutes, four piccolos, three oboes, two English horns, three clarinets 'in A- or B-flat,' two E-flat clarinets, two bass clarinets, three bassoons and two contra-bassoons, ten horns, four Wagner tubas, six trumpets and one bass trumpet, one alto trombone, four tenor trombones, one bass trombone, one contra-bass trombone, one contra-bass tuba, six kettledrums, tenor drum, side-drum, bass-drum, cymbals, triangle, glockenspiel, tamtam, xylophone, rattle, 'some large iron chains,' four harps, celesta, and an amplified body of strings.

The music is set to a cycle of nineteen poems by Jacobsen, translated from the Danish into German by Robert Franz Arnold. The story told in the poems is the medieval tale of King Waldemar's hopeless passion for the Princess Tove. Waldemar IV of Denmark had been forced, for political reasons, to marry Helvig of Schlesvig, but he continued to lavish his devotion upon Tove, to whom he had given as residence his favorite castle at Gurre. 'The ruins of this castle,' it has been said, 'are two miles from Elsinore, and are still shown.'

Wild with jealousy, Queen Helvig brought about the death of Tove. 'The grief of Waldemar was terrible to witness. He uttered many fearful blasphemies, which provoked Divine punishment, and Waldemar was condemned after death to hunt nightly, from dusk to dawn, galloping with his henchmen in a wild chase across the skies.' But Waldemar's love proves to be stronger and more lasting than death and damnation. All nature speaks to him of Tove, and each morning, when the grisly horrors of the nocturnal hunt are past, he finds Tove in the reawakening of the beauty of the world.

The work, as it stands in the score, is in three parts. Part I, beginning with an orchestral introduction, comprises solos for Waldemar, Tove, and the Wood-Dove, in which are set forth the story of the lovers' mutual passion and the story of Tove's death, related in the concluding song of the Wood-Dove. Part II is short, consisting only of the solo in which the anguished Waldemar reproaches God. Part III, the longest and most elaborate in the work, relates the tale of the Wild Hunt and ends with the choral apostrophe to the dawn. It contains solos for Waldemar, the Peasant, and Klaus the Fool; passages for male chorus (Waldemar's vassals, his companions of the ghostly chase). Then follows the monologue for the 'Speaker' with accompanying orchestra, to which Schönberg has given the title, 'The Summer Wind's Wild Hunt'—a poetical nature-revery which prepares the way for the final chorus, with its climactic hymn to the rising sun and its symbolic vision of perpetual renewal.

● FIVE ORCHESTRAL PIECES, OP. 16

Schönberg's *Fünf Orchesterstücke*, composed in 1909, were performed in London at a Queen's Hall Promenade concert, under Sir Henry Wood, on September 3, 1912, and it was then announced that the pieces were played for the first time anywhere. The score was published in 1912, without preface, titles, sub-captions, superscriptions, mottoes, or any other one of the variously sly or candid methods by which a composer avows whatever program he has in mind.

Schönberg's way with these orchestral pieces was a compromise—neither very gratifying nor wholly without suggestiveness. The *Fünf Orchesterstücke* were repeated at a Queen's Hall concert by Sir Henry Wood's players on January 17, 1914; but they were then conducted by Schönberg himself—who had not heard his music, it was said at the time, until he rehearsed the orchestra for that performance. Mrs. Rosa Newmarch wrote the program notes for the second London performance, and in them she said:

Although the pieces are published without any verbal program which might give a clue to their poetic and emotional content, Herr Schönberg has furnished me with the subtitles given on this program [see below], which do not appear in the score—a concession that may prove rather helpful to those who are bewildered by the strangeness of the music, which seeks to express for us 'all that dwells in us subconsciously like a dream; which is a great fluctuant power, and is built upon none of the lines that are familiar to us: which has a rhythm, as the flood has its pulsating rhythm, as all life in us has its rhythm; which has a tonality, but only as the sea or the storm has its tonality; which has harmonies, though we cannot grasp or analyze them, nor can we trace its themes. . . All its technical craft is submerged, made one and indivisible with the content of the work. We can no longer differentiate between technique and idea, because the composer attains to an unresting intermingling of both. There is no working out; any attempt to separate what is inseparable would be to misunderstand this music.'

That, as Tom Sawyer said of the stories told in *Pilgrim's Progress*, is 'interestin'' but tough.' Nor is it easy to put one's hand on one's heart and declare that the titles furnished by Schönberg for the five movements throw an illuminating light upon their expressive intentions. These are his titles (the English translations are those used in London, probably devised by Mrs. Newmarch): I. 'Vorgefühle' ('Presentiments'); II. 'Vergangenes' ('The Past'); III. 'Der wechselnde' Akkord ('The Changing Chord'); IV. 'Péripétie' (Peripetia); V. 'Das obligate Recitativ' ('The Obbligato Recitative').

Schönberg was quoted as saying to a London interviewer that 'he wrote his music to a definite mental scheme, translated into tone, as viewed by him. However, he does not wish the public to take this into account, but simply to listen to his works purely as music, for its own sake.' Apparently, then, his titles were not intended to shed much light on his programmatic intentions— and they seem admirably contrived from that point of view. Perhaps they should recall to faithful Meredithians the sublime declaration of Mrs. Mountstuart Jenkinson in *The Egoist:* 'My remarks are thrown out to be apprehended, not dissected.'

Franz Peter Schubert

1797-1828

S

Schubert was a little man. He stood five feet one in his socks. He had a snub nose. His large head seemed too heavy for his body. He was painfully short-sighted, shy, and socially awkward. Almost anyone who chose could cheat or exploit him. When he died, he left behind him personal effects valued at a little over twelve dollars (reckoning in our money) and some of the loveliest music ever written. A few coats, waistcoats, trousers, shirts, cravats, handkerchiefs, socks, one hat, one towel, one sheet, one mattress, one bolster, one quilt, and a quantity of manuscripts appraised in the official inventory at the present equivalent of about two dollars— that was the extent of his material possessions. Within a year of his death, he had been unable to afford a seventeen-cent dinner, and was selling immortal songs at about the present value of a pack of cigarets. As Sir George Grove observes, 'beside this, the poverty of Mozart was wealth.' Yet Schubert in the midst of this wretchedness turned out masterpieces as easily and casually as a slot-machine turns out stamps. 'When I have done one piece, I begin the next,' he remarked simply to a visitor. In one morning he wrote six of the songs of the *Winterreise.* He composed nearly one thousand works in thirteen years; and at an age when Beethoven, as Sir George reminds us, had produced one symphony, Schubert had written nine. ‡He was in point of fact one of the greatest composers who ever lived; he was potentially the very greatest. The year of his death was the year of the composition of the C major Symphony (No. 9) and the C major String Quintet, and the thought of what he might have achieved, starting from this point, stretches the mind.‡

- SYMPHONY NO. 2, IN B-FLAT MAJOR

Schubert completed this symphony in his nineteenth year. He was at that time an assistant master in his father's school. Schubert's sister Therese told his biographer, Kreissle von Hellborn, that the gentle Franz was strict and ill-tempered as a teacher, and that he often kept his hands in practice on children's ears. His yearly salary was the equivalent of a little under eight dollars (yes—*eight*; not eighty, not even eighteen).

The year in which Schubert finished the Second Symphony was 1815, the most prolific year of his life—a year in which he composed a vast number of works: chamber-music, church music, secular choruses, piano pieces, half-a-dozen operas and melodramas, and 144 songs. The Second Symphony was begun in December 1814; it was completed in March 1815, and its composition virtually coincided with the creation of two incomparable masterpieces in another field—the songs 'Gretchen am Spinnrade' and 'Der Erlkönig'; Schubert was already an amazing genius.

It is undeniable, of course, that the early symphonies which were contemporaneous with these wonderful songs (at least 20 of the 144 dating from 1815 are indispensable) are not on a comparable plane of power and inspiration. Schubert was already a lyric and musico-dramatic genius by the grace of God. He was not yet a great symphonist—the 'Unfinished'. and the great C major lay some years ahead. But it was only organizing power and structural grasp that he lacked at nineteen—incredible inventiveness he had, and a gift of lyric utterance which only Mozart rivaled before him, and no one since.

The Second Symphony is in four movements: an 'Allegro vivace' first movement prefaced by a slow introduction of ten measures; an Andante in E-flat, triple time (a theme and variations); a Minuet in C minor, with a trio in E-flat, and Finale, 'Presto vivace,' in the tonic key.

- SYMPHONY NO. 4, IN C MINOR ('Tragic')

It has long been said that none of the music of this symphony was heard until 1860, when Herbeck, at a concert of the Gesellschaft der Musikfreunde in Vienna, brought forward four symphonic fragments from Schubert's pen that had not seen the light of day—the first and second movements of the 'Tragic' Symphony, the Scherzo of the Sixth Symphony, in C (1818) and the Finale of the Third, in D (1815). But the editor of the Eulenberg edition of the score asserts that the 'Tragic' Symphony was performed on November 19, 1849, at a concert of the Euterpe Society in Vienna.

The autograph, owned by C. F. Peters at the time, was afterward acquired by Nicolas Dumba, a wealthy amateur and music patron of Vienna, who placed it at the disposal of the editors of the Breitkopf & Härtel edition. 'The autograph, which consists of ninety-seven pages, resembles those of Schubert's ripest period in being remarkably free from erasures and corrections. The youth of nineteen was already a quick and accurate worker.' After Dumba's death in 1900, his collection of manuscripts came into the possession of the city of Vienna. The Gesellschaft der Musikfreunde acquired the manuscript symphonies.

The title, 'Tragic,' was given to the symphony by Schubert. Sir George Grove wondered why, and conjectured that Schubert's poverty might have had something to do with the mood that inspired the epithet. Schubert in April 1816—the period of the symphony's composition—had applied for, and lost, the position of chief teacher at the State School of Music in Laibach, near Trieste. The appointment would have brought him a princely salary—about $100 a year.

'The taste of today,' remarked a commentator on this symphony, 'will scarcely find a sufficient infusion of the tragic element in the music to justify the epithet which the composer applied to it. Pathos speaks out of the first movement, and a spirit of lamentation out of the last. The Andante is a soulful song in which Schubert's fondness for the Adonic meter (a combination of dactyls and spondees), so eloquently exemplified in the slow movement of the D minor quartet, already finds expression.'

But Hermann Grabner, in his preface to a modern edition of the score, declares that the title was given by Schubert 'with some reason'; for, 'after the first three joyful symphonies, the opening movement of the Fourth breathes a spirit of sorrow and resignation, though it is not long maintained.' Both the first and last movements, he observes, 'begin in C minor, and pass into C major; while the two middle movements, the Andante in A-flat major and the Minuet in E-flat, bear slight affinity with the tragic mood elsewhere expressed.'

The first movement begins with a slow introduction ('Adagio molto,' C minor, 3-4) opening with a unison C for the full orchestra, fortissimo, which is followed by a melancholy theme for the first violins, accompanied by the other strings. A fermata leads to the main movement, 'Allegro vivace,' 4-4, at first for the strings, piano; and to the strings also is assigned the second theme, in A-flat. The working-out is quite extensive. The movement ends in C major.

The symphony was made famous by its slow movement, the Andante in A-flat major, 2-4—the movement that was first published separately in score. It begins with a typically Schubertian theme for the strings, dolce and pianissimo, to which at the tenth measure the oboe adds its voice. There is a contrasting section, agitated in expression. The two phases of the movement are set off against each other—the tranquil and the disturbed. But at the end, it is the quieter mood that prevails, and the movement ends, *ppp*, on a beautifully orchestrated chord of A-flat major (for two flutes, two oboes, two clarinets, two bassoons, two horns, and strings).

The Minuet ('Allegro vivace,' 3-4), with a Trio in E-flat is remarkable for its chromatic writing. In the Finale (Allegro, C minor, 2-2) we are again impressed by the harmonic daring of the nineteen-year-old genius, and his confident handling of the orchestra—note especially his use of the woodwind. There are some bold modulations in the working-out section, and the music throughout is striking in its freedom and resourcefulness. There is a long and effective coda in C major.

● SYMPHONY NO. 5, IN B-FLAT

This symphony is sometimes known as the symphony 'without trumpets or drums.' It is scored for flute, two oboes, two bassoons, two horns, and strings. It was written, probably, for the small amateur orchestra of a private music society which had developed out of the activities of a string quartet that performed in the house of Schubert's father. Schubert composed for this same aspiring and zealous group, it is supposed, three other of his early symphonies: the Symphony in D major, No. 3 (1815); the 'Tragic,' in C minor, No. 4 (1816); and the 'little' C major, No. 6 (1818).

It was long believed that the score of the Fifth Symphony was lost. The orchestral parts were discovered in Vienna by George Grove and Arthur Sullivan while they were on the hunt for Schubert manuscripts in 1867. The parts were in the possession of Johann Herbeck, the Viennese Court Conductor and Director of the Musikverein concerts, who had, a while before, disinterred the 'Unfinished' Symphony from the dusty archives of Anselm Hüttenbrenner. But the two adventurous Englishmen could not find the score of the B-flat Symphony, which was eventually discovered in the Berlin Royal Library and published in 1882 (an edition for piano, four hands, had been published ten years earlier). There was a performance of the symphony by the Boston Symphony Orchestra, in Boston, on February 10, 1883, under Georg Henschel— probably the first in America.

Sir Donald Tovey has called this symphony 'a pearl of great price.' He remarks with justice of Schubert's earliest instrumental works that are artistically successful that 'no student of any academic institution has ever produced better models of form. At all events, no academic criticism has yet been framed that can pick holes in this little Symphony in B-flat'—'the only possible cavil,' he observes, 'is that Schubert does not seem fond of long developments.'

There are four movements: (I) Allegro; (II) 'Andante con moto'; (III) Minuet and Trio; (IV) Finale: 'Allegro vivace.'

After four introductory bars (Allegro, 2-2), Schubert brings forward his first subject, and his second. The whole movement, remarks Tovey in an affectionate comment, 'is full of Schubert's peculiar delicacy; and its form escapes stiffness like a delightful child overawed into perfect behavior, not by fear of priggishness but by sheer delight in giving pleasure.'

Schubert the lyrist sings in the 'Andante con moto' (E-flat, 6-8), beginning with a theme that seems to have remembered at least the outlines of the Rondo from Mozart's Violin Sonata in F (K. 377). Mozart is again recalled (the Minuet of the G minor Symphony) by the Minuet, in the same key, of this symphony of Schubert, though the latter is a far more elementary affair. There is a trio in G major, the melody sung by the first violins and first bassoon— a dance of rustic character, with the suggestion of a drone-bass.

The Finale ('Allegro vivace,' B-flat major, 2-4) is a blithe and engaging example of first-movement form, with two main themes.

• SYMPHONY NO. 6, IN C MAJOR

Schubert's Sixth Symphony was begun in October 1817, and completed in January 1818. Four years later, Schubert composed the two movements of his 'Unfinished' Symphony. The 'mystic abyss' (as Herbert Peyser has happily called it) 'that yawns between the C major Symphony of 1818 and the B minor of 1822 is a repetition, *mutatis mutandis,* of the creative and emotional cataclysm that took place between Beethoven's Second Symphony and his Third. Schubert in 1822 had become, symphonically, another being. The two completed movements of the B minor have no bonds of connection with Schubert's symphonies of the previous decade save, perhaps, in certain fortuitous resemblances of instrumental combination and timbre.'

Ten years after he had completed the 'little' C major Symphony, No. 6, Schubert composed the great C major that is variously numbered Seventh or Ninth in the procession of his symphonic works.

The Sixth Symphony, like the Fifth, was in all probability composed for Schubert's amateur society *Im Gundelhof* [see notes above]. The first public performance of the work was in Vienna, at a concert of the Gesellschaft der Musikfreunde, December 12, 1828, three weeks and two days after Schubert's death. The performance was from manuscript; the score and parts were not published until 1885.

The work marks a transitional period in Schubert's symphonic style. He was just emerging from the influences of Mozart, Haydn, and Beethoven. The Minuet of the preceding symphony is absent, and in its place is a Scherzo. The four movements consist of an Allegro in C, 2-2, prefaced by a slow introduction; an Andante in F, 2-4; a Scherzo in C, Presto, 3-4; and an 'Allegro moderato' Finale in the tonic key.

Anton Dvořák, writing of Schubert in an essay published in America many years ago, declared of Schubert's early symphonies:

The more I study them, the more I marvel. Though the influence of other masters is apparent in them, Schubert's musical individuality is unmistakable in the character of the melody, in the harmonic progressions, and in the orchestration. . . I conducted his early Fifth Symphony, in B-flat major, and the Sixth, in C major, a dozen times with my orchestral pupils at the National Conservatory of Music [New York]; they shared my pleasure in them, and recognized at once their great beauty. . . Although partly anticipated by Gluck and Mozart, Schubert was one of the first composers to make use of an effect to which Wagner and other later composers owe many of their most beautiful orchestral colors—the employment of the brass not for volume of tone, but played softly, to secure rich and warm tints.

• SYMPHONY NO. 8, IN B MINOR ('Unfinished')

Schubert, who was almost the age of his contemporary, Shelley, composed his B minor Symphony in the year of Shelley's death. Like Shelley, he was too well-beloved of the gods; Shelley died at thirty, Schubert at thirty-one. Almost all of the finer Schubert—his tenderness, his passion, his melancholy, his sense of drama, his magical charm—may be found in the B minor Symphony. It was begun in his twenty-sixth year (in October 1822), and he lived six years longer; yet only the Allegro, the Andante, and fragments of the Scherzo survive.

The music is as spontaneous, as sincere, as affecting, as anything he ever wrote. There is grief in it, and protest. Not many things more dolorous are to be found in that insurpassably woeful threnody, likewise in B minor— Tchaikovsky's 'Pathétique'—than the mournful passage in the first movement of the 'Unfinished' wherein the wailing phrase sung by the violins is imitated by the violas and bassoons. And those tragic outbursts later in the movement are of startling intensity. Schubert's sorrow is graver, more reticent, than Tchaikovsky's: it has nothing of that anguished abandonment which makes the Finale of the 'Pathétique' so overwhelming to those who can still listen to it with unresentful ears. Yet Schubert's grieving in certain moments of this symphony is unmistakable.

There is much else in the 'Unfinished,' however, besides melancholy brooding. The romantic Edmondstoune Duncan, in his devoted study of Schubert, has cheered us all by discovering in this symphony the suggestion of 'salt-flavored breezes,' the 'pulsation of waves,' and 'the freedom and expanse which a wilderness of waters convey to the mind'—though he hastens to say that he does not impute any such pictorial intentions to Schubert. Others, more interested in music than in tonal waves and breezes, have found in the famous 'cello theme of the first movement 'the most charming melody in all music'; and Philip Hale, in an unforgettable essay on Schubert, published many years ago, did not hesitate to say of the first movement of the B minor that 'there is nothing of more complete, well-rounded beauty in the literature of music.'

● SYMPHONY NO. 9, IN C MAJOR

'I hope to be able to send you,' wrote Mendelssohn to the London Philharmonic Society over a century ago, 'a very extraordinary and excellent symphony by Fr. Schubert, the famous composer.' Extraordinary, indeed! So extraordinary that when the worthy players of the Royal Philharmonic Society of London tried over the new work at rehearsal, they laughed loud and long at certain of its features. It is not of record that the players of the Philharmonic Society of New York ridiculed the symphony when they performed it for the first time in America on January 11, 1851, or that they laughed at the reiterated triplet-figure in the Finale, as their older colleagues did. Probably by that time those rushing, tumultuous figures had ceased to be funny and had become sublime.

For sublimity is the note of this symphony at its greatest—especially of the Finale. An accomplished and scholarly Englishman, Sir Donald Tovey, has said of the Finale of the C major that in it 'the grotesque is the veil of the sublime'—an astonishing phrase: for, to many of us, the sublimity of this incomparable movement wears no veil of any sort—certainly none that could be called 'grotesque.' Rather it proceeds in clarity and light, wind-borne, under a wind-swept sky. Where else, except perhaps in the Finale of Beethoven's

Seventh, will you find music with quite the energy and pace and high exuberance that Schubert has compassed here? In this lyric world of wind-swept daylight and of lucid, soaring exultation one finds the often elegiacal Schubert unbound and free, transformed, 'leaping and shining like a mountain water'—and the mountain is in the country of the gods.

In the C major Symphony, the discourse, almost throughout, is like that of a speaker who knows and loves and cunningly employs 'the shape and hue and odor and sweet sound of words.' It is full of surprising and inexhaustible subtleties of design and procedure, of delicate felicities accomplished with so perfect an art that they wear the innocence and spontaneity of natural proc-esses. Consider, as an example among many, a detail in the slow movement even more delectable than that famous incident which so captivated the romantic Schumann, the passage in which 'the horn is calling as though . . . from another sphere': consider that place (it is in the twenty-fourth measure from the opening of the 'Andante con moto') where the song of the oboe modulates from A minor into A major. Nothing, apparently, could be simpler, more unsought, than that change from minor to major; yet how consum-mately artful it is, and how ravishing! And mark the touch of magic—seemingly naïve—that is given to the second (F major) theme in its eighth measure by the D-flat in the 'cellos.

If the Finale, especially, is not the pure, brave ecstasy of tone, then that ecstasy was never captured and released. Here, indeed, as Francis Thompson said of *Prometheus Unbound*, 'poetry is spilt like wine, music runs to drunken waste. The jubilant voices sweep down the wind flight after flight, till we cry for respite from the unrolling splendors.'

Like all authentic masterworks, the C major Symphony has an ever-receding horizon. It gives us the sense of an enchanted familiarity: that sense both of the wonder and the intimacy of the world—the conviction that just beyond the next hill lies some accessible paradise for the pilgrim mind. Schubert's comrade, Holzapfel the paralytic, used to talk exhaustlessly of the friend that he had known, and always he began his reminiscences in the same way: 'He was a little man, but he was a giant . . .' If Schubert had written nothing else but this symphony, his head would be among the stars.

● OVERTURE AND INCIDENTAL MUSIC FROM *Rosamunde*

Schubert's *Rosamunde* music comprises eleven numbers: an overture; three entr'actes; two ballets; a piece for clarinets, horns, and bassoons entitled 'Shepherd's Melody'; a romance for soprano solo, 'Der Vollmond strahlt auf Bergeshöh'n'; a Spirits' Chorus; a Shepherds' Chorus, and a Huntsmen's Chorus.

It is the charmingly inconsequential way of composers, from Bach and Handel down, to shift their works about from one connection to another; and the so-called 'Overture to *Rosamunde*' has really nothing to do with *Rosa-munde, Fürstin von Cypern*, the preposterous drama by Wilhelmine von Chézy for which Schubert wrote music, composing it within the space of five days in the month of December 1823. Play and incidental music were performed at the Theater an der Wien on the 20th of that month, but were shelved after two performances.

The piece which was played as the overture to *Rosamunde* when the drama was produced at Vienna in 1823 had been composed three years before as an overture to Hofmann's melodrama, *Die Zauberharfe* ('The Magic Harp'), and it was heard in connection with that work at Vienna in 1820. When *Rosamunde* was given in 1823, the *Zauberharfe* overture demonstrated the convertibility of most music by serving obligingly as its tonal preface. A four-hand piano arrangement of the overture was published a few years later, but the score was not printed until 1867. The overture that properly belonged to *Rosamunde* afterward appeared as the overture to Schubert's opera on a Spanish subject (the libretto by Schober), *Alfonso und Estrella*, op. 69. If the history of this overture sounds slightly insane, the fault is that of Schubert rather than of Clio.

It may not be inappropriate to present here an outline of Wilhelmine von Chézy's remarkable drama. Here is a paraphrase of Kreissle von Hellborn's summary of the plot:

> Rosamunde, Princess of Cyprus, has been brought up as a shepherdess, in ignorance of her real rank, until she comes of age. Fulgentius, who has been the ruler of Cyprus in the meantime, wishes to marry her, but Rosamunde not only refuses to accept his hand, but accompanies her rejection with words of scorn. Fulgentius, now filled with rage and with hate for the girl whom previously he had loved, casts her into prison, and, through the Prince of Candia, sends her a poisoned letter wherewith to carry his vengeance to the point of death.
>
> The Prince of Candia was, however, in love with Rosamunde, and, in order to be near her, had entered the service of the Cyprian ruler in disguise. He sends another letter to the girl, in which he unfolds the conspiracy against her life, and Rosamunde then feigns sickness. When the fitting opportunity arrives the prince gives back the poisoned letter to Fulgentius, who promptly dies, and the loving couple are free to marry.

Schubert's manuscript of the *Rosamunde* music vanished from sight for forty-four years. In 1868, the orchestral parts were discovered in a dusty cupboard in a house in Vienna by George Grove and Arthur Sullivan; after which the two British discoverers celebrated, it is said, by playing a game of leap-frog about the room.

Robert Schumann

1810-56

S

‡Virgil Thomson has somewhere spoken of the 'manly pathos' of Schumann's music—a happy verbal shaft which reaches the heart of its target. Schumann had the Romantic view of life—that is to say, passion

and sadness were what he chiefly saw and chiefly experienced in it. But he saw and experienced them as a man, with valor and good hope. He was aware of the withered flower, the fallen bird, and the bloody sacrifice on the altar under the noonday sun, but they did not haunt him as they haunted Chopin. No characteristic work of Schumann's ends with anything like the shudder of the last movement of Chopin's B-flat minor Sonata. Are there tears in Schumann's music? One has not heard them. Schumann is often grave, but he does not weep. Having acknowledged of life that 'worse it has given,' he was able to assure himself that 'still I live.' He was worthy of, and fitted for, a long life of devotion and service to music, to his wife and his children, to his friends (who were all who knew him). But fate, in a fit of irresponsible and gratuitous savagery, struck him down, destroying first his mind and then his body. He died insane in his forty-sixth year.‡

● SYMPHONY No. 1, IN B-FLAT MAJOR, OP. 38

'Within the last few days,' wrote Schumann to his friend Wenzel early in 1841, 'I have completed, at least in outline, a labor which kept me in a state of bliss, but also exhausted me. Think of it! A whole symphony—and moreover, a Spring symphony! I can myself scarcely believe it is finished. The filling out of the score remains to be done. Think of the labor which that involves, and help your Schumann.'

In the following year (November 23, 1842) he wrote to Spohr: 'I composed the symphony toward the end of the winter of 1841, under the impulse of that vernal ardor which carries away man even at the most advanced age, and seizes upon him anew every year. I did not aim to describe or portray; but I do believe that the season in which the symphony originated has influenced its form and made it what it is.'

Schumann sent a more explicit commentary to Wilhelm Taubert, who was to produce the symphony in Berlin. 'I should be pleased [he wrote in a letter dated January 10, 1843] if you could imbue your orchestra with something of the mood of Springtime. This I had particularly in mind when I wrote the symphony in February, 1841. I should like to have the very opening trumpet call sound as if it came from on high like a summons to awakening. By what follows the introduction I might then suggest how on all sides the green leaves are sprouting, perhaps how a butterfly appears, and by the Allegro how gradually everything that belongs to Spring bursts forth. But these are fancies which occurred to me after I had completed the work. Regarding the last movement, however, I would say that I imagined it to represent the departure of Spring, and would like to have it played in a manner not too frivolous.'

But Schumann did not publicly avow the true source of his inspiration in composing this symphony. In October 1842, he sent a portrait of himself to his friend Adolph Böttger (1815-70), accompanied by an inscription consisting of the opening measures of the symphony (the phrase for horns and trumpets),

with these words: 'Beginning of a symphony inspired by a poem of Adolph
Böttger. To the poet, in remembrance of Robert Schumann.' According to
Böttger, this is the poem that stimulated Schumann's fancy:

> Du Geist der Wolke, trüb und schwer,
> Fliegst drohend über Land und Meer.
> Dein grauer Schleier deckt im Nu
> Des Himmels klares Auge zu.
> Dein Nebel wallt herauf von fern,
> Und Nacht verhüllt der Liebe Stern!
> Du Geist der Wolke, trüb' und feucht,
> Was hast Du all' mein Glück verscheucht,
> Was rufst Du, Thränen in's Gesicht,
> Und Schatten in der Seele Licht?
> O wende, wende Deinen Lauf—
> Im Thale blüht der Frühling auf!

These stanzas have been translated into prose (we do not know by whom)
as follows:

Thou Spirit of the Cloud, murky and heavy, fliest with menace over land and sea;
thy gray veil covers in a moment the clear eye of heaven; thy mist seethes up from afar,
and Night hides the Star of Love. Thou Spirit of the Cloud, murky and damp, how
thou hast frightened away all my happiness, how thou dost call tears to my face and
shadows into the light of my soul! O turn, O turn thy course—In the valley blooms
the spring!

It is the opinion of Professor Niecks that the last line of the poem ['In the
valley blooms the Spring'] might have been taken by Schumann as his special
point of departure; for the poem as a whole is scarcely jubilant in spirit.

Berthold Litzmann in his *Clara Schumann* declares that the four movements
of the B-flat Symphony, according to Schumann's original intention, were to
have had these motives: 'Frühlingsbeginn' (Spring's Beginning), 'Abend'
(Evening), 'Frohe Gespielen' (Joyful Playing), 'Voller Frühling' (Full Spring).

Clara Schumann, in the diary kept jointly by herself and her husband, wrote
on January 25, 1841: 'Robert has nearly finished his symphony; it was composed chiefly at night. He calls it 'Spring Symphony.' A Spring poem by . . .
gave him the first impulse toward composition.' Böttger's name is omitted
from the above sentence in the diary. Taciturnity was evidently a Schumann
family trait.

The B-flat Symphony was first performed in public under Mendelssohn's
direction in the Gewandhaus, Leipzig, March 31, 1841.

Schumann, like Haydn in his 'Military' Symphony and Beethoven in his
Ninth, dared to invite that orchestral *fille de joie*, the triangle, to his symphonic gathering—a fact which Hanslick may have forgotten when he so
sternly rebuked the Paphian Liszt for a similar impropriety in his E-flat Piano
Concerto.

● SYMPHONY NO. 2, IN C MAJOR, OP. 61

Schumann conceived the C major Symphony at a time of physical and spiritual depression. 'I sketched the symphony,' he wrote, 'while suffering severe physical pain; indeed, I may well call it the struggle of my mind which influenced this, and by which I sought to beat off my disease. The first movement is full of this struggle.' He and Clara had returned to Leipzig from their Russian trip in the spring of 1844—a trip that had brought unhappiness and humiliation to the proud and sensitive composer, who was received merely as the husband of a distinguished pianist. He confided to his diary a note of his 'almost unbearable mortifications, and Clara's attitude towards them!' He was nervously exhausted. He took the waters at Karlsbad, without benefit. Then, with Clara, he visited Dresden. Even in that delectable town he was miserable. Clara wrote that he passed one sleepless night after another, and that in the morning she found him bathed in tears. 'He had given himself up for lost.' His physician noted that 'so soon as he busied himself with intellectual matters he was seized with fits of trembling, fatigue, coldness of the feet, and a state of mental distress culminating in a strange terror of death, which manifested itself in the fear inspired in him by heights, by rooms on an upper story, by all metal instruments, even keys, and by medicines, and the fear of being poisoned.'

Schumann and his wife decided to settle in Dresden—despite the presence there of an obnoxious colleague named Richard Wagner, whose 'restless exuberance' Schumann could not abide. In Dresden, Schumann's anxiety about his health became more and more acute and distressing. He wore himself out with morbid fears, and suffered a form of melancholia that was aggravated by an excited condition of the aural nerves. Yet it was at this time that he completed not only the buoyant and lovely piano concerto, but the Symphony in C major, which his biographer, Wasielewski, speaks of with justice as 'more mature, masculine, powerful, and profound than its predecessors (the symphonies in B-flat and D minor).'

Schumann wrote to Mendelssohn from Dresden in the autumn of 1845 that for days drums and trumpets had been throbbing and blaring in his head —'trumpets in C. . . What will come of it all I do not know.' The C major Symphony came of it. Schumann completed it in 1846. The first performance was at a Gewandhaus concert in Leipzig, under Mendelssohn, on November 5 of that year.

So far as profundity of feeling and felicity of instrumental speech are concerned, it has seemed to many that Schumann equaled nowhere else in his symphonic writing the page that makes this work so treasurous: the fervent Adagio—an utterance of such rich and moving poetry that, listening to it, you cannot help wondering if the bodily and spiritual malaise out of which this loveliness proceeded is not a condition that should occasionally be prayed for by certain composers enjoying perfect health.

Schumann himself seems to have been fairly well pleased with this Adagio; for he said in a letter to G. D. Otten, founder of the Hamburg Musikverein: 'That my melancholy bassoon in the Adagio, which I confess to having introduced at that point with particular pleasure, has not escaped your attention, gives me the greatest satisfaction.' The 'melancholy bassoon' enters in the ninth measure, after the oboe has taken up the opening song of the violins, and the two woodwind instruments continue their duo against the syncopated accompaniment of the violins and violas and the melodious undersong of the basses. As the song (now in the strings) grows more impassioned, you may find yourself inclined to agree with Weingartner that this is 'the best movement in all of Schumann's symphonies.'

But, indeed, this symphony, as a whole, is rich in felicities. The 'motto-theme' of the trumpets, horns, and trombone that opens the 'Sostenuto assai' of the first movement has a curious impressiveness. Wasielewski says that the slow introduction was originally intended for another work, and 'was already composed when Schumann conceived the idea of writing this symphony.' The repetition of this motto-theme is one of the devices used by Schumann to integrate the different movements of the symphony; for not only does this motive occur again in the coda of the first movement (in the trumpets, forte, marcato), as well as at the close of the Scherzo and in the Finale, but a variant of the chief theme of the Adagio is heard in the last movement.

In this admirable Finale there are other features of uncommon interest. As in the Finale of the D minor Symphony, the first theme of the movement does not return after the working-out. The new subject that appears in the oboe reminded Fuller Maitland of one of the songs in Beethoven's cycle, 'An die ferne Geliebte.' Schumann's theme (particularly in its later form, as it is played in C major by the strings, after the fortissimo chord on the dominant, and the fermanta) does suggest 'Nimm sie hin denn diese Lieder'; but the resemblance is not very close. It is more likely that Schumann remembered his own embryonic anticipation of the theme in the Finale of his F major Quartet, op. 41, No. 2, composed three years earlier.

● SYMPHONY NO. 3, IN E-FLAT MAJOR, OP. 97 ('Rhenish')

J. W. von Wasielewski, author, violinist, critic, composer, and concert-master under Schumann at Düsseldorf, 1850-52, wrote as follows in his biography of Schumann regarding the E-flat Symphony, which was composed at Düsseldorf in the last two months of 1850:

'The symphony may properly be called "The Rhenish"; for the idea was first conceived, so the composer said, on seeing the Cathedral at Cologne. During its composition, the master was greatly influenced by the ceremonies attendant upon the installation of Archbishop von Geissel as a Cardinal, which Schumann witnessed in the Cathedral at Cologne. To this fact the symphony probably owes its fourth movement, originally headed, "In the Character of an Accompaniment to a Solemn Ceremony." When the work was published, Schumann omitted the heading. He said: "We must not show our heart to the world: a general impression of a work of art is better; at least, no preposterous comparisons can then be made." '

It was Schumann's intention to portray in the symphony as a whole the joyful folk-life along the Rhine; 'and,' he declared, 'I think I have succeeded.'

Spitta remarks in his biographical account of Schumann that 'the whole symphony is full of vivid pictures of Rhineland life.' In the Finale, especially, there is reason to believe that the composer's mind dwelt on some popular Rhenish festivity—though, toward the close of the movement, there is a reminiscence of the music suggestive of a religious function.

The first performance of the symphony was in Geisler Hall, Düsseldorf, at the sixth concert of the Allgemeine Musikverein, February 6, 1851. Schumann conducted from manuscript. Clara Schumann, a devoted wife but a cool-headed critic, wrote with modified rapture concerning the music. She seems not to have liked that movement which a later time has agreed upon considering the salient feature of the symphony—the 'Cathedral Scene.' 'The fourth movement,' she confessed, 'is the one that at present is least clear to me. It is most artistically made, but I cannot follow it so well; while there is scarcely a measure in the other movements that is not clear to me.'

The first movement of the 'Rhenish' Symphony opens without introduction ('Lebhaft,' E-flat major, 3-4) with a sweeping and heroic theme, announced by the full orchestra, forte, which for some hearers bears a spiritual if not a musical affinity with the opening subject of Brahms' Third Symphony. The rhythm of the initial three measures of Schumann's theme is effectively employed in the evolution of this subject. Oboe and clarinet, accompanied by other woodwinds and low strings, introduce the second theme, of a wistful character (G minor), with the violins and flute adding their voices to its gentle cantilena.

The energetic rhythm of the principal theme returns, there are two *fff* outbursts, a swift subsidence, and we hear the second subject handed from the top to the bottom of the orchestra: the flute sings it, *p*, and is answered in imitation by the 'cellos and double-basses. The movement rises to a high pitch of heroic exultation, with the horns and trumpets wreaking themselves upon the chief theme.

The Scherzo ('Sehr mässig,' C major, 3-4) opens with a theme for violas, 'cellos, and bassoons, accompanied by chords of the violins, horns, trumpets, timpani, and double-basses, which some have declared to be a modified version of the 'Rheinweinlied'—a theme 'of rather ponderous joviality,' which, remarked W. F. Apthorp, 'well suits the drinkers' "Uns ist ganz cannibalisch wohl, als wie fünf hundert Säuen!" in the scene in Auerbach's cellar in Goethe's *Faust*.' There is a more vivacious counter-theme for the strings and woodwind. In the Trio, horns, trumpets, clarinets, and bassoons have a contrasting melody in A minor above a pedal-point on C.

The third movement ('Nicht so schnell,' A-flat major, 4-4), is a lyric interlude between the jovialities of the Scherzo and the solemn pomp of the 'Cathedral Scene.' It is scored only for woodwind, two horns, and strings, and is derived from two themes. The first, sung by a quartet of clarinets and bassoons, piano and dolce, over an accompaniment of violas and pizzicato 'cellos, has suggested to some the air, 'Tu che a Dio,' in *Lucia di Lammermoor*, though the resemblance is not very striking. The second theme is a melody beginning with an ascending phrase in sixteenth notes for the first violins, pianissimo.

The fourth movement is the so-called 'Cathedral Scene' (Feierlich, E-flat major, 4-4). For this movement Schumann added three trombones to his score. The principal thematic material is supplied by the figure announced at once, pianissimo, by trombones and horns, against pizzicati of the strings. There are changes of time signature (to 3-2 and 4-2), and the key of B major has a brief reign; the movement ends in the initial tonality.

It was in this movement that Schumann remembered the impression made upon his mind by the solemn ceremony that he had witnessed in the Cathedral at Cologne upon the occasion of von Geissel's elevation to the Cardinalate.

The Finale of the Symphony (Lebhaft, E-flat major, 2-2) is that which is said to have been suggested by a Rhenish festival. The chief subject opens in the strings, forte, supported at first by woodwind and horns. The second theme (B-flat) is stated by the violins. Some have found in this movement a hint of the Rhine song, 'So leben wir, so leben wir alle Tage.' At the climax, we are reminded of the music of the 'Cathedral Scene,' and there is a brilliant coda.

● SYMPHONY NO. 4, IN D MINOR, OP. 120

In the marriage register of the parish of Schönfeld, near Leipzig, it is recorded that 'Dr. R. Schumann, composer of music, and resident in Leipzig, only remaining lawful son of August Schumann, bookseller, of Zwickau, was joined in marriage with Miss Clara Josephine Wieck, lawful eldest daughter of the first wife of Friedrich Wieck, music-dealer, of Leipzig, on September 12th, Saturday before Dom. XIII. p. Trin. at 10 o'clock a.m.'

That was in the year 1840—the year of the great love songs—and Schumann had passed his thirtieth birthday. He led thenceforth what his biographer Wasielewski describes as 'a more quiet and contemplative life'—a life that was not, however, without activity; for thereafter—until his 'mortal anguish of mind' became an engulfing darkness sixteen years later—Schumann composed four symphonies, commended to the world a talented, tow-headed boy of twenty named Brahms, and assisted the development of that great Romantic movement in music which not even the bright certainties of the neue Sachlichkeit have as yet completely invalidated.

Of Schumann's energetic habits in the course of the next decade, at such times as they were stimulated by his periods of good health, Spitta has assembled some revealing details. In the year 1849, for example, he produced thirty works, most of them considerable in extent. He wrote, at this time, with an almost Schubertian fluency—composing while he walked or stood, indifferent to his surroundings, even when they were of the most disturbing sort. He wrote the song, 'Kennst du das Land,' at Kreischa, near Dresden, surrounded by a group of noisy children; and in a restaurant much frequented by the Greenwich Village set of Dresden, Schumann used to sit alone, his back to the crowd and his face to the wall, happy with his beer and his thoughts, whistling softly to himself and evolving unforgettable music.

After his marriage he entered upon a new phase of his development as a composer; he returned to instrumental music, 'but in another spirit,' as Wasielewski remarks. 'He now grasped the symphonic elements, and showed himself devoted and industrious in this form of composition.' Two years earlier Schumann had written to Dorn: 'I often feel tempted to desert my piano—it's too narrow for my thoughts. I really have very little practice in orchestral music now; still, I hope to master it.' But Wasielewski thinks that this 'sudden conversion to other forms may be explained in another way. He had learned that, to compose with ease, he must master theory.' For Schumann had written sagely: 'If a man wants to compose in free forms, he must first master those binding and current in all ages.'

W. J. Henderson, who has discussed Schumann's music with clairvoyant understanding, remarks that 'his artistic development is so indisputably the result of his life up to this point [1840], that we are not surprised at his next step. The tumult of young love lifted him from the piano to the voice. The consummation of his manhood, in the union with a woman of noble heart and commanding intellect, led him to the orchestra. In 1841 he rushed into the symphonic field, and composed no fewer than three of his orchestral works.'

These were the B-flat Symphony (No. 1, op. 38); the Overture, Scherzo, and Finale (op. 52); and the Symphony in D minor. The latter was written in a little over three months. It was begun at the end of May, according to the diary of Clara Schumann, although the first page of the MS. score is inscribed: June 7, 1841. It was finished September 9, and, in chronological order, follows the Symphony in B flat. On the program of the concert at which it was first performed, at the Gewandhaus, Leipzig, on December 6, 1841, it was announced as Schumann's 'second symphony.' Clara wrote that 'Robert's symphony was not especially well performed'; and its reception was disappointing.

Schumann did not publish the symphony at that time—though it is said that he offered it to a publisher two or three years later as 'Second Symphony, op. 50.' He revised his manuscript in 1851, and he conducted the new version of the symphony at a Düsseldorf Festival in the spring of 1853. The score and parts of the revised version were published late in the same year, with a dedication to Joachim. In the twelve-year interval between the composition of the original draft and the publication of the remodeled version, Schumann had composed and published two other symphonies: the C major (No. 2, op. 61, 1846) and the E flat, or 'Rhenish' (No. 3, op. 97, 1850); so the D minor was issued as No. 4, op. 120, though it is really the second in order of composition.

Henderson, in his essay 'Schumann and the Program-Symphony,' has seen more deeply and sympathetically into the emotional substance of this richly expressive symphony than has any other commentator we know of. He calls the D minor, written at the beginning of the composer's married life, 'Schumann's nuptial hymn, the Io triumphe of love victorious and manhood blessed:' This symphony, intended for performance without pauses between the movements, he views as 'the first symphonic poem—a form which is based upon the irrefutable assertion that "there is no break between two successive emotional states" '; and he draws attention to the fact that it is also integrated by partial community of theme—'nothing more nor less than an approach to the leit-motive system.'

• CONCERTO FOR PIANO AND ORCHESTRA, IN A MINOR, OP. 54

Over a century ago Schumann began what is now the first movement of his
piano concerto, but which was then projected and (in August 1841) completed
as a 'Phantasie in A minor.' Schumann sought to publish the music in that
form, but without success. Four years later he added two more movements,
and on December 4, 1845, Clara Schumann played the complete work from
manuscript at a concert in Dresden, with Ferdinand Hiller (to whom the
score is dedicated) conducting. Schumann's music was then, as we have indicated, ultra-modern, and our timeless friends, the Bourbons of aesthetic
appraisement, behaved in their unchangeable way. 'Labored,' 'utterly extravagant,' were among the epithets suggested by some of Schumann's most lucid
and lovely pages to the mind of the clairvoyant Davison, who adorned English criticism in those incredible days; and he patronized contemptuously the
'praiseworthy efforts of Mme Schumann [who played the work in London,
May 14, 1856] to make her husband's curious rhapsody pass for music.' Pass
for music! Well, it may amuse the gentle ghost of Schumann to realize that
Davison survives for us today chiefly as one of the pressed flowers of Mid-
Victorian obscurantism.

How far removed from us today is this music of Schumann, this music of
the Romantic Age! How far we are from Schumann the dreamer and rhapsodist—the introspective Eusebius and the impassioned Florestan! How unimag-
inably remote are these presences and memories from the music of Hindemith
and Krenek and Varèse, Bartok and Stravinsky!

It is true that some there are who still incline an ear toward these far-
wandering phantoms—some who still are wont to visit, surreptitiously and at
night, those once-enchanted woods, those ancient gardens that sleep so
quietly beneath the hill, where no one walks, where now there lingers only the
fragrance of an old forgotten day. But though we may love that vanishing,
abandoned world, we no longer draw upon it for our creative life. The music
that we make today—as distinguished, perhaps, from the music that we love—
is separated by an untraversible sea and an impenetrable forest from the music
of the Romantic Age. We have learned to write a briefer, sparer, harder music,
which has no tolerance for those cries from the heart, those meditative heights
and despairing depths, those mystical flights and brave adventurings, those
unseemly palterings with sensibility, which characterized the world of the
Romantics.

The music that we make today is cool and astringent and unbemused. It
disdains the poetical as haughtily as a courtesan disdains vulgarity; it repudiates
everything that was imaginative food and drink to the Romantics. But, regener-
ate and untrammeled though we may be, with our bright, clean, ironic, hard-
edged art, there is surely no harm in our living ourselves again into that
legendary dim Atlantis of the musical imagination where Schumann dwelt,
and so incorrigibly dreamed and suffered, trafficking indecently with loveliness.
Perhaps it may not too implacably be held against us if we turn an ear now
and again to catch some echo of the tenderness and passion and sincerity of
this old music, with its warmth of speech, the color and cadence of its sensi-

bility, its fantasy and sweetness and exaltation, its haunted awareness of the mystery of life and of the heart of man.

● Concerto for Violin and Orchestra, in D minor

This concerto, written for Josef Joachim, and dedicated to him, was never publicly performed by the great violinist—for reasons best known to himself. After his death in 1907, the manuscript came into the possession of the Prussian State Library at Berlin, where it was deposited in accordance with a stipulation in Joachim's will to the effect that the concerto should not be published until one hundred years after Schumann's death—which would have resulted in its suppression until 1956. In earlier years, Joachim had played the work in private, and the score was known to certain of his friends—Brahms, Bruch, Carl Halir, and others; but in the latter part of his life, Joachim is said to have refused to play the work even in private, and was reluctant to discuss it.

For thirty years after Joachim's death in 1907, the concerto remained in the Library at Berlin, lost to the world of music, its whereabouts unknown save to a small number of initiates. In 1937, Herr Wilhelm Strecker, head of the publishing house of B. Schotts Söhne, Mainz, persuaded the custodians of the score to consent to its release for publication and performance; and the concerto was thus given to the world from which it had so long been withheld.

From the full and authoritative life of Schumann written by his close friend, Josef Wilhelm von Wasielewski (*Robert Schumann, seine Biographie*—Dresden 1858), one gains some curious sidelights upon the early history of the concerto. According to Wasielewski, Schumann, in the spring of the year in which he composed the concerto, became engrossed in the then popular practice of 'table-tipping,' and, 'with convulsively dilated eyes,' solemnly assured Wasielewski that 'the tables know all.' The all-knowing table even obliged (as Schumann told Ferdinand Hiller) with the rhythm of the opening measures of Beethoven's Fifth Symphony.

Schumann was robbed of sleep, says Wasielewski, 'by spirit-voices whispering in his ear'; and one night in February 1854, he rose from bed, called for a light, and wrote down a theme which he said the spirits of Schubert and Mendelssohn had sent him. It was this theme which Johannes Brahms, after Schumann's death, used as the basis of his Variations for Piano Duet (op. 23); and, oddly enough, it was a somewhat altered form of this same theme (the first six notes are identical) that Schumann himself had used, less than half a year before the 'spirits' imparted it to him, as the theme of the slow movement of the violin concerto.

According to Wasielewski, the symptoms of Schumann's mental ailment had begun to show themselves in 1851, more than two years before the composition of the violin concerto. These symptoms, says Wasielewski, recurred 'often' in 1852 and reappeared in 1853, with 'new ones added.' On February 27, 1854 (less than a fortnight after he wrote down the theme received from 'the spirits of Schubert and Mendelssohn'—that theme which had already served him, in part, for the violin concerto), Schumann's mortal anguish of mind became an engulfing darkness.

This is not the place to repeat in detail, or to discuss, the extraordinary and amazing account—published and vouched for by responsible persons of the highest reputation—according to which the spirits were apparently concerned about the long-suppressed concerto for violin. Briefly, it appears that in 1933, the distinguished Hungarian violinist, Miss Yelly d'Aranyi, grandniece of Joachim, was informed by the spirit of her famous uncle (who had died in 1907), and by the spirit of Schumann himself, of the existence of an unpublished violin concerto by Schumann, which they urged her to find and perform.

When Joachim died, his grandniece, Yelly d'Aranyi, was a violin student in the Royal Academy at Budapest. Why Joachim, during his lifetime, did not inform his grandniece of his intention regarding the disposal of the concerto, instead of waiting to communicate with her after his death by the somewhat laborious route of the spiritistic grapevine—this is among the various mysteries, mundane and supermundane, which cloud the history of the concerto. They cloud it so thickly, indeed, and the stories concerning it are so conflicting, that wary chroniclers would do well to wait until the mists clear away before attempting to recount all the facts in the case.

● CONCERTO FOR 'CELLO AND ORCHESTRA, IN A MINOR, OP. 129

'Last month,' wrote Clara Schumann in her diary of November 16, 1850, 'Robert composed a concerto for violoncello that pleased me very much. It seems to me to be written in true violoncello style.' In October of the following year she wrote further: 'I have played Robert's violoncello concerto again, and thus gave to myself a truly musical and happy hour. The romantic quality, the freshness and the humor, and also the highly interesting interweaving of violoncello and orchestra, are, indeed, wholly ravishing; and what euphony and deep feeling there are in all the melodic passages!' Schumann was then living at Düsseldorf, where he had lately become director of music.

The concerto was not published until August 1854. On Shrove Monday, February 27th, of that year, poor Schumann had attempted suicide by throwing himself from a bridge over the Rhine during an acute attack on melancholia. He was rescued by some boatmen, and at once placed under restaint. He lingered at Endenich for two years—from March 4, 1854, until he died July 29, 1856, in the presence of his devoted Clara.

The scheme of the concerto comprises these movements:

I. 'Nicht zu schnell,' A minor, 4-4.

II. Langsam, F major, 4-4. (This movement leads without pause, by way of an accelerando passage for the 'cello, into the last movement)—

III. 'Sehr lebhaft,' A minor, 2-4.

● OVERTURE TO BYRON's *Manfred*, OP. 115

On a certain evening toward the middle of the last century, Robert Schumann brought home a bottle of champagne with which to celebrate the completion of the 'first section,' as Clara called it, of his music to *Manfred*. He had already finished the overture (on November 4, 1848), and he thought well of it. 'I really consider it,' he wrote, 'one of the finest of my brain children.' The excellent Professor Niecks agrees with him. He considers the *Manfred* Overture not only Schumann's 'greatest achievement as a composer of program-music,' but his greatest 'as a composer generally.' 'One of the most original and grandest orchestral compositions ever conceived, one of the most powerful . . . one of the most sombre soul-portraits ever painted,' is his tribute of it. And then he becomes more specific in his characterization. He points out that the 'somberness is nowhere relieved, although contrast to the dark brooding and the surging agitation of despair is obtained by the tender, longing, regretful recollection of Astarte, the destroyed beloved one. And when at last life ebbs away, we are reminded of Manfred's dying words to the Abbot:

> 'Tis over—my dull eyes can fix thee not;
> But all things swim around me, and the earth
> Heaves, as it were, beneath me. . .
>
> Old man! 'tis not so difficult to die.'

Krehbiel thought that of all Schumann's works this is 'the most profoundly subjective.'

Alexander Scriabin

1872-1915

‡Scriabin was a member of the 'third generation' of Russian composers (the first being represented by Glinka, the second by Tchaikovsky and the Five). He was almost exactly Rachmaninoff's contemporary, and like him was widely acclaimed as a concert pianist. He died, however, in his forty-third year. His compositions may be roughly separated into two groups: in the first are a multitude of piano pieces of Chopinesque character; in the second are more piano pieces and a number of orchestral works that show the influence of certain philosophic, or, more properly, mystical ideas which came to dominate his thinking, and which in his music were related to the development of a highly personal harmonic technique of limited potentiality. His music has in recent times declined in popular favor, but is still occasionally heard.‡

- *The Divine Poem*, OP. 43
- *The Poem of Ecstasy*, OP. 54
- *Prometheus: The Poem of Fire*, OP. 60

The later orchestral works of Scriabin cannot be fully apprehended unless it is borne in mind that for him they represented something much more than adventures in aesthetic expression. Those last symphonic scores of his—*The Divine Poem, The Poem of Ecstasy,* and *Prometheus*—do not primarily aim (in Wagner's phrase) at 'the suscitating of pleasure in beautiful forms.' Nor are they 'program music' in the more familiar sense of the term: music designed to convey those moods and emotions that are common to all men—joy, desire, passion, grief; the contemplation of nature; the delight of the senses in the beauty of the world. Scriabin conceived these orchestral tone poems as mystical rites, and we cannot meet him even half way unless we try to understand his point of view, with as generous an attempt to grant his premises as we can achieve.

The essential fact to bear in mind is that Scriabin was a wholehearted and uncompromising mystic, and that he regarded music as a vehicle for the transfer of religious experience (we are speaking of the mature Scriabin, not of the earlier composer of Chopinesque salon music). He was dubbed by those about him 'the Muscovite seer'; and his friends have testified that, for him, 'Art and Religion were one'—that he employed music as a means for 'the expression of great inner truths.' It was 'the language in which he prophesied.'

Scriabin has been called a Theosophist, and undoubtedly he regarded himself as such. 'He had made himself,' wrote Paul Rosenfeld with truth in his *Musical Portraits*, 'a curious personal religion, a bizarre mixture of Theosophy and Neoplatonism and Bergsonian philosophy—a faith that prescribed transport; and these works [the symphonic poems] were in part conceived as rituals. They were planned as ceremonies of elevation and deification by ecstacy, in which performers and auditors engaged as active and passive celebrants.'

Those whom Scriabin endorsed as his spokesmen have told us that he desired, like Wagner, to unite all the arts in the service of an ideal purpose. But in Scriabin's case this end was not 'the perfect Drama, but the perfect Rite.' In his *Prometheus,* the third and last of these mystical tone poems, he intended that the 'symphony of sounds' should be accompanied by 'a symphony of color-rays'; and to that end he invented a keyboard instrument which he called a *tastiera per luce,* or *clavier à lumières,* by means of which effects of colored light were to be projected upon a screen, synchronizing with the progress of the music, and having a symbolic association with its expressional purposes. At the time of his death he was engaged upon a still more elaborate synthesis: a 'Mystery,' in which the music was to be associated not only with synchronous effects of light, but with perfume and the dance as well.

Scriabin, planning *The Divine Poem,* contemplated music 'such as had never been heard before.' The work was to be a further step toward the consummation of that 'Mystery' of which Scriabin 'now for the first time began to talk in definite terms,' says Alfred J. Swan in his informing book on the composer. 'The mere deification of the creative impulse, which characterized the preceding piano work, no longer satisfied him. He now began to identify this creative impulse with the divine play of the free powers of self-asserting individuality. His spirit was thus passing from struggle, through enjoyment, to divine play. This is the basis of *The Divine Poem.*'

Scriabin's wife made public, with her husband's approval, an interpretation of *The Divine Poem,* according to which the first section of the work ('Allegro, mystérieux, tragique,' C minor, 3-4), following a slow introduction, portrays the struggle between Man enslaved to a personal God and Man who is himself God, but lacking the will to proclaim his divinity. Thus frustrated, he immerses himself in the pleasures of sense, depicted in the second section of the work ('Lento, sublime,' E major, 3-4). But internal divine powers assist him toward liberation, and in the third and last section of the tone poem ('Allegro, avec une joie éclatante,' C major, 4-4) he gives himself up to the joys of 'untrammeled existence.'

Let us turn now to *The Poem of Ecstasy*. In this work, according to Modest Altschuler, who was the composer's intimate friend and confidant, Scriabin 'sought to express something of the emotional side of his philosophy.' Altschuler tells us that the expressional scheme of the *Poem* may be divided into three connected parts: (1) the composer's soul in an 'orgy of love'; (2) 'the realization of a fantastic dream'; (3) Scriabin's apprehension of 'the glory of his own art.' Other witnesses might be summoned, but their testimony would point to the same conclusion: That Scriabin's philosophy, as it is quintessentialized and projected in his symphonic scores, is a curious blend of exalted emotionalism and voluptuous revery. Of genuine spiritual rapture it has almost nothing, and to view Scriabin as a spiritual mystic is to misjudge his qualities.

The composition of the three tone poems occupied Scriabin for about seven years. *The Divine Poem* dates from 1903, *The Poem of Ecstasy* from 1908, and *Prometheus* from 1910. When *Prometheus* was first performed in London, Rosa Newmarch acted as interpreter of Scriabin's mystico-aesthetic doctrines, and her exegesis of *Prometheus* had the approval of the composer. It relates the music not to the familiar Greek myth, but to its theosophical transmogrification: 'The nascent races of mankind, not yet illuminated by the Promethean spark, were physically incomplete, possessing only the shadows of bodies . . . devoid of conscious personality. From this condition they were liberated by the gift of Prometheus—the fire which awakened man's conscious creative power.'

A word should be added concerning Scriabin's original plan for *Prometheus*, to which allusion was made above. The color-keyboard, or *clavier à lumières*, or *tastiera per luce*, with which he purposed to produce effects of colored light in conjunction with the music, has a complete and continuous part to itself, written out in notes on the top staff of the score. When *Prometheus* was performed for the first time, at Moscow on March 15, 1911, the color-keyboard was not ready—or refused to work (history is vague on this point)—and the piece was performed without its accompaniment of colored light. Nor was the device tried in any subsequent performances until *Prometheus* was given for the first time in New York, on March 20, 1915, by Modest Altschuler and the Russian Symphony Orchestra, when the *clavier à lumières* was used in accordance with Scriabin's intention. The result was not encouraging. The effort to watch the 'color symphony' and listen to the music at the same time, in an endeavor to trace an expressional correspondence between the two, proved to be distracting and ungratifying. Nor did the colors seem an inevitable reflection of the moods and emotions summoned by the music.

In addition to the orchestral apparatus itself—an immense one—the score comprises parts for piano, for organ, and for a chorus of mixed voices (without words); but a note inserted by the composer gives authority for the performance of the work without the use of the chorus and the *clavier à lumières*.

Dmitri Shostakovich

1906-

S

Shostakovich, the most prominent and successful of the first generation of Soviet composers, has lived most of his life in Leningrad, the city (then St. Petersburg) of his birth. He was the pupil in composition of the veteran Alexander Glazounoff and of Maximilian Steinberg, the son-in-law of Rimsky-Korsakoff. His works include nine symphonies (of which the Fourth has never been performed), a piano concerto, some chamber and piano music, the opera *Lady Macbeth of Mzensk*, and a number of ballets. ‡He was a lad of eleven when the Bolsheviks, with Lenin at their head, seized power in Russia and proceeded at once to lay the foundations of the first and most successful of modern totalitarian states. Thus from the outset of his career as a composer he has been subjected to teachings and disciplines designed to destroy, in all to whom they are applied (and in Russia they are applied to all), individuality of perception, intellectual curiosity, and imaginative initative. Yet these qualities survive in his music, and give it a distinction (not necessarily of a high order) of its own. Following the production of *Lady Macbeth* Shostakovich was accused of 'bourgeois formalism' and his work was placed under interdiction. His reinstatement in official favor was signalized by the successful performance of his Fifth Symphony in 1937. The charges against him were, however, revived in 1947 (at which time they were also directed against other prominent Soviet composers, notably Prokofieff and Katchaturian), and Shostakovich found it expedient to make a public confession of error and pledge of future good conduct. The concept of 'bourgeois formalism' has never been adequately defined from the point of view of a Western observer, who also finds it difficult to detect its presence in certain of Shostakovich's works and its absence in others. All of Shostakovich's qualities and characteristics appear to be present in some measure in all of his works—even in his epic 'political' symphonies he asserts, from time to time, the witty impertinence, the penchant for satirical observation and comment to which it has been supposed his masters take exception.‡

● SYMPHONY NO. 1, OP. 10

This symphony belongs to Shostakovich's twentieth year. It was issued by the Soviet Publishing Bureau in 1927. There is no key designation on the published score, which is entitled merely: Symphony for Orchestra, op. 10. The instrumentation is for large modern orchestra, including a piano.

The chief theme, which is in two sections, is heard in the Introduction to the first movement (Allegretto, 4-4). The first section of the theme, a brief motive of three notes, is stated by a solo trumpet, *p* and 'con sordino.' A bassoon follows immediately with the second member of the theme—indeed, the theme might be said to consist of three sections: for the bassoon's concluding phrase is also used as a germinating subject in the development of the movement. A clarinet delivers fragments of the theme above a pizzicato figure in the 'cellos. There is a pause, and the first section of the subject is given over to the strings. The main body of the movement begins ('Allegro non troppo'), in a tonality which, after the vagueness of the introductory pages, proves to be F minor, and the different members of the chief theme are now set forth. The second theme, in C minor, is introduced by the flute over pizzicati of the strings, the clarinet takes it up under a trill on E-flat for a solo violin, and it is soon heard in the basses. The mood becomes more and more impassioned, and the motive with the descending chromatics is heard fortissimo from the unison violins, with one of its related sections in the trumpets. Then, for a time, the gentler second theme dominates the musical scene. But the more passionate phrase recurs—in the basses, in the trumpets and, fortissimo, on the four unison horns. But the close is quiet, with the clarinet and 'cellos, pianissimo, recalling the introductory bars.

The second movement is the Scherzo of the symphony. It begins with foreshadowings in the string basses and clarinet (Allegro, 4-4—5-4) of the chief theme, which is heard in A minor at the fourteenth measure from the violins with pizzicato accompaniment. A piano, which is added to the orchestra in this movement, takes the theme, to an accompaniment of cymbals, horns, and basses. A Trio follows, in E minor, 3-4 time, 'meno mosso,' with a subject for two flutes under an inverted pedal E of the second violins, which is sustained for half a hundred measures. The voice of the triangle is also heard in the land. The bassoon, *pp*, brings us back to the main theme of the Scherzo. There is a notable climax, with the subject of the Trio given to the brass, fortissimo (in common time) against the main theme in the strings, woodwind, and piano. The close is quiet.

An oboe solo accompanied by string tremolos begins the expressive song of the slow movement (Lento, D-flat major, 4-4). This chief theme is tinged with a sorrowful chromaticism, and so also is the theme of the Largo at which the music shortly arrives—a passage of deep melancholy, scored at first, pianissimo, for strings alone (with an octave phrase in the bass). An oboe solo adds its voice, in a subject that is soon enunciated forte by the brass in a swiftly reached climax. A clarinet solo, *pp*, brings us back to the theme of the opening, now recalled by a solo violin. We hear this theme in the string basses, with a solo trumpet, muted, repeating softly the earlier oboe melody. The end is reached in a pianissimo passage for divided strings. A drum-roll, crescendo, leads to the Finale.

This Finale, a dramatic and vivid movement, full of abrupt alternations of mood and tempo, begins forte, with a single measure 'Allegro molto' (basses, bassoons, cymbals, tamtam, muted horns, and muted string tremolos), followed by twenty-nine Lento measures of introduction. The movement proper starts off as an 'Allegro molto,' 3-4, in F minor. The exuberant chief theme is delivered by the clarinet, with soft accompaniment of strings and cymbals. Bass strings and piano present it in imitation, and the violins lead it to a fortissimo. A change to A major introduces a new theme, exposed fortissimo by strings and woodwind, but this soon declines to a diminuendo, and leaves the second subject to the soft utterance of a solo violin ('meno mosso'), then to a solo horn. The 'Allegro molto' returns, there is a fortissimo climax, and a pause. Adagio: the kettledrum has a solo, with curious alternations of *fff* and *ppp*, and a solo 'cello, muted, broods upon the second subject (Largo).

The climax of the movement is now approached. The basses repeat the chief subject, under a counter melody for the other strings. This leads to a proclamation of the second theme, in augmentation, by the strings and wood, while the trombones oppose to it the chief subject. A Presto leads to a sonorous close in F major.

● SYMPHONY NO. 3, OP. 20 ('May Day')

Shostakovich's Third Symphony was composed in 1929 and was performed in Russia the following year. It is said to have 'stirred Russian audiences on each successive May Day,' and caused Shostakovich to be spoken of as a 'kind of composer-laureate to the Soviet State.' The score was published by the appropriate agency of the Soviet Government in 1932.

May Day—the first day of May—was chosen as an international Labor holiday by the International Socialist Congress of 1889. It is the day usually selected by Socialist parties, trade unions, and labor organizations for public celebrations of a more or less political character. It is, of course, celebrated with particular emphasis in the USSR. Shostakovich's 'May Day' Symphony (which is in one movement) employs in the final section an 'ad libitum' chorus of mixed voices singing a Russian text which exhorts the proletariat to 'raise the May-Day standard!' recalls, briefly, the downfall of the Tsarist regime in Russia, and extols the Five Year Plan.

The single movement of the symphony (which dispenses with key-signatures) is noteworthy for its looseness of thematic organization. Victor Belaieff has pointed out this peculiarity of Shostakovich's structural method:

It might be described as the negation of thematic development, and consists in the systematic adoption of a method which is the converse of Liszt's 'transformation of themes.' Shostakovich not only refrains in general from repeating a theme in its original or in a transformed version—the accepted custom with symphonic composers—but in writing a theme, he even avoids the repetition of identical *motifs* and melodic turns of phrases. One gets the impression that he wants every bar of his composition to be different from the rest. He applies this method also to the distribution of the parts, striving to attain a completely independent design for each of the orchestral parts in the score.

There is a profusion of themes, many of them declamatory in style, some of popular characters; and they are employed with little regard for traditional form. The melodic structure is prevailingly diatonic; and Shostakovich is almost as fond of scale passages raised to the dignity of thematic material as his Finnish colleague Sibelius—or, for that matter, as Beethoven (though there is a difference).

The symphony starts off with an Allegretto in common time, begun by a clarinet solo which becomes, at the fourteenth measure, a clarinet duo accompanied by pizzicati of the string basses. This leads, through a 'più mosso' passage, to an Allegro section of 198 measures, initiated by the full orchestra, fortissimo, 4-4, with one of the vigorously striding scale passages which are almost a hallmark of the symphony's thematic subject matter. At the peak of a crescendo, all the instruments save the side-drum are withdrawn, and we hear, above a persistent tattoo of the drum, a sort of medley of popular tunes for the brass. The woodwind follows with a complex of other tunes, and the strings add their voices. The pace slackens, and leads to a brief and quiet Andante. The orchestra plays pianissimo almost throughout this section. There is a singular duo for piccolo and first violins, *ppp*, against which the 'cellos and basses mutter an opposing subject. Afterward, the strings play alone ('Lento espressivo') for thirty-eight measures.

The Allegro is resumed, at first in triple time. Much use is made of the characteristic scale passages as thematic patterns. A proclamative phrase is uttered, *fff*, by the four horns in unison. A climax and a swift diminuendo bring another but very brief slow section (Andante—Largo), introduced by a tuba solo above a drum-roll and tremolos of the string basses, and followed by a curious episode in which recitativo passages for trombone soli are interspersed with glissandi of the 'cellos and double basses, afterward of the violins. Descending scale passages in octaves for the orchestra, another recitative for the trombones, and an *fff* cymbal crash, announce the entrance of the choral Finale, Moderato, 4-4.

● Symphony No. 5, op. 47

‡Shostakovich is said to have written his Fifth Symphony in 1937 to celebrate the twentieth anniversary of the Soviet Republic. Shortly before, he had for the first time been subjected to the discipline of adverse criticism in the official press of the Soviet Government. Stalin had attended a performance of his opera *Lady Macbeth of Mzensk* and had left the theater while it was in progress. Not long afterward, an article appeared condemning the composer for 'bourgeois formalism,' his works were withdrawn from the operatic, ballet,

and concert repertoires, and his career as a composer was, to all intents and purposes, at an end, though he was allowed to retain his teaching post at the Leningrad Conservatory. One does not know by what acts of contrition he sought reinstatement in official favor, but he succeeded in obtaining it, and on 21 November 1937 his Fifth Symphony was performed in Leningrad and received with great acclamation.‡

The Fifth Symphony is in four movements: (i) Moderato—'Allegro non troppo'—Largamente, 4-4; (ii) Allegretto, 3-4; (iii) Largo, 4-4; (iv) 'Allegro non troppo,' 4-4. The movements have been described as follows:

The first movement opens with a theme based on chordal intervals, stated alternately in the low and high registers (strings), from which is evolved an extended subject of dramatic and lyrical character. The development involves extensions and evolutions of this material, and what may be called the recapitulation is ushered in by a unison restatement of the initial theme, largamente. The second movement is a Scherzo, with the Ländler-like character of similar movements in Bruckner and Mahler symphonies. The succeeding Largo is a lyrical rhapsody of cumulative intensity—and here the resemblance in method is to certain movements of Sibelius or sections of movements (i.e. the Seventh Symphony). There is a Rondo-Finale in which march rhythms predominate and which, punctuated by reminiscences from themes used in the first movement, rises to a brilliant climax and conclusion.

According to Shostakovich, the theme of the Fifth Symphony is 'the assertion of personality. It is man with all his emotions and experiences that I saw as a focus of design in this work, which is lyrical in conception from beginning to end.'

● CONCERTO FOR PIANO AND ORCHESTRA, OP. 35

This concerto, composed in 1933, was performed for the first time in America at one of Stokowski's Concerts for Youth, under his direction, at the Academy of Music, Philadelphia, December 12, 1934. The solo pianist was Eugene List.

The work is written for piano and an orchestra of strings and trumpet. There are four movements.

The opening movement ('Allegro moderato,' C minor, 4-4) begins with an introductory call for the muted trumpet accompanied by runs of the piano, after which the solo instrument announces the chief theme, a simply constructed subject which completes its initial statement after ten measures. The strings then take it up, and we hear it in the first violins, with a variant of it in the octave basses. The tempo changes to 'Allegro vivace,' and the second theme, based on a fanfare-like motive in E-flat major, is proposed, marcatissimo, by the piano bass, against reiterated staccato chords of the strings. The instruments are soon joined by the trumpet, which has a conspicuous part throughout, and there is much play with this material. The development is brilliant and vivacious.

The last dozen measures, Moderato, lead directly into the slow movement, a Lento in 3-4 time, in which Shostakovich remembers the Phrygian Mode (the third of the Ecclesiastical Modes). The strings alone, muted, give out the principal subject, and expound it through twenty-seven measures in an extended cantilena delivered by the first violins. At the twenty-eighth measure the piano enters with a counter-subject. The intensity of the music's mood is steadily increased to a fortissimo outburst, appassionato. The pace quickens ('più mosso'); there are vehement declamatory phrases for the piano answered by sharply reiterated chords of the orchestra, and the piano surges upward through a succession of octave scale-passages to a *ffff*, Largo. There is a dolorous descent by the solo instrument, diminuendo, to an unresolved suspension. The orchestral strings re-enter softly, preparing the way for a solo of the muted trumpet, which is now heard, piano and espressivo, accompanied by the strings, in a reminiscence of the chief theme of the movement as first stated by the piano. The piano resumes its song, in which it is joined by the strings. The movement ends quietly, on a sustained chord of the orchestra and piano.

The solo instrument begins the third movement, a brief intermezzo of twenty-nine measures (Moderato) which consists essentially of two cadenzas for the solo instrument, the first unaccompanied, the second accompanied, separated by an orchestral interlude of nine measures.

The Finale, which follows without pause, makes a dutiful bow to the rondo form in its ground-plan, though the ancient prescriptions do not estop the composer from amusing himself in his own way. The piano leads off, 'Allegro brio,' C minor, 2-4, with an eight-bar prelude accompanied by the string basses. Then the orchestra alone sets forth the chief theme, an exuberant and infectious subject based on a pattern of repeated notes and an impudent gruppetto in sixteenths. The piano re-enters after twenty-two bars, and soon the trumpet, which has an important part in these concluding activities, adds its voice. A fermata on a fortissimo chord of the orchestra introduces a cadenza for the piano, which is followed by a brilliant coda, Presto, in which the piano very handsomely allows its brother soloist, the trumpet, to have the final word.

Jan Sibelius
1865-

S

Sibelius in his lifetime has become a classic master—a composer to whose music we listen conscious that we are in the presence of something timeless, neither old nor new, independent of fashion, unaffected by the search for novelty and sensation. When we look back over the remarkable succession of works produced by him during his long creative life, especially the seven symphonies, we must recognize that this is music marked by a purity of intentions, an integrity of style, and a mysterious exaltation of spirit, that have few counterparts in the music of the past half century. We hear in it what a profound, inscrutable, yet candid spirit has chosen to tell us of his vision of Nature and the world, and we are inexplicably moved—inexplicably, because the processes of this art are fundamentally mysterious, as Nature is mysterious. Their mysteriousness is part of their inner life and movement; it is of their essence. The thoughts of this tone poet move on the far side of an indefinite boundary. They move as those who go on a secret errand. They are shut away from us by the very clarity and simplicity that deceptively surround them. Their very directness is a cloak. And we shall probably never know quite what they would say to us, or why they stir and haunt us as they do.

● SYMPHONY No. 1, IN E MINOR, OP. 39

This symphony was completed in 1899 and published three years later. Thus Sibelius was thirty-four years old when he made his first essay in the symphonic form, and he had already proved himself a master. Cecil Gray thinks it 'symbolically significant' that this First Symphony should have been written in the last year of the nineteenth century, 'since it is the last of an old line rather than the first of a new': a conclusion reached apparently for the reason that 'the symphony has distinctive affinities, both formal and coloristic, with . . . the romantic symphonies of various predecessors.' The symphony is, undeniably, orthodox in form. It is also the utterance of a personality which was, even in 1899, unprecedented in musical art.

The symphony has the regular four movements of the established tradition, and is scored for an orchestra comprising woodwinds in pairs, four horns, three trumpets, three trombones, tuba, harp, timpani, bass-drum, cymbals, triangle, and strings.

The slow introduction to the first movement ('Andante, ma non troppo,' E minor, 2-2) 'evokes a legendary mood,' remarked Arthur Shepherd, the distinguished American composer, teacher, and critic, in an interesting comment. It is begun by a solo clarinet with a melody twenty-eight measures long, announced over a roll of the timpani (this melody recurs in the Finale of the symphony). Following this introductory passage the bold principal theme is presented by the first violins ('Allegro energico'). A subsidiary portion of the theme is carried on in forceful accents by the woodwinds, leading forward to an eloquent re-statement of the initial period in full power, reaching at length an abrupt turning-point on an F-sharp major chord. A soft string tremolando leads over to a second theme, in sharply rhythmed phrases, presented, conversationally, in the woodwinds and horns. An expressive corollary to this material is projected in long-sustained phrases in the oboe, flutes, and clarinets, in a wide dispersion, which, in its particular timbre, becomes a sort of hallmark of Sibelius' orchestration. The staccato subject reasserts its way through a crescendo and accelerando culminating on a unison cadence in B minor. The development section is notable for its adroit blending of all the thematic material, a fragment or figure of one theme merging into that of another. Highly imaginative is the extended passage of overlapping and converging chromatic scales. A finely achieved crescendo marks the climax of the development, bringing with it the recapitulation with modification and abridgements of the various themes.

The second movement is an 'Andante, ma non troppo lento,' in E-flat major, 2-2 time, begun by a song-like theme, heard in the muted first violins and 'cellos, with a brief refrain in the clarinets, recurring at the phrase intersections. A new theme is presented by the bassoons and carried forward through a rising crescendo by the other woodwinds, culminating in a forte measure for the brass, recalling rhythmically the initial measures of the principal theme. This figure is taken over by the strings and developed briefly but vigorously. A solo 'cello remembers the first theme, beneath repeated pianissimo chords of the woodwind. Then occurs the most poetical and haunting moment of the symphony—a passage in which the horn quartet is heard against a murmurous accompaniment of violins and harp ('molto tranquillo, dolce') with the first horn singing a new theme of extraordinary beauty, both pastoral and melancholy. There is a return to the earlier thematic material, which is developed stormily. The end comes peacefully, with a recurrence of the chief theme, subsiding finally, *ppp*, in the strings, horns, and harp.

The Scherzo is an Allegro in C major, 3-4 time. Announced with vigor and joviality by thrumming chords in the violas and 'cellos (pizzicato), the principal idea of the movement is presented forcefully by the timpani and immediately after by the violins. This motif, which, in the formal sense, becomes only a figure in the phrase-building, dominates, in a large degree, the first and third sections of the movement. Subsidiary ideas are developed with gusto. The Trio ('Lento, ma non troppo,' E major, 3-4) is begun by a new theme in the horns. The movement ends with the pizzicato strumming chords of the beginning.

The Finale is marked 'quasi una fantasia.' 'It begins with an Andante introduction in which the strings recall the melody heard at the beginning of the symphony from the clarinet. The main body of the movement ("Allegro molto," 2-4) projects an agitated theme in the woodwind, which, in detached phrase-form, is bandied about through the different choirs, the material assuming more and more the character of free fantasy as implied in the superscription of the movement. A broad and expressive melody is at length heard in the unison violins ("Andante cantabile"). This is the inevitable foil for the strenuously agitated material of the first part, which returns in a forceful development only to be followed in turn by an eloquent climax on the song theme. The end, on two pizzicato chords of the strings, is reminiscent of the close of the first movement.'

• SYMPHONY NO. 2, IN D MAJOR, OP. 43

Sibelius composed his Second Symphony in 1901-2. It was performed for the first time at Helsingfors, on March 8, 1902, at a concert given under the composer's direction. Theodore Thomas introduced the work to America at a concert of the Chicago Symphony Orchestra on January 2, 1904.

The English critic, Cecil Gray, has characterized succinctly the various movements of this symphony in his compact and vivid study of the Northern master.

If the First Symphony of Sibelius, he writes, 'is the very archetype of the romantic and picturesque symphony of the latter part of the nineteenth century, the Second strikes out a new path altogether. The First is a conclusion, the last of its dynasty and in many ways the best; the Second is the beginning of a new line, and contains the germs of immense and fruitful development.' It is Gray's contention that while the Second Symphony, viewed superficially, appears to conform to the basic structural principles of the nineteenth-century four-movement symphony—as represented, for example, in the symphonic scores of Brahms and Tchaikovsky—it is in fact organized upon new and revolutionary principles. For a full exposition of the nature of these principles, the interested reader is referred to Gray's admirable *Sibelius*.

In his analysis of the Second Symphony, Gray calls attention to the inversion in this work of the usual construction of a first movement. For Sibelius introduces 'thematic fragments in the exposition, building them up into an organic whole in the development section, then dispersing and dissolving the material back into its primary constituents in a brief recapitulation.' 'In this movement,' Gray writes, 'one can detect several distinct groups of thematic germs, none of which can claim the right to be regarded as the most important.' Nor in the second movement ('Tempo andante, ma rubato'), he remarks, does one find the contrast between a lyrical chief subject and a more virile second subject. A second lyrical subject enters, for 'the melancholy, reflective first subject is quite unequal to the task of coping with the violent opposition it arouses.'

The Scherzo (Vivacissimo) is 'more conventional in form and style, apart from the Trio, which is built upon a theme beginning with no fewer than nine repetitions of the same note.' The Finale ('Allegro moderato') follows tradition. 'In these days of cynicism and disillusion,' remarks Gray, 'it is of course the fashion to sneer at the convention of the "happy ending," of which the orthodox symphonic Finale is the musical equivalent, and it is certainly true that most modern attempts to conform to it ring hollow and insincere. We of the present generation simply do not feel like that; we find it difficult to be triumphant, and we have no doubt excellent reasons for it. Yet the fact remains that that is a weakness and a deficiency in us; and there is something of sour grapes in the contemporary attitude towards those artists of an earlier generation who have achieved the state of spiritual serenity, optimism, and repose which makes it possible for them to conclude a work convincingly in this manner. Sibelius is one of them: his triumphant final movements, so far from being due to a mere unthinking acceptance of a formal convention, corresponds to a definite spiritual reality.'

Georg Schneevoigt, the Finnish conductor, a close friend of Sibelius, told Philip Hale that the composer's intention in the Second Symphony was to epitomize the history and character of the Finnish people.

• SYMPHONY NO. 4, IN A MINOR, OP. 63

The first performance of this symphony—in many respects the most strikingly original in the Sibelius canon—is said to have been at Helsingfors in 1911. It was introduced to America by the New York Symphony Society and Walter

Damrosch, on March 2, 1913. When the work was about to be disclosed to the public of the Symphony concerts in Boston (then under the direction of Karl Muck), Olin Downes prepared the following illuminating analysis of the score and published it in *The Boston Post*; subsequently, this exposition was printed by Philip Hale in his notes for the Boston Symphony performances of the symphony on October 24-5, 1913:

I. 'Tempo molto moderato, quasi adagio,' 4-4. Of the four movements of this symphony, the first is freest in its form. There is a somber, lowering introduction. Bold, harsh progressions for the brass lead from an opening that has hovered about from E minor through various minor keys to the key of F-sharp major. This place might be called the opening of the movement proper. The mood is gentle and melancholy. The passage leads in turn to a very curious shifting background in counterpoint for the strings, against which various woodwind instruments call strangely. Later there is a return to the gentle mood of the F-sharp major section, and this brief movement, the first movement of a symphony described as in 'A minor,' comes to an end in the lovely and pastoral key of A major.

II. 'Allegro molto vivace,' 3-4. The scherzo is not less singular, although its form is clear enough. It is wild and restless. The extraordinary juxtapositions of certain instruments and tonalities remain to be heard before the effect can be described. After a curious climax, built chiefly on two notes of one of the themes, a motive shouted repeatedly by many instruments, this movement ends softly and suddenly.

III. 'Il tempo largo,' 4-4. The slow movement has more sheer beauty than any of the others. It commences with dialogue of the wind instruments and the free preluding of various choirs. Then, under a shimmering accompaniment of the upper strings, the 'cellos intone the real theme of the movement, a broad and noble song, almost Bruckner-like in these qualities, which, with some episodic interruptions, is repeatedly proclaimed by the orchestra and always more impressively. The movement ends mysteriously, a C-sharp held by violas and muted horns, with wood and stringed instruments echoing fragments from an earlier passage.

IV. Allegro, 2-2. But of the four movements the last is, perhaps, the most brusque and fantastical. The first phrase of the theme, at once given out by the violins, is scarcely heard again, but the second half of the theme is employed in variation, and a brief motive taken from it is the predominant thought of the movement. This motive consists, first of four notes composed of a triplet and a quarter, followed by a sort of rejoinder of three quarter notes, often sounded on the bells or stopped horns. Then there is the passage where the strings, tremolo, ascend gradually over a vibrating bass, and the flutes and oboes, practically in another key, call eerily. After the clashings of reiterated successive chords of the dominant-seventh and tonic of A-flat, a curious chant in three-part harmony and in march-like rhythm is developed by the woodwind.

Very curious and interesting should this effect be, although not more so than many other passages of the symphony. . . Farther on occurs a passage where the horns and woodwind instruments sustain the chord of C major in its second position, while the strings whirr up and down the scale, the bells ring exultantly, and a trumpet, swelling the initial tone of its figure from *ppp* to *fff*, throws out the fragment of the opening theme previously mentioned. The march-like theme is resumed and developed. The string passage with the off-key cries of the woodwind recurs, rondo fashion, and finally this remarkable movement comes to an end in a most gray and arid manner: a complaint of the oboe (the skip of a seventh), and soft despondent chords from the strings —always softer, always more gray—in the key of A minor.

Cecil Gray has interesting things to say of this symphony:

This symphony is a landmark not merely in Sibelius' own development, but in the history of musical form, representing as it does the farthest point to which the principle of the elimination of non-essentials has been pushed. There is not a superfluous note in the score from beginning to end, and hardly one that is not of thematic origin, although the most careful and minute scrutiny may sometimes be necessary in order to trace the connection between the theme and its ultimate derivatives. Sometimes, indeed, it can only be felt or intuitively apprehended. The scoring, too, is similarly of the utmost restraint and austerity throughout. The modest instrumental requirements of the Third are here still further reduced by the omission of a third trumpet, and only in a few bars in the whole work is the full orchestra employed, the greater part of the action being carried out by a bare handful of instruments.

The complete absence of sensuous appeal in this work, coupled with the exacting demands it makes upon the intelligence of audiences, will always prevent it from becoming popular. For the few, however, it probably constitutes Sibelius' greatest achievement; he has certainly never written anything to surpass it.

● Symphony No. 5, in E-flat major, op. 82

This symphony was played for the first time on February 12, 1921, at Queen's Hall, London, with Sibelius conducting.

It was announced then in London that 'the composer desires his work to be regarded as absolute music, having no direct poetic basis.' The critic of the *Daily Telegraph*, referring to what he called the lack of 'joyousness' in the music, concluded that this could not be attributed to the history of the years between 1914 and 1918, since the work 'was apparently composed before the War.' But Cecil Gray gives the date of its composition as 1915, and says that it was commissioned by the Finnish Government in celebration of the composer's fiftieth birthday, which fell on December 8 of that year.

The symphony is divided into three parts; but the first part comprises two well-defined movements: an opening 'Molto moderato,' which leads without pause into an 'Allegro moderato' which may be viewed as the Scherzo of the symphony. These two linked movements, though they are distinct in mood and character, are integrated by community of theme, after the fashion set by Schumann and popularized by César Franck. The subject which binds them together is a motto-theme of concise and simple outline: the bucolic phrase proclaimed by the first horn in the opening measures over a roll of the timpani ('molto moderato,' E-flat, 12-8). Its first four notes (B-flat, E-flat, F, B-flat, ascending) constitute the thematic seed from which is developed a good part of the substance of the two connected movements. The motto-theme, four times repeated by the three trumpets in unison, introduces the scherzo section of the first part ('Allegro moderato [ma poco a poco stretto],' at first in B major, 3-4), with a curiously Beethovenish theme in a dance rhythm for the woodwind in thirds, the sixth and seventh measures of which recall the motto-theme of the opening.

In the succeeding movement ('Andante mosso, quasi allegretto,' G major, 3-2) the somewhat unpromising theme is developed with much resourcefulness of variation. From a simple and rather naïve subject, foreshadowed by the violas and 'cellos pizzicati against sustained harmonies in the clarinets, bassoons, and horns, and afterward more clearly defined by a pair of flutes playing in thirds and sixths, the composer evolves a series of variations singularly rich in expressiveness (an odd detail is the elaborate use of an appogiatura effect in the flutes and bassoons, as a background against which the strings develop the theme).

The Finale is the crown of the work, and is in many ways the most nobly imagined and nobly eloquent page that Sibelius has yet given us. The violas announce the first subject ('Allegro molto,' E-flat, 2-4) under an agitated figure for the second violins divisi, and the first violins continue it. Woodwind and 'cellos sing a more lyrical theme against a broad and swinging melody for the horns and strings, which is derived from a double-bass figure heard in the preceding movement. A recapitulation of the first theme, misterioso, for the muted and divided strings alone (violins in eight parts), leads to the superb coda—'un pochettino largamente'—in which the music achieves a gradual amplification and heroic emphasis.

• SYMPHONY NO. 7, IN C MAJOR, OP. 105

This symphony was published in 1925, and remains the last in Sibelius' series of symphonies. It is without key designation, but the tonality at the opening of its single extended movement is A minor, and, at the close, its relative key, C major.

The symphony opens with an extended Adagio section of brooding and somber intensity. Its initial subject, an ascending scale passage in A minor, 3-2, for the strings, furnishes the underlying theme of the work. It crops out again and again, as a whole or fragmentarily, and often inverted. In the twenty-second measure it is succeeded by a broadly lyrical theme in C major, sung by the divided violas and 'cellos, joined later by the divided first and second violins. The scale passages return in the string and woodwind, and then we hear from a solo trombone a chant-like melody in C, which will later assume great importance.

The tempo quickens; there are more scale passages; the pace is Vivacissimo, C minor. The strings announce a subject that recalls the mood of the Scherzo of Beethoven's 'Eroica.' There is a rallentando, and a return of the adagio tempo of the beginning. The solo trombone repeats its chant-like phrase against figurations in the strings, and it is joined by the rest of the brass choir. Again the tempo quickens, and an 'Allegro molto moderato' is established. The strings ('poco forte,' C major, 6-4) give out a new melody of folk-line simplicity and breadth; and this is followed by another subject, also in C major, arranged—according to a pattern of which Sibelius is fond—for woodwind doubled in pairs, playing in thirds, fifths, and sixths. This theme is developed by strings and wind, with interjections of the familiar scale passages of the violins.

The key changes to E-flat major, the tempo becomes Vivace. There are ascending and descending antiphonal passages, strings answered by woodwind. The tempo becomes Presto, the key C major. The strings, divided in eight parts, begin a mysteriously portentous passage, at the first triple *p*, with the violas and 'cellos defining an urgent figure against a reiterated pedal G of the violins, basses and timpani. A crescendo, rallentando, is accompanied by a fragment of the basic scale passage, in augmentation, for the horns. The tempo is again Adagio; and now the chant-like C major theme is heard once more from the brass choir, against mounting figurations of the strings. There is a climax, *ff*, for the whole orchestra. The strings are heard alone, 'largamente molto,' in an affetuoso of intense expression. Flute and bassoon in octaves, supported by soft string tremolos, sing a plaint. The strings, dolce, in syncopated rhythm, modulate through seventh chords in A-flat and G to a powerful suspension, fortissimo, on the tonic chord of C major; and this brings to a close the enigmatic, puissant, and strangely moving work.

● CONCERTO FOR VIOLIN AND ORCHESTRA, IN D MINOR, OP. 47

This concerto, dedicated to Ferenc Vecsey, was published in 1905. Mrs. Rosa Newmarch, in her brochure on Sibelius, implies that in its published form the concerto is a revision of an early work. 'We cannot judge it by comparison with its original conception,' she remarks, 'but the Finnish critics consider it to be far more acceptable in its revised form. Sibelius' violin concerto, like that of Tchaikovsky, has been pronounced "impossibly difficult"; but it has not had to wait so long for its interpreter as the Russian concerto waited for Brodsky. Its remarkable originality, and even the new technical difficulties it presents, will commend this work to virtuosi in search of fresh laurels.'

The emotional key for much of the concerto is set by the mood of the opening, with the somberly expressive chief theme heard from the solo violin through a misty accompaniment of muted strings. This opening movement ('Allegro moderato,' D minor) is curiously rugged, dark-hued, rhapsodic, evoking the thought of ancient bardic songs heard against a background of torches or pagan fires in some wild Northern night. It is rich in unaccompanied passages for the solo instrument.

The slow movement ('Adagio di molto,' B-flat major, 4-4) is a lyric meditation of penetrating tenderness, touched with melancholy fervor. The violin sings the simple and heart-felt theme (after a few measures of preluding in thirds by the woodwind), above accompanying chords in the horns and bassoons. Later, the violin weaves expressive arabesques about the song of the orchestra.

The composer is said to have stated that the Finale is a 'Danse macabre,' although it is not so designated in the published score. This movement, a boldly fantastic rondo, opens ('Allegro, ma non tanto,' D major, 3-4) with a daringly reiterated dactyllic rhythm established by the kettledrums and lower strings, above which the violin begins its sinister dance. The key whirls into G minor, with the orchestra (violins and 'cellos) introducing the second theme. The path of the solo instrument, with its obstacle race of leaping octaves across intervals of minor and major ninths, is not strewn with roses in these wild and exciting dance measures.

• TWO LEGENDS FOR ORCHESTRA: *The Swan of Tuonela* AND *Lemminkäinen's Homecoming*, OP. 22

The programmatic basis of this tone poem is to be found in the *Kalevala*, the national epic of Finland—an imaginative source whence Sibelius drew inspiration for many of his most powerful conceptions. In the early and middle 'nineties, when he was almost thirty, he projected, and afterward completed, a cycle of four tone poems, or *Legends*, for orchestra, based on episodes in the *Kalevala*, and comprising these numbers: (1) *Lemminkäinen and the Maidens*; (2) *Lemminkäinen in Tuonela*; (3) *The Swan of Tuonela*; (4) *Lemminkäinen's Homecoming*.

According to Cecil Gray in his book on Sibelius, the music that eventually became the third number of this symphonic tetralogy, *The Swan of Tuonela*, was intended originally as the prelude to an opera which Sibelius, in 1893, planned in collaboration with a Finnish writer named J. H. Erkko. The opera was to be called *The Building of the Boat*, and part of the action was to pass in Tuonela, the Finnish underworld, the abode of the dead. The idea of the opera was abandoned, but the intended prelude survived, and was eventually published in 1901 as *The Swan of Tuonela*.

The Swan of Tuonela: The four symphonic legends derived by Sibelius from material in the *Kalevala* are largely concerned with the adventures of Lemminkäinen, one of the four chief heroes of the epic—'a jovial, reckless personage, always getting into serious scrapes, from which he escapes . . . by his skill in magic. . .' Lemminkäinen, in the course of certain heroic exploits, arrives at the dread river which surrounds the land of Tuonela, the Finnish Hades, the Kingdom of Death. His task is to shoot the swan 'on Tuoni's murky river . . . using but a single arrow.' There he is slain and dismembered by an old enemy; but his mother, through necromantic arts, joins together the fragments of the body and restores her son to life.

The score of Sibelius' tone poem contains this prefatory note:

Tuonela, the kingdom of Death, the Hades of Finnish mythology, is surrounded by a broad river of black water and swift current. On it, in majestic course, floats and sings the Swan of Tuonela.

The melancholy swan-song is heard on the English horn, above an accompaniment of muted strings and a roll on the bass-drum. There is a poignant climax, and then the dolorous song drifts down the river into silence.

Lemminkäinen's Homecoming: When this tone poem, or legend, was first played by the Philharmonic Society on February 1, 1902, the program book remarked that 'the following note, published in the score, will serve to guide the listener through the composition:

"Lemminkäinen is the warrior-hero, the Achilles, of Finnish mythology. His intrepidity and beauty make him the favorite of the women. Exhausted by a long series of wars and combats, he determines to seek his home. He turns his sorrows and cares into warhorses, and sets out. After a journey replete with adventures, he reaches his native land, so full of the recollections of his childhood." '

● Tone Poem, *En Saga*, op. 9

The score of this tone poem, published in 1903, contains no preface, argument, program, or other guide to the composer's meaning; and Sibelius has kept his own counsel concerning the significance of the music. But his biographer, Mrs. Newmarch, tells us that 'although the work unfortunately belongs to that baffling and unsatisfactory class of symphonic poems which composers issue to the world without any frank indication of their literary basis, nevertheless the music certainly suggests the recital of some old tale in which the heroic and pathetic elements are skillfully blended, while the title indicates that it belongs to Scandinavian rather than to Finnish history. The episode with which the work closes, a clarinet solo accompanied by muted strings and an almost inaudible roll of the cymbals (which are struck with the drumsticks), belongs to the most effective pages Sibelius has ever written. The absence of timpani is a peculiar feature of this work.'

Mrs. Newmarch should have had a conference with Walter Niemann; for Dr. Niemann is sure that this symphonic poem is the story of Finland. He perceives in it 'one of the most magnificent, most heart-rending and strongly affecting tone-pictures of our time, in which, as one can perceive easily, Sibelius has set forth in tones for posterity the present lot of his people. We do not need a program for his *Saga* to tell us at every moment what hovered before the composer.'

Nevertheless, hearers less clairaudient than Dr. Niemann may wish that Sibelius had given us some clue to his expressional intentions.

● Tone Poem, *Finlandia*, op. 26

Mrs. Newmarch, literary godmother to Sibelius, quotes the composer as stating with emphasis that he has used no genuine folk tunes in this score. 'There is a mistaken impression abroad,' Sibelius is said to have remarked years ago to Mrs. Newmarch, 'that my themes are often folk-melodies. So far I have never used a theme that was not of my own invention. The thematic material of *Finlandia* (and of *En Saga*) is entirely my own.' Mrs. Newmarch remarks that, like Glinka, 'Sibelius avoids the crude material of the folk-song; but like that great national poet, he is so penetrated by the spirit of his race that he can evolve a national melody calculated to deceive the elect.'

Finlandia, in its assemblage of contrasted moods, expresses agitation, prayerfulness, sorrow, buoyancy, elevation, and a prophetic vision, as it seems, of ultimate national triumph.

The work was composed in 1894. At one of its first performances in this country—by the Russian Symphony Orchestra in 1905—this note on the score was published:

Finlandia, though without explanatory subtitle, seems to set forth an impression of the national spirit and life. The work records the impressions of an exile's return home after a long absence. An agitated, almost angry theme for the brass choir, short and trenchant, begins the introduction, 'Andante sostenuto (alla breve).' This theme is answered by an organ-like response in the woodwind, and then a prayerful passage for strings, as though to reveal the essential earnestness and reasonableness of the Finnish people, even under the stress of national sorrow. This leads to an 'Allegro moderato' episode, in which the restless opening theme is proclaimed by the strings against a very characteristic rhythmic figure, a succession of eight beats, the first strongly accented. With a change to Allegro the movement, looked at as an example of the sonata form, may be said to begin. A broad, cheerful theme by the strings, in A flat, against the persistent rhythm in the brass, is followed by a second subject, introduced by the wood-wind and taken up by the strings, then by the 'cello and first violin. This is peaceful and elevated in character, and might be looked upon as prophetic of ultimate rest and happiness. The development of these musical ideas carries the tone poem to an eloquent conclusion.

● SYMPHONIC FANTASIA, *Pohjola's Daughter*, OP. 49

The programmatic basis of this symphonic poem is to be found in the *Kalevala*, the national epic of Finland. The elements of the *Kalevala* are ancient popular songs, hitherto orally transmitted, that were collected in different parts of Finnish territory, for the most part during the nineteenth century. The first important collection was published in 1822 by Zaccharias Topelius, though fragments of mythical poetry had been known in the eighteenth century. The poem was given its present coherent form in 1835 by the Finnish scholar, Elias Lönnrot (1802-84), one of the founders of modern Finnish literature. Lönnrot, with incredible industry, collected the material in Finland proper, but principally in Russian Karelia eastward to the White Sea. His first edition, which appeared in 1835, contains 12,000 verses, for the first time systematically arranged as a consistent whole. A second edition (1849) containing 23,000 verses, is the best known form of the poem.

The *Kalevala* is written in eight-syllabled trochaic verse, with alliteration, but without rhyme. It is divided into fifty cantos or runes.

The symphonic fantasia, *Pohjola's Daughter*, was published, as op. 49, in 1906. Of the two characters represented in the tone poem, Väinämöinen and Pohjola, the former is one of the chief personages of the *Kalevala*. He has been called 'the Finnish Orpheus—the ideal hero of the race. Profound wisdom and the power of magic song are his special attributes.' He is also described as the 'Son of the Wind and of the Virgin of the Air,' and represented as a vigorous patriarch, a bard of enormous strength and crafty skill.

'Pohjola' is 'the name for the North Country, sometimes identified with Lapland.' Louhi is the mistress of it. 'Her daughter has a complex character. In the *Kalevala* she appears in three phases: as the beautiful and accomplished daughter of the witch; as a timid and shrinking bride, almost a child bride; and as a wicked and heartless peasant-woman.'

Väinämöinen had been borne by an eagle to a spot near the castle of Pohjola. There Louhi received him graciously and promised to reward him with her beautiful daughter if he would forge for her a talisman called the Sampo. He replied that he was unable to do this, but that he would send his brother Ilmarinen (a handsome youth, famous for his craft as a smith). Väinämöinen was then provided with a sledge for his journey home, with the warning not to look above or about him, lest ill-hap befall him.

Väinämöinen, homeward bound on his sledge, comes suddenly upon the maiden Pohjola, seated aloft upon a dazzling rainbow, spinning. The *Kalevala's* description is enticing. Väinämöinen, 'enchanted by her radiant beauty, beseeches her to come down and join him, which she refuses to do except on condition that he will, by means of his magic arts, make for her a boat out of the pieces of her magic spindle. Väinämöinen toils in vain, unable to discover the magic formula, until finally in despair he relinquishes his attempt and, leaping back into his sleigh, continues his homeward journey.'

Bedrich Smetana

1824-84

‡Smetana's father was a gifted musical amateur and encouraged his small son's musical leanings from the earliest age. The development of his talents and his career proceeded without hindrance, and he enjoyed easy successes as pianist, pedagogue, conductor, and teacher. He was associated with the National Theater in Prague from its inception, and was for some years chief conductor of that institution. His original and beautiful music, in which he gave expression to the history and aspirations of the Czech people, then under Austrian rule, was beloved from the start. Yet tragedy clouded the last years of his life; he lost his hearing, and he died insane.‡

● SYMPHONIC CYCLE, *Má Vlast* (My Fatherland)
Smetana, an ardent nationalist and patriot, composed between 1874 and 1879, for the glorification of his country, a cycle of six symphonic poems under the general title, 'My Fatherland' (*Má Vlast*), dedicated to the city of Prague. Their titles and subjects, in brief, are as follows:

I. 'VYSEHRAD': A celebration of the splendid past of the historic citadel, the ancient stronghold of Bohemian kings.
II. 'VLTAVA': The Moldau, and the scenes through which the course of the beloved river passes—forests and meadows, historic edifices, revels of nymphs and naïads.
III. 'SÁRKA': Sárka was 'the noblest of the Bohemian Amazons,' and she slew by a ruse the abhorred male leader—the Knight Ctirad—who had betrayed her. A valley north of Prague is named after her.
IV. 'FROM BOHEMIA'S FIELDS AND GROVES': Music of pastoral and folk-like character, evoking peasant scenes and dances and the rustic loveliness of their surroundings.
V. 'TABOR': The fortress of the Hussites. The music is based on the Hussite chorale, 'You are God's warriors.'

VI. 'Blanik': The name of the mountain on which are sleeping in glorious death the Hussite warriors, awaiting the resurrection which shall restore them to renewed service for the faith.

The second of the series, 'Vltava' ('The Moldau'), is devoted to a celebration of the Moldau. The work was finished late in 1874. The score is prefaced by the following program:

Two springs pour forth their streams in the shade of the Bohemian forest, the one warm and gushing, the other cold and tranquil. Their waves, joyfully flowing over their rocky beds, unite and sparkle in the morning sun. The forest brook, rushing on, becomes the River Moldau, which, with its waters speeding through Bohemia's valleys, grows into a mighty stream. It flows through dense woods from which come the joyous sounds of the chase, and the notes of the hunter's horn are heard ever nearer and nearer.

It flows through emerald meadows and lowlands, where a wedding feast is being celebrated with song and dancing. At night, in its shining waves, wood and water nymphs hold their revels, and in these waves are reflected many a fortress and castle— witnesses of bygone splendor of chivalry, and the vanished martial fame of days that are no more. At the Rapids of St. John the stream speeds on, winding its way through cataracts and hewing the path for its foaming waters through the rocky chasm into the broad river bed, in which it flows on in majestic calm toward Prague, welcomed by time-honored Vysehrad, to disappear in the far distance from the poet's gaze.

The fourth of the symphonic poems in Smetana's cycle, 'From Bohemia's Fields and Groves,' was completed October 18, 1875, and performed for the first time at Zofin in the following December. It was Smetana's intention to compose a symphonic poem which would evoke the life of the Bohemian folk 'at work and while dancing.' When the score was published, it contained the following prefatory program:

On a fine summer day we stand in Bohemia's blessed fields, whose lovely scent of flowers and cool breezes fill us with inspiration. From the general plenitude of enjoy- ment and gladness resounds the natural, blissful tone of country contentment. Far from the human tumult we are led into a shady, quiet grove. Fanned by the light breeze, the lisping of leaves and twigs is wafted farther and louder, until the whole wood resounds with echoes, with which is mingled the twittering song of birds in endless harmony. In this Hymn of Nature sound from afar ecstatic horn-tones. A strong gust of wind interrupts this solemn stillness, and brings to our ear the festal tones of country merry-making: they draw ever nearer, and we find ourselves in the midst of a brilliant feast of the country-folk, who divert themselves with music and dancing and are glad to live. Their gladness and enjoyment of life spread themselves in the shape of the eternally fresh music of the folk, even over the farthest meadows of Bohemia.

The following description of the work was given by Smetana to Dr. V. Zeleny:

At the very beginning, I intended to suggest arrival in the country. . . Thereafter (G major) I imagined the walk of a naïve girl of the fields. Later, in 3-4 time, first violins muted, there is the thought of the splendor of nature in summer at high noon, when the sun falls directly on the head. In the forest, complete shadows; only here and there a luminous ray passes through the treetops. The constant figure (in triplets) repre- sents the twittering of birds. It persists in all the counterpoint that follows when the motive in F major appears in the horns. Here was a great contrapuntal task which I accomplished as if it were mere sport, for I have greatly exercised myself in such things! G minor: it is the festival of the harvest, or in general some peasant holiday.

● OVERTURE AND DANCES FROM *The Bartered Bride*

Smetana, who began to compose operas while the devastating Richard was in his *Meistersinger* period, was plagued by the accusation of 'Wagnerism' directed against himself, and he wrote his *Bartered Bride* as a sort of defiant manifesto flung in the face of an antagonistic public. 'I did not compose it from any ambitious motive,' he said in 1882 at the hundredth performance of the opera in Prague (the first performance was on May 30, 1866, at Prague), 'but rather as a scornful challenge; for after my first opera I was charged with being a Wagnerite, one who could accomplish nothing in a light and popular style.'

Smetana had been totally deaf since 1874. In October 1882, his last opera, *The Devil's Wall*, fell flat in Prague. Smetana was deeply depressed. 'I shall write nothing more,' he said: 'no one wants to hear from me.' And he offered an explanation in the simply pathetic words of Arkel: 'Je suis trop vieux.' His health had been failing, and now his mind began to go. He lost his memory, and was tortured by hallucinations. Early in 1884 he was put away in the asylum at Prague, and in May he died, leaving one of the gayest and most lucid of musical comedies as a legacy of one of the darkest tragedies in modern art.

As for the famous and irresistible overture, it has long been an acknowledged masterwork. The music (which thematically is for the most part derived from the Finale of the second act, the sale of the bride) is the quintessence of merriment. When it first began to appear on concert programs in Germany, it was known as the 'Lustspiel Ouverture' (Comedy Overture); and Hanslick's remark is often quoted: that the piece might well serve as an overture to a comedy of Shakespeare.

The Polka and Furiant occur respectively in the first and second acts of the opera; the 'Dance of the Commedians' occurs in Act 3 and accompanies a pantomime by members of a circus troupe who figure in the action.

Richard Strauss

1864-1949.

S

Strauss, during his last years, found himself in an altered relation to the imaginative and intellectual world about him. Man, says Nietzsche, is something to be surpassed, and Strauss (who knew his Nietzsche) was doubtless resigned to his own participation in the process. Or perhaps he was unaware of it. Certainly he continued to turn out music with unabated assurance. But let us not confuse the Strauss of those later discouraging productions with the Strauss of *Don Juan, Till Eulenspiegel, Don Quixote, Salome, Elektra, Rosenkavalier*—that Strauss who, to the musical youth of the 'nineties, appeared as an intrepid liberator, marching under a splendid banner of revolt; who, by his headlong and unsparing audacities, became at once a prodigious offense in the sight of the orthodox and a prodigious exhilaration to the responsive. Strauss taught his generation a new way of approaching the problem of making music articulate. He showed them how to do two seemingly contradictory things: how to expand and how to concentrate it. He applied it to an immensely widened range of human experience. He seemed to touch life with generous daring, and at every side—at its loveliest and gravest, at its most disordered and crass and ill-favored. He learned how to convey essential experience still drenched in its proper colors, pungent with its veritable odors, rich with all its implications. Toward the end, younger and more daring spirits supplanted him as a controversial issue; he appeared an academic, a conservative, a reactionary; he was, they said, old stuff. Yet we possessed and still possess his abiding virtues unimpaired. Nothing has gone out of the masterpieces he created except what they could most easily spare—the element of surprise. The saliency, the swift energy, the beauty that often overwhelms, the individual voice, the compassionate awareness of human life, and the faculty of conveying it with sensibility and truth and power—these remain.

• TONE POEM, *Don Juan*

The Don Juan of Strauss's music is the protagonist of a dramatic poem by Nikolaus Franz Niembsch von Strehlenau, the Austrian poet who wrote under the name of Nikolaus Lenau. He was born at Csta'd, Hungary, August 13, 1802. He came to America in his thirtieth year and settled on a homestead in Ohio. But the real America of 1832 proved to be somewhat different from that ideal America conceived by the Austrian Romanticist; and after a few months in the United States, Lenau returned to Europe. Four years later he published his *Faust*—a frankly revelatory work. Lenau was distraught by his hopeless passion for Sophie von Löwenthal, the wife of a friend, and much of his finest poetry was inspired by his love for her. He wrote his dramatic poem, *Don Juan*, in 1844. Soon afterward he began to show signs of aberration, and in October of that year he was placed under restraint. He died in the asylum at Oberdöbling, near Vienna, August 22, 1850.

Lenau himself expounded the philosophy of his poem. 'My *Don Juan*,' he said, 'is no hot-blooded man eternally pursuing women. It is the longing in him to find a woman who is to him incarnate womanhood, and to enjoy in one all the women on earth, whom he cannot as individuals possess. Because he does not find her, although he reels from one to another, at last Disgust seizes hold of him, and this Disgust is the Devil that fetches him.'

Thus it will be seen that Lenau's Don Juan was disquieted by that Ideal Beauty which has ever perturbed all poets and mystics of sensuous imagination. He was akin to Michael Robartes, who, in loving a woman, loved not really herself, but rather an immortal and transcendent beauty of which she was the momentary incarnation—

> When my arms press you round, I press
> My heart upon the loveliness
> That has long faded from the world. . .

And what is this, Lenau or Strauss might say to us, but a passion for that 'divine beauty' of Plato, 'pure and clear and unalloyed, not clogged with the pollutions of mortality and all the colors and vanities of human life'?

So, at the end of Strauss's tone poem, after the incandescent ardors of the immemorial quest, bitterness and despair engulf the hero; and in that shuddering passage where the A minor chord of the wind and strings is pierced by the dissonant F of the trumpets, in that last desolate moment, Don Juan sees love 'beautiful like the autumn evening, sorrowful like the autumn evening, fading like the autumn evening.'

● TONE POEM, *Tod und Verklärung* ('Death and Transfiguration'), OP. 24

This score, the third in Strauss's series of tone poems, projects the meditations of a tragic poet brooding with awe and tenderness and passion upon Death in its dual aspects: as the King of Terrors, the 'Gray Henchman of Destiny,' the Old Pander, the minister of anguish and consternation and despair; and as the Great Deliverer—'eloquent, just, and mighty.' And out of this dramatic conception issues music that is at first dolorously wistful, full of the awe, the terror, the agonizing finality of death, and then august and triumphant, 'exulting' (as Blake declared that only music could) 'in immortal thoughts'— assuring us, as he said, that 'the door of death is made of gold.'

The score is prefaced by an unsigned poem. It was written by Strauss's friend and mentor, Alexander Ritter (1833-96), after Ritter had come to know the music, and may be viewed as an authoritative exposition of the imaginative basis of Strauss's tone poem, wholly sufficient as a guide to the emotional significance of the music in its four chief phases: the dreams and childhood memories of the sick man in his delirium; his struggle with death; the brief reprieve, the memories of youth and manhood and lusty effort, the sharp and final struggle and 'the last limit of life'; and (finally) the transfiguration— music of chantings and fulfillments.

Here are Ritter's verses, in a prose version by an anonymous British translator published in London many years ago on the occasion of the first performance there of *Tod und Verklärung*:

A sick man lies upon his mattress in a poor and squalid garret, lit by the flickering glare of a candle burnt almost to its stump. Exhausted by a desperate fight with death, he has sunk into sleep; no sound breaks the silence of approaching dissolution, save the low monotonous ticking of a clock on the wall. A plaintive smile from time to time lights up the man's wan features; at life's last limit, dreams are telling him of childhood's golden days.

But death will not long grant its victim sleep and dreams. Dreadly it plucks at him, and once again begins the strife: desire of life against might of death! A gruesome combat! Neither yet gains the victory; the dying man sinks back upon his couch, and silence reigns once more.

Weary with struggling, reft of sleep, in the delirium of fever he sees his life unrolled before him, stage by stage. First the dawn of childhood, radiant with pure innocence. Next the youth who tests and practices his forces for manhood's fight. And then the man in battle for life's greatest prize: to realize a high ideal, and make it all the higher by his act—this the proud aim that shapes his course. Cold and scornful, the world heaps obstacle after obstacle in his path; deems he the goal at hand, a voice of thunder bids him 'Halt!'—'Let each hindrance be thy ladder,' thinks he. 'Higher, ever higher, mount!' And so he climbs, and so he urges, breathless with hallowed fire. All that his heart had ever longed for, he seeks it still in death's last sweat—seeks, but never finds it! Though now he sees it more and more plainly; though now it looms before him, he yet can ne'er embrace it wholly, ne'er put the last touch to his endeavor. Then sounds the iron stroke of death's chill hammer; breaks the earthly shell in twain; enshrouds the eye with the pall of night.

But now from on high come sounds of triumph; what here on earth he sought in vain, from heaven it greets him: Deliverance, Transfiguration!

- TONE POEM, *Till Eulenspiegels lustige Streiche* ('Till Eulenspiegel's Merry Pranks'), OP. 28

Till Eulenspiegel is supposed to have died in the middle of the fourteenth century. He is the vagabond hero of an old *Volksbuch* whose authorship is attributed to Thomas Murner (1475-1530). Till, according to Murner, was born at Kneithlinger, Brunswick, in 1283, and died of the plague at Mölln, near Lubeck, about 1350. It is said that one may still see there, if one be properly credulous, his tombstone, with an owl and a mirror on it; for, as Krehbiel pointed out, the origin of the name *Eulenspiegel* ('owl's glass,' or 'owl's mirror') is found in an old German proverb: 'Man is as little conscious of his own faults as an ape or an owl, looking into a mirror, is conscious of his ugliness.'

Till's exploits, the stories of which are household tales in Germany, consisted of horseplay and jests that he practiced without discrimination, and, in some instances, with a frank and joyous lack of seemliness which would not bear unexpurgated narration. In Murner's book, Till is sentenced to the gallows, but escapes death at the last moment. Strauss, however, does not let the rogue off, but despatches him on the scaffold.

Strauss declared at the time of the first performance of his work (at Cologne, November 5, 1895—the composition of the score dates from 1894-5) that it was impossible for him to furnish an explanatory program.

Were I to put into words [he added] the thoughts which its several incidents suggested to me, they would seldom suffice, and might even give rise to offense. Let me leave it, therefore, to my hearers to crack the hard nut which the rogue has prepared for them. By way of helping them to a better understanding, it seems sufficient to point out the 'Eulenspiegel' motives, which, in the most manifold disguises, moods, and situations, pervade the whole up to the catastrophe, when, after he has been condemned to death, Till is strung up to the gibbet. For the rest, let them guess at the musical joke which a rogue has offered them.

The themes referred to by Strauss were indicated by him in notation. They are the opening subject of the introduction (violins), the horn melody that follows almost immediately, and the descending interval of a seventh which, portentously sounded, *ff,* by the trombones, tuba, horns, and bassoons near the close of the piece, is suggestive of Till's abrupt end on the scaffold.

That remorseless analyst, Herr Wilhelm Mauke, has supplied for the music an exhaustive program, which, paraphrased and sternly compressed, is as follows:

> Once upon a time there was a prankish rogue, ever up to new tricks, named Till Eulenspiegel. Now he jumps on his horse and gallops into the midst of a crowd of market-women, overturning their wares with a prodigious clatter. Now he lights out with seven-league boots; now conceals himself in a mousehole. Disguised as a priest, 'he drips with unction and morals,' yet out of his toe peeps the scamp. As cavalier he makes love, at first in jest, but soon in earnest, and is rebuffed. He is furious, and swears vengeance on all mankind, but, meeting some 'philistines,' he forgets his wrath and mocks them. At length his hoaxes fail. He is tried in a Court of Justice, and is condemned to hang for his misdeeds; but he still whistles defiantly as he ascends the ladder. Even on the scaffold he jests. Now he swings; he gasps for air; a last convulsion. Till is dead.

But there is an epilogue. It is in the Old World, narrative vein of the opening. Till has become a tale that is told: 'Once upon a time. . .' A merry tale, yet something besides. For there is, in the folk-like quality that spreads its influence over this music both at the beginning and at the end of the piece, something that is inexplicably touching, that deepens its appeal in a curious and indescribable way. The work is a good deal more than a mere humoresque. You may find yourself remembering, as you listen to it, that sudden cry of one of the characters in Bernard Shaw's *Heartbreak House*—though it would not be easy to say precisely what congruity it has with Till and his pranks: 'I have a terrible fear that my heart is broken, and that heartbreak is not like what I thought it was.' Perhaps it is because no great artist, richly sensitive to life, ever completed what he intended as pure comedy without unwittingly, at some point, giving it the accent and the hue of tragedy; as if he remembered or anticipated that subduing comment of Henry James's: 'Everything's terrible in the heart of man.'

The work is a grotesque fretted with golden fire, Rabelais read by lightning —a thing of blended impudence, fantasy, humor, outrageousness; and now and then of a heart-easing naïveté and tenderness, so that the music takes the breath by its sweetness and its pathos. Till becomes a simulacrum of human life, with its fun and fury that bring forgetfulness, its pity and frustration, its flickering beauty that dies and lives and dies again.

• Tone Poem, *Also sprach Zarathustra* ('Thus Spake Zarathustra'), op. 30

'Freely after Friedrich Nietzsche (*frei nach Friedr. Nietzsche*)' reads the subtitle of this tone poem. The reference is to Nietzsche's masterpiece, that superb poetical rhapsody which he thought was a philosophy of life.

Nietzsche wrote *Also sprach Zarathustra* in 1883-5—each part in about ten days. It was conceived some years before, chapter by chapter, in long walks—'with a feeling of inspiration,' wrote Nietzsche to a friend, 'as though each sentence had been shouted in my ear.' He composed it at a breakneck speed of inspiration—or, if one prefers, in a mood of rapturous contempt for the little earth-men who know not the lyric Titanism of those who are at home on mountain-tops, who can stare Eternity out of countenance and 'walk with the moon and stars.' For Nietzsche lived by the light of 'the spirit that hates the dogs of the populace and all that abortive and gloomy breed; the spirit of wild laughter that dances like a tempest as gaily on marshes and sadness as it does on fields.'

The book holds the heart of Nietzsche's doctrine—it is, said James Huneker, his bible, and 'the history of his soul,' with some of Amiel's introspection and some of Baudelaire's morbidity, 'half-mad, yet exhorting, comforting; Hamlet and John Bunyan.' Nietzsche was delighted with the phrase that Brandes invented for his philosophy—'aristocratic radicalism'—and he wrote to the Danish critic in 1887 that it was 'the cleverest thing I have ever read about myself.' Therefore it behooves the heedful to listen attentively when Brandes tells us that Nietzsche's Zarathustra expounds 'the religion of purity': that his wisdom is 'cheerful and dauntless, as that of one who laughed at his birth'; that his nature is 'light and flame.' The eagle and the serpent, who share his mountain cave—the proudest and the wisest of beasts—are, says Brandes, ancient Persian symbols. *Zarathustra* he hailed as 'a book of edification for free spirits.'

The central figure of Nietzsche's rhapsody, and something of the form, were borrowed from the Persian *Avesta*. Nietzsche's Zarathustra is a very distant relative of the founder of the Parsee religion ('Zoroaster' is the Greek form of the name, 'Zarathustra' the Persian form). 'At different periods of his life,' says his sister, 'he would call this haunter of his dreams by different names; "but in the end," he declares in a note on the subject, "I had to do a *Persian* the honor of identifying him with this creature of my fancy." ' The teachings of the two are far from similar: the veritable Zarathustra or Zoroaster, who lived probably about 1000 B.C., and Nietzsche's reanimation of him for his own purposes of mystical window-dressing, are not even brothers under their skin. For whereas the Persian Zarathustra plodded along in company with those ancient doctrines that were founded upon a positive conviction of the unmistakable difference between good and evil, Nietzsche's Zarathustra dances across the mountain peaks in an exuberance of joy over the glad discovery that none can know the difference between the two.

On a fly-leaf of Strauss's score is printed this passage from the preface of Nietzsche's book:

ᴢᴀʀᴀᴛʜᴜsᴛʀᴀ's Pʀᴏʟᴏɢᴜᴇ

When Zarathustra was thirty years old, he left his home and the lake of his home, and went into the mountains. There he enjoyed his spirit and his solitude, and for ten years did not weary of it. But at last his heart changed—and rising one morning with the rosy dawn, he went before the sun, and spake thus unto it: 'Thou great star! What would be thy happiness if thou hadst not those for whom thou shinest! For ten years hast thou climbed hither unto my cave: thou wouldst have wearied of thy light and of the journey, had it not been for me, mine eagle, and my serpent. But we awaited thee every morning, took from thee thine overflow, and blessed thee for it. Lo! I am weary of my wisdom, like the bee that hath gathered too much honey; I need hands outstretched to take it. I would fain bestow and distribute, until the wise have once more become joyous in their folly, and the poor happy in their riches. Therefore must I descend into the deep: as thou doest in the evenings, when thou goest behind the sea, and givest light also to the nether-world, thou exuberant star! Like thee must I go down, as men say, to whom I shall descend. Bless me, then, thou tranquil eye, that canst behold even the greatest happiness without envy! Bless the cup that is about to overflow, that the water may flow golden out of it, and carry everywhere the reflection of thy bliss! Lo! This cup is again going to empty itself, and Zarathustra is again going to be a man.'

Thus began Zarathustra's going-down.

This extract is obviously not intended to correspond to the programmatic scheme of the music. It is a starting point; and, as the various superscriptions printed in the score make clear, the composer begins his discourse at the place where the quotation ends.

Here, in brief, is the implied 'scenario' of the piece, as it is indicated by the captions in the published score—all of them quotations of chapter headings from Nietzsche's book:

Zarathustra faces and greets the sunrise; and we hear in the orchestra a prodigious evocation of the mood of dawn—a mighty opening and flowering of sonorities in a spreading instrumental radiance that begins above an organ-point on C for double-basses, organ, double-bassoon, and bass drum, with four trumpets intoning the solemn motto-theme (C-G-c) that integrates the entire work. The passage culminates in a C major blaze of irradiating splendor for the full orchestra and organ. Then, like the sun which descends at dusk to give light below the rim of the world, Zarathustra too goes down among men to spread illumination, to solve the Riddle of the Universe.

1. 'Oғ ᴛʜᴇ Bᴀᴄᴋᴡᴏʀʟᴅsᴍᴇɴ.' He goes among the 'Backworldsmen'—those benighted ones who seek in religion the solution of the World-Riddle. Zarathustra himself had once been a dweller in that abandoned world. The horns intone Credo in unum deum, and there is a chorale-like passage in A-flat for organ supported chiefly by divided strings.

2. 'Oғ ᴛʜᴇ Gʀᴇᴀᴛ Lᴏɴɢɪɴɢ.' He turns from piety and asceticism, and, as the organ intones the Magnificat and the horns recall the Credo, while the woodwind assume the chromatic hues of desire above the soaring of the strings, his soul 'glows and dreams.'

3. 'Oғ Jᴏʏs ᴀɴᴅ Pᴀssɪᴏɴs.' 'Once hadst thou passions and calledst them evil. But now hast thou only thy virtues.' The far-sweeping chromatic song of the strings descends through showers of harp glissandi.

4. 'GRAVE SONG.' Satiety and despair lay hold of his spirit and he broods upon 'the silent isle . . . the isle of graves.' Oboe and English horn sing mournfully above the 'cello's reminiscence of the music of longing.

5. 'OF SCIENCE.' Zarathustra now turns to learning for solace and illumination, but rejects this also. 'Thou seducest, thou false one—thou subtle one, to unknown desires and deserts.' We hear an amazing fugato, the subject of which contains all the diatonic and chromatic degrees of the scale. 'Strauss seems to present this passage as a bitter satire on the emptiness of dry science.' This, too, proves to be a meal of husks. Zarathustra despairs.

6. 'THE CONVALESCENT.' 'Filled with disgust and rage, he fell down as one dead; and for long he could neither eat nor drink.' But an eagle fetched him berries, grapes, apples, pine-cones, sweet-smelling herbage. He revived, and the animals came and talked with him. 'Speak not further, thou convalescent, but go out where the world waiteth for thee like a garden! Heal thy soul with new songs!' In the music, the nightmare of science is slowly dispelled, and the 'cellos and violas have an upspringing version (*Schnell*) of the Longing theme.

7. 'THE DANCE-SONG.' Zarathustra perceives that he may cleanse himself of the contamination of science only by laughter and dance—that dance of the Cosmos into which all human dreams and moods and longings enter together: religions, passions, aspirations, dismay, exaltation. 'Lift up thy hearts, my brothers! Higher still! and forget not to laugh! I have sanctified laughter. Thou Supermen, learn to laugh!' In the rhythm of a slow waltz, the dance begins in the orchestra after a preluding of woodwind trills.

Night falls, and Zarathustra dreams of love. The orchestra sings a *Nachtlied* of grave and tender beauty. 'Now only do all songs of the loving ones awake. And my soul also is the soul of a loving one. . . 'Tis night—alas, that I have to be light.' The dance bursts forth again: but in the midst of it we hear the stroke of midnight.

8. 'SONG OF THE NIGHT-WANDERER.' In the fourth part of Nietzsche's rhapsody, the strophes are interrupted line by line 'in the manner half of a medieval watchman's chant, half like the hymn of a mystic':

ONE!

O man, take heed!

TWO!

What saith midnight's voice indeed?

THREE!

I slept my sleep.—

FOUR!

From deepest dream I've waked, and plead:

FIVE!

The world is deep,

SIX!

And deeper than the day could read.

SEVEN!

Deep is its woe—,

EIGHT!

Joy—deeper still than grief can be;

NINE!

Woe saith: Hence! Go!
TEN!
But joys all want eternity—,
ELEVEN!
Want deep, profound eternity.
TWELVE!

In the orchestra, the twelve somber bell strokes die into silence, and the piece comes to its famous and mystically enigmatic close in two juxtaposed keys—the woodwind, divided strings, and harp reiterating a high B major triad, the double-basses, pizzicato, sounding the motto-theme C-G-c against a dissonant chord of the trombones. It is the shadow of that ineluctable ghost, the Riddle of the Cosmos.

• TONE POEM, *Don Quixote* (Fantastic Variations on a Theme of Knightly Character), OP. 35

Strauss's *Don Quixote* has been astonishingly misunderstood, strangely undervalued. It has been called 'an intellectual gambol,' 'an exhibit of drollery, which leaves us inwardly cold.' Even Romain Rolland, who is not often unperceptive, sees in it only 'a prank, a musical pleasantry.' Others have found it merely a brilliant and wholly cerebral piece of virtuosity, 'appallingly clever,' 'a grotesque and derisive parody.' It is futile to dispute over such things. Yet the wonder grows, with every hearing of this extraordinary and affecting work, that its tenderness, its sincerity, its pathos, should ever have been misapprehended.

Don Quixote, the sixth of Strauss's tone poems, was composed at Munich in 1897, and stands between *Also sprach Zarathustra* (1896) and *Ein Heldenleben* (1898). The work, true to its subtitle, is in the form, broadly, of a *Tema con Variazione*, with Introduction and Finale. From the programmatic point of view, it is a connected series of tone pictures in which are set forth upon the orchestral screen certain famous episodes from the 'stupendous and memorable history' of Don Quixote de la Mancha—'chastest lover and most valiant knight'—and Sancho Panza, his squire—earthbound, gluttonous, but infinitely faithful. The orchestral score contains no program, and no explanatory notes save two captions printed above the dual portions of the theme, identifying the first part with Don Quixote, the second part with Sancho Panza. But the arrangement for two pianos is generously annotated, each of the divisions of the piece being furnished with verbal clues to the particular aspect of the immortal tale which the music unfolds.

The Introduction, ten variations, and Finale are played without pause. A solo 'cello represents Don Quixote: personifies, dramatizes, and 'enacts' the lovable, crack-brained dreamer, expresses his moods, narrates his deeds, draws his portrait—so far as music can accomplish these things by suggestion and association. Sancho Panza is personified by the bass clarinet and tenor tuba when his theme is first heard; but afterward he is represented by a solo viola.

INTRODUCTION. 'DON QUIXOTE GOES MAD.' The 'renowned gentleman,' Don Quixote de la Mancha—his age bordering upon fifty years, 'square-visaged, a very early riser, and a keen sportsman'—devoted his time to perusing old books of chivalry, having recklessly sold many acres to purchase stories of knight-errantry. Reading from sunset to sunrise, his brain was turned by all that he learned of 'enchantments, battles, single combats, challenges, wounds, courtships, armours, tempests, and impossible absurdities.' In fine, having lost his wits, he conceived it to be expedient and necessary 'that he should commence knight-errant,' and wander through the world, with horse and arms and squire, in quest of adventure, 'and to put in practice whatever he had read to have been done by knights-errant. . . And he hastened to put in execution what he so much desired.'

The opening subject in the woodwind (a foreshadowing of the Knight's theme) is marked 'ritterlich und galant': we may see in this a symbol of knight-errantry; and in the beautiful and touching subject that follows it in the strings, with its wistful ardor and valorous tenderness, a suggestion of the thought of ideal chivalry. The passage ends with some strangely unrelated chords that are associated with the idea of the Knight's bemused wits. He is now deep in the perusal of his beloved romances. Heroic and splendid images pass through his mind. He visions Dulcinea, the Ideal Woman (the oboe evokes her, in a theme that is not easy to forget, accompanied by harp and muted strings divisi). He fancies her beset by giants and rescued by a knight (muted brass). His poor brain is in a whirl; the orchestra becomes mad, chaotic, a confused, fantastic nightmare. The tension increases; the instruments utter insane and wildly muddled things; until finally, 'in some terrible chords that give one the sensation of an overstretched spring snapping violently,' we realize that the Knight is at last quite mad. He has determined on a life of chivalry.

THEME. 'DON QUIXOTE AND SANCHO PANZA.' The two-part theme is announced. Don Quixote is portrayed by a subject, pathetically grandiose, for the solo 'cello (Moderato, D minor, 4-4); Sancho Panza by a burly and grotesquely comic tune first heard on the tenor tuba and bass clarinet. 'The fat shoulders, big paunch, of the good-natured, constant fellow are limned with the startling fidelity that Gustave Doré or Daniel Vièrge attained. . . Strauss's Sancho is very humorous, but your laughter at him is always softened with tears; while the portrait of Quixote has an added touch of pathos in that it invariably suggests the spare, worn frame of the poor, middle-aged Knight. It is true in this as in every other respect.'

VARIATION I. 'THE ADVENTURE WITH THE WINDMILLS.' Don Quixote and his squire sally forth on their quest of chivalric adventure, the Knight inspired by the Ideal Woman of his thoughts, whom he has resolved to call Dulcinea del Toboso (you hear her theme soaring ecstatically in the violins and woodwind). The sight of windmills revolving in the breeze inspires his valor, for to his imagination they are 'monstrous giants' (a ponderous descending figure in the brass, wood, and strings). He charges them, lance in rest, and is tumbled over by the sails, 'in very evil plight.'

VARIATION II. 'THE BATTLE WITH THE SHEEP.' Through a thick cloud of dust, Don Quixote discerns the approach of 'a prodigious army of divers and innumerable nations' on the march, led by the great emperor Alifanfaron, lord of the island of Trapobana, and yet another army coming against them.

Sancho perceives that they are but flocks of sheep. The muted brass bleats pitifully, but Don Quixote charges with stern valor, leaving seven dead in the road; whereupon he is stoned by the shepherds and falls to the ground.

VARIATION III. 'COLLOQUIES OF KNIGHT AND SQUIRE.' The Knight and Sancho discuss the worth of a life of chivalry. Sancho doubts, submitting various proverbs, questions, demands; the Don replies with appeasings, promises, instructions. You hear their themes in dialogue, and, later, sharply opposed. The squire is all for the comforts of reality—he is plain, homespun, sagacious. The Knight, transported by visions and aspirations, expatiates ardently upon the glory of the chivalrous life, while the orchestra in a cantilena of memorable fervor (developed out of the Knight's theme and that of Dulcinea), sings nobly of ideal things. Sancho reverts to his advocacy of the homely and attainable things of reality—we hear a fragment of his motive; but Don Quixote silences him angrily.

VARIATION IV. 'THE ADVENTURE WITH THE PILGRIMS.' The Knight and his squire fall in with a band of pilgrims (a phrase of ecclesiastical character for bassoons and muted brass). Don Quixote imagines them to be miscreants and ruffians. He attacks them and is worsted, falling senseless, while the pilgrims resume their march, chanting as they go. Don Quixote revives slowly, and Sancho, relieved, lies down beside him and sleeps.

VARIATION V. 'THE KNIGHT'S VIGIL.' Don Quixote, after the knightly custom, refrains from sleep, and keeps vigil beside his arms throughout the night, dreaming of Dulcinea (the theme of the Ideal Woman is heard as a horn melody in the bass). This variation is chiefly a long rhapsody for the solo 'cello, adorned with harp glissandi and a rapturous cadenza for muted violins.

VARIATION VI. 'THE FALSE DULCINEA.' The pair meet three country wenches, mounted upon asses, and Sancho Panza assures the Don that one of them, round-visaged and flat-nosed, is his adored lady, Dulcinea del Toboso, arrayed in flaming gold, 'all strings of pearls, all diamonds, all rubies, all cloth of tissue above ten hands deep: their tresses loose about their shoulders are so many sunbeams playing with the wind . . . and they come mounted upon three pie-bellied belfreys.' The Knight corrects him—' "palfreys," you would say, Sancho, not "belfreys" '; to which Sancho replies that there is no great difference. The Knight, seeing that the alleged Dulcinea is only an ugly and common peasant-girl, is horrified and incredulous, and insists that some wicked enchanter has transformed his lady. The orchestra paints the alleged Dulcinea in a richly humorous parody of the Ideal Woman theme (oboes in thirds, with tambourine), while Sancho, through the voice of his solo viola, insists upon the presence of the idealized Dulcinea.

VARIATION VII. 'THE RIDE THROUGH THE AIR.' Sitting blindfolded upon a wooden horse and fanned by huge bellows, the Knight and his squire fancy that they are riding through the air. We hear in the orchestra the whistling of the gale as they take their dizzy imaginary flight (here enters the famous 'wind-machine'); the themes of the Don and of Sancho are borne giddily aloft on the instrumental breeze. A sudden pause on a long-held note of the bassoons jolts the two riders into an awareness of reality.

VARIATION VIII. 'THE VOYAGE IN THE ENCHANTED BOAT.' The Knight, perceiving a small boat, without oars, tied to a tree on the bank of the river Ebro, is convinced that it is miraculously intended for his use, so that he may succor some distressed knight or other person of high degree. They embark, and the orchestra plays a graceful barcarolle. The boat capsizes, but the two reach shore in safety, and offer up thanks for their escape (woodwind and horns, religioso).

VARIATION IX. 'THE COMBAT WITH THE TWO MAGICIANS.' The adventurous pair meet on the road 'two monks of the order of St. Benedict,' mounted upon their dromedaries, 'for the mules whereon they rode were not much less.' The monks wore traveling masks; and, we are assured, 'carried umbrellas.' Behind them comes a coach, and men on horseback. Don Quixote mistakes the monks for magicians who are abducting some fair princess. Obliged to redress this wrong, he attacks them (though Sancho reminds him unkindly of the windmills); but in this battle he is victorious, for the terrified monks take flight. Belligerent passages for the strings, and a churchly duo for bassoons, paint the encounter.

VARIATION X. 'THE DEFEAT OF DON QUIXOTE.' The bachelor, Samson Carrasco, disguised as the 'Knight of the White Moon,' but actually one of Don Quixote's townsmen, does battle with him for the sake of his own good, to cure him of his delusions. The music pictures their joust, beginning with vehement scale-passages in the low strings and woodwind. Don Quixote is vanquished, and is compelled by the conditions of the contest to do the bidding of the victor—which is, that he shall retire home for a year.

And now Don Quixote—humiliated, heart-heavy, despoiled of his acquired glory, the luster of his exploits obscured, his happiness fallen—rides homeward despairingly with his squire. In the orchestra his theme becomes a lament of poignant expressiveness, with the strings sweeping downward in sorrowful chromatics above a basso ostinato of the timpani and bassoons. 'In these long descending wails of the orchestra,' says Ernest Newman (in the chapter on Strauss in his *Studies in Music*), 'you have all the anguish, all the disillusionment of the poor knight painted with an expressiveness, a fidelity, that sets one thinking of visual as well as auditory things. Strauss illustrates the scene as consummately as a pictorial artist could do, and at the same time throws over it the melting melancholy that music alone among the arts can express.'

The English horn sings a pastoral theme. Don Quixote resolves to become a shepherd. 'We will buy sheep,' says he to Sancho, 'and I, calling myself the shepherd Quixotiz, and you the shepherd Panzino, we will range the mountains, the woods, and meadows, singing here and complaining there, drinking the liquid crystal of the fountains, of the limpid brooks, or of the mighty rivers. . . Singing shall furnish pleasure, and complaining yield delight: Apollo shall provide verses, and love conceits. . .' Little by little his reason is restored, his illusions vanish; and this is remarkably indicated in the orchestra by a kind of harmonic and instrumental clarification, a suggestion of increasing serenity and light, of obscurity dispelled.

FINALE. 'DON QUIXOTE'S DEATH.' The knight, once more a sane and wise man, his brain cleared of mists, is dying resignedly in his bed. The music which portrays his end is simple and very peaceful. The touching song of the 'cello ('Sehr ruhig,' D major, 4-4) is gravely tranquil. There is a brief moment of agitation, but the end comes with the chords which, at the beginning, indicated his aberration; but now they are orderly, lucid, and coherent.

George Meredith in his essay 'On the Spirit of Comedy' speaks of that 'laughter of reason refrsehed,' which is 'floriferous, like the magical great gale of the shifty Spring deciding for Summer': and of that sense which perceives the incongruous because it divines at the same time an ultimate harmony. It perceives also the infinite pathos of man's idealism and unconquerable hope. That is what one may rewardingly glean from this matchless characterization by Cervantes and Richard Strauss. For what, after all, is Don Quixote but a symbol of ecstasy flinging down the gauntlet to common life?

● TONE POEM, *Ein Heldenleben* ('A Hero's Life'), OP. 40

Ein Heldenleben is the seventh of those nine uncompanioned tone poems that span the post-Wagnerian generation—from the *Macbeth* of 1886-7 to the *Alpensinfonie* of 1915. It was composed in 1898, and stands between *Don Quixote* (1897) and the *Symphonia Domestica* (1903). The first performance was at Frankfurt-am-Main, under the composer's direction, March 3, 1899.

Strauss has said that in *A Hero's Life* he wished to present, 'not a realistic portrait of a particular historical or poetical figure, but rather a more general and free ideal of great and manly heroism—not the heroism to which one can apply an everyday maxim of valor, with its material and exterior reward, but that heroism which relates to the inward battles of life, and which aspires, through struggle and renouncement, toward the elevation of the soul.'

There is no explanatory guide, preface, or other elucidation printed in the published score; but when Strauss was in this country in 1922 he informed the present annotator that the programmatic significance of the music would be faithfully conveyed by the commentary which follows.

The tone poem is in six connected sections: (1) 'The Hero.' (2) 'The Hero's Adversaries.' (3) 'The Hero's Courtship.' (4) 'The Hero's Battlefield.' (5) 'The Hero's Works of Peace.' (6) 'The Hero's Release from the World,' and the Conclusion.

I. 'THE HERO.' We hear first the chief theme of the Hero: the valorous opening subject for the low strings and horns, joined later by the violins. There are subsidiary themes, picturing different aspects of the Hero's nature— his pride, depth of feeling, inflexibility, sensitiveness, imagination. This section comes to a defiant, heaven-storming close, *fff*, with a hold on the dominant seventh chord of E-flat.

II. 'THE HERO'S ADVERSARIES.' Herein are pictured the Hero's opponents and detractors—an envious and malicious crew, filled with all uncharitableness. Flutes, oboes, piccolo, English horn, clarinets, utter shrill and snarling phrases. There is also a malignly ponderous phrase, in fifths, for tenor and bass tubas, intended to picture the malevolence of the dull-witted among the foe. The theme of the Hero appears in sad and meditative guise. But his dauntless courage soon reasserts itself, and the mocking horde are put to rout.

III. 'The Hero's Courtship.' A solo violin introduces the Hero's beloved. She reveals herself at the start as capricious, an inconsequent trifler, an elaborate coquette. The directions printed above the violin part in the score— 'flippantly,' 'playfully,' 'insolently,' 'sedately,' 'soothingly,' 'angrily,' 'scoldingly,' et cetera—suggest the changing aspects of the emotional scene. But a grave and earnest phrase—heard at first in the 'cellos, double-basses, trombones, and horns—recurs again and again, with the effect of an increasingly fervent appeal, in the dialogue of the two protagonists. And then the orchestra breaks into a love song of heroic sweep and passion. There are rapturous phrases for the strings, gorgeously adorned with glissandi in the harps; the oboe sings an ardently tender song. As the ecstasy subsides, the mocking voices of the foe are heard remotely, like the distant croaking of night birds through an enchanted dream.

IV. 'The Hero's Battlefield.' But suddenly the call to arms is heard, and it may not be ignored. Distant fanfares (trumpets behind the scenes) summon the Hero to the conflict. The orchestra becomes a battlefield; the music 'evokes the picture of countless and waging hosts, of forests of waving spears and clashing blades,' wrote Huneker of this section. Through the dust and uproar we are reminded of the inspiration of the Beloved, which sustains and heartens the champion, whose theme contests for supremacy with that of his adversaries. A triumphant orchestral outburst proclaims at last his victory. Yet he exults alone—the world regards his conquest with cold and cynical indifference.

V. 'The Hero's Works of Peace.' Now begins a celebration of the Hero's victories of peace, suggesting his spiritual evolution and achievements. We hear quotations of themes from Strauss's earlier works: reminiscences of *Tod und Verklärung, Don Quixote, Don Juan, Till Eulenspiegel, Macbeth, Also sprach Zarathustra*, the music-drama *Guntram*, and the exquisite song, 'Traum durch die Dämmerung.' It may be doubted if Strauss has ever written more persuasively than in this example of polyphonic ingenuity, in which an uncanny contrapuntal skill is made to yield subduingly lovely music. Note, for example, the exceeding beauty of that G-flat major passage in which the tenor tuba, violas, and bass clarinet sing the melody of 'Traum durch die Dämmerung' against a theme from *Don Quixote* on the 'cellos, horn, and cor anglais.

VI. 'The Hero's Release from the World,' and the Conclusion. The tubas mutter the uncouth and sinister phrase which voices the dull contempt of the benighted adversaries. Even the glorious achievements of the Hero's brain, his spiritual conquests, have won him only envy and derision. Furiously he rebels, and the orchestra rages. But his anger subsides. Over a persistent tapping of the kettledrum, the cor anglais sings a gentler version of his theme. An agitating memory of storm and strife again disturbs his mood. But the solo violin reminds him of the consoling presence of the beloved one. Peace descends upon the spirit of the Hero. There are pages of tender and exalted beauty, with an intimate dialogue between horn and violin—music of which Philip Hale once dared to say that it was 'worthy of Beethoven in his supreme moments of rapt meditation.' In the trumpets, the chief theme, immensely broadened, rises in solemn majesty to a climax of memorable splendor—a great chord of E-flat major that fills the orchestral heavens with dazzling light. The Finale, majestic and serene, recalls the words of the luminous Shankara: 'For the circling world is like a dream, crowded with desires and hates; in its own time it shines as real, but on wakening it becomes unreal.'

• Sinfonia Domestica, OP. 53

The early history of the 'Domestic' Symphony is, oddly enough, American. Its first performance anywhere was in New York, at Carnegie Hall, under the visiting Strauss himself, by Wetzler's Orchestra (the date was March 21, 1904), and the first authorized information concerning the eagerly awaited novelty was conveyed to the public through the pen of Richard Aldrich, then music critic of *The New York Times*. Shortly before the première Strauss divulged to Aldrich, for publication in the *Times*, his attitude toward his new work, and Aldrich communicated these views as follows:

He wishes it to be taken as music, for what it is, and not as the elaboration of the specific details of a scheme of things. The symphony, he declares, is sufficiently explained by its title, and is to be listened to as the symphonic development of its themes. It is of interest to quote the title, as he wishes it to stand. It is *Sinfonia Domestica* (*meiner lieben Frau und unserm Jungen gewidmet*), op. 53; which is, interpreted, 'Domestic Symphony, dedicated to my dear Wife and our Boy, op. 53.' It bears the descriptive subtitle, *In einem Satze und drei Unterabteilungen: (a) Einleitung und Scherzo; (b) Adagio; (c) Doppelfuge und Finale.* (In one movement and three subdivisions: (a) Introduction and Scherzo; (b) Adagio; (o) Double Fugue and Finale.) It is highly significant that the composer desires these movements to be listened to as the three movements of a composition, substantially, as he declares, in the old symphonic form.

'This time,' says Dr. Strauss, 'I wish my music to be listened to purely as music.'

This certainly was plain enough. But one soon learned that Strauss was up to his old tricks—or that particular trick of offering the public a new work to be listened to 'purely as music,' and afterward permitting the truth to leak out that the work could not be fully understood by listening to it 'purely as music,' followed by the issuing of information which should have been supplied in the first place. For it is obvious that we are getting less than all that the composer put into his score if we must hear it in ignorance of certain ideas and images which shaped the form and substance of the work and made it what it is.

Observe what happened: A year after the première of the 'Domestic' Symphony in New York, the work was played in London, and it was then thought proper to enlighten the public concerning Strauss's expressional intentions in composing his elaborate score. An 'official' description (evidently authorized by the composer) was issued and it was at last possible to know what Strauss had intended to say in his music. One learned that in this 'Domestic' Symphony the three chief themes represent the husband, the wife, and the child. The husband theme is divided into three sections, the first of which is marked 'easy-going,' the second 'meditative,' and the third 'fiery.' The wife's themes are marked 'very lively' and 'full of feeling.' The first section of the symphony, the Introduction, is devoted to an exposition of these themes or groups of themes. On this follows a very characteristic passage which has been interpreted as representing the child in his bath. At the end of the Introduction occur the celebrated comparisons regarding the baby. Above a brief and emphatic ascending figure in the clarinets and muted trumpets is this note in the score: 'The Aunts: Just like his papa!' Oboe, trombone, and horn rejoin in an uncompromising descending phrase which is superscribed: 'The Uncles: Just like his mamma!' The Scherzo is explained as an expression of 'the parents' happiness,' followed by a portrayal of 'the child at play.' Toward the end of this section the music suggestive of the bath recurs. There is a lullaby (sung by the oboe d'amore) and the clock strikes seven (undoubtedly P.M.).

The Adagio, a movement of great polyphonic elaboration and gorgeous orchestral color, is a love scene—succeeded, unfortunately, by 'dreams and cares.' The gradual awakening of the family is portrayed (apparently the Strauss family once followed the bad habit of allowing the child to sleep in the room with its parents). The music becomes increasingly restless. The baby has another bath. That faithful orchestral timepiece, the glockenspiel, strikes seven (A.M.). The Finale is a fugue, based on a version of the theme of the child. The movement is explained as a portrayal of 'a merry argument' with, it is pleasant to note, 'a joyous conclusion.'

- SUITE FROM THE INCIDENTAL MUSIC FOR *Le Bourgeois Gentilhomme*, OP. 60

Max Reinhardt helped Strauss and his inseparable playwright, Hugo von Hofmannsthal, to mount *Der Rosenkavalier* at the Dresden Opera House in 1911. Inspired by the noble emotion of gratitude, poet and musician evolved the happy idea of consorting a play with an opera, and dedicating the resultant offspring to Reinhardt. They chose Molière's delectable *Le Bourgeois Gentilhomme*. Hofmannsthal performed various major operations upon the old play. Basing his adaptation upon the familiar and conscientious eighteenth-century translation of the text made by Bierling, Hofmannsthal freely amended the piece to suit the needs of the collaborators—transposing, suppressing, expanding, as suited his purposes. Strauss not only wrote incidental music for the transformed play, but he composed an entire opera (though, like the maiden's baby, it was only a little one) to take the place of the 'Ballet des Nations' and of the burlesque 'Cérémonie Turque' which were features of Molière's and Lully's original hodge-podge of acting, singing, dancing, and immortal dialogue. The excuse for the insertion of the opera is provided by Monsieur Jourdain's fête given in honor of the Marquise Dorimène, of whom the aspiring bourgeois is enamored. For the entertainment of his guests, Jourdain has planned a performance of an opera by a promising young composer. The opera is *Ariadne auf Naxos*.

Strauss completed his score in 1912, and the combined play-and-opera, dedicated to Reinhardt—who devised the stage settings and costumes—was produced at Stuttgart October 25, 1912. The piece was afterward revamped, and an entirely new form of it emerged from the weariless hands of Strauss and his coadjutors. In 1918, Strauss published a suite for orchestra drawn from his incidental music for the comedy. It comprises nine numbers, and is scored for an orchestra that causes a rubbing of eyes, when one recalls the gigantic instrumental apparatus required for most of Strauss's later works. The orchestra used in this suite needs less than forty players; and the general effect of the writing is often that of somewhat magnified chamber music.

The published score contains a preface in which the somewhat complicated history of the work is lucidly and authoritatively narrated by Richard Specht, Strauss's official biographer. Specht also enumerates the nine numbers of the suite as follows:

(1) the Overture, which paints a satirical portrait of Jourdain, the 'hero' of *Le Bourgeois Gentilhomme*: we see him strutting along—awkward, self-complacent, coarsely jovial, yet inwardly uncertain (note the abrupt modulations). The Overture ends with the charming little song which 'the Composer' improvises in the prologue of *Ariadne auf Naxos*; (2) the solemnly graceful Minuet, whose graceful flute theme seems to conjure up visions of powdered head-dresses, and beauty-spots; (3) the droll, swaggering piece entitled 'The Fencing-Master,' which illustrates with sly humor the bragging instructor and the clumsy attacks, thrusts and guards of his pupil; (4) 'Entrance and Dance of the Tailors'—an amusing and graceful tone picture, comprising a Polonaise; (5) the well-known Minuet of Lully, which Strauss has skilfully adapted; (6) the Courante, strikingly true to the atmosphere of the time; (7) 'Entrance of Cleonte'—also after Lully; (8) Prelude to the Second Act (Intermezzo), a Rococo portrait of delicately charming colors; and, finally (9) 'The Dinner.' This last is a musical bill-of-fare, replete with ingenious allusions—a witty musical illustration of the menu. It opens with a little Entrance March which contains a reference to the short aria of the fencing-master from the *Ariadne* prologue; then follows a reference to Wagner's *Rheingold*, accompanying the serving of the Rhinewine, while an Allegretto illustrates the service of the first dish. The theme of the dancing-master recurs, and a mock-sentimental Andante suggests the conversation of the dinner party; then follows the music which in the ballet accompanies the serving of the roast thrushes, and the suite ends with the whirling dance of the scullions.

- DANCE OF THE SEVEN VEILS AND FINAL SCENE FROM *Salome*, OP. 54

Oscar Wilde wrote his celebrated one-act tragedy, *Salome*, in French. It was published in that language in 1893. The legend is that he devised it for Sarah Bernhardt, but Oscar indignantly denied this. To write a play especially for any actor or actress, he declared, 'is work for the artisan in literature, not for the artist.' In 1894 the play was published in an English translation by Lord Alfred Douglas, and Aubrey Beardsley made pictures for it. When the play was performed at Paris in the original French, at the Nouveau Théâtre, October 28, 1896, it was not Mme Bernhardt, but Mme Lina Munte, who enacted the part of Salome.

Strauss's opera—or 'drama in one act, after the like-named play of Oscar Wilde,' as he styled it—was completed in June 1905. The music was set to a German version of Wilde's text made by Hedwig Lachmann. The libretto omits from Wilde's play the characters of Tigellinus, the young Roman, and 'A Nubian.' Some unessential dialogue is eliminated, and the action of the drama is quickened at various points.

The opera was produced at Dresden, December 9, 1905. It was received with unbounded enthusiasm, and there were thirty-eight recalls for the singers, the conductor, and the composer. Within a year, thirty continental opera houses had staged the music-drama.

On January 22, 1907, *Salome* was produced at the Metropolitan Opera House, New York, by Heinrich Conried, at a special performance thoughtfully arranged by that excellent realist for his own benefit. Olive Fremstad sang the role of Salome. Alfred Hertz conducted. The performance was prefaced by a concert, given by all the singers of the company who were not to appear in the opera. On the Sunday before the public performance, Mr. Conried gave a dress rehearsal, for which about a thousand of the elect received invitations.

After the public performance of January 22, the too-exigent daughter of Herodias was banished, apparently for life, from the Metropolitan. But she found a friend in Mr. Hammerstein, who gave her sanctuary at his Manhattan Opera House two years later. *Salome* was produced on West Thirty-fourth Street, in a French version, on January 28, 1909, with Mary Garden appearing for the first time as the heroine. Miss Garden offered an important innovation. Olive Fremstad, in the Metropolitan production, had entrusted to a substitute the dancing of the famous 'Dance of the Seven Veils.' But Miss Garden attended to that duty herself.

Wilde's chief departure from the Scriptural and legendary originals, in the matter of plot, consists in imputing to Salome a maniacal passion for the Prophet; and her request for his head in payment for her dancing is a voluntary one, unprompted by her mother Herodias. Salome would kiss the mouth of John; and, when her passionate importunities are repulsed, she demands his head, that she may bestow upon his dead lips the kisses which she had burned to give them in life. Wilde has still further altered and amplified the traditional story by bringing the figure of Herod far more prominently into the action. The Tetrarch (a marvelous portrait of neurotic sensuality and superstitious fear, both in the drama and in Strauss's music) is racked by an ill-concealed and ungovernable passion for his step-daughter, Salome, a passion which is turned to horrified revulsion at the close of the drama, when, at the sight of the enraptured princess caressing in the moonlight the severed head of John, he commands the soldiers to crush her beneath their shields.

The scene of Salome's Dance is a moonlit terrace before the palace of Herod, Tetrarch of Galilee. At one side is a gigantic staircase; at the back, an old cistern surrounded by a wall of green bronze. The neurotic Herod cannot take his gaze off his perturbing step-daughter; while his wife Herodias, that most unneighborly of operatic consorts, keeps a balefully suspicious eye on him. Herod has just slipped in the blood of the love-sick suicide, Narraboth, and Herodias has contributed to the general amiability by reminding her spouse that she, of royal race, had condescended to marry the son of a camel driver. Herod informs her that she is a liar, and turns for consolation to Salome, stonily pale and sick with desire—though not for him.

'Dance for me, Salome!' beseeches Herod. But Salome answers that she has no wish to dance. Herod pleads with her: he promises to give her, if she will dance, whatever she may ask. Salome brightens up, and bids him swear it. He swears by his life, his crown, his gods. 'You have sworn, Tetrarch,' she says. 'I have sworn, Salome,' answers Herod. He shivers—there is a chill wind on the terrace, and he hears the beating of mighty wings. . . No—the wind is not cold, he cries: it is hot, and he is suffocating. Unbearably excited, he cries for water, for air.

As slaves bring perfumes and the seven veils, and remove the sandals of Salome in preparation for the dance, the warning voice of Jokanaan is heard from his cistern. Herodias is upset, and would go indoors; but the infatuated Herod declines to move until Salome has performed. 'Do not dance, my daughter!' begs Herodias. But Salome pays no heed to her. 'I am ready, Tetrarch,' she announces.

'The musicians begin a wild dance,' say the stage directions in Strauss's score. Salome remains motionless. The music grows quieter at her command. Then Salome begins to dance the Dance of the Seven Veils.

The principal dance theme is sung by a flute and solo viola. This is combined with Salome's chief motive (flute), and with others of amorous significance. A second dance theme—a passionate and contagious tune—is played by violins, violas, horn, and woodwind. Salome languishes, but soon bestirs herself to new frenzies, and the dance reaches a vertiginous climax with a double fortissimo ('sehr schnell') on a phrase from the motive of *Ecstasy*, with a version of the first dance tune as a tumultuous counter-theme for trumpets and trombones. The scene ends with a prolonged trill and a wild descent of the strings, as Salome lingers for an anticipatory moment by Jokanaan's cistern, then flings herself at the feet of the enraptured Herod.

In the last and climactic scene of Strauss's opera, Salome, having danced for Herod, demands as her promised reward the head of Jokanaan on a silver charger. The horrified Tetrarch, after many evasions, orders that she be given what she asks. Salome, in a maniacal frenzy of impatience, leans over the cistern where the Prophet is confined, awaiting that which is hers, screaming shrill orders to the soldiers, to Herod.

Suddenly, a huge black arm, the arm of the gigantic Negro headsman, is thrust upward from the cistern, bearing on a silver dish the head of Jokanaan. Salome seizes it avidly. Herod, watching from his throne, hides his face with his cloak. Herodias smiles and fans herself. It is the most appalling moment in all opera.

Then Salome, in ungovernable ecstasy, apostrophizes the severed head in music that beggars description—music of shattering intensity and power, exultant, triumphant, beautiful, and strangely piteous.

● *Burleske*, FOR PIANO AND ORCHESTRA, IN D MINOR

This *Burleske* was composed at Meiningen in 1885, when Strauss was twenty-one years old, and while he was still a passionate Brahmsian—though he was soon to entrain for the Liszt-Wagner encampment. The *Burleske*, dedicated to Eugen d'Albert, was published in 1894. The orchestral part is scored for an orchestra of woodwind, horns, trumpets, timpani, and strings, in addition to the piano. Four kettledrums are required. They open the piece ('Allegro vivace,' 3-4) playing a phrase four bars in length—a kind of motto-theme.

The orchestra replies, and the brief dialogue is repeated. The piano alone sets forth the first of the two chief subjects, and later the contrasting theme is also stated by the solo instrument. Throughout the piece the rhythmic and melodic characteristics of the opening timpani phrase recall themselves.

Strauss's early mastery of grotesquerie and humor, as well as of formal structure and instrumentation, is strikingly displayed in this score, so that the hearer is more than once forewarned of the brilliant comedy and craftsmanship of the author of *Till Eulenspiegel*. Huneker found less of humor than of mordant irony in the piece. He noted the apparition of the ghost of Brahms at the beginning of the work, 'the opening bar of the piano being the theme of Brahms' first D minor Ballade. But how different the treatment! Bitter, more sardonic than witty.'

Igor Stravinsky

1882-

S

‡There can be no denying the immense prestige which Igor Stravinsky has enjoyed for the past quarter of a century, and which he still enjoys in undiminished measure. If the adulation of the intellectual audience can stamp a living artist's work with the cachet of immortality, then Stravinsky's music is for the ages. He has been and remains the most fashionable composer of our time and the most widely, if not the most deeply, influential. Yet a curious fate has overtaken many, indeed almost all, of his later works—that long succession of dismayingly disparate 'masterpieces' that he has produced since 1913. Each has had its day in the news and has passed into oblivion. Where, oh where, one asks, are the *Renards*, the *Marvas*, the *Noces* of yesteryear? Gone, one fears (or hopes, as the case may be) with the Schiaparellis, the Mainbochers, the Diors of their date. We must, however, wait to see. Meantime, there is another Stravinsky who exists independent of the mode, the Stravinsky of the *Fire-Bird* and *Petrouchka* and the *Rite of Spring*. It is doubtful if those who today cluster about the feet of the master (a glittering crew) remember him, and possibly Stravinsky himself does not, too clearly— the youthful Igor, fresh from the atelier of Rimsky-Korsakoff, with all the tricks of *Sadko* and *Schéhérazade* and the *Tsar Saltan* up his sleeve, along with a thousand fantasies and audacities of his own, and a surer immortality within his grasp than that which fashion gives and fashion takes away. ‡

● SUITE FROM *L'Oiseau de feu* ('The Fire-Bird')

A false anecdote, says Freeman of Oxford, may be good history; so it is imma-
terial whether Rimsky-Korsakoff did or did not exclaim to his former pupil,
Stravinsky, upon hearing his try-out on the piano of a passage from *L'Oiseau
de feu*, 'Look here, stop playing that horrid thing; otherwise I might begin
to enjoy it!' Rimsky died in June 1908, and it is said Stravinsky did not
begin *L'Oiseau de feu* until the summer of 1909, when he was asked by
Diaghileff to compose the score for a ballet to be based on the old Russian
folk legend of the Fire-Bird, after a scenario by Fokine.

It is possible that *L'Oiseau de feu* may have sounded 'horrid' to the correct
and conventional Rimsky, but it can hardly today seem fearsome to even the
most timorous ears. This music contains few hints of the later, insurgent
Stravinsky; there is in *The Fire-Bird* no portent of the iconoclast of *Le Sacre
du Printemps* and *Le Rossignol*. The Fire-Bird, despite her exotic and fantastical ways, her ingenuities of facture, her distinction of style, her decorative
and brilliant loveliness, yet flies contentedly within the golden cage of musical
tradition.

According to Ralston in his *Russian Folk-Tales*, the Fire-Bird is known in
its native haunts as the *Zhar-Ptitsa*—a name less immediately beguiling to the
non-Slavic fancy than is the picture that Ralston draws of the creature's place
in Russian mythology. Its name, he says, indicates its close connection with
flame or light; for, he tells us, *Zhar* means ' "glowing heart," as of a furnace';
and *Zhar-Ptitsa* means, literally, 'the Glow-Bird.' 'Its appearance corresponds
with its designation. Its feathers blaze with golden or silvery sheen, its eyes
shine like crystal, it dwells in a golden cage. In the depth of the night it flies
into a garden and lights it up as brilliantly as could a thousand burning fires.
A single feather from its tail illuminates a dark room. It feeds upon golden
apples, which have the power of bestowing youth and beauty—or, according
to a Croatian version, on magic grasses.'

Now, continuing our explorations of Russian folklore, we encounter the
monstrous ogre, Kastcheï the Immortal, who exists (again to quote the accommodating Ralston) 'as one of the many incarnations of the Dark Spirit. . .
Sometimes he is described as altogether serpent-like in form; sometimes he
seems to be of a mixed nature, partly human and partly ophidian; but in
some stories he is apparently framed after the fashion of a man. . . He is
called "immortal" or "deathless" because of his superiority to the ordinary
laws of existence. . . Sometimes his "death"—that is, the object with which
his life is indissolubly connected—does not exist within his body. . .'

The action of Stravinsky's ballet, from which this concert suite is extracted,
may be outlined as follows:

Into the domain of the Ogre Kastcheï there wandered one night, after a
long day's hunting, the young Prince Ivan Tsarevitch. In the shadows of an
orchard he discovered a marvelous golden bird, with plumage that shone
through the darkness as if its wings had been dipped in flame. The wondrous
creature was sybaritically engaged in plucking golden apples from a silver tree
when Ivan gleefully laid hold of her; but, melted by her entreaties, he soon

released her, and she flew away, leaving with him, in gratitude, one of her shining plumes.

As the night lifted, Ivan saw that he was in the park of an ancient castle, and, as he looked, there issued from it twelve lovely maidens, and then a thirteenth, who, despite her sinister number, seemed to Ivan infinitely desirable. Hiding himself, he watched the damsels, who he knew at once to be princesses because of the easy grace with which, as to the manner born, they played with the golden apples and danced among the silver trees. When he could no longer restrain himself, he went among them; and then, because he was young and comely, they made him a present of some expensive fruit, and besought him to depart in haste, warning him that he was in the enchanted realm of the maleficent Kastcheï, whose prisoners they were, and whose playful habit it was to turn to stone whatever venturesome travelers he could decoy. But Ivan, with his eyes on the beautiful thirteenth princess, was undismayed, and would not go. So they left him.

Then the prince, made bold by love, flung open the gates of the castle, and out swarmed a grotesque and motley throng of slaves and buffoons, soldiers and freaks, the Kikimoras and the Bolibochki and the two-headed monsters—subjects and satellites of the Ogre—and finally the terrible Kastcheï himself, who sought to work his petrifying spell upon Ivan. But the Fire-Bird's golden feather, which Ivan still carried, proved to be a magic talisman, against which the wicked power of the Ogre could not prevail.

And now the Fire-Bird herself appeared. First she caused the Ogre and his crew to begin a frenzied dance, which grew ever wilder and wilder. When they had fallen to the ground exhausted, the Fire-Bird disclosed to Ivan the absurdly simple secret of Kastcheï's immortality: In a certain casket the Ogre preserved an egg. If the egg were broken, Kastcheï would die. It did not take Ivan long to find the egg and dash it to the ground, whereupon Kastcheï expired, and the castle vanished, and the captive knights who had been turned to stone came to life and joined in the general merrymaking, while Ivan and the Tsarevna, the most beautiful of the Princesses, gazed expectantly into each other's eyes.

Stravinsky's ballet, the scenario and choreography by Fokine, the décor by Bakst and Golovine, was produced by the Diaghileff company at the Paris Opera on June 25, 1910. Stravinsky later arranged music from the ballet as a suite for concert performance. The movements of this suite are as follows:

I. INTRODUCTION, leading into a section called

II. 'THE FIRE-BIRD AND HER DANCE,' which combines some of the music accompanying Ivan's pursuit of the miraculous Bird as prelude to the Dance itself—music of fantastic and captivating grace.

III. 'DANCE OF THE PRINCESSES.' This movement, a 'Khorovode,' or round dance, of charming gravity and stateliness, opens with an introductory passage for two flutes in imitation over an octave F-sharp sustained by the horns. The melody of the dance is first played by the oboe, accompanied by harp chords, and is continued by solo 'cello, clarinet, and bassoon. A second section of the theme is sung by the muted strings.

IV. 'KASTCHEÏ'S INFERNAL DANCE.' This section (introduced by a *sfff* chord of the whole orchestra) is called, in the ballet, 'Infernal Dance of All the Subjects of Kastcheï.' The passionate theme in A major for the strings in unison, *fff*, which appears shortly before the end of the movement, is derived from a subject heard in the ballet as the Princesses play with the golden apples—where, thinks Montagu-Nathan, it hints at their ultimate liberation through the good graces of the Fire-Bird. This movement ends on a crashing chord for all the instruments, followed by a sudden quiet of the orchestra and a brief transitional passage (Andante, *p*) for woodwind, horns, piano and harp, then for divided and muted 'cellos and violas. This leads without pause into the

V. BERCEUSE. In the ballet, this delightful cradle-song, with its opening bassoon solo over an accompaniment of muted strings and harp, follows the Infernal Dance, lulling the Tsarevna into a sleep that will protect her from the evil designs of Kastcheï.

VI. FINALE. This movement, which succeeds the Berceuse without pause, follows, in the ballet, the Death of Kastcheï, and accompanies the breaking of the Sorcerer's spell, the vanishing of his castle, and the revivification of the petrified knights. The movement opens with a horn solo (*p*, 'dolce, cantabile'; 'lento maestoso'), above string tremolos—a melody that at the climax of the Finale is sung with thrilling beauty by all the strings in unison against an ascending scale in the brass. The work ends with the jubilant music that celebrates the release of the Ogre's victims and the happy conclusion of Ivan's adventure.

● *Petrouchka*

According to a note in the score, Stravinsky finished the music of *Petrouchka* at Rome on May 26, 1911. The ballet (entitled, in full, *Petrouchka: Scènes burlesques en 4 Tableaux*), scenario by Alexandre Benois, was produced by the Diaghileff company at the Châtelet, Paris, on June 13 of the same year. The dancers included Nijinski and Karsavina, and Monteux conducted. *Petrouchka* was first performed in America (again by the Diaghileff company) on January 24, 1916, at the Century Theater, New York. The first performance of the music of the ballet as a concert piece was by Monteux, in Paris, in March of 1914.

The scene of the ballet is the Admiralty Square at St. Petersburg, about 1830, during the festival of Shrove-tide. A fair is in progress and the stage is crowded with varied and colorful figures—carnival folk, and all the multitude of types of the Russian people who would be found among the onlookers. Presently a long drum-roll draws attention to the booth of the old Charlatan, who proceeds to demonstrate his magic powers by a truly marvelous example of conjuring. In response to his flute, three lifeless puppets revealed by the opening curtains of his little theater—Petrouchka, the Ballerina, and the Moor—come to life, and to the amazement and delight of the breathless crowd, perform a Russian dance.

The second scene takes us back-stage in the Charlatan's theater. We see Petrouchka kicked into his room by his brutal master, and the door slammed behind him. The poor puppet, brought to life against his will, makes us aware that his ruthless creator has afflicted him with humanity. 'He suffers bitterly,' says Mrs. Rosa Newmarch, in her description of the ballet, 'from his own grotesqueness and ridiculous appearance, and from the fact that he has been made aware of human joys which are utterly beyond his attainment.' Presently he is visited by the Ballerina, and he falls desperately in love with her. But she is indifferent to him—or only a little amused and a little frightened by his antics—and leaves him. The third scene takes us to the quarters of the Moor, who is seen in adoration of his strange Idol, a huge egg. He, too, is visited by the Ballerina, over whom he exerts a sinister fascination. When Petrouchka enters in search of his beloved, the Moor turns on him with murderous intent and pursues him from the room.

In the final scene we are back again in the Admiralty Square, where the carnival is at its height. Suddenly the merrymaking is interrupted by cries of terror, and from the Charlatan's booth Petrouchka emerges, the Moor at his heels, and the Ballerina trying in vain to interpose between the two. Petrouchka falls dead, slain by a stroke of his rival's sword, and for a moment the crowd of merrymaking onlookers fears that a real tragedy has taken place. But the old Charlatan assures them that his puppets are puppets merely, and nothing more, and they gradually disperse. The Charlatan is left alone before his booth—and now, to his amazement and consternation, the ghost of Petrouchka appears above the little booth. The Charlatan drops the sawdust-filled figure of his puppet, and flees in terror.

Stravinsky's score is a masterpiece, a thing of fascinating gaiety and wit and beauty. The rhythmic and instrumental ingenuity of the work is beyond praise. And so is the slyness of its humor, the fidelity and vividness of its characterization. How astonishingly imagined is the combination of piccolos and violin harmonics in Petrouchka's death scene; and the famous hurdy-gurdies of the carnival have lost nothing of their delectable humor. But there is much more than slyness and vividness in the music: there is an astringent melancholy, a deep piteousness, a bitter, straining passion. There is the sense of compassion for all unshapely and broken and frustrate things, a half-mocking tenderness for the poor creatures galvanized by the inscrutable, irresponsible Charlatan. These things are not stressed by the music—there is no hint in it of sentimental musing or rich, romantic grief: they are most subtly contained within the exuberant vivaciousness of the score. Yet they are inescapable, if one listened with more than half an ear.

● *Le Sacre du Printemps*

The full title of Stravinsky's ballet is *Le Sacre du Printemps: Tableaux de la Russie Païenne en Deux Parties*—'The Rite of Spring: Pictures of Pagan Russia, in Two Parts.' It was composed in 1912-13, and was produced by Diaghileff, at the Théâtre des Champs Elysées, Paris, on May 29, 1913, with décor by Nicholas Roerich and choreography by Nijinski. Pierre Monteux conducted. The reception of the work was uproarious, with an obbligato of hissing, catcalls, and fisticuffs, and counter-demonstrations by the well-disposed. The concert version of the music of the ballet was played for the first time, again under Monteux's direction, in Paris on April 4, 1914.

According to the generally accepted interpretation of Stravinsky's ballet, the subject deals with the worship of the forces of Nature by primitive man. On the surface, it is a representation, conceived in terms of the dance, of a prehistoric religious ritual, devoted to the mystical adoration of Spring as the sign of fertility, and culminating in a propitiatory sacrifice. It is perhaps not inappropriate to recall here that one of the principles of what Frazer in *The Golden Bough* calls 'sympathetic magic' (which plays a large part in most systems of superstition) is that 'any effect may be produced by imitating it. . . If it is desired to kill a person, an image of him is made and then destroyed.' The decay of vegetation in winter was readily interpreted by pagan man as an enfeeblement of the impulse of fertility: 'the spirit (he thought) had grown old and weak, and must therefore be renovated by being slain and brought to life in a younger and fresher form. . . Thus the killing of a representative of the tree-spirit in Spring was regarded as a means to promote and quicken the growth of vegetation.'

The subject of the first part is the adoration of the earth; that of the second part is concerned with the sacrifice. The various episodes in each part succeed one another without pause. The two parts are separated by a brief interval.

There is first an Introduction, a section of seventy-five bars in slow tempo, designed to suggest 'the mystery of the physical world in spring.'

Harbingers of Spring. Dances of the Adolescents ('Tempo guisto,' 2-4). The Adolescents perform a rite of incantation, which consists of stamping heavily upon the ground, and the strings reiterate, forte, with unevenly placed accents emphasized by the horns, a chord that is half in A-flat and half in E-natural. Youths and maidens participate in this ceremonial worship of the Earth. Under a charming dance tune (flutes), four trumpets chant a simply harmonized theme which will be heard again later. A mock-abduction, or 'marriage by capture,' follows as part of the ritual, accompanied by an agitated passage (Presto) in rapidly changing meters—9-8, 4-8, 5-8, 12-8, 7-8, et cetera.

Then comes a Horovod, or round dance, entitled 'Spring Rounds,' introduced (Tranquillo, A-flat) by E-flat and bass clarinets with a tune in the style of a Russian folk song, under flute trills, with the time changing constantly. After this brief preluding comes the main portion of the dance, based on the chanting theme previously played by the trumpets ('Sostenuto e pesante,' D-flat, at first in 4-4 time), now scored for woodwind, horns, and strings, later for the full orchestra, *fff*, polytonally harmonized, the rhythm punctuated with earth-shaking drum beats. This section closes with a return of the folk-like tune of the prelude under its accompanying trill.

Another ceremonial follows, a sort of community contest: 'Games of Rival Tribes' ('molto allegro'), in rapidly changing meters. The principal theme is a phrase harmonized for the most part in thirds, at first for muted trumpets and flutes, in G major, against an accompaniment figure (strings pizzicato) in B major. At the close of this section appears the Sage, the most venerable member of the tribe. He is the Celebrant, whose function it is to consecrate the soil for its coming renewal. ('Procession of the Sage.') His entrance is announced by four tubas, bass-drum, timpani, tamtam, low strings, horns, and wood. There is a pause. The Celebrant blesses the soil, and invokes its rejuvenation. 'A Dance of the Earth' (Prestissimo) carries the first part of the ballet to a tumultuous and abrupt conclusion.

The second part opens with an Introduction (Largo) to which Stravinsky gave the title, 'The Pagan Night,' though this does not appear in the score. 'A deep sadness pervades it, but this sadness is physical, not sentimental. . . It is gloomy with the oppression of the vast forces of Nature, pitiful with the helplessness of living creatures in their presence,' observed Edwin Evans. Dark-hued harmonies for flutes and clarinets move above a sustained horn chord, and the strings (harmonics) foreshadow the theme of the following section. Two muted trumpets have a dual motif, for the most part unaccompanied.

The prelude, which is harmonized throughout with extraordinary poignancy, leads to a section headed, 'Mystical Circles of the Adolescents.' Here the maidens dance in a slow and mysterious round, pausing while the sacrificial victim is elected. We hear one of the themes of the Introduction ('Andante con moto'), harmonized in major and minor triads that sound against each other in different octaves (six solo violas), and a second theme played by the bass flute accompanied by divided violins, answered by two clarinets playing in consecutive major-sevenths.

The chosen victim is now glorified (Vivo, 5-8), and the action of the ballet proceeds through scenes of progressive intensity. There is an 'Evocation of the Ancestors' (ponderous chords for the wood and brass, punctuated by ff chords of the strings. A 'Ritual of the Ancestors' is introduced by reiterated chords for the horns and strings pizzicato, emphasized by tambourine, bass drum, and timpani, underlying a theme for the English horn and one for the bass flute. Later there is a new theme for muted trumpets.

Now the elected victim begins her sacrifice; for the final act of propitiation has been demanded, and she must dance herself to death. The music expresses the mystical rapture of this invocation of vernal fertility in rhythms of paroxysmal frenzy. There is nothing in music quite like this frenetic close of *Le Sacre du Printemps*, with its famous alternations of meter—bars of 5-16, 3-16, 2-16, 4-16—and its delirious culmination as the victim falls dead.

Le Sacre du Printemps is essentially a barbaric and stupendous spring song. The spring that is celebrated is not, as Evans has pointed out, the poetic conception that has lured the Romanticists in all ages and all countries, but 'Spring stripped of its literary associations and presented bare, with a naked directness that is the secret of the music's compelling force.' He might have gone further and said that if this music is anything, it is a glorification of Spring as the supreme expression of the creative impulse—a primordial Spring, savage, elemental, ruthless. Music has long been in love with death—the greatest music in the world, indeed, is music of the ecstasy of death. Here, for the first time, is music of the ecstasy of birth, music which makes audible 'that conflict which is forever rending and tearing, not in order to destroy, but in order to emerge. It is not the sound of death battering down and in, but of life hewing and tearing apart, that a new birth may issue out.'

• Symphonie de Psaumes

This work is a setting, for orchestra and chorus, of passages from the Psalms. Stravinsky chose verses from three of the Psalms, using the text of the Vulgate. Upon the first page of the manuscript of the orchestral score, Stravinsky has written, in French, the following 'remarks':

The three parts of this symphony are to be played without pause. The text of the Psalms, which is that of the Vulgate, is to be sung in Latin. The Psalms are: Verses 13 and 14 of XXXVIII, for the First Part of the Symphony; verses 2, 3, and 4 of XXXIX for the Second Part; Psalm CL, in its entirety, for the Third Part. The chorus should be of children's voices. Failing these, women's voices (sopranos and altos) may be substituted [the score contains parts for sopranos, altos, tenors, and basses].

It should be noted that the Psalms and verses set to music by Stravinsky are numbered differently in the Vulgate and in the King James version. Psalm XXXVIII, verses 13-14, of the Vulgate (the text of the first movement) becomes in the English Psalter, Psalm XXXIX, verses 12-13. Psalm XXXIX, verses 2, 3, 4, of the Vulgate (second movement), becomes in the English version Psalm XL, verses 1, 2, 3. Psalm CL (third movement) is the same in the Latin and the English versions.

In the first excerpt, the Psalmist utters his prayer and his entreaty—and makes immortal beauty with the marvelous line, 'Hold not thy peace at my tears.' In the second, he proclaims his joy over the Lord's response, for he has been rescued from the horrible pit and set upon a rock. The third is the magnificent exhortation to praise the Lord with trumpet and psaltery and harp, with timbrel and dance, 'upon the high-sounding cymbals.'

For the three contrasting moods of the symphony—prayer, thanksgiving, praise—Stravinsky has found original utterance. He has foregone the obvious approaches to his text. The musical clichés of lamentation, of thanksgiving, of jubilant praise, have no place in his expressional scheme. He has done what the fructifying artist always does in subjecting to his imagination a standardized theme—has discovered in it fresh aspects and implications, hidden depths and surfaces, has made it yield him what the seventeenth century would have called 'an exalted strangeness.'

'Before I go hence and be no more,' sings the Psalmist at the end of his entreaty; and the long-held notes of Stravinsky's chorus, the grave harmonies of the orchestra, effuse no facile pathos, but an age-old austerity of grief. For the verses of thanksgiving (set at the beginning as an astonishing double fugue) he finds music of intricate and subtle poignance, perhaps the most searching page he has yet given us. The Psalmist recalls the horrors of the pit and of the miry clay, and his anguished waiting for release; and the acid, astringent tones of the woodwind, the spareness and sharpness of the musical idea, its refusal of the easily delectable, mirror the poet's thought. But the most deeply touching of the symphony's moments is that remarkable E-flat passage near the end in which, as you await a mighty outburst at 'Praise him upon the loud cymbals,' the music is suddenly stilled, and the voices, in a page that haunts the ear and mind, evoke the awe of the worshiper before the Sanctuary. And

the concluding Alleluia too is hushed, as at the thought of the supreme benefi-
cence: 'He hath made everything beautiful in his time: also he hath set
eternity in their hearts.'

The orchestra employed by Stravinsky is an unusual one. It is devoid of
violins and violas, and the wind section contains no clarinets. The score calls
for five flutes (one interchangeable with piccolo), four oboes, English horn,
three bassoons, double-bassoon, four horns, five trumpets (including a small
trumpet in D), three trombones, tuba, harp, two pianos, violoncellos, and
double-basses. None of the traditional phrases is used to indicate the pace and
character of the movements. Instead of the conventional Allegro, 'Andante
espressivo,' et cetera, Stravinsky puts his faith in metronomic markings.

The *Symphonie de Psaumes* was composed in 1930—'à la gloire de Dieu,'
as the title page affirms—and is dedicated to the Boston Symphony Orchestra,
for whose fiftieth anniversary it was written. The first performance (owing to
an unexpected postponement of the American première) was at Brussels, by
the Brussels Philharmonic Society, December 13, 1930.

Peter Ilich Tchaikovsky

1840-93

T

‡The reader of Tchaikovsky's letters and diaries receives the impression
that their author must indeed have been the unhappiest of men. He had,
apparently, no defenses against life, and the wounds which it daily in-
flicted upon him bled and bled (for he suffered from a kind of spiritual
hemophilia). 'I wept . . . I wept . . . I wept . . .' This is his constant
refrain. Yet beyond afflicting him with inverted sexuality, with a hypersensitive and hypochondriacal nature, the fates treated him kindly enough.
He was not required to bear for long the burden of poverty—never, in
his case, crushing—which he had accepted when, as a young man of
twenty-three, he resigned his post in the civil service to devote himself
exclusively to music; from his thirty-sixth year until nearly the end of
his life he received a substantial annuity from his patroness Nadejda von
Meck. Nor had he ever cause to complain that his abilities were unrecog-
nized and unrewarded; long before his death his fame was world-wide.
Yet the substance of all that he thought and said and wrote was heartbreak, despair, and death: He affords us a striking illustration of the
essentially subjective nature of human happiness. But while as a man
Tchaikovsky was deplorably, was pitiably weak, as an artist he had, curi-

ously, the strength of ten. He was quite sure that all was vanity and vexation of spirit, but this conviction did not affect his strong sense of his responsibilities as an artist. He could and did subject himself to the severest disciplines with the object of mastering his craft; work was an obligation and a routine from which he never shrank. He produced an enormous amount of music, very little of which lacks distinction in some form and measure, and much of which is among the most popular ever written. Every class of listener must pay him the tribute of admiration and respect: the sincerity of his communication and his mastery of means alike compel it.‡

● SYMPHONY NO. 2, IN C MINOR, OP. 17 ('Little Russia')

In the early seventies of the last century, Tchaikovsky had descended to the writing of musical criticism in order to increase his income (his professorial job, together with the proceeds from the performance and sale of his works, brought him in about $1000 a year). But he maintained his self-respect by continuing to compose. So, in the autumn of 1872, we find him at Moscow, absorbed in the completion of his Second Symphony. 'Modi, my conscience pricks me,' he wrote in November to his devoted brother, Modest. 'That is my punishment for not having written to you for so long. What can I do, when the symphony, which is nearing completion, occupies me so entirely that I can think of nothing else? . . . It will be performed as soon as I can get the parts copied. It seems to me my best work, at least as regards correctness of form, a quality for which I have not thus far distinguished myself.'

During the Christmas holidays, Tchaikovsky went to St. Petersburg and while there he consorted with 'the Invincible Band'—the fire-eating Five (Balakireff, Cui, Moussorgsky, Borodin, Rimsky-Korsakoff), who evidently improved the occasion by subjecting him to some nationalistic propaganda. Tchaikovsky wrote that he was nearly 'torn to pieces' during an evening party at Rimsky's house, and Modest, in his biography of his brother, expresses the belief that it was the influence of the Five that induced Peter Ilich to make use of a Little Russian folksong in the last movement of the C minor Symphony.

Shortly after this, the symphony was performed at a concert of the Imperial Music Society in Moscow. Tchaikovsky wrote Stasoff that it had met 'with great success,' and at a repeat performance, some days later, the composer was recalled after each movement, and was presented with a silver goblet and a laurel wreath. But Tchaikovsky was not satisfied with the work. Years later he wrote to Mrs. von Meck (from Paris, in December 1879) that he was about to take in hand the revision of the symphony, 'of which only the last movement can be left intact.' This resolution was duly carried out. Modest tells us that the alterations were considerable, and that the first movement was entirely rewritten. On February 2, 1881, the symphony was given in its revised version by the Musical Society in St. Petersburg. It was received with acclamation—but, says Modest, 'not a single critic observed the changes in the work, nor the fact that the first movement was entirely new.' Poor souls! they had evidently not been tipped off.

Apparently Tchaikovsky, responding to the goadings of the 'Invincible Band,' injected as much nationalism into his work as his conscience would permit. It was Kashkin who first gave it the name of 'Little Russian' Symphony because, he asserted, 'its chief themes are Little Russian folksongs.' This is most conspicuously true of the first and last movements. In the former, Tchaikovsky uses the Malo-Russian variant of 'Down by Mother Volga,' and the Finale is based on the folksong known as 'The Crane.' The latter is played by the first violins at the beginning of the main movement of the Finale ('Allegro vivo,' C major, 2-4), after twenty-four introductory bars.

The first movement has a long introduction ('Andante sostenuto,' 4-4), filling sixteen pages of the score, in which the solo horn, in a passage of singular and melancholy charm, has the field to itself for the opening eight bars. At the end of this introduction two horns, unaccompanied, lead into the main section—Tchaikovsky the symphonist was indeed good to his horns. The first fiddles, accompanied by the other strings, set forth the folk tune which is the basis of the Allegro. A contrasting theme of typically Tchaikovskian sentiment, a melting cantabile for the oboe, reminds us that Peter Ilich, the dispenser of lyric sweets, is not forgetting his obligations.

In the place of a songful slow movement, we get an 'Andantino marziale' in E-flat major, common time, for the subject of which the thrifty Tchaikovsky went to his opera *Undine*, which he had composed three years before but afterward destroyed. From the tune of a wedding march in the last act of the opera, Tchaikovsky derived the theme of the second movement of his symphony. We hear it on clarinets and bassoons, over a tonic-dominant ostinato of the kettledrums.

The Scherzo is a vivacious and frolicsome page, with a rather naïve trio, initiated by the woodwind and horns. The Finale of the symphony takes us into the heart of Little Russia. Even Cui, who loved not Tchaikovsky, called it 'magnificent.' A noteworthy feature of this movement is the appearance of a perfectly good whole-tone scale, which may be heard in the basses just before the appearance of the second theme in the strings (page 132 of the full score). In this matter, Tchaikovsky anticipated Debussy by a dozen years or so—a fact not without its interest for the student of musical history. In fact, the whole-tone scale as a serious device seems to have made its first earthly appearance in Russia; for Glinka used it in his *Russlan and Ludmilla* overture in 1842, and Dargomijsky employed it twenty-five years later in his opera *The Stone Guest*—although Mozart, who could do amazing and revolutionary things when he felt like it, had anticipated both of them by tucking a whole-tone scale into the Adagio of his *Dorfmusikanten-Serenade*.

● SYMPHONY NO. 3, IN D MAJOR, OP. 29 ('Polish')

Tchaikovsky composed his Third Symphony in less than two months. He began it on June 5, 1875, at Ussovo, and completed it on the following August 1st, at Verbovka. The first performance was on November 7th of that year, at Moscow. The first performance in America was by the Philharmonic Society of New York, under Adolph Neuendorff, at the Academy of Music, February 8, 1879.

Tchaikovsky had finished his B-flat minor Piano Concerto the winter before he composed the Third Symphony. After the completion of the symphony he began work on his ballet, *Swan Lake,* and the following year he sketched his symphonic fantasia, *Francesca da Rimini.*

When the Third Symphony was played at St. Petersburg, under Napravnik's bâton, in 1876, César Cui wrote that at the end of the performance 'the composer was enthusiastically recalled.' 'This symphony,' Cui declared, 'must be taken seriously. The first three movements are the best. The only charm of the fourth movement is its sonority. . . The fifth movement, a polonaise, is the weakest. On the whole the new symphony shows talent. . .' Laroche was better pleased: 'The importance and power of the music,' he wrote, 'the beauty and variety of form, the nobility of style, the originality and rare perfection of technique, all contribute to make this symphony one of the most remarkable musical works produced during the last ten years. Were it to be played in any musical center in Germany, it would raise the name of the Russian musician to a level with those of the most famous symphonic composers of the day.'

Tchaikovsky's chief musical enthusiasm at this time was *Carmen.* When he heard the opera at Paris, in company with his brother Modest, he was so carried away that his brother 'became quite embarrassed.' Later, Tchaikovsky attended the Bayreuth Festival of 1876, where he was astonished to find himself received as a distinguished visitor. 'It appears,' he wrote home, 'that I am not so unknown in Western Europe as I thought.' His days in Bayreuth were 'one long confusion of hospitality.' But Tchaikovsky did not take to the music of the *Ring.* 'After the final note of *Götterdämmerung,*' he wrote, 'I felt as if freed from poison.' The perceptive Mrs. von Meck seems to have shared his feelings. 'How can Wagner . . . compare with you?' she wrote Tchaikovsky in the following year. 'He profanes the art.' But Mrs. von Meck admitted that Wagner had 'great talent.' 'It is lucky,' she added, 'that we are not Germans. . . We can say with impunity, "Thank God, we have no Wagner, but we have Peter Ilich."'

The Third Symphony has five movements: the Introduction (suggesting a funeral march) and 'Allegro brillante'; an 'alla Tedesca'; an Andante; a Scherzo; and a Finale 'alla polacca.' Tchaikovsky himself, in one of his letters, points out that this symphony has two scherzi, of which the 'alla Tedesca' is the first.

● SYMPHONY NO. 4, IN F MINOR, OP. 36

Tchaikovsky's Fourth Symphony is interwoven with the inner history of the composer's relations with two women who most vitally touched his life: the woman whom he never met, never spoke with, yet profoundly and intimately knew; and the spiritual stranger who was for a time his wife.

Tchaikovsky began his Fourth Symphony in the winter of 1876-7. It was about this time that he entered upon his unique friendship with Nadejda von Meck, a rich widow who dwelt in Moscow. Mrs. von Meck deeply admired the music of Tchaikovsky. She made inquiries concerning his pecuniary status, and when she learned that his means were small, and that he was embarrassingly in debt, she sent him, in the summer of 1877, the sum of 3000 rubles. A correspondence had meanwhile begun between them—the first letter from Mrs. von Meck is dated December 30, 1876. She had given Tchaikovsky certain small commissions to execute for her—transcriptions for violin and piano of certain of his works—and for these she paid him liberal honoraria. In the autumn of 1877 she asked him, with many apologies, to permit her to settle on him an annual allowance of 6000 rubles (about $3000 then), in order that he might compose unhampered by material cares. 'If I should want something from you,' she wrote extenuatingly, 'of course you would give it to me, is it not so? Very well, then, we are quits. Do not interfere with my management of your domestic economy, Peter Ilich.'

She attached a peculiar condition to their friendship: she insisted that she and Tchaikovsky must never meet or know one another personally. 'The more you fascinate me,' she wrote, 'the more I shrink from knowing you.' Tchaikovsky accepted the financial settlement, and respected Nadejda's wish concerning the limitations of their intercourse. 'I can only serve you,' he wrote, 'by means of my music. Nadejda Filaretovna, every note which comes from my pen in the future is dedicated to you!' They corresponded frequently, at length, and with the deepest intellectual and spiritual intimacy, but they never met.

This extraordinary friendship, which extended over thirteen years, was abruptly and lamentably ended. In December 1890, Tchaikovsky received a letter from his patroness informing him that she was on the brink of ruin, and that she would be obliged to discontinue his allowance—this, despite the fact that she had more than once declared to him that no matter what occurred, his annuity was assured to him for life. As it happened, this curtailment of his income did not greatly affect Tchaikovsky's financial situation, for he had achieved prosperity with his increasing fame. But he suffered keen anxiety on his friend's account.

Later, it transpired that Mrs. von Meck's fortune was not seriously cut down after all—a turn of events which brought new misery to the hypersensitive Tchaikovsky, who persuaded himself that Mrs. von Meck's announcement had been merely 'an excuse to get rid of him at the first opportunity'; that he had been mistaken in idealizing his relations with his 'best friend'; that her allowance to him had long since ceased to be the expression of a generous impulse. He thought of returning to her in full the money she had settled on him, but feared to mortify her. He endeavored, both frankly and by diplomatic guile, to renew their intercourse; but to no avail. Nadejda took no notice whatever of his attempts to renew their intimacy, either through letters or in response to overtures by Tchaikovsky through mutual acquaintances. He learned that she was ill of 'a terrible nervous disease' which had affected her relations with everyone. Yet no illness or misfortune, it seemed to him, could 'change the sentiments which were expressed in [her] letters.' 'I would sooner,' he declared, 'have believed that the earth would fail me than that our relations should suffer change. But the inconceivable has hap-

pened, and all my ideas of human nature, all my faith in the best in mankind, have been turned upside down.' Two years later, on his death-bed, her
name was constantly and feverishly on his lips. 'In the broken phrases of his
last delirium,' writes Modest Tchaikovsky, 'these words alone were intelligible
to those about him.' Nadejda herself survived Tchaikovsky by only two months.
She died in January 1894.

But to return to the Fourth Symphony. In May 1877, Tchaikovsky wrote to
Mrs. von Meck that he was 'absorbed' in the symphony; and he added that
he was 'in a very nervous, worried, and irritable state.' He explained the reason
two months later. It appears that he had engaged himself, at the behest of a
fantastic conception of chivalry, to a woman 'no longer very young' (Tchaikovsky himself was 37), whom he did not love, who was poor, and of meager
charm—'rather good-looking' was his phrase for her—and with whom he
proposed to live only 'as a devoted and grateful friend.' But Antonina Miliou-
kow (the unfortunate woman's name) loved him 'intensely,' he related, and
had avowed her love, and so he married her. 'The agonies I have endured,'
he confided to his patron, 'defy description. To live for thirty-seven years with
an innate antipathy to matrimony, and then suddenly, by force of circumstance,
to find oneself engaged to a woman with whom one is not in the least in
love—is very painful.'

The wedding took place July 18, 1877. In October, Tchaikovsky fled pre-
cipitately from his new home in Moscow 'in a state bordering upon insanity.'
When his brother Anatol met him at the railroad station in St. Petersburg,
Peter was shockingly distraught, and his face was scarcely recognizable. He
suffered a nervous collapse and was unconscious for two days. His wife returned
to her mother, and a permanent separation followed. It was an expensive
indulgence in chivalry.

In these troubled and difficult months the Fourth Symphony came into
being. It was completed in the winter of 1877-8. 'On none of my works for
orchestra have I expended such love and devotion,' he wrote to Mrs. von Meck.
To Taneieff, he wrote that 'of course' the symphony was program music—'I do
not wish any symphonic work to emanate from me that has nothing to express,
and consists merely of harmonies and a purposeless design of rhythms and
modulations.' As for the Fourth Symphony, there was not, he said, a single
measure in it 'which is not an echo of my intimate spiritual life.' To Mrs.
von Meck, he was more explicit. Writing to her from Florence in March 1888,
he said: 'For our symphony, it is possible to express the contents in words,
and I will tell you, but only you, the significance of the entire work, as well
as of its different movements.' Here is Tchaikovsky's interpretation of the
meaning of the symphony:

I. ('Andante sostenuto; Moderato con anima'): The Introduction is the kernel of the
entire symphony [Tchaikovsky quotes here the opening theme—the ominous and
Draconian phrase for horns and bassoons]. This is Fate, the somber power which pre-
vents the desire for happiness from reaching its goal . . . a force which, like the sword
of Damocles, hangs perpetually over our heads. This force is inescapable and invincible.
There is no other course but to submit and inwardly lament [Tchaikovsky quotes here

the dolorous first theme for violins and 'cellos—'Moderato con anima' (in movimento di valse)—which begins the main body of the movement].

The feeling of depression and hopelessness grows stronger and stronger. Would it not be better to turn away from reality and lull one's self in dreams? [the counter-theme for clarinet—'Moderato assai, quasi andante'—is quoted in this association]. O joy! A sweet and tender dream enfolds me. A serene and radiant presence leads me on [Second theme: flutes and oboes cantabile]. Deeper and deeper the soul is sunk in dreams. All that was dark and joyless is forgotten. . .

No—these are but dreams: roughly we are awakened by Fate. Thus we see that life is only an everlasting alternation of somber reality and fugitive dreams of happiness. Something like this is the program of the first movement.

II. ('Andantino in modo di canzona'): The second movement shows suffering in another stage. It is a feeling of melancholy such as fills one when sitting alone at home, exhausted by work; the book has slipped from one's hand; a swarm of memories fills the mind. How sad to think that so much has been, so much is gone! And yet it is sweet to think of the days of one's youth. We regret the past, yet we have neither the courage nor the desire to begin life anew. We are weary of existence. We would fain rest awhile, recalling happy hours when our young blood pulsed warm through our veins and life brought satisfaction. We remember irreparable loss. But these things are far away. It is sad, yet sweet, to lose ourselves in the past.

III. (Scherzo, 'Pizzicato ostinato': Allegro): No definite feelings find expression in the third movement. These are capricious arabesques, intangible figures which flit through the fancy as if one had drunk wine and were exhilarated. The mood is neither sad nor joyful. We think of nothing, but give free rein to the fancy, which humors itself in evolving the most singular patterns. Suddenly there arises the memory of a drunken peasant and a ribald song. . . Military music passes in the distance.—Such are the disconnected images which flit through the brain as one sinks into slumber. They have nothing to do with reality; they are incomprehensible, bizarre, fragmentary.

IV. (Finale: 'Allegro con fuoco'): Fourth movement. If you can find no pleasures in yourself, look about you. Mix with the people. Observe that the multitude understands how to be merry, how to surrender itself to gaiety. A popular festival is depicted. Scarcely have you forgotten yourself, scarcely have you had time to lose yourself in contemplation of the joy of others, when unwearying Fate again announces its presence. But the multitude pays no heed to you. It does not even spare you a glance, nor note that you are lonely and sad. How merry they all are! And do you still say that the world is steeped in grief? Nay, there is such a thing as joy—simple, vigorous, primitive joy. Rejoice in the happiness of others, and it will still be possible for you to live.

I can tell you no more, dear friend, about the symphony.

● SYMPHONY NO. 5, IN E MINOR, OP. 64

Montaigne observed that he was 'very fond of peasants—they are not educated enough to reason incorrectly.' At Hamburg, in the 'eighties, there were some who would not have sympathized with that view. Tchaikovsky, in his diary of the year 1888, writes with humorous frankness concerning the venerable Theodore Ave-Lallement, an officer of the Hamburg Philharmonic, to whom the Russian's Fifth Symphony is dedicated. 'Herr Lallement,' says Tchaikovsky, 'candidly confessed that many of my works which had been performed in Hamburg were not at all to his taste. . . He thought that I had in me the making of a very good German composer. Almost with tears in his eyes he besought me to leave Russia and settle permanently in Germany, where classical conventions and the traditions of high culture could not fail to correct my faults, which were easily explainable to his mind by the fact of my having been born and educated in a country so unenlightened.' Yet this alleged deficiency of aesthetic sophistication in Tchaikovsky was not perceived by the members of what was once called the Neo-Russian School, the ferocious nationalists of the 'Invincible Band,' the famous Five—Balakireff, César Cui, Rimsky-Korsakoff, Borodin, and Moussorgsky—for whom Tchaikovsky was that deplorable thing, a cosmopolite. Tchaikovsky was tolerated by the Five, as Julian Tiersot observes, only because of his amiable disposition. Rimsky-Korsakoff remarks that 'Tchaikovsky's conservatorial education always raised a barrier between him and us.' Poor Tchaikovsky! But at least they seem not to have said of him what Balakireff said of Moussorgsky: 'His brain is feeble—he has no head.'

Tchaikovsky's Fifth Symphony is separated by ten years from his Fourth, and by five years from his Sixth. It was one of the products of 1888, together with the *Hamlet* Overture and the six songs of op. 65. In June of that year he wrote to Mrs. von Meck that he was 'dreadfully anxious' to prove not only to others, but also to himself, that he was 'not yet *played out* as a composer,' and that he was writing a new symphony. The phrase 'played out' is italicized in Modest Tchaikovsky's quotation of this letter (Mrs. Newmarch's translation); probably Tchaikovsky remembered that those disheartening words had been used half a dozen years before by a Moscow critic in commenting upon his violin concerto. So, in the summer of 1888, Tchaikovsky tended his garden at Frolovskoe and worked, a little downheartedly, upon the E minor Symphony. He 'felt his age,' he says (he was only forty-eight), and was not well; he was too tired to read, or to play in the evening his favorite game of cards. On August 26 he wrote of the symphony as completed.

Tchaikovsky was at first despondent concerning the effect of his new score. His Moscow friends, Taneieff in particular, praised it warmly. But after two performances in St. Petersburg and one in Prague, Tchaikovsky came to the conclusion that the work was a failure. 'There is something repellent, superfluous, patchy, and insincere in it,' he wrote to Mrs. von Meck in December 1888. 'Am I really played out, as they say? Last night I looked through *our* symphony (No. 4). What a difference! How immeasurably superior it is!' He cheered up about the E minor in the following spring, after 'a great success' with it in Hamburg (March 15, 1889), when the symphony was 'magnificently played.' The composer liked his work 'far better' then, and resented the fact that the Russian press continued to ignore him.

Brahms was in Hamburg at the time, and heard a rehearsal of the symphony. Nicholas Kashkin in his Recollections says that Brahms 'did not like the symphony at all,' and that he told Tchaikovsky so with his usual bluntness. Modest Tchaikovsky in his Life of his brother gives a different account; the symphony, he says, 'had pleased [Brahms] on the whole, with the exception of the Finale.' But Tchaikovsky need not have felt, as Modest reports, 'deeply hurt' by the candor of Brahms; for had he not, in a letter written to the Grand Duke Constantine Constantinovitch, five months before, spoken with extreme severity about Brahms—behind his back? 'Is not Brahms,' he had inquired of the Grand Duke, 'in reality a caricature of Beethoven? Is not this pretension to profundity and power detestable, because the content which is poured into the Beethoven mold is not really of any value?' His Imperial Highness, one gathers, ventured to offer a good word for Brahms; for in another letter, written ten days later, Tchaikovsky returned to the attack. He 'could not at all agree with the Grand Duke'; Brahms, he insisted, is 'dry,' 'cold,' and has 'very little melodic invention. . . His depth is not real: *c'est voulu*. . . He lacks the chief thing—beauty.'

Thus do composers, functioning as critics, sometimes add to the gaiety of nations.

The Fifth Symphony, it has been pointed out, bears the strongest internal evidence of having been written to a program. 'The feeling that this is so is mainly due to the recurrence, in each movement, of the theme with which the symphony begins (the opening theme, for clarinets, Andante, E minor, 4-4). This produces a feeling of unity that irresistibly suggests one central controlling purpose. The theme in question is peculiarly somber and fateful. It recurs twice in the following Andante, and again at the end of the waltz that constitutes the third movement. In the Finale, the treatment of it is especially remarkable. It serves, transposed into the major, to commence this movement; it makes more than one reappearance afterwards. But this is not all the thematic filiation this symphony reveals. One of the themes of the second movement—the Andante—also recurs in the Finale, while the opening subject proper of the Finale (following the Introduction) is plainly based on the opening subject of the whole symphony. Lastly, the first subject of the Allegro of the first movement reappears in the major, on the last page but two of the score, to the same accompaniment as in the Allegro. So that—to sum the matter up concisely—the fourth movement contains two themes from the first and one from the second; the third and second movements each contain one theme from the first. No one, probably, will venture to assert that so elaborate a system of thematic repetition as this is due to mere caprice; nor is it easy to see why Tchaikovsky should have indulged in it at all if his object had been merely to write a symphony in four movements. Nothing can be clearer than that the work embodies an emotional sequence of some kind. It is a great pity that we have no definite clew to this; but even on the face of the matter as it now stands the general purport of the symphony is quite plain.' (Ernest Newman.)

● SYMPHONY NO. 6, IN B MINOR, OP. 74 ('Pathétique')

This symphony was performed for the first time anywhere on October 28, 1893, at a concert of the Imperial Russian Musical Society in St. Petersburg. Tchaikovsky conducted. It is remarkable, in view of the subsequent history of the work, that at the first performance the 'Pathétique' made little impression. Even Modest Tchaikovsky, Peter's devoted brother, says that it 'fell rather flat.' Nor were the critics enthusiastic. The reviewer for the *Novoe Vremya* observed that the symphony contained 'much that is clever and resourceful as regards orchestral color, besides grace and delicacy (in the two middle movements), but so far as inspiration is concerned, it stands far below Tchaikovsky's other symphonies.' The gentleman on the *St. Petersburg Viedomosti* found 'the leading subjects' 'neither new nor significant.' The *Syn Otechestra* was reminded of Gounod's *Romeo et Juliette* and of Grieg. Only one lonely soul, he of the *Birjevya Viedomosti*, uttered warm praise of the work.

The work at first did not bear the title 'Pathétique,' nor any other. How it came to be so named is thus related by Modest:

> The morning after the concert I found my brother sitting at the breakfast table with the score of the symphony before him. He had agreed to send the score to [his publisher] that very day, but could not decide upon a title. He did not care to designate it merely by a number, and he had abandoned his original intention of entitling it *A Program Symphony*. 'What would *Program Symphony* mean,' he said, 'if I will not give the program?' I suggested *Tragic* Symphony as an appropriate title, but that did not please him. I left the room while he was still undecided. Suddenly *Pathetic* occurred to me, and I went back to the room and suggested it. I remember, as though it were yesterday, how he exclaimed: 'Bravo, Modi, splendid! *Pathetic!*' And then and there he added to the score, in my presence, the title that will always remain.

Modest thereafter observes casually that this simple account demolishes the theory of Hugo Riemann, who in his thematic analysis of the symphony saw the solution of the title in 'the striking resemblance between the fundamental idea of the work [the somber and heavy-footed opening phrase for the bassoon which, in the Introduction, foreshadows the chief theme of the Allegro] and the chief subject of Beethoven's Sonata Pathétique'—of which, remarks Modest, 'Tchaikovsky never dreamed.' Eight days after the conversation related by Modest, Tchaikovsky was dead of cholera at St. Petersburg.

Vernon Blackburn has said that 'it is in Tchaikovsky's music that you must find him; and there is probably no more tragic musical life than that of Tchaikovsky. His scores teem with vitality . . . yet he always strayed, in the end, to that darkness, that gloom and that despair which found its last utterance in his Sixth Symphony.'

What, precisely, was in Tchaikovsky's mind when he composed this 'Program Symphony'? According to Tchaikovsky's intimate friend, Nicholas Kashkin, 'if the composer had disclosed it to the public, the world would not have regarded the symphony as a kind of legacy from one filled with the presentiment of his own approaching end.' To Kashkin it seems justifiable 'to interpret the overwhelming energy of the third movement and the abysmal sorrow of the Finale in the broader light of a national or historical significance, rather than to narrow them to the expression of an individual experience. If the last movement is intended to be predictive, it is surely of things vaster and issues more fatal than are contained in a mere personal apprehension of death. It speaks rather of a *lamentation large et souffrance inconnue*, and seems to set the seal of finality on all human hopes. Even if we eliminate the purely subjective interest, this autumnal inspiration of Tchaikovsky, in which we hear "the ground whirl of the perished leaves of hope," still remains the most profoundly stirring of his works.'

But Blackburn, who wrote of Tchaikovsky with peculiar understanding and tenderness, saw in this symphony something far more moving than any 'national' or 'historical' utterance. 'It seems to us,' he wrote, 'that in this symphony Tchaikovsky realized his own self with a completeness and with all too sad a feeling that must ever remain unique in the art of the world. . . This wonderful and extraordinary work is a thing that still brings unbidden tears to the eye, that still in the ripeness of its moments seems to read a lesson of sadness and of tolerance which is rare indeed in the pages of musical art, that still shakes the heart and fills up all one's lifelong grief for things that are dead. . .'

Perhaps the day may come again when we shall all be willing to agree that this too-familiar symphony is among the most touching disclosures in art—a thing of deep and terrible sincerity, of an eloquence that at times is overwhelming, that is filled, in its richest moments, with a searching and unforgettable beauty. If ever music drew its breath in pain, it is in certain accessions of passionate grieving that this work contains, when we seem to hear Tchaikovsky say—

Absent thee from felicity awhile;

or when, in other pages of a desperate and fearful gaiety, the music sounds as though Tchaikovsky had hoped to sustain himself and us by that intolerable, that heart-breaking cry—

Death cannot spoil the Spring!

Tchaikovsky dreaded with passionate protest what Sir Thomas Browne called 'the iniquity of oblivion.' He feared the thought of death with a shuddering and increasing terror; and into his most personal and characteristic utterance, the 'Pathétique' (though not only there), he emptied all the dark troubles of his heart—all that he knew of anguished apprehension and foreboding, of grief that is unassuageable, of consternation and despair. Tchaikovsky never divulged the meaning of this singularly affecting music, but its purport is unmistakable. Its burden is the infinite sadness of human life and the crushing finality of death. Tchaikovsky has not here incurred the calm reproach of Krishna: 'Thou hast grieved for those who need no grief'; for his grief is centered upon the tragic frustrations of his own past; his lamentation is for the precious things of the world that he sees slipping irreclaimably from his grasp. This music is saturated with the precise emotion which moved Edgar Allan Poe when he wrote his 'Dream within a Dream':

> I stand amid the roar
> Of a surf-tormented shore,
> And I hold within my hand
> Grains of the golden sand:
> How few! Yet how they creep
> Through my fingers to the deep,
> While I weep, while I weep!
> O God! Can I not grasp
> Them with a tighter clasp?
> O God! Can I not save
> One from the pitiless wave?
> Is all that we see or seem
> But a dream within a dream?

Tchaikovsky, like the ancient poets of China, believed that 'to feel, and in order to feel, to express, all that is poignant and sensitive in man, is in itself a sufficient end'; and much of that poignancy, that sensibility, he imprisoned in music that is indeed in itself a sufficient end: music that is full of the sense of human evanescence—'the pathos of life and death, the long embrace, the hand stretched out in vain, the moment that glides forever away into the shadow of the haunted past.'

It is a strange and impressive experience to listen to the thrice-familiar 'Pathétique' and to realize (as some have long realized) that this symphony, which few musicians will nowadays allow themselves to praise, is after all a towering and lonely masterpiece. Where, indeed, is there anything at all like it?

Tchaikovsky has given us here a score that is excelling and unique because of the poignancy with which it utters that unquietable dread within the human heart. In its moments of terrible despair, in the mighty lamentation of the Finale, Tchaikovsky foresees 'the opening of the nettled lips of graves.' This work is heavy with mortal anguish; and at the end, as the gusts die down in the darkening street, and the light fades, and the long night falls, you know, beyond doubt or contradiction, that you have listened to an utterance that will outlast the years.

● *Manfred* SYMPHONY (After the Dramatic Poem of Byron), OP. 58

Byron, writing to his publisher in 1817, set forth briefly an outline of his dramatic poem, *Manfred*, which he had begun the year before. 'It is,' he wrote, 'in three acts, of a very wild, metaphysical, and inexplicable kind. Almost all of the persons—but two or three—are spirits of the earth and air, or the waters; the scene is in the Alps; the hero is a kind of magician, who is tormented by a species of remorse, the cause of which is left half unexplained. He wanders about invoking these spirits, which appear to him, and are of no use; he at last goes to the very abode of the Evil Principle, in *propria persona*, to evoke a ghost, which appears and gives him an ambiguous and disagreeable answer; and in the third act he is found by an attendant dying in a tower, where he had studied his art.'

Balakireff, impressed with the suitability of Byron's drama for musical treatment, had suggested it to Berlioz; but Berlioz, old and infirm, had not been interested. Balakireff himself found the subject 'not in harmony with his intimate moods,' and was disinclined to write music for it. So, in 1882, he proposed the subject to Tchaikovsky. He even outlined a programmatic scheme for the work. There must be, he said, an *idée fixe*—a motive typifying Manfred, which should recur throughout the symphony. The opening movement was to portray 'Manfred wandering in the Alps,' his life ruined and nothing left him but torturing doubts and recollections of his lost Astarte. The second movement, contrasting with the first, should depict the simple, patriarchal life of Alpine hunters and mountaineers, among whom the gloomy Manfred strays; the third, a fantastic vision of the Alpine fairy dancing in the waterfall; the fourth, a wild orgy in the subterranean cave of Arimanes, with the apparition of Astarte's wraith and the death of Manfred.

Tchaikovsky seems to have been in no hurry to take advantage of Balakireff's proposal. He waited for three years before he set about it, and when he did so, he was apparently anxious to get through with the undertaking. He wrote to Taneieff on June 25, 1885, that he had made up his mind to compose *Manfred* only 'because I shall find no rest until I have redeemed my promise so rashly given to Balakireff in the winter. I do not know how it will turn out, but meantime I am very discontented. It is a thousand times pleasanter to compose without a program. When I write a program symphony, I always feel that I am not paying in sterling coin, but in worthless paper money.'

Tchaikovsky's brother, Modest, says that the actual composition of the score was begun in June. But Peter seems to have made sketches for the music in April of that year. The longer he was occupied with it, the more unhappy he became. 'The work is so difficult and complicated,' he complained to Mrs. von Meck, 'that I myself am for the time being a Manfred.'

On September 21, 1885, he wrote to E. K. Pavlovskaya that the work was finished; although a note in the score gives the date of its completion as December 24, 1885. The first performance was at Moscow, March 23, 1886. Tchaikovsky expressed himself as contented with his symphony. 'I think it is my best orchestral composition,' he wrote to Mrs. von Meck (he had then completed all of his principal orchestral works except the Fifth and Sixth Symphonies, the *Hamlet* Overture, the symphonic ballad *The Voyevode*, and the *Nutcracker* ballet-music.

Tchaikovsky adhered quite faithfully to the programmatic outline supplied to him by Balakireff. Each of the four movements of the symphony is prefaced by a synopsis of the dramatic and poetical contents of the music that is to follow; and this synopsis is virtually an elaboration of Balakireff's scheme— except that Tchaikovsky reversed the order of the second and third movements as proposed by Balakireff, devoting his second movement to the Fairy of the Alps, and his third to the simple life of the mountaineers.

In Tchaikovsky's score, the movements are thus described:

I. Manfred wanders in the Alps. Tortured by the fatal anguish of doubt, racked by remorse and despair, his soul is a prey to sufferings without a name. Neither the occult sciences, whose mysteries he has probed to the bottom, and by means of which the gloomy powers of Hell are subject to him, nor anything in the world, can give him the forgetfulness for which alone he yearns. The memory of the fair Astarte, whom he has loved and lost, eats his heart. Nothing can dispel the curse which weighs on Manfred's soul; and without cessation, without truce, he is abandoned to the tortures of the most atrocious despair.

II. The Fairy of the Alps appears to Manfred beneath the rainbow of the waterfall.

III. Pastorale. Simple, free, and peaceful life of the mountaineers.

IV. The underground palace of Arimanes. Manfred appears in the midst of the Bacchanal. Evocation of the ghost of Astarte. She foretells him the end of his earthly woes. Manfred's death.

● CONCERTO FOR PIANO AND ORCHESTRA, IN B-FLAT MINOR, OP. 23

This most famous of piano concertos was composed, originally, in November and December 1874, and the scoring was completed the following February.

The concerto is thus roughly contemporaneous with Tchaikovsky's opera *Vakoula the Smith* and his Third Symphony. Tchaikovsky submitted the work, on which he had expended much effort, to the critical judgment of his friend Nicholas Rubinstein. Rubinstein detested it, and said so. Tchaikovsky, in a passion of disappointment and anger, destroyed the dedication to Rubinstein, and submitted the work to Hans von Bülow, who thought better of it, and introduced it to the public at (curiously) a concert in Boston, Massachusetts, on October 25, 1875. Tchaikovsky, in the happy foreign way, made merry over the reception of his work by the American troglodytes (though he did not quite call them that). 'A few days ago,' he wrote to Rimsky-Korsakoff in November of 1878, 'I had a letter from Bülow, enclosing a number of American press notices of my concerto. The Americans think that the first movement suffers from "the lack of a central idea around which to assemble such a host of musical fantasias, which make up the breezy and ethereal whole." . . Think what appetites these Americans have: after every performance Bülow was obliged to repeat the entire finale!'

We do not know what ass wrote the offending notice. 'Breezy and ethereal' does seem rather wide of the mark. Yet Tchaikovsky might have been more lenient to the New England cave-dwellers, considering their enthusiasm. He seems himself not to have been wholly of Bülow's opinion of the work, which pronounced it 'perfect,' but to have inclined more and more to the critical view of Rubinstein. Eventually—some thirteen years later—he submitted the concerto to a drastic revision, with particular reference to the writing for the solo instrument (of which Rubinstein had been especially critical). It is in the revised version that the concerto is familiar to us today.

There are three movements: (1) 'Allegro non troppo e molto maestoso' (after a few measures of introduction in the tonic key, there is a modulation to the relative major, and the chief theme of the movement, the most familiar of all Tchaikovsky's melodies, is announced by strings and wind against majestically ascending chords for the piano): (1) 'Allegro con spirito'; (2) 'Andantino semplice'; (3) 'Allegro con fuoco.' Tchaikovsky derived the chief subject of the 'Allegro con spirito' in the first movement from a tune that he heard sung by a blind beggar at a village fair in Kamenko. 'It is curious,' he wrote to Mrs. von Meck, in May 1879, 'that in Little Russia every blind beggar sings exactly the same tune with the same refrain. I have used part of this refrain in my piano concerto.' His brother Modest tells us that for the waltz-like melody played by the violas and 'cellos in the animated section of the second movement, Tchaikovsky 'borrowed the chansonette "Il faut s'amuser, danser, et rire," which brother Anatol and I used to hum early in the 'seventies, in remembrance of a certain charming singer.'

● CONCERTO FOR PIANO AND ORCHESTRA, NO. 2, IN G MAJOR, OP. 44

Five years after Tchaikovsky composed the most famous of his three piano concertos—the first, in B-flat minor, op. 23—he wrote a second, 'more showy' than the first, says Rosa Newmarch; 'less showy,' says James Huneker.

'The sketch of my concerto is finished,' wrote Tchaikovsky from Paris to

Mrs. von Meck on December 15, 1879, 'and I am much pleased with it, especially with the Andante.' According to Modest Tchaikovsky, the concerto was performed for the first time on May 18, (30), 1882, at Moscow. But the concerto had been played half a year before in Boeotian America: Madeline Schiller performed it at a Philharmonic concert in the Academy of Music, New York, under Theodore Thomas, November 12, 1881. The pianist at the Moscow performance was Taneieff. Anton Rubinstein conducted. 'The concerto was received,' says Modest Tchaikovsky, 'with much applause, but it was difficult to determine whether this was intended for the composer or the interpreter.'

The chief theme is proclaimed, forte, by the orchestra alone, and re-uttered by the piano in the ninth measure. After the solo instrument has been left to its own devices for thirty measures, with a concluding dominant-seventh chord thundered out *fff* by the pianist, the orchestra enters in E-flat major with the first part of the second theme (a dialogue for clarinet and horn in imitation), the piano contributing the second section of the theme unaccompanied. The pianist often has the floor in this movement.

The Andante is noteworthy for its treatment of the orchestral accompaniment, in which solo passages for violin and 'cello are conspicuous. The third movement has been characterized as a rondo on four themes. The first of these, in G major, is announced at once by the piano, with a pizzicato string accompaniment; the second, in E minor, is based on a dotted figure for the piano and strings; the third, in the tonic (G major), is initiated by the solo instrument; the fourth is in B minor, for orchestra and piano.

● CONCERTO FOR VIOLIN AND ORCHESTRA, IN D MAJOR, OP. 35

For Tchaikovsky the year 1878 was a rich one. That thirty-eighth year of his life yielded the Fourth Symphony, *Eugene Onegin*, and the Concerto for Violin. These were its major products. In addition, Tchaikovsky turned out six songs, the piano Sonata in G, a choral work (The Liturgy of St. John Chrysostom), the greater part of the First Suite for Orchestra (op. 43), and some odds and ends for piano.

The violin concerto was finished in the spring, at Clarens, overlooking the Lake of Geneva, but it was not heard in public until three years later, when Adolf Brodsky played it at a Philharmonic concert in Vienna, December 4, 1881, with Richter conducting. It was trampled upon with joyous ferocity by the reviewers, almost without exception—out of ten criticisms, only two were sympathetic. It was on this occasion that the Olympian Hanslick assured himself of a lonely immortality by achieving what is probably the most triumphantly offensive piece of critical disparagement on record: that famous passage from his review of the concerto in the *Neue Freie Presse* in which he described the Finale as suggesting 'the brutal, deplorable merriment of a Russian holiday carousal . . . savage, vulgar faces, coarse oaths . . . fusel oil'—and Hanslick went on to a climax of hysterical ferocity which seems incredible as an attempt to characterize Tchaikovsky's gay and brilliant Finale. Tchaikovsky picked up a copy of the *Neue Freie Presse* in a café at Rome, and by chance came upon Hanslick's review. He was horribly hurt. 'To his life's end,' says his brother Modest, 'he never forgot it, and knew it by heart.'

In August of the following year the concerto was played for the first time in Russia, at a concert in Moscow, and a Slavic contemporary of Hanslick's concluded from a hearing of the work that Tchaikovsky was 'played out.' He was, indeed, so wholly 'played out' that the best he could produce during the remaining decade of his life were the Fifth Symphony and the 'Pathétique.'

The concerto is in three movements: (1) 'Allegro moderato'; (2) Canzonetta: Andante; (3) 'Allegro vivacissimo.'

● SERENADE FOR STRINGS, OP. 48

'You can imagine, dear friend,' wrote Tchaikovsky to Nadejda von Meck in October 1880 (from Kamenka), 'that recently my Muse has been benevolent, when I tell you that I have written two long works very rapidly: a Festival Overture [the 1812] and a Serenade in four movements for string orchestra. The overture will be very noisy. I wrote it without much warmth of enthusiasm; therefore it has no great artistic value. The Serenade, on the contrary, I wrote from an inward impulse: I felt it; and I venture to hope that this work is not without artistic qualities.'

In September of the following year Tchaikovsky wrote again to Nadejda concerning this work, for which he evidently had a special fondness: 'I wish with all my heart that you could hear my Serenade properly performed. It loses so much when played on the piano. I think that the middle movements, as played by the strings, would win your sympathy. . . The first movement is my homage to Mozart: it is intended to be an imitation of his style, and I should be delighted if I thought I had in any way approached my model.'

The Serenade was played at the Moscow Conservatory in the year of its composition; but its first public hearing was on January 16, 1882, at Moscow, under Erdmannsdörfer's direction, when it achieved a considerable success.

I. 'PEZZO IN FORMA DI SONATINA.' This, as its title indicates, is a movement in shortened and simplified sonata-form, with an introduction ('Andante non troppo,' 6-8) based on a chorale-like subject that will be found to bear a family resemblance to the folk tune used by Tchaikovsky as the chief theme of his Finale. The main part of the movement is an 'Allegro moderato' in 6-8 time, with the energetic theme announced by the full string band, forte. The broad and imposing theme of the introduction recurs at the end of the movement.

II. WALTZ (Moderato. 'Tempo di valse,' G major, 3-4). The first violins lead off with the principal theme, 'dolce e molto grazioso.'

III. ELEGY ('Larghetto elegiaco,' D major, 3-4). The wistful opening is followed by a more animated middle section; then all the players adjust their mutes and repeat the opening with heightened dolor (there is a faint suggestion of the Finale of the 'Pathétique' in the muted sforzando chords of the violins above the reiterated D of the 'cellos and double-basses).

IV. FINALE ('TEMA RUSSO'). The last movement is based on a Russian folk tune, and, for good measure, Tchaikovsky throws in a second one—the subject of the slow introduction to the Finale (Andante, G major, 2-4), for the muted violins, which is derived from a song that is said to belong to the district of Makariev, in the government of Nijni-Novgorod. It is, we believe, a Volga song—a *chant de haleur*, as Balakireff's French translator calls it. The merry chief theme of the movement begins its main portion, 'Allegro con spirito,' C major, in the first fiddles. This is described by Balakireff as a street song of the district of Kolomna, in the government of Moscow. Just before the close of his Finale, Tchaikovsky recalls, in augmentation, the broad song theme of the introduction of his first movement. But the jolly form of his principal folk tune brings an exuberant end.

• SUITE FOR ORCHESTRA, NO. 1, IN D MINOR, OP. 43

'I am beginning to be proud of my works,' wrote Tchaikovsky to his publisher Jurgenson, from Kamenka, in April 1879, 'now that I see what an extraordinary effect some of them make. Everyone here is crazy over the Andante, and when I played it with my brother as a pianoforte duet, one girl fainted away—this is a fact!! To make the fair sex faint is the highest triumph to which any composer can attain.'

This overwhelming Andante is the third movement of the Suite in D minor, the Intermezzo. The tempo, now marked Andantino, was originally Andante; Tchaikovsky made the change in the second edition of the published score. Whether the lady would have been prostrated by an Andantino as effectively as by an Andante is a point well worth the consideration of such behaviorists as are disposed to regard the art of music as a subject worthy of scientific consideration.

Tchaikovsky made sketches for this suite at Verbovka in the summer of 1878. In November he wrote to his brother Modest: 'Inspiration has come to me, so the sketch of the suite is almost finished. But I am anxious because I left the manuscript of the first three movements in Petersburg, and it may get lost. I wrote the last two movements here. This short and—if I am not mistaken—excellent suite is in five movements.'

In the following year, Tchaikovsky added a sixth movement to his suite, the Divertimento. He wrote Mrs. von Meck that he interpolated this movement in waltz rhythm into the suite 'to avoid rhythmic monotony [all the others were in duple time]. I wrote it actually at one sitting, and spent much less time upon it than upon any other movement. As it turns out, this has not hindered it from giving more pleasure than all the rest.'

The Marche Miniature (No. IV of the suite in its published form) bears this note in the score: 'To be played ("ad libitum") after the Andante' [the Intermezzo].

The six movements are thus devised:

I. Introduction and Fugue: 'Andante sostenuto,' D minor, 4-4; 'Moderato e con anima,' D minor, 4-4. II. Divertimento: 'Allegro moderato,' B-flat major, 3-4. III. Intermezzo: 'Andantino semplice,' D minor, 2-4. IV. Marche Miniature: 'Moderato con moto,' A major, 2-4. V. Scherzo: 'Allegro con moto,' B-flat major, 4-4. VI. Gavotte: Allegro, D major, 4-4.

● Suite for Orchestra, No. 3, in G major, op. 55

Tchaikovsky composed his Third Suite for Orchestra in the spring and summer of 1884. Writing to his publisher from Grandkino, July 2nd, he declared: 'A more inspired work than the new suite has never existed! I have great hopes of the new-born work. Though God knows what I shall say of it a year from now. At least, it has cost me great pains.' He told Taneieff that he had 'wished to make a symphony,' but that 'it did not come to him.' However, 'the name's nothing,' he added. 'At any rate, I am writing a great symphonic work. It will be ready toward the end of the Summer.'

The suite was performed in St. Petersburg, at a concert of the Imperial Society, January 12 (24), 1885, under the direction of Hans von Bülow, 'who conducted without a score, and with electrifying brilliance.' The liberal-minded Hans—classicist, Wagnerite, Brahmsian—was then a convinced Tchaikovskian. 'Toward the end of the 'eighties,' writes Peter's brother, Modest, 'Bülow's enthusiasm for Peter's compositions cooled a little, and he began to wax enthusiastic over the music of Richard Strauss, then at the beginning of his career.'

The suite was immensely successful at its St. Petersburg performance. Modest remarks that no other of Tchaikovsky's works was so enthusiastically received at first. Peter, who was present, wrote Mrs. von Meck: 'Never before have I experienced such a triumph.' He appears to have retained his good opinion of the work, for he selected it as one of the compositions with which to introduce himself in person to New York at the Festival which signalized the opening of Carnegie Hall (then known as 'Music Hall'), in May 1891.

The four movements of the suite are (1) Elegie; (2) Valse melancholique; (3) Scherzo; (4) Theme and Variations. This final movement leads a life of its own in the repertoire, divorced from its associates in the suite. In it, the theme ('Andante con moto,' G major, 4-8) is announced by the first violins, accompanied by the other strings in detached chords, and is followed by twelve variations. In the first, the theme is played pizzicato by all the strings in octaves, while two flutes and two clarinets play counter-themes against it. In the second variation, violins play the melody, broken into rapid passages in thirty-second notes, while the violas, 'cellos, double-basses, flutes, oboes, clarinets, bassoons, and horns join in an accompaniment, the dominant rhythmical figure of which consists of an anapaest—two sixteenths and an eighth. The third variation is given to the woodwinds—three flutes, two clarinets, and two bassoons. In the fourth, the whole orchestra is employed, and the melody is transposed to the key of B minor; a unison of the 'cellos, clarinets, and English horn on the melody is one of its striking features. In the basses, trombones, and bassoons we hear the grim muttering of the *Dies Irae*. The fifth variation is a fugato for strings and wood alone. The sixth is in the style of a tarantella. The seventh is again reserved for the woodwinds, and here we are reminded of the music of the Russian church. The spirit of the Russian folk music, song and dance, now animates the composition and asserts itself to the end. The last variation is a festive polonaise of exceptional sonority and brilliance.

- OVERTURE-FANTASIA, *Romeo and Juliet*

George Moore once speculated in his naïve way upon the question whether Wagner's *Tristan und Isolde* was the imaginative precipitation of a gratified or an ungratified passion. It is an exciting but futile question. The precise extent to which Wagner and Mathilde ignored the conventions has never been established. Moore believed that the character of the music of *Tristan* is testimony on the side of the Moral Order, since all impassioned art is in some degree the product of frustration. If Wagner and Mathilde had been able to accomplish an irrubrical honeymoon remote from the cramping proximity of Richard's wife and Mathilde's husband, would the music of *Tristan* have been the unique conflagration that it is?

So with Tchaikovsky: If Désirée Artôt, the singing-actress, had not thrown Peter over in January 1869, would the music of his *Romeo and Juliet* have exhibited quite the veracious intensity that it does? Tchaikovsky met Désirée in the spring of 1868, in his twenty-eighth year; by the following winter he loved her 'heart and soul,' and they had come to 'an understanding'; in January 1869, Désirée jilted him to mate with a warbler from the Mediterranean. Modest Tchaikovsky assures us that Peter 'bore her no grudge . . . as a woman, she was always dear to his memory.' Later, when Peter heard her at the Moscow Opera, 'he held his opera-glasses to his eyes and never lowered them during the entire performance; but he must have seen very little, for tear after tear rolled down his cheeks.'

It was in the year of Tchaikovsky's jilting by Désirée Artôt that he composed *Romeo and Juliet*. The music was written in the autumn of 1869, rewritten in the summer of 1870, published in 1871, revised and republished in 1881.

The composition of the overture was instigated by Balakireff, redoubtable nationalist and composer of *Thamar* and *Islamey*, who projected the plan of the work, outlined the character of the themes, stirred the creative fancy of the young music-maker. This was in the spring of 1869, when the memory of Désirée must have been achingly vivid. If she kindled the music's flame, she wrought to an admirable end. The score is uneven; but at its best—and its best predominates—it is not only Tchaikovsky raised to the level of authentic genius, but it achieves for a few unforgettable moments a quality of utterance that justifies the heady epithet 'Shakespearian.' There are not many things in modern music more justly and beautifully expressive, more richly poetic, than the exquisite theme for muted and divided strings that projects the mood of the enraptured pair as they watch the coming of the dawn in Juliet's chamber. Here Tchaikovsky outdid himself; here, for a moment, he captured the very hue and accent of Shakespearian loveliness.

The dramatic and emotional structure of the overture adheres in the main to the outline proffered to Tchaikovsky by the enthusiastic Balakireff. There is an introduction of religious character designed—so Kashkin tells us—to suggest the figure of Friar Laurence (churchly harmonies in the clarinets and bassoons, 'Andante non tanto, quasi moderato,' F-sharp minor, 4-4), followed by an 'Allegro giusto' in B minor, intended to depict the conflict of the opposing houses—a tumultuous section full of strife and fury. Then follows the love scene, based on two lyric themes of rich emotional expressiveness which Tchaikovsky used in a fragmentary 'Duo from *Romeo and Juliet*' found among his papers after his death and orchestrated by Taneieff (who also provided an instrumental introduction for the duet constructed of themes from the overture). The love scene is followed by a resumption of the stress and conflict of the first part, against which the solemn warning of Friar Laurence protests in vain. The lovers are again brought before us, with increasing and passionate intensity. There is a great climax; then, after a brief and portentous silence, the piece ends (according to Kashkin) with 'the death of the lovers.' There is a dolorous reminiscence of the ecstatic song of Romeo, now dirge-like and woeful (sung by 'cellos, violins, and bassoon, above drum-beats, with basses pizzicato), then an elegiacal conclusion: a variant of the love song given by the higher strings in unison, with accompaniment of woodwind, horns, and harp.

• FANTASIA FOR ORCHESTRA, *Francesca da Rimini* (After Dante), OP. 32

The loveliest utterances that music ever attained deal with romantic passion in two superlative exhibitions; but neither of these, oddly enough, concerns the immortal case of Paolo and Francesca. Perhaps there have been only three men in the history of music who could have handled that unforgettable tale with adequate power. Wagner, it is superfluous to say, might have given us a *Paolo and Francesca* that would have been a thing of deathless wonder—what, indeed, could not that marvel of marvels have done, if he chose? Richard Strauss in his prime could have shown us a *Paolo and Francesca* that the world would not soon forget; so could Claude Debussy.

Not one of those masters of passionate speech is an Italian; not one is a man of the south. But others than they, who are both men of the South and Italians, have tried their hand at an operatic *Paolo and Francesca*, as it was wholly fitting that Italians should—and have failed in the endeavor. That event does not necessarily prove the unimportance of national relationship in the choice and treatment of an artistic subject. But it is certainly interesting to reflect that whereas we have had the spectacle of a typical Italian composers exhibiting unfitness in an engagement with a typical Italian theme, we can, on the other hand, look elsewhere and see another Italian, Verdi, the rare comedian, handling with felicity and comprehension an unequivocally English theme in his *Falstaff*. No more and no less than that does nationality count in the relation between a musical creator and his subject.

And so it is not surprising that a Russian has given us the only symphonic embodiment of the passion of Francesca and Paolo that is widely current in the concert repertoire of our time—Liszt's treatment of the subject in his 'Dante' Symphony is episodic. The intrinsic musical quality of Tchaikovsky's tone poem is aside from the point. As a projection of the tale that is told in the Fifth Canto of Dante's *Inferno*, the work survives and persists.

Tchaikovsky's score is prefaced by the touching lines from the Fifth Canto of the *Inferno* that enclose the story of Paolo and Francesca's passion, beginning with

. . . Nessun maggior dolore

and ending with

E caddi, come corpo morto cade.

And there is this introductory paraphrase of the argument of the canto:

Dante comes to the second circle of Hell, where are the souls of carnal sinners, whose punishment consists in their being driven incessantly to and fro through the dark air by violent winds. Amongst these tormented souls he encounters Francesca da Rimini, who tells her story.

Here is Francesca's narrative in the admirable English version of John A. Carlyle:

There is no greater pain than to recall a happy time in wretchedness; and this thy teacher knows. But, if thou hast such a desire to learn the first root of our love, I will do as one who weeps and tells.

One day, for pastime, we read of Lancelot, how love constrained him. We were alone and without all suspicion. Several times that reading urged our eyes to meet and changed the color of our faces. But one moment alone it was that overcame us. When we read how the fond smile was kissed by such a lover, he who shall never be divided from me kissed my mouth all trembling. The book, and he who wrote it, was a Galeotto. That day we read in it no further.

Whilst the one spirit thus spake, the other wept so, that I fainted with pity, as if I had been dying; and fell, as a dead body falls.

Tchaikovsky's tone poem begins and ends with an evocation of the dreadful scene which greeted Dante and Virgil as they entered the region of the Second Circle—the buffeting winds, the haunted and sinister air, the wailing of the damned, the appalling gloom and horror. In the middle section of the piece the tempest is subdued at the approach of the two entwined spirits, who come, 'strangely light upon the wind, as doves called by desire'; and we listen, in the poignant stillness, as Francesca 'weeps and tells,' before she and her lover are again engulfed in the malign and clamorous dusk.

● *Marche Slave*, OP. 31

Tchaikovsky composed his *Marche Slave* (or *Russo-Serbian March*, as he sometimes called it) for a concert given at Moscow in November 1877, under Nicholas Rubinstein, for the benefit of soldiers wounded in the war between Turkey and Serbia. He chose appropriately as his principal subject ('Moderato in modo di marcia funèbre,' B-flat minor, 4-4, violas and bassoons) the mournfully beautiful Serbian folk song, 'Sunce jarko nesijas jednako'—which, we are told, means literally: 'Glittering sun, you do not shine the same.' Later appear fragments of the old Russian National Hymn, and this is proudly declaimed at the end by all the orchestral forces.

● *Capriccio Italien*, OP. 45

Tchaikovsky, sojourning at Rome in the winter of 1880, was no happier than usual. He wrote to Mrs. von Meck on February 17 that 'a worm gnaws continually in secret at my heart,' but he did not tell her what it was, though he must have known. 'I sleep badly and do not feel that courage and freshness which I might expect under the circumstances. Only at moments can I conquer my depression. My God! what an incomprehensible and complicated machine the human organism is! We shall never solve the various phenomena of our spiritual and material existence!' Poor Tchaikovsky, with his naked, quivering nerves, and his pathetic inability to face the essential cruelty of existence! He could never meet life on what an ironic contemporary sage calls 'its own terms,' and could never remember that 'its cruelty is as casual as its enchantments . . .'

On February 18, Tchaikovsky wrote that the Carnival was at its height and that, though at first 'this wild folly' did not suit him, he was growing used to it. He added that he was then at work on a new composition, 'an Italian fantasia,' as he then described it, 'based upon folk songs. Thanks to these charming themes, some of which I have taken from collections, and some of which I have heard in the streets, this work will be effective.' He avoided the mistake which Richard Strauss made some years later of incorporating a popular song of the day in *Aus Italien* under the impression that it was a folk song. But living with his brother Modest at the Hotel Constanzi, adjacent to the barracks of the Royal Cuirassiers, he often listened to the bugle calls of the cavalrymen, and one of these signals found its way into the *Italian Caprice*. It may be heard there as the trumpet fanfare which opens the piece.

The *Italian Caprice* is in A major. There is an Introduction ('Andante un poco rubato,' 6-8). The melancholy mood of the first subject (strings) is soon lightened, and Tchaikovsky brings on his folk tunes, their melodies characteristically harmonized in thirds. The Finale of the Caprice is a brilliant and extended tarantella movement.

• 1812: *Ouverture Solonnelle*, OP. 49

Tchaikovsky was unduly modest in his estimate of this overture. He referred to it in his diary as having 'only a patriotic and local significance.' The word 'local' may well provoke a smile; for the event celebrated by the music was nothing less than the repulse of Napoleon's invasion of Russia in 1812.

The Cathedral of the Saviour, in Moscow, was to be consecrated in the summer of 1881, and it was planned to amplify the eccesiastical ceremonies by festivities commemorating the Russian victory. Tchaikovsky was asked by Nicholas Rubinstein to write a piece for the occasion. He composed his overture in 1880, and it was devised originally for performance in the public square in front of the Cathedral, by an orchestra of heaven-storming size, with cannon (to be fired by electric connection from the conductor's stand), an auxiliary brass band, an accompaniment of church bells, et cetera.

The musical symbolism of the overture is not abstruse. There is a theme (that of the slow Introduction) of folk-song character, derived from a Russian hymn, 'God, Preserve Thy People.' The Marseillaise is heard, fragmentarily, though with increasing power; but at the end it is overwhelmed, and the work ends with a triumphant assertion of the folk theme of the introduction, and a thunderous proclamation of the old Russian National Hymn.

● BALLET, *The Nutcracker*, OP. 71

Early in the year 1891 Tchaikovsky was commissioned to write an opera and a ballet for the St. Petersburg Opera House. For the opera he selected a Russian version by Swanzeff of Herz's drama, *King René's Daughter*, which Tchaikovsky turned into a one-act opera with the title of *Iolanthe*. For the subject of the ballet he chose a French version by the elder Dumas of E. T. A. Hoffmann's fairy tale, 'Nussknacker und Mausekönig' ('The Nutcracker and the Mouse-King'), from the collection of stories called *Die Serapions Bruder*. Dumas entitled his version of the tale 'Histoire d'un Casse-Noisette.'

In April 1891, Tchaikovsky made his first and only visit to the United States, assisted at the opening of Carnegie Hall, was tortured by homesickness and upset by too many dinners, and returned to his beloved Russia late in May. Before he sailed for America he had completed the first act of the ballet—though somewhat under protest: for Tchaikovsky, an ardent patriot, was annoyed because the management of the Petrograd Opera had engaged a number of pushing foreign artists who were permitted to sing in French and Italian on a Russian stage. (These outrageous interlopers were Melba and the de Reszkes.) But Tchaikovsky was mollified when he learned that the Tsar entertained a favorable opinion of his opera *Pique-Dame*.

By the end of June he had finished the sketch of the ballet, and he had been made happy by his discovery in Paris of a new orchestral instrument, the célesta, which he described to his publisher Jurgenson as 'something between a piano and a glockenspiel.' It had, he wrote, a 'divinely beautiful' tone and he proposed to make use of it in the ballet. He urged Jurgenson to secure one without delay. 'Have it sent direct to Petersburg,' he wrote, 'but no one there must know about it. I am afraid Rimsky-Korsakoff and Glazounoff might hear of it and make use of it before I do. I expect it to make a tremendous impression.' Tchaikovsky used it in the *Nutcracker* in the 'Danse de la Fée Dragée' (somewhat loosely translated as 'Dance of the Sugar-Plum Fairy').

Tchaikovsky did not finish scoring the music of his ballet until February of the following year (1892), when he conducted at a concert of the Russian Musical Society in St. Petersburg, March 19, 1892, a suite put together from numbers in the score. The new suite was enthusiastically received, and five of the numbers had to be repeated. The ballet itself, completed later in the spring, was given for the first time, together with *Iolanthe*, at the Imperial Opera House, St. Petersburg, December 18, 1892. The Court was present, and seems to have been pleased, though Modest Tchaikovsky in his Life of Peter says that neither the ballet nor the opera achieved more than a *succès d'estime*. The subject was unusual, the lady who impersonated the Sugar-Plum Fairy was homely, and the admirable ballet-master, Petipa, was absent because of illness. 'The delicate beauty of the music did not appeal to the public on a first hearing.'

The scenario of the ballet concerns a wonderful dream that came to little Marie Silberhaus (Tchaikovsky calls her Clair) after the Christmas party at which the presents were dolls that behaved as if they were alive—though Marie herself had received only an ordinary household nutcracker, which apparently had no higher destiny than the destruction of filbert shells. But Marie, after the wise and mysterious fashion of the young, was captivated by the poor crunching thing, and after the candles had been blown out and when the house was dark and still, she climbed out of bed and tiptoed downstairs to look at her toy. Whereupon marvelous things began to happen. The Christmas tree blazed again with light, the toys and sweetmeats were dancing wildly, and the Nutcracker had come to life and was taking part in the festivities. But suddenly a terrific battle began between the tin soldiers, led by the Nutcracker, and an army of mice under the command of their king. The Nutcracker and the Mouse-King clinched, and things looked black for the Nutcracker, whose muscles were naturally a bit lame from his labors at the Christmas dinner. But just at this moment Marie slew the Mouse-King with her slipper, and his army retired in defeat. The Nutcracker was transformed into a glorious young prince, and he and Marie flew away together over the silent, snowy forests to the delectable Kingdom of Sweetmeats and Lollipops. Here they were welcomed by the Sugar-Plum Queen (the Fairy Dragée) with all her Court, and a dance of the Sweetmeats was arranged for the edification of the visiting lovers.

The familiar concert suite arranged from the *Nutcracker* music comprises the following numbers:

I. 'OUVERTURE MINIATURE' ('Allegro giusto,' B-flat major, 2-4).

This prelude to the fairy ballet is scored without the lower bass instruments—the 'cellos and double-basses are not used at all. The chief theme begins at once, pianissimo, in the violins.

II. 'DANSES CARACTERISTIQUES':

(*a*) 'MARCHE' ('Tempo di marcia viva,' G major, 4-4).

In the ballet, the opening scene of the first act is the decorating and lighting of the Christmas tree; then President Silberhaus, who is giving the party, orders the March to be played. Clarinets, horns, and trumpets have the captivating march tune. There is a contrasting trio-like section in E minor.

(*b*) 'DANSE DE LA FÉE DRAGÉE' ('Andante non troppo,' E Minor, 2-4).

This dance is taken from a *pas de deux* in Act II called, in the score, 'Variation II (pour la danseuse).' After four introductory measures, the célesta, which so captivated Tchaikovsky, plays the chief theme, and later exhibits itself in a cadenza.

(*c*) 'TRÉPAK, DANSE RUSSE' ('Tempo di Trépak, molto vivace,' G major, 2-4).

In the second act of the ballet, No. 12 of the score, is a divertissement comprising these dances: Chocolat, Café, Thé, Trépak, and Danse des Mirlitons. In the concert suite they are differently named: Café is changed to Danse arabe, and Thé to Danse chinoise. The Trépak is a national Russian folk dance, of rapid and energetic character, strongly accented. Violins announce the chief dance theme.

(*d*) 'DANSE ARABE' (Allegretto, G minor, 3-8).

Here the Fairy Dragée's dancers remember that Russia and the Orient are neighbors. Above a drone-like double pedal-point for the low strings, a clarinet dreams of Araby. Then the violins enter, 'molto espressivo.'

(*e*) 'DANSE CHINOISE' ('Allegro moderato,' B-flat major, 4-4).

This concise and captivatingly fantastic movement—only thirty-two bars long—is founded on an unchanging accompaniment figure for the bassoons and double-basses pizzicato, above which the flute disports itself capriciously.

(f) 'DANSE DES MIRLITONS' (Andantino, D major, 2-4).

A 'mirliton,' according to the best authorities, makes a noise like a kazoo; and a kazoo, one learns, is merely one of those domestic music producers constructed out of a piece of thin paper and a comb. The mirliton is described as a wooden or cardboard tube with the ends covered by a membrane; a triangular hole is cut in the tube a short distance from each end. 'By singing into one of the holes, a sound is produced not unlike that obtained by singing against a comb wrapped in thin paper.' In other words, it is a kind of toy pipe, and in Tchaikovsky's ballet, the mirlitons were among those present in the divertissement of the second act. The charming first theme of this dance is sung by the flutes, above a pizzicato accompaniment of the strings.

III. 'VALSE DES FLEURS' ('Tempo di valse,' D major, 3-4).

An introduction, with a concluding harp cadenza, leads to the chief waltz theme (for the horns)—one of Tchaikovsky's most famous and ingratiating tunes.

Ralph Vaughan Williams
1872-

V

‡As a young man, Vaughan Williams studied composition with Parry and Stanford, respected British masters. Later, he came under the influence of the German Bruch and the Frenchman Ravel. Of greater effect on the formation of his own style has been his life-long absorption in English folk music, and in the music of the Tudor period. His music—much of it cast in the large orchestral and choral forms—expresses a reserved and reflective nature, an admirable balance of intellectual and emotional forces, and a consistent fastidiousness in the selection and treatment of materials. The rather striking 'modernism' of his latest works seems to be the inevitable outcome of the experience which they communicate.‡

● *A London Symphony*

It may be that Vaughan Williams has something of the expressional duality which Flaubert discerned in himself. 'There are two men in me,' remarked the incomparable Frenchman: 'one a lyricist, a lover of the . . . haunting, the sonorous; the other desires to make the things he describes felt almost in their material nature.' One is aware of a similar dualism at work in *A London Sym-*

phony—or, rather, in Vaughan Williams's apparent attitude toward it. When the work was performed under the direction of Albert Coates, Coates made public an unequivocal, detailed, and admirably vivid exposition of the composer's descriptive purposes. This was signed by Coates, and it is impossible to suppose that he spoke without authority. The published score of the work, however, contains no program or descriptive indication whatever, beyond the title: *A London Symphony*.

Edwin Evans, the accomplished London music critic and essayist, remarked that *A London Symphony* 'is the expression, not of London, but of a Londoner. Its reflective side, which is overwhelmingly predominant, owes its most beautiful moments to its detachment from all that the title might imply on its material side. That is the composer's innate fastidiousness. But the frequent references to the bustling scene in which this minor reflective life has its being are handled with a sympathy so sincere that even occasional vulgarities are touched upon with affection. Add to that a certain diffident reserve which almost brings the flow of musical communicativeness to a premature stop, and you have the Englishman who feels deeply, but is embarrassed when he suddenly discovers that he has been showing it.'

Evans believed that the breadth of canvas necessitated by the subject of *A London Symphony*, with all its thronging and kaleidoscopic evocations, and also Vaughan Williams's impatience of traditional recipes, conditioned the scope and form of the work, with its broad spaces filled with a profusion of material, its developments rich in new incident, and its curtailment of the recapitulations—due to the assumption by modern symphonists, in Evans's view, that the modern listener is a bit fed up on the explicitness of the classic recapitulation, and is more than willing to take it for granted. Vaughan Williams, as compensation, restores his formal balance by an important coda to the first movement, and by the coda-like relation of the Finale to the work as a whole. 'Much of the material is of purely incidental quality. Especially is this the case with such easily recognizable features as the Westminster chimes, the Lavender Cry, and the frequent snatches of tunes having the jovial rhythm which, to the man of the London streets, is the quintessence of musical enjoyment.'

According to the doubtless inspired exegesis of Coates, the Introduction to the first movement of the symphony (Lento, G major, 3-4) pictures a scene at daybreak by the river. 'Old Father Thames flows calm and silent under the heavy gray dawn, deep and thoughtful, shrouded in mystery.' The theme that is associated with the thought of the mysterious and brooding river begins at once in the 'cellos and basses, muted and pianissimo. 'London sleeps, and in the hushed stillness of early morning one hears "Big Ben" (the Westminster chimes) solemnly strike the half hour' (harp and clarinet, thirty-first measure). 'Suddenly the scene changes ('Allegro risoluto,' 2-2); one is on the Strand in the midst of the bustle and turmoil of morning traffic. This is London street life of the early hours—a steady stream of foot passengers hurrying, newspaper boys shouting, messengers whistling, and that most typical sight of London streets, the costermonger, resplendent in pearl buttons, and shouting some coster-song refrain at the top of a raucous voice, returning from Covent Garden

Market, seated on his vegetable barrow, drawn by the inevitable little donkey. Busses, taxis, hawkers, flower-girls—a gay and careless picture, pulsating with life.'

The slow movement (Lento, 4-4) is music of haunting and wistful beauty— music of slow autumnal twilights veiling compassionately the poor pretensions of furtively shabby streets that once had quality and pride. Coates identifies this as 'a picture of that region of London which lies between Holborn and Euston Road, known as Bloomsbury. Dusk is falling. It is the damp and foggy twilight of a late November day.' Violas divisi in three parts, 'cellos in four, basses in two, muted and *ppp*, play successions of gray and dolorous minor triads erected on a series of whole tones; above them the English horn utters a plaint of simple and meditative pathos. 'There is tragedy, too, in Blooms- bury,' says Coates, 'for among the many streets between Holborn and Euston there are alleys where one finds acute poverty and worse. In front of a "pub" whose lights flare through the murky twilight stands an old musician playing the fiddle. His tune is played in the orchestra by the viola. In the distance the "Lavender Cry" is heard: "Sweet lavender; who'll buy sweet lavender?" Up and down the streets the cry goes, now nearer, now further away.' An outburst of passionate melancholy is heard from the full orchestra, and the song of the opening is heard again. The 'Lavender Cry' is heard first on the clarinet, then on the piccolo, through a haze of string tremolos. There is an outburst of pas- sionate melancholy for the full orchestra, and the song of the opening is heard again. 'The gloom deepens and the movement ends with the old musician still playing his pathetic little tune.'

The third movement bears in the score the superscription: Scherzo-Noc- turne. It begins ('Allegro vivace,' 6-8) with pianissimo trills in the woodwind and violins, and we are aware at once that the composer is being what Evans called 'biologically democratic.' Coates tells us that we must now imagine our- selves sitting late on a Saturday night on one of the benches of the Temple Embankment, lying between the Houses of Parliament and Waterloo Bridge. All is quiet, decorous, respectable, on our side of the river; but across the river are the slums; and they are far from quiet. But toward the end 'the music changes suddenly and one feels the Thames flowing silent, mysterious, with a touch of tragedy. One of London's sudden fogs comes down, making Slum- land and its noises seem remote. Again, for a few bars, we feel the Thames flowing through the night, and the picture fades into fog and silence.' We are reminded that the composer's attitude is subjective; for after the bustling ob- jectivity, the raucous humor and rich vulgarity of this popular scene, the musi- cian, once more the contemplative poet, 'turns, so to speak, from his open window, in order to muse upon his theme in the quiet calm of a nocturne.'

The last movement is musical gall and wormwood. It is steeped in tragic bitterness, an acrid draught distilled from the contemplation of wretchedness and pain and savage protest. It deals almost wholly with the crueler aspects of London, the London of the unemployed and the unfortunate. There is an Epilogue in which the river-music of the opening is heard again, sinking slowly into silence, as if the timeless stream were brooding in its everlastingness upon the brief lives that it encircles, and upon their unspeakable aspirations, their 'fears and hopes that wander through eternity.'

A *London Symphony* was composed in 1912-13, and was first performed at Queen's Hall, London, under the direction of Geoffrey Toye, on March 27, 1914.

● FANTASIA ON A THEME BY THOMAS TALLIS, FOR DOUBLE STRING ORCHESTRA

Thomas Tallis, a contemporary of Palestrina and one of the greatest of English composers, has been called 'the father of English cathedral music.' A superb contrapuntist, he wrought magnificently in the spacious and sovereign style of his period. He was organist of Waltham Abbey until the dissolution of the Abbey in 1540, when he was dismissed with twenty shillings for wages and a bonus of twenty more. Thereafter he secured the position of a Gentleman of the Chapel Royal, and retained his place there from his appointment in the reign of Henry VIII until his death in the reign of Queen Elizabeth: an achievement that he owed in part to his talent for conforming to the religious faith and forms of worship which happened to be uppermost at the moment—though it is suspected that his private inclination was toward the Catholic faith.

He wrote in all the musical forms practiced in his day; but the major part of his compositions is vocal church music. He was so great a genius that he could combine the most elaborate subtlety of organization with the most spontaneous and full-throated exercise of the grand style. He could be searchingly tender and intimate, as in the delicately lovely work, *O Lord, give Thy Holy Spirit*, or he could sweep the whole gamut of majestic utterance in his five-part *Absterge Domine* or the famous *O sacrum convivium* from the *Cantiones Sacrae*; and he could toss off such dazzling bravura writing as the splendid and extraordinary forty-part motet, *Spem in alium non habui*, written for eight choirs of five parts each—at once a prodigious tour de force and a nobly beautiful work of art.

In 1567, Tallis wrote eight melodies, each in a different one of the ecclesiastical modes, for the Metrical Psalter of Matthew Parker, Archbishop of Canterbury. This was under the rule of Queen Elizabeth, and so the accommodating Thomas was for the nonce a Protestant. In Tallis's day, different characteristics were assigned to each of the modes. These distinguishing traits were set forth as follows in contemporary verse:

> The first is meeke; deuout to see.
> The second sad: in majesty.
> The third doth rage; and roughly brayth.
> The fourth doth fawne: and flattry playth.
> The fyfth delight: and laugheth the more.
> The sixth bewaileth: it weepeth full sore.
> The seuenth tredeth stoute: in froward race.
> The eyghth goeth milde: in modest pace.

Vaughan Williams chose for his Fantasia (composed for the Gloucester Festival of 1910) the tune which Tallis wrote in the third mode—that mode which the sixteenth century deemed appropriate for 'raging and braying.' Evidently Tallis thought it fittingly expressive, for he used it in setting the second Psalm, 'Why do the heathen rage, and the people imagine a vain thing?' Vaughan Williams's Fantasia on the stalwart old melody is scored for double string orchestra, with four solo strings (two violins, viola, and 'cello). At times the solo parts are heard individually, at times as a single separate choir, and again they are merged with one or other of the two orchestras.

The Tallis theme, purely modal in character, is at first outlined by the lower strings. In its complete form, it is sung by all the second violins and violas and half the 'cellos, against the first violins above and the other 'cellos and basses below in octaves. Then follow free variations which Vaughan Williams has contrived with an extraordinary command of the appropriate mood and style. The somber and archaic harmonization, with its daring yet sensitive use of the cross-relations and dissonantal textures that characterized the writing of Tallis's period, combine to evoke for the imagination a valid musical image of that distant day when English music was indisputably glorious, and need not have been ashamed to hold up its head even in the presence of Palestrina.

Giuseppe Verdi

1813-1901

‡The two unrivaled masters of the lyric theater (after Mozart) were born in 1813 within six months of each other—Wagner on May 22, Verdi on October 10. The Italian outlived his overwhelming contemporary by eighteen years, a period in which he produced two remarkable works— *Otello* and *Falstaff*, both of which testify to the impact on him of Wagner's genius, though their qualities are still those which, native to Verdi, had already established him as the greatest of Italian opera composers. The parallel suggested by the accident of their birth in the same year might be extended through other details selected from the histories of the two men. Almost without exception, the greatest composers have given evidence of their capabilities in early youth; but this was true of neither Verdi nor Wagner. Indeed, Verdi at sixteen was denied a scholarship by the Milan Conservatory on the ground that he showed no special aptitude for music. It is interesting to note, further, that both Verdi, with *Ernani*, and Wagner, with *Tannhäuser*, produced their first viable works in the same year, 1841, and that the composition of Verdi's *Aida* coincided, some thirty years later, with the completion of Wagner's

Ring (the sketch for *Die Götterdämmerung* was finished in 1871). And, finally, that at this point both found their interest engaged by sacred themes—Wagner in his *Parsifal*, and Verdi in his Manzoni Requiem. But a different selection of facts would weaken the force of the parallel, and too much emphasis is not, therefore, to be laid on it. The two men were almost exact contemporaries, they devoted themselves almost exclusively to the same branch of the musical art, but their separate achievements are in no real sense comparable. And it is significant that while, mentioning the year of Verdi's birth, one remembers the birth of Wagner, one does not, when the circumstances are reversed, find oneself reminded of Verdi.‡

● MANZONI REQUIEM

Shortly after the death of Rossini in 1868, a suggestion was made by Verdi that a group of prominent Italian composers join forces in the composition of a Requiem to the memory of their great compatriot. The idea found favor, and the different numbers were assigned and duly prepared. The composers and their contributions were as follows: *Requiem aeternam* (G minor), Buzzola; *Dies Irae* (C minor), Bazzini; *Tuba mirum* (E-flat minor), Pedrotti; *Quid sum miser* (A-flat major), Cagnoni; *Recordare* (F major), Ricci; *Ingemisco* (A minor), Nini; *Confutatis* (D major), Boucheron; *Lacrymosa* (G major, C minor), Coccia; *Domine Jesu* (C major), Gaspari; *Sanctus* (D-flat major), Platania; *Agnus Dei* (F major), Petrella; *Lux aeterna* (A-flat major), Mabellini; *Libera me* (C minor), Verdi.

As might have been expected, the musical result of this collaboration was unprofitable. The patchwork Mass, by reason of an inevitable diversity of conception, workmanship, and style, proved to be a failure artistically, and the project was abandoned. But Verdi's contribution, the *Libera me*, attracted the attention of S. Mazzucato, then teacher of composition at the Milan Conservatory, and he endeavored to persuade Verdi to undertake the composition of the entire Mass himself. Verdi did not at that time respond to the suggestion, but it bore fruit five years later.

Alessandro Manzoni, poet and novelist—author of what has been called 'the most popular lyric in the Italian language,' '*Il Cinque maggio*,' inspired by Napoleon's death, and of the celebrated novel based on the episode of the Innominato, *I Promessi sposi*—died at Milan May 22, 1873, in his eighty-ninth year. Verdi, who had been his friend, was deeply affected. Manzoni, 'whom even his political opponents called a saint,' had seemed to Verdi the ideal of an artist and a man, one whose unassailable honesty and goodness had helped to justify human living. After Manzoni's funeral (his country mourned him with almost regal pomp), Verdi visited quietly and alone the cemetery, and on his return he wrote to the municipal authorities of Milan offering to compose a Requiem Mass in memory of Manzoni, 'and thus,' he said, 'fulfil a great longing.' Verdi was assured of the co-operation of the municipality, which set on foot plans for a patriotic and artistic commemoration. Verdi completed his score within the year, retaining the *Libera me* which he had written as his contribution to the proposed Rossini Requiem.

The Mass was sung for the first time on the anniversary of Manzoni's death, May 22, 1874, at the Chiesa di San Marco, Milan. Stolz, Waldmann, Capponi, and Maini were the solo quartet, and Verdi conducted. There were further performances at La Scala. The Requiem was sung in the course of the following year in Paris and in London. At Vienna it was given four times in the summer of 1875, and filled the theater at every performance, notwithstanding high prices and oppressive heat. According to *Dwight's Journal of Music* (1852-81), the Requiem was first sung in America at St. Ann's Church, New York, October 25, 1874 (with what musical forces the *Journal* does not say). On November 17 of the same year, the Requiem was given 'by Mr. Strakosch's artists' (the Italian Opera Company) at the Academy of Music, New York.

The Requiem was widely hailed as a work of genius, 'remarkable for its union of pure and expressive melody with dramatic power and intensity.' But there were dissenting voices, especially in Germany. Bülow, for example, at first could not abide the work, and condemned it without reservation. But later he altered his views. He confessed that the music had moved him to tears, and he wrote a letter to Verdi frankly avowing his changed opinion. Verdi responded with a letter of rare modesty and magnanimity.

Concerning the charge, frequently heard a half century ago, that Verdi's music was too secular in tone, too dramatic and impassioned, Hanslick (who can scarcely be accused of frivolity) made in his *Musikalische Stationen* the following reply: 'Can the piety of Haydn or Mozart be questioned? Certainly not. And yet a large proportion of their church music appears to us very, very worldly. As compared with the "state-fair" jubilation in many a "Gloria," or with the operatic ornaments in many a "Benedictus" and "Agnus" of these masters, Verdi's Requiem seems truly sacred. . . The main thing is that the composer should combine, with a reverence for his task, a consistency with his own character. This testimonial of honesty must be granted to Verdi. There is not a movement in his Requiem which is superficial, unreal, or frivolous.'

Why indeed should not a musical setting of the Requiem Mass be dramatic, lurid—even theatrical, if you will? Are not the words themselves dramatic, lurid, theatrical enough, in all conscience? Are the basic conceptions that underlie the text—the thoughts, visions, prayers of the believer—are these reserved and sober and austere? The thought of Judgment Day, when the graves shall give up their dead, when the heavens shall be rolled together like a scroll and the world become ashes; the thought of the trumpets of the Resurrection; the thought of the horror of the everlasting darkness, of the fiery lake, of the agonies of damnation; the thought of universal lamentation, supplication, dread: *Mors stupebit et natura, cum resurget creatura, judicanti responsura*—what music could be dramatic, lurid, vehement, theatrical enough to come within speaking distance of such appalling conceptions? When men's imaginations have dared to think of a sun become 'black as sackcloth of hair,' of the moon become as blood, of the cosmos raining fire, of an earth deafened by the thunders of God's wrath, is it possible that any conceivable setting of these things in tones would equal them in wildness and extravagance of passionate fantasy? And what of death and lamentation and dread and anguished supplication—are these things undramatic, calling for reticent dignity of speech? What has the King of Terrors to do with dignity and decorum and seemly ways?

Verdi, the Latin, the southerner, with his bare nerves and quick responsiveness, has naturally reacted to the implications of his subject with the sensibility, the uninhibited emotions, of his race and his type. He has given us a Requiem such as no other composer could have written. The music has extraordinary and multiple virtues—a mysticism essentially Latin, compassionate tenderness, purity of feeling. And above all, overwhelming dramatic power. Who that has heard the work revealingly interpreted can forget the terrifying intensity of the fortissimo 'Allegro agitato' that follows the quiet A major finale of the *Kyrie*, with its proclamation of the Day of Wrath, and that later shatteringly recurs? Who can forget the hushed and overwhelming close that sets the crown of beauty and affectingness on the work: that wonderful decrescendo, with its prayer for security and holy rest and peace at the last—as if the music, breathless with awe, remembered the ancient promise of living fountains of waters, and the end of tears, and the city that needed not the sun.

Antonio Vivaldi

c. 1680-1743

Antonio Vivaldi, one of the outstanding masters of instrumental music in the early eighteenth century—composer, violinist, priest—was director of music to Duke Philip of Hesse at Mantua (some authorities say that his employer was Philip of Hesse-Philippsthal, Ernst Ludwig—but the point seems unimportant). In 1714, he was appointed to the post of violinist at St. Mark's, Venice; and he was also director of music at a girls' conservatory, where he remained till he died. Relatively little of Vivaldi's enormous output of music has been printed. He composed at least eighty concertos for the violin, and thirty-eight operas. His published compositions include twelve trios for two violins and 'cello (op. 1); eighteen violin sonatas with bass (op. 2 and 5); *L'Estro armonico*, twelve concertos for four violins, two violas, 'cello, and organ bass (op. 3); twenty-four for solo violin, two violins *ripieni*, viola, and organ bass (op. 4, 6, and 7); *Le Quattro Stagioni*, twelve concertos for four and five voices (op. 8); *La*

Cetera, six ditto (op. 9); six concertos for flute, violin, viola, 'cello, and organ bass (op. 10); twelve concertos for solo violin, two violins, viola, 'cello, and organ bass (op. 11 and 12).

- *Le Quattro Stagioni* ('The Four Seasons'): FOUR CONCERTI GROSSI FOR STRINGS, OP. 8

Vivaldi's op. 8 was published at Amsterdam about two hundred years ago— the date is not known. Vivaldi issued it under the general title *Il Cimento dell' Armonia e dell' Inventione* ('The Trial of Harmony and Invention'). In its entirety, this work consists of twelve concerti grossi for strings and continuo [see notes, above, on the concerti grossi of Handel]. The first four of the set are the *Quattro Stagione.* Vivaldi in his dedication of the work calls attention to the fact that he presents the concertos thus entitled with four accompanying sonnets, which preface and explain the music. The sonnets are by an anonymous author—possibly by Vivaldi himself, it has been suggested. The four symphonic poems—for such they are—and the four sonnets that accompany and explain them, are entitled (1) 'La Primavera' ('Spring'); (2) 'L'Estate' ('Summer'); (3) 'L'Autunno' ('Autumn'); (4) 'L'Inverno' ('Winter').

What makes the *Stagioni* especially noteworthy is their programmatic explicitness. Each sonnet is divided into lettered lines, and these lines, with their key initials, are repeated in the score at the beginning of those passages of the descriptive music to which they apply. Johann Kuhnau used a somewhat similar device in his six 'Bible Sonatas' for clavier, composed in 1700, when he printed in his score a series of verbal clues to the episodes he was illustrating in his music. Thus he guides us to the precise bar at which Goliath is felled by David's stone, and leaves us in no doubt as to when Jacob is 'amorous and contented.' Richard Strauss did the same thing two centuries later when he printed in the two-piano arrangement of his *Don Quixote* (though not, curiously enough, in the partitur) verbal clues to the successive episodes of the narrative that the music is designed to portray.

Let us see how the scheme works out in the case of the *Four Seasons.* The first of the concertos, 'Spring,' is prefaced in the score by the following lines, with Vivaldi's key letters at the left (the Italian poem is here presented in an English prose version):

(a) Spring is come.
(b) The festive birds salute it with their merry songs.
(c) And the fountains run with a soft murmur under the breath of the zephyrs.
(d) The sky becomes overcast, and thunder and lightning follow.
(e) When calm is restored, the birds resume their singing.
(f) On the flowery meadow, amid the rustling of leaves, sleeps the goatherd with his faithful dog at his side.
(g) To the festal sounds of pastoral piping, nymphs and shepherds dance on their beloved heath to celebrate the coming of radiant Spring.

Now turn to the score of 'Spring.' The music begins, Allegro, E major, 4-4, with a joyous outburst for full orchestra. Above the first bar duly appear Vivaldi's key letter (a) and its corresponding line from the printed poem:

'Spring is come.' Naïve, no doubt; but clear, definite, honest, and unmistakable. By the fourteenth measure, the orchestra has quieted down and all the instruments fall silent except three solo violins, which trill and warble unmistakably beneath the caption (b) with its reference to the 'festive birds.' The joyous spring theme of the opening measures returns briefly, forte, followed by a sudden drop to piano, and the caption (c) makes clear the meaning of a gentle figure in sixteenth-notes for the violins. And now Vivaldi brings on his storm. Under the caption (d) the unison strings sound the formula of repeated notes which for so many years has signified musical rain; the lightning flashes in violin runs; we hear some gentle eighteenth-century thunder. We reach caption (e), and three violins carol above a pedal C-sharp of the 'cellos, and the opening spring song bursts forth from the full orchestra. The Allegro ends.

We reach the letter (f). 'On the flowery meadow . . . sleeps the goatherd.' This caption introduces a Largo in C-sharp minor, 3-4. The solo violin, 'dolce espressivo,' sings above an accompaniment of muted strings. The whole of this brief slow movement is devoted to an evocation of the picture of the tranquil, blossoming meadow, the sleeping shepherd, the lazy, outstretched dog. The final Allegro (the most elaborate movement of the concerto) is summed up by caption (g). This movement not only is captioned by the excerpt from the sonnet; Vivaldi also adds the superscription 'Pastoral Dance.' The opening measures are in the typical manner of the eighteenth-century 'Pastorale.' There are solos for the violins of the concertino, one of them accompanied only by the cembalo (clavier), and a later one—after a change of key to E minor—beginning with an ascending chromatic phrase over a sustained pedal B. The recurring chief theme ends the movement in E, but softly, at the close, as if the jubilant nymphs and shepherds had wearied a little of their play.

In the three other concertos of the *Quattro Stagione* ('Summer,' 'Autumn,' 'Winter'), Vivaldi uses the same method of detailed and explicit indication. In 'Summer' we are reminded of Gombert's 'bird concert' and Jannequin's *Le Chant des oiseaux*—or of Vivaldi's contemporary Handel, with his *Vogel-Arien*. Vivaldi in his 'Summer' summons from his orchestra the song of the cuckoo, of the turtle-dove, and of the goldfinch. He goes even further—he paints for us the slumbering shepherd disturbed in his repose by a swarm of flies!

'Autumn' gives us a festival of Bacchus, and a hunting scene. In 'Winter' the strings shiver with cold; there are suggestions of 'chattering teeth.' (Mozart's father wrote a musical description of a journey by sleigh in which the travelers are represented as shivering with the cold.) Later we cross the ice, 'walking timidly, walking boldly, slipping and falling.' (Vivaldi's strings are here delightfully realistic.) 'The ice breaks up and melts.' The work ends with 'Boreas and all the winds at war'—a tumultuous Finale. But, says the poet cheerfully, 'This is the Winter, and it giveth joy.'

Vivaldi is revealed in these program-concertos as greatly in advance of his time, so far as the details of his tone painting are concerned. He is determined to make his music as expressive as his orchestra of strings and continuo will permit. His frequent dynamic modifications, indicated with great care, his legato and staccato markings, his use of mutes, attest the seriousness with which he approached his task. And he is often felicitous in expression. We shall doubtless find a good many of his expedients naïve and amusing, but we need not adopt toward them the rather toplofty attitude of Sir John Hawkins in his *General History of the Science and Practice of Music* (published at London in 1776). 'The plan of this work,' wrote Sir John of the *Stagione*, must appear very ridiculous.' But he was obliged to admit that it was 'one of the most applauded of Vivaldi's works.'

Who was the first composer to write nature music? Was it Nicola Gombert, of Bruges, whose *Chanson des oiseaux*, a four-part vocal composition printed about the middle of the sixteenth century, is 'a complete bird concert'? And Gombert published other musical celebrations of nature—*En ce mois délicieux; Joyeux verger, Je me'n vois au vert bois; L'été chaud bouilloit*. Was Gombert anticipated by the Bavarian tone poet, Lorenz Lemlin, who sometime during the first half of the sixteenth century published a 'cuckoo' song for six voices which Ambrose in his *Geschichte der Musik* praises as a charming piece *im Volkston*. As for the Frenchman, Clément Jannequin, who followed in the wake of Gombert, everyone has heard of his descriptive vocal music, among which we find a collection of chansons for four voices, *Le Chant des oiseaux*, imitating in words and notes the songs of various birds.

All this music was vocal. It was much later in the sixteenth century—perhaps it was early in the seventeenth—that John Mundy, the Elizabethan and early Stuart virginalist, wrote the Fantasia in which he describes 'Fair Weather,' 'Lightning,' 'Thunder,' 'Calm Weather,' 'A Clear Day,' included as No. 3 in the Fitzwilliam Virginal Book. Nobody knows when Mundy was born—it was probably about 1560. He died in 1630.

Was this the earliest nature music written for an instrument? No one can say. A large part of the early history of instrumental music is concerned with recording more or less determined attempts at nature painting on the part of various composers in various countries of Europe, and it is quite likely that Mundy was anticipated by some composer unchronicled in the books. We know that the beginnings of program music are lost in the tonal mists of the sixteenth century, and much of this early program music was nature music.

From the seventeenth century on, we find an inexhaustible supply of instrumental music—at first for the keyboard, later for the orchestra—devoted to attempted transcriptions of what Henry More called 'the Outworld': 'Forest' symphonies, 'Spring' symphonies; music of running streams, wind, and weather; and one could fill a volume the size of Webster's Unabridged with a history of the imitative bird songs of music. There were orchestral seascapes at least a century before Mendelssohn's 'Hebrides' Overture—as the suite for orchestra entitled *Wassermusik* by George Philipp Telemann, the famous contemporary of Bach (1631-1767), which gives us tone pictures of a calm sea (sustained notes of the oboes), a breeze, rippling waves, 'the amorous Neptune,' 'the playful Naiads,' 'the stormy Aeolus,' et cetera; and there were orchestral landscapes a century and a half before Beethoven's 'Pastoral' Symphony—as the 'Forest Symphonies' (*Sinfonie Boscareccie*) of Don Marco Uccellini, court conductor to the Duke of Modena, composed in 1669 for strings and continuo.

And we have not discussed such operatic nature music as the seascapes in the *Didone* and *Nettuno e Flora festeggianti* of Pietro Francesco Cavalli (1602-76).

But for an example of strikingly elaborate, detailed, and explicit nature music we shall probably not find anything in the records of old music more remarkable than Vivaldi's *Quattro Stagioni*. Indeed, the Italian editors of a modern piano transcription of part of this work describe the *Quattro Stagioni* as 'the first artistically careful example of programmatic descriptive music.'

Richard Wagner

1813-83

‡There is a sense in which Richard Wagner has no place in the pantheon of musicians. The great works he produced are unique in kind as in quality; nothing quite like them has ever come to us from another mind and hand. They are not musical works, strictly speaking, and they are not drama, and they are something more than a combination of the two, employing both music and drama to make a whole which somehow is greater than its parts. The Wagnerian literature is enormous, but in so far as it is criticism, of whatever tendency, it is largely irrelevant, proceeding to its task of explication on the assumption that the *Ring* and *Tristan* and *Die Meistersinger* and *Parsifal* are to be apprehended with the faculties and evaluated with the criteria that we apply to other and quite different expressions of the creative spirit. The bulk of Wagnerian criticism is analytical, and, having separated Wagner's work into its several components, attempts its reconstitution from one component only, usually the music. But Wagner does not make his extraordinarily complex and almost infinitely significant communication to us through his music alone, but through his poetry too (and it is really not such bad poetry as is usually supposed; functionally considered, indeed, it is admirable poetry); and through the attitudes and actions of the characters who speak it; and through the situations of which these attitudes and actions are alternatively cause or effect. It is the merit of the best Wagnerian criticism—Newman's, Gilman's, Mann's—that, passing from analysis to synthesis, it takes into account all of the elements present in these remarkable works—or as many as it can; for critics, after all, have their limitations, though the greatest of artists seem at times to have none—

and attempts their interpretation and appraisal not as music, or as drama, or as music-drama even, but as works of art *sui generis*.

Music from the Wagnerian 'operas' has no place in the concert repertoire, but it is none the less established there, and is not likely to be dislodged. Hence notes on this music which have as little place in the scheme of the book in hand are necessarily included in it. These notes comprise a fractional part of Lawrence Gilman's Wagnerian criticism, and, necessarily, they misrepresent it, barely suggesting its qualities, among which imaginative grasp and communicative intensity, allied at all times with responsible scholarship, are paramount.‡

• Overture to *Rienzi*

Wagner was twenty-five when, seeking to beat Meyerbeer at his own game, he was moved to contrive an opera out of a German version of Bulwer-Lytton's three-volume novel, *Rienzi, the Last of the Tribunes.* He completed his libretto in 1838, and the music for it in 1840. The outcome staggered even his gargantuan appetite for his own music. When he listened to the première of the work at Dresden in 1842, he was dismayed to find that the first two of his five acts had taken as long in performance as the whole of Weber's *Freischütz.* The entire opera lasted from six until midnight. It was, therefore, decided to serve the huge concoction in two portions—the first and second acts on one night, the remaining three on the night following. This seems to have pleased the Royal Family, who had objected to any cuts in the score, but the thrifty Dresden public declined to pay two entrance fees for one opera. So the old arrangement was restored, with various curtailments made by the composer, and the opera proceeded on its triumphal way.

The overture is based on four themes derived from the opera. After the introductory bars, with the swelling trumpet call which moved the incredible Edmund von Hagen to fifty-three pages of symbolic exegesis, the strings play the melody of Rienzi's prayer ('Molto sostenuto e maestoso,' 4-4). This is imposingly worked up; the trumpet call is heard again; and then ('Allegro energico,' 2-2), the full orchestra breaks forth in the Romans' cry for freedom, *Gegrüsst sei hoher Tag,* which the chorus sings at the end of the first act. Now, while the rest of the orchestra is still, the trombones in a fortissimo unison declaim the portentous theme of the battle hymn, *Sancto spirito cavaliere,* from the third act. This is repeated in another key (A major, following C major), and is succeeded by a cantabile phrase for the 'cellos. This phrase leads to a repetition of the Prayer theme in faster tempo. The Battle Hymn is heard again in the brass, and then comes a theme (first violins, oboe, and clarinet) which is derived from the melody sung by Adriano, Irene, and others in the Finale of Act 2. This comprises the thematic subject matter of the overture; the rest is development and recapitulation.

• Overture to *Der Fliegende Holländer*

The Flying Dutchman Overture, like the Venusberg scene in *Tannhäuser*, is a hybrid—fascinating and treasurable, but nevertheless a curious and instructive mixture of musical styles. The greater part of it is early Wagner, powerful but crude. But some of the overture as we possess it is post-*Tristan* Wagner and represents the mature and subtle artist who had traversed *Das Rheingold*, *Die Walküre*, the first two acts of *Siegfried*, and *Tristan und Isolde*.

The Flying Dutchman was completed at Paris in 1841, and was first performed at the Royal Court Theater, Dresden, in January 1843. It was Wagner's fourth opera—he had written only *Die Feen* (1833-4), *Das Liebesverbot* (1835-6) and *Rienzi* (1838-40). Wagner was still a cub, but with a punishing left paw. Most of the Overture to *The Flying Dutchman* remains as Wagner first wrote it in 1841, yet even these pages are extraordinary for their sweep and power. The chief theme of the overture—its opening subject, the theme of the Dutchman, the doomed wanderer—is among the enduring triumphs of the creative imagination, one of those exhibitions of conquering strength and pregnancy of expression which made Wagner the most articulate of composers. That stark and tremendous phrase for the brass, under the empty fifth sustained by strings and woodwind, is saturated with the mood of bleak and inexorable tragedy. It belongs to the class of those great themes, charged with intense and concentrated power, wherewith Wagner was able to achieve his epics of heroes and of gods, sad stories of the death of kings, immortal fables of the heart of man. And though John Runciman found it in his heart to say hard things of the Senta theme, yet he credited Wagner with having evolved from it a variant (that modification of it containing a turn or groupetto in the third bar of the melody) which he called 'one of the most wonderful things in music.'

But admirable as these things are, they remain early Wagner, and they are qualified by interludes of rampant sentimentalism and noisy commonness. If the overture as we know it today were wholly the product of 1841, it would present a much simpler problem to the critical assessor than in fact it does. But in 1852, and again in 1860, Wagner, having grown from a young man of prodigious talent to a middle-aged artist of consummate genius, returned to the score of his *Flying Dutchman* Overture and proceeded to do magical things to it, as he was afterwards to do in the case of the Paris version of his *Tannhäuser*. The ending was transformed, by one of his habitual strokes of genius, from a conventional and empty close to a peroration of exalted beauty. The last five measures were eliminated and ten new ones put in their place. This revised ending (which belongs to the year 1852) begins at the final D of the fortissimo descent of the trombones and tuba under the tumultuous figure in the violins. The music is suddenly stilled. The woodwind and horns, dolce, enter in the key of the subdominant (G major) over harp arpeggios, with a version of the Senta theme. A modulation to G minor introduces an upward sweeping phrase for the violins, and the close of Isolde's 'Liebestod' is suggested by the mood of luminous exaltation.

But still more remarkable are the twenty-one measures which Wagner wrote into the coda of the overture in 1860. They follow the first entry of the harp, twenty-six bars after the crashing diminished-seventh chord and the long silence which mark the climax of the piece. This particular revision of the score was alluded to by Wagner in a letter to Mathilde Wesendonck, written from Paris, March 3, 1860: 'I have made a new close for the overture to *The Flying Dutchman* which pleases me much'; and five weeks later: 'Not until now that I have written Isolde's last transfiguration could I find the right close for *The Flying Dutchman* Overture.' Would that Wagner in his last revision had gone further! A *Flying Dutchman* Overture developed from the greater subjects of the 1841 original, with the added resourcefulness and enhanced imaginative grasp of the master of 1860, would have been a wonderful thing indeed.

And the expressional scheme of *The Flying Dutchman* Overture? Wagner himself wrote an analysis of his work for the program of a Zürich festival concert, given in May 1853. Here it is, in the translation by William Ashton Ellis:

The Flying Dutchman's dreaded ship is scudding before the tempest; it reaches the coast and puts to land, where its captain has been promised healing and redemption; we hear the pitying strains of that foretoken of salvation, which sound like wailings blent with prayer: sullen and bereft of hope, the doomed man listens to them; weary and athirst for death, he comes ashore; while the crew, faint-hearted, and their lives outlived, in silence bring the ship to rest.

How often has the unhappy one passed through the self-same thing! How often has he steered his ship athwart the breakers to the shores of man, where once in every seven years 'twas granted him to land; how often has he dreamt that the end of all his trials was reached, and ah! how often, direly undeceived, has he set sail again upon his wild voyage! To force his own undoing, he has called on flood and storm to arm themselves against him; into the yawning whirlpool has he plunged his ship—but the gulf refused to swallow it; against the beetling headland has he urged it—but the rocks have never wrecked it. All the fearsome perils of the deep, at which he erst had laughed in madcap lust of venture, they now but laugh at him—they harm him not; he's curst to all eternity to hunt the desert seas for spoils that yield him no delight, ne'er to find the only thing that could redeem him!

A stately ship sweeps proudly by; he hears the merry, happy songs of men rejoicing at the near approach of home: anger takes him at this sound of gladness; raging, he rushes onward through the storm, affrights and silences the singers, and puts the joyous crew to flight. Then from the bottom of his misery he cries aloud for ransom. None but a wife can bring him weal! Where, in what distant land, may dwell the rescuer? Where beats a compassionate heart for sufferings so great as his? Where is she who will not flee in horror from him, like these coward men, who, shuddering, cross themselves at his approach?

A ray divides the gloom of night; like a lightning flash it pierces through his tortured soul. It fades, and leaps to life once more: the seaman keeps the lodestar firm in eye, and stoutly steers through waves and billows toward it. What draws him with such might? It is a woman's look, which, full of sad sublimity and divine fellow feeling, shines through to him! A heart has opened its depths to the unmeasured sorrows of the damned: for him must it make offering, to end alike his sorrows and its life. At this divinest sight the fated man breaks down at last, as breaks his ship to atoms: the ocean's trough engulfs it: but he, from out the waves, rises whole and hallowed, led by the redemptress's saving hand to the daybreak of sublimest Love.

TANNHÄUSER

● OVERTURE (Dresden Version)

It is perhaps desirable, from time to time, to remind ourselves of what Wagner really meant to suggest by the music of the *Tannhäuser* Overture. He has
given us his own explanation. Here it is, in a somewhat condensed translation
by William Ashton Ellis (*Wagner's Prose Works*):

At the beginning the orchestra chants the song of the pilgrims, which, as it
approaches, swells into a mighty hymn, but at length recedes. It is twilight; the last
strain of the pilgrim's song is heard. As night comes on, magic sights and sounds appear.
A rosy mist arises, wafting to our ears voluptuous cries of joy; we become aware of the
wild turmoil of a wanton dance.

These are the seductive spells of the 'Venusberg,' which at the hour of night reveal
themselves to those inflamed with sensual desire. Attracted by these allurements, a
human form approaches: it is Tannhäuser, the Minnesinger. Proudly exulting, he trolls
forth his jubilant love song as if to challenge the wanton crew to turn their attention
to himself. Wild shouts respond to his call; the rosy mist surrounds him more closely;
its enrapturing fragrance steals away his senses. Endowed now with supernatural vision,
he perceives in the dim light an unspeakably lovely being; he hears a voice which, with
bewitching sweetness, murmurs a promise of unutterable delights.

It is Venus herself. Heart and soul he burns with desire. Longing inflames his blood;
by an irresistible power he is drawn into the presence of the goddess, and with the
highest rapture sings his song in her praise. Then the wonder of the Venusberg is
revealed to him in its fullest brightness; wild laughter re-echoes on every side; Bacchantes
rush hither and thither in their drunken revels; and, dragging Tannhäuser into their
mad dance, deliver him over to the caresses of the goddess, who, passionately embracing
him, carries him off, drunken with joy. The wild throng then disperses. A voluptuous,
plaintive whirring alone stirs the air.

Day begins to dawn, and now the chant of the returning pilgrims is heard from
afar. As this chant draws closer and closer, as the day drives farther back the night,
that whir and soughing of the air—which had erewhile sounded like the aerial cries
of souls condemned—now rises, too, in ever gladder waves; so that when the sun
ascends at last in splendor, and the Pilgrim's chant proclaims in ecstasy to all the
world, to all that lives and moves thereon, Salvation won, this wave itself swells out
the tidings of sublimest joy. 'Tis the carol of the Venusberg itself, redeemed from the
curse of impiousness, this cry we hear amid the hymn of God. . .

The *Tannhäuser* Overture in this, its most familiar form, is a brilliant set-
piece of conventional tripartite construction, A-B-A, the opening and concluding section utilizing the music of the Pilgrim's Chorus heard in the third act
of the opera, the middle section being derived from the music of the Venusberg scene.

● OVERTURE AND BACCHANALE ('Venusberg Scene') (Paris Version)

Wagner rose from the task of completing *Tristan und Isolde* only to apply
himself, scarcely a year later, to the formidable labor of reconstructing the first
two scenes of *Tannhäuser,* in order to prepare his score for the Paris perform-

ance so handsomely ordered by Napoleon III (to oblige his friend the Princess Metternich; for to Napoleon, Wagner and his *Tannhäuser* were less than nothing. 'Wagner? . . . *Tannhäuser?* I have never heard either name,' he remarked to the Princess).

'I am removing such weak points as I have discovered in the score,' Wagner observes casually in the course of a letter to Liszt, September 13, 1860. 'I am rewriting the great Venus scene, and I hope to improve the effect thereby. The ballet scene also will be entirely new, after a more elaborate plan which I have made for it.'

This so-called 'Paris Version' of the Bacchanale, and the ensuing scene between Venus and Tannhäuser, had a singular genesis, and it encountered a no less singular fate. Consider the circumstances. Here was a musician returning, after fifteen years, to the source of an earlier inspiration. 'You have perhaps never undergone so hard a trial of patience,' wrote Liszt during the summer of 1860, when Wagner was 'once more in the old *Tannhäuser* birth-throes,' 'as the rewriting and restudying of this work, which to you is partly "ein überwundener Standpunkt."' Wagner had, so far as his creative activities were concerned, put *Tannhäuser* out of his mind in 1845; yet now, fifteen years later, he took up again this early score, which he had transcended by a decade and a half of amazing intellectual and aesthetic growth, and, moved by a veritable passion for perfection, remodeled an essential part of it in a spirit of unalloyed artistic enthusiasm.

The act was one of heroic supererogation. So far as the popular reception of the opera was concerned, it would have gone quite as well, even better, indeed, had the old version of the Venusberg scene been used. Wagner gained no favor with the young gentlemen of the Paris Jockey Club by the change: he merely antagonized them by putting in the wrong place the ballet that they required. It was an unheard-of thing that the ballet should occur in any act but the second. The subscribers dined late, and did not reach the opera house until the performance was half over. But Wagner was adamant; he would supply a ballet, if need be, but it must go in the opening scene. In carrying out this decision he had his labors and his pains for nothing—except that the world gained thereby a magnificent musical torso. For what did this insatiable lover of perfection set himself to accomplish? Not only the rewriting of the Bacchanale (there was a short one in the old version of *Tannhäuser*), but the remodeling of practically the entire scene between Tannhäuser and Venus—which resulted merely in placing increased difficulties in the way of a good performance. The original version of that scene was easy, old-fashioned Wagner—the Wagner of 1845. The new music that he wrote for it in 1860 is the subtle, the exacting, the prodigious Wagner of *Tristan und Isolde* (blended with surprising anticipations of *Die Meistersinger, Götterdämmerung,* and even *Parsifal*).

For the Paris version of 1861 Wagner shortened the original overture. He omitted the last 156 measures, and ran the curtailed overture directly into the revised Bacchanale, without pause. Both the Bacchanale and the following scene between Venus and Tannhäuser were greatly amplified; the former was increased from eighteen pages to 56; the latter from 38 to 75: an addition to the original orchestral score of 75 pages. Throughout the 133 pages which now comprise the Bacchanale and the duet, there is scarcely a measure that has not undergone some transformation—harmonic, rhythmic, or orchestral; and there is a liberal infusion of new matter.

So far as the Bacchanale is concerned, this new material is evolved from three new themes—inventions of superb strength and beauty, conceived in the ripened style of *Tristan*. The first of these is the incandescent, downward-rushing violin figure in tumultuous sixteenth and thirty-second notes that has its prototype in the Liebeslust motive first heard at the end of the second act of *Siegfried*. It appears in the Bacchanale, in its final shape, 73 bars after the opening. The second new theme is the glowing phrase, in ascending Tris-tanesque chromatics, that occurs, fortissimo, four bars later, just before the amorous orgy reaches its climax. The third new theme is one of Wagner's most haunting inventions. It is the exquisite phrase in E major, given to a solo violin and solo 'cello, against reiterated chords in triplet rhythm, heard as the apparition of Europa and her escort fade from view, while the Graces resume their languorous dance. This is developed in a lovely chromatic pas-sage, harmonized in thirds, that oddly foreshadows *Götterdämmerung*. It is used again with piercing effect near the conclusion of the Bacchanale; and just before the beginning of the first scene, when Tannhäuser first endeavors to dislodge the burden of his too cloying dreams, it is ingeniously combined with a fragmentary reminiscence of the theme of the Pilgrims—one of those simple but happy effects which Wagner's matured art had taught him how to ac-complish. Out of these motives, and from other material that is not new but has been wonderfully enhanced in potency and beauty by the composer's sorcerous art, Wagner achieves what is probably the most incandescent episode in all music.

For the remodeled Bacchanale, Wagner wrote stage directions as elaborate as any of Bernard Shaw's. They provide a complete and vivid elucidation of the music, even without the choreographic scene which the orchestra was in-tended to accompany and illustrate. Here are Wagner's directions:

The stage represents the interior of the Venusberg, the Hörselberg near Eisenach, a deep, wide grotto, seeming to lose itself in endless distance as it curves around to the right. From a jagged opening through which the daylight wanly glints, a greenish-tinted waterfall dashes down the whole height of the cavern, foaming wildly over rocks; from the basin which receives the water a brook streams toward the farther background, and there expands into a lake in which one sees the forms of bathing Naiads, while Sirens recline upon its brink. On each side of the grotto are jutting crags of weird irregular form, bearing wondrous growths of tropical coral-like vegetation. In the fore-ground, in front of the opening of a cavern that stretches upwards on the left, from which there issues a soft and roseate shimmer, Venus lies stretched upon a sumptuous couch; while before her, his head upon her lap, his harp beside him, half kneels Tann-häuser. Around the couch, in loving interlacement, are grouped the Three Graces. At the side of, and behind the couch, are massed in inextricable confusion knots of sleeping Cupids like children tired of play. The whole foreground glows with a magic flush of ruddy light streaming up from below, through which the emerald green of the cascade and the white of its foam-flecks break with a vivid contrast; while the distant back-ground and the banks of the lake are lit by a haze of blue, like moonshine.

At the rise of the curtain a group of Youths is discovered lying on the crests of the jutting rocks, their wine cups in their hands; in answer to the beckoning glances of the Nymphs they now spring down to meet them. Around the foaming basin of the waterfall, the Nymphs have already commenced the inviting dances which are to lure the young men to them. The couples meet and mingle with each other; seeking, fleeing, and playful teasing make gay the dance. From the farther background there draws near a train of Bacchantes, and dashes through the mazes of the loving pairs, inciting them to wilder revels. With gestures of intoxicated transport, the Bacchantes urge the lovers to ever-waxing riot. Satyrs and Fauns have appeared from the rock-clefts, and force their headlong dance among the Bacchantes and the pairs of lovers. They make confusion worse confounded by their chase after the Nymphs, as the general tumult mounts to the highest pitch of frenzy.

But now, when the madness is at its height, the Three Graces arise in horror. They endeavor to bridle the rage of the dancers, and to drive the groups asunder. Powerless, they fear to be caught themselves in the mad swirl; they turn to the sleeping Cupids, and rouse them to wing their flight on high. The little creatures, opening out their ranks, dart upward like a flock of birds, and occupy in battle array the whole upper region of the grotto, whence they shoot a ceaseless hail of arrows upon the surging crowd below. The wounded, seized by pangs of love, leave off their frenzied dance, and sink down breathless. The Graces claim their wounded for their own, and marshalling the rioters into pairs, they seek by gentle suasion to force them to the background. Fleeing in all directions, the Bacchantes, Satyrs, Fauns, Nymphs, and Youths depart, pursued by a detachment of the Cupids from the height of the cave. An ever-denser rosy mist sinks down; it submerges first the Cupids, then it cloaks the entire background; until, at last, beyond Venus and Tannhäuser, the Three Graces alone are left in sight. These now return to the front; in graceful embrace they approach their mistress, and apprise her of the victory which they have won over the savage passion of the lieges of her realm. Venus motions them her thanks.

The dense mist in the background opens out, and a cloud picture shows the abduction of Europa, who passes over the breast of the blue sea, upon the back of a flower-decked snow-white steer, led by a band of Tritons and Nereids, while from the background is heard the song of the Sirens.

The rosy mists close once more; the picture vanishes, and the Graces describe by a gently moving dance its secret meaning. Again the mist divides. In the soft glamor of the moon Leda appears, outstretched beside a woodland pool; the swan swims toward her, and buries its caressing neck within her bosom. Gradually this picture also fades away. At last the mist rolls off completely, and shows the entire grotto silent and deserted. The Graces, smiling, bend before Venus; then slowly withdraw to the side-cavern. Deepest quiet. Venus and Tannhäuser remain in unchanged posture. [*Translated by W. A. Ellis.*]

William Ashton Ellis, that consummate Wagnerian, begs us to remember that this is 'no vulgar scene of sensual temptation, such as one may witness in the ghastly orgies of *Robert the Devil*; but Venus seems to have stepped from out of the noble poem of Lucretius, in all her classic dignity. The wild passions of untamed natural forces are lashed to fury by the savagery of elemental spirits, until the handmaids of the goddess send forth her mandate and resolve the discord, turning the headlong lust to ordered love, and evolving from the chaos a world of harmony.'

LOHENGRIN

• PRELUDE TO ACT 1

Wagner himself has left us an explanation of the poetic significance of the *Lohengrin* Prelude. Here is a paraphrase of his note:

Out of the clear blue ether of the sky there seems to condense a wonderful yet at first hardly perceptible vision; and out of this there gradually emerges, ever more and more clearly, an angel host, bearing in its midst the sacred Grail. As it approaches earth it pours out exquisite odors, like streams of gold, ravishing the senses of the beholder. The glory of the vision grows and grows until it seems as if the rapture must be shattered and dispersed by the very vehemence of its own expansion. The vision draws nearer, and the climax is reached, when at last the Grail is revealed in all its glorious reality, radiating fiery beams, and shaking the soul with emotion. The beholder sinks to his knees in adoring self-annihilation. The Grail sheds its light upon him, like a benediction, and consecrates him to its service; then the flames die away gradually and the angel host soars up again to the ethereal heights of tender joy, having made pure once more the hearts of men by the sacred blessing of the Grail.

• PRELUDE TO ACT 3

This brief prelude is virtually an independent composition, for it has no thematic connection with the rest of the opera, beyond a slight reminiscence (in the woodwind passages in the middle section) of the scene between Elsa and Ortrud in the preceding act.

Runciman, the Perfect Wagnerite, regarded this introduction as 'the most brilliant that Wagner ever wrote.' 'Here we have,' said he, 'no summary of the Act, no hint of impending disaster and tragedy, but simply a joyous preliminary to the procession that escorts Lohengrin and Elsa to the bridal chamber. It starts off with immense spirit, the music leaping straight up, hesitating a moment on a cross-accent, then with a noisy shake reaching its highest note, and, after a clash of cymbals, sliding off into the more regular rhythm. The melody in the bass that follows, and the more tender strains of the middle portion, are familiar to everyone nowadays—in fact, so familiar that we are likely to overlook the intense originality of the whole thing.'

DAS RHEINGOLD

• ENTRANCE OF THE GODS INTO WALHALLA

Das Rheingold is ceaselessly interesting to the student of Wagner because it marks the transition between the accomplished composer who wrote *Lohengrin* and the unparalleled genius who wrote *Die Walküre*. And here again is a wonder—one of the miracles in the history of the human brain. In 1848 Wagner completed the scoring of *Lohengrin*, an opera by a composer of rare gifts, who could not forget Weber and Marschner and Meyerbeer. Five years later this gifted but scarcely extraordinary music-maker had become a genius of the first order and the most original musical mind in the art of his time. The Wagner of *Lohengrin* had become the Wagner of *Das Rheingold*. A chasm between two different worlds had been bridged; and a new master had been born.

We encounter in *Das Rheingold* not only an unexampled Wagner, but a new region of creative musical thought. The Wagner of *Lohengrin* could not have conceived this music, would not have dared it. And we are in a new world of the imagination, as well as a new world of invention and craftsmanship. Wagner, as Romain Rolland said, carried all Nature in his imagination; and in the music of *Das Rheingold* we confront the Wagner who released without stint his delight and exhilaration in the beauty and terror and endless fascination of the natural world.

The music of this Prologue to the gigantic *Ring* begins in the primordial abyss, in the green, twilit depths of the old river, timeless and immemorial. It ends with lightning and a rainbow and a stormy, tragical, deceptive sunset brightening the faces of the doomed gods; and between, there is music of fire and clouds and mountain heights and subterranean gloom and the roar of wind among primeval hills, and the gathering tempests and the never-absent sense of the wonder and strangeness and magic of the created earth.

The excerpt from *Das Rheingold* known in the concert room as the 'Entrance of the Gods into Walhalla' is derived from the Finale of the music-drama. Fafner has just slain his brother Fasolt in a quarrel over the Ring. The gods stand horror-struck at this visible sign of the instant operation of Alberich's Curse. The world is wrapped in gloom. Donner, the Storm God, unable to endure the pervading depression, decides to clear the atmosphere. He springs to a rocky height, and 'calls the clouds as a shepherd calls his flocks,' swinging his hammer as he utters his mighty shouts, while the mists gather and hide him from view. We hear his great theme in the orchestra thundered out by the brass; there is a swift and overwhelming crescendo, as if all the storms in the universe were coming to a head; the lightning flames and the heavens split. Then suddenly the air clears: from the feet of Donner and Froh, as they stand on the summit, a rainbow bridge of dazzling radiance stretches across the valley to the opposite height, where Valhalla, the troublous castle of the gods, is revealed in all its splendor as it gleams in the rays of the setting sun, while the sublime Valhalla theme sounds with tranquil majesty from the brass under an iridescent accompaniment of strings and harps. As the gods start to walk over the rainbow bridge (all but the cynic Loge, who remains behind, muttering sour comments), the melancholy song of the Rhine-maidens, lamenting their stolen gold, is borne upward from the valley.

DIE WALKÜRE

• The Ride of the Valkyries

The Valkyries, in Scandinavian mythology, were the nine daughters of Odin, whose happy privilege it was to wait upon the heroes in Valhalla and fill with mead their horns at the banquet table of the gods. Also, their duties included the solemn but joyous task of marking for death those heroes who were elected to fall in battle, and afterward to bear them to Valhalla on their horses' backs.

There they were restored to life and vigor, and equipped to fight the battles of Odin against his foes. *Valkyrior*, which some prefer as the plural form of the word, means 'Choosers of the Slain'; and it is in this character that the epic sisterhood appear in Wagner's music-drama.

The scene in *Die Walküre* from which this excerpt is extracted for concert use occurs at the beginning of Act III, and is laid upon the summit of a rocky mountain, high among the clouds, where the formidable maidens are gathering after one of their affrays. Garbed in shining mail, armed with spears and war-shields and mounted on their steeds, they ride wildly through the storm, heralded by lightning, bearing across their saddles the bodies of slain heroes. As the curtain opens, four of the maidens are seen upon the stage. The others are not yet in sight. Their voices are heard in advance of their appearance, shouting the jubilant cry that is their typical theme—a wildly exultant motive, the famous 'Ho-jo-to-Ho!' based upon the intervals of an augmented triad. This is heard together with another subject, the theme of the Ride—one of Wagner's most astonishing inventions: for it is only a bugle-call, unbelievably transformed, which courses exultingly through the orchestra. The shrilling of the wind, the galloping hoofs, the whinnyings of the woodwind, contribute to a tone picture unsurpassed even by Wagner for elemental sweep and power.

• WOTAN'S FAREWELL AND MAGIC FIRE SCENE

The setting is that of the preceding scenes of Act III—a wild mountain height, bordered by dark pine woods, across which a tempest has lately driven its storm winds and flying clouds. Far below are the forest-fringed slopes and valleys, still echoing with the distant thunder and the panic-stricken flight of the Valkyries across the sky. The ancient cedars stand black and gaunt against the sunset, now cleared of storm and cloud, and fading through orange and amethyst and violet into a tranquil evening loveliness. On the open rocky space at the summit, barred with the lengthening shadows of the pines, are two tragic and sorrowful figures—Wotan, uneasy lord of earth and heaven, a struggling and frustrate god, and his dearest child, Brünnhilde, who lies prostrate on the ground before him. She has defied his commands (while fulfilling the secret desire of his heart) by protecting Siegmund, his son, against the god's decree of death, and now she must suffer banishment and degradation.

Brünnhilde's supplication is searching and pitiful. But her pleading cannot avert her punishment, though it wins from Wotan this concession: he will surround the rock on which she is to lie asleep with a towering and dreadful ring of fire, through which only a fearless hero can pass and win her.

So, as the dusk gathers about the mountain-top, and the slanting shadows of the pine trees lengthen at their feet, while the light pales in the west and the mists hide the distant valleys and the blue deepens luminously above, Wotan, his heart breaking, takes leave forever of Brünnhilde—now deprived of her godhead and all its powers. He lays her down in an enchanted sleep, draws her helmet over her closed eyes, and covers her with her long war-shield, to slumber under the lonely firs through many a dawn and moonrise and mountain storm, until she shall be wakened by a hero who, indifferent to

Wotan's spear and to the girdling flames which the god evokes to guard her couch, shall pass unfearful through the blazing hedge. With Loge's terrible fire leaping against the blue-black sky and brightening the armor of the sleeper underneath the pines, Wotan turns his back on that which was more dear to him than anything save pride and power, and disappears slowly down the mountainside.

Here, in the scene of Wotan's Farewell, as in all of Wagner's major writing, is music that meets, with superb and triumphant competence, the ultimate test: for it selects a great, passionate, abidingly human theme—the immemorial pathos of farewell and loss—and treats it with supreme felicity and perfect truth. He had already given us 'the daughter at the father's feet.' Now he gives us, in essence, the most ancient and common of human griefs: the grief of parting and separation—the separation that is terrible in its finality, in the desolation that it foresees.

We watch the old god, weary and proud and sorrowful, as he embraces the beloved daughter that he is never to see again. And as we listen to the over-powering Farewell, and to the epilogue which follows it, that indescribable symphonic pattern woven out of a half-dozen of the most wonderful inventions in all Wagner—the mysterious theme of Erda the Earth-mother, the exquisite Slumber Song, the mighty theme of Siegfried the deliverer, the miraculous evocation of Loge's magic flames, the solemn and haunting theme of Fate, the divinely tender music of the Farewell—as we listen, we know that this is no longer Wotan the lord of earth and heaven, but something less and more: the eternal father among men, a mortal like ourselves, familiar and pitiful, his heart breaking as he looks back upon the treasured dearness that he is never to see again.

Wagner has set these scenes and happenings and emotions to music of such noble height and living fullness of song that it seems, as Charles Doughty said of the poetry of Chaucer, 'as if his vein flowed from the island-wells of Nature herself.' If sheer sublimity, and a depth of sorrowful tenderness that turns the heart to water, are anywhere in music, they are in these infinitely touching pages wherewith Wagner closes the second chapter of his mighty tale of gods and men and destiny, set amid the pageantry of clouds and winds, woods and hills, dawns and sunsets, and the deep places of the earth and sea. These 'ancient streams and far-descended woods' are peopled by gnomes and nixies, giants and gods and heroes, garrulous beasts and prophylactic birds. Yet the true wonder of Wagner's magic fairyland is that it is drenched in the colors of human life.

This great dreamer, who might have been content merely to remain 'sole-sitting by the shores of old Romance,' has done a wonderful and unprecedented thing—he has made this cumbrous and somewhat childish apparatus, over-loaded though it is with metaphysical and symbolistic baggage, the vehicle for music that sweeps the gamut of humanity's inward life: that loves and exults, through the figure of Siegfried, with all that is jocund and unworn and blithe in the souls of men; for whom the tragic struggle of Wotan against himself, the groping passion of Sieglinde, the great-heartedness of Brünnhilde, are timeless symbols of the lives and destinies of men and women. Almost one might say of him (ignoring the caution of Henry James) that he knew, in truth, 'the last word of every human heart.'

SIEGFRIED

• WALDWEBEN ('Forest Murmurs')

Mime has led the adventurous Siegfried on a long and weary hike since nightfall; day is breaking, and they have come to the farthest reach of the woods. Siegfried throws himself on a knoll under a linden tree. They are deep in the forest, at the mouth of the cavern where Fafner lies guarding his provocative hoard. As the dawn slants through the tree trunks and searches out the gloomy entrance to the dragon's cave, Mime proceeds to paint for Siegfried's benefit an elaborately awful portrait of the monstrous *Wurm*—the poison gas that is his breath, his appalling jaws, his thrashing and lethal tail. But Mime admits that the brute has a heart; and this is enough for Siegfried: 'Nothung,' his mighty sword, will find and pierce it. He drives Mime impatiently away, stretches himself out on the warm grass in the shade of the linden, and looks reflectively after the dwarf.

In the orchestra the low strings begin that vague murmuring which is the meditation of the forest captured and made lyrical. Siegfried thinks aloud: That Mime is not his father has been revealed as a joyful certainty; and the woods take on a new and laughing magic for him, now that he is forever rid of the detestable Nibelung. But what, then, was his father like? No doubt like Siegfried himself. Through the green stillness, broken only by the anonymous stirring of the wind in the grass and among the leaves, the music reminds us that Siegfried is a Volsung, while the clarinets recall the mournfully beautiful theme from the first act of *Die Walküre*. And his mother? Surely her eyes were soft and shining like the eyes of a doe—only more lovely. Oh, if he might have seen her—his mother, a mortal's mate! In the orchestra we hear the tender song of the 'cellos that, in the first act, accompanied Siegfried's wistful talk about the pairing of the creatures of the forest; and then, on a solo violin, the ravishing motive of Freia, goddess of youth and love, that clambers upward 'like a dewy branch of wild clematis.'

A wind stirs among the branches, and the rustling of the forest grows louder. Siegfried's attention is attracted by the songs of the birds. There is one just above his head. Siegfried is captivated, and would fashion a reed with which to imitate the song, and thus, perhaps, understand its meaning. It might, he hopes, tell him something of his mother. He springs up, draws his sword, and, cutting a reed, tries in vain to contrive a pipe. (Then, in the opera, follow the encounter with the Dragon, the squabbling of the two Nibelung dwarfs, and the killing of Mime. The music of these incidents is omitted from the concert version.)

Siegfried—hot, weary, despondent, longing for friend or companion—reclines again under the branches and listens for the voice of the Bird, which, in the opera, proves to be a light soprano, uttering the lyric speech of Wagnerland (although in the concert version, of course, the Bird is still only an ad-

mirable orchestral player in a black coat). Siegfried receives news that is indeed
arousing: news of the 'glorious bride' who, sleeping behind a blazing rampart,
awaits the deliverer who knows not fear. The strings burst forth in a phrase
of passionate eagerness, the orchestra remembers Loge's magic flames, the
Siegfried theme sounds exultantly on the horn, and the violins and woodwind
sing the so-called Slumber motive from *Die Walküre*. Siegfried shouts aloud
and springs to his feet, crying for someone to guide him to Brünnhilde's rock;
the infinitely obliging Bird flutters forth, with Siegfried following in high excitement.

DIE GÖTTERDÄMMERUNG

● DAWN MUSIC AND SIEGFRIED'S RHINE JOURNEY

Siegfried (in the preceding opera of the *Ring*) had passed through Brünnhilde's
guarding flames, had wakened her with the traditional kiss, and won her as
his bride. They have dwelt for a while in Brünnhilde's mountain retreat; and
now, in the Prologue of *Die Götterdämmerung*, Brünnhilde is about to send
the hero forth to new deeds of glory, after having endowed him with all the
wisdom that she had acquired from the gods.

The stage setting is that of the Finale of *Siegfried* and of the opening scene
of *Götterdämmerung* (the fate-weaving of the Norns): the summit of the
Valkyries' rock. Morning dawns, and as the daily miracle is accomplished in
the east, Siegfried and Brünnhilde enter from the cave, the hero in full armor.
Brünnhilde urges him forth to fresh exploits. They exchange vows, and Siegfried acquires from his bride that most irksome inhabitant of the Nibelungen
zoo, the recalcitrant steed Grane, in exchange for the curse-bearing Ring;
whereupon the hero begins his Rhine journey, to experience love of another
kind, and black betrayal, and a murderous end. Brünnhilde watches from the
cliff as Siegfried disappears down the mountainside. From afar in the valley
comes the sound of his horn.

This excerpt begins with the orchestral passage that depicts the coming of
the dawn after the portentous night in which the three Norns have played
with the destinies of gods and men. There are few things more wonderful in
all Wagner than this music of daybreak. The compact expressiveness of it is
extraordinary: in fifty measures the music lifts the sun above the mountain
mists, paints with a few swift strokes two of the greatest figures in the Wagnerian epos, and, in the course of achieving this feat, weaves for us a tonal
pattern of overmastering beauty.

We hear first, on the trombones, the solemn motive of Fate. Following this,
the 'cellos develop a melody long-breathed and contemplative. Horns in three-
part harmony foreshadow the transformation of Siegfried's call which limns
the matured hero; and on the clarinet we hear that melody astonishingly derived from one of the oldest and tritest of musical ornaments, the 'turn,'
which Wagner has made into a thing of rapturous tenderness to characterize
Brünnhilde the woman. The taking over of this theme by the violins, at their
first entrance—where the key changes from B-flat to E-flat—is one of those

transporting moments that draw the errant back to Wagner. With this material, the tone poet evokes his dawn and brings on his hero and heroine.

In the concert version, this passage is consorted with the extended interlude descriptive of Siegfried's journey to the Rhine, which connects the Prologue with Act I of *Die Götterdämmerung*—that superb orchestral epic derived from a dozen of the most memorable themes of the tetralogy. The arrangement most frequently heard is one made by Humperdinck, with its abrupt transition from the high point of the Dawn Music to the beginning of the Rhine Journey. But various conductors—notably Toscanini—have made modifications of Humperdinck's arrangement, bridging the gap between the Dawn Music and the Rhine Journey with the music that accompanies the entrance of Siegfried and Brünnhilde, and with the last portion of the ensuing duet—beginning at the point of Brünnhilde's O *heilige Götter!*

- SIEGFRIED'S DEATH AND FUNERAL MUSIC

Siegfried, resting in the woods with the assembled huntsmen—Gunther and Hagen and the vassals—relates to them the tale of his own life and adventures. As his narrative approaches its end, Hagen interrupts the hero to press upon him a horn of wine in which he has mixed a magic brew that removes from Siegfried's mind the cloud that had obscured his memory of Brünnhilde. Siegfried resumes his marvelous tale, describing with gusto his pursuit of the guiding Forest-Bird, his finding of Brünnhilde on the flame-girdled mountain-top, and his waking of the enchanted sleeper by his kiss. As he reaches this exultant climax, two ravens fly up from a bush, and Hagen asks him, 'Can'st read the speech of these ravens, too?' As Siegfried turns to look after them, Hagen thrusts his spear into the hero's back. Siegfried attempts to crush Hagen with his shield, but his strength leaves him, and he falls backward. Then the dying hero, supported by two of the vassals, raises himself slightly, opens his eyes, and sings his last greeting to Brünnhilde.

By one of those supreme strokes of genius wherewith Wagner so often overwhelms us, the first part of Siegfried's greeting to the bride whom he had unwittingly betrayed is set to the music with which Brünnhilde herself had greeted the sun and the day and the glory of the world on that radiant morning when the hero wakened her from her enchanted sleep; while Siegfried's dying vision of the beloved woman is accompanied in the orchestra by an almost intolerably poignant reminiscence of an ecstatic phrase from the great love duet in *Siegfried*. It is by such miracles of inspiration that Wagner's art occasionally tempts us to say that it is transcendent and incomparable.

Siegfried sinks back and dies. And for a few moments the stricken vassals and warriors gathered about him in the darkening woods stand speechless beside the silent figure stretched on its great war-shield. Then, at a gesture from Gunther, the vassals lift the shield with its incredible burden upon their shoulders and bear it in solemn procession over the heights, hidden at last by the mists that rise from the river, while the mightiest death song ever chanted for mortal or for god ascends from the instrumental choir.

This titanic funeral hymn is also an elegy, in which is recalled to us the tragic history of the Volsung race, now come to its end. One by one the immortal themes are passed in review before us, recalling their old associations: the sorrows of the Volsungs, and their noble fortitude; the compassion of Sieglinde, and the love between herself and Siegmund; the Sword; Siegfried; Siegfried the Hero; Brünnhilde; Alberich's cry of triumph; the curse—while around them the Death motive swirls and crashes like a black and devastating flood, and at last sinks into quietness with a murmured recollection of the theme of Siegfried the Hero.

•BRÜNNHILDE'S IMMOLATION

The body of Siegfried, slain by Hagen's spear—in swift fulfillment of the Rhine-Maidens' warning prophecy—lies on its bier in the hall of the Gibichungs beside the Rhine. Gunther, too, is dead, Gutrune distraught; and Hagen has been cowed by the threatening, supernatural gesture of the dead Siegfried as he tries to seize the Ring from the hero's finger. In that moment of spellbound horror, Brünnhilde, veiled and sovereign, no longer wholly of this world, advances with tranquil majesty from the back. Contemplation and revelation have made clear to her the whole vast tangle of fate and sin and tragedy that enmeshed them all. After long contemplation of Siegfried's body, she turns to the awestruck men and women and begins that matchless valedictory, filled with an overmastering eloquence of grief and reproach and prophecy and expiatory passion, which is the dramatic and musical consummation of the Trilogy—that farewell to earth and earthly love and all felicity, with its sublime Requiescat for the distant, perishing god, beside which every other leavetaking in poetry or drama seems dwarfed and limited. She perceives the divine justice of self-sacrifice. Her vision is that of a transfigured seeress proclaiming a new day; and with solemn exaltation she prepares to join her dead hero on the funeral pyre in order that she may fulfill the last necessity which shall bring that day.

She turns toward the back, where Siegfried's body has already been laid upon the flower-strewn pyre, seizes a great firebrand from one of the staring vassals, and hurls it among the logs, which break into sudden flame. Two young men bring forward Grane, her horse. Brünnhilde unbridles him, bends to him affectionately, addresses him. In rising ecstasy, she cries aloud their joint greetings to the dead Siegfried, swings herself onto Grane's back, and together they leap into the pyre.

The flames blaze up, filling the whole space before the hall, as the terrified men and women crowd toward the back. The Rhine overflows, and the Rhine-Maidens are seen swimming forward. Hagen plunges as if mad into the flood, and is drawn beneath the surface by two of the Nixies as the Curse motive is thundered out by three unison trombones. Flosshilde exultantly holds the recovered Ring on high, while the Rhine-Maidens' song is heard from the woodwind. The Valhalla theme is chanted solemnly by the brass, and high in the violins and flutes the motive of Redemption through Love soars above the wreckage of cupidity and the selfish pride of gods. As the hall falls in ruins, an increasing glow in the heavens reveals Valhalla, the assembled divinities and heroes seated within, awaiting majestically their doom. The theme of the

Twilight of the Gods marks their downfall as flames seize upon the castle of the mighty ones; and with a final transfigured repetition of the motive of Redeeming Love in the strings, which marks the passing of the old order and the coming of a new, the great drama is brought to its end.

TRISTAN UND ISOLDE

● PRELUDE AND FINALE ('Liebestod')

Wagner heard his *Tristan* Prelude played for the first time by an orchestra when he conducted it in Paris on January 25, 1860—'after the most unheard-of torment, stress, and toil.' He wrote Mathilde Wesendonck three days later that the occasion was 'nothing more nor less than a festival. The orchestra was already fired to white enthusiasm and hung upon my eye, my fingertip. I was received both by it and by the audience with endless cheers . . . The sensation is quite immense; strange experiences . . . feuilletonists rushing to kiss my hand. I myself was deadbeat. On that night I took my last initiation into suffering: I must trudge on. The flower [*Tristan und Isolde*] has to open to the world.'

At the rehearsals Wagner had found that the Prelude 'was so inscrutably new to the bandsmen' that he had to lead his men from note to note 'as if exploring for gems in a mine.' Bülow, who was present, 'confessed that the performances attempted of this piece in Germany had been taken on trust by the audience, but the music itself had remained entirely unintelligible.' The Parisians, according to Wagner, were more responsive: 'I succeeded,' he wrote, 'in making this Prelude understandable both to orchestra and audience—aye, people assure me it called forth the deepest impression of all.'

Wagner prepared for the first Paris performance of the *Tristan* Prelude (the concert of January 25, 1860) an 'explanation' of the music, and he wrote it out for Mathilde on the back of a manuscript piano transcription of the concert close which he devised at that time for the Prelude (it is this close which is used when the Prelude is played at concerts without the Finale). Wagner's draft of the explanation is dated on his MS. 'December 15, 1859.' This is the familiar and rather extended gloss upon the Prelude that is included in vol. VIII of the collected *Prose Works*. It has appeared upon analytical programs for many years as an interpretation of the original form of the Prelude, to which, of course, it does not apply. But Wagner afterward prepared another explanatory note, to be used when the Prelude (minus its Paris concert ending) was linked with Isolde's death song, the most interesting aspect of which is that it gives the title 'Liebestod' not to the Finale—as we do today—but to the Prelude, while the Finale is called 'Transfiguration' ('Verklärung'). This later explanation, as used upon the program of a Vienna concert conducted by Wagner, December 27, 1863, is as follows:

TRISTAN AND ISOLDE

(a) PRELUDE (LOVE-DEATH)

Tristan as bridal envoy conducts Isolde to his uncle, the King. They love each other. From the first stifled moan of quenchless longing, from the faintest tremor to unpent avowal of a hopeless love, the heart goes through each phase of unvictorious battling with its inner fever, till, swooning back upon itself, it seems extinguished as in death.

(b) FINALE (TRANSFIGURATION)

Yet, what Fate divided for this life, in death revives transfigured: the gate of union opens. Above the corpse of Tristan, dying Isolde sees transcendent consummation of their passionate desire, eternal union in unmeasured realms, nor bond nor barrier, indivisible!

The transference of the term 'Liebestod' from the Prelude to the Finale, for which it has now become synonymous, seems to have been brought about by Liszt, who gave the title to his masterly piano transcription of Isolde's death song. Liszt found the term in the text of the love duet in the second act, where the transported pair sing together the words: *Sehnend verlangter Liebestod!* ('O bitterly burned-for death-by-love!' is Alfred Forman's English rendering. 'Death through stress of love' is Ellis's attempt at an explanation of the word 'Liebestod.') Liszt used the momentous theme to which these words are sung as the introduction to his transcription; but the theme itself, curiously enough, does not occur in that portion of the duet which is virtually identical with the music sung by Isolde over her lover's body—that 'singing and soaring flame' which we know as the 'Liebestod,' both in the opera and in the version for orchestra alone that is now almost invariably linked with the Prelude in the concert room: music so drenched in sorrow and loveliness and exaltation that the world still shares Wagner's own wonder in the presence of it. '*Tristan* is, and remains, a marvel to me,' he wrote candidly to the woman who had inspired it. 'I am more and more unable to understand how I could produce such a thing.' The mystery is still unsolved.

In this Prelude and its companion piece, the Finale, Wagner is at the summit of his genius. The terrible disquiet of the first, the 'high, immortal, proud regret' of the second, its dying fires, its mood of luminous reconciliation, have called forth the greatest that he could give. In the Prelude he has uttered, once and for all, the passionate protest of the human heart against its doom of separateness—not merely and grossly the desire of animal for animal; and in the death song of Isolde he has prisoned forever that ancient wonderment of seers and poets at 'the idleness of tears.' Who that has witnessed the opera's close can dislodge the image of Isolde bending above her dead lover, as the rapturous music utters its dark saying: 'I and this love are one, and I am Death'; or can forget the end of the orchestra's song upon that aureoled B-major chord, while we see the burnished air of evening fade and 'the last bird fly into the last night,' and all desire and all regret become as a quiet fold of dimming sky?

• PRELUDE TO ACT 3

Tristan, wounded and unconscious, lies upon a couch in the courtyard of his ancient castle in Brittany, whither he has been brought from Cornwall by the devoted Kurvenal, who now watches anxiously beside his master in the shade of a great lime tree. At one side rise the dilapidated walls of the castle, at the other side are a parapet and a watch tower, crumbling and neglected. In the background stretches the empty sea. From without is heard the sound of a shepherd's piping—'one of the strangest, saddest melodies ever invented, a melody that seems to have been distilled from all the tears that man in his pain has ever shed.'

The scene is steeped in desolation. There is no movement but the faint stirring of the sultry air in the branches above the two quiet figures beneath the tree—the dying man on his bed of feverish longing, and the sorrowing watcher bent above him; there is no sound but the strange, bitter-sweet, half-wild, half-drowsy piping of the invisible shepherd.

The tune blown by the shepherd is the same melody that accompanies Tristan's despondent soliloquy later in the act, when, after his delirious anticipation of Isolde's approaching ship and that frenzied question of his to the watcher on the parapet—'Kurvenal, dost thou not see it?'—he sinks back in dejection upon his couch, the shepherd's tune playing a counterpoint of infinite sadness to his melancholy brooding.

In the opera, this unforgettable and utterly original tune, charged with old dreams, heavy with remembered griefs, is first heard from the English horn behind the scenes, beginning with the last notes of the orchestral introduction to the act. The introduction itself begins with a wearily drab and heart-heavy transformation of the theme of Desire (for the strings) that now progresses diatonically, instead of chromatically, as if all its old tremulous intensity had been dulled into despondent weariness. The violins, ascending slowly and drearily—wan and lonely as the barren sea—make way for the second subject of the prelude: the motive that is associated with Tristan's sorrow. This theme —one of the most haunting among Wagner's incomparable utterances of grief—is sung by horns and 'cellos (later in the act, it fills with passionate anguish Tristan's despairing cry to Kurvenal: 'What I suffer, thou can'st not suffer!'). This comprises the thematic material of the prelude.

DIE MEISTERSINGER

• PRELUDE

Writing of the spring of 1862 in his autobiography, Wagner tells us that 'the fair season of the year was now approaching, and I was once more seized with a desire for work. As from the balcony of my flat, in a sunset of great splendor, I gazed upon the magnificent spectacle of "Golden" Mayence, with the majestic Rhine pouring along its outskirts in a glory of light, the Prelude to my *Meistersinger* again suddenly made its presence closely and distinctly felt in my soul. . . I wrote down the Prelude exactly as it appears today in the score, containing the clear outlines of the leading themes of the whole drama. I proceeded at once to continue the composition, intending to allow the remaining scenes to follow in due succession.'

Wagner never more completely than in the prelude to his most radiant score achieved what he set out to accomplish. This spacious and magnificent music, endlessly delectable as a pattern of sound, is marvelous in its vivid projection of a recovered past: here, to the life, is medieval Nuremberg, 'with its thousand gable-ends, its fragrant lime trees and gardens, its ancient customs, its processions of the guilds and crafts, its watchman with his horn and lantern calling the hour, its freshness and quaint loveliness by day and its sweetness on soft summer nights.'

Does this overture, as a piece of music detachable from the opera, transcend every other work of Wagner's? Some have thought so, yet there are others who hold out for the *Tristan* Prelude, or for the music that exalts the dead Siegfried. But there are probably few who would maintain that Wagner ever wrote anything more enduringly lovable than the Prelude to *Die Meistersinger*, with its magical blend of gaiety and tenderness, poetry and homespun, richly comforting earthiness, and the immortal wonder of man's unquiet dream of beauty.

● PRELUDE TO ACT 3

Here we have Wagner in one of his profoundest moods—a mood of gravely contemplative meditation, beginning in a vein of sorrowful brooding, closing in a spirit full of benignant calm and resignation. Wagner has given us his own commentary upon the music:

The opening theme, for the 'cellos, has already been heard in the third strophe of Sach's cobbler-song in Act II. There it expressed the bitter cry of the man of resignation who shows the world a cheerful, energetic countenance; that smothered cry was understood by Eva, and so deeply did it pierce her heart that she fain would fly away, only to hear this cheerful-seeming song no longer. Now (in the Introduction to Act III), this motive is played alone (by the 'cellos), and developed (in the other strings) till it dies away in resignation; but forthwith, and as from out the distance, the horns intone the solemn song wherewith Hans Sachs greets Luther and the Reformation, which had won the poet such widespread popularity. After the first strophe the strings again take single phrases of the cobbler-song, very softly and much slower, as though the man were turning his gaze from his handiwork heavenwards, lost in tender musings. Then, with increased sonority, the horns pursue the master's hymn, with which Hans Sachs, in the last scene of the act, is greeted by the populace of Nuremberg. Next reappears the strings' first motive, with grandiose expression of the anguish of a deeply stirred soul; calmed and allayed, it attains the utmost serenity of a blest and peaceful resignation.

This wonderful prelude stands among the great slow movements of music. In it is enshrined the heart of Hans Sachs, for it is he who is the central figure of Wagner's drama. It is his sorrow, his fortitude, his resignation, his magnitude of spirit that are portrayed here with an exalted poetic beauty such as none but Bach or Beethoven, in their loftiest moods of compassionate understanding, would have known how to express.

A great many years have passed since George Bernard Shaw (as he then signed himself) made the momentous discovery that Hans Sachs, the hero of *Die Meistersinger*, is merely 'a widower who cobbles shoes, writes verses, and contents himself with looking on at the sweetheartings of his customers'; which causes you to wonder what Shaw thinks the Prelude to Act III is all about—that matchless revery which, as no less an authority than Wagner himself has told us, 'expresses the anguish of a deeply stirred soul—the bitter cry of the resigned man who presents to the world a composed and cheerful countenance.' The Sachs of Wagner's imagination is, in these intense moments, the man of Hardy's terrible poem, 'I Look into My Glass'—the middle-aged lover with his wintering body shaken in the evening of its days 'with the throbbings of noontide.' It is this element in *Die Meistersinger* that makes it so much more profound and moving a thing than Shaw supposed it to be. He called it 'a work full of health, fun, and happiness' (which, to be sure, it often is), containing 'not a single bar of love music that can be described as passionate.' But perhaps mere lyric ecstasy does not come within Shaw's definition of human passion.

• DANCE OF THE APPRENTICES AND ENTRANCE OF THE MASTERS

When the curtain rises upon the final scene of *Die Meistersinger* we see a green meadow on the banks of the Pegnitz; in the distance, the city of Nuremberg, its walls and towers lit by a dazzling midsummer sun. 'The place is decorated for a holiday. There is an imposing platform with chairs and benches on it for the Mastersingers and judges in the song-contest. Crowds of holidaymakers are on the spot already, more still arrive by the river in bright boats. The various guilds enter with their respective insignia—shoemakers, tailors, bakers. Apprentices and young girls dance together to a measure gay as their fluttering ribbon-knots. Conspicuous among them is David, so forgetful for the moment of Magdalena and himself as to imprint a glowing kiss on his partner's cheek. 'Frivolities stop short with the arrival of the Masters. They assemble on the landing stage; then march in imposing procession to their places on the stand, Kothner waving the banner of the guild, on which is represented King David and his harp. The people acclaim them, cheering and waving their hats. Pogner escorts Eva to the seat of honor. . .'

When all are in their places, a corps of young apprentices, filling the function of heralds, and carrying staffs of office liberally beflowered, call out in Latin the order for silence. Quiet being established, Hans Sachs, spokesman for the occasion, rises. At once the silence is shattered by cheers for the beloved cobbler-poet, cries of joy at sight of him; there is waving of kerchiefs and hats. To show him how everyone knows and loves his works and himself, the populace hails him in an overwhelming chorus, the words of which are from a poem by the historic Hans Sachs himself, greeting Luther and the Reformation.

PARSIFAL

• PRELUDE

The Prelude to *Parsifal* is music of consecration, lofty faith, aspiration, and immeasurable suffering, in which we may discern a signal of that purification through pity and terror whereby we are put in touch with immortal things. Wagner himself has left us an explanation of the inner meaning of this unapproachable page. He wrote it for a private performance of the Prelude at Munich, before King Ludwig II.

The commentary is headed: 'Love—Faith: Hope?' Wagner sets a question mark after the word 'Hope.' 'He does not mean to imply that the Prelude fulfills the hope, but only that it suggests the possibility of it.' But let us proceed with the master's explanation of the Prelude. It reads as follows:

First theme: Love. Take my body, take my blood, in token of our love. [This is the solemn opening theme of the Prelude, sometimes called the motive of the Eucharist, played in unison, at first without accompaniment, by the muted strings and woodwind. It is several times repeated, with and without accompaniment, and is followed by the theme of the Grail, heard from the trumpets and trombones, then from the woodwind. Its concluding phrase, the ascending progression of sixths, was borrowed by Wagner from the celebrated *Amen* of the Saxon liturgy, used in the Court Church at Dresden.]

Second theme: Faith [continues Wagner]—promise of Redemption through Faith. Strong and firm does Faith reveal itself, elevated and resolute even in suffering [the theme of Faith, proclaimed with superb assurance by the brass, follows immediately the pianissimo repetition of the last phrase of the Grail theme by the woodwind]. In answer to the renewed promise, the voice of Faith sounds softly from the distant heights—as though borne on the wings of the snow-white dove—slowly descending, embracing with ever-increasing breadth and fulness the heart of man, filling the world and the whole of nature with mightiest force, then, as though stilled to rest, glancing upward again toward the light of heaven.

Then, from the awe of solitude, arises the lament of loving compassion, the agony, the holy sweat of the Mount of Olives, the divine suffering of Golgotha; the body blanches, the blood streams forth and glows now in the chalice with the heavenly glow of blessing, pouring forth on all that lives and languishes the gracious gift of Redemption through Love. For him we are prepared, for Amfortas, the sinful guardian of the shrine, who, with fearful rue for sin gnawing at his heart, must prostrate himself before the chastisement of the vision of the Grail.

This 'lament' referred to by Wagner is introduced by a roll of the timpani and a tremolo of the basses. Phrases derived from sections of the Eucharist theme become a plaint of overwhelming poignancy; and with this music of infinite sorrow and compassion the Prelude reaches its climax.

'Shall there be redemption from the devouring torments of the soul?' says Wagner's commentary. 'Once again we hear the promise, and—we hope!'

● Transformation Music (Act 1)

This is the orchestral interlude which accompanies the transition from the first scene of *Parsifal*—the wooded glade in the forest—to the scene in the Temple of the Holy Grail. At Bayreuth, this transition is accompanied by the moving scenery whereby Wagner intended to convey the visual illusion of the progress of Gurnemanz and Parsifal as they proceed from the woods to the Temple. Their advance is a strange and impressive one: as they seem to walk to the left, the scene imperceptibly moves from left to right. The forest disappears; a door opens in towering rocky cliffs through which the two pass and are lost to sight; later they are seen again in somber and mysterious passages which they appear to ascend. Long-sustained trombone notes softly swell; the sound of bells draws near. At last they come to a mighty hall, which loses itself overhead in a high vaulted dome, through which alone the light streams down. From the heights above the dome comes the increasing sound of chimes.

This transformation is accompanied in the orchestra by music that at first is a solemn and majestic march, based upon the notes of the Bell theme, but which is soon changed to an utterance of overwhelming poignancy by the appearance of a great phrase, the theme of the Divine Lament for human sin and suffering, which cuts across the orchestra with piercing intensity, until, as the music reaches its tremendous climax, it seems to be giving utterance to the cumulative burden of humanity's immemorial woe, transfixing the spirit with its lancing pity and its grief.

● PRELUDE TO ACT 3

The orchestral introduction to the Third Act of *Parsifal* is music of desolation and weariness. It evokes for us, in the opening measures of the strings, the despair and spiritual decay that have fallen upon the brotherhood of Knights— for, as we learn later from the lips of Gurnemanz, Amfortas, longing for re- lease in death, has refused to unveil the Grail; his aged father, Titurel, has died; and the Knights, deprived of the Grail's miraculous sustenance, are no longer able to perform their deeds of service and of mercy.

The frustrate and disheartening wanderings of Parsifal in his search for Amfortas are suggested by the wearily ascending and descending figures in the first violins, which rise to a plangent outburst with a phrase from the Grail theme, the motive of Kundry's laughter, and that of the Spear. The prelude reaches its climax in a peculiarly sorrowful and tragic version of the theme of Prophecy.

● GOOD FRIDAY SPELL

Parsifal, after long wandering under Kundry's curse, arrives at Monsalvat on Good Friday. He is clad in black armor, his visor down, and he bears the sacred spear. Gurnemanz, now old and sorrowful, gazes in astonishment at the somber figure. He rebukes the Knight for bearing arms upon a holy day. Thereupon Parsifal thrusts his spear into the ground, lays beneath it his sword and shield and helmet, and sinks on his knees in prayer before the sacred weapon. Then Gurnemanz recognizes the praying Knight as the simpleton whom he had dismissed in anger from the temple long years before. Gurne- manz informs him of the evil that has befallen the Knights of the Grail, and Parsifal is overcome with grief. Kundry and Gurnemanz restore him by gentle ministrations, Kundry bathing his feet and drying them with her long hair, while Gurnemanz anoints his head with holy oil, blesses him, and hails him as lord and sovereign of the Grail (it is at this point that the concert excerpt known as the *Good Friday Spell* begins in the orchestra). Parsifal then baptizes Kundry; and she, the humble penitent, bows her head and weeps.

Parsifal turns his head, and gazes in gentle ecstasy upon the sweet peaceful- ness of the spring woods and the meadows radiant in the morning light. 'How fair the meadow is today!' he says to Gurnemanz. 'That is Good Friday's Spell, my lord!' says Gurnemanz; and he explains to Parsifal that the radiant beauty of the landscape is a sign of all Creation's tender gratitude to the Redeemer on this day of sacrifice and love, when the flowers of the field, watered by sacred dews—the tears of all repentant sinners—lift up their heads, and glow with thankfulness and joy.

When Gurnemanz, deeply moved, anoints the head of Parsifal and greets him as sovereign and savior of the Grailhood, we hear, first, at the beginning of this excerpt, Parsifal's own theme, proclaimed majestically in B major by the brass. This is followed by an extraordinary beautiful and expressive version of the motive of Promise, sometimes called the theme of the Guileless Fool, associated with the mystical Prophecy of the coming of the stainless simpleton who, through the enlightenment of compassion, shall deliver the Grailhood from its woe.

The music ascends, through one of those progressive intensifications of which only Wagner knew the secret, to a climax of uplifting grandeur for the full orchestra, culminating in the rising sixths of the Grail theme.

This superb passage—one of the most exalted and magnificent in all Wagner —is followed, after a series of long-held chords, diminuendo, for the wind, by the measures that accompany Parsifal's baptism of Kundry. We hear in the strings and wind, pianissimo, the motive of Baptism, and, succeeding it, the motive of Faith, at first in the woodwind, then in the muted strings. When the baptized Kundry bows her head and weeps, the motive of Faith becomes the dolorous motive of Penitence (muted strings, 'Sehr langsam').

As Parsifal turns and gazes on the tranquil loveliness of the fields and woods, the motive known as that of the Blossoming Meadows is sung by the oboe in B major over a murmuring of muted strings and sustained harmonies of the horns and woodwind: music of ineffable tenderness, yet penetrated with a subtle emotion of remembered pain, as if it were shadowed by the recollection of some assuaged yet unforgettable grief.

● TRANSFORMATION MUSIC (ACT 3)

The Good Friday music is followed by an orchestral interlude which, like that in Act I, accompanies the moving scenery that brings us to the Temple of the Grail. But the music is not the same as that of the corresponding passage in Act I. Titurel has died, and Parsifal is no longer the innocent youth of former days. Therefore the interlude has a new character; it is somber and sad, like a funeral march, and begins with an ostinato figure in 'cellos and basses, borrowed from the music which had previously accompanied Gurnemanz's reference to the funeral of Titurel. Above it we hear the trumpets and trombones in a majestic version of Parsifal's theme, followed by the motive of Herzeleide's Grief. The motive of Desolation, from the prelude to the Third Act, is recalled by strings, woodwind, and horns. Now the bells begin to sound in the Temple, and in the orchestra (double-basses, tuba, and timpani) we hear the reiterated notes of the Bell theme, C, G, A, E. Above them, as the movement nears its climax, trombones, trumpets, and 'cellos intone a mighty phrase that descends by step-like intervals, against the ostinato of the Bell theme. There is a grandiose and imposing climax, fortissimo, on a phrase from the motive of Desolation.

• A FAUST OVERTURE

Wagner, in the forlorn Paris days of his late twenties, when he was eating his
heart out in wretchedness and destitution, composed, as he said, 'out of the
depths of my discontent an orchestral piece which I called "an overture to
Goethe's *Faust*," but which was really intended for the first section of a grand
Faust symphony.' This was in 1840, and Wagner was yet to compose his *Flying
Dutchman*. He describes the sketches and the composition as 'hasty.' Eight
years later he confesses to Liszt that the Overture 'does not please me any
longer,' but that if Liszt wants it he may have it. Liszt gave the overture in
Weimar, with marked success, in May 1852, and afterward he wrote Wagner
a letter full of shrewd criticism and consummate tact:

The work is quite worthy of you; but, if you will allow me to make a remark, I must
confess that I should like either a second middle part or else a quieter and more agree-
ably colored treatment of the present middle part. . . . and—forgive my opinion—the
motive in F is not satisfactory; it wants grace in a certain sense, and is a kind of hybrid
thing, neither fish nor flesh, which stands in no proper relation of contrast to what has
gone before and what follows, and in consequence, impedes the interest. If instead of
this you introduced a soft, tender, melodious part, modulated *à la* Gretchen, I think
I can assure you that your work would gain very much. Think this over and do not be
angry in case I have said something stupid.

Wagner was not angry. He was lamb-like:

You beautifully spotted the lie when I tried to make myself believe that I had composed an overture to *Faust* [he wrote a month later]. You have felt quite justly what is
wanting: the woman is wanting. Perhaps you would at once understand my tone-poem
if I called it *Faust in Solitude*. At that time I intended to write an entire *Faust* Symphony. The first movement, that which is ready, was this *Solitary Faust*, longing,
despairing, cursing. The 'feminine' floats around him as an object of his longing, but
not in its divine reality; and it is just this insufficient image of his longing which he
destroys in his despair. The second movement was to introduce Gretchen, the woman.
I had a theme for her, but it was only a theme. The whole remains unfinished. I wrote
my *Flying Dutchman* instead. This is the whole explanation. If now, from a last
remnant of weakness and vanity, I hesitate to abandon this *Faust* work altogether,
I shall certainly have to remodel it, but only as regards instrumental modulation. The
theme which you desire, I cannot introduce. This would naturally involve an entirely
new composition, for which I have no inclination. If I publish it, I shall give it its
proper title, *Faust in Solitude*, or *The Solitary Faust*: a Tone-Poem for Orchestra.

He did not 'abandon' it. Writing to Liszt from Zürich on January 19, 1855,
he declared: 'I have been taken with a desire to remodel my old *Faust* overture. I have made an entirely new score, have rewritten the instrumentation
throughout, have made many changes, and have given more expansion and importance to the middle portion (second motive). I shall give it in a few days
at a concert here, under the title of A *"Faust" Overture*.'

Four days later, January 23, the Overture in its altered form was played at
Zürich for the first time. Thus a decade and a half elapsed between the first
and second versions of the *Faust* Overture (Wagner had forgotten, apparently,
his clarifying idea of calling the work *Faust in Solitude* or *The Solitary Faust*).

In the interval, he had composed the music of *The Flying Dutchman, Tann-häuser, Lohengrin, Rheingold, Die Walküre.* Yet there is less of the mature Wagner in the remodeled *Faust* than one would expect. A good deal of *The Flying Dutchman* aroma still clings to it. But there is one remarkable exception. Neither Gretchen nor the Devil, it has been noted, appears in the score. But Tristan is there, and so is Isolde; yet they were not born, musically, until almost three years later. Listen to the melody played by the oboes immediately after the entrance of the second theme (the tender flute passage in F major), and you will hear the Love Glance motif from *Tristan und Isolde.*

A brooding and lugubrious phrase for the bass tuba and double-basses opens the slow introduction of the *Faust* Overture. Its concluding four notes form a section of the main theme of the overture, which is foreshadowed by the first violins in the eighth and ninth measures. We hear, immediately after, a complaining phrase for the woodwind (borrowed thirty-four years later by Richard Strauss for his *Death and Transfiguration,* by the way). A faint premonitory hint of the unborn *Tristan* is suggested by a brief chromatic phrase in the strings; there is a wraith from the Kingdom of the Past—a naïve thematic ghost with the composite features of the *Dutchman* and *Lohengrin* (wood and horns); and then the main body of the overture is begun by an extension of the expressive violin phrase, against a harmonic background supplied by the bassoons, horns, and drums ('sehr bewegt,' 2-2). An exceedingly energetic subsidiary theme for the strings, wood, horns and trumpets, and a plaintive tune for the oboe, precede the entrance of the second theme, wherewith the flute evokes that circumambient 'feminine' which, said Wagner, was the object of Faust's unrest—'this insufficient image of his longing which he destroys in his despair.' Then comes the prophetic Love Glance theme from *Tristan* on the oboes and bassoons; and thirty measures further on, in the strings alone, a remarkable anticipation of the chromatic style of the *Tristan* Prelude. The development is extensive and darkly tempestuous. You hear the solitary Faust, 'longing, despairing, cursing.' Yet the close is consolatory. First violins alone play the chief theme. The final note of the phrase, C-sharp, taken over by a solo bassoon and held through four measures, merges very beautifully into a C-sharp major chord of the wood and horns, pianissimo, and a lovely and simple cadence writes the Finis in D major. Has Faust perceived the benignity of solitude?

● *A Siegfried Idyl*

In the summer of 1869 a son was born to Richard Wagner and Cosima von Bülow, who were then living together at Triebschen, on the Lake of Lucerne.

Richard and Cosima, seeking refuge in Switzerland, had discovered Triebschen on the last day of March 1866, while taking a trip on the Lake of Lucerne. They found 'a simple little two-storied house rising on a projecting tongue of land in peaceful, park-like surroundings, among venerable trees,' as Cosima described it in her diary. From the promenade that runs in front of the Kurhaus and the Hotel National, at Lucerne, one can almost discern, among the trees on the peninsula a mile across the lake, the house whence issued such amazing treasures—for at Triebschen, Wagner wrote the *Siegfried Idyl*, and completed *Die Meistersinger, Siegfried*, and the composition sketches of *Die Götterdämmerung*.

On Easter Sunday 1866, Richard and Cosima inspected the villa, and Wagner saw with delight that he had found what he wanted. He at once rented the property—'nobody,' he declared, 'will get me out of here again.' He remained at Triebschen for six years. 'We live here as though in a fairy-tale,' wrote Cosima to King Ludwig. . . 'About midday, our Friend [Wagner] tells me what he has done during the morning (the workroom is upstairs). In the afternoon he roams about the pastures and meadows, and I usually go to meet him. He then spends a little time with me and the children, who are very happy here. In the evening he dictates to me his autobiography. . . He is just hailing me in the distance; am I not right in saying that we are living an idyllic existence and have found sweet forgetfulness of life? We hear nothing but the tinkle of bells as the herds of cattle descend from the high pastures and wander in the meadows which have been cleared among the woods, gazing at us every day in friendly curiosity with their great eyes. . . A strangely happy dream.'

On June 25, 1870, Wagner wrote to his friend Mrs. Wille: 'She [Cosima] has defied every disapprobation and taken upon herself every condemnation. She has borne to me a wonderfully beautiful and vigorous boy, whom I could boldly call "Siegfried"; he is now growing, together with my work, and gives me a new, long life, which at last has attained a meaning. Thus, we get along without the world, from which we have retired entirely. . . But now listen; you will, I trust, approve of the sentiment which leads us to postpone our visit until I can introduce to you the mother of my son as my wedded wife.' (Cosima and Hans von Bülow were divorced July 18, 1870; and on August 25, Cosima and Wagner were married at Lucerne.)

In the following November Wagner wrote to Ferdinand Präger: 'My house is full of children, the children of my wife, but besides there blooms for me a splendid son, strong and beautiful, whom I dare call Siegfried Richard Wagner. Now think what I must feel, that this at last has fallen to my share. I am fifty-seven years old.'

At 4 o'clock on the morning of June 6, 1869, the boy Siegfried was born. Wagner heard a cry from Vreneli, the 'good spirit of the house'—'Ach, Gott in Himmel!' and in his anxious dread imagined the worst. But when he heard Vreneli say, 'Ein Sohn ist da!' a deep emotion swept over him. 'He was surprised,' says Cosima's diary, 'by an incredibly splendid glow as of fire, which blazed upon the orange wallpaper beside the bedroom door with a glow of color such as he had never seen before, and was reflected from my portrait on the wall, so that the picture, covered with glass and surrounded with a narrow golden frame, was transfigured with an unearthly beauty.'

A week later Cosima writes of hearing at sunset the twittering of a bird outside her window. 'Richard calls it Siegfried's bird, for it had announced the child's arrival, and now it is asking after him. That morning Richard brought me sketches of the third act of *Siegfried*' (Wagner was completing the composition of the long-interrupted music-drama when his son was born, although he did not finish the instrumentation until 1871).

Cosima's thirty-third birthday fell on Christmas Day of the year following Siegfried's birth, and Wagner had composed in November 1870 a piece for small orchestra to be played as a surprise to Cosima on Christmas morning. The music was written and rehearsed in secret. The parts were copied by Hans Richter, who assembled and prepared the orchestra in Zürich. On Saturday, December 24, Wagner himself directed the final rehearsal in the hall of the Hotel du Lac at Lucerne. 'On Christmas morning,' wrote Richter many years later, 'the little orchestra took their places on the stairs of Wagner's villa at Triebschen (they had done their tuning in the kitchen). The Master, conducting, stood at the top; below him were the violins, woodwind, horns; at the bottom the 'cello and double-bass.' Beginning promptly at 7:30, Wagner led his players through the première of the exquisite aubade.

The orchestra comprised sixteen instruments (fifteen players): flute, oboe, two clarinets, bassoon, two horns, trumpet, two first violins, two second violins, two violas, one 'cello, one double-bass. Richter himself played one of the two violas, dropping it and taking the trumpet for the few bars allotted to that instrument.

Some have doubted that the performance actually took place on the stairs. But Richter is specific on this point, and even gives in his letter a diagram of the positions of the players on the staircase. The children of the Wagner household called the piece 'die Treppenmusik' (the stairs-music).

Cosima wrote as follows in her diary concerning the events of that Christmas: 'I can give you no idea, my children, about this day, nor about my feelings. I shall only tell you quite barely what happened: As I awoke, my ear caught a sound, which swelled fuller and fuller; no longer could I imagine myself to be dreaming: music was sounding, and such music! When it died away, Richard came into my room with the children and offered me the score of the symphonic birthday poem. I was in tears, but so was all the rest of the household. Richard had arranged his orchestra on the staircase, and thus was our *Triebschen* consecrated forever. . . After lunch the orchestra came into the house downstairs, and now the 'Idyl' was heard once again, to the profound emotion of us all.'

Wagner, remembering the dawn and the evening bird of his son's birthday, wrote on the title page of his manuscript: 'Triebschen Idyl, with Fidi's bird-song and orange sunrise, as symphonic birthday greeting from Richard to Cosima.' 'Fidi' was his nickname for his son.

Wagner had lost no secret of his magic when he wrote the *Siegfried Idyl* (he had traversed that year two acts of *Götterdämmerung*, and was at work on the scoring of *Siegfried*). For his thematic material he drew upon the third act of *Siegfried*, with the addition of the so-called Slumber motive from *Die Walküre*, the little German cradle-song, *Schlafe, Kindchen, Schlafe*, and some episodic matter. The flawless art with which he weaves this new fabric out of old colors and used patterns, turning what might have been a patchwork into a delicate marvel of homogeneity, is endlessly rewarding to the student.

But the most interesting fact concerning the musical subject matter of the

Idyl is that two of its chief themes, which it shares in common with *Siegfried* the music-drama, were originally intended for use in some chamber music (string quartets and trios) that Wagner projected at Starnberg in the summer of 1864, after Cosima had joined him there and when 'all barriers between them were broken down.' The two themes are those from which Wagner evolved the greater part of Brünnhilde's speech in the third act of the music-drama beginning *Ewig war ich, ewig bin ich.* In the *Idyl*, the first of these themes is the exquisite melody for the strings, heard in its complete form beginning at the thirtieth measure (its six opening bars are identical with the form which it has in the music-drama; after that point Wagner treats it differently). The second theme in question is that known to commentators as the World's Treasure motive. It is heard in the music-drama at Brünnhilde's words, *O Siegfried, Herrlicher! Hort der Welt!* In the *Idyl* (where its form is slightly varied) it is introduced by trills and string arpeggios, sixty measures after the appearance of the cradle-song.

John Runciman once declared, with pardonable enthusiasm, that the *Siegfried Idyl* 'is, in a word, the most beautiful thing Wagner ever wrote.' If one does not immediately subscribe to that opinion, there need be no hesitation in affirming that the *Siegfried Idyl* is the most beautiful piece of purely symphonic music that Wagner ever wrote. For in listening to this consummate score, superlatives rise to the lips of the most wary. The *Siegfried Idyl*, indeed, is *sui generis*. It has not its like in all music for blended loveliness, blitheness, poetic charm, and enamoring tenderness.

Wagner—odd as it may seem to those who choose to think of him as essentially a man of the theater, a musician of the footlights—was, in certain of his phases, 'one of the children of revery'; and nothing is more deeply illuminative of his true nature as an artist than such revelations of the stilled depths that we find in him from time to time as he turns from his passionate contemplation of human tragedy, 'when life and its difficulties must have seemed to him like the lessons of an elder boy given to a younger by mistake,' and solaces himself and us with some interlude of rich quietude and appeasement like the *Siegfried Idyl* or the third act Prelude of *Die Meistersinger*—those moments when he is without an equal. Surely, in this vein, he never surpassed the infinitely peaceful close of the *Siegfried Idyl*—that passage in which the murmuring music seems to fall into silence at the thought of the happiness it scarcely dares contemplate. Here Wagner might well have remembered the words of Lamb when he spoke of children as if they were 'things too dear for his possessing.'

Carl Maria von Weber
1786-1826

‡Weber's life, though brief, was in the main a happy one, though he himself did not always think so. He looked back on his childhood as a time of cares and restraints, but one suspects that he was consciously cultivating a fashionable Byronism. Actually, he grew to young manhood in a notably relaxed and bohemian household. His musical training lacked system, but his natural gifts led him to early success and later mastery. He was scarcely more than seventeen years old when he was appointed conductor of the opera in Breslau. His early twenties were spent in the employ of Duke Eugene of Würtemburg and his brother Duke Ludwig. At this time he lived, and doubtless enjoyed, a life of some dissipation, but eventually, circumstances depriving him of a sinecure, he came to his senses, got down to work, married, and enjoyed a brilliant success as a conductor and composer. He produced *Der Freischütz* in 1820, *Euryanthe* in 1823, and *Oberon* in 1826—three works which gave a new direction to the development of German opera—and in the latter year he died, ripe in honors if not in years.‡

● *Konzertstück* FOR PIANO AND ORCHESTRA, OP. 79

Weber's *Konzertstück* (composed in 1821) is program music. Sir Julius Benedict, friend and pupil of Weber, has made it known that a story lies back of the music—a naïvely fantastic romance of chivalry, of crusaders and knights and ladies, forsaken châtelaines and reunited lovers. The tale runs as follows:

The Châtelaine sits alone on her balcony, gazing far away into the distance. Her knight has gone to the Holy Land. Years have passed by; battles have been fought. Is he still alive? Will she ever see him again? Her excited imagination calls up a vision of her husband lying wounded and forsaken on the battlefield. Can she not fly to him, and die by his side? She falls back unconscious. But hark! what notes are those in the distance? Over there in the forest something flashes in the sunlight, nearer and nearer. Knights and squires with the cross of the Crusaders, banners waving, acclamations of the people; and there—it is he. She sinks into his arms. Love is triumphant. Happiness without end. The very woods and waves sing the song of love; a thousand voices proclaim his victory.

The piece is in four sections: a 'Larghetto affettuoso,' F minor, 3-4, leading, by an accellerando for the piano into an 'Allegro passionato,' F minor, 4-4. An adagio passage of five bars is succeeded by a 'Tempo di Marcia,' C major,

4-4. A connecting passage for the piano ('piu mosso') leads to the last part, a Rondo, 'Presto giojoso,' F major, 6-8.

● OVERTURE TO *Der Freischütz*

Weber began the composition of the Overture to *Der Freischütz* on February 22, 1820; he finished it (and with it the whole opera—the overture was written last) on May 13, praising God for its accomplishment; 'to Him alone be the glory,' he wrote handsomely in his diary. The first performance of the opera was at Berlin, on June 18 of the following year, 1821. Four years later it was given in New York, at the Park Theatre: March 2, 1825—and in English.

Weber confided to his diary his pious gratification over the popular success of *Der Freischütz* at its première: 'This evening *Der Freischütz* was given . . . in the Schauspielhaus with incredible enthusiasm. Overture and Bridesmaids' Song encored; out of seventeen pieces, fourteen loudly applauded. All went excellently well. I was called for, and went forward. . . Plenty of garlands of flowers. *Soli Deo gloria.*' But some of the critics injected a sour note. It was asserted that the opera owed the greater part of its success to its 'deviltry and fireworks'; that 'the originality was often monstrous'; that 'the characterization bordered on caricature.' Tieck described the opera as 'the most unmusical row that ever roared upon a stage.' But 'Weber spoke to the popular heart, and its quick, responsive throb lifted him at once to the crest of the wave which soon deluged all Germany,' wrote H. E. Krehbiel in his study of *Der Freischütz*. 'When the curtain fell on the last scene, a new chapter in German art had been opened.'

The Overture to *Der Freischütz* was first performed in public (eight months in advance of the première of the opera itself) at Copenhagen, October 8, 1820, under the direction of the composer. Weber was touring Denmark at the time, acquiring golden snuff-boxes from royalty and falling gaily in love with the Queen—as he wrote blithely to his 'darling Caroline.' He found the Queen 'charming'; but the presented snuff-box seems to have been received with modified rapture, for it is somewhat coldly referred to by Weber's son Max in his biography of his father. 'It might be supposed,' he remarks, 'that a more direct pecuniary recompense would have pleased Weber better.' And Weber wrote to his Caroline: 'It is a fine affair, certainly; but what am I to do with all this sort of thing?'

The concert that was rewarded by a snuff-box took place at court, October 4, four days before the public one. Max Maria von Weber, in his biography of his father, says nothing, oddly enough, about the performance of the *Freischütz* Overture at the public concert of October 8.

The *Freischütz* Overture was pinnacled by Berlioz in a rhapsodic tribute. 'No one dreams of disputing its pre-eminence,' he declared in *A Travers Chants*. And Berlioz, who was as sentimental as a Congressman, could scarcely contain himself in the presence of that moment in the overture which he seems to have regarded as the summit of its inspiration: '. . . the dreamy phrase of the clarinet, accompanied by a tremolo of stringed instruments in the midst of the Allegro of the Overture' [the first part of the second subject, in E-flat major, sixty measures after the beginning of the 'Molto vivace' section]. 'Does it not depict the lonely maiden, the forester's fair betrothed, who, raising her eyes to heaven, mingles her tender lament with the noise of the dark woods agitated by the storm? O Weber!!' Even today, when our response to the romantic emotionalism of such critical drum-beating has become a bit lanquid, Berlioz's enthusiasm seems fully warranted by the expressiveness of that particular passage in the *Freischütz* Overture, and by the deathless beauty and genius of the overture as a whole.

● OVERTURE TO *Euryanthe*

William Foster Apthorp once called the libretto of *Euryanthe* 'the most deplorable that can be imagined.' But he departed from the view of most commentators when he asserted somewhat impatiently that it was not alone the libretto of Helmine von Chezy which interfered with the viability of *Euryanthe*. 'Weber,' he declared, 'betrayed something of the 'prentice hand in his recitatives, he did not fall easily and naturally into the vein, and gave little evidence of that dramatic power which he showed in his grand scenes in *Freischütz* and *Oberon*.' But Apthorp excepted the superb, unfading overture.

As to the much-berated libretto of Helmine von Chezy, Philip Spitta differs energetically from the traditional opinion. He insists that it is 'on the whole a good, and, in some respects, an excellent libretto.' He thinks it absurd to suppose that 'a composer has no sort of responsibility with regard to the words he sets. "Do you suppose that any proper composer will allow a libretto to be put into his hand like an apple?" are Weber's own words. It is, moreover, obvious that a libretto which satisfied a man of such high culture, and a composer of so eminently dramatic organization, could not have been utterly bad. . . *Euryanthe* is an epic procession, an enchanted panorama, representing the life of one special period, that of medieval chivalry. Looked at from this point of view, it can be thoroughly enjoyed.'

The overture, after an energetic and fiery opening ('Allegro marcato, con molto fuoco,' E-flat, 4-4), exhibits a theme for the brass and woodwind derived from Adolar's 'Ich bau' auf Gott und meine Euryanth'' in the first act. The first violins (dolce, B-flat major) propose as the second theme the thrice-familiar melody from Adolar's aria in the second act, *Wehen mir lüfte Ruh'*, sung to the words, *O Seligkeit, dich fass' ich kaum*. After a climax, sempre fortissimo, followed by softly sustained chords for horns and bassoons, there is a pause. Then comes the historic fifteen-measure Largo—that wonderful passage, astonishing in its Wagnerian anticipations, for muted and divided violins, with a tremolo of the violas, which Weber intended as an accompaniment to the disclosure on the stage of the following tableau: 'The interior of Emma's tomb. A kneeling statue of her is beside the coffin, which is surmounted by a twelfth-century *baldacchino* [canopy]. Euryanthe prays by the coffin, while the spirit of Emma hovers overhead. Englantine looks on.'

Weber meant this passage to sound uncanny; you wonder if he suspected how beautiful it was in addition. To our ears, a century later, the strangeness has faded out of it, leaving only its sorrowful loveliness.

The development section of the overture works out, in a fugato (*assai mod-*

erato), an inversion of the theme of the wind instruments. In the recapitulation, the lyrical second theme is sung fortissimo by the full orchestra.

● OVERTURE TO *Oberon*

Weber's son, Max Maria von Weber, wrote as follows concerning the Overture to *Oberon* in his biography of his father:

Although the opera may bear unmistakable traces of weariness and haste, sad marks of the spur applied to the composer's flagging genius, and may thus display Weber's mannerisms more than any other of his works, yet that great symphonic introduction to the whole, the Overture, which was completed only two months before his death, soars triumphantly over the influence of the deadly faintness lying heavy on him, and the pressure of outward circumstances. This Overture is inferior to none of his others in life, fire, freshness, and wealth of ideas. Combined with those of *Der Freischütz* and *Euryanthe*, and his *Jubilee Overture*, it forms a magnificent constellation, each star in which shines with a different light, but yet with co-equal splendor. From first to last, the Overture to *Oberon* is in most intimate sympathy with the subject. Every picture of the drama is mirrored forth in it—the world of elves and spirits; the pomp and pride of chivalry and romance; glowing love struggling against slavery, elemental might, separation, and death; the majesty of Oriental enchantment. It has been asserted that Weber went too far, in this Overture, in his conglomeration of various musical intentions. . . But still the Overture to *Oberon* will always remain a monument of strength to the fame of the dramatic, romantic composer.'

'As a mere matter of record, perhaps not uninteresting as such to Anglo-Saxons,' wrote William Foster Apthorp, 'be it said that Weber, the German, wrote the only modern English opera that can in any way stand in the first class: *Oberon; or, The Elf-King's Oath*.' That was said many years ago. It is still true. For Providence seems to feel that the Anglo-Saxon soul is intended for a more respectable destiny than mere music-making; and *Oberon*, composed by Weber to an English text written by James Robinson Planché, and played for the first time at Covent Garden, London, more than a century ago, remains in a class by itself.

Weber, dying of consumption, but with a feverish eye upon the glittering reward of $5000 which this final operatic enterprise would bring in for his family, completed the music for Planché's absurd libretto at breakneck speed, and on April 12, 1826, conducted the première at Covent Garden. He was 'a shattered machine,' as he gasped out afterward to his friends. But he struggled through eleven more performances of *Oberon* before he died two months later. He had earned his superb honorarium and had accomplished immortal music.

● *Aufforderung zum Tanze* ('Invitation to the Dance'), OP. 65

Weber wrote his *Aufforderung zum Tanze* as a piano piece in 1819, in the early years of his married life, and dedicated it to his wife, Caroline. According to that lady, when Weber first played the piece to her he described as follows the 'program' which he had in mind:

'Bars 1-5, first appearance of the dancer. Bars 5-9, the lady's evasive reply.

Bars 9-13, his more pressing invitation. Bars 13-16, her consent. Bars 16-19, he begins conversation. Bars 19-21, her reply. Bars 21-23, he speaks with greater warmth. Bars 23-25, the sympathetic agreement. Bars 25-27, the dance begins; he addresses her with regard to it. Bars 27-29, her answer. Bars 29-31, they take their places. Bars 31-35, waiting for the commencement of the dance. The dance. The conclusion of the dance, his thanks, her reply, and their retirement.'

The best advice one can offer to the concert-goer, however, is not to try to count the bars, read the program, and listen to the music all at the same time.

Fifteen years after Weber's death, Berlioz orchestrated the piano piece for a *scene de ballet* interpolated into a revival of *Der Freischütz* at the Paris Opera in 1841. He transported the key from D-flat to D in order to make life happier for the orchestra. Half a century later, Felix Weingartner 'recast the piece on polyphonic lines' (in his own words), restored the music to its original key, and wrote his own orchestration.

Jaromir Weinberger
1896-

Weinberger received his earliest musical education in Prague, the city of his birth, under Kricka and Hoffmeister. Afterward he studied in Max Reger's Master Class at the Leipzig Conservatory. In 1922 he crossed the seas to the New World and taught composition and theory at Ithaca, N. Y. When he returned to Czechoslovakia he became Director of the Music School at Eger. But in 1939 he was again in the United States, where he has since resided. He is essentially of the line of Smetana and Dvořák, and his music bears the strong impress of the nationalistic style of those Bohemian masters, even when its subject matter is of English, American, or other non-Bohemian derivation.

● POLKA AND FUGUE FROM *Schwanda*

Weinberger's opera, *Schwanda, the Bagpipe-Player*, produced at the Czech National Theater, Prague, April 27, 1927, achieved a popularity in Europe almost equal to that once enjoyed by Krenek's now obsolescent *Jonny Spielt Auf*. Since its première at Prague in 1927, the opera has had performances on more than one hundred stages, in fourteen languages. The opera was produced at the Metropolitan Opera House November 7, 1931.

Schwanda, der Dudelsackpfeifer, a Volksoper in two acts and five tableaux, text by Milos Kares, in the Czech language, German version by Max Brod, is founded on an old Bohemian legend. The story has been set forth as follows:

Schwanda, the bagpiper of Strakonitz—a typical example of the Czech musician—lives with his young wife Dorota happily on his farm. The famous and infamous robber Babinsky comes and takes Schwanda away into the outer world. He has designs on the beautiful Dorota. Schwanda reaches the bower of Queen Eisherz, plays on his bagpipes, and wins the heart of the Queen. But a wicked magician frustrates his rapprochement between Throne and People by bringing in Dorota, who has followed her husband. Now Schwanda is to be beheaded, but Babinsky appears as rescuer in his hour of need, gives him back his bagpipes which the magician had seized, and tells him to play. As Schwanda begins the *Odzemek*, all are irresistibly moved to dance to the sound of his pipes. They dance, and dance away—first the Queen, then the twelve executioners, the soldiers, and the people. Babinsky remains behind with the couple. Schwanda calls on the Devil to punish him if he has kissed the Queen—and, being taken at his word, goes straight to Hell. So the trapdoor comes into its own again on the stage. Dorota remains true to her husband and dismisses the consoling Babinsky. She sings to him, and, by this, reduces the noble robber to tears.

In Hell the Devil is beguiling himself with a game of patience. Schwanda signs away his soul to the Devil in order to see Dorota again. Once again Babinsky appears as rescuer, and in conclusion Schwanda with his playing vanquishes the Devil's very home-like Hell. Schwanda is reunited with his Dorota, never again to leave her.

So closes this simple affair. The musical development of the chief folk-theme reaches its apotheosis, the song becomes the hymn to the homeland.

As should be the case in all fairy-tales, there is a moral in this play: Schwanda is the type of wandering musician who longs for adventures, and pines for home again after he has learnt that the outside world is far less desirable and kind than his own fireside, and that nothing is to be preferred to the love of a true wife.

Aubry, G. Jean, *French Music Today*. Trans. by Edwin Evans. London: Kegan Paul, Trench, Trubner & Company, Ltd., 1919

Barzun, Jacques, *Berlioz and The Romantic Century*, Boston: Little, Brown & Company, 1950

Bekker, Paul, *Beethoven*. Trans. by M. M. Bozman. London: J. M. Dent & Sons, Ltd., 1925

Berlioz, Hector, *Beethoven's Nine Symphonies: A Critical Study*. Trans. by Edwin Evans. New York: Charles Scribner's Sons, 1913.

—— *Evenings in the Orchestra*. Trans. by Charles E. Toche. New York: Alfred A. Knopf, Inc., 1929.

—— *Memoirs*. Trans. by Rachel Holmes and Eleanor Holmes. Annotated and trans. revised by Ernest Newman. New York: Alfred A. Knopf, Inc., 1932.

—— *Mozart, Weber and Wagner*. Trans. by Edwin Evans. London: William Reeves, 1918(?)

Brahms, Johannes, and Clara Schumann, *Letters of Clara Schumann and Johannes Brahms*. New York: Longmans, Green & Company, 1927

Calvocoressi, Michael, *Musorgsky the Russian Musical Nationalist*. Trans. by A. Eaglefield Hull. London: Kegan Paul, Trench, Trubner & Company, Ltd., 1919

—— and Gerald Abraham, *Masters of Russian Music*. New York: Alfred A. Knopf, Inc., 1936

Chopin, Frederic, *Letters*. Trans. and edited by E. L. Voynich. New York: Alfred A. Knopf, Inc., 1931

(Colles, H. C., ed.), *Grove's Dictionary of Music and Musicians*. Third edition, including revised American supplement. London and New York: The Macmillan Company (v.d.)

—— *Grove's Dictionary of Music and Musicians*. Supplementary volume. London and New York: The Macmillan Company (v.d.)

Cooper, Martin, *Georges Bizet*. London and New York: Oxford University Press, 1938

Cortot, Alfred, *French Piano Music*. Trans. by Hilda Andrews. London and New York: Oxford University Press, 1932

Delius, Clare, *Frederick Delius: Memories of My Brother*. London: Ivor Nicholson & Watson, Ltd., 1935

Deutsch, Otto E., *The Schubert Reader: A Life of Franz Schubert in Letters and Documents*. Trans. by Eric Blom. New York: W. W. Norton & Company, 1947

D'Indy, Vincent, *Beethoven: A Critical Biography*. Trans. by Theodore Baker. New York: G. Schirmer (v.d.)

—— *César Franck*. Trans. from the French. London: John Lane, 1910

Einstein, Alfred, *Mozart: His Character, His Work*. Trans. by Arthur Mendel and Nathan Broder. New York: Oxford University Press, Inc., 1945

Finck, H. T., *Grieg and His Music*. New York: Dodd, Mead & Company, 1929

Flower, Newman, *George Frideric Handel: His Personality and His Times*. New and revised edition. New York: Charles Scribner's Sons, 1948

Forkel, J. S. *Bach*. Notes and appendices by C. S. Terry. London: Constable & Company, 1920

(Foss, Hubert J., ed.), *The Heritage of Music*. London and New York: Oxford University Press, 1927

Fuller-Maitland, J. A., *Brahms*. New York: John Lane Company, 1911

Geiringer, Karl, *Haydn: A Creative Life in Music*. New York: W. W. Norton & Company, 1946

Gilman, Lawrence, *Aspects of Modern Opera*. New York: John Lane Company, 1909

—— *Phases of Modern Music*. New York: Harper & Brothers, 1904

—— *The Music of Tomorrow and Other Studies*. New York: John Lane Company, 1907

—— *Stories of Symphonic Music*. New York: Harper & Brothers, 1907

—— *Toscanini and Great Music*. New York: Farrar & Rinehart, 1938

—— *Wagner's Operas*. New York: Farrar & Rinehart, 1937

Glasenapp, C. F., *Life of Richard Wagner*. Trans. by William Ashton Ellis. London: Kegan Paul, Trench, Trubner & Company, Ltd., 1900

Grace, Harvey, *Organ Works of Bach*. London: Novello & Company, 1922

Gray, Cecil, *Sibelius*. London and New York: Oxford University Press, 1931

—— *A Survey of Contemporary Music*. London and New York: Oxford University Press, 1924

Grove, George, *Beethoven and His Nine Symphonies* (v.p.; v.d.)

Hadow, W. H., *Studies in Modern Music*. London: Seeley & Company, 1902

—— (ed.), *Oxford History of Music*. (7 volumes) London and New York: Oxford University Press (v.d.)

Hale, Philip, *Boston Symphony Programme Notes*. Edited by John N. Burk. New York: Doubleday, Doran & Company, 1935

Henderson, W. J., *Preludes and Studies*. New York: Longmans, Green & Company, 1901

Heseltine, Philip, *Frederick Delius*. London: John Lane, 1923

Huneker, J. G., *Chopin: The Man and His Music*. New York: Charles Scribner's Sons, 1900

—— *Franz Liszt*. New York: Charles Scribner's Sons, 1911

—— *Ivory, Apes and Peacocks*. New York: Charles Scribner's Sons, 1915

—— *Mezzotints in Modern Music*. New York: Charles Scribner's Sons, 1899

—— *Overtones: A Book of Temperaments*. New York: Charles Scribner's Sons, 1910

Jahn, Otto, *Life of Mozart*. Trans. by Pauline D. Townsend. London: Novello, Ewer & Company, 1882.

Kalbeck, Max, *Johannes Brahms*. Berlin: Deutsche Brahms-Gesellschaft, 1908-12

Krehbiel, H. E., *A Book of the Operas* and *A Second Book of the Operas*. New York: The Macmillan Company (v.d.)

—— *Chapters of Opera* and *More Chapters of Opera*. New York: Henry Holt & Company (v.d.)

—— *Studies in the Wagnerian Drama*. New York: Harper & Brothers, 1891

Mahler, Alma Maria, *Gustav Mahler: Memories and Letters*. Trans. by Basil Creighton. New York: The Viking Press, 1946

Maine, Basil, *Elgar: His Life and Works*. London: G. Bell & Sons, Ltd., 1933

Mainwaring, John, *Memoirs of the Life of the Late George Frederic Handel*. London, 1760

May, Florence, *Life of Johannes Brahms*. London: William Reeves (v.d.)

Mendelssohn, Felix, *Letters*. Edited by G. Selden-Goth. New York: Pantheon Books, 1945

Montagu-Nathan, M., *Contemporary Russian Composers*. London: Palmer & Hayward, 1917

Mozart, W. A., *The Letters of Mozart and His Family*. Trans. by Emily Anderson. New York: The Macmillan Company, 1938-

Newman, Ernest, *Gluck and the Opera*. London: Bertram Dobell, 1895

—— *The Life of Richard Wagner*. New York: Alfred A. Knopf, Inc., 1933-46

—— *The Man Liszt*. New York: Charles Scribner's Sons, 1935

—— *Musical Studies*. New York and London: John Lane, 1905

—— *Richard Strauss*. London: John Lane, 1908

—— *The Unconscious Beethoven*. New York: Alfred A. Knopf, Inc., 1927

Newmarch, Rosa, *The Concertgoer's Library of Descriptive Notes*. London and New York: Oxford University Press, 1928-38

—— *Jean Sibelius*. Boston: C. C. Birchard & Company, 1939

—— *The Russian Opera*. New York: E. P. Dutton & Company, Inc., 1914

—— *Tchaikovsky: His Life and Works*. New York: John Lane Company, 1900

Niecks, Frederick, *Robert Schumann*. London: J. M. Dent & Sons Ltd., 1925

Niemann, Walter, *Brahms*. Trans. by Catherine A. Phillips. New York: Alfred A. Knopf, Inc., 1929

Parry, C. H. H., *Johann Sebastian Bach*. New York: G. P. Putnam's Sons, 1909

Pohl, Karl F., *Joseph Haydn*. Leipzig: Breitkopf u. Härtel, 1878

Reich, Willi, *Alban Berg*. Vienna: H. Reichner, 1937

Riemann, Hugo, *Encylopaedic Dictionary of Music*. Philadelphia: Theodore Presser, 1899

—— *Musiklexikon*. Berlin: Max Herses Verlag (v.d.)

Riesimann, Oskar von, *Moussorgsky*. Trans. by Paul England. New York: Alfred A. Knopf, Inc., 1929

Rimsky-Korsakov, Nicholas, *My Musical Life*. Trans. by Judah A. Joffe. New York: Alfred A. Knopf, Inc., 1923

Rolland, Romain, *Beethoven*. Trans. by B. Constance Hull. New York: Harper & Brothers, 1924

—— *Beethoven the Creator*. Trans. by Ernest Newman. New York: Harper & Brothers, 1929

Rolland, Romain, *Handel*. Trans. by A. Eaglefield Hull. New York: Henry Holt & Company, 1916

Rosenfeld, Paul, *Musical Portraits*. New York: Harcourt, Brace & Company, 1920

Runciman, John F., *Richard Wagner, Composer of Operas*. London: G. Bell & Sons, Ltd., 1913

Schindler, Anton F., *Life of Beethoven*. Edited by I. Moscheles. Boston: Oliver Ditson Company, 1841(?)

Scholes, Percy A., *The Oxford Companion to Music*. London and New York: Oxford University Press (v.d.)

Schubert, Franz Peter, *Letters and Other Writings*. Edited by Otto E. Deutsch; trans. by Venetia Savile. New York: Alfred A. Knopf, Inc., 1928

Schumann, Eugenie, *The Schumanns and Johannes Brahms: The Memoirs of the Author*. New York: The Dial Press, 1927

Schweitzer, Albert, *J. S. Bach*. Trans. by Ernest Newman. London and New York: A. & C. Black; The Macmillan Company (v.d.)

Sourek, Otakar, and Paul Stefan, *Dvořák: Leben und Werk*. Vienna: Rolf Passer, 1934

Specht, Richard, *Gustav Mahler*. Stuttgart: Deutsche Verlags-Anstalt, 1925

—— *Johannes Brahms*. Trans. by Eric Blom. New York: E. P. Dutton & Company, 1930

—— *Richard Strauss und Sein Werk*. Leipzig: E. P. Tal, 1921

Spitta, Philipp, *J. S. Bach: His Work and Influence on the Music of Germany*. Trans. by Clara Bell and J. A. Fuller-Maitland. London: Novello & Company, 1899

Stefan, Paul, *Gustav Mahler*. Trans. by T. E. Clark. New York: G. Schirmer, 1913

Sullivan, J. W. N., *Beethoven: His Spiritual Development*. New York: Alfred A. Knopf, Inc., 1927

Tchaikovsky, Modest, *The Life and Letters of Peter Ilich Tchaikovsky*. With an introduction by Rosa Newmarch. London: John Lane, 1906

Tchaikovsky, Peter I., *The Diaries of Tchaikovsky*. Trans., with notes, by Wladimir Lakond. New York: W. W. Norton & Company, 1945

Terry, C. S., *Johann Christian Bach*. London and New York: Oxford University Press, 1929

—— *J. S. Bach: A Biography*. London and New York: Oxford University Press, 1928

—— *The Music of Bach: An Introduction*. London and New York: Oxford University Press, 1933

Thayer, A. W., *The Life of Ludwig van Beethoven*. Trans. by H. E. Krehbiel. New York: G. Schirmer, 1921

Tovey, D. F., *Essays in Musical Analysis*. London and New York: Oxford University Press, 1935-44

Toye, Francis, *Giuseppe Verdi: His Life and Works*. New York: Alfred A. Knopf, Inc., 1931

—— *Rossini: A Study in Tragi-comedy*. New York: Alfred A. Knopf, Inc., 1934

Turner, W. J., *Mozart: The Man and His Works*. New York: Alfred A. Knopf,
    Inc., 1938

Vallas, Léon, *Claude Debussy, His Life and Works*. Trans. by Marie and Grace
    O'Brien. London and New York: Oxford University Press, 1933

Wagner, Richard, *Letters of Richard Wagner*. Selected and edited by Wilhelm
    Altman; trans. by M. M. Bozman. New York: E. P. Dutton & Company,
    1927

——— *My Life*. New York: Dodd, Mead & Company, 1911

——— *Prose Works* (8 volumes). Trans. by William Ashton Ellis. London:
    Kegan Paul, Trench, Trubner & Company, Ltd., 1882-99

Wasielewski, W. J. von, *Life of Robert Schumann*. Trans. by A. L. Alger.
    Boston: Oliver Ditson & Company, 1871

Weber, Max, *Carl Maria von Weber; The Life of an Artist*. Trans. by J. Palmer
    Simpson. Boston: Oliver Ditson & Company, 19-

Whittaker, W. G., *Fugitive Notes upon Some Cantatas and Motets of J. S.
    Bach*. London and New York: Oxford University Press, 1924